COLORADO CAMPING

JOSHUA BERMAN

COLORADO REGIONS

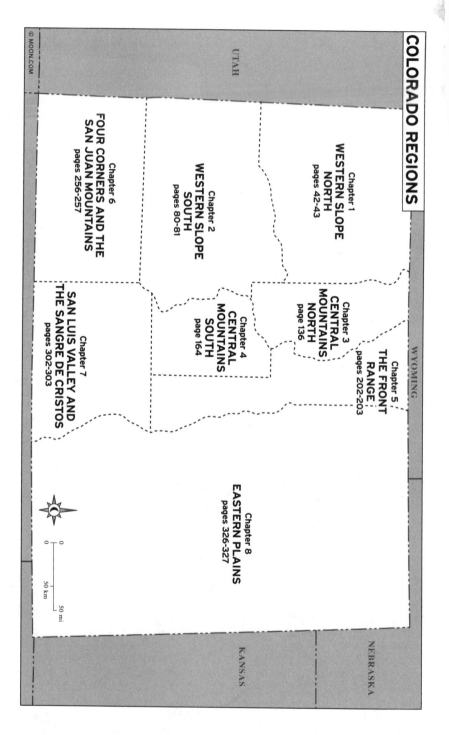

UTAH

WYOMING

NEBRASKA

KANSAS

0
0
50 mi
50 km

Contents

How to Use This Book

ABOUT THE CAMPGROUND PROFILES

The campgrounds are listed in a consistent, easy-to-read format to help you choose the id camping spot. If you already know the name of the specific campground you want to visit, the name of the surrounding geological area or nearby feature (town, national or state par forest, mountain, lake, river, etc.), look it up in the index and turn to the corresponding pag Here is a sample profile:

Campground name and number →

1 SOMEWHERE USA CAMPGROUND

Icons noting activities and facilities at or nearby the campground

General location of the campground in relation to the nearest major town or landmark →

Scenic rating: 10

south of Somewhere USA Lake

Rating of scenic beauty on a scale of 1-10 with 10 the highest rating

Map 1.2, page 4 **BEST (**

Map the campground can be found on and page number the map can be found on →

Each campground in this book begins with a brief overview of its setting. The description typically covers ambience, information about the attractions, and activities popular at the campground.

Symbol indicating that the campground is listed among the author's top picks

Campsites, facilities: This section notes the number of campsites for tents and RVs and indicates whether hookups are available. Facilities such as restrooms, picnic areas, recreation areas, laundry, and dump stations will be addressed, as well as the availability of piped water, showers, playgrounds, stores, and other amenities. The campground's pet policy and wheelchair accessibility is also mentioned here.

Reservations, fees: This section notes whether reservations are accepted, and provides rates for tent sites and RV sites. If there are additional fees for parking or pets, or discounted weekly or seasonal rates, they will also be noted here.

Directions: This section provides mile-by-mile driving directions to the campground from the nearest major town or highway.

Contact: This section provides an address, phone number, and website, if available, for the campground.

ABOUT THE ICONS

The icons in this book are designed to provide at-a-glance information on activities, facilities, and services available on-site or within walking distance of each campground.

- Hiking trails
- Biking trails
- Swimming
- Fishing
- Boating
- Canoeing and/or kayaking
- Winter sports

- Hot springs
- Pets permitted
- Playground
- Wheelchair accessible
- RV sites
- Tent sites

ABOUT THE SCENIC RATING

Each campground profile employs a scenic rating on a scale of 1 to 10, with 1 being the least scenic and 10 being the most scenic. A scenic rating measures only the overall beauty of the campground and environs; it does not take into account noise level, facilities, maintenance, recreation options, or campground management. The setting of a campground with a lower scenic rating may simply not be as picturesque that of as a higher rated campground, however other factors that can influence a trip, such as noise or recreation access, can still affect or enhance your camping trip. Consider both the scenic rating and the profile description before deciding which campground is perfect for you.

MAP SYMBOLS

Expressway		Interstate Freeway		Airfield	
Primary Road		U.S. Highway		Airport	
Secondary Road		State Highway		City/Town	
Unpaved Road		County Highway		Mountain	
Ferry		Lake		Park	
National Border		Dry Lake		Pass	
State Border		Seasonal Lake		State Capital	

INTRODUCTION

Author's Note

The people who come from around the world to experience Colorado's campgrounds come for all kinds of reasons: to hike and mountain bike on the Continental Divide, to four-wheel through ghost towns, to raft raging rivers, to soak in hot springs, fly fish on Gold Medal waters, canoe across reservoirs, tour fall foliage, and to snowshoe and ski. And, of course, they come to camp—that primordial act of sleeping under the stars that unites us all.

In addition to the nearly 500 public and commercial campgrounds listed in *Moon Colorado Camping*, there are thousands of small, simple campsites throughout public lands that are accessible only by hiking or on horseback. These backcountry sites usually require a permit and are beyond the scope of this book, but we'll get you to the trailheads. For some people, their favorite campground *is* the destination. For others, campgrounds are pleasant, but crowded stepping-stones to access their favorite backcountry area or secret hot springs.

As the Denver metro area population continues to swell, snagging a campsite during the summer has become a bit of an art form. If you're able to camp between Sunday and Thursday nights, your site availability skyrockets. Weekends are increasingly difficult if you don't have a reservation. The onset of campsite, camper, and RV-sharing apps and networks helps add more supply to meet the demand, so you may consider trying them out; I've included a few in the first chapter.

Plus, there is so much space. A whopping 35 percent of Colorado—23 million acres!—is public land, including 4 national parks, 8 national monuments, 13 national forests and grasslands, 41 state parks, and 42 designated wilderness areas. Most official campgrounds are in or around these parks and preserves, providing immediate immersion and access. These "frontcountry" campgrounds are the focus of this book. Some are right next to the interstate, others are 50 miles from the nearest town or paved road. As varied as they are, Colorado's campgrounds also serve as buffer zones, concentrating and thus minimizing, human impact on the lands we love.

The campground listings in this book are short and to the point, but also provide some context in the form of recommendations for hiking and biking trails, white-water runs, fishing opportunities, winter sports, and cultural attractions that are accessible from each campground. Each listing also includes practical information on facilities, reservations, and driving directions, as well as a narrative evaluation informed by firsthand knowledge, conversations with camp hosts, fellow campers, and rangers. There are regional maps and "best" lists to facilitate driving and decision-making—and an introduction to basic camping tips. Enjoy!

-Joshua Berman

Best Campgrounds

BEST❶ Climbing Fourteeners
Avalanche, Western Slope South, page 99.
Silver Jack, Western Slope South, page 133.
Halfmoon, Central Mountains North, page 155.
Elbert Creek, Central Mountains South, page 178.
Collegiate Peaks, Central Mountains South, page 190.
Longs Peak, The Front Range, page 228.
Burro Bridge, Four Corners and the San Juan Mountains, page 261.
Molas Lake, Four Corners and the San Juan Mountains, page 268.
North Crestone Creek, San Luis Valley and the Sangre de Cristos, page 307.

BEST❶ Day Hiking
Trappers Lake-Shepherd's Rim, Western Slope North, page 65.
Saddlehorn, Western Slope South, page 89.
Lake Irwin, Western Slope South, page 103.
Silver Queen, Western Slope South, page 107.
Timber Creek, Central Mountains North, page 142.
Gore Creek, Central Mountains North, page 158.
Moraine Park, The Front Range, page 218.
Glacier Basin, The Front Range, page 219.
Pawnee, The Front Range, page 231.
Mueller State Park, The Front Range, page 250.

BEST❶ Fly-Fishing
Hinman Park, Western Slope North, page 53.
Trappers Lake-Cutthroat, Western Slope North, page 66.
Little Maud, Western Slope South, page 84.
Weller, Western Slope South, page 108.
East Portal, Western Slope South, page 111.
Lottis Creek, Western Slope South, page 124.
Blue River, Central Mountains North, page 151.
Cross Creek, Central Mountains South, page 185.
Big South, The Front Range, page 207.
Platte River, The Front Range, page 246.

BEST❶ Hot Springs
Strawberry Park Hot Springs, Western Slope North, page 55.
KOA Steamboat Campground, Western Slope North, page 56.
Sunset Point, Central Mountains North, page 146.
Cottonwood Lake, Central Mountains South, page 192.
Chalk Lake, Central Mountains South, page 195.
Mount Princeton, Central Mountains South, page 195.
Orvis Hot Springs, Four Corners and the San Juan Mountains, page 264.

BEST Weddings

These campgrounds are in scenic locations and have amphitheaters or other facilities for events or outdoor ceremonies. They have group sites for tent and RV camping and sometimes cabins or yurts for guests who don't like sleeping pads. Some campgrounds even have wedding packages and local planners available.

Dunes Group, Eastern Plains, page 333.

BEST❰ White Water

Gates of Lodore, Western Slope North, page 46.
Deerlodge Park, Western Slope North, page 48.
Bogan Flats, Western Slope South, page 100.
East Portal, Western Slope South, page 111.
Blue River, Central Mountains North, page 151.
Ruby Mountain, Central Mountains South, page 193.
Hecla Junction, Central Mountains South, page 196.
Ansel Watrous, The Front Range, page 214.
Echo Canyon Campground, The Front Range, page 253.
River Hill, Four Corners and the San Juan Mountains, page 285.
Bridge, Four Corners and the San Juan Mountains, page 291.

BEST❰ Full-Service Campgrounds

Dutch Hill, Western Slope North, page 51.
Bookcliff, Western Slope South, page 87.
Pa-Co-Chu-Puk, Western Slope South, page 131.
Winding River Resort, Central Mountains North, page 143.
River Run RV Resort, Central Mountains North, page 148.
Reverend's Ridge, The Front Range, page 235.
Cherry Creek State Park, The Front Range, page 240.
Ouray KOA, Four Corners and the San Juan Mountains, page 265.
Dolores River Campground, Four Corners and the San Juan Mountains, page 259.
Castle Lakes Resort, Four Corners and the San Juan Mountains, page 280.
Mosca, San Luis Valley and the Sangre de Cristos, page 307.

BEST❰ Lakeside Campgrounds

Dutch Hill, Western Slope North, page 51.
Deep Lake, Western Slope North, page 75.
Lost Lake, Western Slope South, page 102.
Silver Jack, Western Slope South, page 133.
Arapaho Bay, Central Mountains North, page 147.
May Queen, Central Mountains South, page 172.
Backcountry, Central Mountains South, page 188.
Boat-in, The Front Range, page 215.
Haviland Lake, Four Corners and the San Juan Mountains, page 268.
Teal, Four Corners and the San Juan Mountains, page 289.

Camping Tips

ENJOYING THE OUTDOORS

Most of the campground listings in this guidebook are developed, frontcountry campgrounds designed for tents and RVs. Some of these campgrounds are at the end of long dirt roads through remote forests, and many are along paved roads, offering a standard package of tent pad, picnic table, fire pit, and composting vault toilet. Some campgrounds are secluded, primitive, remote paradises. Others are more like little villages, complete with the hustle and bustle. For some people, frontcountry campgrounds serve only as launching pads for forays deeper into the wilderness. For others, the campground itself is the destination. All types mix easily at Colorado's campgrounds, where the elevation and mountain air seem to make people friendlier. Colorado's campgrounds are varied, but most can accommodate families and some have group facilities and are wheelchair-accessible. As the state's urban centers grow, especially Denver and the Front Range, campgrounds within a few hours' drive are increasingly busy throughout the summer and into the fall. The general trend in Colorado has been toward accepting reservations at more sites and offering additional lodging options like yurts, cabins, and tepees. Another trend is the advent of campsite and camper/RV-sharing apps, which are increasing the number of sites and situations possible.

Campsite Courtesy

The U.S. Forest Service, National Park Service, and Colorado Parks and Wildlife have built campgrounds in nearly every nook and cranny of the state. Some are now managed by private concessionaires. In more remote areas, the campsites may be well spaced and you may have the place all to yourself, but increasingly, campgrounds are crowded or full, especially on weekends, making campsite courtesy more essential than ever. The most common violations of campsite courtesy include noise, litter, and impact on plants or wildlife:

NOISE

Always follow posted quiet hours, usually from 9pm to 6am or 10pm to 7am, especially if you are using a generator. While few things are as enjoyable as listening to musicians strum a guitar or pick a banjo around the campfire, remain respectful of your neighbors and leave the Bluetooth speakers at home. Late arrivers—or early risers—should also be as quiet as possible.

LITTER

Many campgrounds provide bear-proof garbage cans to dispose of the trash you create during your stay. Some don't and you should be prepared to pack out trash when receptacles are not available. Well-meaning campers often leave garbage in the fire rings, but this can attract animals. If in doubt, pack it out. Better yet, make a rule to leave the campsite cleaner than when you found it—and teach your children to do the same.

VANDALISM

Never carve your initials or name into trees, as it leaves them susceptible to disease. Graffiti on picnic tables and vault toilets—or bullet holes in signs—redirects limited funds away from needed campground improvements.

IMPACT

Learn and follow Leave No Trace principles for having as little impact as possible when spending time in the outdoors. Never cut down limbs or branches or remove leaves from trees in and around your site. Respect wildlife by not feeding or harassing animals, even if they visit your campsite. Keep your camp clean of food, especially if you're in bear country, so you don't tempt any animals to visit. Many campsites provide bear-proof storage lockers in which you can fit entire coolers full of food. Use them.

Control your leashed pets at all times and if you can't, leave them with a sitter at home. Many campgrounds prohibit hanging hammocks on trees to help protect the bark.

Camping with Children

For generations, camping has been one of the most affordable family vacations available. It has the potential to be an unforgettable adventure and learning experience for kids of all ages. Infants can go camping—just strap 'em on and bring enough diapers. Toddlers enjoy camping so much, they may get wound up on s'mores and have a hard time going to sleep. Elementary school-age children will unconsciously seize on the myriad of learning opportunities that come from being outdoors, from building fairy houses in the tree roots to participating in the Junior Ranger programs at national parks and monuments. Some tweens and teens will be more difficult to please—be sure to include them in the decision-making process and they're more likely to have fun. Here are some tips for keeping young kids happy:

- Keep trips short and within the physical abilities of a child.
- For babies and toddlers, it's often easier to strap them on your back/belly while you set up and break down camp.
- Include children in the planning process. Show them maps and photos of the destination so they can get excited about the trip. Ask for their input on activities and outings.
- Plan frequent activities, outings, and games, while keeping in mind their short attention spans. For young children, plan naps as well. Be flexible to accommodate weather and moods.
- Keep the campground safe for kids. Be aware of campfire and boiling-water hazards, and educate them on appropriate behavior in the woods and around wildlife. A good rule to teach from a young age is no running in the campground.
- Pack appropriate clothing and gear. Children need layers too, so be sure to bring long underwear, warm layers, rain gear, hats, and sunglasses. Bring a child's backpack with his or her own water and snacks, whistle, first-aid kit, magnifying glass, sunblock and insect repellent, compass and watch, flashlight, hiking map, and notebook.
- Let them help around the campsite with setting up and sweeping out the tent, pumping water, cooking meals, washing dishes, and planning activities.
- Keep it fun so they'll want to go again year after year.

Camping with Pets

Bring your pets only if you can comply with the following rules:

- Keep pets on a leash at all times. Loose pets disturb the homes and habitats of native wildlife, not to mention fellow campers.
- Never leave pets unattended at the campground.
- Don't allow dogs to bark at or intimidate other campers or wildlife.
- Consider using a Bluetooth enabled pet-tracking device like Pawscout, to help quickly find your pet if it runs away.

RULES, REGULATIONS, AND RESERVATIONS

Rules vary between campgrounds, or more accurately, between how various branches of local, state, and federal governments (and their subcontracted concessionaires) manage their campgrounds. *Please note that all fees and rules in this guidebook were current as of Spring 2020 and are subject to change.*

National Parks and Monuments

Colorado has four national parks: Black Canyon of the Gunnison National Park, Great Sand Dunes National Park and Preserve, Mesa Verde National Park, and Rocky Mountain National Park. There are eight national monuments plus a selection of national recreation areas, historic sites, historic trails,

LEAVE NO TRACE

The Leave No Trace Center for Outdoor Ethics (800/332-4100, http://lnt.org) is an international educational program based in Boulder, Colorado that provides resources on how to minimize our impact on the lands we love so much. Follow their tips:

PLAN AHEAD AND PREPARE

- Know the regulations and special concerns for the area you'll visit.
- Prepare for extreme weather, hazards, and emergencies.
- Schedule your trip to avoid times of high use.
- Visit in small groups when possible. Consider splitting larger groups into smaller groups.
- Repackage food to minimize waste.
- Use a map and compass to eliminate the use of marking paint, rock cairns, or flagging.

TRAVEL AND CAMP ON DURABLE SURFACES

- Durable surfaces include established trails and campsites, rock, gravel, dry grasses, or snow.
- Protect riparian areas by camping at least 200 feet from lakes and streams.
- Good campsites are found, not made. Altering a site is not necessary.
- Concentrate use on existing trails and campsites.
- Walk single file in the middle of the trail, even when wet or muddy.
- Keep campsites small. Focus activity in areas where vegetation is absent.
- Disperse use to prevent the creation of campsites and trails.
- Avoid places where impacts are just beginning.

DISPOSE OF WASTE PROPERLY

- Pack it in, pack it out. Inspect your campsite and rest areas for trash or spilled foods. Pack out all trash, leftover food, and litter.
- Deposit solid human waste in "catholes" dug 6 to 8 inches deep, at least 200 feet from water, camp and trails. Cover and disguise the cathole when finished.
- Pack out toilet paper and hygiene products.
- To wash yourself or your dishes, carry water 200 feet away from streams or lakes and use small amounts of biodegradable soap. Scatter strained dishwater.

and national river corridors for good measure. Most allow camping by permit in the backcountry and most offer one or more frontcountry campgrounds. Many of these campgrounds are run by one of several private concessionaires that operate in Colorado, but are very basic. You'll usually find potable running water (but not always), bathrooms, but rarely hookups or electricity. They range from walk-in tent sites to RV parks. Fees and regulations vary, but most campsites are limited to eight people and two vehicles or one vehicle and one camping unit. Stay limits range from 7 days to 14 days. Leashed pets are permitted in campgrounds but are not allowed on trails or in the backcountry. Campfires are only allowed in fire rings and hammocks are prohibited on trees. At smaller campgrounds, trash must be packed out. At most national parks and monuments, you are not allowed to forage for firewood and must purchase firewood locally (to prevent the spread of disease). When fire restrictions are in place, follow them! Quiet hours are enforced by rangers and camp hosts. Permits are required for backcountry camping.

LEAVE WHAT YOU FIND

- Preserve the past: Examine, but do not touch cultural or historic structures and artifacts.
- Leave rocks, plants, and other natural objects as you find them.
- Avoid introducing or transporting nonnative species.
- Do not build structures or furniture, or dig trenches.

MINIMIZE CAMPFIRE IMPACTS

- Campfires can cause lasting impacts to the backcountry. Use a lightweight stove for cooking and enjoy a candle lantern for light.
- Where fires are permitted, use established fire rings, fire pans, or mound fires.
- Keep fires small. Only use sticks from the ground that can be broken by hand.
- Burn all wood and coals to ash, put out campfires completely, then scatter cool ashes.

RESPECT WILDLIFE

- Observe wildlife from a distance. Do not follow or approach them.
- Never feed animals. Feeding wildlife damages their health, alters natural behaviors, and exposes them to predators and other dangers.
- Protect wildlife and your food by storing rations and trash securely.
- Control pets at all times, or leave them at home.
- Avoid wildlife during sensitive times: mating, nesting, raising young, or winter.

BE CONSIDERATE OF OTHER VISITORS

- Respect other visitors and protect the quality of their experience.
- Be courteous. Yield to other users on the trail.
- Step to the downhill side of the trail when encountering pack stock.
- Take breaks and camp away from trails and other visitors.
- Let nature's sounds prevail. Avoid loud voices and noises.

(Copyright: The Leave No Trace Center for Outdoor Ethics.)

Reservations are required at many park campgrounds and can be made on the National Recreation Reservation System at 877/444-6777 or www.recreation.gov. There is a nonrefundable $10 reservation fee. Visitors must also purchase a park pass (price varies between parks and monuments) when entering the park; or you can use an America the Beautiful annual pass ($80), Senior Annual passes ($20), Senior Lifetime Passes ($80), military are free (must be active and have documentation), Every Kid in the Park (EKIP) is a free pass for 4th graders during their 4th grade year only, and they can have up to four adults in the car and no limit on kids.

National Forests

Colorado has 11 national forests and two national grasslands: Arapaho National Forest, Comanche National Grassland, Grand Mesa National Forest, Gunnison National Forest, Pawnee National Grassland, Pike National Forest, Rio Grande National Forest, Roosevelt National Forest, Medicine Bow-Routt National Forest, San Isabel National Forest, San Juan National Forest, Uncompahgre National Forest,

Kids will love the Junior Ranger program, available in National Parks, Monuments, Grasslands, and Historic Sites.

and White River National Forest. It's notable that White River National Forest encompasses 2.3 million acres and is the most visited forest in the United States; it has 11 ski resorts, eight wilderness areas, 10 fourteeners, and 2,500 miles of trails.

Most developed campgrounds in national forests are maintained and operated by private concessionaires, so regulations and fees vary. Campsites are usually limited to six or eight people and two camping units for a maximum stay of 14 consecutive days. Tents must be on pads if provided. Dogs must be leashed in the campground, and leashed or under voice command on trails. Campfires are limited to fire rings. Hammocks and laundry lines cannot be hung from trees. Trash receptacles and bear lockers are frequently provided. Rules are enforced and facilities are cleaned by camp hosts at busy campgrounds. More remote campgrounds are less frequently cleaned and maintained by rangers or camp hosts.

Many USFS campground are first come first served, but many require reservations up to six months in advance, and if you're looking to camp on a weekend, you better book it the full six months in advance. Use the National Recreation Reservation System at 877/444-6777 or www.recreation.gov. For some campgrounds, there is an additional reservation fee of up to $10 per night.

Senior Annual passes are $20 year, Senior Lifetime Passes are $80, Annual Pass is $80, military are free (must be active and have documentation), Every Kid in the Park (EKIP) is a free pass for 4th graders (only during their 4th grade year) who can have up to four adults in the car and no limit on kids. National Forests with entrance fees also accept America the Beautiful National Park and Federal Recreation Lands Passes.

State Parks and Forests

In Colorado, there are 41 state parks, managed by Colorado Parks & Wildlife (CPW). CPW manages more than 4,000 campsites, ranging from primitive backcountry sites for those who desire seclusion to full-hookup sites on the

BEFORE YOU GO

- Learn about the regulations and any special concerns that apply to the area you're going to visit. What are the elevation and projected conditions?
- Obtain maps, permits, and emergency contact numbers in advance.
- Plan your trip and give a copy of your itinerary to a friend. Be clear about where you are going and when you expect to return.
- Plan your meals and do your grocery shopping in advance so that you have a stock of at least a few meals and a few gallons of water in the car.
- Make a checklist for gear, clothing, and food. Check it off as you pack.
- Check the condition of your gear and pack appropriate clothing for weather extremes. In Colorado, this often means being prepared for all four seasons at any time of year.
- Run last-minute errands (including going to the bank and gas station) and pack the car the night before you leave.
- Double-check the weather forecast for any surprises. Check road conditions, closures, and current construction at www.cotrip.org.

shores of massive reservoirs. State park campgrounds usually have potable water and frequently have electrical or full hookups. Flush toilet bathrooms, laundry facilities, and showers are also common. Camping fees include one camping unit for up to six people. A camping unit is defined as one passenger vehicle and two tents, or one motorized vehicle towing a camping trailer and one tent (if space allows). If space permits, one additional passenger vehicle and/or motorcycle may be parked at a campsite. There is a 14-day maximum stay allowed per park during any 45-day period. This may be 14 consecutive days or 14 days spread throughout the 45 days. Parents or guardians must accompany minors. Where pets are allowed, they must be on a six-foot leash unless utilizing one of the two off-leash dog areas at Cherry Creek State Park or Chatfield State Park. Alcoholic beverages are allowed at Colorado's state parks, but bring cans not glass and enjoy responsibly. Quiet hours are from 10 pm to 6 am and are enforced by camp hosts.

Since January 2019, all state park campgrounds are reservation only, which you can make 24/7 at www.cpwshop.com or by calling 800/244-5613 (ReserveAmerica.com has limited functionality for CPW customers). This allows campers to see what is available at the minute they hope to book, eliminating the prior three-day window where reservations could no longer be made and guests had to hope for an open first-come, first-served site. If you have questions about the changes, contact the CPW call center at 303/297-1192. Campers at state parks must also purchase a Daily Park Pass ($8) or an Annual Parks Pass ($80 per vehicle). You can also get an Annual Hangtag pass ($120), which is issued to individuals, not vehicles, and can be moved between vehicles. There are also: Aspen Leaf Passes ($70 per vehicle for Coloradans over 64 and over), Columbine Passes for Disabled Colorado Residents ($14), Disabled Veterans Passes (no cost), Centennial Passes for "income-eligible Colorado residents" ($14), Blue Spruce pass for disabled First Responders (no cost), Individual Daily Passes for walk-in/bike in access to select parks ($4) and Senior Lifetime Passes.

Colorado's state parks hire temporary and volunteer campground hosts. Hosts usually receive a free campsite and utilities in exchange for greeting campers, helping them check in, and keeping the facilities clean. To find out more, visit https://cpw.state.co.us/aboutus/Pages/Temporary-Positions.aspx.

Commercial Campgrounds

In addition to the hundreds of campgrounds on public lands (most of which are managed by private concessionaires), there are numerous private, for-profit campgrounds on private land, including several chains found elsewhere

Follow all posted rules and regulations, especially regarding quiet hours and fire restrictions.

in the country. There are 27 Kampground of America (KOA) campgrounds around Colorado (out of 500 total campgrounds nationwide). I've included a handful of the more pleasant, popular, or strategic Colorado KOAs in this book, but please know there are more out there, especially around bigger population centers (browse them on the KOA app). There are also three franchises of the Jellystone Park Camp Resorts in Colorado (in Larkspur, Estes Park, and Montrose), which are fun for families. Lately there are a few higher priced, modern campgrounds popping up, with glamping tents and cabins, and other amenities; examples are River Run RV Resort in Granby, Echo Canyon Campround near Cañon City, and Platte River Fort Campground in Kersey.

CAMPING GEAR

Colorado is one of the epicenters of the world's outdoor gear industry. Denver hosts the renowned Outdoor Retailer shows throughout the year, and the state is home to scores of companies producing the latest tents, sleeping bags, stoves, climbing gear, and apparel. Visit the

REI Flagship store on the banks of the Platte River in downtown Denver (1416 Platte St., tel. 303/756-3100) to browse the latest camping and hiking gear, much of which is also available for rental.

Tents

Your options range from stringing a tarp between a few trees and crawling under it, to wall tents with integrated lighting and multiple entrances. Before you start looking at tents, ask yourself the following questions:

What time of year and at what altitude will I be camping? Sporting goods and camping gear companies make summer, three-season, and four-season tents, and prices increase dramatically with the number of seasons covered. In my opinion, three-season tents offer the best compromise between price and utility, especially since Colorado weather can easily span three seasons in a single day.

How many people will use this tent? If you are young and childless, a two-person tent will do the trick, with room for your sleeping pad and backpack and/or Labrador. You can

CAMPGROUND SHARING APPS

APPS FOR FINDING CAMPSITES:

Campsite-sharing apps are all the rage, for finding and booking traditional campgrounds on public lands, and also to explore the newly opened world of individuals renting out campgrounds or glamping sites on private land. Here are a few:

- **The Dyrt** (free, Apple iOS and Android) allows you to search, review and reserve campgrounds, based on crowdsourced, user-generated information regarding tent and RV sites, plus a few cabins. The Dyrt maintains an online space "for campers to connect with other campers" and boasts many thousands of reviews, campground photos, and videos for the 1,300 campgrounds it has listed in Colorado (out of some 35,000 total campgrounds nationally). The Dyrt also has direct-booking capability and millions of users.

- **Hipcamp** (free, Apple iOS) is a camping and glamping list with 750 campground listings in Colorado, including private and public campgrounds. *Outside* magazine's article, "Hipcamp Just Made Booking Campsites Way Less Terrible," reports on the company's efforts to keep public lands campground info open and accessible.

- **Campendium** (free, iOS only) is another crowd-sourced database of campgrounds (28,000 nationwide), vetted and reviewed by nearly 200,000 members. They host an online community of campers who share site photos, GPS coordinates, camping fee updates, reviews and reports on local cell carrier coverage. The app has single-tap search for nearby RV parks, campgrounds on public lands, free camping sites, RV hookups, overnight parking, and dump stations.

- **Tentrr** (free, iOS only) specializes in upscale campsites, or "glampsites" on private land, and usually includes most of the gear you'll need, making this service ideal for city-dwellers who don't have their own camping gear. Tentrr also connects you to "CampKeepers," or local hosts with "the inside info on all the secret swimming holes, best nearby adventures and quality local provisions." At most Tentrr sites, you get a canvas tent on a wood platform, wooden camp chairs, fire pit, portable toilet, cookware and a queen-sized air mattress. In addition to glamping, they also list affordable primitive tent sites (which require you to bring your own tent and gear) located on private property.

- **Wikicamps USA** ($2.99, iOS only) is another powerful, crowdsourced database of campgrounds, but it has the added benefit of working offline when there is no cell service. You just have to pre-plot campsites, then download a personalized map onto your device before heading off-grid. Campground searches can be filtered by things like toilets, showers, hookups and pet-friendliness. In addition to basic details, each campground listing has user ratings, user reviews, prices, photos, and a weather forecast.

FOR FINDING FREE CAMPSITES:

Free Campsites (free, Android) is a community-driven platform for finding campgrounds and campsites. **Boondockers Welcome** ($30/year, www.boondockerswelcome.com) is a network of landowners who will let you boondock, or park your RV for free, on their property. Your RV must be self-contained (i.e. all sleeping, eating, cooking and sanitation must happen inside the vehicle, especially a toilet system and a built-in grey water tank). Founder Marianne Edwards calls it, "the driveway equivalent of couch-surfing," which "saves on camping fees, builds community, and beats staying in a Walmart parking lot." Hosts pay nothing and RVers pay a $30 annual subscription for an unlimited number of stays at any of the 44 host locations in Colorado (or the 1,700 host locations across North America).

go even smaller, with a one-person bivvy sack or a netted hammock. If you are family camping with the Brady Bunch, there are tents with multiple rooms, windows, shelves, and even doggy doors.

Will I be car camping or backpacking? It's all about weight. If you're backpacking, you should buy the lightest tent you can afford. Car-camping tents are generally heavier, larger, and less expensive than tents intended for the backcountry (you can take a backpacking tent car camping, but you won't want to take a car-camping tent into the backcountry).

How often and how long will I use this tent? A good tent can last a lifetime if it's regularly maintained and properly stored. If you plan on camping frequently, buy the best tent you can afford. If you only go once or twice a year, save your money for the perfect sleeping bag.

Sleeping Bags and Pads

A sleeping bag doesn't produce heat; it can only trap the heat your body generates. The heat is retained in the air trapped in the bag's insulation. More loft equals more air and that equals more warmth. Sleeping bags are sold by temperature rating, size, and shape, and their prices are determined by type of construction and material. Unless you are doing winter camping or mountaineering, you'll want a general purpose, three-season sleeping bag.

Temperature Rating: This is the lowest temperature at which the bag will keep you warm. Because there's no universal standard, it's determined by individual manufacturers. Therefore, temperature ratings are consistent within brands but not necessarily between brands, and to complicate the matter further, individuals have different sleeping temperatures (women usually sleep colder than men). As a rule of thumb, figure out the coldest temperature that you'll experience and then pick a bag that's rated 10 degrees colder than that. Zero-degree bags are a safe bet for summers and falls at high altitude, and on warm evenings you can always unzip them.

Size and Shape: Most bags now come in regular and long lengths. Extra air in a bag is difficult to heat and adds extra weight, but a small bag can make you claustrophobic. Pick the smallest bag in which you can comfortably sleep. Bags come in three cuts: mummy, rectangular, and semi-rectangular. Mummy bags are the narrowest and most efficient. Rectangular bags have room for tossing and turning but are not very efficient, and semi-rectangular bags are a good compromise between efficiency and comfort. Some companies are also making specific bags for women that are cut to accommodate narrower shoulders, wider hips, and colder sleeping temperatures.

Construction: A quality sleeping bag has a hood with a drawstring (you should be able to draw it tight and still breathe) and a draft collar. Humans lose 50 percent of their body heat through the head, so these features greatly increase the efficiency of a bag. You should be able to wear a hat inside the hood. A good bag also has a comfortable foot box, a sturdy zipper with an insulated flap, and a lifetime warranty. Sleeping bags are built with baffling to keep the insulation material evenly distributed. Baffles should run horizontally across the body. Box, slant, and V-tube baffles have the best heat retention properties.

Materials: A sleeping bag consists of a shell and fill material. The shell is usually a synthetic material with a water-repellent finish. Waterproof shells are not recommended because they trap moisture inside the bag. Fills are down or synthetic, and this can be the hardest decision to make when shopping for a bag. Down is more expensive, but it is superior for the insulation-to-weight ratio. If you are backpacking in a dry climate (most of Colorado), go with down. If you are car camping, synthetic is an excellent alternative. It is bulkier and heavier than down, but it's also less expensive, more durable, and it stays warm when wet (down doesn't). Synthetic fills come in a variety of brand names.

Sleeping Pads: Sleeping pads provide not only cushioning but insulation against the cold

CAMPER AND RV RENTALS

If you don't have your own camper, there are many rental possibilities in Colorado.

In addition to camper/RV sharing apps, there are plenty of rental companies, most based around Denver and the Front Range. Most companies reserve far in advance, and many are booked all summer, so plan ahead.

RV AND CAMPER RENTALS:

•**LazyDays RV** (970/278-1900, Lazydays.com,) Lazydays RV has a variety of campers for rent (or purchase) at its Denver and Loveland locations, from small motorhomes that sleep two people, to larger trailers and motorhomes that can accommodate a large family or group of friends.

•**All Stars RV** (Louviers, 720/348-0404, www.allstarsrv.com) has 35-40 units for rent (22 to 31-feet long) at a lot 6.5 miles south of C-470. They are the Denver dealer for El Monte RV, with pick up or drop off locations around the United States.

•**Colorado Camper Rental** (Denver, 303/443-1422, www.coloradocamperrental.com) has a large selection of towable travel trailers and pop-up campers for rent. They are located one mile east of I-25, off 58th Avenue. Rates are from $82 a day.

• **Colorado Teardrops** (720/432-6817, www.coloradoteardropcamper.com, offers a variety of lightweight teardrop-style trailers. Their trailers are compact enough to be pulled by almost any car, insulated for all four seasons, and spacious enough for a family (larger models feature a queen bed and 2 bunk beds). Rental prices vary, starting at around $85 a day.

• **Rocky Mountain Campervans** (720/593-0433, www.rockymountaincampervans.com) rents Custom Promasters Conversion Campers, Volkswagen Eurovans, Vanagons, and buses outfitted for camping. They operate year-round, even during ski season. Most vehicles have pop-tops, two beds (sleep 4), a sink, a refrigerator, and a stovetop. Rates are roughly $150-290 a night. One-way rentals to or from their second location in Las Vegas, Nevada (or other major cities) are possible, too.

APPS FOR RENTING VANS, CAMPERS, TEARDROPS, AND RVS:

• Outdoorsy (free, iOS) and RVshare (www.rvshare.com, online only) are two of the most popular peer-to-peer RV-sharing networks. Many renters list their vehicle on both sites. Both provide a reliable marketplace for renters and owners to list and book RVs, and both offer 24/7 roadside assistance and travel concierge services for travelers. Simply download the apps, open them up, and start browsing all the available campers in your town.

ground. Some pads come with a converter kit to turn into a camp chair. Sleeping pads come in four types: self-inflating, backpacking air pad, foam pads, and air mattresses. Foam pads are lighter, more durable, and less expensive. Self-inflating pads and backpacking air pads (some models include fill insulation to increase warmth) are more expensive and require more care, but they are a heck of a lot more comfortable. Both types come in a variety of sizes and thicknesses designed for specific activities. Newer pads have integrated foot pumps and instant deflate valves for even quicker setup and takedown.

Cooking Gear and Food

Dehydrated, prepackaged meals (Mountain House and Good To-Go are several brands that cater to campers) are a great choice for saving weight in the backcountry or saving time at the campground—but at roughly $7 per meal, such meals may not be sustainable—especially since you're not really limited by food weight when car camping. Inexpensive grains like pasta, couscous, and oatmeal go a long way. Whatever you're packing, there are a few equipment essentials: lightweight nesting pots, a metal pot grabber, insulated mugs, a lighter and matches, utensil kit, and a strainer so you can do the dishes without leaving behind bits of food. Of course, you'll want your favorite coffee-making device, frying pan, and a "sink," which I make with a few plastic washbasins and a bottle of Pure-Castile Liquid Soap (Dr. Bronner's or Purist are two earth-friendly soaps for washing both dishes and hands). A few dry dishrags are also indispensable.

Cooking over a campfire may be romantic, but in reality it can be difficult, time consuming, and not very efficient. The fire needs to be just right, you need some kind of grill, and your pots will turn black from the carbon. One alternative is to cook with a Dutch oven, an old-school cast-iron cooking pot with thick walls and a snug-fitting lid. Campers who have mastered the slow-cooking Dutch oven method often prepare elaborate layered lasagnas or enchiladas beforehand in the pot, then just place it in the coals at the campsite and kick back until dinner's done.

The most popular option is a camping stove. These range from small, lightweight liquid-gas backpacking stoves to multi-burner tabletop and freestanding car-camping stoves and even barbecues. The middle ground is some type of tabletop unit that fits across the end of a picnic table. Coleman USA, based in Golden, Colorado, is the most long-standing camp stove manufacturer and is constantly tinkering with its windproof line of stoves and portable grills.

Keep in Mind: Windscreens and stove repair kits are extremely useful, as are carrying cases to keep the stove from getting everything else in your backpack dirty or greasy. A stove should have an adjustable flame. Push-button stoves are convenient, but you should always pack a lighter or matches. Never, ever use a stove inside a tent or cabin. Not only are tents flammable, they can also fill up with dangerous carbon monoxide.

Water Treatment

Developed campgrounds usually have safe drinking water but many don't. I've tried to specify all of them in this book, but it's always smart to have 2–5 extra gallons of water in your car, just in case, and some means of treating water from rivers and lakes. The simplest treatment method is to boil it. Boiling river water kills all harmful organisms. The next is a filter, SteriPEN, or iodine tablets. If you're heading into the backcountry, you'll need to treat all your water. Tablets require a little patience and taste a little funny, but they are foolproof and easy to use. Pump filters are used by the majority of backpackers. Ceramic filters are reliable, long lasting, and easy to replace. Be sure to air out your filter between uses.

Navigation

MAP AND COMPASS

An old-fashioned paper map and compass (in addition to the GPS app on your phone) are essential, and make sure you know how to use them. It's a good excuse to take a short course on navigation at your local REI or mountain shop, or check with the nearest orienteering club for classes. Regional maps are often distributed at trailheads and visitors centers, and U.S. Forest Service (USFS) ranger stations have motor vehicle maps of their district and neighboring districts that are essential if you are going off the highway. For a true "lay of the land" map, you'll need a topographic, or topo, map, which uses contour lines to indicate elevation, steepness, and the location of natural features. A topo map combined with a basic compass are essential if you step off the trail or travel into the backcountry. Topo maps come in many scales; the most popular for backpacking is 1:24,000. You can find these at your local mountain shop, order them from the United States Geological Survey, or download them onto your phone or device for offline use. For navigating in the car, a copy of the *Colorado Atlas & Gazetteer* is indispensable. There are some excellent and inexpensive map and tracking apps out there now to add to your arsenal.

GPS

GPS receivers use a system of 24 orbiting satellites operated by the U.S. Department of Defense to triangulate the unit's position. GPS receivers work day and night, rain or shine, although their effectiveness is affected by the gadget's type of antenna, processor chip, software, memory, and screen type. GPS receivers (or your phone via one of many GPS apps) can be used for determining your location and track, navigating from point-to-point, and entering and storing waypoints and routes. GPS receivers are incredibly useful in the backcountry, but always carry a paper map and basic compass for backup. One way to learn how your GPS app/device works is to practice geocaching, an activity available at some of the campgrounds in this book.

CLOTHING
What to Wear

Whether you're car camping for a weekend or traveling into the backcountry for a week, the right clothing can be the difference between a trip you cherish and a disaster you'd like to forget. The key to success is dressing in layers: a base layer that manages moisture, a middle layer for insulation, and an outer layer that protects you from wind and rain. None of these layers should contain cotton, which cannot keep you warm when it gets wet with sweat or rain.

In the summer, when you're most likely to experience hot, sunny days and afternoon thunderstorms, dress to stay cool and dry. Your base layer should include silk or synthetic briefs

Bring the essentials. Plus, welding gloves and an axe are helpful for campfires.

CAMPFIRE SAFETY

Where fires are permitted, use existing fire rings away from large rocks or overhangs.

• Scattered campfire areas can scar the backcountry. If a fire ring is not available, use a camp stove for cooking.

• Where fires are permitted, use existing fire rings away from large rocks or overhangs.

• Don't char rocks by building new fire rings.

• Don't gather firewood anywhere where it is prohibited. This includes most national park campgrounds in Colorado.

• Don't snap branches off live trees. You'll hurt the tree and live wood doesn't burn well.

• Put the fire "dead out" and make sure it's cold before departing. Check by running the top of your hand a few inches over the drowned fire to feel for heat.

• Do remove all trash and food scraps from the fire ring and sprinkle dirt over the site.

• Remember that some forest fires can be started by a campfire that appears to be extinguished. Hot embers burning deep in the pit can cause tree roots to catch fire and burn underground. Check if it's out and check again before leaving.

• Don't bring in firewood from out of state. Colorado Parks & Wildlife warns visitors that bringing firewood can spread pests and diseases. To protect the lands, buy local.

and a sports bra with a mesh tank or tee and lightweight shorts that transport moisture away from your skin. If you are fair skinned, are spending an extended amount of time at high elevations, or are selecting clothing for children, you could also consider base layers with an ultraviolet protection factor (UPF) rating. All fabrics interfere with ultraviolet (UV) radiation transmission to some extent, but clothing with a high UPF rating (between 25 and 50+) uses fiber, construction, dyes, or treatments to increase your protection. If you have any concern about UV radiation, skin cancer, or burning, a long-sleeved, lightweight top, lightweight pants, and a hat with high UPF ratings are essential for summer activities.

You'll also want an insulating layer for cool afternoons and evenings. A lightweight fleece or wool sweater or even a lightweight synthetic or down vest can keep you warm after a storm and once the sun starts to set. If I'm camping at high altitudes, I'll even bring a down sweater. Ultra-thin merino wool is effective, too.

Finally, bring a light shell for when afternoon thunderstorms roll in. A shell should block the wind and keep you dry. Choose your shell based on the weather you expect to encounter, your activity level, and the duration of the trip. When I'm participating in high-energy activities like backcountry skiing or running, a water-resistant/breathable shell or soft shell is often adequate in Colorado's relatively dry winters, but if I expect to be fairly inactive, I prefer an insulated shell.

In the fall or winter, when low temperatures and snow are more likely, dress to stay cool during periods of high activity, warm during periods of low activity, and dry. For a base layer, wear silk, synthetic, or merino wool thermal underwear. Choose light, mid-weight, or expedition-weight garments depending on the season and conditions. For insulation, a merino wool sweater or fleece jacket (possibly with wind proofing) will trap warm air close to your body while transporting moisture away from your skin. If you expect to encounter very cold conditions, don't leave home without a down sweater or vest.

Hiking Shoes and Socks

Many visitors to Colorado's campgrounds enjoy taking to the trails. Before you leave home, think carefully about the kind of footwear you'll need for this trip. Consider the shoe's cut, the upper material and construction, midsole materials, support components, and the outsole. If you are enjoying day hikes in pleasant weather, a low- or mid-cut boot of synthetic and/or split-grain leather can provide protection and breathability. If you expect to spend a lot of time in and out of water, sandals or hybrid shoes like Keens might even be appropriate. If you are a backpacker who's carrying moderate to heavy loads, you're more likely to need a high-cut boot made from full-grain leather or a combination of split-grain leather and synthetic materials, with steel or plastic shanks for support.

Don't forget that your footwear is only as good as the socks inside. Cotton is the kiss of death in both hot and cold weather. Many companies now sells liners, lightweight hiking socks, mid-weight backpacking socks, and mountaineering socks in wool, synthetics, and silk. The best combination of socks depends on your body temperature and activity level. Whenever possible, test your socks out before you take them camping and hiking.

HIKING FOOTCARE

Sore feet and blisters are often an inevitable part of backpacking and camping, but planning ahead can keep them from ruining your trip.

- Make sure your shoes fit well and break them in before hitting the trail.

- Pack the right socks and liners for your activity level. Like shoes, socks are best when test-driven at home.

- Treat hot spots as soon as they appear. You'll need to keep moleskin, blister bandages, or (my personal favorite) duct tape, as well as antibiotic ointment in your first-aid kit in order to treat hot spots appropriately.

- Pack a lightweight pair of comfortable camp shoes so you can give your tired paws a break around the campfire.

- If sore arches, aching heels, or lower-back pain regularly prevent you from enjoying hiking and camping, try store-bought or custom-made inserts for extra support.

CLIMATE AND WEATHER

In Colorado, goes the old saying, if you don't like the weather, wait five minutes. Colorado's weather does change rapidly, not just with time but also with elevation and orientation. Colorado can be split into three topographical areas, each with its own climate patterns. In the east, the high plains slope upwards for 200 miles from Kansas and Nebraska to the base of the foothills, where elevations are 5,000 to 6,500 feet. The foothills rise to 7,000 to 9,000 feet and are backed by the mountain ranges, which climb from 9,000 to over 14,000 feet. This portion of Colorado straddles the highest peaks of the Continental Divide. West of the mountain ranges, a rugged plateau country of mesas and canyons extends to the border with Utah. Much of the state has a high-desert climate.

Seasons

In the eastern plains, the climate features low humidity and precipitation, abundant sunshine, moderate to high winds, and a large daily and seasonal range in temperature. These characteristics result in dry winters with very cold temperatures; windy springs with occasional blizzards; dry summers with hot days, cool nights, and big thunderstorms and hail storms;

COLORADO'S FOURTEENERS

Fourteeners are peaks rising above 14,000 feet of elevation. In Colorado, there are 53 fourteeners—or 54, or 59, depending on who you ask and how you count the saddles between peaks. Yes, true peak-baggers take their mountain-counting seriously. The majority of fourteeners have nontechnical walk-up routes, but some require technical climbing and mountaineering skills. There are numerous guides to take you up many fourteeners safely. The Fourteeners Initiative is also a valuable source of information. The mission of this nonprofit organization is to protect and preserve the integrity of these peaks through stewardship and public education. The **Fourteeners Initiative** (Golden, 303/278-7650, www.14ers.org) offers volunteer opportunities to help preserve and protect these peaks, including field projects, trail maintenance, and the Adopt-a-Peak and Peak Steward programs. The following list groups the fourteeners by mountain range:

- **Front Range:** Longs Peak, Torreys Peak, Grays Peak, Mount Evans, Mount Bierstadt, Pikes Peak.
- **Mosquito Range:** Quandary Peak, Mount Democrat, Mount Lincoln, Mount Bross, Mount Sherman.
- **Sawatch Range:** Mount of the Holy Cross, Mount Massive, Mount Elbert, La Plata Peak, Huron Peak, Missouri Mountain, Mount Belford, Mount Oxford, Mount Harvard, Mount Columbia, Mount Yale, Mount Princeton, Mount Antero, Mount Shavano, Tabeguache Mountain.
- **Sangre de Cristo Range:** Kit Carson Peak, Crestone Peak, Crestone Needle, Humboldt Peak, Ellingwood Point, Little Bear Peak, Blanca Peak, Mount Lindsey, Culebra Peak.
- **Elk Mountains:** Capitol Peak, Snowmass Mountain, North Maroon Peak, South Maroon Peak, Pyramid Peak, Castle Peak.
- **San Juan Mountains:** Wetterhorn Peak, Uncompahgre Peak, Mount Sneffels, San Luis Peak, El Diente Peak, Mount Wilson, Wilson Peak, Handies Peak, Redcloud Peak, Sunshine Peak, Mount Eolus, Sunlight Peak, Windom Peak.

COLORADO'S THIRTEENERS

Fourteeners too trendy for you? Want to avoid the crowds—and that last thousand-foot slog to the summit? Colorado has 832 peaks rising above 13,000 feet of elevation! That'll still get you way above treeline and on top of the world. There are numerous guidebooks out there that focus specifically on hiking these thirteeners. Some of these peaks are more technical than fourteeners, and others are non-technical walk-ups. Three recommended mountains to try are Atlantic Peak, James Peak, and Geissler Peak according to James Dziezynski, author of *Hiking Colorado* (Falcon Guides). All standard mountain and wilderness precautions should be taken for these mountains as you would with fourteeners.

and a dry, comfortable autumn. The corridor along the foothills, where most of Colorado's population is, enjoys milder temperatures than the eastern plains, including warming Chinook winds in the winter.

In the mountains, climate varies dramatically with elevation and orientation. Precipitation increases with elevation and falls mainly on mountaintops and west-facing slopes. Generally, temperatures decrease with elevation, but mountain valleys can experience inversions, which result in colder temperatures at lower elevations. This phenomenon is especially common in the San Luis, Gunnison, Yampa, Eagle, and Fraser Valleys. Wind patterns depend on topography, but tend to be stronger east of the Continental Divide. Strong winds are common above the tree line and may exceed 50 or even 100 miles per hour in the winter. In the summer, afternoon thunderstorms are typical and can include hail, snow, and lightning.

In the canyonlands and plateaus of western Colorado, precipitation decreases and temperatures increase towards Utah. Most precipitation falls in the winters, which feature moderate temperatures at lower elevations. The valleys and canyons can get quite hot in the summers, but a short drive to higher elevation brings cooler temperatures. Wind patterns also depend on local topography, but tend to be less severe than in the mountains.

Winter Camping

Though most of Colorado's developed campgrounds close down in the early fall before the snow starts flying, many stay open into the winter, often at a reduced fee and/or without basic services like running water. If you choose to camp in the winter, whether you're in the frontcountry or backcountry, plan ahead to avoid the two biggest threats: frostbite and hypothermia. Dress in warm layers of wool, fleece, and down, and wear an outer layer that's wind- and waterproof. Choose a four-season tent that will keep out the weather, and take care to keep snow and moisture out of it. (Don't plan on sleeping in an igloo or snow cave unless you have an experienced friend to show you how to do this correctly.) You'll need a high-quality sleeping bag, preferably mummy style with a hood, and a sleeping pad. Plan on sleeping in your long underwear and a warm hat. Eat lots of food! Your body needs calories to burn, especially calories from fat and protein. Finally, travel with a reliable buddy and educate yourself on Colorado's winter weather and hazards. The Colorado Avalanche Information Center is an amazing resource for winter-sports enthusiasts. Follow weather and avalanche forecasts on its website (avalanche.state.co.us) and consider taking a class on avalanche safety.

Desert Camping

You'll find high-desert environments across much of the state, more than you'd expect if you only have pictures of the lush mountain forests in your mind. This may mean high temperatures, low humidity, and very little shade, especially at campgrounds in Dinosaur National Monument, Colorado National Monument, Mesa Verde National Park, and Great Sand Dunes National Park. The biggest challenge of desert camping is the sun; you'll need a hat, sunglasses, sunscreen, lip balm with a sun protection factor (SPF), and plenty of water. Don't plan on finding water once you leave the interstate or the trailhead. Bring everything you need with you. You may be able to go without a tent, but a tarp can be a great source of shade. Be prepared for cold temperatures at night by bringing plenty of warm clothing (yes, you may want that down jacket) and a good sleeping bag. Try acting like the wildlife by adapting crepuscular habits. In other words, be active in the morning and evening when it's cool, and use the hottest hours of the day to rest. Finally, keep an eye on conservation while you're traveling in this delicate ecosystem. Never camp or walk on cryptobiotic soil, a castle-like crust of algae, fungi, moss, and other microscopic organisms that prevent erosion and take hundreds of years to grow.

Weather Fronts

"Everybody out of the river!" I shouted to my family the moment I saw the lightning-driven cold front headed straight toward us. We were camping in Dinosaur National Monument along the Green River, but this scenario could have taken place anywhere in Colorado. Before we'd even dried off and gotten back to our camp, a terrific squall collapsed half of our tent and attempted to toss our 12-by-12-foot shade structure across the river. My wife and I clung to it with all our strength as the rest of our camp was blown apart and the kids scrambled into the car. The temperature plummeted, everything got soaked, and then it all passed as quickly as it came. Colorado storm fronts can move at 30-50 miles per hour and will test all your campcraft skills. Be prepared for sudden changes in the weather throughout the summer months, especially in the afternoon.

WEATHER INDICATORS

- Cows lying in the field are a sign of rain.
- Geese fly low before bad weather arrives.
- Fish bite before rain.
- Smoke stays near the ground before a storm.
- Cottonwoods show the bottom of their leaves before rain.
- Woodpeckers call before rain falls.
- Dew on the grass means it won't rain.
- Rings around the moon are a sign of coming rain.
- Spiders spin long webs on hot, dry days and short webs when bad weather is coming.
- Cloud and lightning icons on your phone's weather app indicate possible afternoon showers.

Cold fronts are associated with high-pressure systems. They contain heavy, dense air that pushes warm air upward ahead of it. In general, the arrival of a cold front brings strong winds, low temperatures, poor visibility, and heavy but brief precipitation, followed by fine weather with occasional showers and clear skies.

Warm fronts are associated with low-pressure systems. They contain warm, light air compared to cold air, which they will overrun. Rising temperatures and continuous rain and snow indicate an approaching warm front. The front is followed by high clouds, intermittent showers, and poor visibility.

CLASSIFYING CLOUDS

Clouds are formed when water droplets condense in the air.

High clouds occur at 16,500-45,000 feet. They include cirrus, cirrostratus, and cirrocumulus. Cirrus clouds are high, thin clouds of ice crystals that are common in the Rocky Mountains.

Middle clouds occur at 6,500-25,000 feet. They include altocumulus, altostratus, and cumulonimbus clouds. Altostratus appear as a thick, gray sheet of clouds. They are common in the Rocky Mountains. When they thicken, rain or snow is approaching quickly.

Low clouds occur from the surface to 6,500 feet. They include stratus, nimbostratus, and stratocumulus clouds. Stratus are low, gray clouds that become fog close to the surface. When they rain, they're called nimbostratus.

Vertical clouds extend from 1,600 feet up. They include cumulus, towering cumulus, and cumulonimbus clouds, often called thunderheads. Cumulus forms at the top of rising air. When they grow rapidly, they become cumulonimbus, which are common in the summer and bring lightning, heavy rain, and high winds.

Orographic clouds are formed by the interaction of air flow and mountainous terrain. They include cap clouds, which "cap" mountain summits, and lenticular clouds. These lens-shaped clouds form when strong winds blow over rugged terrain. They form on the lee side of mountains and ridges, the side sheltered from the wind, and may by stacked in layers like pancakes.

READING THE WEATHER

Storms Approaching: Cirrus clouds thicken from the south or west and become altostratus clouds. Several layers of clouds move in at various altitudes. Lenticular clouds become ragged. A change in wind direction accompanies a rapid temperature change.

Local Thunderstorms: Scattered cumulus clouds grow rapidly in the afternoon. Cumulus or cumulonimbus clouds approach in a line. Large cumulus clouds hang over a summit or ridgeline.

Strong Winds: Blowing snow on ridgelines or peaks. Ragged clouds moving rapidly. Lens-shaped clouds above or on the downwind side of peaks and ridgelines.

Good Weather: A cloudless sky and fog or haze at the valley bottom in the morning. Cumulus clouds appear in the afternoon but do not increase in size or number. Clear skies.

SAFETY AND FIRST AID

In addition to basic safety measures of camping and sleeping outdoors, Colorado's mountain geography, high elevation, and unique environmental hazards add additional necessary layers of awareness and precautions.

First-Aid Training

For first responders, "wilderness" is defined as being one hour or more away from a hospital, which describes many of the campgrounds listed in this book. So even though I'm not taking my family into the backcountry, we may very well find ourselves an hour away from medical care. If you have the time, take a Wilderness First Responder (WFR) class, an intensive, scenario-based course, usually about 60 hours long over 8 straight days. If you can't pull that off, at least take a Wilderness First Aid (WFA) course, often given over a weekend. Find courses near you or via the Wilderness Medicine Institute and the National Outdoor Leadership School (NOLS, www.nols.edu/wmi).

First-Aid Kit

It should go without saying that the knowledge and skills to use what's inside any first-aid kid are as important as everything inside. That said, I like to divide my kit into four compartments for treating the following: (1) cuts, scrapes, and splinters; (2) burns; (3) meds for illnesses, and (4) trauma items like splints, sheers, tape, etc. If you buy a premade kit, spend some time before the trip going through all the contents and creating "what-if" scenarios to

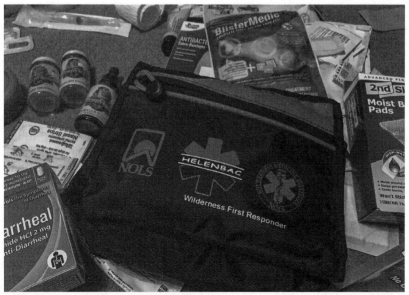

Consider signing up for basic first responder training.

prepare yourself for the real thing. NOLS (see above) sells some excellent kits.

Hunting Season

I love fall. Golden aspen leaves shaking in the wind, the first signs of snow, the crack of rifles in the backcountry. Yes, Colorado attracts hunters from around the world. The state has hunting seasons for deer, elk, pronghorn, bear, mountain goat, bighorn sheep, mountain lion, moose, turkey, prairie chickens, waterfowl, and small game. Seasons vary with location, weapon, and animal. In most areas, big-game seasons begin in September and extend through January. If you're planning a trip to the backcountry in the fall or winter, call Colorado Parks and Wildlife at 303/297-1192 or visit its website, www.cpw.state.co.us, to check on local hunting regulations or to acquire a license. If in doubt, be safe and dress yourself, your kids, and your pets in blaze orange so you're not mistaken for a family of pronghorn.

Wildlife

BEARS

If you're camping in Colorado, you are playing in bear country. Black bears are the smallest and most common bear in North America, and they are the only bear known to live in Colorado at this time. Population estimates range 8,000-12,000. Black bears can live for about 20 years in the wild. They run at speeds up to 35 miles per hour, and they are strong swimmers and climbers.

Black bears vary in size and weight by gender, season, and food supply. Adult males average 275 pounds and adult females average 175 pounds. They are about three feet tall when standing on all fours and five feet tall when standing upright. Black bears can be identified by their tracks, droppings, claw marks on trees, and sound. The most common sounds are woofing and jaw popping. Black bears are solitary animals, but they use trails just as humans do. They are intelligent and curious. They have good vision but rely on smell and hearing to locate food and warn them about danger. In Colorado, the most common black bear habitats are areas of Gambel oak and aspen near clearings with chokecherry and serviceberry bushes. They are omnivorous and will eat anything, from plants, berries, and nuts to carrion and trash.

Most conflicts between bears and humans result from careless handling of food or garbage. Once bears discover that human settlements are a food source, they quickly become pests and often have to be tagged, removed, and sometimes put down. By adhering to the following guidelines, you'll save bears' lives—and possibly your own.

Keep your camp clean. Never leave food or coolers unattended. Keep food out of your tent, and don't eat and sleep in the same clothing. Burn grease off grills and camp stoves and keep your eating area clean.

Store your food and toiletries safely. Store food and coolers in your car trunk or suspended from a tree (at least 10 feet off the ground and four feet from the trunk). Use bear-proof containers when available.

Dispose of garbage properly. Put trash in bear-proof receptacles and pack it out. Never burn or bury food. Bears will dig it up.

Sleep away from food areas. Move a safe distance away from your cooking and food-storage sites to sleep.

Don't surprise bears. Keep kids within sight at all times and keep dogs on a leash. Bears are most active at dawn and dusk, so take care when hiking at these times and in areas with reduced visibility. Talk or sing to avoid surprising them.

Learn more: Go to https://cpw.state.co.us/bears and watch the short videos on what to do if you see a bear.

MOUNTAIN LIONS

The mountain lion is one of North America's biggest cats and an important part of the Rocky Mountain ecosystem. In Colorado, population estimates range 3,000-7,000, but sightings are rare. This powerful predator lives on big game, especially deer, but they will also eat

Bear lockers are safer than storing food in your car.

elk, small mammals, pets, and livestock. They vary in size and weight. Adult males can be up to eight feet in length and weigh 150 pounds on average. Adult females weigh 90 pounds on average.

These solitary animals are most active from dusk to dawn, but they may hunt and travel during the day as well. In Colorado, lions are usually found in areas of piñon, juniper, ponderosa pine, and oak brush, and in areas with large deer populations. Lion and human interactions have increased as both human and lion populations grow, and as the lions' habitats begin to overlap with mountain subdivisions and urban areas. Lion attacks are extremely rare, but if you are traveling in mountain lion country, follow these rules to be safe:

- Make lots of noise when you are out at dusk or dawn.
- Travel in groups.
- Supervise children closely and keep pets on a leash.
- Never approach a mountain lion or its kittens.
- Stay calm if you meet a mountain lion. Stop

or back away slowly. Appear larger by raising your arms or opening a jacket. Pick up small children so that they cannot panic and run.

- Throw stones and speak firmly if a lion acts aggressively. If you are attacked by a lion, fight back. Lions have been driven away by prey that fights back.

SNAKES

The rattlesnake is the only poisonous snake in Colorado. Rattlesnakes live at elevations below 9,000 feet and are easiest to identify by their large triangular heads and the eponymous rattle on the tail. They're easily confused with the nonpoisonous bull snake, which mimics the rattlesnake for its own protection. Rattlesnakes spend the cold months in winter dens and emerge in the spring and summer. They like to bask in the warm sun, especially on hard surfaces like trails and pavement. If you encounter a snake, freeze in place until you know where it is. Then move away slowly until there's at least five feet between you and the snake and leave it alone! Snakebites are actually very rare, and

CAMPSITE SANITATION

There are still a few classic outhouses out there.

• Most campgrounds have composting vault toilets, also called pit toilets. Some are nicer than others, but most campground hosts take great pride in keeping a tidy toilet and you can help them by following all posted campground bathroom rules.

• Do not put any kind of garbage in vault toilets. Trash—such as plastic bags, sanitary napkins, and diapers—cannot be pumped and have to be picked out, piece by piece, by some unfortunate soul.

• If showers are available, bathe quickly so others can use the facilities.

• Use biodegradable soap for washing dishes and cleaning up. Scatter dishwater after food particles have been removed or drain in appointed area.

• Never litter.

• Scour your campsite for even the tiniest bit of trash and any other evidence of your stay. Pack out all the trash you can, even if it's not yours.

• If bathrooms are not available, deposit human waste in catholes dug six to eight inches deep. Cover and disguise the cathole when finished. Make sure this is done at least 75 paces (200 feet) away from any water source.

• Use toilet paper sparingly. Pack it out.

more than one-third of bites are the result of people trying to handle or kill the snake.

ARACHNIDS AND INSECTS

Ticks: These miniature vampires live in brushy areas along fields and woodland edges and like to hitchhike on passing humans and animals. When a tick settles in for a feeding, it can transmit diseases. The most common in Colorado is Colorado tick fever, an acute viral illness characterized by fever, headache, and body aches, as well as lethargy and nausea. The disease is rarely life threatening, and there are no vaccines. Humans contract tick fever from Rocky Mountain wood ticks. Adult ticks emerge in late February or March and are abundant on south-facing brushy slopes. Perform regular tick checks in the mountains and avoid areas of high infestation in April, May, and June. There have been no human cases of Lyme disease in Colorado.

Spiders: Two types of poisonous spiders occur in Colorado—the widow and the brown recluse. Widow spiders like dark, undisturbed sites near the ground, like abandoned animal dens, window wells, and woodpiles. Their bites release a toxin that attacks the nervous system. Fortunately, widow spiders are nonaggressive and are unlikely to attack unless they're in the nest guarding an egg sac. The brown recluse is very rare in Colorado, but it is occasionally transported here from other areas. Its venom damages human cells and can result in an ulcerous lesion that is very slow to heal.

Mosquitoes: These buzzing bloodsuckers were little more than annoying pests until West

Nile virus and several strains of encephalitis were detected as mosquito-borne diseases in Colorado. West Nile virus results in flulike symptoms and, in very rare cases, a more serious brain infection. If you're traveling in an area where mosquitoes are likely to thrive, wear long pants and long sleeves at dawn and dusk and consider using a DEET-based repellent. Citronella-based repellents can be effective for short periods of time, and there are all kinds of mosquito-repelling sticks and candles you can burn.

BARK BEETLES

Any visitor to northern, central, and southern Colorado will notice large stands of red and gray trees. In some areas, especially Summit, Eagle, Grand, Routt, Jackson, and Larimer Counties, it seems as if the whole forest has perished. These forests have been attacked by the mountain pine beetle (or MPB, *Dendroctonus ponderosae*), a native pest that now infects more than 1 million of the state's 1.5 million acres of lodgepole and limber pine forests.

The mountain pine beetle has a year-long life cycle. In the late summer and early fall, the adult insects leave the dead trees in which they developed to seek out large-diameter, mature trees. They burrow into the bark of these new trees, forming a vertical tunnel that becomes the egg gallery. A mating pair lays as many as 75 eggs. When the eggs hatch, the larvae burrow away from the egg gallery and spend the winter and spring feeding on the tree. They are able to survive the winter by metabolizing glycerol, which acts like antifreeze. Additionally, they carry with them blue stain fungi that also attack and kill the trees, staining the sapwood blue in the process. When the weather warms, they transform into pupae, and finally emerge as mature adults in July and August, beginning the cycle anew. The trees they leave behind are usually red or yellow and already dead or dying.

How does a native insect wreak so much havoc? Historically, the MPB infected only mature trees that were already under stress. As epidemic conditions develop, the beetles attack healthy mature trees as well as small-diameter trees. Each infected tree produces enough new adults to kill two or more new trees. In a crowded, high-density forest, the beetles will ultimately attack nearly all of the trees, and once a tree is infected, nothing can be done to save it.

Colorado's forests are more crowded and more mature today than they were 100 years ago due to fire suppression policies. Additionally, a decade-long drought that began in the 1990s stressed the trees, making them more susceptible to attack. Finally, prolonged exposure to extremely cold winter temperatures can kill off the beetle population, but those temperatures haven't occurred in the last decade, so more beetles are surviving the winter than ever before.

The good news is that the outbreak has run its course in many areas. The bad news is that the dead forests pose threats to campers, wildlife, firefighters, and infrastructure. For now, state and national forest service personnel are trying to manage these areas with selective cutting, timber sales, and prescription burns. (The harvested wood, which is just as strong as uninfected wood, carries a unique blue stain that's made it a popular material for furniture and homes.) They are also monitoring the ponderosa pine forests on the Front Range, into which the beetle epidemic has begun to move.

There are many other kinds of bark beetles in Colorado, including the pine engraver (*Ips pini*), which attacks small-diameter lodgepole pine, often in conjunction with the MPB. Another pest that may impact your experience in Colorado is the spruce beetle, which attacks high-elevation Engelmann spruce forests. The beetle has infested large stands of forest in the Rawah Range and the San Juan Mountains around the headwaters of the Rio Grande, and has decimated areas around Wolf Creek Pass, in the Never Summer Range, and on the Grand Mesa.

If you are recreating in a bark-beetle-infected forest, follow these guidelines from the USFS for avoiding falling trees:

CAMPING GEAR CHECKLIST

COOKING GEAR
- Camp stove and extra fuel
- Two pots and nonstick (or cast-iron) pan
- Water jug or plastic "cube," minimum 2 gallons
- Nontoxic dish soap and scrubber
- Set of steel plates, cups, bowls, utensils
- Cooler, ice, drinks
- Itemized food bins, separated by meals, plus a fourth bin for hot drinks and spices
- Kitchen knife, cutting board
- Garbage bags
- One lighter for each camper
- Dish towels and rags
- Two or three plastic bins for washing dishes
- Spatula and stir spoon
- Pot grabber, potholder, can opener
- Salt, pepper, spices
- Matches, stored in resealable bags

GENERAL CAMP GEAR
- Kitchen tarp and/or shade structure
- Axe or hatchet, multi-tool
- Rubber mallet for pounding tent stakes
- Barbecue tongs

- Candles
- Picnic-table cover
- Grill
- Wood or charcoal
- Fire starter (treated bricks or just cardboard)
- Duct tape
- Flashlight and batteries
- Lantern
- Nylon rope for food hang
- Spade for digging cathole
- Toilet paper, baby wipes
- Toothbrush and toothpaste

CAMPING CLOTHES
- Wool or polypropylene long underwear
- Comfortable quick-dry pants
- Gore-Tex parka or jacket
- Rain pants
- Lightweight, breathable shirt
- Lightweight fleece jacket
- Medium-weight fleece vest
- Rain jacket, pants
- Sunglasses
- Swimsuit
- Wide-brimmed hat
- Gloves, scarf, ski cap year-round

- Be aware of your surroundings and avoid dense patches of dead trees. They can fall without warning.
- Stay out of the forest when there are strong winds that could blow down trees. If you are already in the forest when winds kick up, head to a clearing out of reach of any potential falling trees.
- Place tents and park vehicles in areas where they will not be hit if a tree falls.
- When driving in remote areas of the forest, park close to a main road rather than on a spur or one-way section to avoid being trapped if a tree falls across the road.
- Have an ax or chainsaw to remove fallen trees from roads and trails in case you become trapped.
- Do not rely on cell phones for safety, as there is no coverage in many areas of the national forest.

Hazardous Plants

There are many poisonous plants in Colorado, including larkspur, water hemlock, and milkweed. Unless you are grazing on the foliage (or caring for horses), you don't have to worry about most of them, but you could run into poison ivy. Poison ivy (along with poison oak and poison sumac) grows in Colorado up to elevations of around 8,500 feet. Watch for shrubs

SLEEPING GEAR

- Ground tarp
- Pillow (or just roll up your sweater)
- Sleeping bag
- Tent or bivvy bag
- Foam sleeping pad or air mattress
- Whisk broom and dustpan for tent

FIRST AID

- Wound care, bandages, Band Aids
- Plastic syringe for flushing out wounds
- Neosporin/antibacterial cream for cuts
- Roller gauze, sterile gauze pads
- Ace bandage, athletic tape
- After Bite for mosquito bites (before you scratch them)
- Pain reliever of choice
- Biodegradable soap
- Caladryl for poison ivy, oak, or sumac
- Campho-Phenique gel for mosquito bites (after you scratch them)
- Lip balm
- Burn kit
- Personal medications
- Mosquito repellent
- Sunscreen
- Tweezers
- Epsom salts for soaking splinters

FISHING GEAR

- All required permits and licenses
- Fishing reel with fresh line
- Fishing rod
- Knife
- Multi-tool or needle-nose pliers
- Small tackle box with lures, flies, hooks, split shot, snap swivels, and floats

MORE GEAR

- Deck of cards
- Folding chairs
- Guidebooks
- Hammock
- Mountain bike
- Canoe, kayak, or inflatable boat
- Binoculars
- Cotton bandanas
- Notebook and pen
- Roof rack/storage pod
- Heavy-duty picnic blanket
- Welding gloves for the campfire
- S'mores sticks or telescoping spears for fire

that range in height from a few inches to several feet, with a group of three bright green leaves at the top of the stem. The plant contains a pale yellow oil called urushiol, which causes a rash, blisters, and intense itching for one to three weeks. If you (or your dog or kids) are exposed, wash thoroughly with soap and water. Hydrocortisone creams may also help.

Giardia

Giardia is a microscopic organism that causes intestinal disorders. It is widespread in Colorado and occurs in mountain streams and lakes that otherwise look safe and taste good. Symptoms include diarrhea, gas, loss of appetite, stomach cramps, and bloating. They occur a few days to a few weeks after infection and should be treated by a doctor. To avoid giardia infection, treat any water you pull out of a river, creek, or lake either by boiling it, using iodine tablets, or using a water filter or pump.

Sunburn and Heat Illness

Sunburn is the most common danger in Colorado, where high altitudes result in very strong ultraviolet light. In addition to burning, excessive sun exposure can result in heat cramps and heat exhaustion. Protect yourself with a hat, long-sleeved clothing, and sunscreen, and drink lots of fluids. If you or a friend develops the symptoms of heat exhaustion (heavy sweating, fatigue, weakness, dizziness and cold, pale and clammy skin, increased pulse and respiration, normal to slightly elevated temperature, possible fainting, vomiting, confusion, and anxiety), cease physical activity, lie down in a cool place, apply wet, cool cloths, rehydrate slowly, and seek a physician.

Dehydration (and hyponatremia)

Drink water. Drink some more. Make everyone in your group raise their water bottles and drink a toast. Whatever works. Your body requires at least 8-10 cups of water a day, more during hot weather. Drink before you're thirsty. If your urine is dark yellow or orange, you have a headache, or you're nauseated, you could be experiencing dehydration. Drink water and replace your body's electrolytes by eating foods with salt and sugar. Note: Be careful to ingest enough salts and food while you are hydrating, to avoid hyponatremia, a low-sodium condition resulting from excessive fluid intake.

Altitude Sickness

Acute mountain sickness (AMS) is the term applied to a group of symptoms resulting from reduced oxygen levels in the bloodstream, usually after an unacclimatized person makes a rapid ascent to altitudes above 8,000 feet, but it can occur at lower altitudes for some. Anyone can get AMS, even the physically fit. Signs and symptoms include headache, malaise, loss of appetite, shortness of breath, sleeplessness, dizziness, nausea, peripheral edema (swelling of the face or hands), and cyanosis (having a bluish appearance, especially around the mouth). These symptoms will disappear as your body adjusts—or they won't and the only solution is to travel back down the mountain to safer elevations. To avoid AMS, take as long as you can to acclimatize at moderate altitudes. Take it easy and avoid strenuous exercise when you're adjusting. Drink plenty of water, avoid alcohol, and ask your doctor about taking aspirin. If you have a heart condition, lung disease, or

diabetes, consult your physician before traveling in the mountains. If symptoms are severe or if there are signs of confusion or loss of muscle condition, see a doctor immediately.

Lightning Strikes

Colorado ranks third in the nation in lightning casualties, so it's a good idea to learn to protect yourself from this natural threat. Most strikes occur in the early afternoon in thunderstorm season and in open, unprotected areas. Hikers in the high country, on exposed ridges above the tree line, are especially prone to lightning strikes. To protect yourself, follow the 30/30 rule. If the time between the lightning flash and the thunder is less than 30 seconds, seek shelter. Don't resume activities for 30 minutes after the last thunder.

What's a safe location? Buildings designed for year-round use are the safest locations. Avoid open shelters. Once you're inside, avoid metal objects and using water. If there are no safe buildings, wait inside a car with a hardtop roof. Never take shelter under a tree. If you're in an open area, crouch on the balls of your feet, at least as far away from a tree as it is tall. Reduce your contact with the surface as much as possible. If you have a foam sleeping pad or air mattress, sit on that with your heels and bottom touching each other (to form a circuit away from your heart, if a strike occurs nearby).

Hypothermia

Hypothermia is the mental and physical collapse that results from lowered body temperatures. It is caused by exposure to cold, often fiercely enhanced by exposure to water and wind. Symptoms include shivering, slurred speech, forgetfulness, irrational behavior, clumsiness, drowsiness or exhaustion, and a lack of concern about discomfort. Usually companions will notice hypothermia before the victim does.

To prevent hypothermia, stay dry and out of the wind. If you get wet, change clothes, dry off, build a fire and drink hot fluids. Make camp while you still have energy. Always dress in layers and pack adequate clothing for mountain weather and wilderness survival.

If a companion is suffering from hypothermia, seek medical help immediately. Remove wet clothing and replace them with warm, dry clothes or blankets. Give the victim warm, sweet drinks, but avoid caffeine and alcohol. Encourage the victim to move arms and legs to create muscle heat, and if he or she can't do this, place warm bottles in the armpits, groin, and neck and head areas.

Frostbite

Frostbite is the freezing of the deep layers of the skin. The skin becomes numb and hard and turns pale and waxy white. It usually affects the fingers, hands, toes, feet, ears, and nose. The victim should be moved to a warm, dry area, and wet or tight clothing should be removed. Place the affected body part in a warm-water bath and monitor the temperature. Warm the tissue slowly. Warming should take 25-40 minutes. Do not rub the tissue or pour water over it. The affected area may become puffy and blister as it warms. When normal feeling returns, dry and wrap the area and keep it warm. If it becomes cold again, do not warm the area as this could lead to more severe tissue damage.

Lost!

Of course, you will never travel into the outdoors without a good map, a compass, and navigation skills. You will also always carry a whistle, a watch, two-way radios, and an emergency kit, right? If you follow these steps, you probably won't get lost, but if you do, follow this advice from the USFS:

- Pay close attention to your surroundings and landmarks, and relate this to your location on a map.
- Stay calm. Panic is your greatest enemy. Try to remember how you got to your present location.
- Trust your map and compass, and do not walk aimlessly. If you are on a trail, don't leave it.
- Stay put if it is nightfall, if you are injured, or if you are near exhaustion.
- As a last resort, follow a drainage or stream downhill. This can be hard going but will often lead to a trail or road.

WESTERN SLOPE NORTH

The northwest corner of Colorado, referred to here as the Western Slope North region, encompasses a biologically, geologically, and culturally diverse area. It extends from the desert and canyon country in the far corner of the state, east to the Continental Divide and south to the Colorado River. The region includes Dinosaur National Monument in the west and Routt and White River National Forests to the east. In this colorful high plateau country, wide rivers cut rainbow-colored canyons into sandstones and shale laid down by Mesozoic rivers and seas. This land is dotted by mesas, buttes, and badlands, where the piñon, juniper, and sage thrive under blue skies. From plateaus to the alpine lakes, the northern Western Slope merits a long visit full of fishing, hiking, rafting, boating, and, of course, camping. Campgrounds range from remote, free BLM destinations to busy but enjoyable U.S. Forest Service sites and state parks.

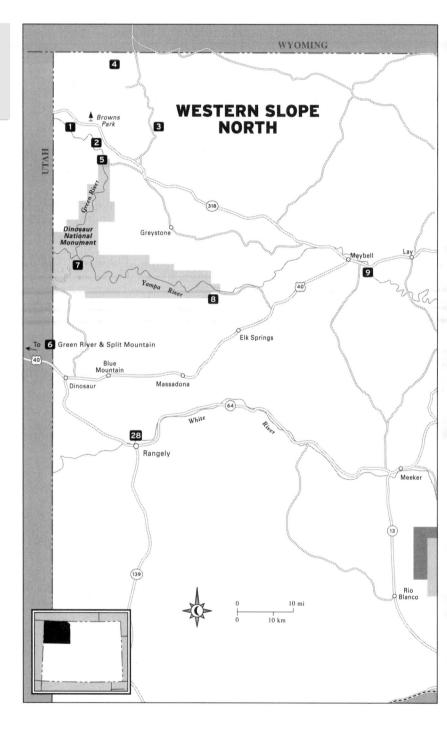

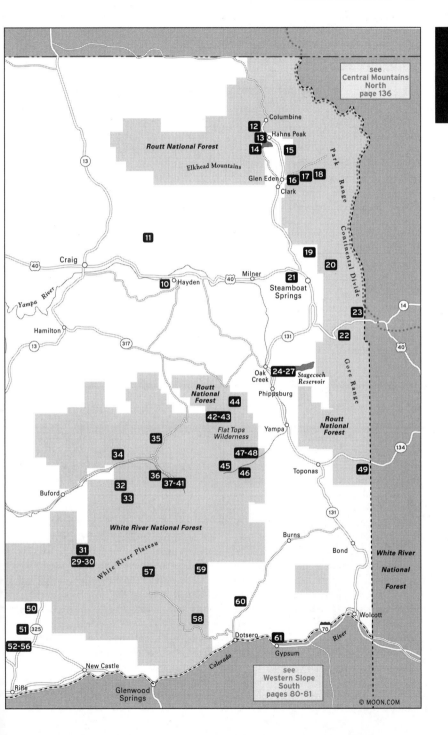

see
Central Mountains
North
page 136

Columbine

12
13   Hahns Peak
14   15

Glen Eden   16   17   18
Clark

Routt National Forest

Elkhead Mountains

11

Craig

40

Yampa River

10   Hayden

Milner   40

19

20

21
Steamboat
Springs

Hamilton

317

13

131

23

22

14

40

Oak
Creek   24-27   Stagecoach
Reservoir
Phippsburg

Routt
National
Forest

44

42-43

Flat Tops
Wilderness

Yampa

Routt
National
Forest

35

47-48

34

45   46

Toponas

134

49

32   36   37-41

33

Buford

131

White River National Forest

Burns

Bond

White River

31

29-30   White River Plateau

National

57   59   Forest

50

60

51   325

58

Wolcott

52-56

Dotsero   61
Gypsum

New Castle

Colorado

70   River

Rifle

Glenwood
Springs

see
Western Slope
South
pages 80-81

© MOON.COM

1 SWINGING BRIDGE

Scenic rating: 9

in Browns Park National Wildlife Refuge

Browns Park, a remote valley that straddles the Colorado, Utah, and Wyoming borders, is miles from nowhere, but if you seek solitude, wildlife, or natural beauty, it is worth the drive. Browns Park was the wintering ground of the Utes and Shoshones because of its mild climate. In the 19th century, the park found favor first with trappers and traders and then with cattle ranchers. With the cattlemen came cattle rustlers. Browns Park soon had a reputation as an outlaw hideout. Most notably, Butch Cassidy and the Wild Bunch hid there between heists. Except for the creation of Dinosaur National Monument and Browns Park National Wildlife Refuge, not much has changed in the last hundred years. Bring all your food, water, fuel, and supplies.

The wildlife refuge was created in 1965 to provide marsh habitat along the Green River for migratory birds. Deer, elk, coyote, and sage grouse are also present. The refuge is surrounded by BLM land and it adjoins Dinosaur National Monument. It's a dream destination for hunters, anglers, and birders who want solitude. Canoes and rafts can put in at the boat ramp. (Boaters who wish to continue into Dinosaur National Monument must secure permits months in advance.) There are also numerous hiking and mountain biking opportunities on the network of trails and 4WD roads, and endless opportunity for backcountry exploration on the BLM land. This campground is named for an old bridge that crosses the river. Cars with a 20-ton limit are allowed on the bridge, but it takes a strong stomach to drive across.

Campsites, facilities: This campground offers primitive dispersed camping for tents and small RVs in a riparian zone. Metal fire rings, vault toilets, a horse corral, and a boat ramp, are available. Generators are prohibited from 10pm-7am and trash must be packed out. Leashed pets are permitted.

Reservations, fees: Reservations are not accepted, and camping is free. Open year-round.

Directions: From the intersection of Highways 40 and 318 (1 mile west of Maybell), take Highway 318 north for 60 miles. Turn left on County Road 83, a well-maintained dirt road. The campground is on the north bank of the Green River in 2.8 miles. To reach the visitors center, continue on Highway 318 for 0.5 mile.

Contact: Browns Park National Wildlife Refuge, 970/365-3613, www.fws.gov/refuge/browns_park.

2 CROOK

Scenic rating: 9

in Browns Park National Wildlife Refuge

This campground's best features are its solitude and its proximity to the Green River, which is wide and wild at this stage on its journey to the Colorado River. In late spring and early summer, the river is flooded with runoff and spring rains. (It can be muddy, too, and therefore not much good for fishing. Conditions vary. Call the National Wildlife Refuge office for an update.) Occasionally, boaters traveling into Dinosaur National Monument will pass by, and in the fall, hunters arrive to look for deer and elk in the surrounding BLM lands. Otherwise, there is almost no traffic in this remote valley. (For more information on Browns Park, see the Swinging Bridge listing in this chapter.)

Campsites, facilities: This campground has dispersed camping for tents and small RVs in a riparian zone. Metal fire rings, vault toilets, picnic tables, and a boat ramp are available. Generators are prohibited from 10pm-7am and trash must be packed out. Leashed pets are permitted.

Reservations, fees: Reservations are

not accepted, and camping is free. Open year-round.

Directions: From the intersection of Highways 40 and 318 (1.0 mile west of Maybell), take Highway 318 north for 52 miles. Turn left at the Browns Park National Wildlife Refuge, an unmarked dirt road. In 1.0 mile, turn right at the fork. The campground is on the left in 0.5 mile. To reach the visitors center, continue on Highway 318 for 8.5 miles.

Contact: Browns Park National Wildlife Refuge, 970/365-3613, www.fws.gov/refuge/browns_park.

3 IRISH CANYON

Scenic rating: 8

in Browns Park

Located in Browns Park, a remote valley with a Wild West history, Irish Canyon is a unique geological feature. Cold Spring Mountain juts 2,500 feet above the valley floor. The entrance to Irish Canyon is at the east end of the mountain, and approaching it feels like stepping back in time. The sensation is fitting—the colorful canyon consists of remnants of the ancient Uinta Mountains, including Red Creek quartzite, which is the oldest rock in Colorado at 2.3 billion years. The canyon receives special environmental protection because of its geology as well as its ecological and archaeological significance. Rare plants such as the Utah piñon-juniper and curl-leaf mountain mahogany grow there, and Native American rock art dating back to AD 400-1100 has been found in the canyon. More recently, this area was home to cattle ranchers and outlaws like Butch Cassidy. The canyon is named for three Irishmen who robbed a Rock Springs, Wyoming, saloon and stopped at the entrance of the canyon to consume their booty. It is still a convenient shortcut to Wyoming.

Most of the visitors to this campground are interested in the wild horse herd located in the Sand Wash basin to the east of the campground. The herd consists of the offspring of Spanish, gaited, North American, and Arabian breeds and the horses come in a wide range of colors, including pintos, grays, whites, blacks, palominos, red and blue roans, bays, and sorrels. Other activities include backcountry hiking on Limestone Ridge, Cold Spring Mountain, Vermillion Canyon, and Vermillion Creek, and mountain biking is possible on the area's primitive roads. Campers should come prepared with plenty of water and a full tank of gas.

The campground is a gravel loop with numerous junipers, piñons, and wildflowers. All of the sites are equally appealing.

Campsites, facilities: There are six sites for tents, but it is possible to park RVs up to 25 feet next to most of the sites. Picnic tables, fire rings, grills, and a vault toilet are provided. Trash must be packed out. Pets are permitted.

Reservations, fees: Reservations are not accepted, and there is no camping fee. Open year-round.

Directions: From the intersection of Highways 40 and 318 (1.0 mile west of Maybell), take Highway 318 north for 42 miles. Turn north on County Road 10N. The campground is in 8.3 miles on the south side of the canyon.

Contact: Bureau of Land Management, Little Snake Field Office in Craig, 970/826-5000, www.co.blm.gov.

4 ROCKY RESERVOIR

Scenic rating: 7

west of Craig

This far-flung, tiny campground is located in a remote area northwest of Irish Canyon, not far from the Wyoming border. It sits at 7,793 feet above sea level in a stunning canyon country between Diamond Mountain and Middle peak. The handful of sites here are on a single small loop at the edge of a forest that leads up to Diamond Peak. Most sites have shade, but bring your own water and all supplies and be prepared for a primitive site. This BLM campground is underutilized most of the year but picks up during hunting season. Hiking opportunities abound but you may be finding your own trail and route.

Campsites, facilities: There are five sites for tents with picnic tables, fire rings, grills, and a vault toilet is provided. Trash must be packed out. Drinking water must be packed in. Pets are permitted.

Reservations, fees: Reservations are not accepted, and there is no camping fee. Open year-round.

Directions: Travel north on Moffat County Road 10N for 8.5 miles to MCR 72. Take MCR 72 west 9.0 miles to BLM road 2014. BLM road 2014 is a primitive road and high clearance is recommended; road is impassable when wet. Head north on BLM 2014 for 1.83 miles to BLM 2015, then turn east 0.5 miles to the campground, turnoff to the right. It's a new campground and does not come up on all the maps. If you're having trouble finding it, punch in 40°57'34.4"N, 108°54'17.4"W, or call the BLM office.

Contact: Bureau of Land Management, Little Snake Field Office in Craig, 970/826-5000, www.co.blm.gov.

5 GATES OF LODORE

Scenic rating: 9

in Dinosaur National Monument

BEST (

At the Gates of Lodore campground, the Green River leaves the high desert and enters the red rock Canyon of Lodore, named by a member of John Wesley Powell's 1869 expedition. The Gates are at the north end of Dinosaur National Monument, in the remote valley of Browns Park, where it is easy to feel like you're camping at the end of the world. Kayaking and rafting groups on the Green River make up most of the traffic at this campground. Watching them pack and repack as they prepare for the Class IV rapids ahead makes for an entertaining morning. (Permits are required for boating the canyon.) There is an easy 0.75-mile nature trail above the Green River with an overlook of the entrance to the canyon.

The campground parallels the river. Sites 11-17 are on the riverbank, and sites 1-10 are in the adjacent meadow. Sites 4-9, 19, and 20 are shaded by large cottonwood trees. When it rains, the dirt turns into mud, so avoid the barest tent sites.

Campsites, facilities: There are 19 sites for tents and RVs up to 35 feet. There are no hookups. Picnic tables, fire rings, and grills are provided. Vault toilets, drinking water, and a boat ramp are available. Trash must be packed out. Leashed pets are permitted in the campground and on the road but are not allowed in the river, on trails, or in the backcountry.

Reservations, fees: Reservations are not accepted. The fee is $10 per night. Cash only. Open year-round, but mid-September-mid-April the drinking water is turned off and camping is $6.

Directions: From the intersection of Highways 40 and 318 (1.0 mile west of Maybell), take Highway 318 north for 40.5 miles. Turn left on County Road 34. Travel west on this dirt road for 7.5 miles to the campground entrance.

Contact: Dinosaur National Monument, 970/374-3000, www.nps.gov/dino.

6 GREEN RIVER

Scenic rating: 7

in Dinosaur National Monument in Utah

This is one of six campgrounds inside Dinosaur National Monument, and one of three on the Utah side. Its location makes it the best base for seeing the more popular attractions of the park, especially the Quarry Exhibit Hall, built around the famous Carnegie Dinosaur Quarry. A river trail leaves from the west side of the campground and there is an amphitheater for ranger programs. Green River campground is about four miles from the visitors center and right on a bend in the mighty Green River. It is a basic, pleasant campground with two loops. A handful of sites have their own river access, including 8, 9, 25, and 27. A few sites are shaded by cottonwood trees, but other sites have little to no shade. Firewood collection is not permitted, but fires are allowed in provided rings when conditions are favorable. There is also a nearby group site, Split Mountain, which is used by commercial rafting groups, Boy Scout troops, school trips, and family reunions ($40 per night, groups of 8 or more).

Campsites, facilities: There are 79 sites for tents and RVs up to 35 feet. There are no hookups. Picnic tables, fire rings, and grills are provided. Flush toilets, drinking water, trash disposal, and recycling are provided. Leashed pets are allowed along roads and in campsites; they are not allowed on most trails or in the backcountry. Check with a ranger for current pet regulations.

Reservations, fees: Reservations are accepted for sites in Loop B at 877/444-6777 or www.recreation.gov. The rest of the sites are first come, first served. The fee is $18 per night. Cash only. Open early April-early-October.

Directions: From the Quarry Visitor Center, near Jensen, Utah, the campground is 5.0 miles east, make a left at the sign.

Contact: Dinosaur National Monument, 970/374-3000, www.nps.gov/dino.

▼ ECHO PARK
🚶‍♀️ 🛶 🐎 ♿ ⛺

Scenic rating: 9
in Dinosaur National Monument

BEST (

Dinosaur National Monument is a 210,000-acre classroom on the history of the earth. There are 23 exposed rock formations in the monument. The most notable, the Morrison Formation, is a treasure trove of plant and animal fossils. In 1909, paleontologist Earl Douglass discovered the dinosaur quarry that most park visitors come to see, but if you leave after just visiting the quarry, you have missed the best of the park. The auto tour from the Canyon Visitors Center to Harpers Corner features colorful canyons and stunning views. The tour takes four hours round-trip, but campers at Echo Park can turn it into a two-day (or more) adventure. Echo Park is located at the confluence of the Green and Yampa Rivers, in the shadow of the impressive Steamboat Rock. In the 1950s, conservation groups defeated a dam proposal at this location. Today, the Yampa is Colorado's most naturally flowing river, with only a few small reservoirs near its headwaters. While enjoying the beautiful scenery at this campground, you can also expect to meet kayakers and rafting groups traveling downriver toward Class IV rapids.

Campsites, facilities: There are 22 sites for tents, four walk-in sites, and one group site. Picnic tables, fire rings, and grills are provided. Vault toilets, drinking water, and a boat ramp are available. Trash must be packed out. Pets are allowed along roads and in campsites, but are not allowed on most trails or in the backcountry. Check with a ranger for current pet information. There is one wheelchair-accessible site.

Reservations, fees: Reservations are not accepted. The fee is $10 per night. The group site (reservation only) accommodates 8-20 people for $15 per night and can be reserved by contacting the park. Cash only. Open year-round, but mid-September-mid-April the drinking water is turned off and camping is $6 (the road may or may not be passable; after a hard rain, the clay road "turns to peanut butter," said one ranger).

Directions: From Dinosaur, drive east on U.S. Highway 40 for 2.0 miles. After the Canyon Visitors Center, turn north onto Harpers Corner Drive/County Road 161. In 25 miles, turn right on Echo Park Road. In 8.0 miles, bear left at the fork and continue 5.0 miles to the campground. Four-wheel-drive and high-clearance vehicles are recommended for this road, which becomes impassable when wet. Call the park headquarters for travel conditions. RVs and trailers are strongly discouraged on this road.

Contact: Dinosaur National Monument, 970/374-3000, www.nps.gov/dino.

8 DEERLODGE PARK
🏃🛶🐴🚐⛺

Scenic rating: 8
in Dinosaur National Monument

BEST (

Deerlodge Park is located at the eastern end of Dinosaur National Monument, in the scenic valley of the Yampa River. (For more information on Dinosaur National Monument, see the Echo Park listing in this chapter.) This campground is mainly used by commercial rafting outfitters and private groups setting out on boat trips. Consequently, its heaviest use occurs during peak river flows, usually in late May and early June. Backcountry hikers may also use this location as a jumping-off point for exploring the park. (Permits are required for boating and backcountry camping.) The campground is very primitive and unpleasant if it's been raining. It can get quite muddy, and only site 7 has gravel to reduce the problem. Sites 1, 3, and 5 are right next to the road.

Campsites, facilities: There are seven shady walk-in sites in the riparian zone. RVs up to 35

feet can park near the camping area, but there are no hookups. Picnic tables, fire rings, and grills are provided at some sites. Vault toilets, drinking water, and a boat ramp are available. Trash must be packed out. Leashed pets are permitted in the campground and on the road but are not allowed in the river, on trails, or in the backcountry.

Reservations, fees: Reservations are not accepted. The fee is $10 per night. Cash only. Open year-round, but October-mid-April the drinking water is turned off and camping is $6 (road may be impassable).

Directions: From Maybell, drive west on U.S. Highway 40 for 17 miles. Drive north on Twelve Mile Gulch Road. The campground entrance is on the right in 12.2 miles. Winter access may be difficult due to snow. Call the park headquarters for travel conditions.

Contact: Dinosaur National Monument, 970/374-3000, www.nps.gov/dino.

9 MAYBELL BRIDGE
🛶🚣🐴🚐⛺

Scenic rating: 4
in Yampa River State Park

Yampa River State Park encompasses a visitors center and campground near Hayden, as well as 13 public access sites along a 134-mile stretch of the Yampa River. Maybell Bridge is one of six primitive campgrounds mainly used for river access. It's also popular with hunters during the season. The Moffat County-Routt County elk herds constitute one-third of Colorado's elk population. Craig (population 5,000) has 500 hotel rooms and every one of those is booked during hunting season. For hunters without reservations, camping is the most reasonable option.

Campsites, facilities: There are 10 sites for tents and RVs up to 30 feet. Sites 5-8 have the best pull-ins for RVs. Picnic tables, grills, tent pads, and trash receptacles are provided. Vault toilets and a boat ramp are available. Campers can use the shower and laundry facilities, back at the Yampa River State Park Headquarters. Leashed pets are permitted.

Reservations, fees: Reservations are not accepted. The fee is $14 per night. Campers must also purchase a vehicle pass ($8) or an Annual Parks Pass ($80). Annual Parks Passes can be purchased at the visitors center near Hayden. Open year-round, weather permitting. Call ahead for road conditions.

Directions: From the intersection of Highways 40 and 13 in Craig, drive west on U.S. Highway 40 for 26.4 miles. Turn left before the bridge across the Yampa, at the Wildlife Viewing Area sign.

Contact: Yampa River State Park, 970/276-2061, www.cpw.state.co.us.

10 YAMPA RIVER STATE PARK HEADQUARTERS

Scenic rating: 4

west of Steamboat Springs

Yampa River State Park encompasses a visitors center and campground near Hayden, as well as 13 public access sites along a 134-mile stretch of the Yampa River. The main campground at the visitors center makes a good base camp for exploring the Elkhead Mountains to the north, or a nice stopover between Dinosaur National Monument and Steamboat Springs. Hunters, anglers, and families enjoy this well-designed facility, which makes the best of its location (between the highway and the Yampa River) with a 1.75-mile nature trail and sheltering groves of cottonwood, willow, and Gambel oak. Despite its proximity to the highway, the campground is quiet and feels almost rural. Summer interpretive programs feature local talent such as storytellers and musicians. The friendly rangers can offer advice on fishing and floating the Yampa. There is one boat ramp at

this location, and a popular 33-mile float trip through Little Yampa Canyon begins at the South Beach access site, which is 25 miles west on U.S. Highway 40 (there are several updated campsites along the way). Another excellent day trip for anglers and wildlife lovers is California Park, located about 20 miles north in Medicine Bow-Routt National Forests. The 8,000-acre park has elk herds and trout streams, but it is closed to motor traffic May 15-July 1 to protect Colorado's largest population of greater sandhill cranes. The campground is a large loop with little shade. Site 29, which sits beneath a giant cottonwood, is the only exception.

Campsites, facilities: There are 35 sites with electrical hookups for RVs of any length and 14 sites for tents only, most have shade. There are also two tepees for rent. Picnic tables, fire rings, grills, sun shelters, and tent pads are provided. Restrooms with flush toilets and showers, laundry facilities, drinking water, a playground, a group picnic area, and dump stations are available. Leashed pets are permitted. Site 9 and all facilities are wheelchair-accessible.

Reservations, fees: Reservations are accepted at 800/244-5613 and at www.cpwshop.com. The fee is $24 per night for tent sites and $32 per night for sites with hookups. Campers must also purchase a vehicle pass ($8) or an Annual Parks Pass ($80). Open May-November.

Directions: From Hayden, drive west on U.S. Highway 40 for three miles. The state park is on the south side of the road.

Contact: Yampa River State Park, 970/276-2061, www.cpw.state.co.us.

11 ELKHEAD RESERVOIR

Scenic rating: 7

north of Craig

This state park 10 miles northeast of Craig in the high desert of the Yampa River Valley has two campgrounds: Bear's Ears, which is located north of the reservoir's dam, and Pronghorn which is located north of the reservoir's boat ramp. Many of these campsites are near the shoreline and accessible by boat. The 900-acre reservoir is popular for boating, swimming, jet skiing, picnicking, hiking, birding, biking, horseback riding, hunting, and fishing.

Campsites, facilities: There are 16 tent sites at Bear's Ears Campground with no hookups and 30 campsites at Pronghorn Campground with hookups.

Picnic tables, fire rings, grills, sun shelters, and tent pads are provided. Restrooms with flush toilets are available. Leashed pets are permitted. There is no dump station here but you can use the one at Yampa River State Park, 12 miles down the road.

Reservations, fees: Reservations are accepted at 800/244-5613 and at www.cpwshop.com. The fee is $22 per night for tent sites and $30 per night for sites with hookups. Campers must also purchase a vehicle pass ($8) or an Annual Parks Pass ($80). Open May-November.

Directions: From Craig, go east on Highway 40 for 7.0 miles, turn left (north) on MCR 29 and continue 4.0 miles. Turn right on MCR 28 to enter park, continue across the dam to reach Bear's Ears Campground.

Contact: 135 County Road 28, Craig, CO, 970/276-2061, elkhead.park@state.co.us.

12 HAHNS PEAK LAKE
🏃 🚴 🛶 ⛺ 🛥 🐴 ♿ 🚐 ⛰

Scenic rating: 7
north of Steamboat Springs

The Hahns Peak Lake campground is a smaller, quieter destination than the busy campgrounds at Steamboat Lake State Park. The narrow lake sits between Nipple Peak to the north and Hahns Peak to the east. Mountain bikers enjoy the Nipple Peak Loop, a combination of Forest Service roads and trails. Hikers can climb Nipple Peak or stick to the West Side Trail along the lake. The campground sits at 8,500 feet of elevation and contains two large loops at the north end of the lake. The sites are about 100 feet apart and have ample room for big families to spread out but not much privacy due to tree removal. The first loop (sites 1-11) is closer to the lake, but the second loop seems to be more popular.

Campsites, facilities: There are 23 single unit sites for tents and RVs up to 40 feet and 3 larger sites for groups. There are no hookups. Sites 1-5, 7, 10, and 11 are pull-through. Picnic tables, grills, and fire rings are provided. Vault toilets are available. Leashed pets are permitted. The facilities are wheelchair-accessible.

Reservations, fees: Reservations are accepted at 877/444-6777 and www.recreation.gov. The fee is $10 per night for a single unit and $20 per night for a double unit. Cash or check only. Open early June-mid-October.

Directions: From Steamboat Springs, take County Road 129 north for 28.3 miles. Turn left on Forest Route 486. The campground is in 2.5 miles.

Contact: Medicine Bow-Routt National Forests, Hahns Peak-Bears Ears District, 970/870-2299, www.fs.usda.gov/mbr.

13 SUNRISE VISTA
🏃 🚴 🛶 ⛺ 🚐 🛥 🐴 🚲 ⛰

Scenic rating: 6
in Steamboat Lake State Park

Steamboat Lake is a 1,053-acre reservoir at the base of Hahns Peak in the heart of the Medicine Bow-Routt National Forests. The surrounding mountains were the traditional hunting grounds of the Utes until 1881, when growing pressure from settlers secured the long-sought exile of the Utes from Colorado to a reservation in eastern Utah. With the original residents gone, this area opened up to a flood of mining and ranching, and it still retains much of that early flavor. The Elk River valley to the south remains ranching land and will stay that way, thanks to progressive landholders and conservation easements.

Steamboat Lake has a party reputation on weekends, but that shouldn't deter anglers, hikers, or mountain bikers. About half of the lake is restricted to wakeless boating; the other half is open to water sports of all kinds. In the quieter coves, and in the creeks that feed the lake, anglers will find cutthroat and rainbow trout. During the summer, hikers can enjoy meadows full of wildflowers, including harebell, mule's ear, lupine, and columbine; hardier souls can climb Hahns Peak or Nipple Peak, or drive to trailheads that climb to the Continental Divide. Be prepared for inclement weather. This area receives vast quantities of precipitation, especially snow.

Sunrise Vista is the larger of the two campgrounds. The campground is on the upswing after severe bark beetle damage from 2004. This campground was previously heavily wooded and fairly private; now all of the sites are sunny and have great views of the lake and mountains. The park continues to plant new trees and grasses and is transplanting mature trees from the surrounding forests as well. The Yarrow loop (sites 97-113) is closest to the water.

Campsites, facilities: There are 113 sites for tents and RVs up to 55 feet. The Larkspur, Lupine, and Yarrow loops (sites 77-113) have electrical hookups. Picnic tables, fire rings, grills, and tent pads are provided. Restrooms with flush toilets, vault toilets, and drinking water are available. The Dutch Hill campground and marina can be reached by a 0.25-mile foot trail and the campground has an amphitheater for educational programs. Campers can use the showers, laundry facilities, and dump stations at Dutch Hill. At the marina, a convenience store, propane gas, vending machines, boat ramp, swim beach, and 10 cabins are available. Leashed pets are permitted.

Reservations, fees: Reservations are required (though you can still find a site by just showing up). Call 800/244-5613 or go to www.cpwshop.com. The fee is $24 per night for sites without hookups and $32 per night for sites with hookups (after October, costs go down to $16 and $24). Campers must also purchase a vehicle pass ($8) or an Annual Parks Pass ($80) or the hangtag option ($120). Open Memorial Day-mid-September.

Directions: From Steamboat Springs, drive north on County Road 129 for about 25 miles. Turn left onto County Road 62, 1.0 mile after the visitors center. The entrance to Sunrise Vista is on the left in 0.4 mile.

Contact: Steamboat Lake State Park, 970/879-3922, www.cpw.state.co.us.

14 DUTCH HILL

Scenic rating: 7
in Steamboat Lake State Park

BEST (

Steamboat Lake attracts hikers, mountain bikers, anglers, water-sports enthusiasts, wildlife lovers, and travelers who are ready to put up their feet and enjoy the view. A normal day at Steamboat Lake includes a hike up Hahns Peak, a dip in the lake, and fishing for rainbow trout. Parents and kids will enjoy the interpretive programs at the visitors center and the five miles of easy trails surrounding the lake. In the winter, there are nine miles of groomed trails around the lake. Dutch Hill is the smaller of the two campgrounds at Steamboat Lake and the more attractive for tent campers. The Bridge Island loop (sites 166-200) is best for tents, is surrounded by water, and offers breathtaking views of Hahns Peak and the Park Range. Sites 181-200 are walk-in tent sites. The Wheeler loop (sites 116-155) has electrical hookups and is popular with RVers. Like Sunrise Vista, this campground has lost all of its trees to the bark beetle.

Campsites, facilities: There are 44 sites for tents and RVs up to 55 feet, in addition to the

Bridge Island 19 hike-in tent sites and 10 cabins. The Wheeler loop (sites 116-155) has electrical hookups. Picnic tables, fire rings, grills, and tent pads are provided. Restrooms with flush toilets and showers, vault toilets, laundry facilities, drinking water, a playground, and dump stations are available. A convenience store, propane gas, vending machines, swim beach, cabins, and a boat ramp are available at the marina. Leashed pets are permitted. Site 135 is wheelchair-accessible.

Reservations, fees: Reservations are required (though you can still find a site by just showing up). Call 800/244-5613 or go to www.cpwshop. com. The fee is $24 per night for sites without hookups and $32 per night for sites with hookups (after October, costs go down to $16 and $24). Campers must also purchase a vehicle pass ($8) or an Annual Parks Pass ($80) or the hangtag option ($120). Open Memorial Day-mid-September. In the winter, 14 sites with electrical hookups are available in the Marina parking lot.

Directions: From Steamboat Springs, drive north on County Road 129 for about 25 miles. One mile after the visitors center, turn left onto County Road 62. The entrance to Dutch Hill is on the left in 1.0 mile.

Contact: Steamboat Lake State Park, 970/879-3922, www.cpw.state.co.us.

15 PEARL LAKE STATE PARK

Scenic rating: 8
north of Steamboat Springs

Pearl Lake is a gem in the state park system. Tucked into a narrow north-south valley at the base of Farwell Mountain, this campground offers scenery and first-rate fishing. On an early summer morning, you could wake up to tendrils of mist curling over the lake, a dusting of snow on the ridgelines, and the sounds of 18-inch trout leaping out of the water. Sadly, the seclusion that the dense forest used to also offer is now gone thanks to selective logging in response to the bark beetle problem, but the views at most sites have improved. Pearl Lake is managed in conjunction with Steamboat Lake to the north, but it is much smaller and attracts a family crowd. There are two loops. The lower loop (sites 24-38) is lakeside, so these sites are most popular, but there is not a bad site in the park. The upper loop (sites 1-23) is located on a gentle hill that is just 200 yards from the lake. Early in the season, the upper sites are preferable during wet weather. There is a short trail to the dam, which connects with the six-mile Coulton Creek Forest Service trail as well as a boat ramp at the south end of the lake. Only wakeless boating is allowed, and anglers must use flies or lures and are restricted to two 18-inch trout per day. The campground is closed in the winter, but the yurts remain available by reservation.

Campsites, facilities: There are 36 sites for tents and RVs up to 55 feet and two yurts available by reservation only. Many sites are pull-through, but there are no hookups. Picnic tables, fire rings, grills, and tent pads, are provided. Restrooms with vault toilets, flush toilets, drinking water, a boat ramp, and a wildlife-viewing deck are available. Showers, a laundry room, interpretive programs, and dump stations are available at nearby Steamboat Lake State Park. Leashed pets are permitted. Site 35 and Yurt 6 are wheelchair-accessible.

Reservations, fees: Reservations are required (though you can still find a site by just showing up). Call 800/244-5613 or go to www.cpwshop. com. The fee is $24 per night for sites without hookups and $32 per night for sites with hookups. Campers must also purchase a vehicle pass ($8) or an Annual Parks Pass ($80) or the hangtag option ($120). Camping is available May-mid-October.

Directions: From Steamboat Springs, go north on County Road 129 for 22.8 miles. Turn right on County Road 209. Follow the signs for 2.0 miles to the park entrance. In 0.3 mile the road

Pearl Lake State Park is a smaller, quieter alternative to nearby Steamboat Lake State Park.

forks. Take the left fork to the campground or the right fork to the boat ramp.

Contact: Pearl Lake State Park, 970/879-3922, www.cpw.state.co.us.

16 HINMAN PARK

Scenic rating: 5

north of Steamboat Springs

BEST (

From Hinman Park, hikers can explore the Mount Zirkel Wilderness, an area of rugged granite peaks and glacial lakes. These mountains were carved by glaciers that left *U*-shaped valleys and high cirques. The South Fork Trail begins near the campground and connects with the Elk Park Trail. This trail crosses three drainages and is the best way to explore the lower elevations of the wilderness. Anglers will enjoy fishing on the Elk River, which the Forest Service has proposed for Wild and Scenic designation. In 2010, the campground underwent a timber sale and cleanup to remove hazard trees, leaving most sites with almost zero shade. Sites 1, 3, and 5 border a meadow. Sites 9, 10, and 12 are on a steep hill that is not ideal for tent camping.

Campsites, facilities: There are 13 sites for tents and RVs up to 22 feet. There are no hookups. Sites 1 and 7 are pull-through. Picnic tables, fire rings, and grills are provided. Vault toilets are available. Leashed pets are permitted.

Reservations, fees: Reservations are not accepted. The fee is $10 per night. Cash or check only. Open mid-June-mid-October.

Directions: From Steamboat Springs, take County Road 129 north for 18 miles. Turn right on County Road 64/Forest Route 400. In 5.5 miles, turn right on Forest Route 440. The campground is on the right in 0.6 mile.

Contact: Medicine Bow-Routt National Forests, Hahns Peak-Bears Ears District, 970/870-2299, www.fs.usda.gov/mbr.

17 HINMAN PARK DISPERSED

🚶 🚴 🛶 🐕 🚐 ⛺

Scenic rating: 7

north of Steamboat Springs

Hinman Park is a little valley hemmed in by the Elk River on one side and rocky outcroppings on the other. The vegetation is mostly sagebrush, with small aspen groves near the outcroppings. Most of the lodgepole and limber pine have died and been removed where they posed a hazard. The north end of this valley has tantalizing views of the Park Range in the Mount Zirkel Wilderness. There are two pull-offs that lead to campsites in the trees near the river. Hikers and bikers can explore the Hinman Creek Trail. Hikers who wish to explore the wilderness area can take the South Fork Trail (near the Hinman Park campground) to the Elk Park Trail, or drive up the road to the Slavonia trailhead. The Elk River has good but challenging fly-fishing.

Campsites, facilities: This is primitive dispersed camping. There are no facilities. Water and toilets are available at the Hinman Park campground. Leashed pets are permitted.

Reservations, fees: Reservations are not accepted, and there is no fee for camping. Open year-round, weather permitting.

Directions: From Steamboat Springs, take County Road 129 north for 18 miles. Turn right on County Road 64/Forest Route 400. Dispersed camping begins in 6.0 miles.

Contact: Medicine Bow-Routt National Forests, Hahns Peak-Bears Ears District, 970/870-2299, www.fs.usda.gov/mbr.

18 SEEDHOUSE

🚶 🛶 🐕 🚐 ⛺

Scenic rating: 6

north of Steamboat Springs

Located in the Elk River valley on the west side of the Park Range, the Seedhouse campground is popular because of its proximity to the Slavonia trailhead, the most heavily used trailhead in the Mount Zirkel Wilderness. Seedhouse is also adjacent to the Wyoming Trail, a 48-mile route from the Summit Lake campground (near Steamboat Springs) into the Medicine Bow Mountains in Wyoming. Anglers can try fly-fishing on the productive Elk River. The campground is a sprawling loop scattered with rocks and boulders left behind by the same glacial activity that carved this valley and the high cirques that are the main attraction of the Park Range. Most of the trees have been removed. The sites are about 30 feet apart. Sites 14 and 15 overlook the Middle Fork of the Elk River.

Campsites, facilities: There are 24 sites for tents and RVs up to 25 feet plus a group site for up to 50 people. There are no hookups. Sites 5, 10, 13, 17, and 24 are pull-through. Picnic tables, fire rings, and grills are provided. Site 1 has an extra-large picnic table. Vault toilets and drinking water are available. Leashed pets are permitted.

Reservations, fees: Reservations are accepted for 15 of the sites (and required for the group site) at 877/444-6777 and www.recreation.gov. The fee is $12 per night or $100 per night for the group site. Cash or check only. Open mid-June-late October.

Directions: From Steamboat Springs, take County Road 129 north for 18 miles. Turn right on County Road 64/Forest Route 400. In 8.5 miles, turn right into the campground.

Contact: Medicine Bow-Routt National Forests, Hahns Peak-Bears Ears District, 970/870-2299, www.fs.usda.gov/mbr.

19 STRAWBERRY PARK HOT SPRINGS

Scenic rating: 8
north of Steamboat Springs

BEST (

Strawberry Park Hot Springs is a series of terraced, seminatural rock pools built into the hillside of a narrow valley. The hot spring pours from the hillside into the pools below. Surrounded by beautiful rock patios, the pools make lounging look like an art form. The architecture of the surrounding buildings, including the brand-new shower house, is modern but fits naturally into the scenery. There are only four tent sites along the creek located 100-300 yards below the main pool; it's a short but steep walk from the pools. A fifth site is on the hill above the shower house. Before soaking, hikers and cyclists can exercise on the Hot Springs Trail, which passes through the campground.

Campsites, facilities: There are five sites for tents. Picnic tables and grills are provided. Flush toilets, showers, and drinking water are available. Pets are prohibited. There are also three covered wagons and six cabins for rent.

Reservations, fees: Reservations are accepted at 970/879-0342 and should be made at least 8-12 weeks in advance. The fee is $65 per night for two people and includes hot springs admission. Cash or check only. Open year-round.

Directions: From Steamboat Springs, go northeast on Third Street. Turn right on Fish Creek Falls Road. Turn left on Amethyst Drive/County Road 36. The road ends in 7.0 miles at the hot springs (the last 1.8 miles are unpaved).

Contact: Strawberry Hot Springs Office, 970/879-0342, www.strawberryhotsprings.com.

There are five tent sites at Strawberry Park Hot Springs.

20 DRY LAKE

Scenic rating: 7

north of Steamboat Springs

This is a great campground for visiting Steamboat Springs and sampling the outstanding hiking and mountain biking of the Park Range. Campers enjoy easy access to the Spring Creek, Fish Creek Falls, and Soda Creek Trails. The campground is also much more affordable than staying at Strawberry Park Hot Springs. During the summer, it can fill up on weekends, so it's best to arrive early for a site. There's been some bark beetle activity at this location, but the aspen, spruce, and fir are still mostly healthy. Sites 6 and 7 are the most private and border a scenic meadow where sheep sometimes graze. In general, sites are 50-100 feet apart, so while privacy is good, they are also close to the campground road. If Dry Lake Campground is full, continue east on Country Road 38. There is dispersed camping plus two more Forest Service campgrounds (Summit Lake and Granite) about 8 and 10 miles beyond Dry Lake up a rough, narrow, twisting road.

Campsites, facilities: There are eight sites for tents and RVs up to 20 feet. There are no hookups. Most sites are pull-through. Picnic tables and fire grates are provided. Vault toilets and trash receptacles are available. Leashed pets are permitted.

Reservations, fees: Reservations are not accepted. The fee is $10 per night. Cash or check only. Open June-October.

Directions: From Steamboat Springs, go northeast on Third Street. Turn right on Fish Creek Falls Road. Turn left on Amethyst Drive/County Road 36. In 2.5 miles, turn right on County Road 38/Forest Route 600. The campground is on the left in 3.3 miles.

Contact: Medicine Bow-Routt National Forests, Hahns Peak District, 970/870-2299, www.fs.usda.gov/mbr.

21 KOA STEAMBOAT CAMPGROUND

Scenic rating: 4

in Steamboat Springs

BEST (

Steamboat Campground is the typical KOA campground with plenty of RVs, cabins, and a sprinkling of tent sites. Campers won't stay here for the scenery, but they will stay here for the abundant recreational opportunities in the area. Steamboat Springs is an outdoor lover's heaven, and the downtown shops and restaurants are fun as well. There are public hot springs right downtown, and a white-water park, hiking and mountain biking trails in Medicine Bow and Medicine Bow-Routt National Forests, boating and fishing on Steamboat Lake and Pearl Lake—and that's just in the summer. In the fall, hunters fill this campground, and in the winter, when the champagne powder starts flying, this could be the most affordable place to stay in town. If you don't have time to take it all in, at least ride the Silver Bullet Gondola up the ski mountain for vistas of the Continental Divide and the Yampa Valley.

Campsites, facilities: There are 80 sites for RVs up to 65 feet and 43 sites for tents only, as well as 11 cabins. Full and partial hookups are available. Picnic tables, fire rings, and grills are provided. Restrooms with flush toilets and showers, a laundry room, drinking water, a pool, a playground, Wi-Fi, propane gas, and dump stations are available. There is also a recreation room, miniature-golf course, horseshoes, a pet walk, bike rentals, and a free bus service into town. Leashed pets are permitted.

Reservations, fees: Reservations are accepted at 800/562-7782. The tent fee is $39 per night for two people. The cost for RVs is $39-52 per night for two people and $58 for full hookups. Each additional person costs $5 per night. Open year-round.

Directions: From downtown Steamboat

Springs, drive west on U.S. Highway 40 for 2.0 miles. The campground is on the south side of the road, after the Snow Bowl Bowling Center. **Contact:** Steamboat Campground, 970/879-0273 or www.koa.com.

22 MEADOWS

Scenic rating: 6
southeast of Steamboat Springs

The Meadows is located between Steamboat Springs and Walden. This part of the Park Range is characterized by low peaks, meandering streams, and large meadows. The campground contains two loops near an open riparian zone. The forest has mostly fallen to the bark beetle. The campground isn't especially scenic, but as a stopover, it stays about half full during the summer. There are no hiking trails nearby.

Campsites, facilities: There are 30 sites for tents and RVs up to 40 feet. There are no hookups. Sites 8, 10, 15, 20, and 25 are pull-through. Picnic tables, fire rings, and grills are provided. Vault toilets are available. Leashed pets are permitted.

Reservations, fees: Reservations are not accepted. The fee is $10 per night. Cash or check only. Open early July-late October.

Directions: From Highway 131 in Steamboat Springs, take U.S. Highway 40 south for 11.4 miles. Turn right on Forest Route 297. The campground is in 0.2 mile.

Contact: Medicine Bow-Routt National Forests, Hahns Peak District, 970/870-2299, www.fs.usda.gov/mbr.

23 DUMONT LAKE

Scenic rating: 8
southeast of Steamboat Springs

Dumont Lake is the best campground on U.S. Highway 40, between Steamboat Springs and Rabbit Ears Pass at an elevation of 9,500 feet. The campground is in a large meadow with abundant wildflowers. In the distance, the smaller peaks of the Park Range, including Walton Peak and Baker Mountain, are visible. Hikers and mountain bikers can walk or drive up Forest Route 311 to the Fish Creek trail, which descends through subalpine meadows, past several lakes, to the popular Fish Creek Falls near Steamboat Springs. The campground is adjacent to a lake (open to electric motors and hand-propelled boats only) and a picnic area. Many trees were removed due to bark beetle damage, but it's still very nice.

Campsites, facilities: There are 22 sites for tents and RVs up to 40 feet. There are no hookups. Sites 1, 2, 5, 7, 8, 16, and 19-21 are pull-through. The nicest and most private sites are 10-15. Picnic tables, fire rings, and grills are provided. Vault toilets and drinking water are available. Leashed pets are permitted.

Reservations, fees: Reservations are accepted at 877/444-6777 and www.recreation.gov. The fee is $12 per night. Cash or check only. Open late June-late October.

Directions: From Highway 131 in Steamboat Springs, take U.S. Highway 40 south for 16.3 miles. Turn left on Forest Route 315. The campground is on the left in 1.2 miles.

Contact: Medicine Bow-Routt National Forests, Hahns Peak-Bears Ears District, 970/870-2299, www.fs.usda.gov/mbr.

24 JUNCTION CITY

Scenic rating: 6

in Stagecoach State Park

Stagecoach Reservoir is named for the vehicles that used to carry passengers and supplies over Yellow Jacket Pass, now County Road 14, between Oak Creek and Steamboat Springs. The 780-acre reservoir is in a river valley green with native grasses, shrubs, and wildflowers. Woodchuck Hill and Green Ridge fill the horizon to the south, and there are glimpses of the Flat Tops to the west. The reservoir is three miles long and home to rainbow trout, as well as some brown and cutthroat. Most visitors come for the fishing and waterskiing. On the south shore, there's a five-mile hiking and biking trail, as well as fishing access and boat ramps. The one-mile Lakeside Trail on the north shore can be connected with the Elk Run Trail by walking on County Road 16 for a short distance. All of the campgrounds are on the north shore, with excellent views of the lake, but traffic noise from Highway 14 is bothersome. Additionally, the campsites are surfaced with a gravel material that is practically impervious to tent stakes. If you don't have a mallet, you'll have to pitch your tent in the grass. It's about a 15-minute drive to Oak Creek, a town with a couple of restaurants and services, and about 25 minutes to Steamboat Springs.

Junction City is adjacent to the wakeless boating area of the reservoir. The boat ramp and swim beach are a short walk away. The habitat is mostly sagebrush, with a few planted trees. Sites 6-12, 16, 17, 19, and 20 are lakeside. Sites 9, 25, and 27 have a few shade trees.

Campsites, facilities: There are 27 sites for tents and RVs up to 35 feet. Electrical hookups are available. Sites 4, 16, 17, 19, 20, 22, 24, and 26 are pull-through. Picnic tables, fire rings, and grills are provided. Flush toilets, drinking water, a picnic area, and a dump station are available. Campers can use the showers at the Pinnacle campground. A convenience store, boat rentals, boat ramp, and swim beach are available at the marina. Leashed pets are permitted.

Reservations, fees: Reservations are accepted at 800/678-2267 and www.cpwshop.com. The fee is $32 per night. Campers must also purchase a vehicle pass ($8) or an Annual Parks Pass ($80). Open May 15-September 30 (though four campsites are open through winter).

Directions: From Steamboat Springs, take U.S. Highway 40 south to Highway 131 south. In about 6.0 miles, turn left on County Road 14. The entrance station is in about 5.0 miles. Turn right 0.4 mile after the entrance station. In 0.3 mile, turn left into the campground.

Contact: Stagecoach State Park, 970/736-2436, www.cpw.state.co.us.

25 PINNACLE

Scenic rating: 4

in Stagecoach State Park

Pinnacle is on a high, flat area on the north shore of three-mile Stagecoach Reservoir, adjacent to a small knob with a short walking trail and a scenic overlook. The campground is essentially an RV park. It has rows of parallel pull-through RV sites that are not suitable for tent camping. Nevertheless, it's a popular campground and quite busy on summer weekends. It's adjacent to the marina, boat ramp, and swim beach. Sites 58-65 have the best lake views. (For more information on Stagecoach State Park, see the Junction City entry in this chapter.)

Campsites, facilities: There are 38 sites (#28-65) for RVs up to 35 feet. There are electrical hookups, and all sites are pull-through. Picnic tables, fire rings, and grills are provided. Restrooms with flush toilets and showers, drinking water, and a dump station are available. A convenience store (Wi-Fi is available on the shaded porch), boat rentals, boat ramp, and a swim beach are available at the marina. Leashed pets are permitted. Site 65 is wheelchair-accessible.

Reservations, fees: Reservations are accepted at 800/678-2267 and www.cpwshop.com. The fee is $32 per night. Campers must also purchase a vehicle pass ($8) or an Annual Parks Pass ($80). Open May 15-September 30. Four sites remain open in the winter (without water) on a first-come, first-served basis.

Directions: From Steamboat Springs, take U.S. Highway 40 south to Highway 131 south. In about 6.0 miles, turn left on County Road 14. The entrance station is in about 5.0 miles. Turn left 0.4 mile after the entrance station. The campground is on the right in 0.1 mile.

Contact: Stagecoach State Park, 970/736-2436, www.cpw.state.co.us.

26 HARDING SPUR
🚶 🚴 ♨ 🎣 🛶 🛥 🏕 🚐 ⛺

Scenic rating: 5
in Stagecoach State Park

Harding parallels a narrow inlet on the north shore of Stagecoach Reservoir. The views aren't as panoramic as at the other campgrounds, but there's also no noise from Highway 14. The campground is in a sagebrush meadow with very few trees and no shade. Sites 66, 67, 69, 72, 74, and 76 are closest to the water. (For more information on Stagecoach State Park, see the Junction City entry in this chapter.)

Campsites, facilities: There are 18 sites (#66-83) for tents and RVs up to 25 feet. There are no hookups or pull-throughs. Picnic tables, fire rings, and grills are provided. Flush toilets, drinking water, and a dump station are available. A convenience store, boat rentals, boat ramp, and swim beach are available at the marina. Leashed pets are permitted.

Reservations, fees: Reservations are accepted at 800/678-2267 and www.cpwshop.com. The

fee is $24 per night. Campers must also purchase a vehicle pass ($8) or an Annual Parks Pass ($80). Open May 15-September 30.

Directions: From Steamboat Springs, take U.S. Highway 40 south to Highway 131 south. In about 6.0 miles, turn left on County Road 14. The entrance station is in about 5.0 miles. Turn left 0.4 mile after the entrance station. The road ends at the campground in 0.2 mile.

Contact: Stagecoach State Park, 970/736-2436, www.cpw.state.co.us.

27 MCKINDLEY
🚶 🚴 ♨ 🎣 🛶 🛥 🏕 ⛺

Scenic rating: 6
in Stagecoach State Park

McKindley is the only tent campground at Stagecoach State Park. This small loop is on a hill overlooking the lake and the other campgrounds. The sites are just 10-20 feet apart, and the vegetation is mostly sagebrush, so there is no shade and very little privacy, but thanks to a small hill in the middle of the loop, campers can see only a couple of sites at a time. (For more information on Stagecoach State Park, see the Junction City entry in this chapter.)

Campsites, facilities: There are nine sites (#66-92) for tents and RVs up to 20 feet and one group site for 45 people. There are no hookups. Sites 91 and 92 are pull-through. Picnic tables, fire rings, and grills are provided. Vault toilets are available. At the marina, a convenience store, boat rentals, boat ramp, swim beach, and restrooms with flush toilets and showers are available. Leashed pets are permitted.

Reservations, fees: Reservations are accepted at 800/678-2267 and www.cpwshop.com. (To reserve the group site, contact the park directly.) The fee is $14 per night. Campers must also purchase a vehicle pass ($8) or an Annual Parks Pass ($80). Open May 15-September 30.

Directions: From Steamboat Springs, take U.S. Highway 40 south to Highway 131 south.

In about 6.0 miles, turn left on County Road 14. The entrance station is in about 5.0 miles. Turn right 0.1 mile after the entrance station and stay to the left up the hill to enter the campground. **Contact:** Stagecoach State Park, 970/736-2436, www.cpw.state.co.us.

28 RANGELY CAMPER PARK

Scenic rating: 3

north of Rangely

This campground is a paved loop in a mature stand of cottonwoods. It is shady and clean, but there is little reason to recommend it. It's a decent stopover for road-weary families, or a base camp for rock hounds and mountain bikers who want to explore the BLM lands that surround this tiny town. In Canyon Pintado, south of Rangely on Highway 139, there are numerous petroglyphs. Highway 139 is the quickest route from Dinosaur to Grand Junction.

Campsites, facilities: There are 23 sites for tents and RVs of any length. Sites 1, 3, 7, 8, 9, and 13-15 have electrical hookups. Picnic tables and grills are provided. Restrooms with flush toilets and showers, drinking water, volleyball court, horseshoe pits, fishing pond, river access and group picnic area, and a dump station are available. Leashed pets are permitted.

Reservations, fees: Reservations are not accepted. The fee is $15 without hookups and $20 with hookups. Cash only. Open May-October.

Directions: From Dinosaur, take Highway 64 south to Rangely. Turn left on Nicholson Avenue and then right on East Rangely Avenue. The campground is at the end of the road.

Contact: Western Rio Blanco Recreation and Park District, 970/675-8211.

29 MEADOW LAKE

Scenic rating: 6

southeast of Meeker

The White River Plateau is a vast landscape of rolling, sage-covered meadows and large stands of quaking aspen. This campground, at an elevation of 9,550 feet, is a popular destination for hunters, OHV owners, snowmobilers, and horseback riders. Meadow Lake also attracts boaters and fishers. The campground sits in a pine forest a short distance from the west end of the lake. There's no host at this campground, so between the OHV riders and the mariachi music, it can be a bit of a party scene. The sites are small and close together. Sites 2, 4, 8, and 9 have the best lake views. Sites 1-7 have the best shade.

Campsites, facilities: There are 10 sites for tents and small RVs. There are no hookups. Picnic tables, fire rings, and grills are provided. Vault toilets are available. Leashed pets are permitted. The fishing pier is wheelchair-accessible.

Reservations, fees: Reservations are not accepted. The fee is $20 per night, plus $6 day use fee for the lake. Cash or check only. Open May-October, road and weather conditions permitting.

Directions: From Buford, go south on County Road 17 for 14.4 miles. Turn left on Forest Route 601. In 5.4 miles, turn right at the fork to access to the campground.

Contact: White River National Forest, Rifle District, 970/625-2371, www.fs.usda.gov/whiteriver.

30 MEADOW RIDGE

Scenic rating: 6

southeast of Meeker

Meadow Ridge sits in a mature evergreen forest on a ridge overlooking Meadow Lake. The sites have ample shade and moderate privacy and are a short walk from the lake and boat ramp, but they do not offer lake views. The sites are larger and farther apart than at Meadow Lake, as well. The presence of a host keeps the party element much smaller than at Meadow Lake, but you are still likely to hear loud music and OHVs late into the night. The lake is stocked and attracts mainly sport fishers.

Campsites, facilities: There are 20 sites for tents and RVs. There are no hookups. Site 11 is pull-through. Picnic tables, fire rings, grills, and tent pads are provided. Vault toilets are available. Leashed pets are permitted. The facilities and some sites are wheelchair-accessible.

Reservations, fees: Reservations are not accepted. The fee is $20 per night, plus $5 day use fee for the lake. Cash or check only. Open May-October, road and weather conditions permitting.

Directions: From Buford, go south on County Road 17 for 14.4 miles. Turn left on Forest Route 601. In 5.4 miles, turn left at the fork to access to the campground.

Contact: White River National Forest, Rifle District, 970/625-2371, www.fs.usda.gov/whiteriver.

31 SOUTH FORK

Scenic rating: 8

southeast of Meeker

The drive to South Fork is a reward in itself.

This is quintessential Colorado terrain. The road follows the south fork of the White River up a wide valley with rock bands and ranch lands. The wide river offers excellent fishing for whitefish, rainbow, and cutthroat, but wait until you're in the campground to fish (the owner of the property before the campground has a reputation for shooting trespassers). Campers can also go hiking on the 26-mile South Fork Trail or visit the Spring Caves, if they aren't closed to protect the bats from white-nose syndrome (an imported fungal disease that has killed millions of bats in North America). Hikers may also see elk, moose, and bighorn sheep. The Hill Creek, Peltier Lake, and Bailey Lake campgrounds are a short drive away.

This is a busy campground that attracts visitors from all over the state. Sites 9, 10, and 11 are the preferred sites because they have excellent shade and border rock outcroppings that are great for scrambling. Tent sites 1 and 2 are about 100 yards down the South Fork Trail across a small bridge.

Campsites, facilities: There are 18 single sites for tents and RVs, including 2 walk-in sites and 3 overflow sites. There are no hookups. Picnic tables, fire rings, and grills are provided. Vault toilets and hitching posts are available. Leashed pets are permitted. The facilities are wheelchair-accessible.

Reservations, fees: Reservations are not accepted. The fee is $20 per night. Cash or check only. Open May-October.

Directions: From Buford, take County Road 17 south for 1.0 mile. Turn left on County Road 10. The road ends at the campground in 10 miles.

Contact: White River National Forest, Blanco District, 970/878-4039, www.fs.usda.gov/whiteriver.

32 EAST MARVINE

[icons]

Scenic rating: 7

east of Meeker

The Flat Tops Scenic Byway is an 82-mile drive (half of it on unpaved roads) through the northern half of the White River Plateau. The drive is scenic, especially at Ripple Creek Pass, but to really enjoy the Flat Tops, one needs to set up camp and hike into the 235,214-acre wilderness. This is an area of subalpine meadows and alpine tundra interrupted by volcanic cliffs and peaks and dotted with picturesque lakes. The East Marvine Trail begins about 2,000 feet below the plateau and climbs through aspen, pine, and spruce-fir forests past Rainbow Lake to the rolling tundra of the plateau. A side trail climbs Big Marvine Peak and offers panoramic vistas of the wilderness. This 10.5-mile trail can be done as an out-and-back day hike or linked with the Marvine Trail for an overnight loop. These trails are very popular pack trips, and the numerous lakes present good fly-fishing opportunities.

The campground at the trailhead is on the east side of the narrow Marvine Creek valley. The sites are shaded by aspen and spruce and overlook a small meadow. It's a short walk to the creek, where anglers can fish for small brookies. This pleasant campground rarely fills up.

Campsites, facilities: There are seven sites for tents and RVs up to 50 feet, plus two equestrian sites with corrals. There are no hookups. Site 1 is pull-through. Picnic tables, fire rings, grills, and trash receptacles are provided. Vault toilets are available, but there is no potable water provided. Leashed pets are permitted.

Reservations, fees: Reservations are not accepted. The fee is $20 per night (plus $5 per night for use of corral). Cash or check only. Open late May-late October.

Directions: From Meeker, take Highway 13 east for less than 2.0 miles. Then take Flat Top Road/County Road 8 east for 29 miles. Turn right on County Road 12. Stay left at the top of the hill and continue 4.8 miles to the campground.

Contact: White River National Forest, Blanco District, 970/878-4039, www.fs.usda.gov/whiteriver.

33 MARVINE

[icons]

Scenic rating: 7

east of Meeker

Like nearby East Marvine, this campground attracts mostly hikers and horseback riders (and elk hunters in season). The East Marvine and Marvine Trails begin 2,000 feet below the plateau and climb through valleys full of aspen and spruce-fir forests to the rolling tundra and picturesque lakes of the plateau. Slide Lake, Pine Island Lake, and Marvine Lakes are all near the trail, offering numerous opportunities for the backcountry angler. Above Marvine Lakes, the trail passes through a ghost forest killed by a budworm epidemic in the 1940s. These dead trees are an important habitat for birds and insects, but snags can be dangerous so hikers should stay on the trail. The East Marvine and Marvine Trails can be hiked separately or turned into an overnight loop.

The campground is in a small valley forested by aspen, spruce, and fir. Sites 1, 2, 4, 8, 17, and 18 are on the edge of a meadow, and the other sites are in the trees. This campground attracts regulars who return every year, many of them with horse trailers in tow. Boy Scout troops also frequent this campground, which is busier than East Marvine. If you bring horses, only certified weed-free forage and bedding are allowed in the campground.

Campsites, facilities: There are 24 sites for tents and RVs up to 60 feet, including four equestrian sites. There are no hookups. Sites 2, 4, 5, 11, 14, 17, and 18 are pull-through. Picnic tables, fire rings, and grills are provided. Vault toilets, drinking water, and horse corrals are available. Leashed pets are permitted.

Reservations, fees: Reservations are not accepted. The fee is $23 per night, plus an extra corral fee of $5 per night. Cash or check only. Open late May-late October.

Directions: From Meeker, take Highway 13 east for less than 2.0 miles. Then take Flat Top Road/County Road 8 east for 29 miles. Turn right on County Road 12. Stay left at the top of the hill. The road ends at the campground in 5.0 miles.

Contact: White River National Forest, Blanco District, 970/878-4039, www.fs.usda.gov/whiteriver.

34 NORTH FORK

Scenic rating: 6

east of Meeker

North Fork is the most accessible campground on the Flat Tops Trail Scenic Byway, an 82-mile driving route through the White River National Forest between Meeker and Yampa. This campground is a convenient stopover, and it appeals to ATV owners, hunters, motorcyclists, and mountain bikers because there's an extensive system of 4WD trails that travel north from the campground. For hikers and horseback riders, the Lost Creek Trail has good trout fishing, and the Lost Park Trail traverses important elk habitat. The more difficult Long Park Trail (open to motorcycles) has views of the White River Valley. It connects with the Deadhorse 4WD Loop. This area has been moderately affected by the bark beetle epidemic because it has a fairly diverse forest. Blocked trails due to deadfall are always a possibility, and the Forest Service recommends that 4WD users carry a chainsaw.

North Fork isn't the most scenic campground in the area, but it's a good place to slather on the mosquito repellent and put your feet up in a hammock. The campground rarely fills up and is usually slow midweek. The sites are widely spaced, and dense underbrush provides ample privacy, while aspen trees offer shade.

Campsites, facilities: There are 28 sites for tents and RVs up to 45 feet. There are no hookups. Picnic tables, fire rings, grills, and some tent pads, and trash receptacles are provided. New vault toilets and drinking water are available. Leashed pets are permitted.

Reservations, fees: Reservations are accepted for some of the sites at 877/444-6777 and www.recreation.gov. The fee is $23 per night (plus $5 per additional vehicle). Cash or check only. Open late May-late October.

Directions: From Meeker, take Highway 13 east for less than 2.0 miles. Then take North Fork Road/County Road 8 east for 32.5 miles. The campground is on the left.

Contact: White River National Forest, Blanco District, 970/878-4039, www.fs.usda.gov/whiteriver.

35 VAUGHAN LAKE

Scenic rating: 7

west of Oak Creek

Vaughan Lake is a small, stocked reservoir on the eastern side of the Flat Tops Scenic Byway. The primitive campground is in an aspen grove overlooking the lake, which is surrounded by meadows and spruce-covered hills. The sites are large and well-spaced, but the spurs are very rough and a few require high clearance. Site 1 is totally isolated and the most scenic. The other sites are near the road. Nearby Ripple Creek Pass has panoramic views of the Flat Top Mountains, formed over millennia by volcanic activity, glacial activity, and erosion.

Campsites, facilities: There are six sites for tents and RVs up to 18 feet. There are no hookups. Site 4 is pull-through. Picnic tables, fire rings, and grills are provided. Vault toilets are available. No potable water provided. Leashed pets are permitted.

Reservations, fees: Reservations are not accepted. The fee is $10 per night. Cash or check only. Open Memorial Day-late September, weather permitting.

Directions: From Oak Creek, take County Road 25 west for 7.0 miles to County Road 132/Forest Route 16 and go right. In 17.5 miles, continue left on County Road 8. The campground is on the right in 7.5 miles.

Contact: Medicine Bow-Routt National Forests, Yampa District, 970/638-4516, www.fs.usda.gov/mbr.

36 HIMES PEAK

Scenic rating: 6

east of Meeker

Himes Peak is on the North Fork of the White River, not far from the famed Trappers Lake area. Himes Peak used to be a lush and shady destination, but the bark beetle has decimated the campground. The sites are 20-50 feet apart and privacy is poor. Anglers and hikers are the most common visitors. The high-use Big Fish Trail leaves from the campground and accesses several fishing spots: Big Fish, Boulder, Gwendolyn, Robinson, McBride, and Doris Lakes. The trail also passes Bessie's Falls and climbs onto the Flat Tops Plateau.

Campsites, facilities: There are 11 sites for tents and RVs up to 36 feet. There are no hookups. Sites 1, 7, and 11 are pull-through. Picnic tables, fire rings, and grills are provided. Vault toilets and water are available. Leashed pets are permitted.

Reservations, fees: Reservations are not accepted. The fee is $20 per night (includes two vehicles). Cash or check only. Open late May-late October.

Directions: From Meeker, take Highway 13 east for less than 2.0 miles. Then take Flat Top Road/County Road 8 east for 39.2 miles. Turn right on Forest Route 205. In 4.3 miles, turn right at the campground sign and continue 0.4 mile to the campground.

Contact: White River National Forest, Blanco District, 970/878-4039, www.fs.usda.gov/whiteriver.

37 TRAPPERS LAKE-HORSE THIEF

Scenic rating: 6

east of Meeker

A drive along the Flat Tops Scenic Byway isn't complete without a side trip to Trappers Lake, the birthplace of the wilderness concept. In 1919, landscape architect Arthur Carhart was sent by the Forest Service to survey the lake for a summer resort. The beauty of the lake ringed by volcanic cliffs inspired him to recommend saving this wilderness in its natural form for all visitors rather than transforming it into a summer destination for a few. The Forest Service heeded his recommendation, marking the genesis of the wilderness movement that Aldo Leopold spearheaded. The north shore has campgrounds and roads, but the rest of the shoreline is wilderness. The trail system around the lake features the Carhart, Stillwater, Trappers Lake, and Wall Lake Trails, which offer numerous opportunities for day hiking and backpacking in the Flat Tops Wilderness. In addition to excellent native trout fishing, these trails access the rolling tundra of the 11,000-foot Flat Tops Plateau, the stunning Chinese Wall, the Devil's Causeway, and panoramic views of the wilderness. The trails also pass through a ghost forest of spruce killed in the 1940s by a budworm epidemic. Hikers should be wary of snags in this area.

There are five campgrounds in a circle on

the north shore of the lake. Horse Thief is the wrangler's campground. It is ringed by the cliffs of the Flat Tops Plateau and the ghost forest. The campground is in a hummocky meadow with many wildflowers. The sites are not private because all of the trees have been cut down due to the bark beetle.

Campsites, facilities: There are five sites for tents and RVs up to 60 feet. There are no hookups. Picnic tables, fire rings, grills, and tent pads are provided. Vault toilets, horse corrals, water, and a dump station are available. Leashed pets are permitted. The facilities are wheelchair-accessible.

Reservations, fees: Reservations are not accepted. The fee is $27 per night. Cash or check only. Open early June-late October.

Directions: From Meeker, take Highway 13 east for less than 2.0 miles. Then take Flat Top Road/County Road 8 east for 39.2 miles. Turn right on Forest Route 205. In 7.5 miles, veer right and cross the one-lane bridge. The campground is on the right, 1.0 mile after the bridge.

Contact: White River National Forest, Blanco District, 970/878-4039, www.fs.usda.gov/whiteriver.

38 TRAPPERS LAKE-SHEPHERD'S RIM

🖈 🛶 ➝ 🎣 🐴 ♿ 🚐 ⛺

Scenic rating: 8

east of Meeker

BEST (

Shepherd's Rim features a striking contrast. Set in a dense spruce-fir forest, the campground is ringed by the ghost forest that a budworm epidemic created in the 1940s. In late summer, the forest floor is covered with wildflowers, so sites with views of the North Fork valley are prized. Sites 7 and 8 have the best views to the west of the Chinese Wall. The campground is flatter than nearby Buck's, and the sites are more private. The Himes Peak trailhead is adjacent. (For more information on Trappers Lake, see

the Trappers Lake-Horse Thief listing in this chapter.)

Campsites, facilities: There are 16 sites for tents and RVs up to 36 feet. There are no hookups. Picnic tables, fire rings, and grills are provided. Sites 1, 3, 5, 7-9, and 12 have tent pads. Vault toilets, water, and a dump station are available. Leashed pets are permitted. Site 2 and the facilities are wheelchair-accessible.

Reservations, fees: Reservations are accepted for a few sites. The fee is $22 per night. Cash or check only. Open early June-late October.

Directions: From Meeker, take Highway 13 east for less than 2.0 miles. Then take Flat Top Road/County Road 8 east for 39.2 miles. Turn right on Forest Route 205. In 7.5 miles, veer right and cross the one-lane bridge. The campground is on the right, 1.2 miles after the bridge.

Contact: White River National Forest, Blanco District, 970/878-4039, www.fs.usda.gov/whiteriver.

39 TRAPPERS LAKE-BUCK'S

🖈 🛶 ➝ 🎣 🐴 🚐 ⛺

Scenic rating: 6

east of Meeker

Buck's is the least appealing of the five campgrounds on the north shore of picturesque Trappers Lake. The campground is in a dense spruce-fir forest, and the sites are close to each other and the campground road. It's a bit hilly, so flat tent sites can be hard to find. The trees obscure views of the surrounding cliffs. Only site 5 offers glimpses of the Flat Tops. (For more information on Trappers Lake, see the Trappers Lake-Horse Thief entry in this chapter.)

Campsites, facilities: There are 10 sites for tents and RVs up to 36 feet. There are no hookups. Sites 1, 3, 7, and 9 are pull-through. Picnic tables, fire rings, and grills, are provided. Sites 3 and 4 have tent pads. Vault toilets, water, and a dump station are available. Leashed pets are permitted.

Reservations, fees: Reservations are not accepted. The fee is $20 per night. Cash or check only. Open early June-early September.

Directions: From Meeker, take Highway 13 east for less than 2.0 miles. Then take Flat Top Road/County Road 8 east for 39.2 miles. Turn right on Forest Route 205. In 7.5 miles, veer right and cross the one-lane bridge. The campground is on the left, 1.1 miles after the bridge.

Contact: White River National Forest, Blanco District, 970/878-4039, www.fs.usda.gov/whiteriver.

40 TRAPPERS LAKE-CUTHROAT

🏃‍♀️ 🛶 🚤 ⛵ 🐎 🚐 ⛺

Scenic rating: 8

east of Meeker

BEST (

Cutthroat and Trapline are identical twins. Adjacent to Trappers Lake, these campgrounds are in a dense spruce-fir forest that obscures the lake but permits glimpses of the volcanic cliffs that ring the lake. The sites are about 50 feet apart and very private. Sites 5, 6, and 7 have the best views. Sites 10 and 11 are runners-up. Cutthroat is the most popular campground at the lake. (For more information on Trappers Lake, see the Trappers Lake-Horse Thief entry in this chapter.)

Campsites, facilities: There are 14 sites for tents and RVs up to 36 feet. There are no hookups. Sites 1, 2, 3, and 12 are pull-through. Picnic tables, fire rings, and grills are provided. Sites 1, 2, 8, and 13 have tent pads. Vault toilets, water, and a dump station are available. Leashed pets are permitted.

Reservations, fees: Reservations are not accepted. The fee is $22 per night (includes two vehicles). Additional vehicles cost $5 per night. Cash or check only. Open early June-late September.

Directions: From Meeker, take Highway 13 east for less than 2.0 miles. Then take Flat Top Road/County Road 8 east for 39.2 miles. Turn right on Forest Route 205. In 7.5 miles, veer right and cross the one-lane bridge. The campground is on the right, 1.3 miles after the bridge.

Contact: White River National Forest, Blanco District, 970/878-4039, www.fs.usda.gov/whiteriver.

41 TRAPPERS LAKE-TRAPLINE

🏃‍♀️ 🛶 🚤 ⛵ 🐎 🚐 ⛺

Scenic rating: 8

east of Meeker

Cutthroat and Trapline are identical twins, except that Cutthroat is more popular. Adjacent to Trappers Lake, these campgrounds are in a dense spruce-fir forest that obscures the lake but permits glimpses of the volcanic cliffs that ring the lake. The sites are about 50 feet apart and very private. They are also flat, so there's room to spread out. (For more information on Trappers Lake, see the Trappers Lake-Horse Thief entry in this chapter.)

Campsites, facilities: There are 13 sites for tents and RVs up to 36 feet. There are no hookups. Site 11 is pull-through. Picnic tables, fire rings, and grills are provided. Sites 1, 2, 4, 7, 8, and 11 have tent pads. Vault toilets, water, and a dump station are available. Leashed pets are permitted.

Reservations, fees: Reservations are not accepted. The fee is $20 per night. Cash or check only. Open early June-late October.

Directions: From Meeker, take Highway 13 east for less than 2.0 miles. Then take Flat Top Road/County Road 8 east for 39.2 miles. Turn right on Forest Route 205. In 7.5 miles, veer right and cross the one-lane bridge. The campground is on the right, 1.3 miles after the bridge. It is the last campground on the circle.

Contact: White River National Forest, Blanco District, 970/878-4039, www.fs.usda.gov/whiteriver.

42 SHERIFF RESERVOIR

Scenic rating: 7

west of Oak Creek

This is a small and remote campground that overlooks a scenic reservoir and has views of Sand Point and the Little Flat Tops. It's an excellent stopover on the Flat Tops Scenic Byway. Visitors can take the Black Mountain and Sand Creek trails into the Flat Tops Wilderness and try fishing on the lake and Trout Creek. This is an older campground so the sites are just 25 feet apart and haven't been updated, but it rarely fills up. Sites 4-6 are closest to the lake and the nicest.

Campsites, facilities: There are six sites for tents and pop-ups. There are no hookups. Picnic tables and fire grates are provided. Vault toilets are available. No potable water provided. Leashed pets are permitted.

Reservations, fees: Reservations are not accepted. The fee is $10 per night. Cash or check only. Open May-September.

Directions: From Steamboat Springs, take Highway 131 south to Phippsburg. Turn right on County Road 15. In 2.7 miles, turn right on County Road 132/North Fork Road. In 9.3 miles, turn left on County Road 95/Forest Route 959. The road ends at the campground in about 5.0 miles.

Contact: Medicine Bow-Routt National Forests, Yampa District, 970/638-4516, www.fs.usda.gov/mbr.

43 TROUT CREEK DISPERSED

Scenic rating: 9

west of Oak Creek

Trout Creek is a beautiful watershed with views of the Little Flat Tops at many sites. There are around 10 dispersed sites along the creek as it climbs to Sheriff Reservoir. Campers will enjoy outstanding privacy, fewer OHVs than at Chapman Reservoir, good fishing on the lake and in the creek and beaver ponds, and great trail access into the Flat Tops Wilderness. The best sites are south of the bridge.

Campsites, facilities: There are approximately 10 sites for tents and RVs. There are no facilities. Leashed pets are permitted.

Reservations, fees: Reservations are not accepted. There is no fee. Open year-round, road and weather conditions permitting.

Directions: From Steamboat Springs, take Highway 131 south to Phippsburg. Turn right on County Road 15. In 2.7 miles, turn right on County Road 132/North Fork Road. In 9.3 miles, turn left on County Road 95/Forest Route 959. The sites are on both sides of the creek up to the reservoir.

Contact: Medicine Bow-Routt National Forests, Yampa District, 970/638-4516, www.fs.usda.gov/mbr.

44 CHAPMAN RESERVOIR

Scenic rating: 7

west of Oak Creek

Chapman Reservoir is not an especially scenic destination, but it does offer views of Sand Point and the northern end of the Little Flat Tops. The campground is popular with OHV owners and is also a good stopover for visitors to the Flat Tops Scenic Byway. The campground sits in an aspen and pine forest and most sites

Summer wildflowers carpet the landscape around Chapman Reservoir.

lack privacy. Sites 1, 3, and 5 overlook the reservoir. Sites 9-12 are grouped around a parking lot removed from the other sites, and make an excellent group site, especially for a group with RVs and OHVs. Site 1 is the best choice in terms of privacy and scenery.

Campsites, facilities: There are 12 sites for tents and RVs. There are no hookups. Site 2 is pull-through. Picnic tables and fire grates are provided. Vault toilets are available. No potable water provided. Leashed pets are permitted. The facilities are wheelchair-accessible.

Reservations, fees: Reservations are not accepted. The fee is $10 per night. Cash or check only. Open late May-November, depending on road and weather conditions.

Directions: From Steamboat Springs, take Highway 131 south to Phippsburg. Turn right on County Road 15. In 2.7 miles, turn right on County Road 132/North Fork Road. In 6.8 miles, turn left on County Road 97/Chapman Reservoir Road. The campground is on the right in 1.3 miles.

Contact: Medicine Bow-Routt National Forests, Yampa District, 970/638-4516, www.fs.usda.gov/mbr.

45 COLD SPRINGS

Scenic rating: 9

west of Yampa

BEST (

This campground is a gem. The Bear River Recreation Area contains 10,000 acres of national forest that abuts the Flat Tops Wilderness, the second-largest wilderness area in the state. The Bear River Area is managed jointly by Medicine Bow-Routt National Forests and the Department of Wildlife, so the fishing in the reservoirs (Stillwater, Bear Lake, and Yamcolo) and the river has an excellent reputation. Cold Springs is the most remote of the three campgrounds in this area, but it's also the most rewarding. This little loop is high up the Bear River valley, and every site has views of the Flat Tops and the stunning Chinese Wall, a 600-1,000-foot cliff. Equally impressive is the

Devil's Causeway, a rock ridge that divides the Williams Fork and Bear River drainages. It's about 50 feet long and four feet across at its narrowest and requires a tough stomach to scramble across. The East Fork Trail accesses this area and can be turned into an overnight loop with the Stillwater Trail. In addition to fishing on the reservoir, the river, and the alpine lakes, the campground has a beautiful little fishing pond fed by two cascades, which is adjacent to several of the campsites. The campground fills up on weekends but is very slow midweek. It attracts regulars who enjoy the hiking and fishing.

Campsites, facilities: There are five sites for tents and RVs up to 20 feet. There are no hookups. Sites 1, 3, and 5 are pull-through. Picnic tables, fire rings, and grills are provided. Vault toilets and drinking water are available. Leashed pets are permitted.

Reservations, fees: Reservations are not accepted. The fee is $10 per night. Cash or check only. Open mid-June-late October.

Directions: From Yampa, take County Road 7/Forest Route 900 south for 16.6 miles. Turn right into the campground.

Contact: Medicine Bow-Routt National Forests, Yampa District, 970/638-4516, www.fs.usda.gov/mbr.

46 HORSESHOE

Scenic rating: 8

west of Yampa

Horseshoe is in the Bear River Recreation Area, which contains 10,000 acres of national forest that adjoin the Flat Tops Wilderness, the second-largest wilderness area in the state. The Bear River Area is managed jointly by Medicine Bow-Routt National Forests and the Department of Wildlife, so the fishing in the reservoirs (Stillwater, Bear Lake, and Yamcolo) and the river has an excellent reputation. At 10,000 feet, Horseshoe offers high-altitude camping for tents and small RVs. The views aren't as amazing as at Cold Springs, but they are still a tantalizing glimpse at the volcanic cliffs of the Flat Tops. The loop is right next to the road, and the small sites are 25-50 feet apart. Privacy could be a problem, but this campground is not heavily used. Several trails begin between the campground and Stillwater Reservoir, including the East Fork Trail, which climbs to the Devil's Causeway, a rock ridge that's 1,500 feet high and four feet wide at its narrowest. Hikers can also take the North Derby and Bear River Trails into the wilderness.

Campsites, facilities: There are seven sites for tents and RVs up to 25 feet. There are no hookups. Sites 6 and 7 are pull-through. Picnic tables, fire rings, and grills are provided. Vault toilets and drinking water are available. Leashed pets are permitted.

Reservations, fees: Reservations are not accepted. The fee is $10 per night. Cash or check only. Open Memorial Day-late September.

Directions: From Yampa, take County Road 7/Forest Route 900 south for 16.2 miles. Turn right into the campground.

Contact: Medicine Bow-Routt National Forests, Yampa District, 970/638-4516, www.fs.usda.gov/mbr.

47 BEAR LAKE

Scenic rating: 9

west of Yampa

Bear Lake is a lovely lake in the Bear River valley, not far from the Flat Tops Wilderness area, the second-largest wilderness area in the state. The lake is enclosed by the volcanic cliffs of the Flat Tops, and the valley is lush with aspen, spruce, and fir. The area is managed jointly by Medicine Bow-Routt National Forests and the Division of Wildlife, so the trout fishery has an excellent reputation. Bear Lake is open to electric and hand-powered boats, and there is a boat ramp on Yamcolo Reservoir for larger boats. The Mandall Lakes Trail begins opposite the campground and climbs onto the Flat Tops Plateau. Several more trails begin at Stillwater Reservoir.

The campground was renovated in 2003 and is the best campground in the valley for families and RVs. It's divided into two wooded loops. There has been some hazard-tree removal. The east loop (sites 24-43) has more aspens. The sites are 50-75 feet apart and fairly private. Sites 13, 34, and 35 are double units. Site 33 is a triple unit. Sites 14-18, 26, 28, 33, and 34 have the best views of the Flat Tops.

Campsites, facilities: There are 43 sites for tents and RVs up to 30 feet, including four double sites, one triple site, and two walk-in tent sites not mentioned on the website. There are no hookups. Sites 11, 17, 18, 25, and 26 are pull-through. Picnic tables, grills, grill tables, fire rings, and tent pads are provided. Vault toilets, drinking water, and a fishing pier are available. Leashed pets are permitted. Site 3 and the facilities are wheelchair-accessible.

Reservations, fees: Reservations are not accepted. The fee is $10 per night for a single site, $20 per night for a double, and $30 per night for a triple. Cash or check only. Open Memorial Day-late September.

Directions: From Yampa, take County Road 7/Forest Route 900 south for 13.5 miles. Turn left and continue 0.5 mile through the day-use area to the campground.

Contact: Medicine Bow-Routt National Forests, Yampa District, 970/638-4516, www. fs.usda.gov/mbr.

48 BEAR RIVER DISPERSED

Scenic rating: 9

west of Yampa

Dispersed camping is so popular in the 10,000-acre Bear River Recreation Area that the Forest

dispersed campsite in the Medicine Bow-Routt National Forests

Service has developed a system for managing the sites. For a small fee, you can camp away from the crowds with a grill and fire ring to boot. There are 32 sites from the Forest Service boundary to the Cold Springs campground, a distance of about 12 miles. Settings range from sagebrush flats to meadows to aspen groves and spruce-fir forests where there has been some hazard-tree removal. Sites 16-23 are near the Yamcolo Reservoir, and sites 24-26 are near Bear Lake. The views improve the higher you go. The Bear River is an excellent trout fishery, with lake fishing on the Yamcolo, Bear Lake, and Stillwater Reservoirs and backcountry fishing on alpine lakes in the Flat Tops Wilderness, which adjoins the recreation area. The fly-fishing is excellent on the rivers and streams. The 200 miles of hiking trails in the wilderness area are accessible from several trailheads near Stillwater Reservoir.

Campsites, facilities: There are 32 dispersed sites for tents and RVs up to 60 feet. Picnic tables, fire rings, and grills are provided at all sites. Leashed pets are permitted.

Reservations, fees: Reservations are not accepted. The fee is $5 per night. Cash or check only. Open mid-June-late October.

Directions: From Yampa, take County Road 7/Forest Route 900 south for 13 miles. Dispersed camping extends from the Forest Service boundary to Cold Springs campground.

Contact: Medicine Bow-Routt National Forests, Yampa District, 970/638-4516, www.fs.usda.gov/mbr.

49 BLACKTAIL CREEK
🚴 🐕 🚙 ⛺

Scenic rating: 6
east of Yampa

BEST (

Blacktail Creek is on the west side of the Gore Range, just a mile from Gore Pass (elevation 9,527 feet). The Lynx Pass-Gore Pass area is very popular with mountain bikers. Several mountain bike routes (on trails and Forest Service roads) explore the large, open meadows and forested ridgelines that characterize this region. Popular routes include the Morrison Divide and Tepee Creek Trails and the Rock Creek, Gore Pass, and Gore Creek Loops. (Trail descriptions and maps are available from the Forest Service.) Moose may be sighted near streams. Highway 134 is also very popular with road cyclists. The campground is in a forest of aspen and spruce near the headwaters of Blacktail Creek. It was heavily impacted by bark beetles and many trees were removed, but it remains a popular destination. Sites have partial shade and are 75-100 feet apart. This campground is popular, but still has ample room for a big family to spread out.

Campsites, facilities: There are eight sites for tents and RVs up to 18 feet. There are no hookups. Picnic tables, fire rings, and grills are provided. Vault toilets are available, but there is no potable water. Leashed pets are permitted.

Reservations, fees: Reservations are not accepted. The fee is $10 per night. Cash or check only. Open Memorial Day-late September.

Directions: From Yampa, take Highway 131 south for 9.0 miles. Go east on Highway 134 for 14.5 miles. The campground is on the right.

Contact: Medicine Bow-Routt National Forests, Yampa District, 970/638-4516, www.fs.usda.gov/mbr.

50 RIFLE MOUNTAIN PARK
👫 🐕 🚙 ⛺

Scenic rating: 6
north of Rifle

Rifle Mountain Park is a world-class rock-climbing destination with more than 250 bolted routes and a beginner's area. Most of the campers at this park are rock climbers, which explains why the underwhelming campground fills up so frequently. The campsites are dispersed along the east and west banks of

East Rifle Creek and a few sites are located up Huffman and Sawmill Gulch. The sites largely improve as you travel upstream. Sites 9, 19, 25, and 26 are most appealing. Campers who have never climbed can contact Rifle Recreation (970/665-6570) about instructional classes at the park, or just go for a hike on Rifle Creek Trail.

Campsites, facilities: There are 31 sites for tents and pop-ups. There are no hookups. Picnic tables, fire rings, and grills are provided. Vault toilets are available. Leashed pets are permitted.

Reservations, fees: Camping is first come, first served. Reservations are accepted for the Community House and Group Area at 970/665-6570. The fee is $15 per night for two cars and two tents, plus $5 for a day pass. Cash or check only. Open year-round.

Directions: From Rifle, take Highway 13 north. Turn right on County Road 325. Continue about 12 miles to the park entrance. The camping begins 1.7 miles past the entrance.

Contact: City of Rifle, Recreation Office, 970/665-6570, www.rifelco.org.

51 RIFLE FALLS STATE PARK

Scenic rating: 8

north of Rifle

BEST (

First impressions at Rifle Falls State Park are not very striking, but if you explore a little, you'll find a triple waterfall and caves riddling the limestone cliffs behind the falls. This is a unique destination, with more to offer than the arid canyon and red cliffs initially indicate. Consequently, the campground is full every weekend during the summer and reservations are essential. In addition to visiting the falls, campers can go hiking, mountain biking, or snowshoeing on three trails, or try fishing for brook and rainbow trout in East Rifle Creek. Weddings also take place at the falls.

Sites 1-13 have electric hookups and are best suited for RVs due to their proximity to the road and each other. Sites 10-13 are a good choice for a larger group. The tent sites (14-20) are right on the creek and offer excellent privacy and shade.

Campsites, facilities: There are 13 sites for tents and RVs up to 40 feet, plus 7 walk-in tent sites. Electric hookups are available. Sites 4-9 are pull-through. Picnic tables, fire rings, grills, and shelters are provided. Vault toilets and drinking water are available. Leashed pets are permitted. There are also a number of cabins and a yurt for rent. Site 2 and the facilities are wheelchair-accessible.

Reservations, fees: Reservations are accepted at 800/678-2267 and www.cpwshop.com. The fee is $26-36 per night. Campers must also purchase a vehicle pass ($8) or an Annual Parks Pass ($80). Cash, check, and credit cards are accepted. Open year-round.

Directions: From Rifle, take Highway 13 north. Turn right on County Road 325. Continue about 10 miles to the park entrance on the right.

Contact: Rifle Falls State Park, 970/625-1607, www.cpw.state.co.us.

52 COTTONWOOD

Scenic rating: 6

in Rifle Gap State Park

Rifle Gap State Park is a very popular destination thanks to its proximity to I-70, the 360-acre reservoir, and the campground renovations that took place in 2007. The park now has five campgrounds along the lake's north shore, each one designed to appeal to a slightly different group. Fishing and water sports are the most popular activities at the park. Swimming is limited to the swim beach and is prohibited some years when lake levels drop too low. Winter visitors can try ice fishing and cross-country skiing.

Cottonwood is the second-smallest campground at the park. It's very close to the water and a few cottonwoods offer shade, but this windy site is best suited for RV camping. The views of the Grand Hogback and the reservoir are excellent.

Campsites, facilities: There are eight sites for tents and RVs up to 40 feet. Water and electrical hookups are available. Picnic tables, fire rings, grills, shelters, and tent pads are provided. Flush toilets, showers, drinking water, and dump stations are available. A group picnic area is available by reservation. Leashed pets are permitted. Site 3 and the facilities are wheelchair-accessible.

Reservations, fees: Reservations are accepted at 800/678-2267 and www.cpwshop.com. A basic site is $28 per night. Campers must also purchase a vehicle pass ($8) or an Annual Parks Pass ($80). Cash, check, and credit cards are accepted. Open year-round.

Directions: From Rifle, take Highway 13 north. Turn right on County Road 325. Continue 5.8 miles to the park entrance on the left and follow the signs to the campground.

Contact: Rifle Gap State Park, 970/625-1607, www.cpw.state.co.us.

53 LAKEVIEW

Scenic rating: 6

in Rifle Gap State Park

Lakeview is the largest campground at Rifle Gap State Park. (For more information on Rifle Gap State Park, see the Cottonwood entry in this chapter.)

It's a terraced hillside with paved sites for RVs and a loop for walk-in tent camping. Most sites have excellent views of the Grand Hogback and the reservoir, but the piñon-juniper vegetation doesn't provide any shade. The boat

ramp is a short drive away and winter visitors will find excellent access to cross-country skiing and ice-fishing opportunities. The walk-in sites (30-54) are 50 to 100 feet apart and have some of the best views.

Campsites, facilities: There are 46 sites for tents and RVs up to 40 feet, including 15 walk-in tent sites. Full hookups and pull-throughs are available. Picnic tables, fire rings, grills, shelters, and tent pads are provided. Vault toilets, flush toilets, showers, drinking water, and dump stations are available. Leashed pets are permitted. Sites 26, 34, and the facilities are wheelchair-accessible.

Reservations, fees: Reservations are accepted at 800/678-2267 and www.cpwshop.com. The fee is $38 per night. Campers must also purchase a vehicle pass ($8) or an Annual Parks Pass ($80). Cash, check, and credit cards are accepted. Open year-round.

Directions: From Rifle, take Highway 13 north. Turn right on County Road 325. Continue 5.8 miles to the park entrance on the left and follow the signs to the campground.

Contact: Rifle Gap State Park, 970/625-1607, www.cpw.state.co.us.

54 CEDAR

Scenic rating: 6

in Rifle Gap State Park

Cedar is a small loop with excellent views located very close to the reservoir at Rifle Gap State Park. It has better boating access than both Cottonwood and Lakeview, and winter visitors may try cross-country skiing on the trail system when weather conditions permit. (For more information on Rifle Gap State Park, see the Cottonwood entry in this chapter.) The sites are close together, but sites 61 and 69 offer the most privacy.

Campsites, facilities: There are 15 sites for tents and RVs up to 40 feet. Electrical hookups are available. Sites 63 and 64 are pull-through. Picnic tables, fire rings, grills, shelters, and tent pads are provided. Vault toilets and drinking water are available. Leashed pets are permitted. Sites 62, 65, and the facilities are wheelchair-accessible.

Reservations, fees: Reservations are accepted at 800/678-2267 and www.cpwshop.com. The fee is $28 per night. Campers must also purchase a vehicle pass ($8) or an Annual Parks Pass ($80). Cash, check, and credit cards are accepted. Open year-round.

Directions: From Rifle, take Highway 13 north. Turn right on County Road 325. Continue 5.8 miles to the park entrance on the left and follow the signs to the campground.

Contact: Rifle Gap State Park, 970/625-1607, www.cpw.state.co.us.

55 SAGE

Scenic rating: 6

in Rifle Gap State Park

Sage is the only campground at Rifle Gap State Park that allows OHV operation. Campers can ride their vehicles onto the adjacent BLM property. The campground is located very close to the boat ramp and 0.7 mile from the swim beach. The swim beach is a small sandy area in a cove at the western tip of the lake. It has picnic shelters, volleyball courts, and shade trees. In the campground, sites 81, 83, and 84 have the best views of the hogbacks and the lake. Winter visitors can try ice fishing on the lake or cross-country skiing on the trail system when there's enough snow. (For more information on Rifle Gap State Park, see the Cottonwood entry in this chapter.)

Campsites, facilities: There are 15 sites for tents and RVs up to 40 feet. There are no hook-ups but most sites are pull-through. Picnic tables, fire rings, grills, shelters, and tent pads are provided. Vault toilets and drinking water are

available. The swim beach and boat ramp are nearby. Leashed pets are permitted. Site 70 and the facilities are wheelchair-accessible.

Reservations, fees: Reservations are accepted at 800/678-2267 and www.cpwshop.com. The fee is $22 per night. Campers must also purchase a vehicle pass ($8) or an Annual Parks Pass ($80). Cash, check, and credit cards are accepted. Open year-round.

Directions: From Rifle, take Highway 13 north. Turn right on County Road 325. Continue 5.8 miles to the park entrance on the left and follow the signs to the campground.

Contact: Rifle Gap State Park, 970/625-1607, www.cpw.state.co.us.

56 PINYON

Scenic rating: 7

in Rifle Gap State Park

Pinyon is the smallest of the five campgrounds at Rifle Gap State Park. (For more information on Rifle Gap State Park, see the Cottonwood entry in this chapter.) It's centrally located, with easy access to the swim beach and the boat ramp for anglers and water-sports enthusiasts. In the winter, adventurous campers may enjoy ice fishing when water levels permit. The sites are small and close together, but the piñon trees provide excellent shade and more privacy than at most of the campgrounds at Rifle Gap. This would make an excellent group destination. Site 87 has the best views.

Campsites, facilities: There are five sites for tents and RVs up to 28 feet. There are no hookups. Picnic tables, fire rings, and grills are provided. Vault toilets and drinking water are available. The swim beach and boat ramp are nearby. Leashed pets are permitted.

Reservations, fees: Reservations are accepted at 800/678-2267 and www.cpwshop.com. The fee is $22 per night. Campers must also purchase a vehicle pass ($8) or an Annual Parks

Pass ($80). Cash, check, and credit cards are accepted. Open year-round.

Directions: From Rifle, take Highway 13 north. Turn right on County Road 325. Continue 5.8 miles to the park entrance on the left and follow the signs to the campground.

Contact: Rifle Gap State Park, 970/625-1607, www.cpw.state.co.us.

57 DEEP LAKE

Scenic rating: 8

north of Glenwood Springs

The White River Plateau is an area of rolling subalpine meadows and alpine tundra dotted with small scenic lakes and interspersed with spruce-fir forests and aspen groves. This area is unique in Colorado for its openness. It's also home to thriving elk herds and the 235,000-acre Flat Tops Wilderness. Deep Lake is a high-alpine campground on the southern edge of the plateau, far from the trails of the wilderness area, which makes it popular with four-wheelers and ATV owners, and the lake attracts anglers as well as electric and hand-powered boats. The campground contains two loops on the east side of Deep Lake with excellent scenery: rolling meadows, a steep canyon, spruce-fir stands with minimal bark beetle impact, and wildflowers. The sites are 50-75 feet apart in meadows and trees. Privacy varies widely with the number of trees. Sites 9, 28, 30-32, and A-C have the best lake views.

Campsites, facilities: There are 37 sites for tents and RVs up to 36 feet. There are no hookups. Sites 6, 17, 18, 20, and 21 are pull-through. Picnic tables, fire rings and grills are provided. Trash pickup is available through mid-September, and then must be packed out. A gravel boat ramp and wheelchair-accessible vault toilets are available. Leashed pets are permitted.

Reservations, fees: Reservations are not

accepted. The fee is $6 per night. Cash or check only. Open early July-mid-September.

Directions: From Glenwood Springs, take I-70 east to Exit 133. Go north on County Road 301 for 1.6 miles. Turn left on Coffee Pot Road/Forest Route 600. The campground is on the right in 28.5 miles.

Contact: White River National Forest, Eagle-Holy Cross District, 970/827-5715, www.fs.usda.gov/whiteriver.

58 COFFEE POT SPRING DISPERSED

Scenic rating: 7

north of Glenwood Springs

Coffee Pot Spring was changed to dispersed camping in 2017. It is on the southern edge of the White River Plateau, far from the trails of the wilderness area, which makes it popular with ATV owners. Several 4WD roads begin nearby. The nearest hiking trail, Broken Rib, is three miles up Coffee Pot Road. The nearby Deep Creek Overlook is simply amazing. From the top of the plateau, you can look down a deep canyon with walls of sandstone and shale. The campground is a small loop on a sloping meadow full of colorful wildflowers. The campsites are on the edge of an aspen grove. Sites 5-8 and 10 are in the trees, and the other sites are in the meadow. (For more information on the White River Plateau, see the Deep Lake listing in this chapter.)

Campsites, facilities: There are 10 old sites for tents and RVs up to 30 feet. There are no hookups, no drinking water, and no bathrooms. Picnic tables, fire rings, and grills are provided. Leashed pets are permitted.

Reservations, fees: Reservations are not accepted. There is no fee.

Directions: From Glenwood Springs, take I-70 east to Exit 133. Go north on County Road 301 for 1.6 miles. Turn left on Coffee Pot Road/

Forest Route 600. The campground is on the left in 16.6 miles.

Contact: White River National Forest, Eagle-Holy Cross District, 970/827-5715, www.fs.usda.gov/whiteriver.

59 SWEETWATER LAKE

Scenic rating: 8

north of Glenwood Springs

At an elevation of 7,700 feet, Sweetwater Lake is a lovely, low-altitude destination on the eastern edge of the White River Plateau that is rarely crowded. The campground is at the east end of the lake and has impressive views of Sweetwater Canyon. The fishing for trout is good, and electric- and hand-powered boats are allowed in the lake. There is also an extensive network of trails departing from the campground and at the end of Sweetwater Road: Ute Trail climbs to Deep Lake, Cross Creek connects to Sweetwater, and Turret Creek heads north into the Flat Tops Wilderness. Generally, these trails feature gradual climbs through sagebrush and scrub oak hills, aspen groves, pine forests, and subalpine meadows to the Shingle and Turret Peaks area in the Flat Tops Wilderness. There is excellent wildflower viewing, and the Cross Creek Trail provides access to a small cave with pictographs drawn by the Utes about 200 years ago. Many of these trails were originally Ute hunting trails. A short scenic overlook trail has nice views of the lake and waterfall.

The campground is on a steep hill overlooking the lake. The terraced sites are screened by scrub oak, but they are small and close to the campground road. Sites 3, 4, 8, and 9 are walk-in sites. Sites 8-10 have wonderful lake views.

Campsites, facilities: There are 9 sites for tents and RVs up to 30 feet. There are no hookups. Site 7 is pull-through. Picnic tables, fire rings, and grills are provided. Drinking water is not available at the campground but is available at the Sweetwater Lake Resort. Leashed pets are permitted. Wheelchair-accessible vault toilets are available.

Reservations, fees: Reservations are not accepted. The fee is $8 per night. Cash or check only. Open early May-November.

Directions: From I-70, take the Dotsero exit (Exit 133). Go north on County Road 301 for 6.9 miles. Go west on Sweetwater Road/County Road 40 for 10 miles. Turn left on an unmarked road. The campground is in 0.2 mile.

Contact: White River National Forest, Eagle-Holy Cross District, 970/328-6388 or 970/827-5715, www.fs.usda.gov/whiteriver.

60 LYONS GULCH

Scenic rating: 4

north of Dotsero

Located in Lyons Gulch Recreation Site, this campground is on the west bank of the Colorado River, screened from the road by cottonwood, Gambel oak, wild rose, and willow. Rafters and kayakers can float 2.2 miles from the Cottonwood Island put-in to Lyons Gulch, or put in at Lyons Gulch and float 3.8 miles to the Dotsero take-out. There are scenic views up the valley, and it's a treat when the train passes on the tracks across the river, but proximity to the road limits this campground to a stopover. The restroom is closed November 15th to May 15th and you may not dig your own cat holes due to the proximity to the river. Their website says, "Do not camp in this location during heavy rains due to mud slides and flooding."

Campsites, facilities: There are five sites more appropriate for tent than RV camping, including one large group site. Picnic tables, fire rings, and grills are provided. Vault toilets are available. Leashed pets are permitted.

Reservations, fees: Camping is free, and reservations are not accepted. Open year-round, but sometimes closed during high snowfalls.

Directions: From I-70, take the Dotsero exit (Exit 133). Go north on County Road 301 for 4.0 miles. The campground entrance is on the right.

Contact: Bureau of Land Management, Colorado River Valley Field Office in Silt, 970/876-9000, www.co.blm.gov.

61 GYPSUM

🛶 ⛵ 🐕 ♿ 🚐 ⛺

Scenic rating: 4

east of Glenwood Springs

Located in Gypsum Recreation Site, Gypsum is a BLM campground on the shores of the Eagle River, about five miles upstream of the confluence with the Colorado River. The campground is a humble, inexpensive stopover. Accessibility is the biggest plus and the biggest drawback. Convenience, and the absence of a camp host, makes this campground a prime site for weekend parties. If you need to stop here, the best sites are 1 and 2. They're located in a large cottonwood grove on the riverbank. Activities here include fishing and river running. Rafters and novice kayakers frequently boat from Edwards to Eagle, but the river can be run to Dotsero, as well.

Campsites, facilities: There are six sites for tents and RVs up to 35 feet, including two large sites for groups. There are no hookups or pull-throughs. Picnic tables, fire rings, grills, vault toilets, and trash disposal are provided. Leashed pets are permitted.

Reservations, fees: Reservations are not accepted. The fee is $10 per night. Cash or check only. Open mid-May-mid-November.

Directions: From Glenwood Springs, take I-70 to Exit 140/Gypsum and turn south. From the roundabout, take the frontage road west for about 1.5 miles and turn left into the campground.

Contact: Bureau of Land Management, Colorado River Valley Field Office in Silt, 970/876-9000, www.co.blm.gov.

WESTERN SLOPE SOUTH

The Western Slope South region encompasses the Uncompahgre Plateau, Colorado National Monument, and Black Ridge Canyons Wilderness near the Utah border. It also includes Grand Mesa, a high, unique plateau of forests and lakes—and plenty of campgrounds. Backcountry desert experiences through canyon systems abound, and include boating the Colorado River. The city of Grand Junction, at the confluence of the Colorado and Gunnison Rivers, is the biggest population center in the area. You've also got the White River National Forest with 10 fourteeners and eight wilderness areas on the east side of this region; to the south, the Maroon Bells-Snowmass Wilderness has backpacking loops over nine 12,000-foot passes and six fourteeners. Black Canyon of the Gunnison National Park is the deepest, narrowest canyon in the country with campgrounds on the North and South Rims. Just east of the park is Curecanti National Recreation Area, and to the north, the West Elk Mountains. This area also includes the stunning mountain lake campgrounds around Crested Butte and the legendary dispersed camping of Taylor Park.

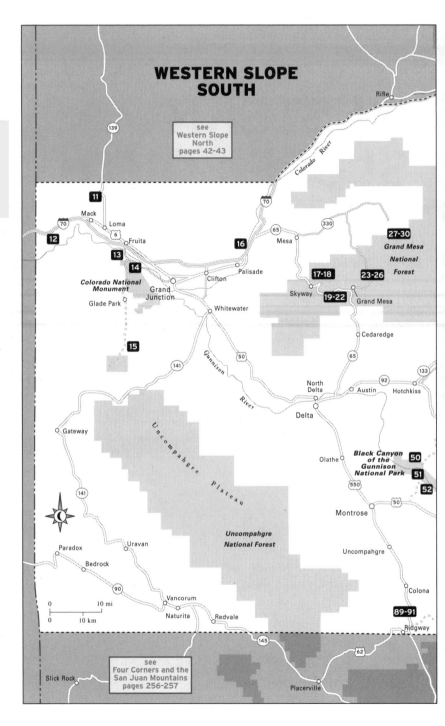

WESTERN SLOPE SOUTH

see
Western Slope
North
pages 42-43

Rifle

Colorado River

139

11

Mack

Loma

70

6

Fruita

12

13

14

Clifton

Palisade

16

Mesa

65

330

27-30

Grand Mesa

National

17-18   **23-26**   *Forest*

Skyway

19-22   Grand Mesa

*Colorado National
Monument*

Grand
Junction

Glade Park

Whitewater

Cedaredge

15

141

50

65

Gunnison

River

North
Delta   Austin   Hotchkiss

92   133

Delta

Gateway

U n c o m p a h g r e   P l a t e a u

Black Canyon
of the
Gunnison
National Park   **50**

Olathe   **51**

550   **52**

50

Montrose

*Uncompahgre
National Forest*

141

Paradox   Uravan

Bedrock

Uncompahgre

90

Vancorum

Naturita   Redvale

Colona

89-91

145

Ridgway

62

0   10 mi

0   10 km

see
Four Corners and the
San Juan Mountains
pages 256-257

Slick Rock

Placerville

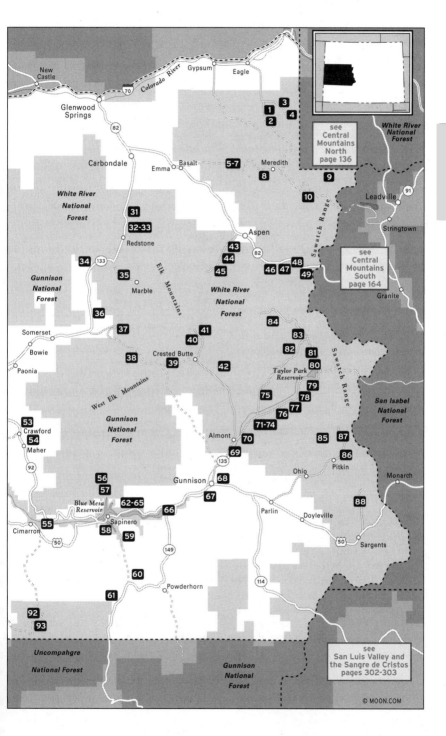

© MOON.COM

1 ELK RUN

Scenic rating: 7

in Sylvan Lake State Park

Note: Most of Sylvan Lake State Park was closed for several years during dam reconstruction, but expected to fully open in the summer of 2020. Sylvan Lake doesn't look like much on the map, but this beautiful little reservoir, tucked into a narrow valley and surrounded by national forest, is famous with anglers. The 40-acre lake is full of brook, brown, and rainbow trout. The small boat ramp and still waters are perfect for launching a canoe. Elk, mule deer, beaver, and hummingbirds also live around the lake, and the wildflowers are outstanding. There are several options for hikers and mountain bikers. A short, level trail circles the lake, and there are more nearby trails on East and West Brush Creek. Hikers and bikers can also try Sneve Gulch Trail, which begins in the parking lot and climbs 2.5 miles to an overlook with views of the lake. And fortunately, unlike Summit County, the impact of the bark beetle epidemic has been marginal so far. You can rent a canoe for the day as well.

Elk Run is the larger of the two campgrounds. It has two gravel loops. The top loop, sites 1-17, has slightly better views of the lake. There are very few trees in the campground, but the sites are far enough apart (50-100 feet) to afford some privacy. Sites 25, 27, 29, and 30 are next to the creek.

Campsites, facilities: There are 34 sites for tents and RVs up to 35 feet. There are no hookups. Half of the sites are pull-through. Picnic tables, fire rings, and grills are provided. Restrooms with flush toilets and showers, drinking water, a group camping area for up to 60 people, a boat ramp, and dump stations, are available. Leashed pets are permitted. Sites 13 and 16 are wheelchair-accessible.

Reservations, fees: Reservations are required at 800/244-5613 or www.cpwshop.com.

(To reserve the group site, contact the park directly.) The fee is $28 per night for up to six people. There is an additional $10 reservation fee. Campers must also purchase a vehicle pass ($8) or an Annual Parks Pass ($80). Open year-round, or until there is too much snow to get through.

Directions: In Eagle, take Capitol Street south through town for 1.2 miles. Turn left on Brush Creek Road/County Road 307. The visitors center is in 9.6 miles. Bear right at the fork, and the campground entrance is in 5.0 miles. After the self-service station, turn left to enter Fisherman's Paradise or right to enter Elk Run.

Contact: Sylvan Lake State Park, 970/328-2021, www.cpw.state.co.us.

2 FISHERMAN'S PARADISE

Scenic rating: 6

in Sylvan Lake State Park

Fisherman's Paradise is a long, narrow grass strip overlooking fabulous Sylvan Lake. The views are unbeatable, but privacy is in very short supply, so it's really only suitable for RVs. For avid anglers, the exposure is a small price to pay to have the 40-acre lake so close. Sailboats, electric boats, and hand-powered boats can all use the boat ramp. Hiking and mountain biking trails encircle the lake and explore East and West Brush Creek and the surrounding White River National Forest. The wildlife and wildflower viewing are also excellent. This is a truly idyllic place to while away a weekend, but it's not a secret. Reservations are a necessity during summer weekends.

Campsites, facilities: There are 12 sites for RVs up to 35 feet, nine cabins, and three yurts. There are no hookups or pull-through sites. Picnic tables, fire rings, and grills are provided. Vault toilets, drinking water, a boat ramp, and dump stations are available. Showers are available at nearby Elk Run. Leashed pets are permitted. Site 46 is wheelchair-accessible.

Reservations, fees: Reservations are accepted (and highly recommended) at 800/244-5613 or www.cpwshop.com. The fee is $28 per night for up to six people. There is an additional $10 reservation fee. Campers must also purchase a vehicle pass ($8) or an Annual Parks Pass ($80). Open year-round.

Directions: In Eagle, take Capitol Street south through town for 1.2 miles. Turn left on Brush Creek Road/County Road 307. The visitors center is in 9.6 miles. Bear right at the fork, and the campground entrance is in 5.0 miles. After the self-service station, turn left to enter Fisherman's Paradise or right to enter Elk Run.

Contact: Sylvan Lake State Park, 970/328-2021, www.cpw.state.co.us.

3 YEOMAN PARK

Scenic rating: 8

south of Eagle

Yeoman Park deserves a long visit from RV and tent campers alike. The campground is at 9,400 feet, on the edge of a wetland meadow with an active beaver colony, and lies partly within a mature spruce forest. The campground is far enough from the crowds to feel like a secret, but it's still easily accessible by passenger car. Adults love the beauty of this quiet valley, and kids love chasing butterflies and exploring the wetlands and observing the beaver colony. (The only drawback is the occasional early morning ATV activity.) There's brook and rainbow trout fishing on East Brush Creek, and two short trails (Browns Loop and the wheelchair-accessible Yeoman Park Discovery Trail) begin at the campground. Two longer trails also begin

here. The Ironedge and Lake Charles Trails can be combined into an 11.5-mile loop with views of the Elk Range, the Fryingpan Wilderness, Castle Peak, and the Flat Tops. Anglers should bring their poles. Cutthroat trout can be found in both Lake Charles and Mystic Island Lake. This campground can also serve as a jumping-off point for a trip into the 10th Mountain Hut system.

Loop A (sites 1-15) sits on the border of an evergreen forest and a wide meadow. Site 1, at the end of the loop, is the most private, and it's next to the Discovery Trail. Sites 6, 8, 9, and 11 have beautiful views of the valley. Loop B (sites 16-24) also occupies the border between forest and meadow, but the sites are more varied. Site 19 is a walk-in tent site on a hill, with good views of the creek. Sites 20-22 are very exposed, but they also have the best views in the campground of Craig Peak to the south.

Campsites, facilities: There are 24 sites for tents and RVs up to 30 feet. There are no hookups. Sites 4, 5, 9, 12, 13, and 20 are pull-through. Picnic tables, fire rings, and grills are provided. Tent pads are available at 11 sites. Vault toilets and a fishing platform are available. Leashed pets are permitted. The facilities are wheelchair-accessible.

Reservations, fees: Reservations are not accepted. The fee is $8 per night (includes two vehicles). Additional vehicles cost $5 per night. Cash or check only. Open late May-early October.

Directions: In Eagle, take Capitol Street south through town for 1.2 miles. Turn left on Brush Creek Road/County Road 307. Bear left at the fork onto East Brush Creek Road/Forest Route 415. In 6.0 miles, turn right and cross the bridge to enter the campground.

Contact: White River National Forest, Eagle-Holy Cross District, 970/328-6388 or 970/827-5715, www.fs.usda.gov/whiteriver.

4 FULFORD CAVE
🚶 🚲 🐾 🚙 ⛰

Scenic rating: 7

south of Eagle

A 0.7-mile trail climbs from the campground to the entrance of Fulford Cave, the eighth-largest cave in Colorado. Spelunkers will discover crevices and pillars, stalactites and stalagmites, narrow gorges, and running water. The hiking is also excellent. Hikers can access the Ironedge and Lake Charles Trails, which can be combined into an 11.5-mile loop with views of the Elk Range, the Fryingpan Wilderness, Castle Peak, and the Flat Tops. Anglers should bring their poles. Cutthroat trout can be found in both Lake Charles and Mystic Island Lake. The camping isn't half bad either. The campground is a small loop in an aspen grove high above East Brush Creek. Sites 1 and 4 are next to the drop-off to the creek. Sites 2-4 are very close together, but there are rarely crowds at this remote campground. Site 6 is the most private site, but it doesn't have a tent pad. Site 4 has a double-sized tent pad.

Campsites, facilities: There are seven sites for tents and RVs up to 20 feet. There are no hookups or pull-throughs. Picnic tables, fire rings, grills, and tent pads are provided. Vault toilets are available. Leashed pets are permitted.

Reservations, fees: Reservations are not accepted. The fee is $8 per night (includes two vehicles). Additional vehicles cost $5 per night. Cash or check only. Open late May-early October.

Directions: In Eagle, take Capitol Street south through town for 1.2 miles. Turn left on Brush Creek Road/County Road 307. Bear left at the fork onto East Brush Creek Road/Forest Route 415. In 6.3 miles, stay right at the fork. The campground is in 1.0 mile. The road is narrow and badly rutted for the last mile.

Contact: White River National Forest, Eagle-Holy Cross District, 970/328-6388 or 970/827-5715, www.fs.usda.gov/whiteriver.

5 LITTLE MAUD
🚲 🚤 ⚓ 🐾 🚙 ⛰

Scenic rating: 6

at Ruedi Reservoir

BEST (

Located just east of Basalt, Ruedi Reservoir is a 1,000-acre body of water in the Fryingpan Valley, surrounded by steep, thickly forested slopes at 7,800 feet elevation. It's a popular weekend destination for boaters and sailors. There is also good fishing for rainbow, brown, and mackinaw trout. There are two trails nearby for hiking and mountain biking. Ruedi Trail climbs steeply eight miles to the top of Red Table Mountain and has great views of the Fryingpan Valley and the Hunter-Fryingpan Wilderness area. The Rocky Fork Trail follows Rocky Fork Creek for 7.5 miles and offers good stream fishing.

Little Maud is the first of three campgrounds in the Ruedi Complex. It is a midsized loop with aspen and spruce in the outer campsites and an open meadow in the center. A small creek runs near the campground. The sites are about 50 feet apart, and there is not much shade. Sites 7-11 have good views of the lake. The campground fills up on the weekends.

Campsites, facilities: There are 22 sites for tents and RVs up to 40 feet. There are no hookups. Picnic tables, fire rings, and grills are provided. Flush toilets, drinking water, a boat ramp, and dump stations are available. Leashed pets are permitted.

Reservations, fees: Reservations are accepted at 877/444-6777 and www.recreation.gov. The fee is $26 per night. Cash or check only. Open late May-early September.

Directions: From Basalt, take Fryingpan Road east for 14.7 miles. Turn right at the Ruedi Creek sign and then left down the hill to the first campground on the right.

Contact: White River National Forest, Sopris District, 970/963-2266, www.fs.usda.gov/whiteriver.

6 MOLLIE B

Scenic rating: 6

at Ruedi Reservoir

Mollie B is the second of three campgrounds in the Ruedi Complex and the closest to the lake. (For more information on the reservoir, see the Little Maud listing in this chapter.) The campground is in a meadow with a creek. The sites are 30-50 feet apart, and there is very little shade except at sites 25, 26, 28, and 30, which are in a small aspen grove. Sites 33-37 are next to the shore.

Campsites, facilities: There are 26 sites for tents and RVs up to 60 feet. There are no hookups. Sites 26, 34, and 46 are pull-through. Picnic tables, fire rings, and grills are provided. Flush toilets, drinking water, a boat ramp, and dump stations ($10 fee), are available. Leashed pets are permitted. Site 27 is wheelchair-accessible.

Reservations, fees: Reservations are accepted at 877/444-6777 and www.recreation.gov. The fee is $26 per night. Cash or check only. Open late May-mid September.

Directions: From Basalt, take Fryingpan Road east for 14.7 miles. Turn right at the Ruedi Creek sign and then left down the hill to the second campground.

Contact: White River National Forest, Sopris District, 970/963-2266, www.fs.usda.gov/whiteriver.

7 LITTLE MATTIE

Scenic rating: 6

at Ruedi Reservoir

Little Mattie is the last of three campgrounds in the Ruedi Complex and the farthest from the lake. (For more information on the reservoir, see the Little Maud listing in this chapter.) The other campgrounds are loops, but Little Mattie is a long lollipop that parallels Pond Creek. It has a lot more vegetation than the other campgrounds. Site 1 has a great view of the lake. Sites 2-4 are in dense thickets. Sites 15-19 are in a pleasant aspen grove.

Campsites, facilities: There are 19 sites for tents and RVs up to 22 feet. There are no hookups. Sites 7-9 are pull-through. Picnic tables, fire rings, and grills are provided. Vault toilets and drinking water are available. Dump stations and a boat ramp are available at Little Maud. Leashed pets are permitted.

Reservations, fees: Reservations are not accepted. The fee is $23 per night. Cash or check only. Open late May-mid October.

Directions: From Basalt, take Fryingpan Road east for 14.7 miles. Turn right at the Ruedi Creek sign and then left down the hill 1.0 mile to the last campground.

Contact: White River National Forest, Sopris District, 970/963-2266, www.fs.usda.gov/whiteriver.

8 DEARHAMER

Scenic rating: 4

at Ruedi Reservoir

Dearhamer is a small loop at the east end of Ruedi Reservoir. (For more information on the reservoir, see the Little Maud listing in this chapter.) The sites are just 10-20 feet apart. There are some cottonwoods for shade, but no privacy. Mostly RVers use this campground. It's also a good campground for anglers who want to fish on the reservoir and the river. The Fryingpan, a Gold Medal river, enters the reservoir next to the campground. The Miller Divide Trail begins near the campground. Open to hiking and mountain biking (but not motorized vehicles), the trail traverses four miles to Rocky Fork Creek and offers excellent views of the Fryingpan Valley. This is also prime elk and deer habitat.

Campsites, facilities: There are 12 sites for tents and RVs up to 35 feet. Picnic tables, fire rings, and grills are provided. Vault toilets, drinking water, and a small boat ramp are available. Leashed pets are permitted.

Reservations, fees: Reservations are not accepted. The fee is $24 per night. Cash or check only. Open late May-late September.

Directions: From Basalt, take Fryingpan Road east for 22.6 miles. Make a sharp right at the end of the reservoir and then bear right immediately into the campground.

Contact: White River National Forest, Sopris District, 970/963-2266, www.fs.usda.gov/whiteriver.

9 ELK WALLOW

Scenic rating: 8

east of Ruedi Reservoir

Situated in a wide valley on the North Fork of Mormon Creek, Elk Wallow's primary attraction is remoteness. This small, primitive campground overlooks a series of beaver ponds and offers excellent wildlife-watching. Bighorn sheep, bald eagles, waterfowl, deer, and elk live in this valley. A short drive up the road is the boundary of the Holy Cross Wilderness and the south end of the Tellurium Lake Trail. The campground is in a small evergreen forest and has a big granite outcropping that's perfect for stargazing. The sites are shaded and 30-50 feet apart. There is ample privacy.

Campsites, facilities: There are seven sites for tents and RVs up to 22 feet. There are no hookups or pull-through sites. Picnic tables, fire rings, grills, and vault toilets are provided. Drinking water is not available. Trash must be packed out. Leashed pets are permitted.

Reservations, fees: Reservations are not accepted. The fee is $15 per night. Cash or check only. Open late May-late October.

Directions: From Basalt, take Fryingpan Road east for 26.8 miles. Turn left onto Forest Route 501. In 3.0 miles, turn right into the campground. There is no sign.

Contact: White River National Forest, Sopris District, 970/963-2266, www.fs.usda.gov/whiteriver.

10 CHAPMAN

Scenic rating: 7

east of Ruedi Reservoir

This extra-large campground feels much smaller than it is because many of the loops are not visible to each other. This is a pretty, peaceful campground with lots of butterflies, birds, and wildflowers. There has been more selective cutting due to the bark beetle here than at other nearby campgrounds, but overall it's still shady and offers good privacy. The diminutive Chapman Reservoir is good for fishing, hand-powered boats, and swimming. The fishing is excellent on the Fryingpan, a Gold Medal river. There is a one-mile nature trail for hiking.

Chapman fills up on holidays, but during the rest of the summer there are always first-come, first-served sites available. Loop A (sites 1-6) is on a hill in an evergreen forest. All of the sites are walk-ins. Loop B (7-9) are also walk-in sites. Loop C (10-14) is a small loop between the river and a meadow. Site 14 is walk-in. Loop D (15-22) is the least private loop, but it is also right next to the river. Loop E (23-41) is in an evergreen forest next to the pond. Loops F, G, and H are on the far side of the river. In Loop F (42-56), most sites are in a meadow, and there are some next to the river. Loop G (57-70) combines the river, aspen groves, and a meadow. Loop H (71-83) is in an evergreen forest next to the river and offers views of Seller Peak and Wildcat Mountain. There are lots of trees and privacy.

The group site is a long walk from the rest of the campground. It offers dispersed tent camping in an evergreen forest and can accommodate up to 75 people ($200 per night). It is very private and scenic, with views of the Sawatch Range, and it has a picnic area and horseshoe pits. This is the perfect destination for a family reunion. The group site is available by reservation only and is usually booked every summer weekend.

Campsites, facilities: There are 84 sites for tents and RVs up to 60 feet. There are no hookups. There are pull-through sites in Loops G and H. Picnic tables, fire rings, and grills are provided. Vault toilets and drinking water are available. Leashed pets are permitted.

Reservations, fees: Reservations are accepted at 877/444-6777 and www.recreation.gov. The fee is $25 per night. Cash or check only. Open late May-late September.

Directions: From Basalt, take Fryingpan Road east for 33.2 miles. Make a soft right into the campground.

Contact: White River National Forest, Sopris District, 970/963-2266, www.fs.usda.gov/whiteriver.

11 BOOKCLIFF

Scenic rating: 5
in Highline Lake State Park

BEST (

Highline Lake is a reservoir in the flat agricultural town of Loma. The park has a following of regulars who enjoy the roomy campsites, which are large enough to set up several tents and a volleyball net. The camping area is grassy and shaded by mature trees. Except for the Book Cliffs to the north, the scenery is not impressive, but this is an ideal weekend trip or stopover for families with small children. Kids can romp on the sandy swimming beach or go mountain biking on the flat 3.5-mile trail that circles the lake. Water sports and fishing are also popular pastimes. There are two lakes for

fishing: Highline Lake, which has largemouth bass and bluegill, and the smaller Mack Mesa Lake, which has trout. Mountain bikers who are exploring the adjacent BLM lands will appreciate the facilities and convenience of this park, and birders can use the two wildlife kiosks to look for over 200 species that frequent the park. Winter sports include ice fishing and waterfowl hunting.

Campsites, facilities: There are 31 sites for tents and RVs up to 40 feet and a group site for up to 100 campers. There are no hookups. Picnic tables and grills are provided. Restrooms with flush toilets and showers, laundry facilities, drinking water, a playground, vending machines, a boat ramp, and dump stations are available. In the summer, there is a small store at the visitors center. The group picnic area is available by reservation. Leashed pets are permitted. Site 22 is wheelchair-accessible.

Reservations, fees: Reservations are required; call 800/244-5613 or go to www.cpwshop.com. The fee is $25 per night from April through October, $14 November through March. The group site costs $120 for the first 30 campers and $18 per night for each additional 10 campers. Campers must also purchase a vehicle pass ($8) or an Annual Parks Pass ($80). Open year-round.

Directions: From Grand Junction, drive west on I-70 to Loma. Go north on Highway 139 for 5.0 miles. Turn left on Q Road. In 1.3 miles, turn right on 11.8 Road. The park entrance is in 1.3 miles.

Contact: Highline Lake State Park, 970/858-7208, www.cpw.state.co.us.

12 RABBIT VALLEY

Scenic rating: 8
in McInnis Canyons National Conservation Area

BEST (

The McInnis Canyons NCA encompasses the

northern canyon lands of the Uncompahgre Plateau as they descend to the Colorado River. Visitors to this area will find the high desert and colorful landforms that one usually associates with southern Utah, but there are no visitors centers or manicured trails here. The adventure is in the backcountry—in remote destinations like Rattlesnake Canyon, Horsethief Canyon, and Ruby Canyon. Most of the visitors to this area are mountain bikers, rafters, and ATVers. The Rabbit Valley campground is a stop on Kokopelli's Trail, a 142-mile mountain bike trail from Loma, Colorado, to Moab, Utah. This trail is technically challenging and requires a lot of preparation and planning. For bikers who want a taste of the trail, there are several shorter loops in the area. Trail conditions and maps are available at the bike shops in Fruita, which is also the last place to stock up on water and biking gear. Visitors who don't want to enter the backcountry can try the Trail Through Time on the north side of the interstate. This 1.5-mile hiking trail tours a working dinosaur quarry. There are two more primitive campgrounds in Rabbit Valley (Castle Rocks and Knowles Canyon), but these are only accessible by 4WD vehicles.

Campsites, facilities: This is a primitive campground, but there are plans to expand and improve it as well as Castle Rocks and Knowles Canyon. For now, there are five walk-in tent sites around a large dirt parking lot. Small RVs can access this area, but the road is very rough and high-clearance vehicles are recommended. Picnic tables, fire rings, grills, and vault toilets are provided. Leashed pets are permitted.

Reservations, fees: Camping is free. Reservations are not accepted. Open year-round.

Directions: From Grand Junction, take I-70 west to Exit 2. At the top of the ramp, turn south. From the Rabbit Valley Recreation Management Area sign, proceed 0.5 mile to a fork. Take the right fork. The campground is on the right in 0.6 mile.

Contact: Bureau of Land Management, Grand Junction Field Office, 970/224-3000, co.blm. gov.

13 FRUITA SECTION

Scenic rating: 4

in James M. Robb Colorado River State Park

This is a modern park and the campground caters mostly to RVs. It is a large, flat loop with very little privacy, but the walk-in tent sites are partially screened by landscaping. Families and retirees love this park because of the facilities and the convenience. It is next to the highway and less than a mile from the entrance to Colorado National Monument. It is also walking distance to the Dinosaur Journey Museum. Hiking opportunities abound in the monument, and there are endless mountain bike trails in the surrounding BLM lands. Grand Junction and the Grand Valley wineries are an easy day trip, and the Grand Mesa Scenic Byway is also nearby. Adventurous souls can schedule horseback riding and rafting trips with local outfitters. It's also a great stopover on the road to Utah.

Campsites, facilities: There are 63 sites, including 22 full hookups, 22 electric hookups, 13 walk-in tent sites with tent pads, and a group camping area that can accommodate 36 people. Picnic tables, fire rings, grills, and shelters are provided. Restrooms with flush toilets and showers, vault toilets, laundry facilities, drinking water, a playground, and dump stations are available. There is also a group picnic area, small fishing lake, and amphitheater. Leashed pets are permitted. Most sites are wheelchair-accessible.

Reservations, fees: Reservations are accepted at 800/244-5613 or www.cpwshop. com. The tent fee is $21 per night. The RV fee is $30-35 per night. Group camping costs $120 per night and can be reserved by calling the park. Campers must also purchase a vehicle pass ($8) or an Annual Parks Pass ($80). Open year-round.

Directions: From Grand Junction, take I-70 west to Exit 19/Fruita. Go south on Highway 340 for one mile. The park entrance is on the right.

Contact: James M. Robb Colorado River State Park, 970/434-3388, www.cpw.state.co.us.

14 SADDLEHORN

🚶 ❄ 🏕 ♿ 🚐 ⛺

Scenic rating: 9

in Colorado National Monument

BEST (

Colorado National Monument is one of Colorado's secret destinations. Most Coloradans drive by the monument on their way to Utah, never realizing that the canyons and rock monuments they're seeking are just south of the interstate. As a result, the park is usually not crowded, and there's usually space for late arrivals in this first-come, first-served campground. It sometimes fills up with school groups in April and May, and then quiets down for the hot months. Late August through October is the best time to visit. The monument protects 32 square miles of canyons and plateaus on the northern end of the Uncompahgre Uplift. The high country here rises 2,000 feet above the Colorado River and the towns of Fruita and Grand Junction. As you may guess, the views are spectacular. Visitors can spend hours at the overlooks watching the weather move across the Grand Valley and the Book Cliffs to the north. It's a paradise for photographers and hikers. There are seven trails that are less than a mile long, and six backcountry trails that are four to nine miles long. The most popular is Monument Canyon Trail, which descends 600 feet through layers of Mesozoic sandstone and passes the Coke Ovens monoliths. There

are campfire programs and guided walks for visitors who want to learn more about the geology and ecology of the park. The trails are open to cross-country skiing in the winter. Mountain biking is not allowed in the park, but the monument is surrounded by BLM land, with world-class mountain bike trails.

Colorado National Monument is also an excellent destination for an outdoors wedding. There are four locations available, but the most popular is the Book Cliffs viewing area, which has truly spectacular views. Special use permits must be purchased in advance and can accommodate from 50-250 people. Sometimes, the Grand Junction astronomy club sets up telescopes at the campground and invites campers to join them.

Campsites, facilities: There are 80 sites for tents and RVs up to 40 feet. The most attractive sites are on the outside of Loops A and B; these sites have more privacy and better views. In the C Loop, sites 79 and 80 have the best views of the monuments below. There are no hookups. Picnic tables and charcoal grills are provided. Wood fires are prohibited in the park. Restrooms with flush toilets and drinking water are available in the summer. Leashed pets are permitted in the campground but are not allowed on trails. A wheelchair-accessible campsite is available on request.

Reservations, fees: Reservations are accepted in Loop B. The fee is $22 per night for up to seven people. Cash or check only. The park entrance fee is $11 per vehicle (good for seven days). Loop A campsites are open year-round.

Directions: From Grand Junction, take I-70 west to Exit 19/Fruita. Go south on Highway 340. In 2.4 miles, turn right on Rim Rock Road. The campground entrance is on the left in 4.0 miles.

Contact: Colorado National Monument, 970/858-3617, www.nps.gov/colm.

15 MUD SPRINGS

Scenic rating: 8

south of Colorado National Monument

Mud Springs is on Pinyon Mesa, a part of the 100-mile-long Uncompahgre Plateau. The campground is on BLM land, just north of the Grand Mesa National Forest, in a setting of meadows and aspen groves. Cool breezes and afternoon showers make this the perfect place to escape the heat of the canyonlands to the north. This is a popular destination for church groups, wedding parties, family reunions, handicap organizations, and scouting troops, all of which benefit from the remote location. There isn't a bad campsite here. They are all very private and screened by aspen. The surrounding land is crisscrossed by 4WD roads and pack trails that are also suitable for hiking and mountain biking. Fishing is available at the Enoch and Fruita Reservoirs located four miles north of the campground. (Swimming is not recommended because of ranching activities in the area.) Glade Park is the last place to buy supplies or, surprisingly, watch a movie. During the summer, the Glade Park Volunteer Fire Station shows movies under the stars on Friday nights for $1 per person. All proceeds benefit the fire station.

Campsites, facilities: There are 14 sites for tents and RVs up to 30 feet and two group sites. There are no hookups. Picnic tables, fire rings, grills, and a horse corral are provided. Vault toilets and drinking water are available. Leashed pets are permitted. The facilities and group sites are wheelchair-accessible.

Reservations, fees: Reservations are not accepted. The fee is $14 per night. Cash only. Open mid-May-mid-October.

Directions: From the Colorado National Monument visitors center, take Rim Rock Road south for 6.6 miles. At the "Glade Springs 5 mi." sign, turn right. At 4.8 miles, you will pass the Glade Park Store and Post Office. Continue straight on Glade Park Road for another 7.0 miles to the campground entrance on the right.

sunrise from Saddlehorn campground in Colorado National Monument

Contact: Bureau of Land Management, Grand Junction Field Office, 970/244-3000, www.co.blm.gov.

16 ISLAND ACRES SECTION

Scenic rating: 4

in James M. Robb Colorado River State Park

James M. Robb Colorado River State Park actually consists of five sections along the Colorado River from the campground at Fruita (the western anchor) to Island Acres (the eastern anchor). The middle three sections are for day use only. The scenery changes dramatically on the drive from Fruita, at the base of Colorado National Monument in the Grand Valley, through the crumbling hills and sandstone cliffs carved by the river. Island Acres is surrounded by the Little Books Cliff Wild Horse Range, where the BLM manages a herd of more than 300 wild horses. It's in a deep canyon, just a hundred yards from the interstate, so it's a convenient stopover with deluxe facilities. It has three stocked fishing ponds and a swim beach, as well as a short trail for hiking and biking. Grand Junction and the Grand Valley wineries are an easy day trip, and the Grand Mesa Scenic Byway begins nearby. Kayakers take over when the river hits 20,000 cubic feet per second and enormous waves occur upstream of Cameo dam. In the winter, the campground and lakes are open for ice fishing and ice-skating.

There are three loops between the interstate and the river. Loop A (sites 1-34) has electric hookups and more shade trees than the other loops. Loop B (sites 35-40) is for tent camping only. The sites are very close together and not appealing. Loops C and D (sites 41-80) are closest to the highway and have few mature shade trees. The sites are about 30 feet apart. There is limited privacy and shade.

Campsites, facilities: There are 6 tent-only sites and 74 sites for tents and RVs of any size. Sites 1-34 have electric hookups, and sites 41-80 have full hookups. Picnic tables, fire rings, and grills are provided at all sites. Some sites have sun shelters and tent pads. Restrooms with flush toilets and showers, vault toilets, a laundry room, drinking water, pay phones, vending machines, a playground, and dump stations, are available. There is also a group picnic area, swim beach, stocked fishing ponds, and interpretive programs. Leashed pets are permitted. Sites 17-19, 39, 41, 56, and 80 and the facilities are wheelchair-accessible.

Reservations, fees: Reservations are accepted at 800/244-5613 or www.cpwshop.com. The tent fee is $21 per night. The RV fee is $30-35 per night. Campers must also purchase a vehicle pass ($8) or an Annual Parks Pass ($80). Open year-round.

Directions: From Grand Junction, take I-70 east to Exit 49. Go north on the Frontage Road for 0.3 mile to the campground entrance.

Contact: James M. Robb Colorado River State Park, 970/434-3388, www.cpw.state.co.us.

17 JUMBO

Scenic rating: 7

on Grand Mesa

Grand Mesa is exactly what the name describes—a huge mesa that's about 50 miles across and 4,000 feet tall. The mesa was once part of an enormous basin that filled with 5,000 feet of shale, limestone, and sandstone. Volcanic activity covered the basin with 400 feet of basalt, and then the whole Colorado Plateau uplifted. After the uplift, the surrounding sediments that weren't capped by basalt eroded away. Weaknesses in the underlying sediments made the basalt unstable, resulting in cracks and depressions that became lakes. Glaciers added to those cracks and depressions, helping to create the 300 ponds, lakes, and reservoirs that speckle the Grand Mesa today.

The Utes tell a very different story to explain the lakes. Their legend says that Grand Mesa was once home to an enormous eagle that swept down on misbehaving children and carried them away. The eagle took a chief's son, and the chief climbed up to the nest to retrieve his son. The boy was gone, so the chief took the eagle's eggs and threw them into the jaws of a giant serpent. The eagle attacked the serpent, tearing it to pieces in the air. Where the pieces of the serpent fell, they left holes that later became the lakes.

The Grand Mesa Scenic Byway passes through five life zones on its way to the top of the mesa: Lower Sonoran, Upper Sonoran, Lower Montane, Montane, and Subalpine. The top of the mesa is mostly covered with spruce-fir forests interspersed with small meadows and hundreds of small lakes and reservoirs. The mesa receives huge amounts of snow, making it one of the lushest environments on the western slope. Five major creeks drain the mesa: Plateau, Buzzard, Kannah, Surface, and LeRoux. Settlers began developing the mesa for irrigation in the 1880s, and today it remains an important source of water for farming and power utilities. The mesa is a patchwork of public and private property, and there are several vacation lodges and developed areas on the mesa.

As you might expect, fishing reigns on the mesa. There are rainbow, cutthroat, brook, brown, and lake trout. The majority of ponds and lakes are stocked. Boating regulations vary, but most boating is limited to hand-powered boats and electric motors. Swimming is not recommended because of the water temperatures and the amount of hooks in the water. Four-wheeling and ATVs are also extremely popular on the mesa. A network of 4WD roads crisscrosses the forest and provides access to remote lakes.

Supplies are available at Mesa Lakes, Ward Lake, and Twin Lakes, but bring plenty of insect repellent. In the words of one camp host, "The mosquitoes are free." And there are lots of them. There is also plenty of pavement in the campground for kids to ride bikes.

Campsites, facilities: There are 21 electric and five nonelectric sites for tents and RVs up to 60 feet (and a few cabins). There are no pull-through sites. Sites 25 and 26 are walk-in tent sites. Sites 17 and 24 are double-wide. Picnic tables, fire rings, and grills are provided. Vault toilets and drinking water are available. Leashed pets are permitted. There are four wheelchair-accessible sites.

Reservations, fees: Reservations are accepted at 877/444-6777 and www.recreation.gov. The fee is $18 per night for a nonelectric site and $22 per night for an electric site. Cash or check only. Open early June-late September.

Directions: From I-70, take Highway 65 east for 25 miles. Turn right at Jumbo Reservoir and right again to enter the campground.

Contact: Grand Mesa National Forest, 970/874-6600, www.fs.usda.gov/gmug.

18 SPRUCE GROVE

Scenic rating: 6

on Grand Mesa

Spruce Grove is in the Mesa Lakes area on the west side of the mesa, at nearly 10,000 feet elevation. As one of the only campgrounds that's not on a lake, it tends to be less crowded than nearby Jumbo. It's a gravel loop in a dense spruce-fir forest about 150 yards from the highway. Sites 1, 2, and 13-16 are within sight of the road. Sites 1-6 have a gentle slope that makes it hard to find tent sites, but sites 7-16 are flat. (For more information on Grand Mesa, see the Jumbo listing in this chapter.)

Campsites, facilities: There are 16 sites for tents and RVs up to 48 feet. There are no hookups. Sites 1, 2, and 5-16 are pull-through. Picnic tables, fire rings, and grills are provided.

Vault toilets and drinking water are available. Leashed pets are permitted.

Reservations, fees: Reservations are not accepted. The fee is $12 per night. Cash or check only. Open late June-late September.

Directions: From I-70, take Highway 65 east for 25.7 miles. The campground entrance is on the right.

Contact: Grand Mesa National Forest, 970/874-6600, www.fs.usda.gov/gmug.

19 ISLAND LAKE

Scenic rating: 6

on Grand Mesa

Island Lake is one of the larger lakes on the mesa and is the site of a visitors center. Its north shore is rimmed by a high rock ridge called Crag Crest, and the campground at the western tip overlooks meadows that slope away to the south. The campground is separated from the water by the road, but it's a short walk to the boat ramp and fishing pier. The majority of sites are shaded by spruce and fir trees; other sites border a large meadow. Mountain bikers and ATV riders can take Forest Route 115 from the campground to Granby Reservoir and beyond. It's a short drive to the west trailhead for the Crag Crest National Recreation Trail. This 10.3-mile loop traverses the "crest" of the mesa and has panoramic views of the Book and Roan Cliffs to the north, the West Elk and San Juan Mountains to the east and south, and the Uncompahgre Plateau and La Sal Mountains to the west. (For more information on Grand Mesa, see the Jumbo listing in this chapter.)

Campsites, facilities: The campground was completely renovated in 2009 and mainly serves RVers. There are 39 sites for tents and RVs up to 45 feet. Sites 2, 3, 6, 7, and 8 have electric hookups. Sites 2, 3, 5, 9, 11, 13, and 14 are pull-through. Sites 18, 19, and 20 are designed for larger groups. Picnic tables, fire rings, and grills are provided. Vault toilets, water, fishing pier, fish-cleaning station, and a boat ramp are available. Leashed pets are permitted.

Reservations, fees: Reservations are accepted at 877/444-6777 and www.recreation.gov. The fee is $18 per night for nonelectric sites and $22 per night for electric sites. Cash or check only. Open mid-June-Labor Day.

Directions: From I-70, take Highway 65 east for 33.3 miles. Turn right at the Island Lake sign and continue 0.6 mile downhill. The campground is on the right.

Contact: Grand Mesa National Forest, 970/874-6600, www.fs.usda.gov/gmug.

20 LITTLE BEAR

Scenic rating: 7

on Grand Mesa

Little Bear is the second campground on lovely Island Lake and the more scenic one. It's strung along the south shore of the lake, in a spruce-fir forest scattered with boulders probably left behind by a glacier. Like most of the Grand Mesa campgrounds, Little Bear isn't very busy during the week, but it fills up on weekends. Sites 10-12, 14, 19, 22, 23, and 25-27 have excellent lake views. Sites 28-30 are also next to the lake, but the dam obstructs their views. From the Island Lake campground, ATVs and mountain bikes can take Forest Route 115 to Granby Reservoir and beyond. It's a short drive to the west trailhead for the Crag Crest National Recreation Trail. This 10.3-mile loop traverses the "crest" of the mesa and has panoramic views of the Book and Roan Cliffs to the north, the West Elk and San Juan Mountains to the east and south, and the Uncompahgre Plateau and La Sal Mountains to the west. (For more information on Grand Mesa, see the Jumbo entry in this chapter.)

Campsites, facilities: There are 36 sites for tents and RVs up to 50 feet. There are no

hookups. Sites 3, 4, 6, 16, 20, 24, 29, and 30 are pull-through. Picnic tables, fire rings, and grills are provided. Vault toilets, drinking water, fish-cleaning station, fishing pier, and a boat ramp are available. Leashed pets are permitted. One handicap-accessible site is available.

Reservations, fees: Reservations are not accepted. The fee is $16 per night. Cash or check only. Open mid-June-Labor Day.

Directions: From I-70, take Highway 65 east for 34.5 miles. Turn right on Forest Route 116. The campground is on the right in 0.8 mile.

Contact: Grand Mesa National Forest, 970/874-6600, www.fs.usda.gov/gmug.

21 WARD LAKE

Scenic rating: 8

on Grand Mesa

Ward Lake is a medium-sized lake surrounded by spruce-fir forests that go right down to the water. Although there is a lodge at one end, only one private residence is visible from the campground. The campground is in a mature but thin forest with lots of wildflowers (and mosquitoes). This is a very popular campground on weekends. The visitors center and Discovery Trail are within walking distance. In the winter, cross-country skiing trails circle Deep Slough and Ward Creek Reservoirs. Sites 6-11 and 14-27 have lake views. Sites 8, 9, 22, 23, 25, and 26 are right on the shore. Sites 1-3, 5, 12, and 13 are near the road. (For more information on Grand Mesa, see the Jumbo entry in this chapter.)

Campsites, facilities: There are 27 sites for tents and RVs up to 45 feet. There are no hookups. Some sites are pull-through. Picnic tables, fire rings, and grills are provided. There is no water. Vault toilets, and a boat ramp are available. Leashed pets are permitted.

Reservations, fees: Reservations are not accepted. The fee is $16 per night. Cash or check only. Open early June-late September.

Directions: From I-70, take Highway 65 east for 34.6 miles. Turn left on Forest Route 121. The campground is on the right in 0.5 mile.

Contact: Grand Mesa National Forest, 970/874-6600, www.fs.usda.gov/gmug.

22 COBBETT LAKE

Scenic rating: 6

on Grand Mesa

This is a small campground on the shore of a small lake, but it attracts big RVs and it's busy all summer. Only nonmotorized boats are allowed on Cobbett Lake. Sites 1-3, 5, 7, and 8 are next to the lake, but they are also very close together. Sites 16-20 overlook a smaller lake to the north, but they are also close together. At the visitors center across the lake, there is a short interpretive hiking trail, and the west trailhead of the Crag Crest National Recreation Trail is a short drive away. This 10.3-mile loop traverses the "crest" of the mesa and has panoramic views of the Book and Roan Cliffs to the north, the West Elk and San Juan Mountains to the east and south, and the Uncompahgre Plateau and La Sal Mountains to the west. Half of the loop is open to mountain bikes and horses. (For more information on Grand Mesa, see the Jumbo entry in this chapter.)

Campsites, facilities: There are 20 sites for tents and RVs up to 42 feet. There are no hookups. Sites 8, 10, 15, and 18 are pull-through. Picnic tables, fire rings, grills, and vault toilets are provided. There is no water. Leashed pets are permitted.

Reservations, fees: Reservations are accepted at 877/444-6777 and www.recreation.gov. The fee is $16 per night. Additional vehicles cost $6 per night. There is an $8 reservation fee. Cash or check only. Open mid-June-late September.

Directions: From I-70, take Highway 65 east

for 34.5 miles. The campground entrance is on the left before the lake.

Contact: Grand Mesa National Forest, 970/874-6600, www.fs.usda.gov/gmug.

23 COTTONWOOD LAKE

Scenic rating: 6

on Grand Mesa

This popular little campground is on a gently sloping hillside surrounded by young stands of aspen. Since a timber sale in 2005, this campground has recovered nicely and enjoys lots of shade from a spruce-fir forest. The sites are very close together, and there are no lake views. Cottonwood Lake and the boat ramp are within walking distance. (For more information on Grand Mesa, see the Jumbo listing in this chapter.)

Campsites, facilities: There are 25 sites for tents and RVs up to 42 feet. There are no hookups. Picnic tables, fire rings, and grills, are provided. Vault toilets are available. Leashed pets are permitted. Water is provided by a solar-powered pump. RVs and camp trailers cannot fill their water tanks from the campground faucets due to the poor recovery of the well. Water tanks should be filled up in Buena Vista prior to visiting the campground.

Reservations, fees: Reservations are not accepted. The fee is $14 per night. Cash or check only. Open early July-Labor Day.

Directions: From I-70, take Highway 65 east for 34.6 miles. Turn left on Forest Route 121. In 11.5 miles, turn left on Forest Route 257. The campground is on the left in 5.0 miles.

Contact: Grand Mesa National Forest, 970/874-6600, www.fs.usda.gov/gmug.

24 BIG CREEK

Scenic rating: 7

on Grand Mesa

This campground is on the west shore of Big Creek Reservoir, a large lake with views of Leon Peak, the highest point on the mesa. This part of the mesa receives more precipitation than the western half, as well as fewer visitors. Campers who do drive out here usually stay for four or five days. Most sites are in a spruce-fir forest. Sites 1, 2, 4-9, 12, 13, and 15 have lake views. Sites 13, 14, 16-18, and 24-26 border a large meadow. (For more information on Grand Mesa, see the Jumbo listing in this chapter.)

Campsites, facilities: There are 26 sites for tents and RVs up to 33 feet. There are no hookups. Sites 9, 11, 12, 17, and 24 are pull-through. Picnic tables, fire rings, and grills are provided. Vault toilets are available. Leashed pets are permitted.

Reservations, fees: Reservations are not accepted. The fee is $14 per night. Cash or check only. Open mid-June-Labor Day.

Directions: From I-70, take Highway 65 east for 34.6 miles. Turn left on Forest Route 121. The campground is on the left in 9.3 miles.

Contact: Grand Mesa National Forest, 970/874-6600, www.fs.usda.gov/gmug.

25 CRAG CREST

Scenic rating: 8

on Grand Mesa

Crag Crest is on the north shore of Eggleston Lake, the largest lake on the mesa, more than 10,000 feet above sea level. It was a pretty, hilly spot with excellent views and moderate privacy. It's a great campground for hikers because it's adjacent to the eastern trailhead of the Crag Crest National Recreation Trail.

This 10.3-mile loop traverses the "crest" of the mesa and has panoramic views of the Book and Roan Cliffs to the north, the West Elk and San Juan Mountains to the east and south, and the Uncompahgre Plateau and La Sal Mountains to the west. Half of the loop is open to mountain bikes and horses. (For more information on Grand Mesa, see the Jumbo listing in this chapter.)

Campsites, facilities: There are 11 sites for tents and RVs up to 27 feet. There are no hookups. Picnic tables, fire rings, and grills are provided. Vault toilets are available. Leashed pets are permitted.

Reservations, fees: Reservations are not accepted. The fee is $12 per night. Cash or check only. Open mid-June-Labor Day.

Directions: From I-70, take Highway 65 east for 34.6 miles. Turn left on Forest Route 121. The campground is on the left in 3.4 miles.

Contact: Grand Mesa National Forest, 970/874-6600, www.fs.usda.gov/gmug.

26 WEIR AND JOHNSON

Scenic rating: 6

on Grand Mesa

This campground is on the east side of the mesa beneath Leon Peak, the highest point on the mesa. The campground receives heavy precipitation, so there are usually pockets of snow on the ground until mid-July. It's in a lush sprucefir forest between Weir and Johnson and Sackett Reservoirs. Sackett is closed to motorized boats. Trail 717 climbs to Loon Lake and other ponds. The sites are just 20-50 feet apart, and the campground is usually busy despite its remote location. Sites 5-7 are walk-in sites on the shore. (For more information on Grand Mesa, see the Jumbo listing in this chapter.)

Campsites, facilities: There are 12 sites for tents and RVs up to 33 feet. There are no hookups. Picnic tables, fire rings, and grills are provided. Vault toilets are available. There is no water. Leashed pets are permitted.

Reservations, fees: Reservations are not accepted. The fee is $14 per night. Cash or check only. Open mid-June-Labor Day.

Directions: From I-70, take Highway 65 east for 34.6 miles. Turn left on Forest Route 121. In 8.7 miles, turn right on Forest Route 126. The campground is in 2.7 miles.

Contact: Grand Mesa National Forest, 970/874-6600, www.fs.usda.gov/gmug.

27 EARLY SETTLERS

Scenic rating: 6

in Vega State Park

BEST (

The main attraction at Vega State Park is the 900-acre reservoir at an elevation of 8,000 feet. Vega means "meadow" in Spanish, and the land under the reservoir was once fertile ranchlands. The surrounding hillsides slope gently out of the lake, facilitating fishing access and hiking. To the south, the Grand Mesa rises 2,000 feet above the lake and provides endless four-wheeling and mountain biking opportunities. From the campground, bikes and ATVs can take Park Creek Road into Grand Mesa National Forest. Hikers can take an easy trail along the shore to the Aspen Grove campground. The lake offers good trout fishing and waterskiing, sailing, and windsurfing. Every Friday and Saturday evening the park offers a free nature program at the visitors center and a nature program geared toward kids on Saturday or Sunday afternoon.

Early Settlers is a large paved loop in a meadow of wheat and wildflowers at the west end of the lake. It is the most modern and the busiest campground at the park. There are very few trees, and privacy is poor for tent campers. All of the sites have nice views of the hills to the north, but the lakeside sites (111-114, 117, 118, 120, and 122) are the best.

Campsites, facilities: There are 33 sites for

tents and RVs up to 40 feet. Water and electrical hookups and pull-through sites are available. Picnic tables, grills, fire rings, and tent pads are provided. Sites 101, 104, 106, 108-111, 119, 124, 127, 129, and 132 have sun shelters. Restrooms with flush toilets and showers, vault toilets, drinking water, a playground, group picnic area, a boat ramp, and dump stations, are available. Horse corrals are available for rent near the Pioneer cabins for $10 per horse per night (reservations required). Leashed pets are permitted. Sites 101, 104, and 119 and the facilities are wheelchair-accessible.

Reservations, fees: Make reservations at 800/244-5613 or www.cpwshop.com. The fee is $30 per night. Campers must also purchase a vehicle pass ($8) or an Annual Parks Pass ($80). Most of the campground is open late spring-late fall, but the park tries to keep some sites open year-round, weather permitting. Winter campers should call in advance to determine availability.

Directions: From Mesa, take Highway 330 east to Collbran. Continue on 330E for 6.5 miles. Turn right on County Road 64.5 and continue 3.3 miles to the entrance station. Take the first right after the station. The campground is on the left in 1.0 mile.

Contact: Vega State Park, 970/487-3407, www.cpw.state.co.us.

28 PIONEER

Scenic rating: 8

in Vega State Park

Pioneer is a real treat for tent campers. This loop of walk-in tent sites (50-300 feet from the parking lot) is on a hillside overlooking Vega Reservoir, and it winds through dense bushes and scrub oaks with pockets of wildflowers. The sites are well screened from each other and many have excellent views of the lake. On the other side of the parking lot, there is an ATV staging area for Park Creek Road, which climbs into Grand Mesa National Forest. This route is very popular with mountain bikers. Hikers and anglers can take a trail from the Early Settlers campground to Aspen Grove. The lake has good trout fishing. It's also a popular water-sports destination. The five cabins at this campground are open year-round and are very popular in the winter, when the lake is open to ice-skating and ice fishing, and cross-country skiers and snowmobilers enjoy exploring Grand Mesa. (For more information on Vega State Park, see the Early Settlers listing in this chapter.)

Campsites, facilities: There are 10 walk-in tent sites and five rustic cabins. Sites 134 and 135 and the facilities are wheelchair-accessible. Picnic tables, fire rings, grills, tent pads, and wheelbarrows are provided. Vault toilets and drinking water are available at the campground. Restrooms with flush toilets and showers, a playground, and a boat ramp are available at the Early Settlers campground. Horse corrals are available for rent near the cabins for $10 per horse per night (reservations required). Leashed pets are permitted.

Reservations, fees: Reservations are accepted at 800/244-5613 or www.cpwshop.com. The fee is $20 per night for campsites, $90 for cabins. Campers must also purchase a vehicle pass ($8) or an Annual Parks Pass ($80). The tent sites are open late spring-late fall, and the cabins are open year-round.

Directions: From Collbran, take County Road 330E east for 6.5 miles. Turn right on Country Road 64.5 and continue 3.3 miles to the entrance station. Take the first right after the station. The campground is on the right in 1.0 mile.

Contact: Vega State Park, 970/487-3407, www.cpw.state.co.us.

29 ASPEN GROVE

Scenic rating: 7

in Vega State Park

Aspen Grove is a pleasant campground on the eastern end of the 900-acre reservoir, at the base of the Grand Mesa. The campground has two loops separated by a group picnic area with a large pavilion. The first loop (sites 200-208) is in an open meadow close to the water. The second loop (sites 209-227) is in a dense thicket of tall bushes and scattered trees. The first has better views, and the second is much more private. Sites 200, 201, 202, 204, and 205 are closest to the lake. Because there are no hookups, this campground is much less popular than Early Settlers, but it's an excellent choice for both tent campers and RVers. A foot trail connects the two campgrounds, and mountain bikers and ATVers can take forest roads into Grand Mesa National Forest. The lake has good rainbow trout fishing, and canoes and kayaks can be carried down to the water. (For more information on Vega State Park, see the Early Settlers entry in this chapter.)

Campsites, facilities: There are 27 sites for tents and RVs up to 35 feet. There are no hookups, but most sites are pull-through. Picnic tables, fire rings, grills, and tent pads are provided. Sites 200, 203, 212, and 214 have sun shelters. Vault toilets, drinking water, and a group picnic area are available. Restrooms with flush toilets and showers and a dump station are available at the Early Settlers campground. Leashed pets are permitted. Sites 203, 212, and 214 and the facilities are wheelchair-accessible.

Reservations, fees: Reservations are accepted at 800/244-5613 or www.cpwshop.com. The fee is $20 per night. Campers must also purchase a vehicle pass ($8) or an Annual Parks Pass ($80). Open late spring-late fall.

Directions: From Collbran, take County Road 330E east for 6.5 miles. Turn right on Country Road 64.5 and continue 3.3 miles to the entrance station. Take the first right after the station. The campground is on the left in 2.8 miles.

Contact: Vega State Park, 970/487-3407, www.cpw.state.co.us.

30 OAK POINT

Scenic rating: 6

in Vega State Park

On the north shore of 900-acre Vega Reservoir, Oak Point is the only campground in the park with views of Grand Mesa towering 2,000 feet above the lake. Except for this feature, it's the least appealing of the campgrounds in the park. It hasn't been renovated, so the sites are smaller and closer together than at the other campgrounds. There are three distinct areas in this long loop along the shore. Some sites are surrounded by Gambel oak, but sites 301-324 and 333-337 are in a meadow with no shade and limited privacy. Sites 306, 307, 309-313, 327, and 332-336 are lakeside. Anglers and water-sports enthusiasts will appreciate the boat ramp at the campground. The lake has good fishing for rainbow trout and some cutthroat. (For more information on Vega State Park, see the Early Settlers entry in this chapter.)

Campsites, facilities: There are 39 sites for tents and RVs up to 25 feet. Some sites are not suitable for tents when water levels are high (call to make sure). There are no hookups or pull-throughs. Picnic tables, fire rings, and grills are provided. Vault toilets, drinking water, a boat ramp, and a dump station (by the visitors center on the other side of the lake) are available. Leashed pets are permitted.

Reservations, fees: Reservations are accepted at 800/244-5613 or www.cpwshop.com. The fee is $20 per night. Campers must also purchase a vehicle pass ($8) or an Annual Parks Pass ($80). Open late spring-late fall.

Directions: From Collbran, take County Road

330E east for 6.5 miles. Turn right on Country Road 64.5 and continue 3.3 miles to the entrance station. The campground is on the right 2.0 miles after the station.

Contact: Vega State Park, 970/487-3407, www.cpw.state.co.us.

31 AVALANCHE

Scenic rating: 9

south of Carbondale

BEST (

Avalanche is a small campground in a stunning setting on Avalanche Creek at the base of Mount Sopris and at the western entrance to the Maroon Bells-Snowmass Wilderness Area. This area doesn't have the Aspen crowds, but it does have hiking, backpacking, and trail-riding access to the Maroon Bells and some gorgeous wildflower meadows in late summer. The popular Avalanche Lake Trail begins at the campground and travels 11 miles to an alpine lake in the shadow of Capitol Peak (14,130 feet). This trail connects to the Hell Roaring Creek, East Creek, and Capitol Creek Trails.

The primitive campground is a small loop beside Avalanche Creek in a forest of evergreens and cottonwoods that has been minimally impacted by bark beetles. Most of the sites are quite large and 50-100 feet apart. Sites 1-6 and 11-13 are next to the creek. Sites 11-13 are overflow sites, so they are a long way from the toilets, but they are next to a meadow and have great views. Site 7 is the smallest and least-appealing site.

Campsites, facilities: There are six sites for tents and RVs up to 16 feet. There are no hookups. Picnic tables, fire rings, and grills are provided. Vault toilets and drinking water are available. Leashed pets are permitted.

Reservations, fees: Reservations are not accepted. There is no fee, but donations are accepted. Open late May-late October.

Directions: From Carbondale, take Highway 133 south for 10.5 miles. Turn left on Avalanche Creek Road/County Road 10. In 1.8 miles, there is a shallow ford that passenger cars can usually cross, but drivers should check the water levels first. The road ends about 1.0 mile past the ford at the campground. This is a narrow dirt road, which is not recommended for trailers longer than 16 feet.

Contact: White River National Forest, Sopris District, 970/963-2266, www.fs.usda.gov/whiteriver.

32 REDSTONE I

Scenic rating: 6

south of Carbondale

Redstone is a clean and pleasant stopover on the way to or from Carbondale. The two loops, Algiers and Osgood, are terraced, slightly wooded, and well screened from the highway. Redstone I is more spacious and has better views than Redstone II. This is one of the few national forest campgrounds in this area with hookups and showers, so it's very popular with RVers. The main activities are fishing on the Crystal River and shopping or eating in Redstone. Redstone, population 200, was founded by utopian industrialist John Cleveland Osgood, who built an inn to house his single employees and cottages for his married employees. The inn and many of the cottages have been preserved. This cute town is full of shops and cafes and is a pleasant one-mile walk from the campground. Advanced kayakers can paddle the Class III-IV section of the Crystal River from Marble to Redstone when water levels permit. A mile north of the campground there's a small, natural hot spring just off the road, or at nearby Avalanche Ranch Hot Springs.

Campsites, facilities: There are 17 sites for tents and RVs up to 60 feet. Water and electric hookups are available at all sites. Sites 10, 17, and 20 are pull-through, and sites 1, 2, 6, 7, 18, and 19 are double sites. Picnic tables, fire rings, grills, and tent pads are provided. Restrooms with flush toilets and showers, vault toilets, drinking water, a playground, and horseshoe pits are available. Leashed pets are permitted.

Reservations, fees: Reservations are accepted at 877/444-6777 and www.recreation.gov. The fee is $34 per night, plus $5 for hookups. Cash or check only. Open late May-late October.

Directions: From Carbondale, take Highway 133 south for 14.3 miles. Turn left on County Road 3. Redstone I is on the left and Redstone II is on the right.

Contact: White River National Forest, Sopris District, 970/963-2266, www.fs.usda.gov/whiteriver.

33 REDSTONE II

Scenic rating: 6

south of Carbondale

Redstone II is very similar to Redstone I (see the listing in this chapter). It's a terraced loop on a hill overlooking the Crystal River and Highway 133. There is some traffic noise from the road, but the wooded site is fairly well screened. The sites are 20-30 feet apart and not very private, but they are large and clean. The main activities are fishing and shopping.

Campsites, facilities: There are 19 sites for tents and RVs up to 40 feet. There are no hookups. Sites 3, 4, 8, 10, and 13-15 are pull-through. Sites 3, 4, 14, and 15 are double sites. Picnic tables, fire rings, grills, and tent pads are provided. Vault toilets, showers, and drinking water are available. Leashed pets are permitted.

Reservations, fees: Reservations are accepted at 877/444-6777 and www.recreation.gov. The fee is $30 per night. Cash or check only. Open late May-late September.

Directions: From Carbondale, take Highway 133 south for 14.3 miles. Turn left on County

Road 3. Redstone I is on the left and Redstone II is on the right.

Contact: White River National Forest, 970/945-2521, www.fs.usda.gov/whiteriver.

34 MCCLURE PASS

Scenic rating: 6

south of Carbondale

McClure is a half-forgotten campground in the Gunnison National Forest, about a half-hour drive from Carbondale. It's a pretty campground full of quaking aspen and the bubbling sounds of Lee Creek. There's not much to do here except sit back, relax, and enjoy the solitude. The sites are large, flat, and heavily wooded. Site 1 has views of Sheep Mountain and the Muddy Creek valley.

Campsites, facilities: There are eight sites for tents and RVs up to 35 feet. Two sites are pull-through. There are no hookups and no drinking water. Picnic tables, fire rings, and grills are provided. Vault toilets are available. Trash must be packed out. Leashed pets are permitted.

Reservations, fees: Reservations are not accepted and camping is free. Open Memorial Day-September.

Directions: From Carbondale, drive south on Highway 133. The campground is on the left 1.6 miles after McClure Pass.

Contact: Gunnison National Forest, Paonia District, 970/527-4131, www.fs.usda.gov/gmug.

35 BOGAN FLATS

Scenic rating: 8

south of Carbondale

BEST (

Bogan Flats is in a beautiful location on the banks of the Crystal River, between the Maroon Bells-Snowmass and Raggeds Wilderness areas.

There are two main attractions: fly-fishing on the Crystal River and visiting the historic town of Marble (five miles away). The Marble Quarry produced the stone for the Lincoln Memorial and the Tomb of the Unknown Soldier. Local artists still use this pure-white stone for sculptures. The nearest hiking trail is the nine-mile Raspberry Creek Loop, which begins in Marble. Jeep trails for four-wheeling and mountain biking are also accessible in Marble. Advanced kayakers can boat the Class III-IV section of the Crystal from Marble to Redstone.

This campground is packed on weekends, so make reservations if possible. The sites are about 50 feet apart, and many are wooded. Sites 1-9, 12, 13, 15-19, 21, and 23-26 are next to the river. Sites 1-5 have views of Ragged Peak. Sites 12 and 15 are very large. The group site is upstream of the main campground. It is very private and an excellent group destination.

Campsites, facilities: There are 35 sites for tents and RVs up to 40 feet and one group site. There are no hookups. Sites 6, 19, 24, and 31 are pull-through. Picnic tables, fire rings, and grills are provided. Vault toilets and drinking water are available. Leashed pets are permitted. Sites 24 and 28 are wheelchair-accessible.

Reservations, fees: Reservations are accepted at 877/444-6777 and www.recreation.gov. The fee is $25 per night. The group site costs $135 per night, for up to 50 people. Cash or check only. Open late May-late October.

Directions: From Carbondale, take Highway 133 south. Turn left on Forest Route 314. In 1.5 miles, make a sharp left into the campground.

Contact: White River National Forest, Sopris District, 970/963-2266, www.fs.usda.gov/whiteriver.

36 PAONIA STATE PARK

Scenic rating: 5

north of Paonia

Paonia State Park features a 334-acre reservoir in a narrow valley with views of the Ragged Mountains. The nearest hiking is in the Raggeds Wilderness area, accessible via County Road 12, which intersects Highway 133 beneath the dam. During runoff, Muddy Creek earns its name, making fishing impossible. When the water clears, anglers fish for northern pike from the shore and boats.

There are two primitive loops with a total of 13 campsites. Spruce Loop is north of the reservoir, between Muddy Creek and Highway 133, in a mature spruce grove. It has ample shade and well-spaced sites. Sites 8-10, 14, and 15 are next to the creek. The Hawsapple Loop is on the other side of the creek. There's not much shade except at site 7, which is secluded in a small grove of trees. Sites 5 and 6 are on the waterfront, and boats can moor at Site 6. Sites 5-7 also have views of Mount Gunnison.

Campsites, facilities: There are a total of 13 primitive sites for tents and RVs up to 35 feet. There are no hookups, and no drinking water. Picnic tables, fire rings, and vault toilets are provided. Leashed pets are permitted. Site 1 is wheelchair-accessible.

Reservations, fees: Reservations are accepted at 800/244-5613 or www.cpwshop.com. The fee is $18 per night. Cash or check only. Campers must also purchase a Daily Park Pass ($8) or an Annual Pass ($80). Open May-September.

Directions: From the intersection of Highway 133 and Highway 187 in Paonia, take Highway 133 north for 20 miles. Turn right at the campground sign.

Contact: Crawford State Park, 970/921-5721, www.cpw.state.co.us.

37 ERICKSON SPRINGS
🏃 🛶 🐕 ♿ 🚐 ⛺

Scenic rating: 7
east of Paonia

Erickson Springs is a pleasant stopover on the West Elk Loop Scenic Byway, with the bonus of an amazing hiking trail out the back door. The 16-mile Dark Canyon Trail traverses the Raggeds Wilderness, and the trailhead is just up the road from the campground. The first portion along Anthracite Creek offers excellent stream fishing and numerous waterfalls. After climbing the Devils Stairway (1,200 feet in less than a mile), the trail enters Horse Ranch Park, an area of quaking aspen stands and meadows full of wildflowers. Connecting trails access the town of Marble and Oh-Be-Joyful Pass.

The campground is separated from Anthracite Creek by the road, but it's a beautiful, overgrown mess of wildflowers, cottonwoods, spruce, and brush. The vegetation offers a lot of privacy, and the sites are well spaced and shaded. The only sites without shade are 11 and 12.

Campsites, facilities: There are 18 sites for tents and RVs up to 35 feet. There are no hookups. Sites 2, 3, 5, 7, 11, and 13 are pull-through. Picnic tables, fire rings, grills, and tent pads are provided. Vault toilets and drinking water are available. Leashed pets are permitted. Four sites are wheelchair-accessible.

Reservations, fees: Reservations are not accepted. The fee is $14 per night. Cash or check only. Open May-September.

Directions: From Highway 135 in Crested Butte, take Whiterock Avenue/County Road 12 west for 18.7 miles. Before the bridge, turn right at the campground sign. The entrance is on the right in 0.25 mile.

Contact: Gunnison National Forest, Paonia District, 970/527-4131, www.fs.usda.gov/gmug.

38 LOST LAKE
🏃 🚴 🛶 🚤 🐕 🚐 ⛺

Scenic rating: 9
west of Crested Butte

BEST (

Lost Lake is on the West Elk Loop Scenic Byway, and whether you're coming from Paonia or Crested Butte, it's worth every minute of the drive because you usually have to hike to reach a place like Lost Lake. This subalpine lake sits in a cirque at the base of East Beckwith Mountain, between the Raggeds and West Elk Wilderness areas. The campground is in a forest of aspen, spruce, and fir on the north shore of the lake, and many of the sites have amazing views of the Beckwith Mountains. Campers enjoy fishing and boating on the lake, as well as hiking and mountain biking on the Three Lakes Trail. This 2.1-mile trail circles Lost Lake and offers great views of the Ruby Range. It connects to the Beckwith Pass Trail, which hikers can take through aspen stands and parks full of wildflowers into the West Elk Wilderness.

The Forest Service renovated this campground in 2010, adding four sites, potable water, new tables, tent pads, grills, and toilets, as well as developing the other side of the lake for horse use. The sites are 100-200 feet apart and very private. This is a very popular campground. The best way to get a spot is to arrive midweek. Sites 6, 8, and 10 are the most requested for their views and lake access. The horse sites are actually "dual use," so you can tent camp there as well.

Campsites, facilities: There are three double sites and 11 single sites for tents and RVs up to 36 feet. On the other side of the lake there are five additional dual use sites for tents or horse trailers. There are no hookups. Some sites are pull-through. Picnic tables, fire rings, grills, and tent pads are provided. Vault toilets and water are available. Leashed pets are permitted.

Reservations, fees: Reservations are currently not accepted. The fee is $20 per night for single sites or horse sites, $36 per night for double sites. Cash or check only. Open mid-June-October.

Directions: From Highway 135 in Crested Butte, take Whiterock Avenue/County Road 12 west for 9.7 miles. Turn left on Forest Route 706. The campground is on the left in 2.4 miles.

Contact: Gunnison National Forest, Paonia District, 970/527-4131, www.fs.usda.gov/gmug.

39 LAKE IRWIN

Scenic rating: 8

west of Crested Butte

BEST (

At 10,300 feet, on the edge of the Raggeds Wilderness, Lake Irwin is in a jaw-dropping setting. The campground sits on the northern tip of the reservoir, in a spruce and fir forest, and offers views of the Ruby Range, Anthracite Range, and Mount Axtell, among other peaks. Hikers with strong lungs will have a heyday. The Dyke Trail leaves from the western shore of the lake and climbs to meet the Silver Basin Trail in the Raggeds Wilderness. The trail is open to mountain bikes until it enters the wilderness area. After that, it travels through pristine high mountain basins where a long loop is possible by connecting with the Dark Canyon Trail. The Scarp Ridge Trail is also accessible. The lake is stocked with rainbow trout and there are native brookies. But there's one problem: Lake Irwin is no secret, and the campground is packed all summer long. With a few exceptions, the sites are small and very close together, so the camping is cramped.

The following sites have great views: 1, 2, 11-18, 30, and 31. Sites 1-6, 8, and 10 overlook the lake. The best sites for privacy and scenery are 10-12.

Campsites, facilities: There are 32 sites for tents and RVs up to 50 feet. There are no hookups. Sites 2, 8, 12, 20, and 31 are pull-through. Picnic tables, fire rings, and grills are provided. Vault toilets and drinking water are available. Leashed pets are permitted.

Reservations, fees: Reservations are accepted

Lost Lake and the Beckwith Mountains from Lost Lake Campground

for 19 of the sites at 877/444-6777 and www. recreation.gov. The fee is $18 per night. Cash or check only. Open mid-June-mid-September.

Directions: From Highway 135 in Crested Butte, take Whiterock Avenue/County Road 12 west for 6.8 miles. Turn right on Forest Route 826. The campground is on the right in 2.6 miles.

Contact: Gunnison National Forest, 970/874-6600, www.fs.usda.gov/gmug.

40 OH-BE-JOYFUL
🚶 🛶 ♨ 🐕 ⛺

Scenic rating: 9
north of Crested Butte

Oh-Be-Joyful, besides having the best campground name in Colorado, is a tent camping gem. It offers free, dispersed camping in an evergreen grove on the east bank of the Slate River, upstream of the confluence with Oh-Be-Joyful Creek. Understandably, it's very popular, and all of the designated sites are full for most of July and August. Hikers can take the Oh-Be-Joyful Creek Trail up to Oh-Be-Joyful Pass and down into Buck Basin, Swan Basin, Silver Basin, and Gold Basin. These pristine basins are in the Raggeds Wilderness and offer unparalleled scenery and wildflowers. This is backpacking paradise. Expert kayakers boat the creek and the river when the levels are right, but this is a very advanced run. Mountain bikers might explore the Forest Service roads, but, because of the wilderness area, there are no bike trails nearby.

BLM reports that the campground is undergoing development that will add a number of new sites.

Campsites, facilities: There are currently 47 sites for tents and RVs; overflow dispersed camping is allowed if you can find a site, but they are in the process of developing this. There are no hookups or pull-throughs. Picnic tables, fire rings, and grills are provided. Vault toilets are available. Trash must be packed out. Leashed pets are permitted.

Reservations, fees: The fee is $10 per night, $5 for an overflow site, and $30 for the group site. Reservations are not accepted. Open year-round, unless blocked by snow.

Directions: From Elk Avenue in Crested Butte, take Gothic Road north for 0.8 mile. Turn left on Forest Route 734/Slate River Road. In 4.6 miles, turn left at the Oh-Be-Joyful sign onto Forest Route 754. The campground is about a quarter mile down this 4WD road.

Contact: Bureau of Land Management, Gunnison Field Office, 970/642-4940, www.co.blm.gov.

41 GOTHIC
🚶 🚴 🛶 🐕 🚐 ⛺

Scenic rating: 9
north of Crested Butte

This itsy-bitsy campground is in a stunning location on the East River between Avery Peak and Gothic Mountain, north of the historic town of Gothic and a few miles south of the Maroon Bells-Snowmass Wilderness. Crested Butte is the Wildflower Capital of Colorado, and the drive to Gothic campground explains the designation. It's gorgeous. Bring a camera and you will have hours of enjoyment in fields of purple, yellow, and red wildflowers. As if that weren't enough, Gothic Natural Area, a virgin stand of Engelmann spruce, is just up the road. On the way there, you'll pass the Washington Gulch trailhead, which ascends Rock Creek through beautiful scenery. The town of Gothic is now the home of the Rocky Mountain Biological Laboratory. To take part in an "Exploration Experience," visit its website at www.rmbl.org. Mountain bikers can take Gothic Road up to Scholfield Pass. You'll share the way with four-wheelers, but the rough road deters many visitors. Fly-fishing is excellent on the East River.

The four campsites are in a stand of Engelmann spruce beside a small creek. The trees provide shade and privacy, and the sites are about 100 feet apart. They can only accommodate tents, pop-ups, and very small RVs. You might be the lone camper on a weekday in July, but arrive early on weekends to secure a spot.

Campsites, facilities: There are four sites for tents and RVs up to 20 feet. There are no hookups or pull-throughs. Picnic tables, fire rings, grills, and tent pads are provided. Vault toilets are available. Leashed pets are permitted.

Reservations, fees: Reservations are not accepted. The fee is $12 per night. Cash or check only. Open mid-June-mid-September.

Directions: From the Town Hall in Mount Crested Butte, take Gothic Road/County Road 317 north for 6.4 miles. The campground is on the left. The road is deeply rutted for the last 100 feet before the campground.

Contact: Gunnison National Forest, 970/874-6600, www.fs.usda.gov/gmug.

42 CEMENT CREEK

Scenic rating: 7

southeast of Crested Butte

Cement Creek is the most accessible campground in the Crested Butte area. This small loop occupies a clearing on the banks of Cement Creek, in the shadow of Cement Mountain. The campground is more open and sunny than many canyon campgrounds and has a profusion of wild roses. It's usually quiet, but it always fills up on weekends, mostly with mountain bikers. Several trails on the north side of the road access the Elk Mountains. Walrod Gulch begins nearby and connects with Double Top Trail, which in turn connects to Block and Tackle and Hunter Hill Trails. Several challenging mountain bike loops can be made on the flanks of Double Top Mountain. Skiers might be interested to know that Cement

Creek was the site of Pioneer Ski Area, one of Colorado's first ski mountains. It operated 1939-1952. The chairlift was partly assembled from trams from nearby mines.

Sites 2-9 are next to the creek and shaded. Site 9 is a walk-in. Sites 11-13 are in the clearing. The roomy sites can easily accommodate large family groups.

Campsites, facilities: There are 12 sites for tents and RVs up to 26 feet, including 1 walk-in tent site. There are no hookups. Sites 2, 3, and 4 are pull-through. Picnic tables, fire rings, grills, and tent pads are provided. Vault toilets available. There is no drinking water, but you can treat the local spring or creek water. Leashed pets are permitted.

Reservations, fees: Reservations are not accepted. The fee is $14 per night. Cash or check only. Open mid-May-mid-September.

Directions: From Gunnison, take Highway 135 north. Turn right on Forest Route 740/Cement Creek Road, 10.5 miles after Almont. The campground is on the right in 3.7 miles.

Contact: Gunnison National Forest, 970/874-6600, www.fs.usda.gov/gmug.

43 SILVER BAR

Scenic rating: 8

near Aspen

The Maroon Bells are among the most photographed mountains in the country because of their beauty and accessibility. The Maroon Creek valley, formed by glaciers and landslides, provides easy access to a wilderness area with nine passes, six fourteeners, and countless wildflower-filled meadows and alpine lakes. Hundreds of thousands of tourists visit the Maroon Bells every summer for picnics, hiking, backpacking, and trail riding. To reduce the impact on the valley, the road is closed to passenger cars during the day from mid-June-September. A public bus takes visitors from the

Aspen Highlands Ski Area to Maroon Lake and other popular trailheads. Additionally, because there are only three campgrounds in the valley, with a total of 24 campsites, reservations are *highly* recommended from mid-June-late August.

There is a reservation system in place for Conundrum hot springs dispersed camping and tickets go very quickly. If you do not have a permit for Conundrum you can still enjoy the hot springs while passing through; you can camp outside a two-mile radius in any direction from the springs. Otherwise, cross your fingers for one of these nearby campgrounds.

All of the trails in the valley begin a short drive away from the campgrounds. The easiest day hikes range from 1.0-3.6 miles round-trip. They are the Maroon Lake, Falls Loop, Maroon Creek, and Crater Lake Trails. Longer backpacking trails are the Maroon-Snowmass, East Maroon, and West Maroon Trails, which feature high passes, alpine lakes, and mountain meadows. The Maroon Bells are composed of fragile shale and siltstone, which breaks easily, making them famous for their treachery. Experienced mountaineers have died while attempting to climb these fourteeners—be cautious while hiking in these mountains. Maroon Lake is stocked with trout and is a popular fly-fishing destination. Road cyclists should not miss the long ascent up Maroon Creek Road.

Silver Bar is the smallest and most overlooked campground on the road. It doesn't have views of the peaks, but there is plenty of privacy in this campground designed mainly for tents. Site 4 is the least private spot, but it also receives the most sunshine early in the morning, which is a big plus.

Campsites, facilities: There are four sites for tents only. Sites 1-3 are short walk-ins. There are no hookups or pull-through sites. Picnic tables, grills, fire rings, trash disposal, and tent pads are provided. Vault toilets and drinking water are available. Leashed pets are permitted.

Reservations, fees: Reservations are accepted at 877/444-6777 and www.recreation.gov. The fee is $15 per night. Campers must purchase a $5 vehicle pass (good for five days). Cash or check only. Open late May-late October.

Directions: From the Aspen roundabout, take Maroon Creek Road south for 4.6 miles. The campground is on the left across from the entrance station. Stop at the entrance station to purchase a car pass.

Contact: White River National Forest, 970/925-3445, www.fs.usda.gov/whiteriver.

44 SILVER BELL
🏃 🏊 🎣 🚐 ⛰️

Scenic rating: 9
near Aspen

Silver Bell is the middle campground in the beautiful Maroon Creek valley. Between the creek and the views of the Maroon Bells, this is a jaw-dropping location. Sites 1-10 are next to the water. Sites 1-4 are very private walk-ins with excellent views. Sites 8-13 are walk-in sites at the end of the campground. They are more exposed to the weather and less private, but they also have the best views of the Bells. Sites 1, 5, and 7 can accommodate RVs. Site 14, right next to the road, is the worst site. (For more information on the Maroon Bells, see the Silver Bar listing in this chapter.)

Campsites, facilities: There are 14 sites for tents and RVs up to 30 feet. Sites 1-4 and 8-13 are walk-in. Picnic tables, fire rings, grills, and tent pads are provided. Vault toilets, trash disposal, and drinking water are available. Leashed pets are permitted.

Reservations, fees: Reservations are accepted for four of the sites at 877/444-6777 and www.recreation.gov; the remaining sites are first come, first served. The fee is $15 per night and campers must purchase a $5 vehicle pass (good for five days). Cash or check only. Open late May-early October.

Directions: From the Aspen roundabout, take Maroon Creek Road south for 4.6 miles to the entrance station. After purchasing a car pass, continue 0.3 mile to the campground on the left.

Contact: White River National Forest, 970/925-3445, www.fs.usda.gov/whiteriver.

45 SILVER QUEEN

Scenic rating: 9

near Aspen

BEST (

Silver Queen, the last campground on Maroon Creek Road, is a quiet, relaxing destination. This small campground in an aspen grove is surrounded by red cliffs and offers amazing views of the Bells. Site 1 is near the entry but very private. Sites 2 and 3 are near the creek and also very private. Site 4, next to the toilet in the middle of the loop, is the worst site. Sites 5 and 6 have the best views of the peaks. (For more information on the Maroon Bells, see the Silver Bar listing in this chapter.)

Campsites, facilities: There are six sites for tents and RVs up to 30 feet. Picnic tables, fire rings, grills, and tent pads are provided. Vault toilets and drinking water are available. Leashed pets are permitted.

Reservations, fees: Reservations are accepted at 877/444-6777 and www.recreation.gov. The fee is $15 per night and campers must purchase a $5 vehicle pass (good for five days). Cash or check only. Open late May-late September.

Directions: From the Aspen roundabout, take Maroon Creek Road south for 4.6 miles to the entrance station. After purchasing a car pass, continue 1.0 mile to the campground on the left.

Contact: White River National Forest, 970/925-3445, www.fs.usda.gov/whiteriver.

46 DIFFICULT

Scenic rating: 7

near Aspen

Aspen is flooded during the summer with tourists from around the country and the world, and the hype is justified. The Maroon Bells-Snowmass, Collegiate Peaks, and Hunter-Fryingpan Wilderness areas are all accessible from town. In a state famous for hiking, Aspen has some of the best trails around. For a small taste, try the Difficult Creek Trail, which leaves from the picnic area. Fishing is also excellent on the Roaring Fork, a designated Gold Medal river. And don't miss the drive up to Independence Pass (elevation 12,095 feet) or a visit to the ghost town of Independence. The campgrounds on Highway 82 are also the best place to stay if you're planning a visit to the Maroon Bells but didn't manage to make a reservation six months ahead of time. Set up camp here and explore the area. Difficult is the largest public campground near Aspen. It contains two paved loops in an aspen and cottonwood grove. The sites are about 30 feet apart. They can feel cramped, but dense vegetation (including wild roses) provides ample privacy.

Campsites, facilities: There are 46 sites for tents and RVs up to 40 feet and one group site for 50 people. There are no hookups. Sites 5-7, 11, 14, and 17 are pull-through. Picnic tables, fire rings, grills, and bear lockers, are provided. Vault toilets and drinking water are available. Leashed pets are permitted.

Reservations, fees: Reservations are required at 877/444-6777 and www.recreation.gov. The fee is $26 per night. The group site costs $85 per night. Cash or check only. Open late May-early October.

Directions: In Aspen, from the Independence Pass sign at the east end of town, drive east on Highway 82 for 4.3 miles and turn right into the campground.

Contact: White River National Forest, 970/925-3445, www.fs.usda.gov/whiteriver.

47 WELLER

Scenic rating: 8

near Aspen

 BEST (

Weller is on Highway 82, about halfway up Independence Pass. This is a good starting place for road cyclists who want to bike the pass but aren't ready for the whole climb. Anglers can fish on the Roaring Fork, a Gold Medal river, and on Weller Lake. The Weller Lake Trail is about a half-mile long and begins on the other side of the highway. Many more hiking trails are available nearby in the Hunter-Fryingpan and Collegiate Peaks wildernesses areas. Nearby Weller Slab is a popular Aspen rock-climbing area with routes ranging in difficulty from 5.7 to 5.10. The campground is a small paved loop in a beautiful aspen grove with well-spaced, wooded sites. This is a quiet, relaxing location to pitch your tent.

Campsites, facilities: There are 11 sites for tents and RVs up to 14 feet. Site 5 is wheelchair-accessible. There are no pull-throughs, and this campground is not recommended for large RVs or trailers. There are no hookups. Picnic tables, fire rings, and grills are provided. Vault toilets are available and water may be available. Leashed pets are permitted.

Reservations, fees: Reservations are not accepted. The fee is $23 per night. Cash or check only. Open mid-May-mid-September.

Directions: In Aspen, from the Independence Pass sign at the east end of town, drive east on Highway 82 for 7.3 miles and turn left into the campground.

Contact: White River National Forest, 970/925-3445, www.fs.usda.gov/whiteriver.

48 LINCOLN GULCH

Scenic rating: 8

near Aspen

Lincoln Gulch is at the northern edge of the Collegiate Peaks Wilderness, which encompasses eight fourteeners, more than any other wilderness area in Colorado. Lincoln Creek Road penetrates 10 miles into the wilderness and remains open to bikes and vehicles. Several trails are accessible from this road, including the New York Creek, Tabor Creek, Petroleum Lake, and Grizzly Lake Trails. Grizzly Lake is a 3.6-mile trail to an alpine lake at the foot of Grizzly Peak, a former volcano on the Continental Divide. Lincoln Creek Road to Ruby, an old mining camp, is a moderately challenging mountain bike ride. Local climbers frequent the cliff near the campground, which has 5.8-5.11 routes.

At first sight, Lincoln Gulch is not very impressive, but there's more than meets the eye at this small campground with interesting rock formations. Maybe it's the solitude, maybe it's the setting, but there's a little bit of magic in the air. The sites are large but not very private because of the clearing in the middle of the loop. Fortunately, Lincoln Gulch rarely fills up. Sites 1 and 2 are next to the creek. Sites 5 and 7 are the best spots.

Campsites, facilities: There are seven sites for tents and trailers up to 16 feet. There are no hookups. Picnic tables, fire rings, grills, vault toilets, and drinking water are provided. Leashed pets are permitted.

Reservations, fees: Reservations are not accepted. The fee is $22 per night. Cash or check only. Open mid-May-mid-September.

Directions: In Aspen, from the Independence Pass sign at the east end of town, drive east on Highway 82 for 9.2 miles. Turn right on Lincoln Creek Road/Forest Route 106. It is 0.4 mile downhill to the campground. This road is very rough and narrow, with steep drop-offs.

Trailers and RVs are not recommended, and 4WD is a must if the road is muddy or wet.
Contact: White River National Forest, 970/925-3445, www.fs.usda.gov/whiteriver.

49 LOST MAN

Scenic rating: 8

near Aspen

Just four miles from Independence Pass, Lost Man is a great base camp for exploring the Aspen area. Lost Man Trail begins across the road and traverses nine miles of the rugged Hunter-Fryingpan Wilderness. (This trail is an arc, which connects at both ends with Highway 82 and requires a short shuttle.) The serrated 13,000-foot peaks and forested valleys of this area don't receive the heavy traffic of the Maroon Bells Wilderness, but they are very rewarding for hikers and backpackers. Campers can also explore the ghost town of Independence, two miles up Highway 82, where the Aspen mining boom started on July 4, 1879, with the discovery of the Independence gold lode. Anglers can try their luck on the Roaring Fork River.

The campground is a small gravel loop in a pine forest. It is heavily wooded, and the sites are 50-100 feet apart. Site 1 is next to the entrance and has no privacy. Sites 3 and 4 are next to the creek. Site 7, over 100 feet from the road, is the most private campsite. At an elevation of 10,500 feet, Lost Man is cool all summer and is the last campground on this road to open.
Campsites, facilities: There are 11 sites for tents and RVs up to 16 feet. There are no hookups. Sites 7 and 8 are pull-through. Picnic tables, vault toilets, and drinking water are provided. Leashed pets are permitted.
Reservations, fees: Reservations are not accepted. The fee is $22 per night. Cash or check only. Open mid-June-mid-September.
Directions: In Aspen, from the Independence

Pass sign at the east end of town, drive east on Highway 82 for 13 miles. The campground is on the right, across from the Lost Man trailhead.
Contact: White River National Forest, 970/925-3445, www.fs.usda.gov/whiteriver.

50 NORTH RIM

Scenic rating: 8

in Black Canyon of the Gunnison National Park

North Rim campground is much smaller than the South Rim facility; it is also more popular because of the spectacular views, especially at sunrise or sunset. (For more information on the Black Canyon, see the South Rim listing in this chapter.) The North Rim Drive has six overlooks and takes 2-3 hours to drive; the campground is about a two-hour drive from the main visitors center. There are three hiking trails on the North Rim. The longest trail in the park, North Vista, begins at the campground and travels west to Exclamation Point (3 miles round-trip) and then Green Mountain (7 miles round-trip). Bring your camera to capture the panoramic vistas and inner-canyon views. Intrepid hikers can explore the inner canyon via S.O.B. Draw, Long Draw, and Slide Draw. These steep, strenuous scrambles drop 1,800 feet in one mile. Wildlife viewing is excellent, especially for bird-watchers who might see peregrine falcons, canyon wrens, great horned owls, and mountain bluebirds. The campground is a small loop in a piñon-sage habitat. It occasionally fills up during the summer, but midweek there's plenty of solitude. As in most national parks, you are not allowed to forage for firewood or kindling inside the park. Assuming there are no fire restrictions, you can pick up a bundle at "Last Chance Firewood" at the corner store on Highway 50 and the turnoff to the park.
Campsites, facilities: There are 13 sites for tents and RVs up to 35 feet. There are no

hookups. Picnic tables, grills, and vault toilets are provided. Drinking water is available mid-May-mid-September. Leashed pets are permitted.

Reservations, fees: Reservations are not accepted. The nightly fee is $16. Cash or check only. Campers must also purchase a park pass ($20 per car, $15 per motorcycle) or one of the Interagency Annual Passes. Open spring-fall. An annual pass to Black Canyon of the Gunnison National Park is available at the entrance station for $40.

Directions: From Crawford, take 38.50 Drive west to Amber Road. Turn right on Amber Road and in less than 1.0 mile turn left on Black Canyon Road/North Rim Drive. In 10 miles, stop at the park entrance station and then follow the signs one mile to the campground.

Contact: Black Canyon of the Gunnison National Park, 970/249-1914 ext. 423 for Visitor Center, www.nps.gov/blca.

51 SOUTH RIM

Scenic rating: 8

in Black Canyon of the Gunnison National Park

Geologist Wallace Hansen wrote: "Some are longer, some are deeper, some are narrower, and a few have walls as steep. But no other canyon in North America combines the depth, narrowness, sheerness, and somber countenance of the Black Canyon of the Gunnison." It took the Gunnison River two million years to carve the 48-mile canyon out of Precambrian gneiss. On average, the river drops 96 feet per mile through the park, and before the dams upstream of the park were built, it was laden with rocks and debris that helped carve the canyon. Most visitors only peer over the rim at the colorful cliffs and spires; an intrepid few go rafting or kayaking on the Gunny. The National Park Service offers 90-minute boat tours on an upper part of the canyon through Morrow

Point Reservoir (contact Morrow Point Boat Tours). Hiking in the park is limited due to the steep walls of the canyon. Most hikers will explore the Rim Rock, Oak Flat, Cedar Point, and Warner Point Trails, which range 1-3 miles round-trip. An excellent half-day trip from the campground involves driving the South Rim Road, stopping at the overlooks, and stretching your legs on the nature trails. Intrepid hikers can head into the inner canyon on the Gunnison, Timichi, and Warner Routes. These are very steep, difficult scrambles. Fishing is available at East Portal. Winter sports include cross-country skiing and snowshoeing on South Rim Road.

This campground, at 8,320-foot elevation, is densely wooded with Gambel oak and serviceberry. As a result, the sites are very private, especially in Loop C and a few sites in Loop A, which has many walk-in sites. Loop B is by reservation only and offers the only electric hookups in the park, so it attracts mostly RVs. Loop C has the most shade and features views of the mountains. This campground rarely fills up, although reservations are recommended on holidays. As in most national parks, you are not allowed to forage for firewood or kindling inside the park. Assuming there are no fire restrictions, you can pick up a bundle at "Last Chance Firewood" at the corner store on Highway 50 and the turnoff to the park.

Campsites, facilities: There are 88 sites for tents and RVs up to 37 feet. Electric hookups are available in Loop B, and pull-through sites are available in all three loops. Picnic tables and grills are provided at all sites. Tent pads are provided in Loop B. Vault toilets, drinking water (mid-May-mid-September), for gray water, an amphitheater, and campfire programs, and dump stations are available. Leashed pets are permitted. A21 and B1 and the facilities are wheelchair-accessible.

Reservations, fees: Reservations are accepted for Loops A and B at 877/444-6777 and www.recreation.gov. The nightly fee is $22 in Loop B and $16 in Loops A and C. There is

the Black Canyon of the Gunnison, seen from the South Rim

an additional $3 per night fee for reservations made online. Cash, checks, and credit cards are accepted. Campers must also purchase a park pass ($20 per car, $15 per motorcycle) or one of the Interagency Annual Passes. Open spring-fall. An annual pass to Black Canyon of the Gunnison National Park is available at the entrance station for $40.

Loop A is open year-round. Loops B and C are open spring-fall.

Directions: From Montrose, take U.S. Highway 50 east for 7.5 miles. Turn north on Highway 347. The entrance station is in 5.8 miles, and the campground entrance is on the right, 0.2 mile after the station.

Contact: Black Canyon of the Gunnison National Park, 970/249-1914 ext. 423 for Visitor Center; Morrow Point Boat Tours at 970/641-2337 ext. 205 or cure_info@nps.gov; www.nps.gov/blca.

52 EAST PORTAL

Scenic rating: 7
in Curecanti National Recreation Area

BEST (

Curecanti National Recreation Area is adjacent to the national park and contains three reservoirs: Blue Mesa, Morrow Point, and Crystal. Blue Mesa is the main storage reservoir, Morrow Point Dam generates power, and Crystal Dam moderates the releases from Morrow Point. East Portal campground is located at about 6,500-feet in elevation, downstream of Crystal Dam, making it the western-most campground in Curecanti (but it must be accessed through the Black Canyon of the Gunnison National Park). From 700 yards below the dam to the North Fork, the Gunnison River is considered Gold Medal water. Anglers can fish for brown and rainbow trout in nearly absolute solitude. An unmaintained trail from the end of the campground reaches about a half-mile into the inner canyon. It's great for fishing access and a nice short trail for families with kids. Expert kayakers put in here for a 27-mile adventure down the Black Canyon to Gunnison Forks. Permits are required for kayaking and overnight backcountry use.

The campground has two loops. The first is a small, gravel loop with five sites. There is some shade but no privacy. The second loop, "The Bowl," has 10 walk-in sites in a grove of box elder and narrowleaf cottonwood. The sites are close together, but the combination of shade and limited use makes it very pleasant.

Campsites, facilities: There are five sites for tents and RVs and 10 walk-in tent sites. Vehicles longer than 22 feet (including the trailer) are prohibited on East Portal Road because of the steep 16% grade and sharp, narrow curves. Picnic tables, fire rings, grills, and tent pads are provided. Vault toilets and drinking water are available. Leashed pets are permitted.

Reservations, fees: Reservations are not accepted. The fee is $16 per night. Cash or check only. Campers must also purchase a park pass or Interagency Annual Pass. Open spring-fall.

Directions: From Montrose, take U.S. Highway 50 east for 7.5 miles. Turn north on Highway 347. The entrance station is in 5.8 miles. After the station, turn right on East Portal Road. This is a long, steep, very narrow road with 16 percent grades. Vehicles longer than 22 feet (including the trailer) are prohibited. In 5.3 miles, turn left at the campground sign. The road ends at the campground.

Contact: Curecanti National Recreation Area, 970/641-2337, www.nps.gov/cure.

53 CLEAR FORK

Scenic rating: 7

in Crawford State Park

Crawford State Park is in an agricultural valley with a mild climate located 12 miles north of the Black Canyon of the Gunnison. The park includes 337 acres of land and a 400-acre reservoir. It's a weekend getaway for locals and a convenient stopover on the West Elk Scenic Byway Loop. When the reservoir is full, the park is packed on the weekends, mostly with families. A 0.5-mile trail connects Clear Fork to the sandy swimming beach, and another trail connects the campgrounds. The lake is stocked with largemouth bass and catfish. Water sports include waterskiing, scuba diving, and boating. Winter sports include ice fishing, cross-country skiing, and snowshoeing.

Clear Fork is a lakeside loop with very few trees. The five tent-only sites (50-54) and sites 63-66 are in the middle of the loop and about 20 feet apart without trees or shade. Sites 55-59 are very small. Sites 46-49 are on the shore. Sites 46, 60, and 61 are very large and perfect for big family groups.

Campsites, facilities: There are 21 sites for tents and RVs up to 35 feet, including five tent-only sites. There are no hookups. Sites 63-65 are pull-through. Picnic tables, grills, and fire rings are provided at all sites. Sun shelters are provided at sites 46-49 and 60-63. Drinking water and restrooms with flush toilets and showers are available. Dump stations and a boat ramp are available at Iron Creek campground. Leashed pets are permitted. Sites 62 and 63 are wheelchair-accessible.

Reservations, fees: Reservations are accepted at 800/244-5613 or www.cpwshop.com. The fee is $16 per night. Campers must also purchase a Daily Park Pass ($8) or an Annual Parks Pass ($80). Open year-round.

Directions: From Crawford, take Highway 92 south for 1.5 miles. The campground entrance is on the right.

Contact: Crawford State Park, 970/921-5721, www.cpw.state.co.us.

54 IRON CREEK

Scenic rating: 7

in Crawford State Park

Crawford is a small state park that's popular with families because of the swimming beach, lake fishing, and gravel trails. A one-mile trail connects Iron Creek to the swimming beach and the other campground. The lake is stocked with largemouth bass and catfish. Water sports include waterskiing, scuba diving, and boating. The campgrounds were renovated in 1997, and they still look very new. Iron Creek is a loop on a small peninsula in a sagebrush habitat. There are excellent views of Needle Rock, Castle Rock, and Saddle Mountain. The sites are 50 feet apart; sun shelters provide most of the privacy. Sites 20, 22, 24, 26, 28, 30, 32, 34, 35, 37, 39, and 41 are lakefront sites, but a steep embankment limits access to the lake.

Campsites, facilities: There are 45 sites for tents and RVs up to 35 feet. Full hookups are available at all sites. Half of the sites are pull-through. Picnic tables, fire rings, grills, and tent pads are provided at all sites. Sun shelters are provided at sites 1, 2, 6, 7, 10, 14, 33-35, and 44. Restrooms with flush toilets and showers, drinking water, dump stations, and a boat ramp are available. Leashed pets are permitted. Sites 1, 33-36, and 44 are wheelchair-accessible.

Reservations, fees: Reservations are accepted at 800/244-5613 or www.cpwshop.com. The fee is $20 per night. Campers must also purchase a Daily Park Pass ($8) or an Annual Parks Pass ($80). Open April-late October.

Directions: From Crawford, take Highway 92 south for 2.0 miles. The campground entrance is on the right.

Contact: Crawford State Park, 970/921-5721, www.cpw.state.co.us.

55 CIMARRON

Scenic rating: 5

in Curecanti National Recreation Area

Cimarron is the only campground in Curecanti that offers access to Crystal Reservoir and the Cimarron River. Hand-powered boats can be carried down to the reservoir via the Mesa Creek Trail, a 0.8-mile trail with a footbridge across the reservoir that provides access to the north shore. (Boaters should inquire at the visitors center about dam releases, which can cause strong currents.) Fishing on the reservoir includes rainbow, brown, brook, and cutthroat trout, as well as kokanee salmon and yellow perch. Kids and history buffs will enjoy the outdoor exhibit at the (unstaffed) visitors center, which includes corrals and stock cars from the Denver and Rio Grande Narrow Gauge Railroad and panels that explain the early importance of the railroad to the ranching communities of the West.

The campground is at an elevation of 6,895 feet and is surrounded by badlands and a granite ridge. The sites in this loop are about 25 feet apart. There is not much shade, privacy, or scenery, but the campground consistently attracts a small crowd of anglers.

Campsites, facilities: There are 21 sites for tents and RVs up to 30 feet. Sites 12, 15, 17, 19, and 21 are pull-through. There are no hookups. Picnic tables, grills, vault toilets, and drinking water are provided. Leashed pets are permitted.

Reservations, fees: Reservations are not accepted. The fee is $16 per night. Cash or check only. Open spring-fall.

Directions: From Montrose, take U.S. Highway 50 east for 19.3 miles. In Cimarron, turn left at the Cimarron Campground sign. The campground is across the bridge on the left.

Contact: Curecanti National Recreation Area, 970/641-2337, www.nps.gov/cure.

56 SOAP CREEK

Scenic rating: 7
north of Curecanti National Recreation Area

Soap Creek is a remote and scenic campground. It provides southern access to the West Elk Wilderness area, which, despite its size (176,092 acres), is mostly used only by hunters in the fall. Trail 451 leads from the campground into the mountains and reaches Cow Creek in 2 miles, West Elk Creek in 13 miles, and Rainbow Lake in 18 miles. The campground is a gravel loop in a mature pine forest. Sites are 10-50 feet apart and heavily wooded. Sites on the outside of the loop are more private. Sites 3-5, 7, 9, 10, and 12-14 are next to Soap Creek, which offers good trout fishing. With a decent pair of binoculars, campers can spot mountain goats on the dramatic cliffs of Pearson Point. Site 17 has especially good views of the point.

Campsites, facilities: There are 16 sites for tents and RVs up to 55 feet, plus 5 walk-in tent sites. There are no hookups. Sites 9 and 10 are pull-through. Picnic tables, fire rings, and grills are provided at all sites. The walk-in sites have tent pads. Vault toilets, drinking water, and a horse corral are available. Leashed pets are permitted.

Reservations, fees: Reservations are not accepted. The fee is $12 per night. Cash or check only. Open mid-May-mid-September.

Directions: From the intersection of U.S. Highway 50 and Highway 92, go west on Highway 92 for 1.5 miles. Turn right on Soap Creek Road. (This dirt road can be hazardous after precipitation.) In 8.8 miles, turn right at the tent sign and continue downhill for 1.7 miles to the campground.

Contact: Gunnison National Forest, 970/874-6600, www.fs.usda.gov/gmug.

57 PONDEROSA

Scenic rating: 6
in Curecanti National Recreation Area

Ponderosa is a big surprise after the stark landscape and mega-campgrounds of the Blue Mesa Reservoir. Located at the northern tip of the Soap Creek Arm of Blue Mesa Reservoir, Ponderosa has three loops at different levels in the canyon. The environment changes dramatically from sagebrush at lake level to a ponderosa pine forest at the highest loop. Most of the campground has excellent views of the cliffs looming over the reservoir. Sites 1-7 are high above the water in a loop around the horse corral. Horse riders can access the West Elk Wilderness area via Forest Route 721/Trail 443. Sites 8-29 are closer to the water. Sites 11-16 and 26-28 are walk-in tent sites. Sites 8-23 are also good tent sites. Sites 24-29 are closest to the water, but they lack privacy and shade.

Campsites, facilities: There are 19 sites for tents and RVs up to 30 feet and 9 walk-in sites. There are no hookups. Some sites have extra parking available. Picnic tables, grills, vault toilets, and drinking water are provided. A boat ramp and horse corral are available. Leashed pets are permitted.

Reservations, fees: Reservations are not accepted. The fee is $16 per night. Cash or check only. Open spring-fall.

Directions: From the intersection of U.S. Highway 50 and Highway 92, go west on Highway 92 for 1.5 miles. Turn right on Soap Creek Road. The campground is on the right in 7.0 miles. This dirt road is hazardous when muddy.

Contact: Curecanti National Recreation Area, 970/641-2337, www.nps.gov/cure.

58 LAKE FORK

Scenic rating: 4

in Curecanti National Recreation Area

Curecanti National Recreation Area contains three reservoirs: Blue Mesa, Morrow Point, and Crystal. Blue Mesa Reservoir is the uppermost reservoir and the largest body of water in Colorado. It is 20 miles long and has 96 miles of shoreline and a capacity of 941,000 acre feet. Stocked with over four million fish a year, the reservoir has some of the best deepwater fishing in the state. Lake trout and kokanee salmon thrive in the cold, deep waters. Boating, waterskiing, and windsurfing are also popular. (Personal watercraft is prohibited.) The reservoir contrasts boldly with the surrounding landscape of arid mesas and canyons. The weather can be harsh, and strong winds are common. Boaters should be alert for storms.

Another attraction is the Morrow Point Boat Tours, accessible via the Pine Creek Trail, which is a short drive from the Lake Fork campground. On the tour, park rangers interpret the geology and history of the area. The tour operates twice daily (except Tuesdays) from Memorial Day-Labor Day. Reservations are required.

There are a few tent sites at Lake Fork, but the campground is designed for RVs and boaters. It is basically a large parking lot with picnic tables. It's quite exposed and windblown, and there is no privacy.

Campsites, facilities: There are 85 sites for RVs of any length and 5 walk-in tent sites (52-56). Sites 1-14 can also accommodate tents, but there is zero shade. There are 16 pull-through sites and no hookups. Picnic tables, grills, and windscreens are provided. Restrooms with flush toilets and showers, vault toilets, dump stations, a boat ramp, fish-cleaning station, and amphitheater are available. Leashed pets are permitted.

Reservations, fees: Reservations are accepted for the upper and middle sections at 877/444-6777 orwww.recreation.gov. The fee is $16 per night plus $3 per night if reserved. Open late spring-fall. Most sites and facilities are wheelchair-accessible.

Directions: From Montrose, take U.S. Highway 50 east for 36.7 miles. Turn left on Highway 92. In 0.2 mile, turn right into the campground.

Contact: Curecanti National Recreation Area, 970/641-2337, www.nps.gov/cure.

59 GATEVIEW

Scenic rating: 6

in Curecanti National Recreation Area

Gateview is in a craggy canyon of volcanic tuff and Precambrian granite, on a steep slope above the south end of the Lake Fork of the Gunnison. A short trail behind the toilets climbs up to the tent sites, which are surrounded by ponderosa pine, Gambel oak, and sagebrush. Except for the roaring of the river and the occasional jackrabbit or bighorn sheep, silence reigns in this canyon, and this remote campground sees little use. Most visitors are kayakers or anglers. The river offers excellent trout fishing for seven miles downstream of the campground, and the white-water run from Red Bridge campground to Gateview campground has Class III-IV boating with some good play spots. Hand-powered boats can be carried down a short trail to the Lake Fork Arm of Blue Mesa Reservoir. Campers may also be interested in the history of settlement in this valley. The first narrow gauge railroad passed through this canyon in 1889 on its way to Lake City. Nearby communities like Powderhorn and Gateview thrived until the last train in 1933.

Campsites, facilities: There are six walk-in tent sites. Picnic tables, fire rings, grills, and food lockers are provided. Vault toilets and drinking water are available. Leashed pets are permitted.

Reservations, fees: Camping is free and reservations are not accepted. Open spring-fall.

Directions: From Lake City, take Highway 149 north for 20.6 miles. Turn left on County Road 25 at Powderhorn. The campground is on the right in 7.2 miles.

Contact: Curecanti National Recreation Area, 970/641-2337, www.nps.gov/cure.

60 RED BRIDGE

Scenic rating: 6

north of Lake City

Red Bridge is a classic BLM campground: small, remote, and quiet, with good recreation nearby. The campground is in a spruce grove on the east bank of the Lake Fork of the Gunnison on a well-traveled road that leads to a subdivision. The scenery includes glimpses of Cinnamon Ridge and a lush valley bottom surrounded by arid hills. The river offers excellent trout fishing for two miles upstream and five miles downstream of the campground, and the white-water run from Red Bridge to Gateview campground has Class III-IV boating with some good play spots. The river used to be boatable from The Gate to Red Bridge, but private landowners have put up obstacles that may make this route impassable. Check with the BLM for current conditions.

Sites 3-7 are in a spruce grove beside the river. There is plenty of shade but no privacy because the sites are right next to each other. Sites 1 and 2 across the road and have no shade. This campground fills up on the weekends with families and anglers.

Campsites, facilities: There are seven sites for tents and RVs up to 20 feet. There are no hookups or pull-through sites. Picnic tables, fire rings, and grills are provided. One vault toilet is available. Trash must be packed out.

Leashed pets are permitted. Facilities are wheelchair-accessible.

Reservations, fees: Reservations are not accepted. The fee is $5 per night. Open year-round, weather permitting.

Directions: From Lake City, take Highway 149 north for 20.6 miles. Turn left on County Road 25. The campground is on the left in 2.3 miles.

Contact: Bureau of Land Management, Gunnison Field Office, 970/642-4940, www.co.blm.gov.

61 THE GATE

Scenic rating: 5

north of Lake City

The Gate is an easy-to-miss stopover on the road between Gunnison and Lake City. It's a small campground, right on the Lake Fork of the Gunnison River and just upstream of the geologic feature for which it's named. The river runs through volcanic tuff that has fractured into fascinating cliff shapes. There is decent trout fishing for two miles upstream from the campground. The river used to be a mellow Class II white-water run from The Gate to Red Bridge, but private landowners have built obstacles to prevent access, so boaters should check with the BLM before getting on the river. The campground is in a grove of spruce trees and willow bushes. Sites 1, 7, and 8 have the most shade.

Campsites, facilities: There are eight sites for tents and RVs up to 21 feet. There are no hookups or pull-through sites. Picnic tables, fire rings, and grills are provided. Vault toilets are available. Trash must be packed out. Leashed pets are permitted.

Reservations, fees: Reservations are not accepted. The fee is $5 per night. Open year-round, weather permitting.

Directions: From Lake City, take Highway 149

north for about 15 miles. The campground is on the left.

Contact: Bureau of Land Management, Gunnison Field Office, 970/642-4940, www.co.blm.gov.

62 RED CREEK

Scenic rating: 4
in Curecanti National Recreation Area

Red Creek is the smallest campground at Curecanti and it's rarely used, in part because there is no fishing or boating available at the campground. The individual site is a small dirt spot beside the river and is not very appealing. At the end of the road, there is a large gravel parking lot and stairs that lead downhill to dispersed tent camping in a cottonwood grove beside the creek. There is not a lot of flat space for pitching a tent. The main activity here is backcountry hiking in Sapinero Wildlife Area. Gunnison National Forest and several pack trails can be accessed via Red Creek Road.

Campsites, facilities: There is one individual tent site and one group tent site that accommodates up to 25 people. Picnic tables, grills, vault toilets, and drinking water are provided. Leashed pets are permitted.

Reservations, fees: Reservations are accepted for the group site at 877/444-6777 and www.recreation.gov. The individual fee is $16 per night. The group fee is $28 per night. Open spring-fall.

Directions: From Gunnison, take U.S. Highway 50 west for about 19 miles. Turn right at the Red Creek sign. Bear left at the fork into the campground. The individual sites are on the left beside the creek. The group site is 1.0 mile past the gate.

Contact: Curecanti National Recreation Area, 970/641-2337, www.nps.gov/cure.

63 DRY GULCH

Scenic rating: 4
in Curecanti National Recreation Area

Dry Gulch offers tent camping in a large cottonwood grove beside an intermittent stream. It is small and not very appealing, but it may be attractive to horse owners who want to explore the BLM lands north of the campground. Windsurfers will appreciate the proximity to the Blue Mesa windsurfing area, about a mile east on U.S. Highway 50. The sites are 15-30 feet apart. There is not much privacy, but there are also very few visitors here.

Campsites, facilities: There are nine tent sites. Picnic tables, fire rings, and grills are provided. Vault toilets, drinking water, and a horse corral are available. Leashed pets are permitted.

Reservations, fees: Reservations are not accepted. The fee is $16 per night. Cash or check only. Open spring-fall.

Directions: From Gunnison, take U.S. Highway 50 west for about 17 miles. Turn right at the Dry Gulch sign.

Contact: Curecanti National Recreation Area, 970/641-2337, www.nps.gov/cure.

64 EAST ELK CREEK GROUP

Scenic rating: 5
in Curecanti National Recreation Area

East Elk Creek is the best group site in Curecanti. It offers dispersed tent camping in a large cottonwood grove. After the stark landscape of Blue Mesa, this green hollow feels like an oasis. It's very sheltered and shady and is a great place for kids to play. Fishing access is available a short walk away on a small arm of the reservoir. The windsurfing area is also nearby. North of the campground are some very interesting rock formations. There are no hiking trails in this area, but backcountry scrambling is an option.

Campsites, facilities: There is one group site for up to 50 people. A picnic shelter and tables, grills, vault toilets, and drinking water are provided. Leashed pets are permitted.

Reservations, fees: Reservations are required and are accepted at 877/444-6777 and www.recreation.gov. The fee is $53 per night. Open spring-fall.

Directions: From Gunnison, take U.S. Highway 50 west for about 16.5 miles. Turn right at the East Elk Creek sign. The campground is on the far side of the creek in 0.5 mile.

Contact: Curecanti National Recreation Area, 970/641-2337, www.nps.gov/cure.

65 ELK CREEK

Scenic rating: 5
in Curecanti National Recreation Area

Curecanti National Recreation Area contains three reservoirs: Blue Mesa, Morrow Point, and Crystal. Elk Creek is located between the Cebolla and Iola Basins of Blue Mesa Reservoir. (For more information on Blue Mesa Reservoir, see the Lake Fork listing earlier in this chapter.) This is the biggest campground in Curecanti at an elevation of 7,540 feet. The location and facilities are perfect for water-sports enthusiasts and anglers who usually troll the deep waters for kokanee salmon and lake trout. Ice fishing continues in the winter on Iola Basin. Snowmobiling, ice-skating, and cross-country skiing are also available on the frozen surface of Blue Mesa. (Check with park rangers for ice conditions.)

The campground is surrounded by sagebrush and mesa country, which contributes to beautiful sunsets, when the arid mesas are outlined against the dark-blue sky. The sites are 30-50 feet apart. There are no trees and very little privacy. For tent campers, the walk-in sites are close to the water and slightly downhill (and out of sight) of the RV area, but with little shade. Pappy's Restaurant serves up good burgers and fish-and-chips.

Campsites, facilities: There are 141 sites for tents and RVs of any length and 15 walk-in tent sites. Loop D has electric hookups and 6 pull-through sites. Picnic tables, fire rings, and grills are provided. Restrooms with flush toilets and coin-operated showers (at the marina), vault toilets, drinking water, a restaurant, naturalist programs, a marina and boat ramp, and dump stations are available. Leashed pets are permitted. Most facilities are wheelchair-accessible.

Reservations, fees: Reservations are accepted for Loops A and D at 877/444-6777 and www.recreation.gov. The fee is $16 per night or $22 per night for sites with electricity plus $3 per night for reservations. Open year-round.

Directions: From Gunnison, take U.S. Highway 50 west for about 16 miles. Turn left at the Elk Creek Visitor Center.

Contact: Curecanti National Recreation Area, 970/641-2337, www.nps.gov/cure.

66 STEVENS CREEK

Scenic rating: 6
in Curecanti National Recreation Area

Stevens Creek overlooks the Iola Basin of Blue Mesa Reservoir. (For more information on Blue Mesa Reservoir, see the Lake Fork listing earlier in this chapter.) This is mesa and sagebrush country. It's arid and the weather can be harsh, but the reservoir is irresistible to boaters and anglers looking for trout and kokanee salmon. Fly-fishing is available on the Gunnison, two miles east of the campground. Hikers can drive four miles east to the Cooper Ranch and Neversink Trails, which offer good bird-watching and more river access.

Stevens Creek is smaller and quieter than its massive neighbor Elk Creek. It has good RV camping and the best tent camping on Blue Mesa Reservoir. Loop A is the middle loop and thus the least private. Loop C is on a separate peninsula and is the most private. Sites 1-11 overlook the water. Loop B is occasionally closed to protect breeding birds.

Campsites, facilities: There are 53 sites for tents and RVs up to 40 feet. There are no hookups or pull-through sites. Picnic tables, fire rings, grills, and tent pads are provided. Vault toilets, drinking water, fish-cleaning station, dog walk, and a boat ramp are available. Leashed pets are permitted. Most facilities are wheelchair-accessible.

Reservations, fees: Reservations are accepted at 877/444-6777 and www.recreation.gov. The fee is $16 per night plus $3 per night for reservations. Open spring-fall.

Directions: From Gunnison, take U.S. Highway 50 west for about 12 miles. Turn left at the Stevens Creek sign, before the Blue Mesa RV Park.

Contact: Curecanti National Recreation Area, 970/641-2337, www.nps.gov/cure.

67 GUNNISON KOA

Scenic rating: 3

in Gunnison

The Gunnison KOA, located southwest of downtown, contains two grassy loops ringed by cottonwoods with a large pond for fishing and paddleboats. This campground is a bit off the beaten path, so it's not as busy as many KOAs, but the sites are very crowded together. The back loop has nice views of nearby cliffs, and sites 38-48 border the pond. Tent camping is available in the middle of the loops and the outer edge of the pavilion loop, with little-to-no privacy. Gunnison is a destination city with a mild climate and excellent recreation opportunities, including 750 miles of single track for mountain bikers. Surrounded by national

forest, visitors also have access to rafting, fishing, hiking, sightseeing, and shopping for antlers or cowboy hats.

Campsites, facilities: There are 88 sites for RVs up to 45 feet and 28 tent sites. Full and partial hookups and 50 amp double-wide sites are available, and many sites are pull-through. Picnic tables, fire rings, and grills are provided. New restrooms with flush toilets and showers, laundry facilities, drinking water, a new playground, and propane gas, and dump stations are available. There is also a store, horseshoe pits, shuffleboard, stocked fishing ponds, bike rentals, paddleboat rentals, and a boat ramp. Tent cabins are also available. Leashed pets are permitted.

Reservations, fees: Reservations are accepted at 800/562-1248. The tent fee is $30 per night for two people plus taxes. The RV fee is $45-75 per night for two people. The KOA Value Kard is accepted. Open May 1-October 1.

Directions: From Highway 135 in Gunnison, take U.S. Highway 50 west for 1.0 mile. Turn left on County Road 38. The campground is on the right in 0.5 mile.

Contact: Gunnison KOA, 970/641-1358, www. gunnisonkoa.com.

68 TALL TEXAN

Scenic rating: 3

in Gunnison

Tall Texan is just two miles north of downtown Gunnison and offers easy access to Gunnison National Forest, Crested Butte, and Taylor Park Reservoir. The location and mild climate keep this campground busy all summer long. The campground is in a cottonwood grove across the street from the Gunnison River. Like most RV parks, the sites are on top of each other. The tent sites are on a grassy strip next to the playground. There is no privacy here, but plenty of shade. The majority of residents seem to be kids and snowbirds.

Campsites, facilities: There are 97 sites for RVs up to 40 feet and six tent sites. Full and partial hookups and pull-throughs are available. Picnic tables and fire rings are provided. Restrooms with flush toilets and showers, laundry facilities, drinking water, a convenience store, playground, and propane are available. Wi-Fi, cable TV, a game room, cabins a pavilion, and dump stations are also available. Leashed pets are permitted.

Reservations, fees: Reservations are accepted at 970/641-2927. The tent fee is $29 plus tax per night for two people. The RV fee is $49-59 plus tax per night for two people; cabins cost $99 per night. Each additional person costs $2 per night. Weekly and monthly rates are also available. Open May 1-October 15.

Directions: From Main Street in Gunnison, take Highway 135 north for 2.5 miles. Turn right on County Road 11. The campground is on the right in 0.1 mile.

Contact: Tall Texan Campground, 970/641-2927, www.gunnisonrvpark.com.

69 ALMONT

Scenic rating: 6

northeast of Gunnison

Almont is a historic stagecoach town turned fishing and rafting resort. In the summer, there are hordes of Midwesterners and Texans in wet shorts and swimsuits returning from rafting trips on the Taylor and Gunnison Rivers. The campground is on the banks of the Gunnison, less than a mile downstream of the town. With the incessant hum of traffic and pretty but not spectacular scenery, it's just a stopover between Gunnison and Crested Butte. Rainbow and brown trout inhabit the river, but even anglers are likely to prefer the roomier campsites in Taylor Canyon. Sites 6-10 are for tents only.

Sites 6, 9, and 10 are down by the river and more private. Site 3 is the best RV site.

Campsites, facilities: There are five sites for RVs up to 35 feet and five tent-only sites. There are no hookups. Site 3 is pull-through. Picnic tables, fire rings, grills, and drinking water, are provided. Vault toilets are available. Leashed pets are permitted.

Reservations, fees: Reservations are not accepted. The fee is $10 per night. Cash or check only. Open mid-May-mid-September.

Directions: From Main Street in Gunnison, take Highway 135 north for 9.3 miles. Turn right at the Almont sign.

Contact: Gunnison National Forest, 970/874-6600, www.fs.usda.gov/gmug.

70 CITY MOUNTAIN PARK

Scenic rating: 5

northeast of Gunnison

This campground is within the Almont Triangle, an area of south-facing hills that are a critical habitat for bighorn sheep, elk, and mule deer in the winter, when it's possible to sight bighorn sheep in the cliffs across from the viewing area in the campground. The campsites are located beneath a similar cliff face in a forest of spruce and aspen. The highway separates the campground from the Taylor River. The small sites are 15-30 feet apart and not far from the road, but this is a comfortable stopover, with excellent fishing and white-water opportunities nearby. The Lower Taylor, from South Bank to Almont, is a Class II-III run that's perfect for advanced beginners. Sites 3-5 are closest to the parking lot.

Campsites, facilities: There are 11 walk-in sites for tents. There are no hookups. Picnic tables, fire rings, grills, and tent pads are provided. Vault toilets and drinking water are available. Leashed pets are permitted.

Reservations, fees: Reservations are not

accepted. The fee is $7 per night. Cash or check only. Open early May-early October.

Directions: From Main Street in Gunnison, take Highway 135 north 10.2 miles to Almont. Turn right on Forest Route 742. The campground is on the right in 2.9 miles.

Contact: Gunnison Parks and Recreation, 970/641-8060, www.gunnisonrec.com.

71 GRANITE

Scenic rating: 6

northeast of Gunnison

Granite is in a small clearing of sagebrush and pine trees between the Gunnison River and the highway. There are fascinating cliffs across the road, and heaps of wildflowers, but there's also a ton of traffic noise. Nonetheless, this campground can be full all weekend because of the white water and fishing in the area. The Taylor is an excellent trout fishery, and the white water from the South Bank put-in to Almont is a mellow Class II-III that's perfect for beginners. The nearest hiking and mountain biking trail begins at the North Bank campground. Trail 424 travels nine miles into the Doctor Park area. In the campground, privacy is limited. Site 1 is farthest from the parking lot, but it's also very close to the road. Site 2, the nicest site in the campground, has lots of shade and privacy. Sites 3 and 6 also have shade and some privacy. Sites 4 and 5 are completely exposed and very close to the parking lot.

Campsites, facilities: There are six walk-in tent sites. Picnic tables, fire rings, and grills are provided. Vault toilets are available. Leashed pets are permitted.

Reservations, fees: Reservations are not accepted. The fee is $12 per night. Cash or check only. Open mid-May-mid-September.

Directions: From Main Street in Gunnison, take Highway 135 north for 10.2 miles. In Almont, turn right on Forest Route 742. The campground is on the right in 7.4 miles.

Contact: Gunnison National Forest, 970/874-6600, www.fs.usda.gov/gmug.

72 NORTH BANK

Scenic rating: 7

northeast of Gunnison

Like all of the Taylor Canyon sites, you can't get away from the sound of road traffic at North Bank, especially since they improved the highway. Still, this campground is full on weekends with rafters, kayakers, and anglers. The stretch of white water from the South Bank put-in to Almont is an easy Class II-III that's perfect for beginners. The five-mile stretch above South Bank is more challenging. Anglers can fish from the campground for about a mile in each direction. The Doctor Park Trail begins in the parking lot and is open to both hikers and mountain bikers. The sites are 25-50 feet apart and not large. Sites 1, 3, and 5-7 are next to the river. Sites 9-16 are in a loop that's away from the road and very shady. It's the best area for tent campers.

Campsites, facilities: There are 16 sites for tents and RVs up to 44 feet. There are no hookups. Sites 1-7 and 15-17 are pull-through. Picnic tables, fire rings, and grills are provided. Vault toilets and drinking water are available. Leashed pets are permitted.

Reservations, fees: Reservations are not accepted. The fee is $14 per night. Cash or check only. Open mid-May-mid-September.

Directions: From Main Street in Gunnison, take Highway 135 north for 10.2 miles. In Almont, turn right on Forest Route 742. The campground is on the left in 7.6 miles.

Contact: Gunnison National Forest, 970/874-6600, www.fs.usda.gov/gmug.

You see all kinds of camping rigs in Colorado's campgrounds.

73 ONE MILE

Scenic rating: 6

northeast of Gunnison

One Mile is on a steep slope above the highway and the Gunnison River. As one of the few campgrounds with electricity in Taylor Canyon, it's very popular with RVers, so reservations are recommended on weekends. Tent campers still have to pay the hookup fee, so the host usually refers them to other campgrounds. Overall, this is a quiet campground, with many anglers who go to sleep early to get up to fish at dawn. One Mile is a paved loop in a forest of pine, aspen, and wild roses with several resident hummingbirds (and Texans). Like all of the Taylor Canyon campgrounds, its main drawback is traffic noise, but fortunately none of the sites is really visible from the road and vice versa. The canyon is popular with kayakers, rafters, and anglers. Trout fishing is excellent, although much of the river is on private property, so anglers should watch for signs. The white water ranges from tough Class IIIs to mellow Class IIs. Guided rafting trips are available at Three Rivers Resort. Hiking and mountain biking are available on Doctor Park Trail, which begins at nearby North Bank campground, across from the South Bank river access. The sites are large and 50-100 feet apart. Sites 24 and 25, at the end of the loop, have the most privacy.

Campsites, facilities: There are 25 sites for tents and RVs up to 58 feet. Electric hookups are available at all sites thanks to an upgrade in 2009. Sites 2, 4, 6, 8, 9, and 13-19 are pull-through. Picnic tables, fire rings, grills, and lantern hooks are provided. Tent pads are provided at sites 3, 10, 15, 16, 18, and 23-25. Vault toilets and drinking water are available. Leashed pets are permitted. Site 21 and the facilities are wheelchair-accessible.

Reservations, fees: Reservations are accepted for about half the sites at 877/444-6777 and www.recreation.gov. The fee is $18 per night plus an additional $6 fee for electricity. Cash or check only. Open mid-May-late September.

Directions: From Main Street in Gunnison,

take Highway 135 north for 10.2 miles. In Almont, turn right on Forest Route 742. The campground is on the right in 8.3 miles.
Contact: Gunnison National Forest, 970/874-6600, www.fs.usda.gov/gmug.

take Highway 135 north for 10.2 miles. In Almont, turn right on Forest Route 742. The campground is on the left in 8.8 miles.
Contact: Gunnison National Forest, 970/874-6600, www.fs.usda.gov/gmug.

74 ROSY LANE

Scenic rating: 8
northeast of Gunnison

For scenery, privacy, and river access, Rosy Lane is the best campground in Taylor Canyon. Many of the campers are regulars who return every summer for the peace and quiet and good fishing. Hiking, mountain biking, and white water are available a little over a mile downstream at the North Bank campground and South Bank river access. The campground is a paved loop in a forest of pine, spruce, and aspen beside the Taylor River. Across the river, there are impressive granite cliffs with so much mica in them that, according to former camp host Ray Zimball, "on a full moon you could read a newspaper by the light." Sites 3-9, 11, 13, and 14 are by the river. Sites 1, 2, and 15-19 are near the highway. Site 14 is a family site, with two picnic tables and fire rings. Sites 4-7 are the best tent sites.

Campsites, facilities: There are 19 sites for tents and RVs up to 45 feet. Sites 3, 4, 5, 8, the facilities, and the fishing trail are wheelchair-accessible. There are no hookups. Sites 1, 2, 4, 6, 13, 15, and 17-19 are pull-through. Picnic tables, fire rings, and grills are provided. Tent pads are provided at sites 3-5, which are right on the river. Vault toilets and drinking water are available. Leashed pets are permitted.

Reservations, fees: Reservations are accepted for 10 of the sites, at 877/444-6777 and www.recreation.gov. The fee is $18 per night, plus $6 electric hookup fee. Cash or check only. Open mid-May-mid-September.

Directions: From Main Street in Gunnison,

75 SPRING CREEK

Scenic rating: 6
northeast of Gunnison

Spring Creek is a pretty little canyon campground located near Gunnison. It's a convenient stopover or a nice weekend destination. Although the campground is very close to the road, noise is not as much of a problem here as in Taylor Canyon because Spring Creek sees a lot less traffic, in part because of the washboard road. The fly-fishing on Spring Creek is excellent. Public access begins at the campground and extends upstream for 10 miles. Rainbow, brown, brook, and native cutthroat trout are found in the numerous pools, some of them right next to the campground. The campground is a loop beside the creek, forested with spruce, pine, and aspen. Sites 1-3, 5-7, and 9-11 all have adequate shade. Sites 11 and 12 are next to the road. The rest of the sites border the creek.

Campsites, facilities: There are 12 sites for tents and RVs up to 30 feet. There are no hookups. Sites 2, 3, 6, 7, 11, and 12 are pull-through. Picnic tables, fire rings, and grills are provided. Vault toilets are available, but there is no drinking water. Leashed pets are permitted.

Reservations, fees: Reservations are not accepted. The fee is $14 per night. Cash or check only. Open mid-May-mid-September.

Directions: From Main Street in Gunnison, take Highway 135 north to Almont. Turn right on County Road 742, and in about 10 miles, left on Forest Route 744. The campground is on the right in 1.8 miles.

Contact: Gunnison National Forest, 970/874-6600, www.fs.usda.gov/gmug.

76 LODGEPOLE
🚶‍♂️ 🏊 ⛴ 🦌 🚐 ⛺

Scenic rating: 5
northeast of Gunnison

As the name suggests, Lodgepole campground is in a lodgepole pine forest. It is cool and shady, but the pines do not provide much privacy. All campsites are visible from the road and vice versa, and the road separates the campground from the river. The traffic noise and lack of privacy make this campground my last choice in the canyon. If you do have to stay here, sites 6-8 are farthest from the road. Site 10 is the best site because huge boulders shield it from the cars. Public fishing access begins at Lodgepole and extends upstream to Lottis Creek campground. The 12-mile Summerville Trail begins 1 mile downstream and climbs into the Fossil Ridge Wilderness. Kayakers can put in on this stretch of river as well.

Campsites, facilities: There are 15 sites for tents and RVs up to 40 feet. There are no hookups. Sites 7 and 10-14 are pull-through. Picnic tables, fire rings, and grills are provided. Vault toilets and drinking water are available. Leashed pets are permitted.

Reservations, fees: Reservations are accepted at 877/444-6777 and www.recreation.gov. The fee is $16 per night. Cash or check only. Open mid-May-mid-September.

Directions: From Main Street in Gunnison, take Highway 135 north for 10.2 miles. In Almont, turn right on Forest Route 742. The campground is on the right in 14.3 miles.

Contact: Gunnison National Forest, 970/874-6600, www.fs.usda.gov/gmug.

77 COLD SPRING
🏊 ⛴ 🦌 ⛺

Scenic rating: 5
northeast of Gunnison

Cold Springs is a little nicer than its neighbor, Lodgepole, but they share the same problem: proximity to the road. During the day, campers can anticipate lots of traffic noise. All of the sites are visible from the road and vice versa. However, Cold Springs has denser vegetation than Lodgepole, including wild roses, which helps the sites feel more private. Sites 1, 3, and 6 are next to the road. Sites 4 and 5 are the best sites. From Lodgepole campground to Lottis Creek campground, the river is open to public access. The fishing is excellent, although wading can be difficult. Kayakers can put in on this stretch of river as well.

Campsites, facilities: There are six sites for tents. Small pop-up campers can also fit in the spurs, but trailers are not recommended. There are no hookups. Site 5 is pull-through. Picnic tables, fire rings, and grills are provided. Vault toilets are available. Leashed pets are permitted.

Reservations, fees: Reservations are not accepted. The fee is $10 per night. Cash or check only. Open mid-May-mid-September.

Directions: From Main Street in Gunnison, take Highway 135 north for 10.2 miles. In Almont, turn right on Forest Route 742. The campground is on the right in 15.4 miles.

Contact: Gunnison National Forest, 970/874-6600, www.fs.usda.gov/gmug.

78 LOTTIS CREEK
🚶‍♂️ 🏊 🦌 ♿ 🚐 ⛺

Scenic rating: 7
northeast of Gunnison

BEST (

Lottis Creek flows from the Fossil Ridge area into the Taylor River. The campground is the last one in the canyon before entering Taylor

Park. It was completely renovated and expanded in 2012 and is very tent-friendly, with 10 sites about 100 feet apart in a wooded area. Across Lottis Creek, you'll find 23 sites in the Union Loop and 15 sites in Baldy, plus a group site that can accommodate up to 50 people. This campground is popular with families and anglers. Hikers also stay here and use the South Lottis Creek Trail, which begins in the campground, to explore the Fossil Ridge Wilderness, or you can continue hiking to Union Park.

The highway traffic noise at this campground is less pronounced than at other sites in the canyon.

Campsites, facilities: There are 48 sites for tents and RVs up to 48 feet and one group site for up to 50 campers. Electrical hookups are available and there are numerous pull-through sites. Picnic tables, fire rings, and grills are provided. Vault toilets, drinking water, and a small amphitheater with electricity are available. Leashed pets are permitted. Each loop has one or two wheelchair-accessible sites and facilities.

Reservations, fees: Reservations are accepted for a little more than half the sites at 877/444-6777 and www.recreation.gov. The fee is $18 per night with a $6 fee for electricity. Cash or check only. Open mid-May-mid-September.

Directions: From Main Street in Gunnison, take Highway 135 north for 10.2 miles. In Almont, turn right on Forest Route 742. The campground is on the right in 16.7 miles.

Contact: Gunnison National Forest, 970/874-6600, www.fs.usda.gov/gmug.

79 LAKEVIEW

Scenic rating: 8

northeast of Gunnison

The broad basin of Taylor Park was once the summer hunting grounds of the Utes, who called it the "Valley of the Gods." In the late 1800s, it saw numerous gold towns boom and bust. The dam was completed in 1937, and since then, the 2,033-surface-acre reservoir has provided irrigation water to the Uncompahgre Valley, as well as recreation opportunities. At an elevation of 9,000 feet, the park is worth a visit whether or not you have time to camp. The impressive Sawatch Range forms the eastern boundary of the park, and the Taylor River and numerous creeks meander through the bottomlands. There is a new trailhead that leaves from the campground and continues all the way to Union Park.

Lakeview is a large campground that's very popular with RVers, though there are plenty of private, shady spots for tents, too. Situated on a steep hill overlooking the reservoir and the Sawatch Range, the campground offers amazing views, but you'll most likely be sharing them with plenty of neighbors. There are four loops. The first loop (sites 47-68) is the electrical loop, and it has very few trees. The second and third loops (sites 1-29) are in a coniferous forest, but many sites still have great views. The last loop is highest on the hill. It's heavily wooded and seems to attract a lot of campers, although there are no views of the park. Campsites 2, 28, 29, 45, and 46 have the most impressive vistas.

Campsites, facilities: There are 68 sites for tents and RVs up to 60 feet. Electrical hookups are available at sites 47-68, and many sites are pull-through. Picnic tables, fire rings, grills, tent pads, and lantern posts are provided. Vault toilets and drinking water are available. A marina with a boat ramp and boat rentals is 0.2 mile down the road. Leashed pets are permitted. Twenty sites are wheelchair-accessible.

Reservations, fees: Reservations are accepted for 36 of the sites at 877/444-6777 and www.recreation.gov. The fee is $18 per night and there's a $6 fee for electricity. Cash or check only. Open mid-May-mid-September (sometimes October).

Directions: From Main Street in Gunnison, take Highway 135 north for 10.2 miles. In Almont, turn right on Forest Route 742 and drive up Taylor Canyon to the reservoir. The campground is 1.4 miles past the dam on the right.

Contact: Gunnison National Forest, 970/874-6600, www.fs.usda.gov/gmug.

80 RIVERS END

Scenic rating: 6

northeast of Gunnison

Rivers End is at the inlet of 2,033-surface-acre Taylor Reservoir. Anglers will be very happy at this campground. The stream fishing is excellent from the inlet up, especially at Italian Creek, and the stocked lake contains rainbow, brook, brown, lake, and cutthroat trout, as well as kokanee salmon. This area is also very popular with four-wheelers. The campground consists of three small loops on a rise above the river. There are zero trees or shade and the area is very windblown, but the views of the Sawatch Range are jaw dropping from every campsite. Sites 10-18 also have views of the lake. Bring a tarp to provide shade, and your camera so you can capture the sunsets.

Campsites, facilities: There are 18 sites for tents and RVs up to 45 feet. There are no hookups. Sites 10-18 are pull-through. Picnic tables, fire rings, and grills are provided. Vault toilets and drinking water are available. Leashed pets are permitted.

Reservations, fees: Reservations are not accepted. The fee is $14 per night. Cash or check only. Open mid-May-mid-September.

Directions: From Main Street in Gunnison, take Highway 135 north for 10.2 miles. In Almont, turn right on Forest Route 742 and drive up Taylor Canyon to the reservoir. The campground is 6.3 miles past the dam on the right.

Contact: Gunnison National Forest, 970/874-6600, www.fs.usda.gov/gmug.

Lakeview campground, at the top of Taylor Canyon, lives up to its name in a grand way.

81 DINNER STATION

Scenic rating: 9

northeast of Gunnison

BEST (

This is the kind of campground that people visit as children and return to every year for the rest of their lives. It's perfect. On one side, the lovely Taylor River flows by. On the other, the Sawatch Range looms impressively above Taylor Park. Most of the campsites are in a coniferous forest that provides ample privacy and shade. The fishing is excellent. Four-wheeling is the second most popular pastime. There are seemingly endless Forest Service routes in the park and the surrounding mountains. Hiking and mountain biking trails are accessible within a 15-minute drive.

Sites 0-5, 7, 11, 12, 13, and 17-22 are by the river. Sites 17-22 are not in the woods, so they have limited shade and privacy but excellent views. The views are also excellent from sites 0-5 and 13-16.

Campsites, facilities: There are 22 sites for tents and RVs up to 45 feet. There are no hookups. Sites 0, 1, 2, 11, and 12 are pull-through. Picnic tables, fire rings, and grills are provided. Vault toilets and drinking water are available. Leashed pets are permitted.

Reservations, fees: Reservations are accepted at 877/444-6777 and www.recreation.gov. The fee is $16 per night. Cash or check only. Open mid-May-mid-September.

Directions: From Main Street in Gunnison, take Highway 135 north for 10.2 miles. In Almont, turn right on Forest Route 742 and drive up Taylor Canyon to the reservoir. The campground is 10.2 miles past the dam on the left.

Contact: Gunnison National Forest, 970/874-6600, www.fs.usda.gov/gmug.

82 MOSCA

Scenic rating: 6

northeast of Gunnison

Mosca is on the western shore of Spring Creek Reservoir, a small but scenic lake in the Elk Mountains that allows boats without motors. The campground contains several small loops on steep, forested hills. Fishing and canoeing on the lake make this a great family destination, but if you crave a little solitude, Mosca isn't for you. The campground is packed with families in July and August (despite the washboard road) and the sites are small and fairly close together. Sites 6-9 are for tents only and are right on the water. Sites 11 and 13 are also close to the water. Sites 8 and 9 are short walkins. Sites 3, 10, and 13 are family sites.

Campsites, facilities: There are 16 sites for tents and RVs up to 45 feet. There are no hookups. Sites 2, 4-7, 11, and 13-15 are pull-throughs. Picnic tables, fire rings, and grills are provided. There is no drinking water. Vault toilets are available. Leashed pets are permitted.

Reservations, fees: Reservations are not accepted. The fee is $14 per night. Cash or check only. Open mid-May-September.

Directions: From Gunnison, take Highway 135 north to Almont. Turn right on Forest Route 742 and then left on Forest Route 744. The campground is on the right in 11.3 miles.

Contact: Gunnison National Forest, 970/874-6600, www.fs.usda.gov/gmug.

83 NORTH TAYLOR PARK DISPERSED

Scenic rating: 10

northeast of Gunnison

At an elevation of 9,500 feet, Taylor Park is a broad basin rimmed by the Sawatch Range and brimming with the scent of sagebrush. In 1937, a 2,033-surface-acre reservoir was completed in the park to provide irrigation water to the Uncompahgre Valley. Many visitors stay at the designated campgrounds (Lakeview, Rivers End, Dinner Station, and Dorchester), but almost as many prefer dispersed camping. From Italian Creek to the end of Forest Route 742, there are about 75 primitive campsites along the creeks and in the forests of the park. These campers come for the first-rate fly-fishing and the four-wheeling. A volunteer attendant at the Dorchester cabin can offer information on camping and fishing regulations as well as the history of the park.

Campsites, facilities: There are about 75 dispersed primitive sites for tents and RVs. Campers must stay at least 100 feet from the river and cannot create new sites. Vault toilets are available at Pothole Reservoir. Leashed pets are permitted.

Reservations, fees: There is no fee for dispersed camping, but campers are limited to 14 days. Some local campgrounds charge a $5 fee for dispersed campers to use their dumpsters.

Directions: From Main Street in Gunnison, take Highway 135 north for 10.2 miles. In Almont, turn right on Forest Route 742 and drive up Taylor Canyon to the reservoir. The dispersed camping begins north of the inlet and campers must stay at least 100 feet clear of the river.

Contact: Gunnison National Forest, 970/874-6600, www.fs.usda.gov/gmug.

84 DORCHESTER

Scenic rating: 9

northeast of Gunnison

Dorchester is the most remote campground in Taylor Park, and consequently the least used. It occupies the border between a coniferous forest and the expanse of sagebrush that characterizes most of the park. The campsites have shade and privacy plus excellent views of the Sawatch Range. Sites 9 and 10 overlook the Taylor River and are truly stunning. Mostly hikers, tent campers, and a few anglers come to this very quiet campground. Trail 760 ascends from the campground to Lily Pond and is open to hikers and mountain bikers. Another popular hike or multiday backpack trip is the Timberline Trail, which begins near Pothole Reservoir and follows the timberline for 31 miles to Mirror Lake. The trail is the western border of the Collegiate Peaks Wilderness, but because it's not in the wilderness, it's open to bikers and motorized traffic.

Campsites, facilities: There are 10 sites for tents and RVs up to 44 feet. There are no hookups or pull-throughs. Picnic tables, fire rings, and grills are provided. Vault toilets are available but no drinking water. Leashed pets are permitted.

Reservations, fees: Reservations are not accepted. Camping is free, but donations are accepted and go toward campground maintenance. Open early June-September.

Directions: From Main Street in Gunnison, take Highway 135 north for 10.2 miles. In Almont, turn right on Forest Route 742 and drive up Taylor Canyon to the reservoir. The campground is 17 miles past the dam on the left.

Contact: Gunnison National Forest, 970/874-6600, www.fs.usda.gov/gmug.

85 GOLD CREEK

Scenic rating: 8

east of Gunnison

It's a long drive to Gold Creek, but the tantalizing views of the Fossil Ridge Wilderness area will please every hiker and backpacker. The South Lottis Trail follows South Lottis Creek to the Lamphier Lakes, where good fishing is available, and continues over Gunsight Pass to the Taylor Park area. Hikers and anglers can also follow the Fossil Ridge Trail for four miles to Boulder Lake. Mountain bikers can follow the Fairview Peak Trail to an altitude of 13,200 feet and then continue into the Taylor Park area. Horseback riders also use this campground frequently. The wooded campsites have Gold Creek on one side and a small meadow on the other. Sites 1 and 2 are practically on top of each other, as are 3 and 4. Walk-in sites 5 and 6 are about 100 feet from the loop and are forested. Horse trailers and corrals can be set up across the road.

Campsites, facilities: There are four sites for tents and short RVs and two sites for tents only. There are no hookups, services, or pull-throughs. Picnic tables, fire rings, and grills are provided. Vault toilets are available. No drinking water; pack it in, pack it out. Leashed pets are permitted.

Reservations, fees: Reservations are not accepted and camping is free, but feel free to drop something in the donation tube for campground maintenance. Open mid-May–mid-September.

Directions: From Gunnison, take U.S. Highway 50 east to County Road 76. Go north on County Road 76 for 8.7 miles to Ohio City. Turn left on Forest Route 771. The road ends at the campground in 6.8 miles. The last 1.5 miles are rough but do not require 4WD.

Contact: Gunnison National Forest, 970/874-6600, www.fs.usda.gov/gmug.

86 PITKIN

Scenic rating: 6

east of Gunnison

Located in the Sawatch Range, on the west side of the Continental Divide, Pitkin is considered an ATV mecca. A network of Forest Service roads extends from this revived railroad town into the mining district to the north. Popular destinations are the Alpine Tunnel,

historic Dorchester ranger outpost, at the entrance to the campground

Cumberland Pass, and the ghost town of Tincup. (The Alpine Tunnel is a railroad tunnel through the Continental Divide that was built in 1881 and abandoned in 1910.) Anglers can fish on Quartz Creek or take the kids to the fishing pond across the street. The mild weather also attracts many vacationers, especially west Texans, who can drive to Pitkin in a day. This campground is a short walk from town, where campers can pick up ice cream and other summer necessities. It's in a spruce-fir forest on the banks of Quartz Creek. The large sites are 50-100 feet apart. Except for ATV traffic, it's a quiet place. Sites 10-14 are on the creek and reserved mainly for tents. Sites 1 and 4 are also on the creek and can accommodate RVs.

Campsites, facilities: There are 22 sites for tents and RVs up to 50 feet. There are no hookups. Sites 8, 9, and 15-23 are pull-through. Picnic tables, fire rings, grills, and lantern posts are provided at all sites. Tent pads are provided at sites 5-14. Vault toilets, drinking water, a very small amphitheater, and a gray-water dump station are available. Leashed pets are permitted. Site 21 and the facilities are wheelchair-accessible.

Reservations, fees: Reservations are not accepted. The fee is $16 per night. Cash or check only. Open mid-May-mid-September.

Directions: From the Silver Plume General Store in Pitkin, drive east on Forest Route 765. The campground is on the right in 0.5 mile.

Contact: Gunnison National Forest, 970/874-6600, www.fs.usda.gov/gmug.

87 QUARTZ

Scenic rating: 7

east of Gunnison

The area around the tiny community of Pitkin is very popular with ATV owners and Texans. Forest Service roads explore ghost towns and the Continental Divide, and the weather is very

mild. Quartz campground, on the banks of North Quartz Creek, is popular with tent and pop-up campers, and it sees a lot less use than Pitkin campground. It's in a forest of aspen, spruce, and fir, and its main features are wilderness and solitude. The small sites are about 50 feet apart. Sites 1-5 are next to the open wetland area along the creek. Site 10 has the most privacy.

Campsites, facilities: There are 10 sites for tents and short RVs. There are no hookups or pull-throughs. Picnic tables, fire rings, and grills are provided. Vault toilets are available. No drinking water. Leashed pets are permitted.

Reservations, fees: Reservations are not accepted. The fee is $10 per night. Cash or check only. Open Memorial Day-Labor Day.

Directions: From the Silver Plume General Store in Pitkin, drive north on Forest Route 765. The campground is on the right in 3.6 miles.

Contact: Gunnison National Forest, 970/874-6600, www.fs.usda.gov/gmug.

88 SNOWBLIND

Scenic rating: 7

east of Gunnison

Hardly anyone knows about Snowblind, which contributes immensely to the charm of this little campground on the banks of Tomichi Creek. Few people visit this remote area between Gunnison and Monarch Pass, but the open meadows and scenic vistas from nearby Waunita Pass are beautiful. Those who do visit this campground can set up camp in one of four loops and spend a week or two without neighbors. Hikers and mountain bikers can explore the Canyon Creek and Horseshoe Creek Trails, which climb to Stella Mountain and Tomichi Pass. Mountain bikers can explore the Old Monarch Pass Road. Waunita Hot Springs, 7.5 miles to the west, are open to the public in the fall. Sites 4-7, 16-18, and 19-21 are next to the creek, which offers fair fishing. Sites 22 and 23 are next to the road.

Campsites, facilities: There are 23 sites for tents and short RVs. There are no hookups or pull-throughs. Picnic tables, fire rings, and grills are provided. Vault toilets and drinking water are available. Leashed pets are permitted.

Reservations, fees: Reservations are not accepted. The fee is $12 per night. Cash or check only. Open mid-May–mid-September.

Directions: From Gunnison, take U.S. Highway 50 east to Sargents. From Sargents, continue east for 1.3 miles and turn north on Forest Route 888. The campground is on the left in 7.8 miles.

Contact: Gunnison National Forest, 970/874-6600, www.fs.usda.gov/gmug.

89 PA-CO-CHU-PUK

Scenic rating: 6

in Ridgway State Park

BEST (

Ridgway is a popular destination with residents and out-of-staters because it is the northwestern gateway to the San Juans. From here, campers can make day trips to Telluride, Silverton, Durango, Mesa Verde National Park, Black Canyon of the Gunnison, and Colorado National Monument. And when campers don't feel like driving, they can enjoy water sports and fishing on the park's 1,000-surface-acre reservoir and the Uncompahgre Reservoir. There are also 14 miles of maintained gravel and concrete trails in the park. As a bonus, the park stays fairly cool all summer because of its altitude (6,650 feet) and frequent afternoon thunderstorms.

Pa-Co-Chu-Puk is one of three campgrounds at Ridgway. It is at the north end of the park, beneath the dam. Loop F (200-236) and Loop G (237-280) are the RV loops. They are located in a barren meadow without shade trees and are almost identical except that Loop G is closer to the river. Sites 200-215 are very close to the highway. Loop H (281-295), which contains the walk-in tent sites, is fantastic. This loop is on a hill across the river in a mature ponderosa pine forest. It is cool and shady, and all of the sites are fairly private. Carts are provided at the parking lot to help campers carry in their gear.

Campsites, facilities: There are 14 walk-in tent sites and 81 sites with full hookups for tents and RVs up to 40 feet. Sites 200-280 have full hook-ups. Picnic tables, fire rings, grills, and tent pads are provided. Restrooms with flush toilets and showers, vault toilets, a laundry room, drinking water, a playground are available. Vending machines, a group picnic area, fish-cleaning station, pay phones, volleyball courts, horseshoe pits, and campfire programs are also available. Dump stations are provided at the south entrance of the park. Leashed pets are permitted. The facilities, most trails, and sites 230, 280, and 281 are wheelchair-accessible.

Reservations, fees: Reservations are accepted (and recommended on weekends) at 800/244-5613 or www.cpwshop.com. The fee is $24 per night for tents and $32 per night for RV sites with electric. Yurts are $90. Campers must also purchase a vehicle pass ($8) or an Annual Parks Pass ($80). Open mid-May–mid-October.

Directions: From the intersection of Highways 50 and 550 in Montrose, drive south on U.S. Highway 550 for 18.4 miles. Turn right at the Ridgway State Park entrance. After purchasing a camping permit at the entrance station, bear right into the campground.

Contact: Ridgway State Park, 970/626-5822, www.cpw.state.co.us.

90 ELK RIDGE

Scenic rating: 7

in Ridgway State Park

BEST (

Ridgway is a very popular state park because of its convenient location, balmy weather, and variety of family-oriented activities. Elk Ridge is one of three campgrounds at Ridgway, and since it is the most popular, reservations are highly recommended. It is situated at the south end of the park on top of a hill overlooking the 1,000-acre reservoir in a piñon-juniper forest. Fishing opportunities include stocked rainbow trout, native brown trout, and kokanee salmon. Waterskiing, sailing, stand-up paddleboarding, and personal watercraft are all allowed on the lake. Three maintained hiking trails are accessible from the campground, and the swim beach is a 0.7-mile walk downhill. The campground is divided into two loops: Loop D (80-118) and Loop E (119-187). Sites 80-95 offer glimpses of the water through the trees. Sites 134-165 and 184-186 have great views of snow-clad Mount Sneffels to the south. The hike-in tent sites (151-160) also have good views of the San Juans, but they are not as private as many of the RV spots. Additionally, there are steep drop-offs near these sites, so they are not recommended for campers with small kids.

Campsites, facilities: There are 10 walk-in tent sites and 97 sites with electric hookups for tents and RVs up to 40 feet. Picnic tables, fire rings, grills, and tent pads are provided. Restrooms with flush toilets and showers, vault toilets, laundry facilities, drinking water, a playground, dump stations are available. At the marina, vending machines, fish-cleaning stations, pay phones, and a boat ramp are available. Naturalist programs are offered at the visitors center. Leashed pets are permitted. The facilities, most trails, and sites 105 and 107 are wheelchair-accessible.

Reservations, fees: Reservations are accepted (and recommended on weekends) at 800/244-5613 or www.cpwshop.com. The fee is $24 per night for tents and $32 per night for RV sites with electric. Yurts are $90. Campers must also purchase a vehicle pass ($8) or an Annual Parks Pass ($80). Open mid-May-mid-October.

Directions: From the intersection of Highways 50 and 550 in Montrose, drive south on U.S. Highway 550 for 22 miles. Turn right at the second Ridgway State Park entrance. After purchasing a camping permit at the entrance station, make the first left and drive up the hill into the campground.

Contact: Ridgway State Park, 970/626-5822, www.cpw.state.co.us.

91 DAKOTA TERRACES

Scenic rating: 6

in Ridgway State Park

BEST (

Ridgway is a very popular state park because of its convenient location, balmy weather, and variety of family-oriented activities. Dakota Terraces, at the southern entrance, is one of three campgrounds at the park. What it lacks in privacy (there is none) it makes up for in lake access. It is a short stroll from the campground to the swim beach and marina. Anglers will find stocked rainbow trout, native brown trout, and kokanee salmon in the lake, and watersports enthusiasts can enjoy waterskiing, riding personal watercraft, and sailing. There are also 14 miles of maintained gravel and concrete trails in the park. As a bonus, the park stays fairly cool all summer because of its altitude (6,650 feet) and frequent afternoon thunderstorms. Dakota Terraces is divided into three loops. Loop A (1-25) is the most attractive loop because it has great views of the San Juans to the west, and mature trees shelter several campsites. Loop B (26-55) and Loop C (56-79) are not as appealing. Loop C does not have mountain views, and it is closest to the highway. There are also 14 miles of maintained gravel and concrete trails in the park open to hiking, biking, and cross-country skiing.

Campsites, facilities: There are 76 sites with electric hookups for tents and RVs up to 40 feet and three yurts. Picnic tables, fire rings, grills, and tent pads are provided. Sun shelters are provided at sites 4, 6, 8, 9, 25, 35, 38, 40, 42, 46, 49, and 78. Restrooms with flush toilets and showers, vault toilets, laundry facilities, drinking water, a playground, dump stations are available. At the marina, vending machines, fish-cleaning stations, pay phones, and boat ramp are available. Naturalist programs are offered at the visitors center. Leashed pets are permitted. The facilities, most trails, and sites 44 and 46 are wheelchair-accessible.

Reservations, fees: Reservations are accepted (and recommended on weekends) at 800/244-5613 or www.cpwshop.com. The fee is $24 per night for tents and $32 per night for RV sites with electric. Yurts are $90 per night and sleep up to six people. Campers must also purchase a vehicle pass ($8) or an Annual Parks Pass ($80). Open year-round.

Directions: From the intersection of Highways 50 and 550 in Montrose, drive south on U.S. Highway 550 for 22 miles. Turn right at the second Ridgway State Park entrance. After purchasing a camping permit at the entrance station, make the first right into the campground.

Contact: Ridgway State Park, 970/626-5822, www.cpw.state.co.us.

92 BEAVER LAKE

Scenic rating: 6

southeast of Montrose

Beaver Lake is a quiet campground beside a fishing pond. There are two loops in an evergreen and aspen forest. The sites are small and some feel cramped, but this is a good campground for families with small kids who will enjoy learning to fish on Beaver Lake. A gravel trail around the lake facilitates fishing access, and hand-powered boats are allowed on the lake. Anglers can also cast for trout in Cimarron River. The fishing is best below the Silver Jack dam. Hikers, mountain bikers, and four-wheelers can explore Alpine and Middle Fork Trail. (For more information on these trails, see the Silver Jack listing in this chapter.) There are views of Cimarron Ridge from the campground, but not from the actual campsites. The best sites are 6-11, and sites 6 and 9 overlook the pond. Sites 1-5 are shaded but smaller.

Campsites, facilities: There are 11 sites for tents and RVs up to 25 feet and 1 walk-in site. There are no hookups. Picnic tables, fire rings, and grills are provided. Vault toilets are available. Leashed pets are permitted.

Reservations, fees: Reservations are not accepted. The fee is $12 per night. Cash or check only. Open May-early October.

Directions: From Montrose, drive east on U.S. Highway 50 for 20 miles. Turn south on Cimarron Road/Forest Route 858. This winding dirt road is passable for passenger cars most of the summer. In 15.7 miles, turn right at the campground sign.

Contact: Uncompahgre National Forest, Ouray District, 970/240-5300, www.fs.usda.gov/gmug.

93 SILVER JACK

Scenic rating: 9

southeast of Montrose

BEST (

Silver Jack is a little-known treasure in the Uncompahgre National Forest near the Silver Jack Reservoir dam, and the views from the overlook of Courthouse Peak, Turret Peak, and Cimarron Ridge are breathtaking. The campground contains three paved loops (Ouray, Chipeta, and Sapinero) in a dense aspen forest, but it feels much smaller because the loops are so well hidden from each other. The sites are 50-100 feet apart. In Ouray Loop, sites 8-12 have excellent views of Cimarron Ridge. Activities include nonmotorized boating and fishing for trout on the 250-acre reservoir, plus hiking, mountain biking, horseback riding, and four-wheeling in the national forest. The Alpine Trail begins just past the campground and traverses 17 miles on the flat-top ridges of High Mesa and Big Park to Alpine Guard Station. The Middle Fork Trail begins 5 miles past the campground at the end of Middle Fork Road in the Uncompahgre Wilderness. Most of the 10-mile trail climbs gently alongside the Middle Fork of the Cimarron before climbing steeply to meet the East Fork Trail. Both trails are scenic and lightly used.

Campsites, facilities: There are 60 sites for tents and RVs up to 53 feet. Sites 4, 18, 21, and 41 are wheelchair-accessible. Many sites are pull-through, but there are no hookups. Picnic tables, fire rings, grills are provided. Vault toilets and drinking water are available. Leashed pets are permitted.

Reservations, fees: Reservations are not accepted, except for the group loop (www. recreation.gov). The fee is $14 per night for single sites and $130-230 for the group site. Cash or check only. Open May-mid-October.

Directions: From Montrose, drive east on U.S. Highway 50 for 20 miles. Turn south on Cimarron Road/Forest Route 858. This winding dirt road is passable for passenger cars most of the summer. In 17 miles, turn right at the Silver Jack sign. The campground is the first left.

Contact: Uncompahgre National Forest, Ouray District, 970/240-5300, www.fs.usda. gov/gmug.

CENTRAL MOUNTAINS NORTH

This swath of Rocky Mountains contains North Park and Middle Park, the western half of Rocky Mountain National Park, and the high peaks and deep reservoirs of Summit County. Hikers, bikers, horseback riders, and four-wheelers visit in summer and fall, while skiers, snowboarders, and snowmobilers take over in winter and spring. Highlights include Colorado State Forest, Grand County, the headwaters of the Colorado River, Indian Peaks Wilderness, and Arapaho National Recreation Area. Many of these campgrounds are close enough to Denver that they are packed all summer and reservations are usually necessary. Grand County also includes the Fraser Valley and the resort town of Winter Park, a great skiing and mountain biking mecca. The Continental Divide separates Grand and Summit Counties, and includes parts of Eagle County, with camping and fly-fishing along the Eagle River.

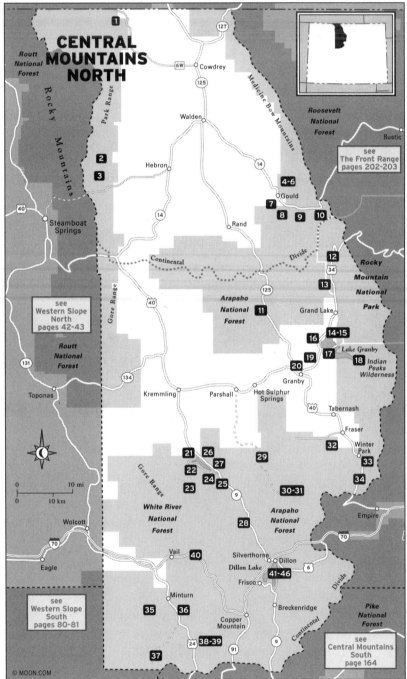

1 BIG CREEK LAKES

Scenic rating: 7

northwest of Walden

This campground is a remote destination on the shores of Colorado's second-largest natural lake. It sits in a pocket of the Park Range foothills at 9,000 feet, and features views of Red Elephant Mountain. The BLM lands to the north and east of the campground are a popular ATV destination. To the west, Seven Lakes Trail provides access to the impressive Mount Zirkel Wilderness area. Campers enjoy fishing for lake trout, splake, and tiger muskie. This campground was the first in the district to be logged for bark beetle kill. Consequently, it's had several years to recover and the west side of the campground (sites 1-45) appears quite healthy. The east side (sites 46-54) was closed in 2010 for logging but continues to recover and grow back.

Sites 1-17 are closer to the water, but the trees are thinner here so there's also less privacy than in the upper loop, where the trees are dense and the sites are 50-100 feet apart. Sites 1-7 are lakeside. Sites 19-22 have excellent lake views. Sites 43-45 are in a small loop by the boat ramp and are an excellent choice for groups.

Campsites, facilities: There are 54 sites for tents and RVs up to 50 feet. There are no hookups. Pull-throughs are available. The facilities are wheelchair-accessible. Picnic tables, fire rings, and grills, are provided. Vault toilets, drinking water, a boat ramp, chapel, and corral are available. Leashed pets are permitted.

Reservations, fees: Reservations for 24 of the sites are accepted at 877/444-6777 and www.recreation.gov. The fee is $10 per night. Cash or check only. Open late May-late September.

Directions: From Walden, drive north on Highway 125 about 9.5 miles. In Cowdrey, turn left on County Road 6W. In 19 miles, turn left on County Road 6A/Forest Route 600. In 4.8 miles, stay left at the fork. The campground is in 0.8 mile.

Contact: Medicine Bow-Routt National Forests, Park District, 970/723-2700, www.fs.usda.gov/mbr.

2 TEAL LAKE

Scenic rating: 6

southwest of Walden

Teal Lake is on the west side of North Park, one of Colorado's four large intermountain valleys. North Park is ringed by the Park Range, Front Range, and the Rabbit Ears Range. Teal Lake is on the eastern flank of the Park Range, just outside the Mount Zirkel Wilderness, a rugged landscape bisected by the Continental Divide. The Newcomb Creek Trail begins nearby and climbs the north flank of Round Mountain to the Continental Divide Trail. The campground is on the northern tip of Teal Lake, a small stocked lake surrounded by lodgepole pines. This forest has been hard-hit by the bark beetle and the campground closed in 2010 for extensive tree removal. It's now a meadow-like loop completely clear-cut of infected trees. The large campsites are about 50 feet apart. The campground can fill up on weekends, but it's quiet midweek. Most campers are there for fishing and four-wheeling. Sites 1, 3, 4, and 8 are lakeside.

Campsites, facilities: There are 17 sites for tents and RVs up to 25 feet. There are no hookups. Sites 1, 3, 4, 9, 11, 13, 16, and 17 are pull-through. Sites 4 and 11 and the facilities are wheelchair-accessible. Picnic tables, fire rings, and grills are provided. Vault toilets, drinking water, and a boat ramp are available. Leashed pets are permitted.

Reservations, fees: Reservations are not accepted for the single sites, but are mandatory for the group site at 877/444-6777 and www.

recreation.gov. The fee is $10 per night. Cash or check only. Open early June-late September. **Directions:** From Walden, take Highway 14 west. At Hebron, turn right on County Road 24. In 11.3 miles, turn right on Forest Route 615. The campground is on the right in 2.8 miles. The Forest Service will continue to remove hazard trees along these roadways for several years. Contact the district to ask about delays.

Contact: Medicine Bow-Routt National Forests, Park District, 970/723-2700, www. fs.usda.gov/mbr.

■3 HIDDEN LAKES

🛶🚐🏕🏕⛺

Scenic rating: 6

southwest of Walden

Hidden Lakes is on the west side of North Park, one of Colorado's four large intermountain valleys. North Park is ringed by the Park Range, Front Range, and the Rabbit Ears Range. Hidden Lake, on the east side of the Park Range, is part of a chain of small lakes surrounded by a lodgepole forest that has been hard-hit by the bark beetle outbreak. The campground itself is in mostly spruce trees, so there is plenty of shade. The lake has a gentle shore that's excellent for fishing. The sites are about 50 feet apart. The lakeside sites (1-4) are large and appealing. The other sites are small and close to the road.

Campsites, facilities: There are nine sites for tents and RVs up to 22 feet. There are no hookups. Sites 1, 7, and 8 are pull-through. Picnic tables, fire rings, and grills are provided. Vault toilets and drinking water are available. Trash must be packed out. Leashed pets are permitted.

Reservations, fees: Reservations are not accepted. The fee is $10 per night. Cash or check only. Open June-Labor Day.

Directions: From Walden, take Highway 14 west. At Hebron, turn right on County Road

24/Forest Route 60 and go west for 12 miles. Turn left on Forest Route 20. The campground is on the left in 4.3 miles. The Forest Service will continue to remove hazard trees along these roadways for several years. Contact the district to ask about delays.

Contact: Medicine Bow-Routt National Forests, Park District, 970/723-2700, www. fs.usda.gov/mbr.

■4 NORTH MICHIGAN

🥾🛶🚐🏊🏕🏕♿🚐⛺

Scenic rating: 7

in State Forest State Park

State Forest State Park contains 71,000 acres on the west side of the Medicine Bow Mountains and ranges in altitude from 8,500 to 12,000 feet. The forest is managed for recreation, logging, and wildlife. Colorado Parks and Wildlife manages the recreational opportunities in the forest, including the campgrounds. Visitors come for the hiking, fishing, mountain biking, wakeless boating, and four-wheeling, and to see the thriving moose herd. In 1978, 36 moose were relocated to North Park, and the herd is now about 600 strong. Hikers and bikers will want to drive to the Montgomery Pass and Ruby Jewel trailheads. Winter visitors can enjoy snowshoeing and cross-country skiing. The campground also has a geocaching program. Visitors who want to try out the high-tech hide-and-seek can check out GPS units at the Moose Visitor Center for $10 per day.

Sadly, all of the campgrounds in the park have been affected by the bark beetle epidemic and campers may want to call for current conditions before visiting. There isn't much shade in any of the campgrounds, so come prepared. North Michigan campground has two loops on opposite sides of the North Michigan Reservoir. The north loop (sites 201-213) is stretched along the whole north shore of the lake and includes 13 campsites and six cabins. Sites 201-205 are next to the dam and road and not very unappealing. Sites 206-213 are on the shore near the middle of the lake. Sites 207-209 are for tents only and are on a small spur at the east end of the lake. The other loop is on the south shore of the lake. Sites 214-241 are separated from the lake by the forest. Sites 242-248 have great views of the ridgeline.

Campsites, facilities: There are 48 sites for tents and RVs up to 35 feet. Sites 211, 213, 215, 217, 219, 221, 222, and 225 are for tents only. Sites 221 and 237-241 are pull-through. There are also six cabins for rent. Picnic tables, fire rings, and grills are provided. Tent pads are provided at the tent-only sites. Vault toilets, drinking water (on the north side), and two boat ramps are available. Leashed pets are permitted. Site 207 and the facilities are wheelchair-accessible.

Reservations, fees: Reservations are required at 800/244-5613 and www.cpwshop.com. The fee is $28 per night for basic tent sites. Campers must also purchase a vehicle pass ($8) or Annual Parks Pass ($80). Credit cards are accepted at the visitors center. Open year-round.

Directions: From Walden, take Highway 14 east for 19.3 miles. Turn left on County Road 41. To reach the south loop, turn right in 1.2 miles. To reach the north loop, stay straight for another mile.

Contact: State Forest State Park, 970/723-8366, www.cpw.state.co.us.

5 BOCKMAN

Scenic rating: 7

in State Forest State Park

Bockman is located in the Colorado State Forest, on the west side of the Medicine Bow Mountains. It's the former site of the Bockman Lumber Camp, the largest logging camp in Colorado's history. The campground's forest has been clear-cut due to the bark beetle

outbreak, but it's already beginning to recover by turning into a meadow full of grasses, shrubbery, and young trees. It also has great views of the Medicine Bow. It's a short walk to a wetland, where anglers can fish in the beaver ponds. Hikers will want to drive to the Montgomery Pass and Ruby Jewel trailheads, but bikers can take the forest routes to those trails. The sites are about 75 feet apart. (For more information on Colorado State Forest, see the North Michigan listing in this chapter.)

Campsites, facilities: There are 52 sites for tents and RVs up to 35 feet and one group area with 6 sites. There are 13 pull-through sites but no hookups. Picnic tables, fire rings, grills, and tent pads are provided. Vault toilets and a horse corral are available. Leashed pets are permitted. The facilities are wheelchair-accessible.

Reservations, fees: Reservations are required at 800/244-5613 and www.cpwshop.com. The fee is $28 per night. Campers must also purchase a vehicle pass ($8) or Annual Parks Pass ($80). Credit cards are accepted at the visitors center. Open early June-late September.

Directions: From Walden, take Highway 14 east for 19.3 miles. Turn left on County Road 41. In 3.7 miles, turn right at Bockman sign. The campground is in 1.2 miles.

Contact: State Forest State Park, 970/723-8366, www.cpw.state.co.us.

6 STATE FOREST STATE PARK DISPERSED

Scenic rating: 9

near Gould

State Forest State Park offers about 40 dispersed vehicle camping sites in selected areas of the park, along County Road 41. (There used to be more, but they lost about 20 sites due to tree damage and removal.) The quality of each site and activities available vary, but these sites are a great option for self-sufficient campers who want to escape the crowds at developed camp-grounds. Some sites require 4WD. Campers should plan on stopping at the visitors center on Highway 14 for a map of the sites and current conditions as well as the most recent moose sightings. Site 421 is one of the most attractive because it still has trees and it provides access to the Ruby Jewel area. Sites 432-439 are an excellent choice for groups. Sites 469-485 provide access to horse corrals and are preferred by horseback riders. (For more information on the State Forest, see the North Michigan entry in this chapter.)

Campsites, facilities: There are 60 sites for tents and RVs, but the exact number varies annually due to bark beetle closures. There are no hookups. Fire rings are provided. Leashed pets are permitted.

Reservations, fees: Reservations are not accepted. The fee is $18 per night. Campers must also purchase a vehicle pass ($8) or Annual Parks Pass ($80). Credit cards are accepted at the visitors center. Open May-October, weather permitting.

Directions: From Walden, take Highway 14 southeast to Gould. The visitors center is about one mile past Gould on the south side of the highway. Stop in for a map of dispersed sites.

Contact: State Forest State Park, 970/723-8366, www.cpw.state.co.us.

7 ASPEN

Scenic rating: 6

near Gould

North Park is one of four large intermountain valleys in Colorado. (The others are Middle Park, South Park, and the San Luis Valley.) North Park is enclosed by the Front Range to the east, the Park Range to the west, and the Rabbit Ears Range to the south. Wyoming lies to the north. The Michigan, Canadian, Illinois, and North Platte Rivers flow through this

fertile ranching valley. Aspen Campground is in the southeast corner of the valley, in the Medicine Bow-Routt National Forests, near the Colorado State Forest State Park, at about 9,300 feet. The state park campgrounds are quite busy all summer, so campers who want a small, quiet destination head over to Aspen. This is a small, meadow-like loop surrounded by aspen and it borders a wetland. It's popular with hunters and ATV owners because of its proximity to BLM land and the Arapaho National Wildlife Refuge.

Campsites, facilities: There are just seven sites for tents and RVs up to 20 feet. There are no hookups. Picnic tables, fire rings, and grills are provided. Vault toilets and drinking water are available. Leashed pets are permitted.

Reservations, fees: Reservations are not accepted. The fee is $10 per night. Cash or check only. Open late May-late September.

Directions: From Walden, take Highway 14 southeast to Gould. Turn right on County Road 21/Forest Route 740. In 0.7 mile, turn right at the fork. The campground is on the right in less than 0.1 mile.

Contact: Medicine Bow-Routt National Forests, Park District, 970/723-2700, www.fs.usda.gov/mbr.

8 PINES

Scenic rating: 5

near Gould

Pines is in the southeast corner of North Park, one of four large intermountain valleys in Colorado. (The others are Middle Park, South Park, and the San Luis Valley.) North Park is enclosed by the Front Range to the east, the Park Range to the west, and the Rabbit Ears Range to the south. Wyoming lies to the north. The Michigan, Canadian, Illinois, and North Platte Rivers flow through this fertile ranching valley and provide habitat for waterfowl and migratory birds. The Pines is near the Arapaho National Wildlife Refuge and a large amount of BLM land, so it's popular with hunters and ATV owners. The campground is a small dirt loop beside the South Fork of the Michigan River. The site lost quite a few trees to the bark beetles but is recovering nicely. There are no views from the campground, but the park is quite scenic. Sites 1-4 are next to the river.

Campsites, facilities: There are 11 sites for tents and RVs up to 50 feet. There are no hookups. Sites 4, 6, and 9 are pull-through. Picnic tables, fire rings, and grills are provided. Vault toilets and drinking water are available. Leashed pets are permitted.

Reservations, fees: Reservations are not accepted. The fee is $10 per night. Cash or check only. Open late May-late September.

Directions: From Walden, take Highway 14 southeast to Gould. Turn right on County Road 21/Forest Route 740. The campground is on the left in 3 miles. The Forest Service will continue to remove hazard trees along these roadways for several years. Contact the district to ask about delays.

Contact: Medicine Bow-Routt National Forests, Park District, 970/723-2700, www. fs.usda.gov/mbr.

9 RANGER LAKES
🚶 🎣 🚤 ⛵ 🦌 ♿ 🚐 ⛺

Scenic rating: 6
in State Forest State Park

Ranger Lakes is one of the most popular campgrounds in the Colorado State Forest because of the electric hookups and the short walk to Ranger Lakes fishing area, but return visitors may be surprised to discover that this campground has suffered the most from the bark beetle epidemic. On the bright side, all of the sites now have great views of the Nokhu Crags and there are better wildlife-viewing opportunities than before, especially in the evening.

Visitors to this campground enjoy easy access to the highway and the moose-viewing areas near Cameron Pass. (For more information on State Forest State Park, see the North Michigan listing earlier in this chapter.) The sites are just 10-30 feet apart. Sites 112-131 are especially close together.

Campsites, facilities: There are 32 sites for tents and RVs up to 40 feet. Electric hookups are available. Picnic tables, grills, fire rings, and tent pads are provided. Vault toilets, drinking water, an amphitheater, campfire programs, and dump stations, are available. Leashed pets are permitted. Site 107 and the facilities are wheelchair-accessible.

Reservations, fees: Reservations are required at 800/244-5613 and www.cpwshop.com. The fee is $28 for tent sites, $36 per night for electric hookups. Campers must also purchase a vehicle pass ($8) or Annual Parks Pass ($80). Credit cards are accepted at the visitors center. Open early June-late September.

Directions: From Walden, take Highway 14 east to Gould. The campground is 1 mile after the visitors center on the right.

Contact: State Forest State Park, 970/723-8366, www.cpw.state.co.us.

10 CRAGS
🚶 🚴 🐕 🚐 ⛺

Scenic rating: 6
in State Forest State Park

Crags (named for the stunning rock formations of the Nokhu Crags) is about two miles west of Cameron Pass on the road to Lake Agnes. This is the most primitive campground in the Colorado State Forest, a year-round destination for hikers, bikers, and skiers. Hikers and bikers can explore the Michigan Ditch and American Lakes Trails. From Lake Agnes and Michigan Lakes, hikers can continue south into the Never Summer Wilderness and Rocky Mountain National Park. (For more information on

Colorado State Forest, see the North Michigan listing earlier in this chapter.)

The campground is in a dense spruce-fir forest. The road is not recommended for RVs, so it's mostly tent campers who use the campground. The sites are small but fairly private. Sites 9, 10, 18, and 20 are practically on top of one another. Sites 16 and 17 have views of Cameron Pass.

Campsites, facilities: There are 26 sites for tents. Picnic tables, fire rings, and grills are provided. Vault toilets and drinking water are available. Leashed pets are permitted.

Reservations, fees: Reservations are not accepted. The fee is $28 per night. Campers must also purchase a vehicle pass ($8) or Annual Parks Pass ($80). Credit cards are accepted at the visitors center. Open early July -September.

Directions: From Walden, take Highway 14 east for about 30 miles. Turn right at the Crags sign and follow the signs 1.5 miles to the campground.

Contact: State Forest State Park, 970/723-8366, www.cpw.state.co.us.

11 DENVER CREEK

Scenic rating: 5
north of Granby

This campground, at a cool 8,800-foot elevation, mainly attracts residents of the Front Range who are seeking a respite from summer heat. There are two loops in a lodgepole forest that have been heavily impacted by the bark beetle epidemic. As a result, the campground has been clear-cut, so there is no shade and poor privacy. There are two loops. The second loop, on the west side of the road alongside meandering Willow Creek, is more popular. The first loop is on the east side of the road and sites 1-3 have pretty views down the valley. There are no trails nearby, and fishing is fair to poor depending on the time of year.

Campsites, facilities: There are 22 sites for tents and RVs up to 45 feet. There are no hookups. Sites 5 and 11 are pull-through. Picnic tables, fire rings, and grills are provided. Sites 3 and 8 have tent pads. Vault toilets and drinking water are available. Leashed pets are permitted.

Reservations, fees: Reservations are not accepted. The fee is $21 per night. Cash or check only. Open late May-late September.

Directions: From Granby, take U.S. Highway 40 north to Highway 125 north. The campground is on the right in 12.5 miles.

Contact: Arapaho National Forest, Sulphur District, 970/887-4100, www.fs.usda.gov/arp.

12 TIMBER CREEK

Scenic rating: 6
in Rocky Mountain National Park

BEST (

Rocky Mountain National Park is a renowned destination for hikers, climbers, and wildlife lovers. The park contains more than 350 miles of hiking trails and 118 peaks over 10,000 feet. One-third of the park is above tree line, so the majority of trails climb to mountain lakes and ridgelines with fabulous views of this glaciated landscape. The park also has the highest continuous paved highway in the country, Trail Ridge Road. A trip to the park isn't complete without a drive along this route, which traverses the park and crosses the Continental Divide. With so many attractions, Rocky Mountain is a busy destination in the summer, but the crowds thin out dramatically in the fall and winter. Winter sports here include snowshoeing, cross-country skiing, and mountaineering.

Timber Creek is the only frontcountry campground on the west side of the park at an elevation of 9,800 feet. It has four loops near the Colorado River, with views of Baker Mountain, Mount Stratus, and Mount Nimbus. The campground used to be in a dense lodgepole pine forest but it has been clear-cut due to the bark beetle epidemic, so there is very little privacy or shade. From the campground, hikers can take the Colorado Trail to Lulu City (the remains of an old mining town) and La Poudre Pass. Fishing is restricted on the river to protect a growing population of greenback cutthroat trout. There are four loops in the campground: Aspen, Beaver, Columbine, and Dogwood. Dogwood (sites 76-100) is for tents only. Sites 29-34, 58-62, and 90-96 are very close to the road.

Campsites, facilities: There are 98 sites for tents and RVs up to 30 feet, including several dozen tent-only sites. There are no hookups. Sites 5, 7, 19, 41, 60, 68, 69, and 74 are pull-through. Picnic tables, fire rings, grills, and tent pads are provided. Vault toilets, drinking water, service sinks, and campfire programs are available. Leashed pets are permitted in the campground but are not allowed on trails. Sites 22, 24, 26, and 39 are wheelchair-accessible.

Reservations, fees: Reservations are not accepted, all sites are first-come first served. The fee is $26 per night when the water is on. Campers must also purchase a vehicle day pass ($25), a weeklong pass ($35), annual park pass ($70), or Interagency Annual America the Beautiful Pass ($80). Credit card, cash, or check. Open only in summer and early fall.

Directions: From Grand Lake, take U.S. Highway 34 north for 9.8 miles. The campground entrance is on the left.

Contact: Rocky Mountain National Park, 970/586-1206, www.nps.gov/romo.

13 WINDING RIVER RESORT
🏃 🚴 🛶 🐕 ⛹ 🚐 ⛺

Scenic rating: 7
in Grand Lake

BEST (

Winding River is a long-standing destination for families and snowbirds looking for a full-service campground with access to Rocky Mountain National Park. The campground is adjacent to the west side of the park, next to the Colorado River. The loops are dispersed in a former lodgepole/aspen forest. Most of the lodgepole have been removed due to the bark beetle outbreak, but the aspen are faring well. Hikers and horseback riders will enjoy the trail access, including the Continental Scenic Divide, Valley, Supply, and River Trails. The campground is also a 2-minute drive from the park entrance and just a bit farther to the fishing and boating opportunities on Grand Lake and Shadow Mountain Lake.

Campsites, facilities: There are 107 sites for tents and RVs up to 45 feet, 27 tent-only sites, eight cabins, and two lodge rooms. Full and partial hookups are available. You can also stay in cabins (from $75/night) and Conestoga wagons ($135/night plus tax). Standard sites have picnic tables and fire rings. Restrooms with flush toilets and showers, drinking water, and dump stations are provided. A laundry room, convenience store, playground, horse corrals, animal farm, softball, volleyball, baseball, horseshoes, trail rides, disc golf, ice-cream socials, hay rides, and chuck wagon breakfasts (on weekends) are available. Leashed pets are permitted.

Reservations, fees: Reservations are accepted at 970/627-3215 and www.windingriverresort. com. The tent fee is $40 per night for two people, and the RV fee is $52-60 per night (includes two people). Additional people over the age of 4 cost a few extra dollars per night. Open May 15-September 30.

Directions: From Grand Lake, take U.S. Highway 34 north for 1.4 miles. Turn left on County Road 120, just across from the visitors center to the park. The resort is on the left in 1.4 miles.

Contact: Winding River Resort, 970/627-3215, www.windingriverresort.com.

14 CUTTHROAT BAY GROUP

Scenic rating: 7

on Lake Granby

Cutthroat Bay is an attractive group campsite on the north shore of Lake Granby. There's something for the whole family here: fishing, boating, hiking, wildlife viewing, sightseeing, and trail riding. Rocky Mountain National Park is a short drive away, and the Indian Peaks Wilderness beckons hardy hikers. (There are no trails from the campground because the surrounding land is private property.) The campground is on a hill overlooking the lake. It was clear-cut in 2008 for hazard-tree removal and the Forest Service has already planted three-foot lodgepole and seedlings. There is a scenic overlook with amazing views of the high peaks of the Continental Divide. There are two group sites with picnic pavilions and plenty of room for large groups to spread out (up to 50 campers per site). (For more information on Lake Granby, see the Stillwater listing in this chapter.)

Campsites, facilities: There are two group sites with tent camping for up to 50 people. The parking area can accommodate RVs up to 32 feet. There are no hookups. Picnic tables, fire rings, grills, and tent pads are provided. Vault toilets, drinking water, picnic pavilions, lantern hooks, and horseshoe pits are available. Leashed pets are permitted.

Reservations, fees: Reservations are required at 877/444-6777 and www.recreation. gov. The fee is $115 per night. Vehicles must also have a daily pass ($5) for the Arapaho National Recreation Area. Open late May-early September.

Directions: From Granby, take U.S. Highway 34 north for 9.9 miles. Turn right on County Road 64. The campground is on the right in 0.3 mile.

Contact: Arapaho National Forest, Sulphur District, 970/887-4100, www.fs.usda.gov/arp.

15 GREEN RIDGE

Scenic rating: 6

on Lake Granby

Green Ridge is at the south end of Shadow Mountain Lake, not far from impressive Lake Granby. The campground has been clear-cut due to bark beetles so there's no shade, but it now has nice views of the mountains. The dam is an easy fishing spot for kids. Wakeless boating is allowed on the lake. Hikers will be pleased to find that a Continental Divide trailhead is nearby. There are two loops with sites 10-25 feet apart. Sites 61-74 are on the edge of the forest, next to a pretty valley. (For more information on the Lake Granby area, see the Stillwater listing in this chapter.)

Campsites, facilities: There are 77 sites for tents and RVs up to 35 feet. Sites 18-22 are walk-in sites and have some shade. There are no hookups. Sites 7, 10, 24, 29, 31, 41, and 52 are pull-through. Picnic tables, fire rings, grills, and tent pads are provided. Vault toilets, drinking water, bear lockers, an amphitheater, and a boat ramp are available. The facilities are wheelchair-accessible. Leashed pets are permitted.

Reservations, fees: Reservations are accepted at 877/444-6777 and www.recreation. gov. Single sites are $23 per night and double sites are $46 per night. Vehicles must also have a daily pass ($5) for the Arapaho National Recreation Area. Cash or check only. Open mid-May-late September, some sites open until late October with reduced services.

Directions: From Granby, take U.S. Highway 34 north for 11.7 miles. Turn right on County Road 66. The campground is on the left in 1.3 miles.

Contact: Arapaho National Forest, Sulphur District, 970/887-4100, www.fs.usda.gov/arp.

16 STILLWATER

Scenic rating: 7

on Lake Granby

Lake Granby is part of the Arapaho National Recreation Area, a 36,000-acre district that contains four other major lakes: Shadow Mountain Reservoir, Monarch Lake, Willow Creek Reservoir, and Meadow Creek Reservoir. The Lake Granby area adjoins Rocky Mountain National Park and the Indian Peaks Wilderness, making it the vacation equivalent of a grand slam. The campgrounds around the lakes are busy throughout July and August. It's possible to find a site midweek, but reservations are highly recommended on weekends. The stocked lake has record mackinaw and kokanee salmon, as well as some rainbow and cutthroat trout. Anglers can fish from boats or from the shore in many areas. There are several hiking trails on the east side of the lake, but none on the west side. In the fall, hunters flock to the lake for the waterfowl and big game.

Stillwater is the largest and most modern campground at Lake Granby, with 22 electrical sites and hot showers. It has three loops on a small promontory with amazing views of the Indian Peaks. It can be a maze, but if you find a site on the lakeshore, it's a great place to spend a week with the family. The sites are 10-25 feet apart, with a few exceptions. The campground was clear-cut in 2008 due to the bark beetle outbreak, and although some trees are coming back, it's still pretty bare overall. All of the sites have lake views. The least appealing sites (0-10) overlook the boat ramp and parking lot.

Campsites, facilities: There are 129 sites for tents and RVs up to 40 feet. Sites 24-29, 32-35, 56-58, 67-75, 111-118, and 120-122 are walk-ins. Water and electrical hookups are available at 20 sites. Sites 2, 3, 9, 84-86, and 95 are pull-through. Sites 41, 42, and 86 are double sites. Picnic tables, fire rings, grills, and tent pads are provided. Restrooms with flush toilets and showers, drinking water, an amphitheater, a

Green Ridge campground on Lake Granby

boat ramp, pay phone, and dump stations are available. Leashed pets are permitted. Sites 29, 32, and 121 are wheelchair-accessible.

Reservations, fees: Reservations are accepted at 877/444-6777 and www.recreation. gov. Single sites are $26 per night, premium lakefront sites are $31 per night, double sites are $52 per night, and sites with hookups are $39 per night. Cash or check only. Vehicles must also have a daily pass ($5) for the Arapaho National Recreation Area, payable by credit card in the self-service kiosk. Open mid-May-late September, some sites open until late October with reduced services.

Directions: From Granby, take U.S. Highway 34 north for 8.5 miles and turn right into the campground.

Contact: Arapaho National Forest, Sulphur District, 970/887-4100, www.fs.usda.gov/arp.

Arapaho National Recreation Area fees can be paid at these vending kiosks.

17 SUNSET POINT

Scenic rating: 7
on Lake Granby

BEST(

Sunset Point is near the dam on the south shore of Lake Granby. This first-come, first-served campground doesn't have the awesome views of Stillwater and Lakeview, but it is a comfortable location for late arrivals and it is the most forested of the campgrounds around the lake. It's also the closest campground in the area to Hot Sulphur Springs for campers looking to visit the hot springs. The campground is in a lodgepole pine forest that provides privacy and shade. There is a short but steep slope down to the water. The following sites are lakeside: 1-4, 6, 7, 10, 11, 17, 18, 20, and 21. (For more information on Lake Granby, see the Stillwater listing earlier in this chapter.)

Campsites, facilities: There are 25 sites for tents and RVs up to 46 feet. Sites 14-16 are walk-in tent sites. Sites 9, 19, 23, and 25 are doubles. There are no hookups. Picnic tables, fire rings, grills, tent pads, and lantern posts are provided. Vault toilets, drinking water, a boat ramp, and dump stations are available. Leashed pets are permitted. The facilities are wheelchair-accessible.

Reservations, fees: Reservations are not accepted. A single site costs $26 per night, and a double site costs $52 per night. Cash or check only. Vehicles must also have a daily pass ($5) for the Arapaho National Recreation Area, payable by credit card in the self-service kiosk. Open mid-May-early September.

Directions: From Granby, take U.S. Highway 34 north for 5.4 miles. Turn right on Forest Route 125/Arapaho Bay Road. In 0.9 mile, turn left at the Sunset Point Complex sign. The campground is on the left in 0.2 mile.

Contact: Arapaho National Forest, Sulphur District, 970/887-4100, www.fs.usda.gov/arp.

18 ARAPAHO BAY

🏃 🏊 ⛴ 🎣 🎿 🐕 ♿ 🚐 ⛺

Scenic rating: 8

on Lake Granby

BEST (

Arapaho Bay is on the eastern tip of the long arm of Lake Granby, beneath the magnificent Indian Peaks. This wilderness area contains 110 miles of trails, 18 miles of the Continental Divide, and nearly 50 high-altitude lakes, as well as a few ice fields—remnants of the glaciers that carved the serrated ridgelines. Because of its proximity to Denver and Boulder, the trails on the eastern side are extremely busy in the summer (so busy that the Forest Service requires permits for backcountry camping), but the west side is much quieter. The Roaring Fork, Monarch Lake, and Strawberry Lake Trails begin near the campground and connect with the Buchanan Pass, Cascade Creek, and Continental Divide Trails, making several overnight loops possible. Anglers will be as happy as hikers. They can fish for mackinaw or kokanee salmon from the shore or by boat.

Arapaho Bay is the most remote and attractive of the four campgrounds around the lake. It has three loops. The Big Rock Loop (sites 1-22) is the least impressive. Many of the sites are by the road, and there are no views, but this loop is also the most forested of the three, so it provides the best shade. The Moraine Loop (sites 23-51) is 0.5 mile away and dramatically different. It is closer to the lake, and all of the sites have good views, thanks in part to clearcutting for the bark beetle outbreak. Sites 25-33 are lakeside. Sites 30-33 have their own small loop and are great for groups. The Roaring Fork Loop (sites 52-84) is even better. The views are awesome and a hilly topography makes the sites more private, but it was also clear-cut in 2009. Sites 55, 57-62, 64-66, and 70-78 overlook the water.

Campsites, facilities: There are 84 sites for tents and RVs up to 40 feet. Sites 57-62 and 64-66 are walk-in sites. Sites 69, 71, and 73 are

doubles. There are no hookups. Picnic tables, fire rings, grills, and tent pads are provided. Vault toilets, drinking water, and a boat ramp are available. Leashed pets are permitted. The facilities are wheelchair-accessible.

Reservations, fees: Reservations are accepted at 877/444-6777 and www.recreation. gov. A single site costs $23 per night, and a double site costs $46 per night. Vehicles must also have a daily pass ($5) for the Arapaho National Recreation Area. Open mid-May-mid-September, and sites 1-7 of the Big Rock Loop are open year-round without snow removal.

Directions: From Granby, take U.S. Highway 34 north for 5.4 miles. Turn right on Forest Route 125/Arapaho Bay Road. The campground is on the left in 8.7 miles.

Contact: Arapaho National Forest, Sulphur District, 970/887-4100, www.fs.usda.gov/arp.

19 WILLOW CREEK

🏃 🏊 ⛴ 🎣 🐕 ♿ 🚐 ⛺

Scenic rating: 7

near Lake Granby

Willow Creek Reservoir is part of the Arapaho National Recreation Area, a 36,000-acre district that contains four other major lakes: Shadow Mountain Lake, Monarch Lake, Lake Granby, and Meadow Creek Reservoir. Willow Creek is much quieter than the busy campgrounds on the shores of Lake Granby. The views aren't quite as spectacular, but the tips of the Indian Peaks are visible to the east, and the lake is surrounded by hills covered in sagebrush, pine, and aspen. There has been some tree removal here, but there are still a lot of mature pine and aspen. The lake is also home to several pairs of osprey every year. The campground is on the south shore of the lake, and sites are about 50 feet apart and have partial shade. A trail around the lake provides easy fishing access. Sites 1 and 4 are very close to the road. Sites 13-15, 19, 24, 26, 28, and 30-32 have the best lake views.

Campsites, facilities: There are 34 sites for tents and RVs up to 40 feet and one group site with four tent pads, which accommodates about 20 people. Sites 2, 6, and 32 are doubles. There are no hookups. Picnic tables, fire rings, grills, tent pads, lantern hooks, and food lockers are provided. Vault toilets, drinking water, and a boat ramp are available. Leashed pets are permitted. The facilities are wheelchair-accessible.

Reservations, fees: Reservations are not accepted. The fee is $23 per night for a single site and $46 per night for a double site. The group site costs $91/night. Vehicles must also have a daily pass ($5) for the Arapaho National Recreation Area. Cash or check only. Open mid-May-mid-November.

Directions: From Granby, take U.S. Highway 34 north for 5.2 miles. Turn left on County Road 40. In 2.6 miles, turn left at the dam. The campground is on the right in 1.0 mile.

Contact: Arapaho National Forest, Sulphur District, 970/887-4100, www.fs.usda.gov/arp.

20 RIVER RUN RV RESORT

Scenic rating: 7

in Granby

This is one of the most modern, amenity-filled campgrounds in Colorado. They opened in the summer of 2019 as an "RV, camping, cabin rental, and glamping resort." The property is located next to the Colorado River on the west side of Granby; campers head to nearby Grand Lake, Rocky Mountain National Park, Winter Park Resort, and other outdoor attractions. The property is part of the Signature Sun RV Resort network and the Granby location has on-site fishing, SUP and kayaking on the river, a pool, and two restaurants. There is a general store, shuttles to nearby attractions, WiFi, three hot tubs, bocce ball courts, a yoga lawn, amphitheater, fire pits, playground, and an off-leash dog park. River Run has a putting green, mini-bowling, golf cart rental, an arcade, and laundry facilities.

Campsites, facilities: There are more than 400 RV, camping, and vacation rental sites. In addition to tent and RV sites, you can sleep in a covered Conestoga wagon, in a yurt, in an "adventure tent," or in a fully furnished cabin with kitchen. RV guests get spacious parking pads with full hookups, pull-through availability, and plenty of room for slide-outs.

Reservations, fees: Reservations are accepted at 888/814-7202 or www.RiverRunRVResort. com. Tent sites and glamping rates had still not been determined at the time of publishing; RV sites are $61-92/night, plus taxes, depending on the season; furnished cabins are $130-289 per night.

Directions: Located in Granby, just off Highway 34, and just north of where Highway 34 meets Highway 40.

Contact: Address is 1051 Summit Trail, Granby. Go to www.RiverRunRVResort.com, tel. 970/557-0200 or 888/814-7202.

21 WILLOWS

Scenic rating: 6

on Green Mountain Reservoir

Green Mountain Reservoir is on the Blue River, between the Williams Fork Mountains and the Gore Range, one of the most striking of Colorado's mountain ranges. The mountains create a rain shadow, so the land around the lake is high desert, at about 8,000 feet in elevation. The reservoir is five miles long and holds over 2,000 surface acres of water. Personal watercraft and water skis are allowed at Green Mountain (but not nearby Dillon Reservoir), so this lake attracts a big water-sports crowd. There are no official trails around the lake, but hikers can drive to nearby Lower Cataract Lake to hike the Surprise and Eaglesmere Trails in the north end of the Eagles Nest Wilderness.

Willows offers dispersed camping along the north end of the reservoir. It's a madhouse on weekends, with RVs, ATVs, and personal watercraft zipping in and out of the campground. Extended families encamp for the weekend, many of them almost on top of each other. If you love solitude, head elsewhere. If you want to play in the water and don't mind a scene, this is your place.

Campsites, facilities: There are approximately 25 sites for tents and RVs of any length. Fire rings, dumpsters, and vault toilets are available. Leashed pets are permitted.

Reservations, fees: Reservations are not accepted. The fee is $18 per night. Cash or check only. Open May-October.

Directions: From Silverthorne, take Highway 9 north for 17.5 miles. Turn left on Heeney Road. The campground is on the right in 9.8 miles.

Contact: White River National Forest, Dillon District, 970/468-5400, www.fs.usda.gov/whiteriver.

22 ELLIOT CREEK

Scenic rating: 5

on Green Mountain Reservoir

Green Mountain Reservoir is on the Blue River, between the Williams Fork Mountains and the Gore Range, one of the most striking of Colorado's mountain ranges. Since the mountains create a rain shadow, the land around the lake is high desert. The five-mile-long reservoir attracts a big water-sports crowd. There are no official trails around the lake, but hikers can drive to nearby Lower Cataract Lake to hike the Surprise and Eaglesmere Trails in the north end of the Eagles Nest Wilderness. Elliot Creek has primitive camping near the dam at the northwest corner of the lake, with views of the dam, the Williams Fork Mountains, and Green Mountain. The sites are dispersed in three levels along a steep shore. Some sites are shaded by evergreens and cottonwoods, others are in the sagebrush flats, and others are right next to a large parking lot. This campground attracts large groups and young people. It's a party scene on weekends.

Campsites, facilities: There are approximately 24 sites for tents and RVs. Vault toilets are available. Leashed pets are permitted.

Reservations, fees: Reservations are not accepted. The fee is $18 per night. Cash or check only. Open May-October.

Directions: From Silverthorne, take Highway 9 north for 17.5 miles. Turn left on Heeney Road. The campground is on the right in 8.0 miles.

Contact: White River National Forest, Dillon District, 970/468-5400, www.fs.usda.gov/whiteriver.

23 CATARACT CREEK

Scenic rating: 9

west of Green Mountain Reservoir

Cataract Creek is a rare gem in a region of oversized and overcrowded campgrounds. This tiny campground overlooks the lovely Cataract Creek valley (almost free of development) and the Williams Fork Mountains. The sites are large and shaded by mature spruce, fir, and aspen, but they still have good views (except site 5). They're also very private. Several trails begin at Lower Cataract Lake, including a 2.3-mile loop around the lake and the Surprise and Eaglesmere Trails. The Surprise Trail is one of the most popular routes into the Eagles Nest Wilderness. It travels through spruce forests, past lakes and wetlands, with views of the Gore Range. There are side trips to alpine lakes and the crest of the Gore Range. Predictably, this campground is very popular. If you're visiting on a summer weekend, arrive on Wednesday or Thursday to bag a spot.

Campsites, facilities: There are only five sites for tents and RVs up to 21 feet. Picnic tables, fire rings, and grills are provided. A vault toilet is available. Leashed pets are permitted.

Reservations, fees: Reservations are not accepted. The fee is $18 per night. Cash or check only. Open late May-October.

Directions: From Silverthorne, take Highway 9 north for 17.5 miles. Turn left on Heeney Road. In 5.3 miles, turn left on Cataract Creek Road. The campground is on the left in 2.2 miles. Parts of the road are rough and narrow.

Contact: White River National Forest, Dillon District, 970/468-5400, www.fs.usda.gov/whiteriver.

24 PRAIRIE POINT

Scenic rating: 4

on Green Mountain Reservoir

Prairie Point is on the east shore of Green Mountain Reservoir, a five-mile-long reservoir on the Blue River, between the Williams Fork Mountains and the Gore Range. The lake attracts mainly water-sports enthusiasts, but the Blue River is also a Gold Medal fishery. There are no official trails around the lake, but hikers can drive to nearby Lower Cataract Lake to hike the Surprise and Eaglesmere Trails in the north end of the Eagles Nest Wilderness. The campground has views of the foothills of the Williams Fork and the tips of the Gore Range. It's in a high-desert setting, with a few cottonwoods and willows along the shore. This campground has designated sites, so it's much calmer than neighboring Cow Creek and more of a family campground, but it still lacks privacy because the sites are just 10 feet apart.

Campsites, facilities: There are 22 sites for tents and RVs up to 20 feet. Picnic tables, fire rings, and grills are provided. Vault toilets are available. Leashed pets are permitted.

Reservations, fees: Reservations are not accepted. The fee is $18 per night. Cash or check only. Open May-October.

Directions: From Silverthorne, take Highway 9 north for 19.1 miles. The campground is on the left.

Contact: White River National Forest, Dillon District, 970/468-5400, www.fs.usda.gov/whiteriver.

25 MCDONALD FLATS

Scenic rating: 4

on Green Mountain Reservoir

On the west shore of Green Mountain Reservoir, McDonald Flats is very exposed, and has views of the Williams Fork Mountains and the highway. It is a very popular weekend destination, especially for water-sports enthusiasts, but is more of a family campground than some of the others at the lake. The reservoir is almost five miles long and has over 2,000 surface acres. Water-skiers and personal watercraft take over the lake on weekends. Anglers may have better luck on the Blue River, a Gold Medal fishery, or at nearby Dillon Reservoir. The campground is in the sagebrush flats, so there is no shade or privacy, and sites are very close together. Sites 10-12 are closest to the water and the most private. The views are not as good at this campground as on the east shore, but it's smaller and quieter than those campgrounds.

Campsites, facilities: There are 12 sites for tents and RVs up to 21 feet. Picnic tables, fire rings, grills, and dumpsters are provided. Vault toilets, pay phones, and a boat ramp are available. Leashed pets are permitted.

Reservations, fees: Reservations are not accepted. The fee is $18 per night. Cash or check only. Open May-October.

Directions: From Silverthorne, take Highway 9 north for 17.5 miles. Turn left on Heeney Road. The campground is on the right in 2.0 miles.

Contact: White River National Forest, Dillon District, 970/468-5400, www.fs.usda.gov/whiteriver.

26 COW CREEK SOUTH

Scenic rating: 5

on Green Mountain Reservoir

Cow Creek South is on the east shore of Green Mountain Reservoir, a five-mile-long reservoir with over 2,000 surface acres of water. The lake is so popular because personal watercraft are allowed on Green Mountain Reservoir but not at nearby Dillon Reservoir. Personalwatercraft owners can put in at the boat ramp and then moor near their campsite. There are no official trails around the lake, but hikers can drive to nearby Lower Cataract Lake to hike the Surprise and Eaglesmere Trails in the north end of the Eagles Nest Wilderness. This is the only campground on the reservoir that accepts reservations and the only one with a campground host. Like the others, Cow Creek South is in a high-desert setting, so there are few trees, but there are excellent views of the Gore Range to the west and Green Mountain.

Campsites, facilities: There are 32 sites for tents and RVs up to 35 feet. Fire rings, lantern hooks, and vault toilets are available. There is no firewood for sale and no potable water. Leashed pets are permitted.

Reservations, fees: Reservations are accepted for Cow Creek South at 877/444-6777 and www.recreation.gov. Reservations are not accepted for Cow Creek North. The fee is $18 per night. Cash or check only. Open May-October.

Directions: From Silverthorne, take Highway 9 north for 23.4 for Cow Creek South and 23.7 miles for Cow Creek North. The campgrounds are on the left.

Contact: White River National Forest, Dillon District, 970/468-5400, www.fs.usda.gov/whiteriver.

27 COW CREEK NORTH

Scenic rating: 5

on Green Mountain Reservoir

Cow Creek North is on the east shore of Green Mountain Reservoir. The campground is a popular shade-free loop of a dozen sites (sometimes more). On weekends, when one group of RVs and tents blends into the next, it's difficult to tell how many groups are there. Personalwatercraft owners can put in at the boat ramp and then moor near their campsite, or you can drive around the reservoir to Heeney and rent a boat there.

Campsites, facilities: There are 15 sites for tents and RVs. Fire rings and vault toilets are available. Leashed pets are permitted.

Reservations, fees: Reservations are not accepted. The fee is $18 per night. Cash or check only. Open May-October.

Directions: From Silverthorne, take Highway 9 north for 23.7 miles. The campground is on the left.

Contact: White River National Forest, Dillon District, 970/468-5400, www.fs.usda.gov/whiteriver.

28 BLUE RIVER

Scenic rating: 6

north of Dillon

BEST (

Between Dillon Reservoir and Green Mountain Reservoir, the Blue River is a Gold Medal trout stream. This little campground on the west bank is popular with anglers and families looking to enjoy the shopping in Silverthorne and Frisco. In addition to fishing, kayakers will find three miles of Class III water on the Blue River below the campground. There are three loops. The upper loop (sites 1-4) is right by the highway and has limited shade. The middle loop is a little lower and has more privacy, but everyone heads for the lower loop beside the river. This loop is shaded by aspen, pine, and cottonwood. The campground closed in 2010 for limited removal of spruce and pine impacted by the bark beetle. Sites 10, 12-15, and 17-20 are right on the water. The sites are small, and this campground is very busy on weekends.

Campsites, facilities: There are 25 sites for tents and RVs up to 25 feet. Picnic tables, fire rings, and grills are provided. Site 19 has a tent pad. Vault toilets are available. Leashed pets are permitted. The facilities are wheelchair-accessible.

Reservations, fees: Reservations are not accepted. The fee is $20 per night. Cash or check only. Open late May-early September.

Directions: From Silverthorne, take Highway 9 north for 8.5 miles. The campground is on the right.

Contact: White River National Forest, Dillon District, 970/468-5400, www.fs.usda.gov/whiteriver.

29 HORSESHOE

Scenic rating: 5
south of Hot Sulphur Springs

Horseshoe campground sits between the Williams Fork Mountains to the west and the Vasquez Mountains to the east. Bark beetles have been very active in this area. The campground is small and not especially scenic, but ATV riders love the network of Forest Service roads in the Vasquez Mountains, and backpackers appreciate the proximity to Byers Peak Wilderness and Ptarmigan Peak Wilderness. Williams Peak Trail is the nearest hiking and pack trail.

The campground is on the west bank of the Williams Fork River in a coniferous forest that has mostly been cut in the campground. Sites 2-5 are riverside and somewhat shaded. The

sites are 30-60 feet apart. Weekdays are quiet, but weekends can be busy, with a four-wheeling crowd.

Campsites, facilities: There are seven sites for tents and RVs up to 50 feet. There are no hookups. Sites 1, 4, and 5 are pull-through. Picnic tables, fire rings, and grills are provided. Vault toilets are available. Trash must be packed out. Leashed pets are permitted.

Reservations, fees: Reservations are not accepted. The fee is $18 per night. Cash or check only. Open mid-June-late October.

Directions: From Hot Sulphur Springs, take U.S. Highway 40 west for 4.5 miles. Turn left on County Road 3/Forest Route 138. In 15.5 miles, turn left on Forest Route 139. The campground is on the left before the bridge.

Contact: Arapaho National Forest, Sulphur District, 970/887-4100, www.fs.usda.gov/whiteriver.

30 SOUTH FORK

Scenic rating: 6
south of Hot Sulphur Springs

South Fork campground is in the Williams Fork Valley between the Williams Fork Mountains to the west and the Vasquez Mountains to the east, upstream of the large Henderson Mill site. This campground has experienced a lot of bark beetle activity and the trees have been clear-cut. The sites are only 25-50 feet apart, so privacy and shade are poor. However, riders and hikers will continue to use this campground for its proximity to the Byers Peak Wilderness. The Darling Creek Trail begins nearby and climbs six miles to the Continental Divide and St. Louis Divide Trail. The South Fork Loop also begins nearby in the Sugarloaf campground. This 27-mile trail is the most popular in the valley with backpackers, riders, and mountain bikers.

Campsites, facilities: There are 21 sites

for tents and RVs up to 23 feet. There are no hookups. Sites 5, 6, 9, 12, 17, and 19 are pull-through. There is also a group site for up to 25 people ($55).Picnic tables, fire rings, and grills are provided. Vault toilets, drinking water, and two horse corrals are available. Leashed pets are permitted. The facilities are wheelchair-accessible.

Reservations, fees: Reservations are not accepted. The fee is $19 per night. Cash or check only. Open mid-June-late October.

Directions: From Hot Sulphur Springs, take U.S. Highway 40 west for 4.5 miles. Turn left on County Road 3/Forest Route 138. In 18.2 miles, stay left on Forest Route 138/County Road 30. In 5.6 miles, turn left and go through the tunnel, then veer right. The campground is on the right in 0.1 mile.

Contact: Arapaho National Forest, Sulphur District, 970/887-4100, www.fs.usda.gov/arp.

31 SUGARLOAF

🚶 🚴 🛶 🐴 ♿ 🚌 ⛺

Scenic rating: 6
south of Hot Sulphur Springs

Sugarloaf is the most attractive campground in the Williams Fork Valley and the most remote. Located on the South Fork of the Williams River, the campground is in a lodgepole forest that has been decimated by the bark beetle epidemic. Like nearby South Fork, this campground has been clear-cut. The sites are 30-60 feet apart. A wheelchair-accessible boardwalk provides fishing access on the river. The 27-mile South Fork Loop begins and ends in the campground and offers challenging backpacking and riding trips.

Campsites, facilities: There are 11 sites for tents and RVs up to 23 feet. There are no hookups. Site 10 is pull-through. Picnic tables, fire rings, grills, and tent pads are provided. Vault toilets and horseshoe pits are available. There

is no potable water. Leashed pets are permitted. The facilities are wheelchair-accessible.

Reservations, fees: Reservations are not accepted. The fee is $19 per night. Cash or check only. Open mid-June-late October.

Directions: From Hot Sulphur Springs, take U.S. Highway 40 west for 4.5 miles. Turn left on County Road 3/Forest Route 138. In 18.2 miles, stay left on Forest Route 138/County Road 30. In 5.6 miles, turn left and go through the tunnel, then veer right. The road ends in 0.6 mile at the campground.

Contact: Arapaho National Forest, Sulphur District, 970/887-4100, www.fs.usda.gov/arp.

32 ST. LOUIS CREEK

🚶 🚴 🛶 🐴 ♿ 🚌 ⛺

Scenic rating: 4
near Fraser

St. Louis Creek is in the Fraser Experimental Forest, a 20,000-acre biosphere reserve where scientists have spent 65 years studying subalpine forests in the Rocky Mountains. This campground is busy all summer, with mountain bikers and hikers of all ages. The Fraser Valley has an extensive trail network between Fraser and Winter Park and in the Winter Park Resort. Bikers can take a dirt trail from the campground into Fraser and beyond. Hikers enjoy ridge hiking in the Byers Peak Wilderness. The 8.6-mile Byers Peak Trail is a difficult but rewarding route that begins near the campground. Hikers can also set off for Creekside Flume, Bottle Pass, or seven miles each way to St. Louis Lake. Families love this campground for creek access, for flat roads where the kids can ride their bikes, and for ample fort-building material.

The campground loop is in a lodgepole pine forest where bark beetle damage forced officials to completely clear-cut the campground. The views of Mt. Byers are awesome. The shade? There's not so much. The campground is also very flat and the sites are 25-50 feet apart, so there's not much privacy. Nevertheless, it's busy on weekends, so arrive early. Sites 8, 10, 12, 13, and 15 are creek side; sites 9 and 17 are tent-only; and site 17 is the only site with trees. The rest of the campground is being actively replanted, with new pines and aspen coming in nicely.

Campsites, facilities: There are 17 sites for tents and RVs up to 40 feet (or more at a couple of sites). There are no hookups. Sites 4, 6, 10, and 11 are pull-through. Picnic tables, fire rings, and grills are provided. Vault toilets and drinking water are available. Leashed pets are permitted. Site 17 and the facilities are wheelchair-accessible.

Reservations, fees: Reservations are not accepted. The fee is $22 per night. Cash or check only. Open late May-late September.

Directions: From Fraser, take County Road 73 west for 4.0 miles. The campground is on the left.

Contact: Arapaho National Forest, Sulphur District, 970/887-4100, www.fs.usda.gov/arp.

33 IDLEWILD

🥾 🚴 ⛴ 🐕 ♿ 🚐 ⛺

Scenic rating: 4

near Winter Park

BEST (

Idlewild is just outside of Winter Park, so even though it sits right on Highway 40 and the train tracks, it is packed throughout July and August. The sites by the river are quite nice, but the rest are a bit crowded, though there is plenty of shade. The Fraser River Trail runs through the campground and connects to an extensive network of mountain biking trails, including the ski runs in Winter Park Resort. Hikers can explore the Byers Peak and Vasquez Peak Wilderness areas, part of a 100,000-acre roadless area. Several trailheads are a short drive away. The campground is divided into an upper and lower loop. The upper loop (sites 16-25) is

very close to the busy highway, and the sites are on a hill, so there's limited tent space. The lower loop (sites 6-25) is in a spruce-fir forest beside the river and the trail. Although bark beetles have been active in this area, the forest around the campground is diverse, so there has been only moderate tree removal.

Campsites, facilities: There are 26 sites for tents and RVs up to 30 feet. There are no hookups. Sites 2, 5, and 18 are pull-through. Picnic tables, fire rings, grills, bear lockers, and tent pads are provided. Vault toilets and drinking water are available. Leashed pets are permitted. The facilities are wheelchair-accessible.

Reservations, fees: Reservations are not accepted. The fee is $22 per night. Cash or check only. Open late May-early September.

Directions: From the Winter Park visitors center, drive south on U.S. Highway 40 for 1.0 mile. The campground entrance is on the left (before the Winter Park Ski Area north entrance).

Contact: Arapaho National Forest, Sulphur District, 970/887-4100, www.fs.usda.gov/arp.

34 ROBBER'S ROOST

⛴ 🐕 ♿ 🚐 ⛺

Scenic rating: 6

near Winter Park

Robber's Roost is a stopover campground on the road to Winter Park. It's in a thick, shady spruce-fir forest adjacent to the Fraser River on U.S. Highway 40 at nearly 10,000 feet. The diversity of the forest and the campground's high altitude have kept the bark beetle activity lower than at other nearby campgrounds. There is a lot of traffic noise. The only activity at the campground is fishing, but the Fraser Valley's extensive trail network attracts hordes of mountain bikers. This campground is very busy in the summer and usually full on weekends. Sites 6-10 are farthest from the road. The sites are about 30 feet apart. There is lots of shade but limited privacy.

Berthoud Pass accesses Winter Park and the northern Central Mountains.

Campsites, facilities: There are 11 sites for tents and RVs up to 25 feet. There are no hook-ups. Site 11 is pull-through. Picnic tables, fire rings, grills, and bear lockers are provided. Vault toilets are available. Leashed pets are permitted. The facilities are wheelchair-accessible.

Reservations, fees: Reservations are not accepted. The fee is $20 per night. Cash or check only. Open late June-early September.

Directions: From the Winter Park visitors center, drive south on U.S. Highway 40 for 6.8 miles. The campground entrance is on the left.

Contact: Arapaho National Forest, Sulphur District, 970/887-4100, www.fs.usda.gov/arp.

35 HALFMOON

Scenic rating: 7

south of Minturn

BEST (

This high-altitude (10,300 feet!) campground is used, for the most part, by hikers and backpackers exploring the Holy Cross Wilderness

area. The Holy Cross Wilderness contains five glacial valleys and the landmark Mount of the Holy Cross. First photographed and painted in 1873 by members of the Hayden Expedition, this mountain draws hordes of visitors every summer who want to see the snowy cross on its north face. From the campground, you can hike to the summit of Mount of the Holy Cross at 14,009 feet above sea level. In 1924, a shelter was built on Notch Mountain to accommodate the pilgrims. The shelter is still accessible via the Notch Mountain Trail, which climbs 3,000 feet in five miles. Campers at Halfmoon can take the Fall Creek Trail to the Notch Mountain Trail, or they can take the Halfmoon Pass Trail to explore the wilderness. The 3.75-mile trail features views of the Sawatch Range, Mount of the Holy Cross, the Gore Range, and the Mosquito Range. If possible, visit midweek when traffic is moderate.

The campground is a small loop in a dense, diverse forest beside Fall Creek. The Forest Service has removed some lodgepole pines, but privacy is still good. Sites 1, 6, and 7 are closest to the creek.

Campsites, facilities: There are seven sites for tents. There are no hookups or pull-throughs. Picnic tables and fire rings are provided. Vault toilets are available and are wheelchair-accessible. Trash must be packed out. Leashed pets are permitted.

Reservations, fees: Reservations are not accepted. The fee is $15 per night. Cash or check only. Open late June-early October.

Directions: From Vail, take I-70 west for five miles to Exit 171. Go south on U.S. Highway 24. In 4.7 miles, turn right on Tigiwon Road/Forest Route 707. In 8.4 miles, the road ends at the Halfmoon Pass trailhead. Just before the parking area, turn left into the campground. The narrow and potted road is very difficult for trailers; high-clearance vehicles are recommended, but not required.

Contact: White River National Forest, Holy Cross District, 970/827-5715, www.fs.usda.gov/whiteriver.

36 HORNSILVER

Scenic rating: 5

south of Minturn

Hornsilver is a clean, convenient stopover on the Top of the Rockies Scenic Byway, a 75-mile Y-shaped travel route. The first section, Dowd Junction to Leadville, features the historic mining towns of Minturn, Gilman, and Redcliff, and access to the Holy Cross Wilderness. Hornsilver is about halfway between Dowd Junction and Leadville. The campground loop occupies a flat area about 20 feet above the highway. Traffic is audible but not heavy. The large sites are about 30 feet apart. The Forest Service has clear-cut this campground due to bark beetle and windthrow, but has been planting new trees since 2011.

Campsites, facilities: There are seven sites for tents and RVs up to 30 feet. There are no hookups or pull-throughs. Picnic tables, grills, fire rings, and tent pads are provided. Vault toilets are available. Leashed pets are permitted.

Reservations, fees: Reservations are not accepted. The fee is $19 per night. Cash or check only. Open late May-early September.

Directions: From Vail, take I-70 west for 5.0 miles to Exit 171. Go south on U.S. Highway 24. The campground is on the left in 11.5 miles, just after Homestake Picnic Area.

Contact: White River National Forest, Holy Cross District, 970/827-5715, www.fs.usda.gov/whiteriver.

37 GOLD PARK

Scenic rating: 7

south of Minturn

The long drive to get to Gold Park deters many campers, but there seems to be a regular following. The campground can accommodate RVs, but it attracts mostly tent campers and families with young children. Situated in an old-growth pine forest next to Homestake Creek, every site has plenty of flat space for pitching pavilion-size tents, and there's no shortage of shade. It's possible to fish from the campground, but the fish are tiny. Anglers will have more luck driving downstream and working their way up to the campground or driving up to Homestake Reservoir. Several hiking trails begin a short drive away, including the Whitney Lake, Missouri Lakes, and Fancy Pass Trails, all of which explore the Holy Cross Wilderness. Four-wheeling is also a popular pastime. The Holy Cross Jeep Trail is one of the toughest roads in Colorado. Forest Route 704 is an easier road to the ghost town.

Campsites, facilities: There are 11 sites for tents and RVs up to 40 feet. Picnic tables, fire rings, and grills are provided. Vault toilets are available. Leashed pets are permitted.

Reservations, fees: Reservations are not

accepted. The fee is $21 per night. Cash or check only. Open late May-early September.

Directions: From Vail, take I-70 west for 5 miles to Exit 171. Go south on U.S. Highway 24. In 12.7 miles, turn right on Homestake Road/Forest Route 703. Continue 7.0 miles to the campground entrance on the left. This is a wide gravel road with a lot of washboarding.

Contact: White River National Forest, Holy Cross District, 970/827-5715, www.fs.usda.gov/whiteriver.

38 CAMP HALE MEMORIAL

Scenic rating: 8

south of Minturn

During World War II, Eagle Park was the site of Camp Hale, the training grounds of the elite 10th Mountain Division, the only specialized mountain/ski soldiers in the United States Army. Up to 14,000 soldiers lived in this valley and trained in the surrounding mountains, developing mountaineering and cold-weather survival skills that they used to battle the Germans in the Italian Alps. After the war, members of the 10th Mountain Division returned to Colorado and founded the first recreational ski resorts. Little remains of the base, but interpretive displays help visitors imagine life in this valley during the war.

The campground is at the south end of the park and is fairly open thanks to bark beetles. It offers expansive views of the valley and surrounding ridgelines. You could spend a whole day just watching the clouds go by, or go fishing on the Eagle River or hiking or mountain biking on the Colorado Trail. All of the sites are large and spaced about 100 feet apart. The campground is usually full on weekends, but five sites are first come, first served.

Campsites, facilities: There are 21 sites for tents and RVs up to 60 feet. There are no hookups or pull-throughs. Picnic tables, fire rings, and grills are provided. Vault toilets are available. Leashed pets are permitted. The facilities are wheelchair-accessible.

Reservations, fees: Reservations are accepted at 877/444-6777 and www.recreation.gov. The fee is $21 per night. Cash or check only. Open late May-mid-September.

Directions: From Vail, take I-70 west for 5.0 miles to Exit 171. Go south on U.S. Highway 24. In 16.6 miles, turn left at the Camp Hale Memorial sign. Turn left at the stone gate and drive 0.2 mile to the *T*-intersection. Turn right on B Street and continue 1.2 miles to the fee station.

Contact: White River National Forest, Holy Cross District, 970/827-5715, www.fs.usda.gov/whiteriver.

39 CAMP HALE EAST FORK GROUP

Scenic rating: 7

south of Minturn

This is a very private group campground, perfect for church groups, Scout groups, and family reunions. The access road Forest Route 726 is also part of the Colorado Trail, which is open to hikers, bikers, and ATV riders. The campground is in a narrow valley beside the East Fork of the Eagle River, which is just a creek at this point. Campers can go fishing here or in Eagle Park, the site of Camp Hale, a World War II training base for the 10th Mountain Division. Rock climbing is also available on the east side of Eagle Park. The campground used to sit in a lodgepole forest, but hundreds of trees have been removed from the outskirts due to bark beetle. The Forest Service is using pesticides and pheromones to try to save the remaining trees.

Campsites, facilities: This is a group site with dispersed tent camping for up to 200 people. Small RVs (up to 45 feet) can also access the site. The facilities are wheelchair-accessible. Picnic tables, grills, and fire rings are provided. Vault toilets are available. Leashed pets are permitted.

Reservations, fees: Reservations are required and can be made at 877/444-6777 and www.recreation.gov. The fee is $210 per night. Open late May-early September.

Directions: From Vail, take I-70 west for 5.0 miles to Exit 171. Go south on U.S. Highway 24 for about 19 miles. After the South Fork bridge, turn left into a large gravel pullout. Forest Route 726 is at the end of the pullout (there is no sign). Drive north for 3.0 miles and then make a sharp left into the campground.

Contact: White River National Forest, Holy Cross District, 970/827-5715, www.fs.usda.gov/whiteriver.

40 GORE CREEK

Scenic rating: 6

near Vail

BEST (

Gore Creek campground isn't especially scenic, but it has two things going for it: proximity to Vail and the Eagles Nest Wilderness. It's a perfect destination for enjoying the town (including numerous summer festivals) and exploring Eagles Nest, one of the most easily accessible wilderness areas. From I-70, there's no hint of the beauty and wildness that await just north of the campground, but the adjacent trailheads climb steeply through lush valleys that dead end at alpine lakes beneath the serrated ridges of the Gore Range. The Deluge Lake Trail is a four-mile ascent (one of the steepest in Eagles Nest) with views of the Vail Valley and Gore Range. The Gore Creek Trail climbs for 6.5 miles to Gore Lake and Red Buffalo Pass, where it connects with the Gore Range Trail. Gore

Creek is the most popular trail in the area, so you can expect company in the summer. Both of these trails are closed to bikes, but mountain bikers can follow Bighorn Road to its terminus and the Two Elk trailhead. This National Scenic Trail has panoramic views of the Gore and Sawatch Ranges and passes by the back bowls of Vail. There is fair fishing for brook and cutthroat trout in Gore Creek. Downstream of Exit 180, Gore Creek is a Class III-IV white-water run with numerous play spots. On Saturday afternoons, the Forest Service offers interpretive programs in a small amphitheater.

The campground is a gravel loop beside Gore Creek. Although there has been a significant bark beetle impact here, the forest was diverse, so many spruce, fir, and aspen remain and provide decent shade. Most of the sites are 50 feet apart and screened from each other but not from the road. Sites 9-14, 16, and 17 are creekside. This is a migratory area for black bears, and the Forest Service has occasionally temporarily closed the campground due to bear problems. However, new bear lockers and bear-proof trash cans have been installed to help reduce that hazard.

Campsites, facilities: There are 25 sites for tents and RVs up to 35 feet. There are no hookups. Picnic tables, fire rings, and grills are provided. Vault toilets are available. Leashed pets are permitted. The facilities are wheelchair-accessible.

Reservations, fees: Reservations are accepted for 15 of the sites, at 877/444-6777 and www.recreation.gov. The fee is $23 per night. Cash or check only. Open late May-mid-September.

Directions: From Exit 180 in Vail, take Bighorn Road east for 2.3 miles and turn left into the campground.

Contact: White River National Forest, Holy Cross District, 970/827-5715, www.fs.usda.gov/whiteriver.

41 HEATON BAY

Scenic rating: 6

on Dillon Reservoir

Located in the heart of Summit County, Dillon Reservoir is an extremely popular summer destination. It has 24.5 miles of shoreline and 3,300 surface acres of water open to boating and windsurfing (but not personal watercraft and swimming). There are four boat ramps, and hiking and biking trails circle the lake and connect the campgrounds to the towns of Silverthorne, Frisco, and Dillon. Three rivers feed the reservoir: the Snake River, Blue River, and Tenmile Creek. Tenmile Creek has Class III-V white water for creek kayakers for about four miles upstream of the reservoir. The valley is ringed by impressive peaks, including the Gore Range, the Williams Fork Mountains, and the Tenmile Range. The Eagles Nest and Ptarmigan Peak wilderness areas offer some of the best high-altitude hiking in the state, and the Continental Divide snakes along the south horizon.

You can faintly hear the nearby interstate, but it's pretty hidden and sounds like a little white noise overall.

Heaton Bay is on the north shore of the reservoir. It used to enjoy a lodgepole forest, but that's been clear-cut and the Forest Service is now working on planting new trees, which are coming up nicely. There are five loops with 10-25 sites in each loop, plus a small sixth loop for tents only. The sites are close together, with very little privacy, but some back onto moose and elk habitat and are walking distance from the lake. Loop C has water and electric hookups and attracts big RVs. Loop D is reserved for tent camping. Sites 18, 19, 21, 43, 44, and 48-52 are lakeside.

Campsites, facilities: There are 81 sites for tents and RVs up to 50 feet, plus 6 tent-only sites in Loop F. Sites 3, 4, 9, 12, 25, 37, 66, and 71 are pull-through. Picnic tables, fire rings, and grills are provided. Sites 10 and 55-72 have tent pads. Vault toilets and drinking water are available. Leashed pets are permitted. Site 10 and the facilities are wheelchair-accessible.

Reservations, fees: Reservations are accepted for Loops A, B, C, and E at 877/444-6777 and www.recreation.gov. The fee is $24 per night for sites without hookups and $29 per night for sites with hookups. Cash or check only. Open late May-early October.

Directions: From I-70, take Frisco exit 203. At the first traffic light, turn left on Dillon Dam Road. The campground is on the right in 2.2 miles.

Contact: White River National Forest, Dillon District, 970/468-5400, www.fs.usda.gov/whiteriver.

42 LOWRY

Scenic rating: 4

on Dillon Reservoir

There are six campgrounds around the 24 miles of shoreline at Dillon Reservoir. Lowry is the only one that's up the slope and not on the water, but it's a short drive to the boat ramps and fishing access. Bike trails circle the lake and connect the campground with the towns of Silverthorne, Dillon, and Frisco. On nearby Sapphire Point, there is a short hiking trail and great views of the lake and mountains. The campground used to be part of Lowry Air Force Base. It hasn't been renovated, so the sites are small and close together. The forest here was totally clear-cut, so there is no shade and very little privacy. Nevertheless, the campground is full on summer weekends. (For more information on Dillon Reservoir, see the Heaton Bay listing in this chapter.)

Campsites, facilities: There are 24 sites for tents and RVs up to 40 feet. Sites 2-24 have electric hookups. Sites 7, 16, and 20 are pull-through. Picnic tables, fire rings, and grills are provided. Vault toilets are available. Leashed pets are permitted.

Reservations, fees: Reservations are accepted for sites 1-14 at 877/444-6777 and www.recreation.gov. The fee is $23 per night for sites without hookups and $28 per night for sites with hookups. Cash or check only. Open late May-early September.

Directions: From Main Street in Frisco, take Summit Boulevard/Highway 9 south for 3.1 miles. Turn left on Swan Mountain Road/Summit High School Road. The campground entrance is on the right in 3.1 miles.

Contact: White River National Forest, Dillon District, 970/468-5400, www.fs.usda.gov/whiteriver.

43 PEAK ONE

Scenic rating: 6

on Dillon Reservoir

Peak One shares a peninsula on the south shore of Dillon Reservoir with the Frisco Nordic Center and Recreation Area. The Crown Point Trail connects the peninsula to the trail network that circles the lake. This family campground has three loops that were clear-cut in 2007. The sites are 20-50 feet apart and offer very little privacy but excellent views. Sites 41-60 and 68-70 are close to the water. (For more information on Dillon Reservoir, see the Heaton Bay listing in this chapter.)

Campsites, facilities: There are 79 sites for tents and RVs up to 50 feet. Sites 2, 21, 72, and 76 are pull-through. Picnic tables, grills, and fire rings are provided. Vault toilets, drinking water, and an amphitheater are available. A skate park and ball fields are available by reservation at the Nordic Center. Leashed pets are permitted.

Reservations, fees: Reservations are accepted for Loop B at 877/444-6777 and www.

recreation.gov. The fee is $24 per night. Cash or check only. Open late May-early September.

Directions: From Main Street in Frisco, take Summit Boulevard/Highway 9 south for 1.1 miles. Turn left on Peninsula Drive. The campground is on the left in 1.0 mile.

Contact: White River National Forest, Dillon District, 970/468-5400, www.fs.usda.gov/whiteriver.

44 PINE COVE

Scenic rating: 6

on Dillon Reservoir

Pine Cove shares a peninsula with the Peak One campground and Frisco Nordic Center and Recreation Area. This campground is for boaters and late arrivals. It's a parking lot with tent camping on the sandy shoreline. The sites are just 10 feet apart and all of the trees were removed, so privacy is very poor. Sites 1-16 are on the water. The best feature is the views of the surrounding peaks. The long ridgelines and bare peaks of the Gore Range, Tenmile Range, and Williams Fork Mountains scream Colorado. The Crown Point Trail connects the campground with the trails that circle the lake and connect Frisco, Dillon, and Silverthorne. (For more information on Dillon Reservoir, see the Heaton Bay listing in this chapter.)

Campsites, facilities: There are 32 sites for tents and RVs up to 40 feet. There are no hookups. Picnic tables, fire rings, and grills are provided. Vault toilets and a boat ramp are available. Leashed pets are permitted.

Reservations, fees: Reservations are not accepted. The fee is $22 per night. Cash or check only. Open late May-early September.

Directions: From Main Street in Frisco, take Summit Boulevard/Highway 9 south for 1.1 miles. Turn left on Peninsula Drive. The campground is on the left in 1.2 miles.

Contact: White River National Forest, Dillon

District, 970/468-5400, www.fs.usda.gov/whiteriver.

45 PROSPECTOR

Scenic rating: 6

on Dillon Reservoir

Located on the southeast shore of Dillon Reservoir, Prospector is a busy, sprawling campground full of families. With five loops, it's a bit of a maze. The sites are close together and the campground was clear-cut in 2009, so there is really no privacy, though there are some trees in spots. The Windy Point Trail connects the campground to the shoreline, but none of the campsites are right on the water. Nearby Sapphire Point has excellent views of the lake and the surrounding mountains. (For more information on Dillon Reservoir, see the Heaton Bay listing in this chapter.)

Campsites, facilities: There are 107 sites for tents and RVs up to 32 feet. There are no hookups. Sites 1, 2, 6-11, 14-19, 22, 23, 25, 37, 41, 55, 58, 70, 103, and 105 are pull-through. Picnic tables, fire rings, and grills are provided. Site 40 has a tent pad. Vault toilets are available. Leashed pets are permitted.

Reservations, fees: Reservations are accepted at 877/444-6777 and www.recreation.gov. The fee is $23 per night. Cash or check only. Open late May-mid-September.

Directions: From Main Street in Frisco, take Summit Boulevard/Highway 9 south for 3.1 miles. Turn left on Swan Mountain Road/Summit High School Road. In 3.0 miles, turn left at the campground sign and continue 0.5 mile to the fee station.

Contact: White River National Forest, Dillon District, 970/468-5400, www.fs.usda.gov/whiteriver.

46 WINDY POINT GROUP

Scenic rating: 6

on Dillon Reservoir

BEST (

Windy Point is a group campground on the southeast shore of Dillon Reservoir. Thanks to clear-cutting, privacy is poor, but the panoramic views are amazing. The Windy Point Trail connects the campground to the shore. (For more information on Dillon Reservoir, see the Heaton Bay listing in this chapter.)

Campsites, facilities: There are two group sites for tent camping for 100 people each. The lake site has a covered pavilion for 95 people. The other site is more rustic. RVs can park in the parking lot. Picnic tables, fire rings, and grills are provided. Vault toilets and a picnic pavilion are available. Leashed pets are permitted. The facilities are wheelchair-accessible.

Reservations, fees: Reservations are required and accepted at 877/444-6777 and www.recreation.gov. The fee is $215-265 per night. Open late May-early September.

Directions: From Main Street in Frisco, take Summit Boulevard/Highway 9 south for 3.1 miles. Turn left on Swan Mountain Road/Summit High School Road. The gated entry is in 3.0 miles. The campground is 0.5 mile past the gate.

Contact: White River National Forest, Dillon District, 970/468-5400, www.fs.usda.gov/whiteriver.

CENTRAL MOUNTAINS SOUTH

Soaring mountains, roiling rivers, and friendly little towns characterize central Colorado. Leadville is a perfect base for summiting some of Colorado's highest peaks, including Mount Elbert and Mount Massive. The numerous high-altitude campgrounds around Turquoise Lake have impressive views of the Sawatch Range, while campers at Twin Lakes Reservoir can enjoy the drive to Independence Pass. The Colorado Trail circumnavigates the lake, providing hiking and mountain biking. South of Twin Lakes, the Arkansas River enters Chaffee County. Around Salida, hikers can join the Colorado and Continental Divide Trails or the Rainbow Trail along the Sangre de Cristos. Visitors to South Park head for Eleven Mile State Park, with nine campgrounds. And then there are the hot springs! Look for campgrounds near Mt. Princeton hot springs, and a few others in Salida and San Luis Valley.

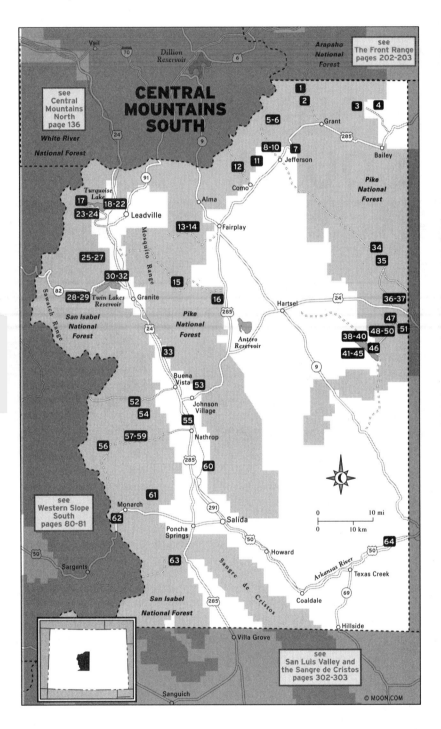

1 GENEVA PARK

Scenic rating: 6

north of Grant

This campground consists of a large loop in a lodgepole pine forest on the quiet side of Guanella Pass, at an elevation of 9,815 feet. The area has a history of mining. In the 1850s, prospectors moved into the basin and worked at three nearby mines. Mining ceased by 1900, and no trace remains of the towns. The campsites here are 30-60 feet apart, and privacy is moderate. Geneva Creek is a short walk away, but fishing is poor and there are no trails near the campground. Sites 1-3 have views of the area around the pass.

Campsites, facilities: There are 26 sites for tents and RVs up to 20 feet, seven of them for tents only. There are no hookups. Site 26 is pull-through. Picnic tables, fire rings, and grills are provided. Vault toilets and a water pump are available. Leashed pets are permitted.

Reservations, fees: Reservations are not accepted. The fee is $22 per night for two vehicles. Cash or check only. Open late May-early September.

Directions: From Grant, take County Road 62 north 6.8 miles. Turn left on Forest Route 119. The campground is on the left in 0.3 mile.

Contact: Pike and San Isabel National Forests, South Platte District, 303/275-5610, www.fs.usda.gov/psicc.

2 BURNING BEAR

Scenic rating: 7

north of Grant

Geneva Basin is a lovely, wide, green valley on the west side of Mount Evans Wilderness. Burning Bear is a small loop on the edge of the valley that blends into a thin forest of pine,

spruce, and fir. The sites are 50-100 feet apart, and privacy is moderate. Hikers can take the Abyss Trail up Scott Gomer Creek to Abyss Lake, at the base of the fourteeners Mount Evans and Mount Bierstadt. Bighorn sheep and mountain goats are frequently sighted in this area, which is notable as being one of the few areas of arctic tundra south of the Arctic Circle. Hikers can also make a loop by connecting Abyss Trail, Rosalie Trail, and Threemile Creek Trail. Mountain bikers can explore Bear Creek Trail. Winter visitors enjoy cross-country skiing and snowshoeing.

Campsites, facilities: There are 13 sites for tents and RVs up to 20 feet. There are no hookups. Site 1 is pull-through. Picnic tables, fire rings, and grills are provided. Vault toilets and drinking water are available. Leashed pets are permitted.

Reservations, fees: Reservations are not accepted. The fee is $22 per night for two vehicles. Cash or check only. Open year-round, but only the first five miles of the road are plowed in the winter.

Directions: From Grant, take County Road 62 north for 5.4 miles. Turn right into the campground.

Contact: Pike and San Isabel National Forests, South Platte District, 303/275-5610, www.fs.usda.gov/psicc.

3 DEER CREEK

Scenic rating: 6

north of Bailey

The only exceptional feature of the Deer Creek campground is its proximity to the Mount Evans Wilderness, which begins 1.5 miles away and is accessible via Trails 603 and 636. Campers can hike into the wilderness in the summer, and ski in the winter. It is about six miles from the trailhead to Beartrack Lakes, a string of lakes created by glacial activity around

Mount Evans. The lakes are an excellent overnight destination. The campground, which sits at 9,168 feet above sea level, is a small, quiet loop in an open forest of pine, spruce, fir, and aspen. The sites are 20-50 feet apart. Sites 3-5 and 10-12 are creekside.

Campsites, facilities: There are 13 sites for tents and RVs up to 20 feet. Picnic tables, fire rings, and grills are provided. Vault toilets and drinking water are available. Leashed pets are permitted.

Reservations, fees: Reservations are not accepted. The fee is $22 per night for two vehicles. Cash or check only. Open year-round.

Directions: From Bailey, take U.S. Highway 285 east about 3.0 miles and turn north on County Road 43. At 6.8 miles, stay left at the fork. The campground is in another 1.3 miles, on the left.

Contact: Pike and San Isabel National Forests, South Platte District, 303/275-5610, www. fs.usda.gov/psicc.

4 MERIDIAN
🚶 🐴 🚐 ⛺

Scenic rating: 6

north of Bailey

Meridian is a dirt loop in a forest of ponderosa pine with scattered aspen at an elevation of 9,000 feet. The campground has a slight slope and lots of sunshine. The sites are 50-100 feet apart. The campground is almost empty on weekdays, but it can fill up with locals on weekends. There is not a lot of privacy, but the large sites can easily accommodate multiple tents. Trail 604 begins nearby and climbs into the Mount Evans Wilderness area, where it intersects Cub Creek Trail. The wilderness area is famous for the fourteeners Mount Evans and Mount Bierstadt and healthy populations of bighorn sheep and mountain goats.

Campsites, facilities: There are 18 sites for tents and RVs up to 20 feet. Picnic tables, fire rings, and grills are provided. Vault toilets and drinking water are available. Leashed pets are permitted.

Reservations, fees: Reservations are not accepted. The fee is $22 per night for up to two vehicles. Cash or check only. Open late May-early September.

Directions: From Bailey, take U.S. Highway 285 east about 3.0 miles and turn north on County Road 43. At 6.8 miles, stay right at the fork on County Road 47. The campground is on the left in 0.9 mile.

Contact: Pike and San Isabel National Forests, South Platte District, 303/275-5610, www. fs.usda.gov/psicc.

5 HALL VALLEY
🚶 🚲 🏂 🐴 🚐 ⛺

Scenic rating: 7

west of Grant

This campground is in a scenic little valley at 9,900 feet, with aspen groves and views of Handcart Peak. The rough road deters many campers, but it's a worthwhile destination. Most of the sites are in the spruce-fir forest beside the creek. They are private and shaded. Sites 3, 8, and 9 are in the meadow. Hikers and bikers can take the Gibson Lake Trail 2.5 miles to remote Gibson Lake, in the shadow of Whale Peak. Mountain bikers and ATV owners can also take Forest Route 121 to Webster Pass.

Campsites, facilities: There are nine sites for tents and RVs up to 30 feet. Picnic tables, fire rings, and grills are provided. Vault toilets and drinking water are available. Trash must be packed out. Leashed pets are permitted.

Reservations, fees: Reservations are not accepted. The fee is $22 per night. Cash or check only. Open year-round, but winter road conditions may limit access.

Directions: From Grant, take U.S. Highway 285 west about 3.0 miles to County Road 60 and turn right. Continue north for 5.2 miles.

The last 0.5-mile requires high clearance. The campground entrance is on the left.

Contact: Pike and San Isabel National Forests, South Platte District, 303/275-5610, www.fs.usda.gov/psicc.

6 HANDCART

Scenic rating: 7

west of Grant

Handcart is a shaded, quiet tent-only campground on the banks of the Lake Fork of the South Platte River. Located in a mature spruce-fir forest, the campground offers privacy and solitude. The Gibson Lake Trail begins in the campground and climbs gradually for 2.5 miles to Gibson Lake in the cirque below Whale Peak. In the late 1800s, this area was home to mining towns and prospectors, but little remains of the old ghost towns. Four-wheelers and mountain bikers can take Forest Route 121 to Webster Pass. All of the sites are walk-ins, but sites 9 and 10 are close to the parking lot. Sites 1-3 and 6-8 are creekside. Sites 6-8 are the most attractive.

Campsites, facilities: There are 10 sites for tents only. Picnic tables, fire rings, and grills are provided. Vault toilets and drinking water are available. Trash must be packed out. Leashed pets are permitted.

Reservations, fees: Reservations are not accepted. The fee is $22 per night for up to two vehicles. Cash or check only. Open late May-early September.

Directions: From Grant, take U.S. Highway 285 west about 3.0 miles and head north on County Road 60 for 4.8 miles. The road is rough but does not require high clearance. The campground is on the left.

Contact: Pike and San Isabel National Forests, South Platte District, 303/275-5610, www.fs.usda.gov/psicc.

7 KENOSHA PASS

Scenic rating: 7

north of Jefferson

Location is the best feature of Kenosha Pass campground, "The Gateway to South Park," which welcomes you at the cool elevation of 10,000 feet. This road was an important route into the Rockies for the Utes and the miners. The Denver, South Park, and Pacific Railroad carried supplies and tourists to the early settlements in South Park. The railroad is gone, but the highway is still the fastest route from Denver into the southern Rockies. The campground is a convenient stopover, and it's popular with hikers and mountain bikers who want to explore the Colorado Trail, which passes through the campground and continues west across the Continental Divide into Summit County. The main campground is a figure eight in a spruce-fir forest that has had mild bark beetle activity. The sites are about 60 feet apart. Across the highway, an old picnic area has been turned into an additional campground. This loop is mostly forested with aspen, and the sites are much closer together. Twin Cone Road leads east from the campground to dispersed camping. Traffic is audible from both loops.

Campsites, facilities: There are 25 sites for tents and RVs up to 24 feet. There are no hookups. Sites 3 and 22 are pull-through. Picnic tables, fire rings, and grills are provided. Vault toilets and drinking water are available. Leashed pets are permitted.

Reservations, fees: Reservations are not accepted. The fee is $22 per night for up to two vehicles. Cash or check only. Open late May-early September.

Directions: From Grant, take U.S. Highway 285 west about 7.0 miles to Kenosha Pass. The campground entrance is on the right.

Contact: Pike and San Isabel National Forests, South Platte District, 303/275-5610, www.fs.usda.gov/psicc.

8 LODGEPOLE

🚶 🚴 🛶 🏕 ♿ � 🏕

Scenic rating: 7

north of Jefferson

Lodgepole is in the Jefferson Creek Recreation Area, a popular weekend destination for anglers and families. So far, bark beetle impact in this area has been mild, but the Forest Service expects it to intensify over the next decade as it travels over from the west. There has been some hazard-tree removal, and these activities will continue as the epidemic worsens.

Lodgepole is the least appealing of the three campgrounds on this road because it's farthest from the lake and the least scenic. The best feature is the Colorado Trail, which passes through the campground and continues west across the Continental Divide and down into Summit County. The campground is a large loop in a coniferous forest surrounded by pine-covered hills and one rocky crag. The road separates the campground from the creek. Sites 2, 5, and 32-35 are near the road. The sites are 20-50 feet apart.

Campsites, facilities: There are 34 sites for tents and RVs up to 30 feet. There are no hookups. Sites 6, 8, and 27 are pull-through. Picnic tables, fire rings, and grills are provided. Vault toilets and drinking water are available. Leashed pets are permitted. The facilities are wheelchair-accessible.

Reservations, fees: Reservations are accepted at 877/444-6777 and www.recreation.gov. The fee is $17 per night plus a $6 day use fee. Cash or check only. Open early May-early October.

Directions: From Jefferson, take County Road 35 north for 2.0 miles. Turn right on County Road 37. The campground entrance is on the left in 2.5 miles.

Contact: Pike and San Isabel National Forests, South Park District, 719/836-2031, www. fs.usda.gov/psicc.

9 ASPEN

🚶 🚴 🛶 🏕 ♿ 🚗 🏕

Scenic rating: 7

north of Jefferson

Aspen is the second campground in Jefferson Creek Recreation Area, a popular weekend destination for families and anglers. The campground is at 9,900 feet and about two miles from Jefferson Lake, but fishing is available on the creek and in the beaver ponds. The Colorado Trail passes through the campground and offers hiking and mountain biking over the Continental Divide. The campground is a small loop in a spruce-fir forest with scattered aspen and wildflowers. There has been some hazard-tree removal here, and there will be more as the bark beetle epidemic worsens. Sites 1 and 2 are next to the road. Sites 4-6 are creekside. Sites 5-8 are the best sites; they're large and sheltered by aspen. The campground is about half-full midweek. Reservations are highly recommended on weekends.

Campsites, facilities: There are 12 sites for tents and RVs up to 25 feet. There are no hookups. Site 1 is pull-through. Picnic tables, fire rings, and grills are provided. Vault toilets and drinking water are available. Leashed pets are permitted. The facilities are wheelchair-accessible.

Reservations, fees: Reservations are accepted at 877/444-6777 and www.recreation.gov. The fee is $17 per night plus a $6 day use fee. Cash or check only. Open early May-early October.

Directions: From Jefferson, take County Road 35 north for 2.0 miles. Turn right on County Road 37. The campground entrance is on the right in 2.7 miles.

Contact: Pike and San Isabel National Forests, South Park District, 719/836-2031, www. fs.usda.gov/psicc.

10 JEFFERSON CREEK

Scenic rating: 6

north of Jefferson

Jefferson Creek is the last campground on the road to Jefferson Lake, a small reservoir with excellent trout fishing at 10,100 feet above sea level. The campground is about a mile from the lake. Fishing is also possible on the creek. Hiking and mountain biking are available on 3.5-mile West Jefferson Trail and on the Colorado Trail, which climbs to the Continental Divide. The campground is a small lollipop in a spruce-fir forest, which has so far only been mildly affected by bark beetles. The sites are about 30 feet apart, and privacy is poor. The campground is not as popular as Aspen, but reservations are recommended on weekends.

Campsites, facilities: There are 17 sites for tents and RVs up to 25 feet. There are no hookups. Site 12 is pull-through. Picnic tables, fire rings, and grills are provided. Vault toilets and drinking water are available. Leashed pets are permitted. The facilities are wheelchair-accessible.

Reservations, fees: Reservations are accepted at 877/444-6777 and www.recreation.gov. The fee is $17 per night plus a $6 day use fee. Cash or check only. Open early May-early October.

Directions: From Jefferson, take County Road 35 north for 2.0 miles. Turn right on County Road 37. The campground entrance is on the left in 3.6 miles.

Contact: Pike and San Isabel National Forests, South Park District, 719/836-2031, www.fs.usda.gov/psicc.

11 MICHIGAN CREEK

Scenic rating: 8

north of Jefferson

This campground consists of a big meadow ringed by aspen and bordered by Michigan Creek on one side. Most sites have views of the Continental Divide to the west. Sites 6-13 sit in or around the meadow. Sites 6-10 are also sheltered by aspen. Sites 1-5 have the best shade. The sites are about 100 feet apart and fairly private. This campground is popular with mountain bikers and ATV owners; forest routes climb to Georgia Pass and panoramic views of South Park. Fishing is also available on Michigan Creek. This campground has had mild bark beetle activity, but the Forest Service expects it to worsen and will continue to remove trees as necessary.

Campsites, facilities: There are 12 sites for tents and RVs up to 25 feet. There are no hookups. Sites 4 and 5 are pull-through. Picnic tables, fire rings, grills, and tent pads are provided. Vault toilets are available. Trash must be packed out. Leashed pets are permitted.

Reservations, fees: Reservations are not accepted. The fee is $15 per night or $20 per night for a double site (sites 1 and 8). Cash or check only. Open early May-early October.

Directions: From Jefferson, take County Road 35 north for 3.0 miles. Turn right on County Road 54. The campground is on the left in 3.0 miles.

Contact: Pike and San Isabel National Forests, South Park District, 719/836-2031, www.fs.usda.gov/psicc.

12 SELKIRK

Scenic rating: 7

north of Como

Selkirk is an excellent destination campground for history buffs, mountain bikers, and four-wheelers. The campground is on the road to Boreas Pass, a former railroad route from South Park into Breckenridge. Nearby Como was a mining and railroad town and has become a self-reliant community of artists. Mountain bikers and ATV riders will enjoy the ride up to Boreas Pass and panoramic views of Summit County and South Park. Anglers can fish for trout on Tarryall Creek. The campground loop is in a mature spruce-fir forest. This area has had mild bark beetle activity, but the Forest Service expects it to worsen and will continue to remove trees as necessary. The sites are about 50 feet apart. Sites 7 and 8 are closest to the creek and the beaver pond. The campground is usually empty midweek and rarely fills up.

Campsites, facilities: There are 15 sites for tents and RVs up to 25 feet. There are no hookups. Picnic tables, fire rings, and grills are provided. Vault toilets are available. Trash must be packed out. Leashed pets are permitted.

Reservations, fees: Reservations are not accepted. The fee is $15 per night. Cash or check only. Open early May-early October.

Directions: In Como, turn north on County Road 33. In 3.8 miles, turn right on Forest Route 33. In 3.5 miles, turn left on Forest Route 406. The campground is in 1.5 miles.

Contact: Pike and San Isabel National Forests, South Park District, 719/836-2031, www.fs.usda.gov/psicc.

13 FOURMILE

Scenic rating: 9

south of Fairplay

The road up Fourmile Creek to the Horseshoe Mine is an interesting historic tour of the mining area that served the Last Chance, Hilltop, and Dauntless Mines. The road has amazing views of the Continental Divide and South Park. The cirque below Horseshoe Mountain is an almost perfect half-circle. Mountain bikers can head up Fourmile Creek Road or take Forest Route 423 to the ghost town Sacramento. Hikers should stretch their legs on the 1.6-mile Limber Grove Trail. The trail passes by a living pine that's over 1,500 years old. Fishing is available on Fourmile Creek. The campground is in a spruce-fir forest in the shadow of Sheep Mountain. The Forest Service expects the diverse forest and high altitude to offer this campground some protection as the bark beetle epidemic spreads into this area. The sites are about 75 feet apart. This campground is rarely used, so privacy is excellent. Site 1 has the best views down the valley. The campground is at a stunning 10,760-foot elevation.

Campsites, facilities: There are 14 sites for tents and RVs up to 22 feet. There are no hookups. Picnic tables, fire rings, and grills are provided. Vault toilets and drinking water are available. Leashed pets are permitted.

Reservations, fees: Reservations are not accepted. The fee is $17 per night. Cash or check only. Open early May-early October.

Directions: From Fairplay, take U.S. Highway 285 south for 1.2 miles. Turn right on County Road 18. The campground is on the right in 7.9 miles.

Contact: Pike and San Isabel National Forests, South Park District, 719/836-2031, www.fs.usda.gov/psicc.

14 HORSESHOE
🏃 🚴 🏊 🐾 🚙 ⛺

Scenic rating: 8

south of Fairplay

Fourmile Creek Road is a historic tour through a mining district that boomed in the late 1880s and went bust in the early 1900s. The 1.6-mile Limber Grove Trail connects Horseshoe and Fourmile campgrounds, and passes by a living pine that's over 1,500 years old. Mountain bikers can travel up Fourmile Creek Road to Leavick townsite and views of South Park and the Continental Divide. The campground loop is in a spruce-fir forest with abundant young aspen next to a small meadow and the creek. Hopefully, the diverse forest and high altitude will offer this campground some protection as the bark beetle impact spreads into this area. The sites are about 60 feet apart and a little less private than at Fourmile. Sites 1 and 2 have the best views. Sites 9-11 are walk-ins. Sites 18 and 19 are next to the meadow and have views of the road.

Campsites, facilities: There are 19 sites for tents and RVs up to 25 feet. There are no hookups. Site 5 is pull-through. Picnic tables, fire rings, and grills are provided. Vault toilets and drinking water are available. Trash must be packed out. Leashed pets are permitted.

Reservations, fees: Reservations are accepted at 877/444-6777 and www.recreation.gov. The fee is $17 per night. Cash or check only. Open early May-early October.

Directions: From Fairplay, take U.S. Highway 285 south for 1.2 miles. Turn right on County Road 18. The campground is on the left in 6.7 miles.

Contact: Pike and San Isabel National Forests, South Park District, 719/836-2031, www.fs.usda.gov/psicc.

15 WESTON PASS
🏃 🏊 🐾 🚙 ⛺

Scenic rating: 9

south of Fairplay

It's a long drive to Weston Pass, but this remote campground at 10,200 feet is a worthwhile destination for hikers interested in exploring the Buffalo Peaks Wilderness. With only 43,410 acres and no fourteeners, this wilderness area receives fewer visitors than the Collegiate Peaks Wilderness across the Arkansas River valley. The wilderness is dominated by the volcanic domes of East and West Buffalo Peaks, which are surrounded by open meadows and gentle forests. From the campground, hikers can make a 12-mile loop by connecting the trails along Rich Creek and Rough and Tumbling Creek. Fishing is possible on the South Fork of South Platte and in the numerous beaver ponds along local creeks. The campground is a lollipop in a spruce-fir forest with a few scattered aspen and mild bark beetle activity so far. The sites are 30-60 feet apart. Sites 5, 7-9, and 12 overlook the creek and the road.

Campsites, facilities: There are 14 sites for tents and RVs up to 25 feet. There are no hookups. Picnic tables and grills are provided. Vault toilets and drinking water are available. Trash must be packed out. Leashed pets are permitted.

Reservations, fees: Reservations are not accepted. The fee is $15 per night. Cash or check only. Open late May-early October, weather permitting.

Directions: From Fairplay, take U.S. Highway 285 south for 4.7 miles. Turn right on County Road 5. The campground is on the left in 11.2 miles.

Contact: Pike and San Isabel National Forests, South Park District, 719/836-2031, www.fs.usda.gov/psicc.

16 BUFFALO SPRINGS

Scenic rating: 6

south of Fairplay

Buffalo Springs is in a small, arid valley a few miles from the Buffalo Peaks Wilderness. The high domes of East and West Buffalo Peaks are impressive landmarks in South Park and the Arkansas River valley. The campground is a large loop in a mature forest of pine, spruce, and fir, with scattered aspen. Many trees have been removed due to the bark beetle epidemic and hazard-tree removal will continue in this area as necessary. There are no trails near the campground, so it is mainly a stopover between Fairplay and Salida, or a destination for snowbirds.

Campsites, facilities: There are 18 sites for tents and RVs up to 30 feet. There are no hookups. Sites 7 and 18 are pull-through. Picnic tables, fire rings, and grills are provided. Vault toilets and drinking water are available. Leashed pets are permitted.

Reservations, fees: Reservations are accepted at 877/444-6777 and www.recreation.gov. The fee is $17 per night. Cash or check only. Open early May-late September.

Directions: From Fairplay, take U.S. Highway 285 south for 13 miles. Turn right on County Road 76/Forest Route 431. The campground is on the left in 0.8 mile.

Contact: Pike and San Isabel National Forests, South Park District, 719/836-2031, www.fs.usda.gov/psicc.

17 MAY QUEEN

Scenic rating: 9

Turquoise Lake

BEST (

May Queen is the only campground at the west end of Turquoise Lake and it is truly special. The views are as spectacular as they are on the east side, but the bedlam is missing. This campground, at nearly 10,000 feet in elevation, also has the best access to the hiking opportunities in the Holy Cross and Mount Massive wilderness areas as well as the Colorado Trail, which passes by the campground entrance. Four-wheelers and ATV riders enjoy driving up Hagerman Pass, but ATVs cannot unload in the campground due to road restrictions (which keeps the campground very quiet). Canoes and kayaks can be carried down to the lake. The nearest boat ramp is the Matchless Ramp, about six miles away. (For more information on Turquoise Lake and activities, see the Belle of Colorado listing in this chapter.)

There are 12 walk-in tent sites. Most of them are widely distributed away from the road in a coniferous forest, but sites 4, 6, and 21-23 are too close to the road and lack privacy. The following tent and RV sites lack trees but they have fantastic views: 10, 12, 13, 15, 17, and 22. Sites 21-23 are close to the lake.

Campsites, facilities: There are 17 sites for tents and RVs up to 32 feet and 12 walk-in tent sites. There are no hookups. Sites 10-17, 19, 20, and 22 are pull-through. Picnic tables, fire rings, and grills are provided. Tent pads are provided at sites 10-13, 16, 17, 19, 20, and 22. Vault toilets and drinking water are available. Leashed pets are permitted. Facilities are wheelchair-accessible.

Reservations, fees: Reservations are accepted at 877/444-6777 and www.recreation.gov. The fee is $24 per night for up to two vehicles. Cash or check only. Open Memorial Day-Labor Day.

Directions: In Leadville, from the intersection of U.S. Highway 24 and 6th Street, drive south on 6th Street. Turn right on McWethy Road/County Road 4 and follow this road for 1.0 mile. Turn right on County Road 9 (unmarked) and in 1.5 miles turn left on another unmarked road. In 0.5 mile, turn right on Forest Route 104. In 7.5 miles, turn left at the May Queen sign and continue downhill 0.5 mile to the fee station.

Contact: Pike and San Isabel National Forests, Leadville District, 719/486-0749, www.fs.usda. gov/psicc.

18 BELLE OF COLORADO

Scenic rating: 8

on Turquoise Lake

Turquoise Lake is a 780-surface-acre reservoir on the Lake Fork of the Arkansas River. The setting is absolutely spectacular. On the west half of the lake, the shores climb steeply to the Continental Divide. On the east half, the land rises gently toward Leadville, a National Historic Landmark District. To the south, the tallest peaks in Colorado, Mount Massive and Mount Elbert, tower over the valley. They are inside the Mount Massive Wilderness area, and trails on the north side of the lake head into the Holy Cross Wilderness.

Turquoise Lake has it all: fishing, boating, swimming, water sports, hiking, mountain biking, fourteeners, and four-wheeling. The lake is stocked with rainbow trout and kokanee salmon and contains brown, cutthroat, brook, and lake trout. There are a few sandy beaches for frigid swimming and three boat ramps. The Turquoise Lake Trail, which circles the lake, is accessible from every campground and is popular with hikers, bikers, horseback riders, and even strollers (but it's not paved). The Colorado Trail passes within a mile of the inlet. The Hagerman Pass Road is a major four-wheeling and ATV destination, and it crosses the Continental Divide Trail. There is enough to do to fill a whole summer, but be warned—it's no secret. The eight campgrounds are busy (and packed on the weekends) from June to August. If you want privacy, stay away. If you don't mind the crowds, then bring the family, a hammock, and your fishing pole.

Belle of Colorado is the first campground on the east side and my personal favorite. It's the smallest and quietest campground on the lake, and every campsite is a short walk away from the water. It's also one of the only first-come, first-served campgrounds in the area, so you can show up on Friday and still bag a site. Like all of the other campgrounds (except May Queen), it's in a lodgepole pine forest that affords lots of shade and glimpses of shimmering water, but not heaps of privacy. Campers can choose between proximity to their cars and proximity to the lake. Sites 1, 6, 8, 9, 13, 18, and 19 are close to the road. Sites 2-4, 7, 11, 15, 16, and 17 are close to the water.

Campsites, facilities: There are 19 walk-in sites for tents. Picnic tables, fire rings, and grills are provided. Flush toilets and drinking water are available. Leashed pets are permitted.

Reservations, fees: Reservations are not accepted. The fee is $24 per night for up to two vehicles. Open Memorial Day-Labor Day.

Directions: In Leadville, from the intersection of U.S. Highway 24 and 6th Street, drive south on 6th Street. Turn right on McWethy Road/County Road 4 and follow this road for 1.0 mile. Turn right on County Road 9 (unmarked) and in 1.5 miles turn left on another unmarked road. In 0.5 mile, turn right on Forest Route 104. In 0.1 mile, turn left at the Belle of Colorado sign.

Contact: Pike and San Isabel National Forests, Leadville District, 719/486-0749, www.fs.usda. gov/psicc.

19 FATHER DYER

Scenic rating: 7

on Turquoise Lake

Father Dyer is upslope of popular Baby Doe. It's neither as scenic nor appealing as Baby Doe, but it's much quieter. It's a fairly flat campground in a lodgepole pine forest, which provides plenty of shade. The sites are 20-50 feet apart, and most of them are very close to the campground road. The following sites are removed from the road and more private: 6, 10, 11, 14, 16, 17, 21, 22, and 25. There is a footpath to the lake (between sites 16 and 17), so fishing and swimming are accessible, but it's a little too far to comfortably carry a canoe or kayak. (For more information on Turquoise Lake, see the Belle of Colorado listing earlier in this chapter.)

Campsites, facilities: There are 26 sites for tents and RVs up to 32 feet. There are no hookups. Sites 2, 8, 11, 12, 16, and 26 are pull-through. Picnic tables, fire rings, and grills are provided. Flush toilets and drinking water are available. The Tabor Boat Ramp is a half-mile away. Leashed pets are permitted.

Reservations, fees: Reservations are accepted at 877/444-6777 and www.recreation.gov. The fee is $24 per night for up to two vehicles. Cash or check only. Open Memorial Day-Labor Day.

Directions: In Leadville, from the intersection of U.S. Highway 24 and 6th Street, drive south on 6th Street. Turn right on McWethy Road/County Road 4 and follow this road for 1.0 mile. Turn right on County Road 9 (unmarked) and in 1.5 miles turn left on another unmarked road. In 0.5 mile, turn right on Forest Route 104. In 0.7 mile, turn left at the Baby Doe sign and in 0.1 mile turn right into the campground.

Contact: Pike and San Isabel National Forests, Leadville District, 719/486-0749, www.fs.usda.gov/psicc.

20 BABY DOE

Scenic rating: 6

on Turquoise Lake

Baby Doe is the hub of the activity at Turquoise Lake. One camp host called the weekend scene "bedlam." The campground is so popular because it has a sandy beach that's easily accessible from all of the sites. There are two loops in a lodgepole pine forest, which provides ample shade. The bottom loop (sites 1-27) is closer to

the lake, and sites 4, 6, 8, 10, 11, and 14 are just a stone's throw from the beach. The top loop (sites 28-50) is terraced into three levels, which offer glimpses of water through the trees. If you are visiting on the weekend, reservations are highly recommended. (For more information on Turquoise Lake and activities in the area, see the Belle of Colorado listing earlier in this chapter.)

Campsites, facilities: There are 50 sites for tents and RVs up to 32 feet. There are no hookups. Site 24 is pull-through. Picnic tables, fire rings, and grills are provided. Tent pads are provided at sites 4, 7, 11, 28, and 41. Flush toilets and drinking water are available. The Tabor Boat Ramp is a mile away. Leashed pets are permitted. Facilities are wheelchair-accessible.

Reservations, fees: Reservations are accepted at 877/444-6777 and www.recreation.gov. The fee is $24–26 per night. Cash or check only. Open Memorial Day-Labor Day.

Directions: In Leadville, from the intersection of U.S. Highway 24 and 6th Street, drive south on 6th Street. Turn right on McWethy Road/County Road 4 and follow this road for 1.0 mile. Turn right on County Road 9 (unmarked) and in 1.5 miles turn left on another unmarked road. In 0.5 mile, turn right on Forest Route 104. In 0.7 mile, turn left at the Baby Doe sign and continue downhill 0.5 mile to the fee station.

Contact: Pike and San Isabel National Forests, Leadville District, 719/486-0749, www.fs.usda.gov/psicc.

21 TABOR

Scenic rating: 4

on Turquoise Lake

Tabor, adjacent to the boat ramp, looks more like a parking lot than a campground. It's busy during Leadville Boom Days in August, but otherwise there is very little traffic. The campsites are around the edge of two large parking lots. Sites 1-8 are on a narrow strip of land between the upper parking lot and the road. Sites 9 and 10 are on the opposite side of this parking lot and are quieter. Sites 11-15 are RV sites. They are numbered on the fence along the lower edge of the bottom parking lot. They have stairs down to the rocky beach, but there are no flat sites for tents. The campground is adjacent to the Lady of the Lake picnic area and boat ramp. (For more information on Turquoise Lake, see the Belle of Colorado listing earlier in this chapter.)

Campsites, facilities: There are 20 sites for tents and RVs up to 37 feet. There are no hookups or pull-throughs. Picnic tables, fire rings, and grills are provided at sites 1-10. Flush toilets, drinking water, picnic area, and a boat ramp are available. Leashed pets are permitted. The facilities are wheelchair-accessible.

Reservations, fees: Reservations are not accepted. The fee is $24 per night. Cash or check only. Open Memorial Day-Labor Day.

Directions: In Leadville, from the intersection of U.S. Highway 24 and 6th Street, drive south on 6th Street. Turn right on McWethy Road/County Road 4 and follow this road for 1.0 mile. Turn right on County Road 9 (unmarked) and in 1.5 miles turn left on another unmarked road. In 0.5 mile, turn right on Forest Route 104. In 1.2 miles, turn left at the Tabor sign and in 0.1 mile turn right into the campground.

Contact: Pike and San Isabel National Forests, Leadville District, 719/486-0749, www.fs.usda.gov/psicc.

22 PRINTER BOY GROUP
🐕 🚐 ⛺

Scenic rating: 7

on Turquoise Lake

Printer Boy is a favorite location for family reunions and other groups. Like the other Turquoise Lake campgrounds, it's in a hilly lodgepole pine forest, but it's about a two-mile drive to the water. The campground can accommodate four groups at a time, situated around a common area, with excellent recreational and cooking facilities. Sites 1 and 4 accommodate groups up to 75, and sites 2 and 3 can host groups up to 35. Nearby activities will keep every group member happy. There is a hiking and mountain biking trail around the lake. More trails access the Mount Massive and Holy Cross wilderness areas, and ambitious hikers can try several nearby fourteeners. There are three boat ramps on the lake, which contains kokanee salmon and rainbow, brown, and lake trout. History buffs and shoppers will love Leadville, a National Historic Landmark District. (For more information on Turquoise Lake and nearby activities, see the Belle of Colorado listing earlier in this chapter.)

Campsites, facilities: There are four group sites with walk-in tent camping and parking areas for RVs up to 32 feet. There are no hookups or pull-throughs. Picnic tables, fire rings, and grills are provided. Flush toilets, drinking water, volleyball, softball, horseshoe pits, and a community cookhouse and picnic area are available. Leashed pets are permitted.

Reservations, fees: Reservations are required and are accepted at 877/444-6777 and www.recreation.gov. The fee is $60-100 depending on group size and which site you choose. Open Memorial Day-Labor Day.

Directions: In Leadville, from the intersection of U.S. Highway 24 and 6th Street, drive south on 6th Street. Turn right on McWethy Road/County Road 4 and follow this road for 1.0 mile. Turn right on County Road 9 (unmarked) and in 1.5 miles turn left on another unmarked road. In 0.5 mile turn right on Forest Route 104. In 3.0 miles turn right into the campground.

Contact: Pike and San Isabel National Forests, Leadville District, 719/486-0749, www.fs.usda.gov/psicc.

23 SILVER DOLLAR

🚶 🚴 ⛵ 🏊 🛶 🎣 🐴 🚐 ⛺

Scenic rating: 7

on Turquoise Lake

Like almost all of the Turquoise Lake campgrounds, Silver Dollar sprawls through a lodgepole pine forest on the hilly shores of the lake. Unlike the other campgrounds, the narrow road and short spurs deter many RV drivers, so this campground tends to be quieter than the campgrounds to the north. Most sites are near the road, but they are grouped in threes and fours, so it doesn't feel like you're surrounded. As a result, these sites feel more private than at many of the other campgrounds. Sites 3, 4, and 13 have the most privacy. A foot trail to the lake begins next to site 18. (For more information on Turquoise Lake, see the Belle of Colorado listing earlier in this chapter.)

Campsites, facilities: There are 43 sites for tents and RVs up to 22 feet. There are no hookups or pull-throughs. Picnic tables, fire rings, and grills are provided. Tent pads are provided at sites 1, 2, 8, 13-16, 24, 27, 33, 37, 40, 42, and 43. Flush toilets, drinking water, a picnic area, and a boat ramp are available. Leashed pets are permitted.

Reservations, fees: Reservations are accepted at 877/444-6777 and www.recreation.gov. The fee is $24 per night. Cash or check only. Open Memorial Day-Labor Day.

Directions: In Leadville, from the intersection of U.S. Highway 24 and 6th Street, drive south on 6th Street. Turn right on McWethy Road/County Road 4 and follow this road for 1.0 mile. Turn right on County Road 9 (unmarked) and in 1.5 miles turn left on another unmarked road. In 0.5 mile, turn left on Forest Route 104. In 1.5 miles, turn right at the Matchless Boat Ramp sign. The fee station is straight ahead in 0.7 mile. Loop B is on the left, and Loop A is on the right.

Contact: Pike and San Isabel National Forests, Leadville District, 719/486-0749, www.fs.usda.gov/psicc.

24 MOLLY BROWN

🚶 🚴 ⛵ 🏊 🛶 🎣 🐴 ♿ 🚐 ⛺

Scenic rating: 8

on Turquoise Lake

Like almost all of the Turquoise Lake campgrounds, Molly Brown sprawls through a lodgepole pine forest on the hilly shores of the lake. The sites are 50-100 feet apart, and most of them are close to the road. There are two paved loops. Loop A (sites 27-49) does not have water access so campers have to walk to Loop B to reach the shore. Sites 35-38, 41, and 44 are on the outside of the loop and have the most privacy. In Loop B, sites 2-16 are on the bottom of the loop and have views of the water. Site 4, 6, 8, 10, 12, and 13 are separated from the shore by a few trees. These are very popular sites and usually require reservations. The Turquoise Lake Trail, which circles the lake, is accessible to hikers and bikers. Anglers can fish from the beach, carry boats down to the water, or drive 1.5 miles to the Matchless Boat Ramp. (For more information on Turquoise Lake, see the Belle of Colorado listing earlier in this chapter.)

Campsites, facilities: There are 49 sites for tents and RVs up to 32 feet. There are no hookups or pull-throughs. Picnic tables, fire rings, and grills are provided. Flush toilets, drinking water, and a dump station are available. Leashed pets are permitted. Facilities are wheelchair-accessible.

Reservations, fees: Reservations are accepted at 877/444-6777 and www.recreation.gov. The fee is $24-26 per night. Cash or check only. Open Memorial Day-Labor Day.

Directions: In Leadville, from the intersection of U.S. Highway 24 and 6th Street, drive south on 6th Street. Turn right on McWethy Road/County Road 4 and follow this road for 1.0 mile. Turn right on County Road 9 (unmarked) and in 1.5 miles turn left on another unmarked road. In 0.5 mile, turn left on Forest Route 104. In 0.3 mile, turn right at the Molly Brown sign. The fee station is in 0.5 mile. Loop A is on the left, and Loop B is on the right.

Contact: Pike and San Isabel National Forests, Leadville District, 719/486-0749, www.fs.usda.gov/psicc.

25 HALFMOON EAST

Scenic rating: 8

south of Leadville

Halfmoon East has a group of regulars from southern Colorado who return every few weeks. Most of them are Golden Age pass holders, so it's a quiet campground. The Mount Elbert, Mount Massive, and Colorado Trails are nearby, but most of these campers just make the short hike to Emerald Lake, which is stocked with trout. Hand-powered and electric motorboats are allowed on the lake. The campground is in a coniferous forest beside Elbert Creek. All of the sites are just 10-30 feet from the lake. Sites 1 and 4 are walk-ins. Site 1 is below the road and has the most privacy.

Campsites, facilities: There are six sites for tents and RVs up to 16 feet. There are no hookups or pull-throughs. Picnic tables, fire rings, and grills are provided. Vault toilets are available, but no drinking water. Leashed pets are permitted.

Reservations, fees: Reservations are not accepted. The fee is $20 per night. Cash or check only. Open Memorial Day-Labor Day.

Directions: From U.S. Highway 24 and 6th Street in Leadville, take U.S. 24 south 4.0 miles. Turn right on Highway 300. In 0.8 mile, turn left on Halfmoon Road. In 1.2 miles, turn right on County Road 11. The campground is on the right in 4.0 miles. This dirt road has potholes and washboarding but does not require 4WD.

Contact: Pike and San Isabel National Forests, Leadville District, 719/486-0749, www.fs.usda.gov/psicc.

26 HALFMOON WEST

Scenic rating: 8

south of Leadville

Like Elbert Creek, Halfmoon West is a quiet campground surrounded by excellent recreational opportunities, but it's barely used. The only busy time is in August during the Leadville 100 ultramarathon, when the campground is turned into a medical station. Halfmoon Road is the first climb, and any runners who can't pass a medical exam are not allowed to continue. The rest of the year, this campground is virtually unused. It contains three loops in a lodgepole pine forest. The sites are large and mostly far apart from each other. The first loop (sites 1-4) is very close to the road. The second loop (sites 5-11) affords more privacy. The back loop (sites 12-16) is on a hill above the rest of the campground. These are the most secluded sites in the campground.

Campsites, facilities: There are 16 sites for tents and RVs up to 16 feet. There are no hookups. Site 14 is pull-through. Picnic tables, fire rings, and grills are provided. Vault toilets are available, but no drinking water. Leashed pets are permitted.

Reservations, fees: Reservations are not accepted. The fee is $20 per night. Cash or check only. Open Memorial Day-Labor Day.

Directions: From U.S. Highway 24 and 6th Street in Leadville, take U.S. 24 south 4.0 miles. Turn right on Highway 300. In 0.8 mile, turn left on Halfmoon Road. In 1.2 miles, turn right on County Road 11. The campground is on the left in 4.1 miles. This dirt road has potholes and washboarding but does not require 4WD.

Contact: Pike and San Isabel National Forests, Leadville District, 719/486-0749, www.fs.usda.gov/psicc.

27 ELBERT CREEK

🥾 🚲 🛶 🚐 🛶 🦌 🚗 ⛺

Scenic rating: 8

south of Leadville

BEST (

Elbert Creek is a quiet campground surrounded by outstanding recreational opportunities. Most of the campers at Elbert Creek are here to climb Colorado's highest peaks, Mount Elbert and Mount Massive. They go to bed early, get up early, hike all day, and leave the next day. A few campers stay to enjoy mountain biking on the South Halfmoon Creek and Mount Champion Trails or fishing on Emerald Lake, which is stocked with trout. It's also a stopover on the Colorado Trail. The only time this campground is full is on holiday weekends. It parallels Elbert Creek, and the sites are large and spaced about 60-100 feet apart. The coniferous forest is not dense, but there is adequate privacy. Sites 1, 4, 7, 8, 10, 13, and 14 are next to the road. Sites 2, 5, 6, 9, 11, 12, and 15-17 are next to the creek. Site 17 is the only site with views of the Continental Divide.

Campsites, facilities: There are 17 sites for tents and RVs up to 16 feet. There are no hookups or pull-throughs. Picnic tables, fire rings, and grills are provided. Vault toilets and drinking water are available. Leashed pets are permitted.

Reservations, fees: Reservations are not accepted. The fee is $20 per night. Cash or check only. Open Memorial Day-Labor Day.

Directions: From U.S. Highway 24 and 6th Street in Leadville, take U.S. 24 south 4.0 miles. Turn right on Highway 300. In 0.8 mile, turn left on Halfmoon Road. In 1.2 miles, turn right on County Road 11. The campground is on the right in 5.0 miles. This dirt road has potholes and washboarding but does not require 4WD.

Contact: Pike and San Isabel National Forests, Leadville District, 719/486-0749, www.fs.usda.gov/psicc.

28 TWIN PEAKS

🥾 🚲 🦌 🚗 ⛺

Scenic rating: 7

near Twin Lakes Reservoir

The Twin Peaks campground and neighboring Parry Peak campground are about five miles upstream from Twin Lakes and all the activity there. Travelers frequently use these campgrounds as a stopover on their way up Independence Pass, but they're not bad for campers who want a quiet vacation near Twin Lakes. Twin Peaks contains two gravel loops between the highway and Lake Creek. The sites are 50-100 feet apart and are forested with pine and aspen. Sites 14, 16, 18, 19, 22, and 23 are next to the creek. Walk-in sites 34-37 are also next to the creek. Sites 6, 27, 29, and 31-33 are next to the road. Traffic can be quite heavy in July and August. From the Parry Peak campground, hikers and mountain bikers can take the Interlocken Loop Trail to Twin Lakes and the Colorado Trail. The Black Cloud trailhead is one mile upstream. This trail climbs 4.4 miles to the summit of Mount Elbert.

Campsites, facilities: There are 33 sites for tents and RVs up to 32 feet and four walk-in tent sites. There are no hookups or pull-throughs. Picnic tables, fire rings, and grills are provided. Vault toilets and drinking water are available. Leashed pets are permitted.

Reservations, fees: Reservations are not accepted. The fee is $23 per night. Cash or check only. Open Memorial Day-Labor Day.

Directions: From the intersection of U.S. Highway 24 and 6th Street in Leadville, take U.S. 24 south for 15 miles. Turn right on Highway 82. In 10 miles, turn left into the campground.

Contact: Pike and San Isabel National Forests, Leadville District, 719/486-0749, www.fs.usda.gov/psicc.

29 PARRY PEAK

🥾 🚲 🐴 🚐 ⛺

Scenic rating: 7

near Twin Lakes Reservoir

Parry Peak is in a flat area below the highway, so there's less traffic noise than at Twin Peaks, but the sites are closer together. The campground has two loops on both sides of Lake Creek. The habitat is subalpine spruce and fir, with some sagebrush. Sites 1, 4, 5, and 7 are very close to the road. Sites 16-26 are across the bridge in an aspen grove. They are great for both tent and RV camping. Sites 14, 16, and 24-26 are next to the creek. Sites 35 and 26 are walk-in tent sites. Hikers and mountain bikers can take the Interlocken Loop Trail to Twin Lakes and the Colorado Trail.

Campsites, facilities: There are 26 sites for tents and RVs up to 32 feet. There are no hookups. Sites 6, 8, and 20 are pull-through. Picnic tables, fire rings, and grills are provided. Tent pads are provided at sites 6, 8-11, 14, 16-18, and 22-24. Vault toilets and drinking water are available. Leashed pets are permitted.

Reservations, fees: Reservations are not accepted. The fee is $22 per night. Cash or check only. Open Memorial Day-Labor Day.

Directions: From the intersection of U.S. Highway 24 and 6th Street in Leadville, take U.S. 24 south for 15 miles. Turn right on Highway 82. In 9.0 miles, turn left into the campground.

Contact: Pike and San Isabel National Forests, Leadville District, 719/486-0749, www.fs.usda.gov/psicc.

30 WHITESTAR

🥾 🚲 🏊 🛶 ⛵ 🐴 🚐 ⛺

Scenic rating: 8

on Twin Lakes Reservoir

Whitestar is a huge campground, but it doesn't feel that big because the three loops are completely separated from each other. Most of the campers are tourists heading over Independence Pass and southern Colorado residents who enjoy fishing. The campground is full on the weekends with boaters and anglers. If you want a good campsite, make a reservation. (For more information on Twin Lakes, see the Dexter Point listing later in this chapter.)

Sage Loop (sites 1-28) is right on the water and offers outstanding views of Twin Peaks, Mount Hope, and Quail Mountain. It's an arid habitat of sagebrush and pine, and shade and privacy are in short supply. Sites 6, 7, 10, 12, and 16 are closest to the water. Site 3 has a lot of shade.

Ridge Loop (sites 30-45) feels cramped, but there is more shade than in Sage Loop. It's a first-come, first-served area on a ridge overlooking Twin Lakes, but only a few sites (33, 35, 37, and 38) have good views. Sites 36-38 are walk-in. Sites 30, 31, 35, 37, 38, 43, and 44 have tent pads.

Valley Loop (sites 46-66) is farthest from the water and the least crowded of the three loops. The habitat is sagebrush, with some pine and aspen in a shallow dell. Sites 46, 48, 51, and 60-66 are shaded. Sites 63-66 are walk-in tent sites. Site 54 has nice views across the Arkansas River valley.

Campsites, facilities: There are 66 sites for tents and RVs up to 32 feet. There are no hookups. Sites 25, 56, and 59 are pull-through. Picnic tables, fire rings, and grills are provided at all sites. Tent pads are provided in the Sage Loop and at some sites in the Ridge Loop. Vault toilets, drinking water from hand pumps, lantern poles, a boat ramp, and a dump station are available. Leashed pets are permitted.

Reservations, fees: Reservations are accepted for the Sage and Valley Loops at 877/444-6777 and www.recreation.gov. The fee is $24 per night. Cash or check only. Open Memorial Day-late September.

Directions: From the intersection of U.S. Highway 24 and 6th Street in Leadville, take

U.S. 24 south for 15 miles. Turn right on Highway 82. In 5.5 miles, turn left into the campground.

Contact: Pike and San Isabel National Forests, Leadville District, 719/486-0749, www.fs.usda.gov/psicc.

31 LAKEVIEW
👫 🚴 🏊 🛶 🚤 🐕 🚐 ⛺

Scenic rating: 8

on Twin Lakes Reservoir

Lakeview contains eight terraced loops on a steep hill overlooking Twin Lakes. Each loop has its own personality. This campground is popular with tent campers and pop-up owners. The Colorado Trail passes by the campground, and hikers and mountain bikers can take it to the Mount Elbert and Interlocken Loop Trails. Fishing, boating, and swimming are a mile away at Twin Lakes. (For more information on Twin Lakes, see the Dexter Point listing in this chapter.)

Loop A has 14 sites in a young, dense pine forest. It can be hard to find enough flat spots for several tents, but sites 7-9, 12, and 14 have tent pads. Site 10 has views of Twin Peaks. Loop B has five sites, all with views of Twin Peaks and Twin Lakes. Sites 2 and 5 have tent pads. Loop C has eight sites packed tightly together. There is no privacy or views. Sites 3 and 8 have tent pads. Loop D has seven cozy sites in an aspen grove. It's great for large-group reservations. Sites 2 and 4-6 have good views. Loop E is my favorite. There are 13 roomy sites, most with excellent views. Site 9 is the best. Loop F is equally inviting but smaller and more private. Sites 3 and 6 have good views. Loop G is in a more mature pine forest. Sites 1, 2, 4, and 6 have good views. Loop H is similar to Loop G, but it's next to the Colorado and Mount Elbert Trails. Sites 3, 7, and 10 have good views.

Campsites, facilities: There are 59 sites for tents and RVs up to 32 feet. There are no hookups. Site C2 is pull-through. Picnic tables, fire rings, grills, and some tent pads are provided. Vault toilets and drinking water are available. Leashed pets are permitted.

Reservations, fees: Reservations are accepted at 877/444-6777 and www.recreation.gov. The fee is $23 per night. Cash or check only. Open Memorial Day-Labor Day.

Directions: From the intersection of U.S. Highway 24 and 6th Street in Leadville, take U.S. 24 south for 15 miles. Turn right on Highway 82. In 4.0 miles, turn right on County Road 24. In 1.0 mile, turn left into the campground.

Contact: Pike and San Isabel National Forests, Leadville District, 719/486-0749, www.fs.usda.gov/psicc.

32 DEXTER
👫 🚴 🏊 🛶 🚤 🐕 🚐 ⛺

Scenic rating: 6

on Twin Lakes Reservoir

The Twin Lakes Reservoir is at the foot of Mount Elbert in the Arkansas River valley. It's been a popular summer vacation destination since the 1860s, when a resort was built on the shore of Colorado's largest glaciated lake. In the late 1890s, a dam was built and the lake became a reservoir. Today, it's a summer destination for boaters, water-sports enthusiasts, anglers, hikers, and mountain bikers. The scenery and recreation are outstanding, but the weekend crowds can be overwhelming.

Dexter (or "Dexter Point") is a campground for boaters and desperate campers who can't find a spot anywhere else at the popular Twin Lakes reservoir. The campground is a large gravel parking lot surrounded by sagebrush. On the lakeside, there are 12 walk-in tent sites with picnic tables, grills, and fire rings. A few sites are on a hill overlooking the lake and have excellent views. Sites 12-24 are on the far side of the parking lot and do not have tables or tent sites. They are strictly for RV camping. Hikers and mountain bikers have access to the 12-mile Interlocken Loop around the lake.

Campsites, facilities: There are 12 sites for tents and 12 sites for RVs up to 37 feet. There are no hookups. Picnic tables, fire rings, and grills are provided at sites 1-12. Vault toilets and a boat ramp are available. Leashed pets are permitted.

Reservations, fees: Reservations are not accepted. The fee is $20 per night. Cash or check only. Open Memorial Day-Labor Day.

Directions: From the intersection of U.S. Highway 24 and 6th Street in Leadville, take U.S. 24 south for 15 miles. Turn right on Highway 82. In 2.3 miles, turn left into the campground.

Contact: Pike and San Isabel National Forests, Leadville District, 719/486-0749, www.fs.usda.gov/psicc.

33 RAILROAD BRIDGE

Scenic rating: 7

north of Buena Vista

The Arkansas Headwaters Recreation Area stretches from the headwaters of the Arkansas River (at Fremont Pass and Tennessee Pass) all the way to Lake Pueblo State Park. It contains some of the finest white water in the state, as well as views of the Collegiate Peaks and portions of the Sawatch Range. From Leadville to Salida, the semiarid Arkansas River valley has endless vistas of fourteeners and fascinating weather patterns. Buena Vista and Salida, with their restaurants, art galleries, bars, and sports stores, are great towns to hang out in for a weekend.

Colorado State Parks manages six campgrounds on the river, all of which are reservation only. Railroad Bridge is the northernmost of the six. Located at the take-out for the Numbers, a classic Class IV white-water run,

this campground is not quite as swamped with commercial rafting companies as other campgrounds farther downstream. Railroad Bridge is also the put-in for the mellower Fractions/Frog Rock Run. Campers who are lucky enough to snag a walk-in site (sites 9-14) or sites 7 and 8 will be content. Sites 1-6 are less appealing, lacking shade and privacy. Some campers still try their hand at gold panning in the river here.

Campsites, facilities: There are 14 sites for tents and RVs up to 40 feet and six tent-only sites. There are no hookups. Sites 1, 2, and 4 are pull-through. Picnic tables, fire rings, grills, and tent pads are provided. Vault toilets, changing rooms, a group picnic area, and a boat ramp are available. Trash must be packed out. Leashed pets are permitted. Site 3 and the facilities are wheelchair-accessible.

Reservations, fees: Reservations are required; make them at 800/244-5613 or www.cpwshop.com. The fee is $28 per night. Campers must also purchase a vehicle pass ($8) or an Annual Parks Pass ($80). Open year-round.

Directions: In Buena Vista, drive east on Main Street. Turn left on Colorado Avenue. In 6.2 miles, turn left into the campground.

Contact: Arkansas Headwaters Recreation Area, 719/539-7289, www.cpw.state.co.us.

34 TWIN EAGLES

Scenic rating: 6

north of Lake George

Twin Eagles sits at an elevation of 8,600 feet beside the southwestern boundary of the Lost Creek Wilderness, a landscape of granite domes and buttresses. There are three mountain ranges in the wilderness: Tarryall Mountains, Kenosha Mountains, and Platte River Mountains. The mountains are covered in dense forests and open parks. Twin Eagles is an afterthought of a campground at the Twin

Eagles trailhead. From this location, hikers heading into the wilderness have several options. They can complete a 16-mile loop around Lake Park, which has some of the best views in the wilderness, or they can head north on the Brookside-McCurdy Trail. This 31-mile trail traverses the entire length of the wilderness and crosses all three mountain ranges. It can be connected with several other trails to make a loop hike.

Campsites, facilities: There are nine sites for tents and RVs up to 22 feet; a few sites are walk-in. There are no hookups. Picnic tables, fire rings, and grills d are provided. Vault toilets are available. Trash must be packed out and there is no potable water. Leashed pets are permitted.

Reservations, fees: Reservations are not accepted. The fee is $15 per night plus a $3 trailhead parking fee. Cash or check only. Open year-round.

Directions: From Woodland Park, take U.S. Highway 24 west to Lake George. Go north on County Road 77 for 16.2 miles. Turn right at the trailhead sign.

Contact: Pike and San Isabel National Forests, South Park District, 719/836-2031, www.fs.usda.gov/psicc.

35 SPRUCE GROVE

Scenic rating: 7

north of Lake George

Spruce Grove is larger and nicer than nearby Twin Eagles. The campground sits on Tarryall Creek in a small park with granite outcroppings and views of South Tarryall Peak. The sites are in the willows beside the creek or in the meadow at the base of a granite cliff. There are scattered pine trees but not much shade. This is a high-use campground on weekends. Many visitors are there to explore the Lost Creek Wilderness, a 120,000-acre landscape of granite domes and spires with three mountain ranges

and numerous high-altitude parks. From the Twin Eagles trailhead hikers can complete a 16-mile loop around Lost Park or head north on the Brookside-McCurdy Trail, a 31-mile route that traverses the length of the wilderness. The area is home to a healthy bighorn population, as well as bear, mountain lion, and elk.

Campsites, facilities: There are 27 sites for tents and RVs up to 35 feet. Sites 3-10 are walk-ins. There are no hookups. Sites 22, 25, and 27 are pull-through. Picnic tables, fire rings, grills, and tent pads are provided. Vault toilets and a drinking water pump are available. Leashed pets are permitted.

Reservations, fees: Reservations are accepted at 877/444-6777 and www.recreation.gov. The fee is $17 per night. Cash or check only. Open early May-early October.

Directions: From Woodland Park, take U.S. Highway 24 west to Lake George. Go north on County Road 77 for 13.7 miles. Turn right at the campground sign and then right after the cattle guard.

Contact: Pike and San Isabel National Forests, South Park District, 719/836-2031, www.fs.usda.gov/psicc.

36 ROUND MOUNTAIN

Scenic rating: 5

west of Lake George

Round Mountain is a stopover campground between Colorado Springs and South Park. The campground is on a low hill in a forest of scattered pines and grassland. The sites are about 100 feet apart around a large gravel loop. ATV owners make up most of the traffic at this campground. They can explore a network of Jeep trails in the Puma Hills and Tarryall Mountains. There are no hiking or biking trails nearby.

Campsites, facilities: There are 16 sites for tents and RVs up to 35 feet. There are no

hookups. Picnic tables, fire rings, and grills are provided. Vault toilets and drinking water are available. Trash must be packed out. Leashed pets are permitted.

Reservations, fees: Reservations are accepted at 877/444-6777 and www.recreation.gov. The fee is $17 per night. Cash or check only. Open early May-early October (or earlier).

Directions: From Woodland Park, take U.S. Highway 24 west to Lake George. The campground is 5.7 miles west of Lake George on the north side of the highway.

Contact: Pike and San Isabel National Forests, South Park District, 719/836-2031, www. fs.usda.gov/psicc.

37 HAPPY MEADOWS
🏊 🐕 🚐 ⛺

Scenic rating: 6
north of Lake George

Happy Meadows is a dirt bike and fishing destination north of the popular Eleven Mile Recreation Area. The campground is in a valley on the South Platte River, surrounded by forested ridgelines and rocky outcroppings. Privacy is fair to poor in this small campground. Sites 1, 2, 4, and 7-10 are creekside, and sites 7-8 and 9-10 are buddy sites. In addition to fishing on the river, anglers can drive to Eleven Mile for lake fishing or to the nearby Lost Creek Wilderness for backcountry hiking and climbing.

Campsites, facilities: There are 10 sites for tents and RVs up to 20 feet. There are no hookups. Picnic tables, fire rings, and grills are provided. Vault toilets and drinking water (hand pump) are available. Leashed pets are permitted.

Reservations, fees: Reservations are accepted at 877/444-6777 and www.recreation.gov. The fee is $17 per night. Cash or check only. Open early May-early October.

Directions: From Woodland Park, take U.S.

Highway 24 west to Lake George. Go north on County Road 77 for 1.3 miles. Turn right at the campground sign. The campground is on the right in 1.0 mile.

Contact: Pike and San Isabel National Forests, South Park District, 719/836-2031, www. fs.usda.gov/psicc.

38 ROCKY RIDGE
🏊 🚣 🏊 ❄️ 🐕 ♿ 🚐 ⛺

Scenic rating: 6
in Eleven Mile State Park

Eleven Mile State Park is an angler's paradise surrounded by Pike and San Isabel National Forests. Located on the southern edge of South Park, the 3,400-surface-acre reservoir is fed by the South Platte River as well as Cross, Prudence, Union, Balm-of-Gilead, Simms, and Spring Creeks. These creeks drain Thirtynine Mile Mountain to the south and the Tarryall Mountains to the north. Every spot in the park offers scenic vistas of the lake, the grasslands, and the mountains, which seem to change constantly with time of day and season. The views and recreational opportunities make this park a year-round destination. The lake offers trophy fishing for kokanee salmon, cutthroat, rainbow trout, northern pike, and carp. Water sports include boating, windsurfing, and personal-watercraft riding (but swimming is prohibited). Winter visitors go ice fishing, ice-skating, ice boating, and cross-country skiing. The park also has five miles of trails open to hiking, biking, and riding, including a 1.4-mile interpretive trail. The climate is arid and subalpine, so trees are few and far between, clinging to spots of soil around boulders and outcroppings. There are nine campgrounds at the park. They all have excellent views but little shade and shelter so plan accordingly.

Rocky Ridge is the largest and most developed of the campgrounds with five loops. Loops C and E have the most shade. Loop A (sites 1-10) is closest to the campers' services building. It has hookups but no views and mainly attracts RVs. Loop B (sites 11-26) also has electric hookups. It's in a low spot that obscures the other loops, but the lake is still visible. Loop C (sites 27-73) surrounds a granite outcropping. It has great views and some shade at sites 28, 33, 44, 47, 53, 56, and 73. Loop D (sites 74-99) is very flat. It has views but no shade or privacy. Loop E (sites 100-144) also has large boulders and outcroppings, but it's farthest from the lake. The walk-in sites (117-120) are more private and have shade.

Campsites, facilities: There are 144 sites for tents and RVs up to 35 feet. Sites 117-120 are walk-in tent sites. Sites 1-26 and 74-99 have electric hookups. Picnic tables, fire rings, and grills are provided. Restrooms with flush toilets and showers, vault toilets, laundry facilities, drinking water, and new dump stations are available. At nearby North Shore campground, there is a marina with rentals and a boat ramp, a playground, and amphitheater. Leashed pets are permitted. Sites 1 and 2 and the facilities are wheelchair-accessible.

Reservations, fees: Reservations are accepted at 800/244-5613 or www.cpwshop.com (calling from the Denver area, dial 303/470-1144). The fee is $28 per night for basic, $36 for electric. Campers must also purchase a vehicle pass ($8) or Annual Parks Pass ($80). Loop A is open year-round. The other loops are open from late spring to early fall.

Directions: From Lake George, take County Road 90 south for 4.1 miles. Turn left on County Road 92. The park office is in 6.0 miles. The campground is behind the park office.

Contact: Eleven Mile State Park, 719/748-3401, www.cpw.state.co.us.

39 NORTH SHORE

Scenic rating: 6

in Eleven Mile State Park

North Shore is the campground for avid boaters and anglers. Located next to the marina, it has fantastic views of the lake and surrounding mountains but very little protection from the strong winds and intense sunshine that are typical of this park. There are almost no trees in this campground because the arid, subalpine climate does not provide adequate soil. Most of the sites are on grassland interrupted by granite outcroppings. Loop A (sites 201-217) is next to the parking lot and is the least appealing. Loop B (sites 218-239) is a little hillier and rockier than the other loops. Loop C (sites 240-249) is on a rocky promontory overlooking the lake. Loop D and Loop E (sites 250-281) are surrounded by short, dry grass. (For more information on Eleven Mile State Park, see the Rocky Ridge listing in this chapter.)

Campsites, facilities: There are 81 sites for tents and RVs up to 45 feet. Site 239 is wheelchair-accessible. There are no hookups. Sites 226, 228, 229, 240-243, 245, 251, 254, 256, 265, and 266 are pull-through. Picnic tables, fire rings, and grills are provided. Vault toilets, drinking water, a marina with a boat ramp and rentals, a playground, and an amphitheater are available. Restrooms with flush toilets and showers, laundry facilities, and dump stations are available at the park office, a short drive away. Leashed pets are permitted.

Reservations, fees: Reservations are accepted at 800/244-5613 or www.cpwshop.com. The fee is $28 per night. Campers must also purchase a vehicle pass ($8) or Annual Parks Pass ($80). Open year-round.

Directions: From Lake George, take County Road 90 south for 4.1 miles. Turn left on County Road 92. The park office is in 6.0 miles. The campground is across from the park office.

Contact: Eleven Mile State Park, 719/748-3401, www.cpw.state.co.us.

40 STOLL MOUNTAIN

Scenic rating: 6

in Eleven Mile State Park

Stoll Mountain is on the north shore of Eleven Mile Reservoir, about halfway between the park office and Spinney Mountain State Park. This is the smallest campground on the north shore, and for that reason, it's attractive to some campers and unattractive to others. It has two gravel loops close to the water, and the gentle shoreline is perfect for fishing from the shore and launching canoes. The views are amazing, but there is no privacy. The campground is in a shortgrass prairie with absolutely no trees, and the sites are just 15-30 feet apart. Mostly small RVs and pop-ups use this campground. Sites 305-308 and 319-325 are closest to the water. (For more information on Eleven Mile State Park, see the Rocky Ridge listing in this chapter.)

Campsites, facilities: There are 25 sites for tents and RVs up to 35 feet. There are no hookups. Sites 313, 316, and 320-323 are pull-through. Picnic tables, fire rings, and grills are provided. Sites 311, 313, and 315 have sun shelters. Vault toilets and drinking water are available. Restrooms with flush toilets and showers, laundry facilities, and dump stations, are available 2.5 miles down the road at the park office. Leashed pets are permitted.

Reservations, fees: Reservations are accepted at 800/244-5613 or www.cpwshop.com. The fee is $28 per night. Campers must also purchase a vehicle pass ($8) or Annual Parks Pass ($80). Open year-round.

Directions: From Lake George, take County Road 90 south for 4.1 miles. Turn left on County Road 92. The park office is in 6.0 miles, and the campground is on the left 1.9 miles past the park office.

Contact: Eleven Mile State Park, 719/748-3401, www.cpw.state.co.us.

41 CROSS CREEK

Scenic rating: 7

in Eleven Mile State Park

BEST (

There are five small campgrounds on the south shore of massive Eleven Mile Canyon Reservoir. Cross Creek is at the west end of the lake, near the South Platte inlet, so anglers can try river and lake fishing at this location. The campground is protected by a low ridge to the south, and it has great views of Spinney Mountain to the west and the Tarryall Range to the north. The landscape is rolling grasslands, and there isn't a tree in sight. The nearest boat ramp is about six miles away, but canoes can launch from the shoreline. There are two loops. The second loop (sites 408-415) is next to Cross Creek and close to the ridge. Walk-in sites 411 and 412 are about 150 feet away from the rest of the campground. (For more information on Eleven Mile State Park, see the Rocky Ridge listing earlier in this chapter.)

Campsites, facilities: There are 15 sites for tents and RVs up to 35 feet. Sites 411 and 412 are walk-in tent sites. There are no hookups. Sites 408 and 414 are pull-through. Picnic tables, fire rings, and grills are provided. Vault toilets and drinking water are available. Leashed pets are permitted.

Reservations, fees: Reservations are accepted at 800/244-5613 or www.cpwshop.com. The fee is $28 per night. Campers must also purchase a vehicle pass ($8) or Annual Parks Pass ($80). Open year-round.

Directions: From Lake George, take County Road 90 south for 4.1 miles. Turn left on County Road 92. The park office is in 6.0 miles. From the office, drive west on County Road 92

for 5.3 miles. Turn left on County Road 59. The campground is on the left in 2.8 miles.
Contact: Eleven Mile State Park, 719/748-3401, www.cpw.state.co.us.

42 LAZY BOY

Scenic rating: 6

in Eleven Mile State Park

There are five small campgrounds on the south shore of Eleven Mile Reservoir. Lazy Boy and Rocking Chair are on a promontory near the middle of the lake. They are located on an arid, grassy plain without trees or shade, but the views of the Tarryall Range and the 3,400-surface-acre lake are outstanding. Lazy Boy has two loops. The first loop (sites 501-507) is close to the water and a walkway to an island that is closed to protect nesting birds. The second loop (sites 508-514) is farther from the water, near the anglers' parking. (For more information on Eleven Mile State Park, see the Rocky Ridge listing earlier in this chapter.)

Campsites, facilities: There are 14 sites for tents and RVs up to 35 feet. There are no hookups. Sites 501-503, 506, and 507 are pull-through. Picnic tables, fire rings, and grills are provided. Vault toilets and drinking water are available. Leashed pets are permitted.

Reservations, fees: Reservations are accepted at 800/244-5613 or www.cpwshop.com. The fee is $28 per night. Campers must also purchase a vehicle pass ($8) or Annual Parks Pass ($80). Open year-round.

Directions: From Lake George, take County Road 90 south for 4.1 miles. Turn left on County Road 92. The park office is in 6.0 miles. From the office, drive west on County Road 92 for 5.3 miles. Turn left on County Road 59. In 5.5 miles, turn left at the campground sign. In 0.3 mile, turn left at the stop sign. The campground is in 0.4 mile.

Contact: Eleven Mile State Park, 719/748-3401, www.cpw.state.co.us.

43 ROCKING CHAIR

Scenic rating: 6

in Eleven Mile State Park

There are five small campgrounds on the south shore of Eleven Mile Reservoir. Lazy Boy and Rocking Chair are on a promontory near the middle of the lake. They are located on an arid, grassy plain without trees or shade, but Rocking Chair has 360-degree views of the Tarryall Range, Thirtynine Mile Mountain, and the lake. The nearest boat ramp is at Witcher Cove, but the gentle shoreline is open to fishing and launching hand-powered boats. Rocking Chair has two loops. The first loop (sites 601-609) is closest to the water. Only self-contained camping units are allowed at the second loop (sites 610-613) because there is no vault toilet. (For more information on Eleven Mile State Park, see the Rocky Ridge listing earlier in this chapter.)

Campsites, facilities: There are 13 sites for tents and RVs up to 35 feet. There are no hookups. Site 601 is pull-through. Picnic tables, fire rings, and grills are provided. Sites 604 and 609 have sun shelters. Vault toilets and drinking water are available. Leashed pets are permitted.

Reservations, fees: Reservations are accepted at 800/244-5613 or www.cpwshop.com. The fee is $28 per night. Campers must also purchase a vehicle pass ($8) or Annual Parks Pass ($80). Open year-round.

Directions: From Lake George, take County Road 90 south for 4.1 miles. Turn left on County Road 92. The park office is in 6.0 miles. From the office, drive west on County Road 92 for 5.3 miles. Turn left on County Road 59. In 5.5 miles, turn left at the campground sign. In 0.3 mile, turn right at the stop sign. The campground is in 0.4 mile.

Contact: Eleven Mile State Park, 719/748-3401, www.cpw.state.co.us.

44 HOWBERT POINT

Scenic rating: 6

in Eleven Mile State Park

Howbert Point is on a small promontory near the middle of Eleven Mile Reservoir. The campground is on an arid grassland, with views of the east end of the lake and the Tarryall Range. There are no trees, and the sites are just 10-20 feet apart, so privacy is in short supply. Sites 709 and 710 are slightly apart from the rest of the campground and are the most appealing. The nearest boat ramp is two miles away, at Witcher Cove. (For more information on Eleven Mile State Park, see the Rocky Ridge listing earlier in this chapter.)

Campsites, facilities: There are 10 sites for tents and RVs up to 35 feet. There are no hookups. Picnic tables, fire rings, and grills are provided. Vault toilets and drinking water are available. Leashed pets are permitted. Facilities are wheelchair-accessible.

Reservations, fees: Reservations are accepted at 800/244-5613 or www.cpwshop.com. The fee is $28 per night. Campers must also purchase a vehicle pass ($8) or Annual Parks Pass ($80). Open year-round.

Directions: From Lake George, take County Road 90 south for 4.1 miles. Turn left on County Road 92. The park office is in 6.0 miles. From the office, drive west on County Road 92 for 5.3 miles. Turn left on County Road 59. The campground is on the left in 7.0 miles.

Contact: Eleven Mile State Park, 719/748-3401, www.cpw.state.co.us.

45 WITCHER'S COVE

Scenic rating: 7

in Eleven Mile State Park

There are five campgrounds on the south shore of Eleven Mile Reservoir. At the east end of the lake, Witcher's Cove sprawls along the shoreline, allowing more privacy than at most of the other campgrounds. The views include the rocky north shore and the Tarryall Range. Sites 802 and 803 are close to the boat ramp and slightly separate from the rest of the campground. Sites 804-807 are surrounded by short grass prairie with granite outcroppings. Sites 809-812 are on a slight rise with awesome views. Sites 818-822 are in a small loop almost a mile from the first sites. They are close to the water and have good views. (For more information on Eleven Mile State Park, see the Rocky Ridge listing earlier in this chapter.)

Campsites, facilities: There are 22 sites for tents and RVs up to 35 feet. There are no hookups. Sites 801, 809, and 810 are pull-through. Picnic tables, fire rings, and grills are provided. Vault toilets, drinking water, a boat ramp, and dump stations, are available. Leashed pets are permitted.

Reservations, fees: Reservations are accepted at 800/244-5613 or www.cpwshop.com. The fee is $28 per night. Campers must also purchase a vehicle pass ($8) or Annual Parks Pass ($80). Open year-round.

Directions: From Lake George, take County Road 90 south for 4.1 miles. Turn left on County Road 92. The park office is in 6.0 miles. From the office, drive west on County Road 92 for 5.3 miles. Turn left on County Road 59. In 8.5 miles, turn left at the Witcher Cove sign.

Contact: Eleven Mile State Park, 719/748-3401, www.cpw.state.co.us.

46 BACKCOUNTRY
🏃 🚴 🛶 ⛵ 🚣 ❄ 🐕 ⛺

Scenic rating: 9
in Eleven Mile State Park

BEST (

Backcountry is one of the best features of Eleven Mile State Park. Designed for walk-in and boat-in tent camping, this campground is on a rocky promontory between Corral Cove and Fresh Water Cove on the north shore of Eleven Mile Reservoir. Granite outcroppings and pine, spruce, aspen, and fir trees interrupt the grassland that dominates the rest of the park. Corral Cove is considered one of the most beautiful locations in the park, especially at sunrise and sunset. The sites are grouped in twos and threes, and are screened and shaded by trees and boulders. Most of them have excellent views of the south shore and east end of the lake. Sites 910, 911, 916, and 922 are alone and have the most privacy. In addition to fishing, campers can enjoy hiking and biking on the five miles of trails on the promontory, including the 1.5-mile Coyote Ridge Interpretive Trail. Midland, the longest trail, circumnavigates a large wetland. (For more information on Eleven Mile State Park, see the Rocky Ridge listing earlier in this chapter.)

Campsites, facilities: There are 25 walk-in and boat-in tent sites. Hike-in sites are about 0.5-0.75 mile in. Picnic tables, fire rings, and grills are provided. Vault toilets and drinking water are available. Leashed pets are permitted.

Reservations, fees: Reservations are accepted at 800/244-5613 or www.cpwshop.com. The fee is $28 per night. Campers must also purchase a vehicle pass ($8) or Annual Parks Pass ($80). Open year-round.

Directions: From Lake George, take County Road 90 south for 4.1 miles. Turn left on County Road 92. The park office is in 6.0 miles. Turn left out of the parking lot. In 0.3 mile, turn right at the Coyote Ridge sign. The parking area is in 0.4 mile.

Contact: Eleven Mile State Park, 719/748-3401, www.cpw.state.co.us.

47 RIVERSIDE
🛶 🏕 🚐 ⛺

Scenic rating: 5
south of Lake George

Eleven Mile Canyon is a surprising find in the gentle rolling hills east of South Park. From Eleven Mile Canyon Reservoir to the town of Lake George, the South Platte River descends 500 feet, carving a narrow, wild canyon out of Pikes Peak granite. The steep walls, huge boulders, and cascading river are a dramatic sight, and when the water is high enough, anglers will find good fishing along the banks.

Riverside is the first of four campgrounds in the canyon. Fishing access is excellent, but like all of these campgrounds, Riverside is squeezed into a narrow area between the canyon walls and the river, so the sites are close to each other and the road. The RV sites in the meadow have minimal privacy. Tent campers will be pleasantly surprised, however, by walk-in sites located among pine trees on a slight hill.

Campsites, facilities: There are 19 sites for tents and RVs up to 30 feet. Sites 2-6 and 14-19 are walk-in. There are no hookups. Sites 10 and 13 are pull-through. Picnic tables, fire rings, and grills are provided. Vault toilets and drinking water are available. Leashed pets are permitted.

Reservations, fees: Reservations are accepted at 877/444-6777 and www.recreation.gov. The fee is $17 per night. Cash or check only. Open early May-early October.

Directions: From Woodland Park, take U.S. Highway 24 west to Lake George. Go south on County Road 96. The fee station is in 1.0 mile. The campground is on the left 1.0 mile after the station.

Contact: Pike and San Isabel National Forests,

South Park District, 719/836-2031, www. fs.usda.gov/psicc.

48 SPRINGER GULCH

Scenic rating: 6

south of Lake George

There are four campgrounds in Eleven Mile Canyon. The second, Springer Gulch, is farthest from the river, but it's also very scenic. Sites 1-3 are near the road and lack shade, but the other sites are in a narrow gulch decked with pine trees and huge granite boulders. It's a great place for rock scrambling, and it has more shade than the other campgrounds. Sites 7-10, at the back of the campground, are the most appealing. (For more information on Eleven Mile Canyon, see the Riverside listing in this chapter.)

Campsites, facilities: There are 15 sites for tents and RVs up to 25 feet. There are no hookups. Picnic tables, fire rings, and grills are provided. Vault toilets and drinking water are available. Leashed pets are permitted.

Reservations, fees: Reservations are accepted at 877/444-6777 and www.recreation.gov. The fee is $17 per night. Cash or check only. Open early May-early October.

Directions: From Woodland Park, take U.S. Highway 24 west to Lake George. Go south on County Road 96. The fee station is in 1.0 mile. The campground is on the right 5.5 miles after the station.

Contact: Pike and San Isabel National Forests, South Park District, 719/836-2031, www. fs.usda.gov/psicc.

49 COVE

Scenic rating: 6

south of Lake George

The third campground in Eleven Mile Canyon, Cove, is small and sweet at an elevation of 9,000 feet. Set in a slight widening of the canyon, Cove has four riverside sites. Site 1 is a walk-in with privacy and the best river access. Sites 3 and 4 are located next to one of the granite outcroppings that characterize the canyon and are screened by trees and boulders. Site 2 is closest to the road and the least appealing. Because of its size, this campground is very popular, and reservations are highly recommended. (For more information on Eleven Mile Canyon, see the Riverside listing in this chapter.)

Campsites, facilities: There are four sites for tents and RVs up to 16 feet. There are no hookups. Picnic tables, fire rings, and grills are provided. Vault toilets and drinking water are available. Leashed pets are permitted.

Reservations, fees: Reservations are accepted at 877/444-6777 and www.recreation.gov. The fee is $17 per night. Cash or check only. Open early May-early October.

Directions: From Woodland Park, take U.S. Highway 24 west to Lake George. Go south on County Road 96. The fee station is in 1.0 mile. The campground is on the right 8.1 miles after the station.

Contact: Pike and San Isabel National Forests, South Park District, 719/836-2031, www. fs.usda.gov/psicc.

50 SPILLWAY

Scenic rating: 7

south of Lake George

Spillway is the last and largest campground in Eleven Mile Canyon. The scenery is dramatic.

It includes the dam, surrounded by tall granite cliffs, and the boulders and outcroppings that form the mouth of the canyon. A 0.5-mile trail climbs steeply to an overlook with panoramic views of the reservoir and the Tarryall Mountains. The sites are fairly close together, and the campground is usually busy. Sites 3-6 and 11-13 are walk-ins. Sites 13 and 14 have enviable views of the river. Sites 16-18, 20, 22, and 24 are also close to the water. (For more information on Eleven Mile Canyon, see the Riverside listing in this chapter.)

Campsites, facilities: There are 24 sites for tents and RVs up to 25 feet. There are no hookups. Sites 17-18, 20, 22, and 24 are pull-through. Picnic tables, fire rings, and grills are provided. Vault toilets, drinking water, and an amphitheater are available. Leashed pets are permitted.

Reservations, fees: Reservations are accepted at 877/444-6777 and www.recreation.gov. The fee is $17 per night. Cash or check only. Open early May-early October.

Directions: From Woodland Park, take U.S. Highway 24 west to Lake George. Go south on County Road 96. The fee station is in 1.0 mile. The campground is on the right 8.4 miles after the station.

Contact: Pike and San Isabel National Forests, South Park District, 719/836-2031, www.fs.usda.gov/psicc.

51 BLUE MOUNTAIN
🏃 🏕 �car 🏕

Scenic rating: 6
south of Lake George

Blue Mountain is a small, quiet campground slightly removed from the tumult of Eleven Mile Canyon and Eleven Mile State Park. The campground is in a dense pine forest on a slightly rolling landscape at an elevation of about 8,200 feet. Sites 1, 10, and 19-21 have nice views of the surrounding valley and the ridgelines of the Tarryall Mountains to the

north. The Hard Rock Trail leads from the campground to a canyon overlook. Fishing is a short drive away in the canyon and at the state park. Campers also take day trips to the mining museums and casinos of Cripple Creek and Victor. Florissant Fossil Beds National Monument is also nearby. Visitors can see the fossilized remains of plants, insects, and small mammals preserved in ash that fell on the ancient lake bed. The ash probably came from the Thirtynine Mile volcanic field at the southern end of South Park. Although quiet midweek, this campground usually fills up by Friday night.

Campsites, facilities: There are 21 sites for tents and RVs up to 25 feet. There are no hookups. Sites 2 and 19 are pull-through. Picnic tables, fire rings, and grills are provided. Vault toilets are available. There is no drinking water. Leashed pets are permitted.

Reservations, fees: Reservations are accepted at 877/444-6777 and www.recreation.gov. The fee is $17 per night. Cash or check only. Open early May-early October.

Directions: From Woodland Park, take U.S. Highway 24 west to Lake George. Go south on County Road 96. In 0.9 mile, turn left on County Road 61. The campground is on the right in 0.6 mile.

Contact: Pike and San Isabel National Forests, South Park District, 719/836-2031, www.fs.usda.gov/psicc.

52 COLLEGIATE PEAKS
🏃 🚶 🏕 �car 🏕

Scenic rating: 8
west of Buena Vista

BEST (

Collegiate Peaks is halfway between Buena Vista and Cottonwood Pass (elevation 12,126 feet). It's an ideal base camp for hikers interested in summiting Mount Yale, Mount Harvard, and Mount Columbia. The Colorado Trail passes less than two miles south of the campground, and the Browns Pass Trail, which connects to the Mount Yale and Hartenstein Lake Trails, begins nearby. Middle Cottonwood Creek borders the campground and offers good trout fishing. The campground is popular with tent and RV campers and is very busy on weekends and holidays. Most of the sites are in a spruce-fir forest. The roomy sites are about 100 feet apart. The back loop (sites 24-34) is in a young aspen grove, and the sites are closer together. Sites 29 and 31 have views up the valley. The following sites are next to the creek: 8, 10, 12, 15, 16, 19, 20, 22, 29, 31, 33, A, B, D, E, G, I, and J.

Campsites, facilities: There are 56 sites for tents and RVs up to 50 feet. There are no hookups. Sites O and 14 are pull-through. Picnic tables, fire rings, and grills are provided. Vault toilets and drinking water are available. Leashed pets are permitted.

Reservations, fees: Reservations are accepted (and highly recommended) at 877/444-6777 and www.recreation.gov. The fee is $20 per night. Cash or check only. Open late May-early September.

Directions: From Buena Vista, take Cottonwood Pass Road/County Road 306 west for 11 miles. The campground entrance is on the left.

Contact: Pike and San Isabel National Forests, Salida District, 719/539-3591, www.fs.usda.gov/psicc.

53 BUENA VISTA KOA

Scenic rating: 6

east of Buena Vista

Located a few miles east of Johnson Village, the Buena Vista KOA has been here since 1965 and completely lives up to its name, with incredible westward views of Mount Princeton and the Collegiate Range. It's used as both a stopover and a base camp, as there are endless outdoor activities in this area. Campers

sunset behind the Collegiate Peaks from Buena Vista KOA

whitewater rafting on the Arkansas River

usually spend their days rafting the Arkansas River, driving up to ghost towns, or heading to Princeton Hot Springs. It's also popular with family groups. The tent sites at the west end of the campground have the best views and some nice rock features. On the downside, there is no river access and minimal shade overall (a few piñon pines); on the plus side, there is foot access to trails on neighboring BLM land and some very nice services at the campground.

Campsites, facilities: There are 42 sites for tents and RVs up to 85 feet and 27 tent-only sites. There are a couple of nice cabins and wall tents as well. Picnic tables and fire grills are provided. Restrooms with showers, a laundry room, an RV dump station, a playground, and Internet access are available. Facilities include a rec room, a sand volleyball court, basketball, and horseshoes. Breakfast is served summer mornings in the Cook Shack. Leashed pets are permitted.

Reservations, fees: Reservations are accepted at 800/562-2672. The fee is $37 per night for a tent site for two people. A site with full hookups

is $55-60 per night (cabins from $75). Cash or check only. Open year round.

Directions: South of Buena Vista, take Highway 24 to turn east onto US 24/285. Continue 1.3 miles and turn left (north) on CR 303.

Contact: Buena Vista KOA, 27700 County Road 303, 800/562-2672 or 719/395-8318, www.koa.com.

54 COTTONWOOD LAKE

Scenic rating: 8

west of Buena Vista

BEST (

Cottonwood Lake has enough activities to keep the whole family happy. The lake and South Cottonwood Creek offer good fishing and hand-powered boating. The Colorado Trail, open to hikers and bikers, is a short drive away. ATV riding and four-wheeling are very popular north of the lake. Plus, it's 18.3 miles from Mount Princeton Hot Springs Resort, perfect for soaking those tired muscles. The campground is a large gravel loop in an aspen grove on a hill that slopes toward the lake. The large sites are terraced and many have stairs. The sites on the top of the loop have good views and more privacy. Those on the bottom of the loop are close to the road and ATV traffic.

Campsites, facilities: There are 24 sites for tents and RVs up to 35 feet. There are no hookups. Picnic tables, fire rings, grills, lantern posts, and tent pads are provided. Vault toilets and drinking water are available. Leashed pets are permitted.

Reservations, fees: Reservations are not accepted. The fee is $22 per night. Cash or check only. Open late May-early September.

Directions: From Buena Vista, take Cottonwood Pass Road/County Road 306 west for seven miles. Turn left on Forest Route 344. The campground is on the right in 4.0 miles.

Contact: Pike and San Isabel National Forests, Salida District, 719/539-3591, www.fs.usda.gov/psicc.

55 RUBY MOUNTAIN

Scenic rating: 8

south of Buena Vista

BEST (

The Arkansas Headwaters Recreation Area stretches from the headwaters of the Arkansas River (at Fremont Pass and Tennessee Pass) all the way to Lake Pueblo State Park. Colorado State Parks manages six campgrounds on the Arkansas River; Ruby Mountain is the second of the six. Like the other campgrounds, it attracts heaps of kayakers and rafters. Ruby Mountain is a put-in for Brown's Canyon, possibly the most popular Class III run in all of Colorado. (Brown's Canyon was designated a National Monument in 2015.) But Ruby Mountain also appeals to hikers, mountain bikers, and ATV riders interested in exploring

the BLM-managed Four Mile Recreation Area. With all this recreation, the campground can be quite a scene on summer weekends, but the views of Mount Princeton and Mount Antero are absolutely stunning and worth every overheard conversation. The campground is a popular site for small weddings and "adventure weddings" (the entire party boards boats to go rafting after the ceremony). Campers should bring a tarp for shade. If you're not lucky enough to get a spot on the river, it can get very hot on a sunny day.

Sites 1-8 have great views but no shade. Sites 5-7 also have excellent views, and they are terraced and have a little more privacy. Sites 12-14 are right next to the parking lot and should be avoided. Sites 15-20 are walk-in sites beside the river in the shade of the cottonwoods. Sites 21 and 22 are in a small canyon a short walk from the river. These secluded sites have heaps of privacy and shade.

Campsites, facilities: There are 22 sites for tents and RVs up to 40 feet and six tent-only sites. There are no hookups. Site 9 is pull-through. Picnic tables, fire rings, grills, and tent pads are provided. Vault toilets, changing rooms, a small amphitheater, and a boat ramp are available. Trash must be packed out. Leashed pets are permitted. Site 11 and the facilities are wheelchair-accessible.

Reservations, fees: Reservations are required; make them at 800/244-5613 or www.cpwshop.com. The fee is $28 per night. Campers must also purchase a vehicle pass ($8) or an Annual Parks Pass ($80). Open year-round.

Directions: In Buena Vista, from the intersection of U.S. Highway 24 and Cottonwood Pass Road, travel south on Highway 24 for 5.9 miles. Turn left on County Road 301. In 0.5 mile, turn right on County Road 300. The Ruby Mountain Recreation Site is on the right in 2.3 miles.

Contact: Arkansas Headwaters Recreation Area, 719/539-7289, www.cpw.state.co.us.

56 IRON CITY

Scenic rating: 7

west of Buena Vista

BEST (

Iron City is the highest of the four campgrounds on the road to St. Elmo. The distance deters many campers, but it is very popular with ATV riders who can unload their vehicles in this campground but not at the others. Mountain bikers will also love this location. The network of forest roads and trails provides access to alpine valleys and the Continental Divide. To many mountain bikers, these lung-busting rides are as good as it gets. Hikers should take advantage of the 6.5-mile Poplar Gulch Trail, which offers vistas of the Sawatch Range. There is good fishing in Chalk Creek between Alpine Lake and St. Elmo, especially in the western branch. The well-preserved ghost town of St. Elmo is just up the road, and it's a very popular tourist destination. Except for toilets and water, the campground is undeveloped and attracts mostly tent campers. The campsites overlook Chalk Creek, but the bank is steep, so flat space can be hard to find. Sites 13 and 15 are the largest sites.

Campsites, facilities: There are 15 sites for tents and RVs up to 25 feet. Picnic tables, fire rings, and grills are provided. New vault toilets and drinking water are available. Leashed pets are permitted. The facilities are wheelchair-accessible.

Reservations, fees: Reservations are not accepted. The fee is $20 per night. Cash or check only. Open late May-early September.

Directions: From Buena Vista, take Cottonwood Pass Road west for 0.7 mile. Turn south on County Road 321. In 8.0 miles, turn right on County Road 162. In 11.2 miles, make a very sharp right onto Forest Route 292. The campground is in 1.0 mile. High clearance vehicles are recommended.

Contact: Pike and San Isabel National Forests, Salida District, 719/539-3591, www.fs.usda.gov/psicc.

57 CASCADE

Scenic rating: 8

west of Buena Vista

Cascade is the highest developed campground on the road to St. Elmo. A dense spruce and aspen forest offers more privacy than either Chalk Lake or Mount Princeton, but the creek is across the road. Hiking, mountain biking, and four-wheeling are all available nearby, but there are no trails accessible from the campground, and ATVs cannot unload in the campground. Nevertheless, this is a very popular family-oriented campground, and reservations are highly recommended throughout the summer. All of the sites have ample shade except for sites 16 and 17, which have the best views. Site 18 is very close to the road.

Campsites, facilities: There are 21 sites for tents and RVs up to 54 feet. There are no hookups. Site 10 is pull-through. Picnic tables, fire rings, grills, and tent pads are provided. Vault toilets and drinking water are available. Leashed pets are permitted. Site 15 and the facilities are wheelchair-accessible.

Reservations, fees: Reservations are accepted (and highly recommended) at 877/444-6777 and www.recreation.gov. The fee is $22 per night. Cash or check only. Open late May-late September.

Directions: From Buena Vista, take Cottonwood Pass Road west for 0.7 mile. Turn south on County Road 321. In 8.0 miles, turn right on County Road 162. In 5.1 miles turn left into the campground.

Contact: Pike and San Isabel National Forests, Salida District, 719/539-3591, www.fs.usda.gov/psicc.

58 CHALK LAKE

🚶 🚴 🛶 🐕 ♿ 🚐 ⛺

Scenic rating: 7

west of Buena Vista

BEST (

Chalk Lake campground is in a peaceful grove of ponderosa pines and cottonwoods on the banks of Chalk Creek. It's the best destination on the road to St. Elmo for tent campers because there are nine walk-in tent sites (11-15 and 6-9) beside the creek. They are close together, so privacy is limited, but the road and the mayhem just disappear. Sites 3-5 are also near the creek, but they share one long tent pad right next to the parking spaces. Sites 16-21 are close to the road and have little or no shade. Site 2 is the best one for RVs. There are several hiking and mountain biking opportunities nearby. The 0.5-mile trail to Agnes Vail Falls begins across the road. The Narrow Gauge Trail connects to the Colorado Trail. Mountain bikers should also explore the forest roads and trails above the historic town of St. Elmo. Kids enjoy pulling brook trout out of the creek. The campground is located 4.4 miles west of Mount Princeton Hot Springs Resort, where you can soak the day away.

Campsites, facilities: There are 10 sites for tents and RVs up to 30 feet and 8 walk-in tent sites. There are no hookups or pull-throughs. Picnic tables, fire rings, grills, and tent pads are provided. Vault toilets and drinking water are available. Leashed pets are permitted. Sites 1, 17, and 18 and the facilities are wheelchair-accessible.

Reservations, fees: Reservations are accepted (and highly recommended) at 877/444-6777 and www.recreation.gov. The fee is $22 per night. Cash or check only. Open late May-late September.

Directions: From Buena Vista, take Cottonwood Pass Road west for 0.7 mile. Turn south on County Road 321. In 8.0 miles, turn right on County Road 162. In 4.3 miles, turn left into the campground.

Contact: Pike and San Isabel National Forests, Salida District, 719/539-3591, www.fs.usda.gov/psicc.

59 MOUNT PRINCETON

🚶 🚴 🛶 🐕 ♿ 🚐 ⛺

Scenic rating: 7

west of Buena Vista

BEST (

Mount Princeton is the first campground on the road to St. Elmo in the Chalk Creek Canyon, and it fills up fast with both tent and RV campers. There are many hiking and mountain biking opportunities nearby, and the surrounding cliffs are home to bighorn sheep and mountain goats, which the very observant camper could spot. Campers shouldn't miss the family-oriented Mount Princeton Hot Springs, four miles down the road. The landscape is fairly arid, and the ponderosa pines provide some shade but limited privacy. There has been selective hazard-tree removal here. Nonetheless, this campground is booked almost every night of the summer, so be sure to plan ahead and make reservations.

Campsites, facilities: There are 17 sites for tents and RVs up to 45 feet. There are no hookups. Picnic tables, fire rings, grills, and tent pads are provided. Vault toilets and drinking water are available. Leashed pets are permitted. Two sites and the facilities are wheelchair-accessible.

Reservations, fees: Reservations are accepted (and highly recommended) at 877/444-6777 and www.recreation.gov. The fee is $22 per night. Cash or check only. Open late May-late September.

Directions: From Buena Vista, take Cottonwood Pass Road west for 0.7 mile. Turn south on County Road 321. In 8.0 miles, turn right on County Road 162. In 3.9 miles, turn left into the campground.

Contact: Pike and San Isabel National Forests,

Hecla Junction, just above a major rafting takeout on the Arkansas River

Salida District, 719/539-3591, www.fs.usda.gov/psicc.

60 HECLA JUNCTION

Scenic rating: 6

south of Buena Vista

BEST (

Hecla Junction, aka the International Harbor of Hecla, is the third of six campgrounds managed by the State Parks system on the Arkansas River. It is the take-out for Brown's Canyon, a very popular Class III run, and one of only two campgrounds open to commercial groups. Hecla campground is slightly removed from the hustle and bustle of the parking lot and boat ramp, perched on a shadeless bluff above the river with some piñon-juniper vegetation. From the campground, anglers can hike up or down the river for excellent fishing, especially in the evening when the rafts are gone. Sites 1-4 and 6-12 overlook the river. Sites 5 and 19 are in the middle of the campground and have no privacy.

Sites 3, 6, 11, and 13 have partial shade. Bring a tarp in case you don't bag a site with shade.

Campsites, facilities: There are 23 sites for tents and RVs up to 40 feet. There are no hookups. Site 13 is pull-through. Picnic tables, fire rings, grills, and tent pads are provided. Vault toilets, changing rooms, and a boat ramp are available. Trash must be packed out. Leashed pets are permitted. Site 8 and the facilities are wheelchair-accessible.

Reservations, fees: Reservations are required; make them at 800/244-5613 or www.cpwshop.com. The fee is $28 per night. Campers must also purchase a vehicle pass ($8) or an Annual Parks Pass ($80). Open year-round.

Directions: From the junction of Highways 285 and 291, drive north on U.S. Highway 285 for 1.4 miles. Turn right onto County Road 194. The campground is in 2.7 miles, past the parking lot and boat ramp area. The road is narrow and steep.

Contact: Arkansas Headwaters Recreation Area, 719/539-7289, www.cpw.state.co.us.

61 ANGEL OF SHAVANO

🏃 🚴 🛶 🐕 🚐 ⛺

Scenic rating: 7

west of Salida

Shavano appeals to hikers and campers looking for a small, primitive campground near the Collegiate Peaks. Except for a few regulars who like the seclusion, very few people know this campground is here, so it's never full. If you can't find a spot at popular Monarch Park, Shavano is a decent backup, although it's a little out of the way for a stopover. The Colorado Trail passes through camp, and the Mount Shavano trailhead is across the road. There is a small beaver pond for fishing or, if you have 4WD, you can drive six miles to the North Fork Reservoir for some alpine fishing. On weekends, a ranger leads scavenger hunts for kids.

The setting is a young spruce and aspen forest beside the North Fork of the Arkansas, which is a small creek at this elevation. At some sites, it's hard to find enough flat space for more than one tent. The best sites for space and privacy are beside the creek: 6, 8, 10, 12, and 14. Site 3 is also very large. Site 6 is in a small aspen grove near the creek and is quite pretty.

Campsites, facilities: There are 20 sites for tents and RVs up to 35 feet and one group site for tent camping. There are no hookups. Sites 6, 12, 14, and 17 are pull-through. Picnic tables, fire rings, and grills are provided. Vault toilets and drinking water are available. Leashed pets are permitted.

Reservations, fees: Reservations are not accepted for the main campground but are required for the group site and can be made at 877/444-6777 and www.recreation.gov. The fee is $20 per night for single sites, and for the group site the fee is $60 to $110 depending on group size. Open late May-mid-September.

Directions: From the intersection of U.S. Highways 50 and 285 in Poncha Springs, take U.S. 50 west for 6.8 miles. In Maysville, turn right on County Road 240. The campground is on the left in four miles.

Contact: Pike and Isabel National Forests, Salida District, 719/539-3591, www.fs.usda.gov/psicc.

62 MONARCH PARK

🏃 🚴 🛶 🐕 🚐 ⛺

Scenic rating: 9

west of Salida

BEST (

Monarch Park is a busy campground for some very good reasons. The setting is beautiful—a subalpine spruce forest at about 10,500 feet in a park with several creeks, beaver ponds, and views of Taylor Mountain. It's also just three miles from the top of Monarch Pass and the Continental Divide Trail. Visitors can take a tram or hike to the summit for vistas that stretch as far as Pikes Peak to the east and Utah to the west. The Monarch Crest Trail traverses 12 miles from Monarch Pass to Marshall Pass. Another 28 miles of single track are accessible on the Rainbow Trail, making this loop one of the best advanced fat-tire rides in this part of the state. Hiking and mountain biking are also available across the highway from the campground entrance. Trail 1417 climbs steeply for 1.6 miles to Waterdog Lakes, which contain good-sized cutthroat trout. Kids love fishing on the beaver ponds, which have been enhanced by the Department of Wildlife to improve fish habitat.

There has been selective hazard-tree removal here, but the mature spruce forest still provides plenty of shade at all of the sites. The sites are large enough for several tents and are spaced 30-60 feet apart. The creekside sites go first: 4-8, 10-13, 15, 17, 19, 21, 24, 26, 28-30, 32, 34, and 36. Sites 2, 22, 23, and 38 have impressive views of Taylor Mountain. Sites 4 and 5 are in a dead-end spur, which provides lots of privacy. Site 4 is walk-in.

Campsites, facilities: There are 38 sites for

tents and RVs up to 45 feet. There are no hook-ups. Sites 24 and 25 are pull-through. Picnic tables, fire rings, and grills are provided. Vault toilets and drinking water are available. Leashed pets are permitted.

Reservations, fees: Reservations are accepted at 877/444-6777 and www.recreation.gov. The fee is $20 per night. Cash or check only. Open mid-June-early September.

Directions: From the intersection of U.S. Highways 50 and 285 in Poncha Springs, take U.S. 50 west for 15.3 miles. Turn left on Forest Route 231. The road ends at the campground in 1.0 mile.

Contact: Pike and San Isabel National Forests, Salida District, 719/539-3591, www.fs.usda.gov/psicc.

rings, and grills are provided. New vault toilets and drinking water are available. Leashed pets are permitted. The facilities and the fishing pier are wheelchair-accessible.

Reservations, fees: Reservations are accepted at 877/444-6777 and www.recreation.gov. The fee is $22 per night. Cash or check only. Open late May-late September.

Directions: From the intersection of U.S. Highways 50 and 285 in Poncha Springs, take U.S. 285 south for 5.0 miles. Turn right on Forest Route 200. In 2.3 miles, turn right on O'Haver Lake Road, which is very narrow and winding. The campground entrance is in 1.3 miles.

Contact: Pike and San Isabel National Forests, Salida District, 719/539-3591, www.fs.usda.gov/psicc.

63 O'HAVER LAKE

Scenic rating: 7

south of Poncha Springs

O'Haver Lake is on the flanks of Mount Ouray, at an elevation of 8,700 feet. This small lake is a fishing favorite with kids. It is usually stocked, and the still waters just beckon canoes. ATV riding is also a common pastime, especially on the road to Marshall Pass and the Colorado Trail. The Marshall Pass Road is also considered an excellent beginning mountain bike trail. Hikers have to drive to the nearest trail-head, Starvation Creek. The campground encircles one half of the lake. All of the sites are within 50 yards of the water, but the lakeside sites are most popular: 8, 10, 11, 12, 15A, 16, 19, 20, 23-26, 28, and 29. The habitat is a mixed sage and ponderosa forest, which provides decent shade at most sites. This is a very popular weekend destination, so reservations are recommended.

Campsites, facilities: There are 29 sites for tents and RVs up to 45 feet. There are no hook-ups. Site 26 is pull-through. Picnic tables, fire

64 FIVE POINTS

Scenic rating: 5

east of Texas Creek

Five Points is in the McIntyre Hills, on the south bank of the Arkansas River, Colorado's premier white-water run. Five Points is the most eastern of the six campgrounds managed by the State Parks system on the Arkansas River. This stretch of the river—from Pinnacle Rock to Parkdale—is a popular Class III-IV run that's easy to scout from the highway. A foot-path under the highway connects the campground with the day-use area. The campground is not especially appealing, but bighorn sheep are sometimes sighted on the surrounding hills. Sites 1-3, 15, 16, 18, and 20 are next to the road. The only sites with shade are 4, 14, and 15. There is very little privacy.

Campsites, facilities: There are 20 sites for tents and RVs up to 40 feet. are no hookups. Picnic tables, fire rings, grills, and tent pads are provided. Vault toilets, drinking water, and an observation deck are available. Trash must be packed out. Leashed pets are permitted. Site 10 and the facilities are wheelchair-accessible. There

Reservations, fees: Reservations are required; make them at 800/244-5613 or www.cpwshop.com. The fee is $28 per night. Campers must also purchase a vehicle pass ($8) or an Annual Parks Pass ($80). Open year-round.

Directions: From Cañon City, take U.S. Highway 50 west for 19 miles. The campground is on the left at mile marker 260.

Contact: Arkansas Headwaters Recreation Area, 719/539-7289, www.cpw.state.co.us.

THE FRONT RANGE

The Front Range includes the urban centers of Fort
Collins, Longmont, Boulder, Golden, Denver, Colorado Springs, and Pueblo. The
Cache la Poudre River, Colorado's only National Wild and Scenic River, offers
excellent camping, while Boulder's Flatirons provide world-famous hiking and
climbing. Just 25 miles west, the Indian Peaks Wilderness holds more than 100
miles of trails, including the Continental Divide Trail. Rocky Mountain National
Park has 355 miles of trails and 114 peaks more than 10,000 feet high. Colorado
Springs, Pikes Peak, and the Garden of the Gods are popular attractions. Florissant Fossil Beds National Monument and Mueller State Park are the primary
attractions west of Pikes Peak. South, the campgrounds at Lake Pueblo State
Park are packed to capacity in summer.

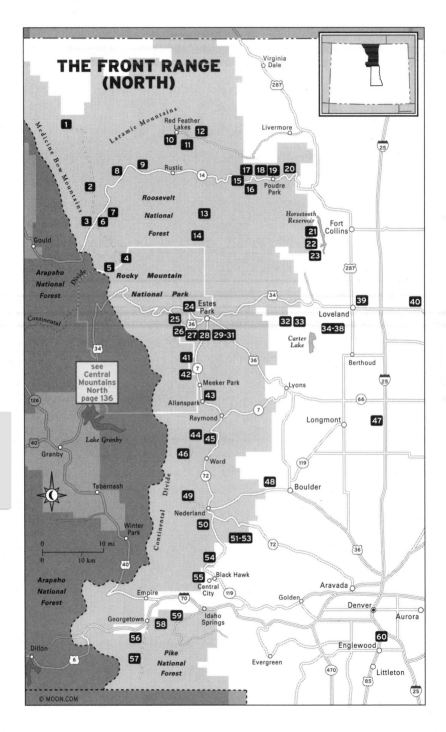

THE FRONT RANGE (NORTH)

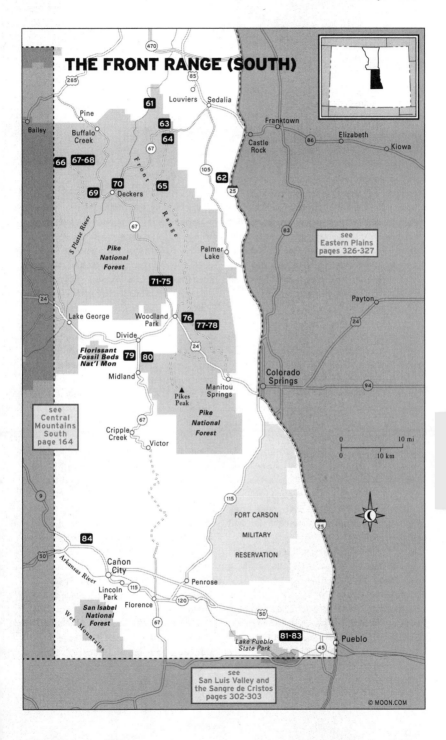

THE FRONT RANGE (SOUTH)

470
285
85
61 Louviers Sedalia
Pine Franktown
Bailey Buffalo 86 Elizabeth
Creek Castle Kiowa
63 Rock
64
67
66 67-68 105
62
69 70 65 25
Deckers
67 83
Palmer
Lake see
Eastern Plains
pages 326-327
Pike
National
Forest Payton
71-75 24
24
Lake George Woodland 76
Park 77-78
Divide
24
Florissant 79 80
Fossil Beds
Nat'l Mon Midland Colorado
Pikes Manitou Springs
Peak Springs 94
Pike
National
Forest
Cripple
Creek 67
Victor
9
115
FORT CARSON
MILITARY
RESERVATION
84 25
50 Cañon
City
Lincoln 115 Penrose
Park
Florence 120
San Isabel 67
National 50
Forest
81-83
Lake Pueblo 45 Pueblo
State Park

see
Central
Mountains
South
page 164

S Platte River
Front Range
Arkansas River
Wet Mountains

0 ____ 10 mi
0 ____ 10 km

see
San Luis Valley and
the Sangre de Cristos
pages 302-303

© MOON.COM

1 BROWNS PARK

Scenic rating: 5

north of Poudre Canyon

Browns Park is in the Laramie River valley, adjacent to the Rawah Wilderness, an area of granite peaks and remote valleys. The campground is a dirt loop in a lodgepole and aspen forest. The sites are just 20-50 feet apart. The campground is a long drive from the Front Range, but it's fairly busy on weekends, with a diverse crowd of old couples, young couples, and serious backpackers. Most campers are there for the hiking. The McIntyre and Link Trails begin at the campground and climb about seven miles to the Medicine Bow Trail on the crest of the Medicine Bow Mountains. The views of North Park and the Laramie River valley are outstanding. These trails can be turned into an overnight loop or combined with other trails for a longer route.

This area has been very heavily impacted by bark beetles and logging will continue for many years. Visitors should contact the Forest Service in advance to learn about campground, trailhead, and road closures.

Campsites, facilities: There are 28 sites for tents and RVs up to 60 feet. There are no hookups. Site 28 is pull-through. Picnic tables, fire rings, grills, and tent pads are provided. Vault toilets are available. There is no water; bring your own. Trash must be packed out. Leashed pets are permitted.

Reservations, fees: Reservations are not accepted. The fee is $18 per night. Cash or check only. Open June-November.

Directions: From Fort Collins, take U.S. Highway 287 north to Ted's Place and take Highway 14 west for 51.7 miles. Turn right on County Road 103/Laramie River Road and drive north for 15.8 miles. Turn left on County Road 190. The campground is on the left in 2.5 miles.

Contact: Arapaho and Roosevelt National Forest, Canyon Lakes District, 970/295-6700, www.fs.fed.us/arp.

2 TUNNEL

Scenic rating: 6

north of Poudre Canyon

Tunnel is a big, sprawling campground on the west bank of the Laramie River, at 8,300' elevation, and adjacent to the Rawah Wilderness, which is 73,000 acres in the Mummy Range, an area of granite peaks and glacial lakes. From the campground, the West Branch Trail climbs through aspen and pine to Grassy Pass and the Rawah Lakes Basin. Campers can also go fishing on the river, and biking and four-wheeling in the Arapaho and Roosevelt National Forest. The campground was in a thin pine forest, but bark beetles have been very active and many trees were removed. The forest is starting to recover and there is now considerable shade again. Sites are just 25 feet apart, so privacy is poor. Sites 4, 10, 20, 21, 24, and 25 are riverside (24 and 25 are the most private).

Campsites, facilities: There are 49 sites for tents and RVs up to 70 feet. There are no hookups. Sites 3, 4, 21, and 35 are pull-through. Picnic tables, fire rings, grills, and tent pads are provided. Vault toilets and drinking water are available. Leashed pets are permitted.

Reservations, fees: Reservations are not accepted. The fee is $22 per night. Cash or check only. Open May-October.

Directions: From Fort Collins, take U.S. Highway 287 north to Ted's Place and take Highway 14 west for 51.7 miles. Turn right on County Road 103/Laramie River Road. The campground is on the left in 6.5 miles.

Contact: Arapaho and Roosevelt National Forest, Canyon Lakes District, 970/295-6700, www.fs.fed.us/arp.

❸ CHAMBERS LAKE
🏃 🛶 🐕 🚗 ⛺

Scenic rating: 7
in Poudre Canyon

At 9,200 feet, Chambers Lake is a high-altitude reservoir surrounded by Roosevelt National Forest. From the campground, hikers can take Blue Lake Trail north for seven miles through the Rawah Wilderness to the West Fork Trail. This route offers panoramic views of the Mummy Range and Rocky Mountain National Park. It is the most popular trail in the Rawah.

This large campground has two paved loops in a coniferous forest on the south shore of Chambers Lake. Bark beetles have been active here and the Forest Service has had to spray and remove many trees. The sites are 20-40 feet apart, and privacy varies from fair to poor. The lower loop (sites 1-20) is not very appealing. The upper loop (sites 21-51) overlooks the lake and surrounding mountains from a high ridge. Sites 21, 23, 32, 34, 37, and 41-51 have the best views of the lake.

Campsites, facilities: There are 45 sites for tents and RVs up to 45 feet and seven walk-in tent sites (sites 45-51). Sites 6, 7, 9, 24, 25, 31, 34, 35, and 38 are doubles. There are no hookups. Picnic tables, fire rings, grills, and tent pads are provided. Vault toilets, drinking water, and a playground, and a boat ramp are available. Leashed pets are permitted.

Reservations, fees: Reservations are accepted at 877/444-6777 and www.recreation.gov. The fee is $24 per night for a single or $48 per night for a double. Cash or check only. Open late June-early October.

Directions: From Fort Collins, take U.S. Highway 287 north to Ted's Place and take Highway 14 west for 52.5 miles. Turn right at the Chambers Lake sign. The campground is in 0.6 mile.

Contact: Arapaho and Roosevelt National Forest, Canyon Lakes District, 970/295-6700, www.fs.fed.us/arp.

❹ LONG DRAW
🏃 🐕 ♿ 🚗 ⛺

Scenic rating: 6
south of Poudre Canyon

Long Draw is a small loop in a conifer forest at just over 10,000 feet, where many trees have been removed due to bark beetles. The sites are small and tightly packed. In the fall, this campground is popular with hunters. Campers can go hiking on the Big South and Corral Creek Trails. The Big South travels through the Comanche Peak Wilderness area, a stunning landscape of dense forests and glaciated peaks. There are no views from the campsites, nor is there direct access to the reservoir, which is a bit farther up the road, but the area is beautiful. There is dispersed camping along the road up to the reservoir, though most of the trees along the road have been clear-cut.

Campsites, facilities: There are 25 sites for tents and RVs up to 55 feet, including three double sites. There are no hookups. Site 9 is pull-through. Picnic tables, fire rings, and grills are provided. Vault toilets and drinking water are available. Trash must be packed out. Leashed pets are permitted. The facilities are wheelchair-accessible.

Reservations, fees: Reservations are not accepted. The fee is $20 per night for a single site and $40 per night for a double site. Cash or check only. Open July-November.

Directions: From Fort Collins, take U.S. Highway 287 north to Ted's Place and take Highway 14 west for 53.9 miles. Turn left on Long Draw Road. The campground is on the left in 8.8 miles.

Contact: Arapaho and Roosevelt National Forest, Canyon Lakes District, 970/295-6700, www.fs.fed.us/arp.

5 GRANDVIEW

Scenic rating: 10

south of Poudre Canyon

Grandview occupies an enviable location between the Neota Wilderness and Rocky Mountain National Park. The campground is at an elevation of 10,220 feet, at the south end of Long Draw Reservoir in a conifer forest on a steep shore. Unfortunately, bark beetles have been active here and the Forest Service has had to remove trees. However, the campground remains small, cozy, and off the beaten track. The large reservoir, wide wetland, and surrounding ridgelines are impressive. Campers can go fishing or carry a boat down to the reservoir. The nearest hiking trails are Neota Creek and La Poudre Pass Trails, which begin at the end of Long Draw Road. Neota Creek Trail is an unmaintained track through wetlands to the base of Iron Mountain. La Poudre Pass Trail enters Rocky Mountain National Park and meets up with the Colorado River.

Campsites, facilities: There are nine sites for tents only. There are no hookups. Picnic tables, fire rings, and grills are provided. Vault toilets and drinking water are available. Trash must be packed out. Leashed pets are permitted.

Reservations, fees: Reservations are not accepted. The fee is $20 per night. Cash or check only. Open July-November.

Directions: From Fort Collins, take U.S. Highway 287 north to Ted's Place and take Highway 14 west for 53.9 miles. Turn left on Long Draw Road. The campground is on the left in 11.9 miles (about 30 minutes driving on an unpaved road).

Contact: Arapaho and Roosevelt National Forest, Canyon Lakes District, 970/295-6700, www.fs.fed.us/arp.

near Long Draw Reservoir

6 ASPEN GLEN

Scenic rating: 7

in Poudre Canyon

Aspen Glen is a small loop in a spruce-fir and aspen forest on Joe Wright Creek. The campground is surrounded by the rocky ridges of the Upper Poudre Canyon. There is a fair amount of traffic noise, but the sites are large and well spaced. Site 6 has the most privacy. The campground is less than a mile away from the Big South trailhead. This 10-mile trail travels into the Comanche Peak Wilderness along the Big South Fork of the Poudre, a tantalizing trout stream characterized by frequent cascades and pools.

Campsites, facilities: There are nine sites for tents and RVs up to 35 feet. There are no hookups. Site 4 is pull-through. Picnic tables, fire rings, grills, and tent pads are provided. Vault toilets and drinking water are available. Leashed pets are permitted.

Reservations, fees: Reservations are not accepted. The fee is $19 per night. Cash or check only. Open May-October.

Directions: From Fort Collins, take U.S. Highway 287 north to Ted's Place and take Highway 14 west for 50.2 miles. The campground is on the right.

Contact: Arapaho and Roosevelt National Forest, Canyon Lakes District, 970/295-6700, www.fs.fed.us/arp.

7 BIG SOUTH

Scenic rating: 6

in Poudre Canyon

BEST (

Big South is a tiny campground at the junction of the Big South Fork and the main fork of the Cache la Poudre River. The campground is right across the river from the Big South trailhead, where hikers can begin a 10-mile trek into the Comanche Peak Wilderness, which encompasses about 67,000 acres of spruce-fir forests and granite peaks in the Mummy Range. The scenic cascades and pools of the Big South are extremely popular with anglers and hikers. The Big South is also a Class V white-water route for steep-creek boaters.

Campsites, facilities: There are four sites for tents and RVs up to 30 feet. There are no hookups. Picnic tables, fire rings, and grills are provided. Vault toilets are available. Leashed pets are permitted.

Reservations, fees: Reservations are not accepted. The fee is $19 per night. Cash or check only. Open May-October.

Directions: From Fort Collins, take U.S. Highway 287 north to Ted's Place and take Highway 14 west for 49 miles. The campground is on the left.

Contact: Arapaho and Roosevelt National Forest, Canyon Lakes District, 970/295-6700, www.fs.fed.us/arp.

8 SLEEPING ELEPHANT

Scenic rating: 6

in Poudre Canyon

Sleeping Elephant is a small loop separated from the river by the highway. The impressive granite summit of Sleeping Elephant Mountain towers over the far bank. This older campground is basically a stopover. The sites are in a forest of aspen and spruce and spaced about 30 feet apart, with many trees between the sites. The nearest hiking trail is Roaring Creek, about three miles downstream. The river has excellent trout fishing but much of the surrounding land is private.

Campsites, facilities: There are 15 sites for tents and RVs up to 20 feet. There are no hookups. Picnic tables, fire rings, and grills are provided. Vault toilets and drinking water are available. Leashed pets are permitted. The facilities are wheelchair-accessible.

Reservations, fees: Reservations are not accepted. The fee is $19 per night. Cash or check only. Open May-September.

Directions: From Fort Collins, take U.S. Highway 287 north to Ted's Place and take Highway 14 west for 44 miles. The campground is on the right.

Contact: Arapaho and Roosevelt National Forest, Canyon Lakes District, 970/295-6700, www.fs.fed.us/arp.

9 BIG BEND

Scenic rating: 6

in Poudre Canyon

Big Bend doesn't suffer from the rambunctious summer crowds that the downstream campgrounds receive, and it can lay claim to one of the grandest sites on the Cache la Poudre River. The canyon opens up here and the formerly narrow river becomes braided. As you might guess from the number of anglers casting up and down the river, it's prime trout habitat. If you don't enjoy fishing, bring your binoculars and try spotting bighorn sheep in the meadow that borders the campground or on the steep hillsides across the road. In early spring, ewes and lambs are often seen munching on western wheatgrass and sulphur flower. Hunting and disease had eliminated bighorn sheep from the canyon by 1900, but the Department of Wildlife reintroduced them in 1950 and the population continues to recover. You can also spot bighorn on the scenic Roaring Creek Trail. The trailhead is 0.5 mile west of the campground. The one thing Big Bend can't boast about is privacy. There are few trees separating the drive-in sites, and even the walk-in sites are close to the road.

Campsites, facilities: There are five sites for tents and RVs up to 20 feet and three walk-in tent sites (sites 7, 8, 9). There are no hookups.

Picnic tables, fire rings, and grills are provided. Vault toilets and drinking water (until late September) are available. Leashed pets are permitted.

Reservations, fees: Reservations are not accepted. The fee is $19 per night, or less when the water is off. Cash or check only. Open year-round.

Directions: From Fort Collins, take U.S. Highway 287 north to Ted's Place and take Highway 14 west for 40.2 miles. The campground is on the left.

Contact: Arapaho and Roosevelt National Forest, Canyon Lakes District, 970/295-6700, www.fs.fed.us/arp.

10 BELLAIRE LAKE

Scenic rating: 6

at Red Feather Lakes

Bellaire is a small lake surrounded by the granite outcroppings and rolling hills of the Red Feather Lakes region. The sandy shore is excellent for shore fishing, and there's a wheelchair-accessible fishing pier and day-use area. The lake and campground were surrounded by lodgepole pine, but bark beetles have been active and there has been quite a bit of hazard-tree removal, which will continue as necessary. It remains a very popular destination, however. Most visitors enjoy fishing and boating (hand-powered only), as well as day trips to Wyoming and the Cache la Poudre canyon. The campground has two loops, with large sites spaced 25-50 feet apart. The back loop (sites 23-27) is smaller and quieter than the front loop, which is very popular with families and RVers. Loop A has electric hookups, but Loop B does not.

Campsites, facilities: There are 26 sites for tents and RVs up to 75 feet. Electric hookups are available at sites 1-22. Sites 14, 18, 20, and 26 are doubles; site 4 is a triple. Sites 8 and 10 are pull-throughs. Picnic tables, fire rings, grills, and

tent pads are provided. Flush toilets and drinking water are available. Leashed pets are permitted. The facilities are wheelchair-accessible.
Reservations, fees: Reservations are accepted at 877/444-6777 and www.recreation.gov. Fees are $24 per night for a nonelectric site and $32 per night for electric sites. Cash or check only. Open June-October.
Directions: From Fort Collins, take U.S. Highway 287 north for about 21 miles. Go west on Red Feather Lakes Road/County Road 74E for 34.1 miles and turn left on County Road 162. In 2.1 miles, turn right on Forest Route 163. In 0.4 mile, turn left on Forest Route 163A. The campground is in 0.3 mile.
Contact: Arapaho and Roosevelt National Forest, Canyon Lakes District, 970/295-6700, www.fs.fed.us/arp.

11 WEST LAKE

Scenic rating: 6

at Red Feather Lakes

The Red Feather Lakes area is surprisingly popular. There are no soaring mountains here, but the rolling hills and low ridgelines covered in grasslands and ponderosa pine and numerous fishing lakes attract a devoted following of weekend campers. West Lake campground has two loops on the south shore of a small, stocked lake. The sites are about 30 feet apart and trees have been removed due to bark beetles (although not to the same extent as Bellaire Lake). Privacy is poor, and this campground mostly attracts RVs. Sites 6, 7, 9, 10, 12, 14, 15, 17, 18, 20, 23, and 25-28 have lake views. Site 35 is on a small knoll with 360-degree views. There is a fishing trail around the lake, which is open to hand-powered boats. Sites 8, 14, 16, and 21 are double sites.
Campsites, facilities: There are 35 sites for tents and RVs up to 50 feet. Sites 1-5 are walkins. Electric hookups are available. Picnic

tables, fire rings, grills, and tent pads are provided. Vault toilets, drinking water, and a boat ramp are available. Leashed pets are permitted. The facilities are wheelchair-accessible.
Reservations, fees: Reservations are not accepted for sites 29-36, but are highly recommended for all other sites at 877/444-6777 and www.recreation.gov. Fees are $24 per night for a nonelectric site and $32 per night for electric sites. Cash or check only. Open May-September.
Directions: From Fort Collins, take U.S. Highway 287 north for about 21 miles. Go west on Red Feather Lakes Road/County Road 74E for 22.4 miles and turn right at the West Lake sign.
Contact: Arapaho and Roosevelt National Forest, Canyon Lakes District, 970/295-6700, www.fs.fed.us/arp.

12 DOWDY LAKE

Scenic rating: 6

at Red Feather Lakes

The campground has five loops around the south and west shores of the lake. Most sites have lake views. Some trees have been removed due to bark beetle impact and sites are just 10-20 feet apart, so privacy is poor, especially on weekends when the campground fills up. Sites 2, 7, 8, 50, 51, 53, and 54 are doubles. Hikers and bikers can take an old logging road to the Mount Margaret Trail, an easy four-mile hike or mountain bike ride to a rocky peak. In the winter, the Mount Margaret Trail is open for cross-country skiing and snowshoeing. (For more information on the Red Feather Lakes area, see the West Lake entry in this chapter.)
Campsites, facilities: There are 62 sites for tents and RVs up to 70 feet. Sites 12-21 are walk-ins. Picnic tables, fire rings, grills, and tent pads are provided. Vault toilets, drinking

water (until late September), and a boat ramp are available. Leashed pets are permitted.

Reservations, fees: Reservations are accepted at 877/444-6777 and www.recreation.gov. Fees are $24 per night for a nonelectric site, and $32 per night for electric sites. Cash or check only. Open year-round.

Directions: From Fort Collins, take U.S. Highway 287 north for about 21 miles. Go west on Red Feather Lakes Road/County Road 74E for 22.7 miles and turn right on Dowdy Lake Road. The campground is on the right in 0.6 mile.

Contact: Arapaho and Roosevelt National Forest, Canyon Lakes District, 970/295-6700, www.fs.fed.us/arp.

13 JACK'S GULCH

Scenic rating: 7

in Pingree Park

Jack's Gulch is on the eastern boundary of the Comanche Peak Wilderness. The campground was built in 1995 to reduce the impact of recreation on the Little South Fork of the Cache la Poudre and is one of the best bets for last-minute campers who don't have a reservation. There are no trailheads at the campground, but it's a short drive to the Flowers, Fish Creek, and Little Beaver Trails. The area is also popular with ATV owners and hunters. The campground is in a ponderosa pine forest with scattered meadows and aspen. Bark beetles have been active here, although the impact is much more mild than in the northern reaches of the Poudre Canyon. The walk-in sites are especially attractive. The Paintbrush Loop has modern, roomy equestrian sites. There is plenty of dispersed camping along Flowers Road on the drive in to the campground.

Campsites, facilities: There are 55 sites for tents and RVs up to 80 feet, 10 walk-in tent sites, and five equestrian sites. There is also a group

site. Electric hookups are available at sites 1-27 and the group site. Picnic tables, fire rings, grills, and tent pads are provided. Vault toilets, drinking water, corrals, and a small amphitheater are available. Each equestrian site has four horse stalls. Leashed pets are permitted. Most sites and facilities are wheelchair-accessible.

Reservations, fees: Reservations are not accepted for the main campground, with the exception of sites 57 and 58, the group site, and the equestrian sites, which can be reserved at 877/444-6777 and www.recreation.gov. The fee is $24 per night for a nonelectric site and $32 per night for an electric site. The group site is $187 per night and equestrian sites are $37 per night. Cash or check only. Open May-November.

Directions: From Fort Collins, take U.S. Highway 287 north to Ted's Place and take Highway 14 west for 26.5 miles. Turn left on Pingree Park Road/County Road 63E. In 6.3 miles, turn right into Jack's Gulch Recreation Area. The main loop is on the left, and the group and equestrian loops are on the right.

Contact: Arapaho and Roosevelt National Forest, Canyon Lakes District, 970/295-6700, www.fs.fed.us/arp.

14 TOM BENNETT

Scenic rating: 6

in Pingree Park

Tom Bennett campground is a few turns in the road before the entrance to Pingree Park Campus of Colorado State University, a research site that once belonged to a homesteading family. Their house and several outhouses have been preserved and restored. The site offers an interesting glance into the lonely lives of the pioneers in this region. The campground is a cramped affair in a patchy lodgepole forest beside a small creek, where some trees have been removed due to bark beetles. The privacy and scenery are poor at most sites, but some shade has returned. The campground serves as an overnight destination for hikers and families whose kids hang out and splash in the creek. Three trails begin nearby: Beaver Creek, Emmaline Lake, and Stormy Peaks Pass. Emmaline Lake Trail climbs through the Comanche Peak Wilderness to the Cirque and Emmaline Lakes basin. The views merit an overnight trip. Stormy Peaks Pass is equally impressive.

Campsites, facilities: There are 12 sites for tents and RVs up to 25 feet. Site 6 is pull-through. Picnic tables, fire rings, and grills are provided. Vault toilets are available. Leashed pets are permitted.

Reservations, fees: Reservations are not accepted. The fee is $15 per night. Cash or check only. Open May-October.

Directions: From Fort Collins, take U.S. Highway 287 north to Ted's Place and take Highway 14 west for 26.5 miles. Turn left on Pingree Park Road/County Road 63E. In 15.8 miles, turn right on Forest Route 145. The campground is on the left at the bottom of the hill.

Contact: Arapaho and Roosevelt National Forest, Canyon Lakes District, 970/295-6700, www.fs.fed.us/arp.

15 KELLY FLATS

Scenic rating: 7

in Poudre Canyon

Kelly Flats straddles both banks of the wild Cache la Poudre River at 6,600-foot elevation. This campground is a great destination for families because the river widens and slows as it flows across a nice gravel bar here. Anglers can fish for trout on this excellent fishery, and kayakers and rafters can take to the river. Upstream of the campground, the Lower and Upper Rustic runs offer scenic Class III

boating. The lower Poudre is tougher and closer to the highway.

The campground has three spurs. In the first spur, sites 1-6 are in a meadow with no trees. These are the least-popular sites. Sites 9-13 are for tents only. Sites 20-30 are across the river. Every site (except 7) is riverside; sites 15-17, 20, and 21 are walk-ins. There has been some tree removal here, but nothing as dramatic as farther up canyon.

Campsites, facilities: There are 29 sites for tents and RVs up to 65 feet. Sites 15, 17, 20, and 21 are walk-ins. There are no hookups. Picnic tables, fire rings, grills, and tent pads are provided. Vault toilets and drinking water are available. Leashed pets are permitted. The facilities are wheelchair-accessible.

Reservations, fees: Reservations are not accepted. The fee is $24 per night. Cash or check only. Open May-October.

Directions: From Fort Collins, take U.S. Highway 287 north to Ted's Place and take Highway 14 west for 25.4 miles. The campground is on the left.

Contact: Arapaho and Roosevelt National Forest, Canyon Lakes District, 970/295-6700, www.fs.fed.us/arp.

16 MOUNTAIN PARK

Scenic rating: 6

in Poudre Canyon

Mountain Park is the largest campground on the Cache la Poudre River. As Colorado's only Wild and Scenic River, the Poudre attracts hordes of campers all summer long with excellent fishing, white-water, and hiking opportunities. Mountain Park is one of the most popular campgrounds, in part because it has hookups, and it's adjacent to the Mount McConnell Trail, the only trail in the Cache la Poudre Wilderness area. This strenuous four-mile loop climbs 1,300 feet to an overlook of the Little South Fork canyon, even wilder and more rugged than the main fork. The trail also has sweeping views of the Mummy Range and Storm Peaks. It's a must-do for visitors to the Poudre.

The campground has four loops and a group area in a pine forest on the south bank of the river. The sites are just 15-30 feet apart, so privacy is poor, but shade is excellent. The campground is packed all summer with snowbirds and families. The Bear and McConnell Loops (sites 1-32) have electric hookups. The Crown and Comanche Loops (sites 33-57) are riverside, but they are also within sight of the road. The group site can be used for events (there was a wedding going on when I visited).

Campsites, facilities: There are 57 sites for tents and RVs up to 45 feet and 1 group site. Electric hookups are available at sites 1-32. Sites 31-33 are pull-through. Sites 24, 37, 38, 40, and 42 are doubles. Picnic tables, fire rings, grills, and tent pads are provided. Showers, vault toilets, drinking water, horseshoe pits, volleyball courts, a playground, and an amphitheater are available. Leashed pets are permitted. The facilities are wheelchair-accessible.

Reservations, fees: Reservations are accepted for sites 1-16, 19-28, and 30-32 at 877/444-6777 and www.recreation.gov. The tent fee is $24 per night for a single site and $48 per night for a double, nonelectric site. Electric sites are $32 per night (or $64 per night for a double). The group site is $145 per night and can accommodate 10 RVs and 30 tents (or a maximum of 100 people). Cash or check only. Open May-September.

Directions: From Fort Collins, take U.S. Highway 287 north to Ted's Place and take Highway 14 west for 23.5 miles. Turn left and cross the river. The campground is on the left.

Contact: Arapaho and Roosevelt National Forest, Canyon Lakes District, 970/295-6700, www.fs.fed.us/arp.

17 DUTCH GEORGE FLATS

Scenic rating: 6

in Poudre Canyon

Dutch George is a popular campground beside the Cache la Poudre, Colorado's only Wild and Scenic River. The campground is across from the Cache la Poudre Wilderness area, an almost impenetrable area of granite gorges and rocky creeks. Anglers fish for trout on the main fork of the Poudre and on the Little South Fork. There is river running above and below the campground. Most sites have views of Sheep Mountain. The riverside sites, 1-13 and 19-21, are shaded by cottonwoods; sites 19-21 are the most private. Sites 14-18 are too close to the road and lack shade and privacy. Sites 10 and 13 are double sites.

Campsites, facilities: There are 20 sites for tents and RVs up to 70 feet. Sites 8-15 are walk-ins. There are no hookups. Sites 8, 13, and 15 are pull-through. Picnic tables, fire rings, grills, and tent pads are provided. Vault toilets and drinking water are available. Leashed pets are permitted. The facilities are wheelchair-accessible.

Reservations, fees: Reservations are not accepted. The fee is $23 per night. Cash or check only. Open May-October.

Directions: From Fort Collins, take U.S. Highway 287 north to Ted's Place and take Highway 14 west. The campground is on the left in 21.6 miles.

Contact: Arapaho and Roosevelt National Forest, Canyon Lakes District, 970/295-6700, www.fs.fed.us/arp.

18 UPPER AND LOWER NARROWS

Scenic rating: 7

in Poudre Canyon

The Narrows is named for the gnarly Class IV-V white-water run that begins just downstream of the campground. Only advanced kayakers can tackle this run, which becomes unsafe for boating when the Cache la Poudre is swollen. The river is the only designated Wild and Scenic River in Colorado; the waters are also protected by the wilderness area to the south of the river. The river has carved a deep gorge through the granite of the Front Range. The wilderness area is almost impenetrable. There is only one four-mile loop trail into the wilderness, but anglers have created a strenuous-use trail up the Little South Fork of the Poudre. Fishing and white water are the primary attractions on this stretch of the canyon.

The campground has two loops at a place where the canyon widens. The upper loop (sites 1-7) is next to the put-in. The sites are exposed to the road and each other. The lower loop (sites 8-15) has walk-in tent sites in a grove of ponderosa pines. The sites are about 25 feet apart. Shade is good and privacy is fair. Sites 1-6 and 11-15 are riverside.

Campsites, facilities: There are 15 sites for tents and RVs up to 30 feet. Sites 8-15 are walk-ins. There are no hookups. Picnic tables, fire rings, grills, and tent pads are provided. Vault toilets and drinking water (until late September) are available. Leashed pets are permitted. The facilities are wheelchair-accessible.

Reservations, fees: Reservations are not accepted. The fee is $23 per night. Cash or check only. Open May-October.

Directions: From Fort Collins, take U.S. Highway 287 north to Ted's Place and take Highway 14 west. The lower campground is on the left in 20.3 miles. The upper campground is on the left in 20.5 miles.

Contact: Arapaho and Roosevelt National Forest, Canyon Lakes District, 970/295-6700, www.fs.fed.us/arp.

19 STOVE PRAIRIE

Scenic rating: 6

in Poudre Canyon

The Cache la Poudre is Colorado's only Wild and Scenic River, a designation that has helped to protect superior fishing and white water on the upper stretches of the river. According to legend, the river was named by a group of fur trappers who had to lighten their load when they hit a snowstorm in the canyon. They were told to "cache la poudre" or "hide the powder" in the banks. Today, trappers have been replaced by rafters and kayakers. Stove Prairie is just downstream of the Upper Landing and Steven's Gulch put-ins at the beginning of the Upper Mishawaka run. This three-mile section is a classic Class IV run. Boaters can take out at the Mishawaka Inn and grab a burger, or keep running down the Lower Mishawaka and Poudre Park runs.

The campground is a small loop in a wide spot of the canyon. The walk-in sites are in a grove of cottonwoods and pine trees by the river. The drive-in sites are grouped around a meadow. They lack shade and privacy.

Campsites, facilities: There are nine sites for tents and RVs up to 55 feet. Sites 3-6 are walk-ins. There are no hookups. Picnic tables, fire rings, grills, and tent pads are provided. Vault toilets and drinking water are available. Leashed pets are permitted.

Reservations, fees: Reservations are not accepted. The fee is $23 per night. Cash or check only. Open mid-May-late October.

Directions: From Fort Collins, take U.S. Highway 287 north to Ted's Place. Take Highway 14 west for 16.8 miles. The campground is on the right.

campsite at Stove Prairie on Colorado's only designated Wild and Scenic River

Contact: Arapaho and Roosevelt National Forest, Canyon Lakes District, 970/295-6700, www.fs.fed.us/arp.

20 ANSEL WATROUS

Scenic rating: 6

in Poudre Canyon

BEST (

From Memorial Day-Labor Day, Ansel Watrous is a hotbed of activity. As the easternmost campground on Colorado's only National Wild and Scenic River, Ansel Watrous fills up fast and early with rafters, kayakers, anglers, families, and groupies. It's the perfect base camp for an early morning launch, and if you don't have your own boat, there are three rafting companies in Fort Collins to choose from. Rafting begins in May and ends in August, when the river nearly dries up. The best times to go are early in the season, when the snowmelt is cold but abundant. If you prefer to stay on dry land, you can watch the rafters from the porch of

the Mishawaka Inn, a short walk upstream. The "Mish" serves the best burgers in the canyon, and it's a popular concert venue, favored by the likes of String Cheese Incident, Yonder Mountain, and Indigo Girls. The Greyrock trailhead is located four miles to the east. This strenuous trail summits Greyrock Mountain at 7,613 feet. The climb is worth it for the views of the plains and the Front Range. The easier 4.7-mile Young Gulch Trail begins across from the campground. It's open to bikes as well as hikers.

Ansel Watrous has two loops sandwiched between the highway and the river, so the sound of traffic is constant on a summer day. The two loops are separated by a short drive on the road. Tall pines provide shade but not much privacy because the sites are just 15-20 feet apart. Trails lead down to the water and a nice swimming hole at the lower loop. Sites 1-10 and 14-19 are riverside sites.

Campsites, facilities: There are 19 sites for tents and RVs up to 33 feet. Sites 8-10 are walk-ins. There are no hookups. Picnic tables, fire rings, grills, and tent pads are provided. Vault toilets and drinking water (year-round in the lower loop) are available. Leashed pets are permitted. The facilities are wheelchair-accessible.

Reservations, fees: Reservations are accepted at 877/444-6777 and www.recreation.gov. The fee is $23 per night. Cash or check only. Open year-round.

Directions: From Fort Collins, take U.S. Highway 287 north to Ted's Place. Take Highway 14 west for 12.6 miles. The campground is on the right.

Contact: Arapaho and Roosevelt National Forest, Canyon Lakes District, 970/295-6700, www.fs.fed.us/arp.

21 BOAT-IN

Scenic rating: 9

west of Fort Collins

BEST (

Horsetooth Reservoir features 15 popular boat-in sites tucked into the coves on the lake's western shore. These sites offer all the recreational opportunities of the developed campgrounds at Inlet Bay and South Bay, plus the outstanding scenery and solitude of more remote destinations. The views of the hogbacks, Horsetooth Rock, and Lory State Park are impressive, and campers will find that they can swim here more easily than elsewhere on the reservoir, where swimming is restricted due to motorboat traffic. Horsetooth is also a popular fishing destination for white bass and walleye, although a consumption advisory has been issued by the Department of Wildlife due to high mercury levels in the lake. (For more information on Horsetooth Reservoir, see the South Bay entry in this chapter.)

Dixon Cove, Quarry Cove, and the main shore (sites 1-8) are most popular with families. South and North Eltuck Coves (sites 11-14) have a reputation for being the party coves. The northern campsites (9-15) offer access to hiking and biking trails in Lory State Park.

Campsites, facilities: There are 15 boat-in sites for tent camping. There are no hookups. Fire rings are provided. Vault toilets are available at sites 1, 2, and 5-10. Trash must be packed out. Leashed pets are permitted.

Reservations, fees: Reservations are recommended and accepted at www.larimercamping. com or 800/397-7795. The fee is $25-38 per night. Campers must also purchase a daily pass ($8) or an annual pass ($90 for Larimer County residents, $120 for nonresidents, $65 for senior citizens, and $10 for disabled veterans). Cash or check only. Open year-round.

Directions: These are boat-in sites. To access the boat ramps on Horsetooth Reservoir, take Harmony Road/County Road 38E west from Fort Collins around the southern end of the reservoir to South Bay or Inlet Bay. Or, take LaPorte Ave west, turn right on Overland Trail, left on Bingham Hill, left on County Road 23, and right on Satanka Trail to Satanka Cove.

Contact: Larimer County Department of Natural Resources, 970/679-4570, www. larimer.org/naturalresources.

22 INLET BAY

Scenic rating: 5

west of Fort Collins

BEST (

Inlet Bay is on the west shore of Horsetooth Reservoir, which is known for its fishing, boating, water-sports, and scuba-diving opportunities. (For more information on Horsetooth Reservoir, see the South Bay entry in this chapter.) This campground mainly serves RVers and boaters, but also offers easy access to the 15-mile Blue Sky Trail, which connects Devil's Backbone near Loveland to the Horsetooth Mountain Open Space and is very popular with mountain bikers. Hikers and bikers will enjoy the trail system in nearby Soderberg Open Space and Horsetooth Mountain Park, as well. Anglers are most likely to catch walleye and bass, but may not want to eat them due to high mercury levels in the lake. There is less traffic here than at nearby South Bay, but the campground also borders a residential area, so this is not a wilderness experience. There are two loops separated by the boat ramp and marina. In the first loop, sites 1-26, all of the sites, overlook the water. The second loop, sites 27-54, are closer to Soderberg Open Space and to the road. **Campsites, facilities:** There are 54 sites for tents and RVs up to 60 feet. Electric hookups are available at all sites and most sites are pull-through. Picnic tables, fire rings, and grills are provided. Shelters are available at sites 7 and 16. Flush toilets, showers, vault toilets, drinking water, and dump stations are available. A boat ramp and boat rentals are available nearby. Leashed pets are permitted. Sites 8, 26, 50, and the facilities are wheelchair-accessible.

Reservations, fees: Reservations are recommended and accepted at www.larimercamping. com or 800/397-7795. The fee is $20-30 per night for nonelectric sites and $20-48 for electric sites. Campers must also purchase a daily pass ($8) or an annual pass ($90 for Larimer County residents, $120 for nonresidents, $65 for senior citizens, and $10 for disabled veterans). Cash or check only. Open year-round.

Directions: From the intersection of Harmony Road/County Road 38E and College Avenue/Highway 287 in Fort Collins, take Harmony Road west for 8.0 miles. Turn right on Shoreline Drive. The campground entrance is on the right in 0.3 miles.

Contact: Larimer County Department of Natural Resources, 970/679-4570, www. larimer.org/naturalresources.

23 SOUTH BAY

🚶 🚴� 🛶 ⛵ 🛥️ 🎣 🐕 ♿ 🚐 ⛺

Scenic rating: 5

west of Fort Collins

Horsetooth Reservoir is a 6.5-mile-long reservoir nestled in the foothills near Fort Collins.

It's named for Horsetooth Rock, a prominent local landmark. According to local legend, the rock is the remains of the heart of an evil giant, cut in two by a powerful Native American chief to protect his people. Horsetooth Mountain Park's mild climate and 29 miles of trails make it a year-round destination for hiking and biking. The reservoir is also a year-round destination for fishing, boating, rock climbing, and scuba diving.

As the name indicates, South Bay sits at the southern end of the reservoir. The views of the hogbacks and the lake can be impressive, but County Road 38E, which wraps around the lake and the campground, guarantees a constant hum of traffic, and the space can feel claustrophobic depending on your camping preferences. Nevertheless, this campground is extremely popular with the boating crowd and reservations are essential on summer weekends. Water levels fluctuate, but many families take advantage of the campground's proximity to the water by parking their boats on the shoreline near their campsite. Cottonwoods, pines, and Russian olives provide limited shade. The sites are 25-50 feet apart and privacy is poor. There are essentially six distinct loops in the campground, and most sites are more suitable for RVs than tents. Sites 1, 2, 16, 18, 20, 23, 25, and 28-33 have the best lake views and are farthest from the road. Sites 46-49 are closest to CR38E. Sites 50-60 are underneath a power line.

Campsites, facilities: There are 78 sites for tents and RVs up to 80 feet and seven cabins. You can also rent a classic Airstream trailer for the night ($99). Sites 13 and 14 are walk-in tent sites. Electric hookups are available at most sites, and sites 5-12 and 74-81 have full hookups. Picnic tables, fire rings, grills, and tent pads are provided. Flush toilets, showers, vault toilets, drinking water, and dump stations are available. A boat ramp and swimming beach are accessible nearby. Leashed pets are permitted. Sites 41-43 and the facilities are wheelchair-accessible.

Reservations, fees: Reservations are recommended and accepted at www.larimercamping.com and 800/397-7795. The fee is $20-30 per night for nonelectric sites and $20-48 for electric sites. Campers must also purchase a daily pass ($8) or an annual pass ($90 for Larimer County residents, $120 for nonresidents, $65 for senior citizens, and $10 for disabled veterans). Cash or check only. Open year-round.

Directions: From the intersection of Harmony Road/County Road 38E and College Avenue/Highway 287 in Fort Collins, take Harmony Road west for 6.5 miles. Just past the southern tip of Horsetooth Reservoir, turn right into the park entrance and follow the signs to the campground in 0.3 mile.

Contact: Larimer County Department of Natural Resources, 970/679-4570, www.larimer.org/naturalresources.

24 ASPENGLEN

Scenic rating: 8
in Rocky Mountain National Park

Rocky Mountain National Park is a renowned destination for hikers, climbers, and wildlife lovers, with more than 350 miles of hiking trails and 118 peaks over 10,000 feet, including Longs Peak, Colorado's most frequently climbed fourteener. The park celebrated its 100-year anniversary in 2015. One-third of the park is above tree line, so the majority of trails climb to mountain lakes and ridgelines with fabulous views of this glaciated landscape. The park also has the highest continuous paved highway in the country, Trail Ridge Road. A trip to the park isn't complete without a drive along this route, which traverses the park and crosses the Continental Divide. With so many attractions, Rocky Mountain is a busy destination in the summer, but the crowds thin out dramatically in the fall and winter.

There are four frontcountry campgrounds

on the east side of the park and one on the west side. Aspenglen is the smallest and quietest campground for tents and RVs, but the views aren't as spectacular as at Moraine Park and Glacier Basin. It also retains one of the healthiest forests of the park's five campgrounds. The Horseshoe Park and Deer Mountain Trails are accessible from the campground, and the Lawn Lake trailhead is a short drive away. Horseshoe Park is a popular location for viewing elk and bighorn sheep. Though the campground feels remote, it is only a five-minute drive from the Fall River park entrance and the visitors center, gift shop, restaurant, and stables.

The campground has four loops with 52 sites. Loop A (sites 1-5 and A-E) has both drive-in and walk-in tent sites. Several of the six walk-in sites are across the old Fall River channel and have views of Bighorn Mountain. Loop B (6-20) has drive-in sites shaded by tall ponderosa pines with views of Bighorn Mountain; site 14 is particularly nice. Generators are not allowed in Loops A and B. Loop C (21-50) is for both tents and RVs; generators are allowed, but only during a few hours in the morning and afternoon. Sites 31-34 and 50 are in a small draw without views. Sites 35-49 are in a meadow with views of Bighorn Mountain; privacy is poor, so mostly RVs use this loop.

Campsites, facilities: There are 52 sites for tents and RVs up to 30 feet, including 10 sites for tents only. Picnic tables, fire rings, grills, and tent pads are provided. Flush toilets, drinking water, dishwashing sinks, food lockers, campfire programs, an amphitheater, and a riding stable are available. Leashed pets are permitted in the campground, but pets are not allowed on trails. The facilities are wheelchair-accessible.

Reservations, fees: Reservations are accepted at 877/444-6777 and www.recreation.gov. The fee is $26 per night. Campers must also purchase a vehicle day pass ($25), a weeklong pass ($35), annual park pass ($70), or Interagency Annual America the Beautiful Pass ($80). Credit card, cash, or check. Open only in summer and early fall. Camping in the park is limited to seven nights total park-wide from early June-late September. Open late May-late September.

Directions: From Estes Park, take U.S. Highway 34 west to the Fall River entrance station. In 0.1 mile, turn left at the Aspenglen sign. The campground is in 0.5 mile.

Contact: Rocky Mountain National Park, 970/586-1206, www.nps.gov/romo.

25 MORAINE PARK

Scenic rating: 8

in Rocky Mountain National Park

BEST (

Moraine Park is the largest of the four campgrounds on the east side of Rocky Mountain National Park. (For more information on the park, see the Aspenglen listing in this chapter.) The setting is incredible—the campground is next to an open, grassy parkland enclosed on three sides by the high peaks of the Continental Divide. The campground is like a small village, busy with RVs coming and going, and everyone from toddlers to senior citizens running around—but the crowds are worth the setting, and many sites do offer amazing space and privacy. For hikers, the Fern Lake and Cub Lake trailheads are nearby and can be done as short out-and-backs or turned into a loop of about 14 miles with the Bear Lake Trail, providing a tour of the park's many ecosystems. Anglers can fish for native trout on the Big Thompson River. In winter, there are excellent cross-country skiing and snowshoeing in the park, but visitors should be prepared for frigid temperatures and howling winds. Book a trail ride at Moraine Park Stables (970/586-2327, www.Ride.RMNP. com), just over the rise from Loop D, so you can walk to your morning ride after breakfast.

The campground has five loops in a montane habitat, with tall ponderosa pines and scattered aspen providing fair shade and excellent views.

It's worth noting that the designated group sites are near the bus stops and high-traffic area and are not the best. Loop A (1-140) attracts tents and RVs of all sizes. Loop B (170-225) is more cramped and attracts mostly RVs, with some tents. Most of the sites in Loop C (226-247) have nice views. Loop D (141-169), the only non-generator loop, is best for tent campers and has several wonderful walk-in sites. This loop has excellent views and beautiful granite rock features for the kids to climb.

Campsites, facilities: There are 244 sites for tents and RVs up to 45 feet. In the winter, group sites are available for tent-camping groups of up to 40 people. There are no hookups. Sites 129, 219, 226, 238, 239, and 242 are pull-through. Picnic tables, fire rings, grills, and tent pads are provided. Flush toilets, drinking water, dishwashing sinks, dump stations, pay phones at the ranger station, bear lockers, campfire programs, and an amphitheater are available. Water is not available in the winter, when only 77 sites remain open. Leashed pets are permitted but are not allowed on trails.

Reservations, fees: Reservations are accepted from late May-late September at 877/444-6777 and www.recreation.gov. The rest of the year, sites are first come, first served. The fee is $26 per night, or $18 per night when the water is off during the winter; $3 per person at the winter group sites. Campers must also purchase a vehicle day pass ($25), a weeklong pass ($35), annual park pass ($70), or Interagency Annual America the Beautiful Pass ($80). Credit card, cash, or checks are accepted. Camping in the park is limited to seven nights total park-wide early June-late September. Open year-round (only Loop B sites are open in winter).

Directions: From Estes Park, take U.S. Highway 36 west to the Beaver Meadow entrance station. In 0.2 mile, turn left on Bear Lake Road. In 1.2 miles, turn right at the campground sign.

Contact: Rocky Mountain National Park, 970/586-1206, www.nps.gov/romo.

Rocky Mountain National Park has plenty of campgrounds, but reserve far in advance.

26 GLACIER BASIN

Scenic rating: 6
in Rocky Mountain National Park

BEST (

Glacier Basin is a sprawling frontcountry campground on the east side of Rocky Mountain National Park. (For more information on the park, see the Aspenglen listing in this chapter.) The basin is surrounded by the peaks of the Continental Divide, including Longs Peak, Storm Peak, Half Mountain, Taylor Peak, Otis Peak, and Flattop Mountain. There are numerous hiking trails, too. The Sprague Lake, Storm Pass, and Bierstadt Lake Trails begin nearby, and a trail connects the campground to the YMCA.

The campground has four loops and 13 group sites. About half of the campground took a hard hit from bark beetle activity a few years ago; as a result, parts of Loops C, D, and the group loop have been clear-cut. On the bright side, these loops now have stunning 270-degree views of the surrounding peaks and night sky, and there are plenty of baby pine and aspen trees sprouting up in the wake of the beetle impact. Loops A and B are still in a dense lodgepole forest. The sites throughout the campground are just 15-30 feet apart, so privacy is poor to moderate. There is no shade in the clear-cut loops, but excellent shade in Loops A and B and parts of C.

Campsites, facilities: There are 150 sites for tents and RVs up to 35 feet. There are also 13 group sites for tents only. Some of the group sites accommodate up to 40 people. Picnic tables, fire rings, grills, and tent pads are provided. Flush toilets, drinking water, dishwashing sinks, food lockers, emergency phone, campfire programs, an amphitheater, a shuttle bus, a riding stable, and dump stations, are available. Leashed pets are permitted, but pets are not allowed on trails. Sites 33, 35, 60, and 61 and the facilities are wheelchair-accessible.

Reservations, fees: Reservations are recommended for Loops A, B, and D at 877/444-6777 and www.recreation.gov. Loop C is first come, first served. The fee is $26 per night. The group sites are $3 per person per night. Campers must also purchase a vehicle day pass ($25), a week-long pass ($35), annual park pass ($70), or Interagency Annual America the Beautiful Pass ($80). Credit card, cash, or check. Camping in the park is limited to seven nights total park-wide early June-late September. Open late May-early September.

Directions: From Estes Park, take U.S. Highway 36 west to the Beaver Meadow entrance station. In 0.2 mile, turn left on Bear Lake Road. In 4.8 miles, turn left at the Glacier Basin sign.

Contact: Rocky Mountain National Park, 970/586-1206, www.nps.gov/romo.

27 ESTES PARK CAMPGROUND AT EAST PORTAL

Scenic rating: 7

south of Estes Park

Estes Park is the gateway to Rocky Mountain National Park, one of the crown jewels of the national park system. The campgrounds in the park are usually full, so latecomers without reservations often have to look outside the park to find a good campsite. Fortunately, Estes Valley Recreation and Park District offers two campgrounds that are a short distance from town and the park, one at Mary's Lake and another at East Portal. Both campgrounds are served by a free shuttle service into town and the park.

East Portal feels more remote than Mary's Lake. With an elevation of about 8,300 feet and proximity to the national park border, it offers excellent views of the several mountain ranges in the park, plus easy access to the Glacier Basin area via the East Portal trail (a one-hour climb to Sprague Lake). Bring your fishing pole to take advantage of the park's native trout population. There are two loops at this hillside campground set on a rather narrow, pitched road. Sites 1-32 are most suitable

for tent camping, located in a lodgepole forest with good shade and moderate privacy. Sites 65-70 are RV sites with excellent views. Like Mary's Lake, this campground would benefit from some renovations.

Campsites, facilities: There are 70 sites for tents and RVs up to 22 feet, including 35 tent sites. Some sites have electricity and full hook-ups. Picnic tables, fire rings, and some tent pads are provided. Flush toilets, showers, drinking water, dump stations, are available. There is a swing set and climbing wall for kids. Leashed pets are permitted. Sites 32, 45, 65, and 70 and facilities are wheelchair-accessible.

Reservations, fees: Reservations are accepted at Reserve America, 800/964-7806 or www.reserveamerica.com. The fee is $35 per night for a basic site and $45-55 per night for an RV site with water, electric, and full hookup. Cash, check, and credit cards are accepted. Open mid-May-mid-October, depending on weather.

Directions: From Highways 34 and 36 in downtown Estes Park, take Highway 36/Moraine Park Road west for 2.0 miles. Turn left on County Road 66/Tunnel Road toward YMCA of the Rockies. In 3.2 miles (you'll pass the YMCA on your right) the road ends at the campground.

Contact: Estes Valley Recreation and Park District, 970/586-4188, www.evrpd.com.

28 ESTES PARK CAMPGROUND AT MARY'S LAKE

Scenic rating: 5

south of Estes Park

Mary's Lake attracts everyone from snowbirds who live full-time in their RVs to tent campers who are prepping for (or recovering from) a long trip into the backcountry. The campground offers decent views of the surrounding peaks, including Ram's Horn and Gianttrack

Mountains to the west and Lilly Mountain to the south, as well as the residential sprawl of Estes Park down the valley. There are no views of nearby Mary's Lake, which is closed to boating and swimming because the reservoir's water levels fluctuate so much on a daily basis that whirlpools make the water unsafe for anything except fishing. The nearest hiking trails are a short drive away at Lilly Lake and Twin Sisters. Much of the campground is a large RV lot, and elsewhere the scattered ponderosa do not provide much privacy. The sites with the best views and privacy are 66-76, and 135. Tent sites 65-80 and 91-93 aren't bad either, with more shade.

Campsites, facilities: There are 141 sites for tents and RVs up to 50 feet, including 60 tent-only sites (maximum of 6 people per site). Electricity and full hookups are available. Picnic tables, fire rings, and grills are provided. Tent pads are provided at the tent sites. Flush toilets, showers, drinking water, laundry facilities, a store, a tiny pool, a playground, propane, Wi-Fi, a game room, a basketball hoop, and dump stations are available. Leashed pets are permitted. Sites 44, 46, 62, 63, 77, and 140 and facilities are wheelchair-accessible.

Reservations, fees: Reservations are accepted at Reserve America, 800/964-7806 or www.reserveamerica.com. The fee is $35 per night for a basic site and $45-55 per night for an RV site with hookups. Cash, check, and credit cards are accepted. Open early May-early October.

Directions: From the intersection of Highways 34 and 36 in downtown Estes Park, take Highway 36/Moraine Road west for 1.9 miles. Turn left on County Road 67/Mary's Lake Road. The campground is on the left before the dam in 1.6 miles.

Contact: Estes Valley Recreation and Park District, 970/577-1026, www.evrpd.com.

29 HERMIT'S HOLLOW

Scenic rating: 8

southeast of Estes Park

Hermit Park Open Space is a gem. Located just two miles from Estes Park, it feels like a world apart. The area was originally settled as a result of the 1862 Homestead Act and is named for Dutch Louie, a squatter who built a cabin in the park in 1910. Until 2007, the park was a privately owned retreat for Agilent Technologies and Hewlett Packard, which helps to explain the fairly pristine conditions. The park ranges in elevation from 7,880 feet to nearly 9,000 feet and features landscape meadows, wetlands, ponderosa pine, Douglas fir, and aspen. The most prominent landmark is Kruger Rock. A 2.75-mile hike to the top rewards hikers with views of the Mummy Range and Longs Peak. The one-mile Homestead Meadows connector trail will take hikers and bikers to a historic area with eight original homesteads. This destination is no secret—reservations are highly recommended on summer weekends, but you can have your pick on weekdays. There are also 15 rustic cabins available for rent in the park. Hermit Park also has excellent facilities for weddings and group events, including special group campsites at Granite Gulch.

Hermit's Hollow is a beautiful campground in a forest of pine, fir, and aspen with interesting rock outcroppings. The only unattractive sites are 28 and 29. Sites 1-6 and 14-16 have outstanding views. Sites 17, 18, 22, 24, 25, 28, and 29 are also in excellent locations with ample privacy. There is a camper cabin with propane lights, heat, and a cook stove that is available year-round.

Campsites, facilities: There are 42 sites for tents and small RVs up to 20 feet and 11 walk-in tent sites. There are no hookups and generators are not allowed. Pull-throughs are available. Picnic tables, fire rings, and grills are provided. Vault toilets, drinking water, and a dump station are available. Leashed pets are permitted. There is a separate group pavilion site for up to 125 people.

Reservations, fees: Reservations are accepted at www.larimercamping.com and 800/397-7795. Nonelectric sites are $30-45 per night and the equestrian site is $40-60 per night, depending on the season. The camper cabin is $100-150 per night. Campers must also purchase a daily pass ($9) or an annual pass ($90 for Larimer County residents, $120 for nonresidents, $65 for senior citizens, and $10 for disabled veterans). Cash, check, and credit cards are accepted. Open March-December 20, weather permitting.

Directions: From the intersection of Highways 34 and 36 in downtown Estes Park, take Highway 36 east 3.8 miles. Turn right at the sign for Hermit Park. The campground is about 1.2 miles past the office, where you must check in and buy your vehicle pass.

Contact: Larimer County Department of Natural Resources, 970/619-4570, www.larimer.org/naturalresources.

30 BOBCAT

Scenic rating: 7

southeast of Estes Park

Bobcat is the second-largest campground in scenic Hermit Park (for more information on Hermit Park, see the Hermit's Hollow entry in this chapter) and is the most appropriate one for RVs. Many sites are just 10 feet apart. Sites 1-9 border a meadow surrounded by aspen and some pine. There's not much shade in this loop. Sites 10-39 are in a more wooded loop. Sites 19, 20, 23-25, and 29 have the best privacy. Site 18 has the best views. Hikers and bikers can enjoy the nearby Kruger Rock trail and the group day use area, where weddings regularly take place.

Campsites, facilities: There are 39 sites for tents and RVs up to 40 feet. There are no

hookups. Picnic tables, fire rings, and grills are provided. Vault toilets and drinking water are available. A day use area with a picnic pavilion and volleyball court is available nearby. Leashed pets are permitted.

Reservations, fees: Reservations are accepted at www.larimercamping.com and 800/397-7795. The fee is $30-45 per night. Campers must also purchase a daily pass ($9) or an annual pass ($90 for Larimer County residents, $120 for nonresidents, $65 for senior citizens, and $10 for disabled veterans). Cash, check, and credit cards are accepted. Open March-December, weather permitting.

Directions: From the intersection of Highways 34 and 36 in downtown Estes Park, take Highway 36 east 3.8 miles. Turn right at the sign for Hermit Park. The campground is on the left about 1.5 miles past the office.

Contact: Larimer County Department of Natural Resources, 970/679-4570, www.larimer.org/naturalresources.

31 KRUGER

Scenic rating: 8

southeast of Estes Park

Kruger is a small campground exclusively for equestrian campers (for more information on Hermit Park, see the Hermit's Hollow entry in this chapter), set in a small loop of aspens and pine with views of an adjoining meadow. All sites have basic facilities for horses and trailers.

Campsites, facilities: There are five sites for trailers and RVs up to 35 feet. There are no hookups or pull-throughs. Picnic tables, fire rings, and grills are provided. Vault toilets and drinking water are available. Leashed pets are permitted.

Reservations, fees: Reservations are accepted at www.larimercamping.com and 800/397-7795. The fee is $40-60 per night. Campers must also purchase a daily pass ($9) or an annual pass ($90 for Larimer County residents, $120 for nonresidents, $65 for senior citizens, and $10 for disabled veterans). Cash, check, and credit cards are accepted. Open March-late December, weather permitting.

Directions: From the intersection of Highways 34 and 36 in downtown Estes Park, take Highway 36 east 3.8 miles. Turn right at the sign for Hermit Park. The campground is about 1.9 miles past the office.

Contact: Larimer County Department of Natural Resources, 970/679-4570, www.larimer.org/naturalresources.

32 PINEWOOD RESERVOIR

Scenic rating: 8

west of Loveland

Like nearby Carter Lake, Flatiron Reservoir, and Horsetooth Reservoir, Pinewood Reservoir is part of the Colorado-Big Thompson Project, which diverts water from the west slope to the east slope for drinking, irrigation, and hydropower generation. The lake itself is uninspiring, but the location is beautiful. Situated at 6,580 feet, the surrounding land consists of meadows, stands of pine, and rocky outcroppings and includes the landmark Blue Mountain. Hikers, bikers, and snowshoers can explore the Blue Mountain, Shoshone, and Besant Point trails in the Ramsay-Shockey Open Space. Trout and tiger muskie fishing is possible on the 100-acre lake and so is wakeless boating.

The campground was remodeled in 2014 and has three loops. Sites 2-4 are adjacent to the parking lot at the south end of the lake, next to the Blue Mountain trailhead. Sites 5-15 are right on the road, near the middle of the lake and with little shade, but sites 7-9 have beautiful views over the lake. Sites 17-27, at the top of the drive, are all walk-in tent sites on a forested knoll with excellent privacy and views.

Campsites, facilities: There are 27 sites for tents and RVs up to 32 feet, including 11 walk-in tent sites. Site 24 is pull-through. There are

campsite at Pinewood Reservoir

no hookups. Site P2-P4 are wheelchair-accessible. Picnic tables, fire rings, and grills are provided. Vault toilets, drinking water, and a boat ramp are available. Leashed pets are permitted.

Reservations, fees: Reservations are recommended and accepted at www.larimercamping.com and 800/397-7795. The fee is $20-30 per night for nonelectric sites and $20-48 per night for electric sites, depending on the season. Campers must also purchase a daily pass ($9) or an annual pass ($90 for Larimer County residents, $120 for nonresidents, $65 for senior citizens, and $10 for disabled veterans). Cash or check only. Open year-round, weather permitting.

Directions: From Loveland, take Highway 34 west and turn south on County Road 29. In 2.0 miles, turn right on County Road 18E. Continue for 6.5 miles up a very steep road. There are three entrances to the campground on the left.

Contact: Larimer County Department of Natural Resources, 970/619-4570, www.larimer.org/naturalresources.

33 FLATIRON RESERVOIR

Scenic rating: 5

west of Loveland

Flatiron Reservoir provides drinking and irrigation water as well as hydropower to the Front Range. It's a popular destination for fishing and family RV camping. At just 47 acres, it's often a backup for campers who want to go boating or swimming on nearby Carter Lake, but couldn't find a spot. The most attractive attribute of this campground is the impressive views of Flatiron Mountain. There are some mature pines and cottonwoods, but privacy and shade are in short supply here. Sites 6, 10, 11, 18, 19, 26, 33, and 37 have the best shade. Sites 12-14, 16, 18, 20-24, 26, and 27 are on the lakeshore.

Sites 26 and 27 are the most private, located at the end of the loop.

Campsites, facilities: There are 37 sites for tents and RVs up to 80 feet and three tepees (sites FT1, FT2, and FT3). Sites 35-37 are walk-in tent sites. Most sites are pull-through and include electric hookups. Picnic tables, fire rings, grills are provided. Shelters are provided at sites 15 and 17. Vault toilets, drinking water, and a group picnic shelter are available. Leashed pets are permitted.Site 19, the facilities, and the fishing pier are wheelchair-accessible.

Reservations, fees: Reservations are recommended and accepted at www.larimercamping.com and 800/397-7795. The fee is $20-30 per night for nonelectric sites and $20-48 per night for electric sites, depending on the season. Tepee sites are $45-68 per night. Campers must also purchase a daily pass ($9) or an annual pass ($90 for Larimer County residents, $120 for nonresidents, $65 for senior citizens, and $10 for disabled veterans). Cash or check only. Open year-round.

Directions: From Loveland, take Highway 34 west and turn south on County Road 29. In 2.0 miles, turn right on County Road 18E. In 2.6 miles, turn left on Flatiron Reservoir Road.

Contact: Larimer County Department of Natural Resources, 970/619-4570, www.larimer.org/naturalresources.

34 NORTH PINES

Scenic rating: 7

southwest of Loveland

Carter Lake is a reservoir in the foothills southwest of Loveland that draws continuous summer crowds for sailing, waterskiing, and swimming, while anglers fish for walleye, trout, kokanee salmon, and largemouth bass. The reservoir is a part of the Colorado-Big Thompson Project, which takes water from the west slope to the east slope to meet the growing demands of the Front Range population. The lake is about a mile wide and three miles long. It's a scenic destination, especially on a summer day when sailboats dot the surface.

There are five campgrounds at Carter Lake. North Pines is the smallest, with four sites located on a hillside overlooking the north end of the lake and boat ramp parking lot. Small sites are scattered throughout a thin pine forest and are most suitable for tent camping; privacy is moderate. The three-mile Sundance Trail connects North Pines with South Shore campground. There is a bar, restaurant, and supply store up the road at the park's north entrance.

Campsites, facilities: There are four sites for tents and RVs up to 56 feet. There are no hookups. Site 3 is pull-through. Picnic tables, fire rings, grills, , and tent pads are provided. Vault toilets, drinking water, and a boat ramp are available. Leashed pets are permitted.

Reservations, fees: Reservations are recommended and accepted at www.larimercamping. com and 800/397-7795. The fee is $20-30 per night. Campers must also purchase a daily pass ($9) or an annual pass ($90 for Larimer County residents, $120 for nonresidents, $65 for senior citizens, and $10 for disabled veterans). Open year-round.

Directions: From Loveland, take Highway 34 west and turn south on County Road 29. In 2.0 miles, turn right on County Road 18E. The park entrance is on the left in 2.0 miles. Continue 1.5 miles to the campground on the right.

Contact: Larimer County Department of Natural Resources, 970/679-4570, www. larimer.org/naturalresources.

35 EAGLE

Scenic rating: 7

southwest of Loveland

Eagle is the largest campground at Carter Lake,

and is quite popular due to its proximity to the marina and boat ramp. Visitors will enjoy sailing and fishing for walleye on the lake, but should consult with the consumption advisory published by the Department of Wildlife before eating their catch. (For more information on Carter Lake, see the North Pines entry in this chapter.) The campground is divided into four loops. Meadow View (sites 1-10) and Golden (sites 11-22) are the most appealing, with ample shade, moderate privacy, and some lake views. Sites 4-10 have the best views. Talon (sites 23-37) has tent pads and a playground but fewer trees, and Dam View (38-49) is in a meadow below the dam and the least appealing of the loops.

Campsites, facilities: There are 49 sites for tents and RVs up to 80 feet. Electric hookups and pull-throughs are available. Picnic tables, fire rings, and grills are provided. Flush toilets, showers, and drinking water are available. A playground is located near Talon Loop and the boat ramp and store are accessible at the marina on the other side of County Road 31. Leashed pets are permitted. Site 19 and the facilities are wheelchair-accessible.

Reservations, fees: Reservations are recommended and accepted at www.larimercamping. com and 800/397-7795. The fee is $20-30 per night for nonelectric sites and $20-48 per night for electric sites, depending on the season. Campers must also purchase a daily pass ($9) or an annual pass ($90 for Larimer County residents, $120 for nonresidents, $65 for senior citizens, and $10 for disabled veterans). Open year-round.

Directions: From Loveland, take Highway 34 west and turn south on County Road 29. In 2.0 miles, turn right on County Road 18E. The park entrance is on the left in 2.0 miles. In 1.7 miles, turn left on Prairie Way. Stay right at the fork to enter the campground.

Contact: Larimer County Department of Natural Resources, 970/679-4570, www. larimer.org/naturalresources.

36 BIG THOMPSON
🚣 🏕 ♿ 🚐 ⛺

Scenic rating: 5

southwest of Loveland

Big Thompson occupies a bluff overlooking the north end of Carter Lake. (For more information on Carter Lake, see the North Pines entry in this chapter.) It's an arid and windy location with a few cottonwoods and pines. Privacy is poor and there is no shade. The most appealing feature is the excellent views of the ridgeline west of the lake. The exposed sites are more comfortable for RV camping than tent camping. Boating and fishing access are available 0.5 mile away at the marina, and hiking is available at Eagle campground.

Campsites, facilities: There are eight sites for tents and RVs up to 48 feet. All sites are pull-through but there are no hookups. Picnic tables, fire rings, and grills are provided. Vault toilets and drinking water are available. Leashed pets are permitted. Site 4 and the facilities are wheelchair-accessible.

Reservations, fees: Reservations are recommended and accepted at www.larimercamping. com and 800/397-7795. The fee is $20-30 per night for nonelectric sites and $20-48 per night for electric sites, depending on the season. Campers must also purchase a daily pass ($9) or an annual pass ($90 for Larimer County residents, $120 for nonresidents, $65 for senior citizens, and $10 for disabled veterans). Open year-round.

Directions: From Loveland, take Highway 34 west and turn south on County Road 29. In 2.0 miles, turn right on County Road 18E. The park entrance is on the left in 2.0 miles. Continue 2.2 miles to the campground on the right.

Contact: Larimer County Department of Natural Resources, 970/679-4570, www. larimer.org/naturalresources.

37 CARTER KNOLLS
🚣 🚣 🏕 🚐 ⛺

Scenic rating: 6

southwest of Loveland

Carter Knolls is a campground for tents and small RVs on the eastern shore of Carter Lake. (For more information on this reservoir, see the North Pines entry in this chapter.) It has excellent views of the peaks on the far side of the lake, but it is very exposed. The sites are 50 feet apart, but privacy and shade are both poor. Fortunately, it's a short walk from the swim beach, so campers with children are often drawn to this campground.

Campsites, facilities: There are seven sites for tents and RVs up to 20 feet. Sites 8 and 9 are walk-ins. There are no hookups. Site 5 is pull-through. Picnic tables, fire rings, grills, and tent pads are provided. Sites 2, 6, and 9 have shelters. Vault toilets and drinking water are available. Leashed pets are permitted.

Reservations, fees: Reservations are recommended and accepted at www.larimercamping. com and 800/397-7795. The fee is $20-30 per night for nonelectric sites and $20-48 per night for electric sites, depending on the season. Campers must also purchase a daily pass ($9) or an annual pass ($90 for Larimer County residents, $120 for nonresidents, $65 for senior citizens, and $10 for disabled veterans). Open year-round.

Directions: From Loveland, take Highway 34 west and turn south on County Road 29. In 2.0 miles, turn right on County Road 18E. The park entrance is on the left in 2.0 miles. Continue 3.2 miles to the campground on the right.

Contact: Larimer County Department of Natural Resources, 970/679-4570, www. larimer.org/naturalresources.

38 SOUTH SHORE

Scenic rating: 6

southwest of Loveland

South Shore is one of the most popular campgrounds at Carter Lake, especially for family reunions and other groups who take advantage of the day use area at the campground. (For more information on Carter Lake, see the North Pines entry in this chapter.) Campers can also enjoy the three-mile Sundance Trail, which ends at North Pines campground, and the boat ramp, as well as fishing from the shore for trout, walleye, bass, and kokanee salmon.

Shade and privacy are both sparse at this campground, which has cottonwoods and some pines but not much vegetation. Site 8 has the best privacy, and sites 10 and 12 have the best shade. Sites 3, 5, 7, 8, and 17-21 have nice views of the lake. Walk-in sites 23-25 are in a forest of pine trees and also have excellent views.

Campsites, facilities: There are 30 sites for tents and RVs up to 60 feet. Sites 22-25, 29, and 30 are walk-ins. Electric hookups and pull-throughs are available. Picnic tables, fire rings, and grills are provided. Sites 10 and 12 and the walk-in sites have tent pads. Vault toilets, drinking water, and a group day-use area with horseshoe pits and a volleyball court are available. Leashed pets are permitted. Sites 1-3, the trail, and the facilities are wheelchair-accessible.

Reservations, fees: Reservations are recommended and accepted at www.larimercamping. com and 800/397-7795. The fee is $20-30 per night for nonelectric sites and $20-48 per night for electric sites, depending on the season. Campers must also purchase a daily pass ($9) or an annual pass ($90 for Larimer County residents, $120 for nonresidents, $65 for senior citizens, and $10 for disabled veterans). Open year-round.

Directions: From Loveland, take Highway 34 west and turn south on County Road 29. In 2.0

miles, turn right on County Road 18E. The park entrance is on the left in 2.0 miles. In 4.6 miles, turn right onto County Road 31. The campground is on the right in 1.0 mile.

Contact: Larimer County Department of Natural Resources, 970/679-4570, www. larimer.org/naturalresources.

39 COTTONWOOD

Scenic rating: 4

in Boyd Lake State Park

Boyd Lake is a water-sports haven and a busy summer destination. The park is on the western edge of the plains; to the west, Longs Peak and the Indian Peaks dominate the horizon. The 1,700-surface-acre lake is open to boating, windsurfing, waterskiing, and swimming. A busy multiuse trail circles the lake, and the wetlands are open to wildlife viewing and waterfowl hunting. Anglers catch bass, catfish, perch, crappie, walleye, and trout. Winter activities include ice fishing and cross-country skiing.

The campground is on the western shore. With six identical paved loops, it's a mega complex. Privacy is poor (the sites are just 10 feet apart), but the campground is extremely popular on weekends, so reservations are highly recommended. Many sites have partial shade, and a few sites have lake views. Loop A is closest to the swim beach. Loop F has more mature trees and it borders a grassland, so it's a little more quiet and private than the other loops.

Campsites, facilities: There are 148 sites for tents and RVs up to 40 feet. Electric hookups are available at all sites, and all sites are paved and pull-through. Picnic tables, fire rings, and grills are provided. Restrooms with flush toilets and showers, drinking water, a laundry room, boat ramp, a group fire pit with regular programs, a marina with rentals, horseshoe pits, a basketball court, and dump stations are available.

Leashed pets are permitted. Sites 47, 76, 97, and 131 and the facilities are wheelchair-accessible.

Reservations, fees: Reservations are highly recommended at 800/244-5613 and www. cpwshop.com. The fee is $36 per night. Campers must also purchase a vehicle pass ($9) or Annual Parks Pass ($80). Open year-round.

Directions: From I-25, take Exit 257/U.S. Highway 34 west for 3.4 miles. Turn north on Madison Avenue. In 1.5 miles, turn right on 37th Street. The park entrance is on the right in 1.0 mile.

Contact: Boyd Lake State Park, 970/669-1739, www.cpw.state.co.us.

40 PLATTE RIVER FORT EVENT CENTER AND CAMPGROUND

Scenic rating: 7

near Greeley

Platte River Fort Event Center and Campground is a unique property just outside Kersey, Colorado. The main lodge is a replica of Bent's Old Fort National Historic Monument in La Junta, five hours to the south, itself a reconstructed 1840s fur trading post. This northern Colorado version also has a 235-acre working cattle ranch, a farmhouse for rent, a barbecue joint in the barn, and a new campground. There are tent sites, RV sites, and six onion-shaped Lotus Belle glamping tents on grassy bank of the South Platte River. The tents are in a flat, lush floodplain, separated from the main lodge by a 1-minute drive past the Longhorn cattle herd. The location means river sounds and wildlife, but also some bugs and the sounds of nearby highways. There are some watersports, like SUP and tubing, available on the river. Campers have some access to the main lodge, where there is a coffee and doughnut shop, additional rooms, and also Hank's Bar & Grill, with barbecue and smoked meats,

and a patio bar with stunning views of the Continental Divide. They have occasional live music, bar specials, barn dances, lawn games, and hayrides. It's about one hour to Denver to the south, or to Rocky Mountain National Park to the west, or Cheyenne to the north; and only 25 miles to Pawnee National Grasslands, making this an interesting crossroads spot.

Campsites, facilities: The tents are on wood platforms and spaced about 50 feet apart, providing plenty of privacy; inside they're spacious and rounded like a yurt, with beds and basic furniture, and electricity. At the moment, the bathroom is just a shared port-a-potty near the river sites.

Reservations, fees: Reservations are recommended. Glamping tents/yurts are $75/night on weekdays, $99 on weekends; tent and RV/trailer sites are $30/night. Rooms at the fort start at $149.

Directions: An hour's drive north from Denver, located on the north side of Highway 34, just east of Greeley.

Contact: Highway 34, Greeley, 80631; www. platteriverfort.com, 970/590-4414.

41 LONGS PEAK

Scenic rating: 9

in Rocky Mountain National Park

BEST (

There are four frontcountry campgrounds on the east side of Rocky Mountain National Park. (For more information on the park, see the Aspenglen listing in this chapter.) Longs Peak is the smallest and is the sole tent-only campground (sleeping in vehicles is prohibited). This is also the starting point for the challenging ascent of Longs Peak (14,259 feet). Climbers typically begin at 3am to complete the 12- to 15-hour trek. The only nontechnical route, the Keyhole, is about 16 miles round-trip and can be treacherous. Many hikers are turned back by strong winds, thunderstorms, and ice, and there are a couple of fatalities nearly every summer. Still, Longs Peak remains the most climbed fourteener in the state.

The campground is a single small loop in a dense lodgepole forest. The sites are just 10-20 feet apart. There is plenty of camaraderie and little privacy, but this is a fun, cozy campground. Sites 1, 3, 4, 6, 8, 9, and 11 have views of Sheep Mountain.

Campsites, facilities: There are 26 tent sites. Picnic tables, fire rings, grills, and tent pads are provided. Wheelchair-accessible vault toilets, drinking water, an emergency phone at the ranger station, and food lockers are available. Water is not available from mid-September–mid-May (sometimes later). Leashed pets are permitted.

Reservations, fees: Reservations are not accepted. Sites are first come, first served. The fee is $26 per night (or sometimes free when the water is shut off). Check-in time is at 1pm and checkout is at noon. Campers must also purchase a vehicle day pass ($25), a weeklong pass ($35), annual park pass ($70), or Interagency Annual America the Beautiful Pass ($80). Credit card, cash, and checks are accepted. Camping in the park is limited to seven nights total park-wide early June-late September. Open late May through November 1 (or sometimes year-round, weather permitting).

Directions: From U.S. Highway 36 in Estes Park, take Highway 7 south for 9.0 miles. Turn right at the Longs Peak sign. Go uphill 0.9 mile to the campground.

Contact: Rocky Mountain National Park, 970/586-1206, www.nps.gov/romo.

42 MEEKER

Scenic rating: 5

south of Estes Park

Meeker is a campground au naturel. Although this is the least-developed campground near Rocky Mountain National Park, it usually fills up on Friday and Saturday nights. It has the

campsite at Platte River Fort

cheapest rates in town and attracts mainly off-site day users and tent campers. It has three loops in a thin pine forest. Sites 1-5 are walk-ins near the busy highway. Sites 6-8 are in an aspen grove that is also near the highway. The back loop (sites 15-29) requires a high-clearance vehicle to access, but it's the best place to camp. Sites 17-19, 21, and 24 have views of Sheep Mountain. Sites 27-29 are especially rocky, but they also have views of Mount Meeker.

Campsites, facilities: There are 29 sites for tents and small RVs. There are no hookups. Sites 1-5 and 9 are pull-through. Fire rings, grills, and plastic portable toilets are provided. Leashed pets are permitted.

Reservations, fees: Reservations are not accepted. The fee is $13 per night. Cash or check only. Open May-September.

Directions: From Estes Park, take Highway 7 south for 11 miles. The campground is on the right about a half-mile before the town of Meeker.

Contact: Arapaho and Roosevelt National Forest, Boulder District, 303/541-2500, www.fs.usda.gov/arp.

43 OLIVE RIDGE
🚶‍♂️ 🐕 🚐 ⛺

Scenic rating: 7

south of Estes Park

Olive Ridge is just outside the southeast corner of Rocky Mountain National Park, at the entryway to the Wild Basin, a vast, wildlife-rich area of dense woods, tumbling streams, and high cirques. From the Wild Basin trailhead, hikers can follow St. Vrain Creek to Ouzel Lake (an excellent fishing destination), Bluebird Lake, and Thunder Lake. This large, pleasant campground is in a pine forest with scattered boulders. The sites are 30-50 feet apart and are practically identical, with a few exceptions, though there is plenty of shade and some rock features. Sites 37, 39, and 40 have views of the

Wild Basin. Site 38 is closest to the highway. Sites 50 and 52 have views of the valley. Sites 26 and 40 are a little larger.

Campsites, facilities: There are 56 sites for tents and RVs up to 55 feet. There are no hookups. Picnic tables, fire rings, grills, and tent pads are provided. There are also vault toilets and drinking water. Leashed pets are permitted.

Reservations, fees: Reservations are required for all sites except 38, 41, and 42 at 877/444-6777 and www.recreation.gov. The fee is $23 per night. Cash or check only. Open May-September.

Directions: From Lyons, take Highway 7 west to Allenspark. Continue 1.3 miles past Allenspark and turn left at the campground sign, and then another left to reach the fee station.

Contact: Arapaho and Roosevelt National Forest, Boulder District, 303/541-2500, www.fs.usda.gov/arp.

44 CAMP DICK
🚶‍♂️ 🚲 🛶 🐎 ♿ 🚐 ⛺

Scenic rating: 8

north of Ward

Camp Dick is a popular destination for families and hikers. The Buchanan Pass Trail runs from the campground into the heart of the Indian Peaks Wilderness, where serrated peaks and alpine lakes await the hardy hiker. The campground consists of two loops in a meadow ringed by an aspen, pine, and spruce forest beside the Middle St. Vrain Creek. The diversity of the forest has kept the bark beetle activity here to a minimum. Mountain bikers and ATV riders can explore the Bunce School Road, Coney Flats Road, and South Vrain Road. Anglers can pick brookies out of the Middle St. Vrain Creek. Most sites are close to the road and not screened, so privacy is poor, but modern facilities and great hiking bring in the crowd. Half of the sites are first come, first served, but those fill up by Thursday; arrive early if you don't have a reservation. Sites 1, 3, 4, 7-10, and 12-16 are creekside. Sites 1, 2, 3, and 4 are walk-ins. There are nine double sites; site 38 is particularly nice. Sites 7, 8, 24, 26, and 28 are in a middle island in the loop and do not have shade.

Campsites, facilities: There are 39 sites for tents and RVs up to 50 feet. There are no hookups. Site 16 is pull-through. Picnic tables, fire rings, grills, and tent pads are provided. Vault toilets, bear lockers, and drinking water are available. Leashed pets are permitted. The facilities are wheelchair-accessible.

Reservations, fees: Reservations are accepted (and highly recommended) at 877/444-6777 and www.recreation.gov. The fee is $23 per night, $46 for double sites. Cash or check only. Open May-October.

Directions: From Lyons, travel southwest on Colorado 7 about 20 miles, then turn south on the Peak to Peak Scenic Byway until the turnoff to Peaceful Valley on the right; from there, take County Road 92 west for 0.8 mile to Camp Dick.

Contact: Arapaho and Roosevelt National Forest, Boulder District, 303/541-2500, www.fs.usda.gov/arp.

45 PEACEFUL VALLEY

Scenic rating: 7

north of Ward

Peaceful Valley is a great campground for R&R. It's about four miles east of the Indian Peaks Wilderness boundary. From nearby Camp Dick, hikers can take the Buchanan Pass Trail into the wilderness to the Middle St. Vrain Trail, the St. Vrain Glaciers, Red Deer Lake, and Buchanan Pass. These are challenging hikes and many require a night in the backcountry. Because of the popularity of the

wilderness, permits are required for backcountry camping. Mountain bikers and ATV riders can explore the Bunce School Road, Coney Flats Road, and Old South St. Vrain Road. Anglers can pick brookies out of the Middle St. Vrain Creek.

The campground is in a spruce-fir forest on the banks of the creek. The diversity of this forest has kept bark beetle activity to a minimum. The road runs through the middle of the campground, so it can be very busy on the weekends, when every site is full. About half of the sites are first come, first served, but they're usually full by Thursday. Sites 1-3, 7, 8, and 11-14 are creekside. Sites 11-14 are walk-ins with views up the valley. Site 17 is a double site and can accommodate up to 12 people.

Campsites, facilities: There are 17 sites for tents and RVs up to 40 feet. There are no hookups. Picnic tables, fire rings, grills, bear lockers, and tent pads are provided. Vault toilets and drinking water are available. Leashed pets are permitted. The facilities are wheelchair-accessible.

Reservations, fees: Reservations are accepted (and highly recommended) at 877/444-6777 and www.recreation.gov. The fee is $23 per night (double sites are $46 per night). Cash or check only. Open May-October.

Directions: From Lyons, travel southwest on Colorado 7 about 20 miles, then turn south on the Peak to Peak Scenic Byway until the turnoff to Peaceful Valley on your right, take County Road 92 west for 0.2 mile to the campground.

Contact: Arapaho and Roosevelt National Forest, Boulder District, 303/541-2500, www.fs.usda.gov/arp.

46 PAWNEE

Scenic rating: 8

west of Ward

BEST (

Pawnee is the best campground for accessing

the Indian Peaks Wilderness from the east side, not to mention it has some of the very best scenery of any national forest campground. Predictably, it's incredibly popular and reservations are highly recommended on weekends. The campground is on the shore of Lake Brainard, in a basin ringed by Pawnee Peak, Mount Toll, Mount Audubon, Paiute Peak, Shoshone Peak, and Navajo Peak—each over 12,000 feet. The campground is at a breathtaking elevation of about 10,400 feet. The Navajo and Isabelle glaciers are visible on these jagged peaks. The Mount Audubon, Mitchell and Blue Lakes, Pawnee Pass, and Beaver Creek Trails are all accessible from the two trailheads at the campground. Pawnee Pass is on the Continental Divide. There is also good trout fishing on Brainard and Red Rock Lakes, which are open to hand-powered boats.

Campsites, facilities: There are 47 sites for tents, campers, trailers, and RVs up to 45 feet, plus 8 walk-in tent sites. There are also some double sites that can accommodate up to 16 people and a rental cabin that is maintained by the Colorado Mountain Club. There are no hookups and no electricity. Picnic tables, fire rings, grills, and tent pads are provided. Vault toilets and drinking water are available. Leashed pets are permitted.

Reservations, fees: Reservations are accepted (and highly recommended) at 877/444-6777 and www.recreation.gov. The fee is $23 per night ($46 per night for double sites). Cash or check only. Campers must also purchase a Brainard Lake Recreation Fee three-day pass for $12 for passenger vehicles and RVs or buy an American Land & Leisure Season Pass for $66 for the summer. Cash or check only. Open July-September.

Directions: From Ward, take County Road 102 west for 4.8 miles. The campground is on the right.

Contact: Arapaho and Roosevelt National Forest, Boulder District, 303/541-2500, www.fs.usda.gov/arp.

Pawnee campground at Brainard Lake

47 ST. VRAIN STATE PARK

🏕🚴🛶🎣🐕♿🚐⛺

Scenic rating: 3

in Longmont

St. Vrain State Park is a series of ponds, paths, and picnic areas on the floodplain of the St. Vrain River, with 236 acres of water, 604 acres of recreational land, and a nice view of the mountains to the west. Located next to the interstate, the park is readily accessible to locals, Denverites, and travelers passing through. Despite truck traffic noise, it's still a popular afternoon fishing hole for residents of Longmont, area birders, and weekend campers looking for a quick getaway. The three stocked ponds are open to hand-powered boats; Blue Heron Reservoir allows 10-horsepower trawling motors. There are four nature trails, each about one mile long. The campground facilities are comprised of eight loops on or near the banks of the fishing ponds. The Pelican Pond Loop (sites 6-24) is best for tent sites and has the most shade.

Campsites, facilities: There are 87 sites for tents and RVs up to 55 feet. Water and electric hookups are available at sites 1-41 and full hookups are available at sites 42-87. Picnic tables, fire rings, grills, afternoon shade structures, and concrete pads are provided. Flush toilets, showers, drinking water, a meeting room, and dump stations are available. Leashed pets are permitted. Sites 37, 57, and 76, the facilities, and the fishing pier are wheelchair-accessible.

Reservations, fees: Reservations are accepted at 800/244-5613 and www.cpwshop.com. The fee is $36-41 per night. Campers must also purchase a vehicle pass ($8) or Annual Parks Pass ($80). Open year-round.

Directions: From I-25, take Highway 119 west for 1.1 miles. Turn right on County Road 7/County Road 24.5. The park entrance is in 0.9 mile.

Contact: St. Vrain State Park, 303/678-9402, www.cpw.state.co.us.

48 BOULDER ADVENTURE LODGE

🏕🚴🛶🎣⛷🐕♿⛺

Scenic rating: 8

west of Boulder

The Boulder Adventure Lodge, or A-Lodge, is minutes from downtown Boulder (2.5 miles from Pearl Street), at the beginning of Four Mile Canyon. The lodge was recently renovated and re-imagined as a combination hotel, hostel, campground, and adventure center. In addition to a range of accommodations (27 rooms, a 12-bed hostel, and 3-bedroom cabin), A-Lodge has a handful of tent platforms for camping and also car camping spots for campervans. All guests have access to a lobby and lounge building, bathrooms, craft beers on tap, a meeting room, two-story fireplace, beer garden, and pleasant outdoor balcony. There are two hiking trails accessible from the property, nearby climbing, fishing, and biking in Boulder Canyon, and they have two Mercedes Sprinter Adventure Vans for rent (built out by Titan Vans with queen bed, induction stove, 300 watts of solar power, running water, sink, bike racks, ski racks, lighting, and lots of storage). A-Lodge also has a swimming pool, lawn games, community hang spaces, slack-lines, and space for yoga classes, meetings, talks, retreats, and events. The front desk can help you book local adventures like fly fishing, snowshoeing, and guided rock climbing.

Campsites, facilities: There are four tent campsites on wood platforms built into the wooded slope behind the main lodge. The sites have bear boxes, plus access to showers and bathrooms, grills, free cold breakfast, and Wi-Fi. Car camping sites are for vans, airstreams, and conversion vehicles under 24 feet only (no RVs or generators allowed); they are essentially parking spots next to the creek with access to electricity, shower, bathrooms, and the rest of the property.

Reservations, fees: Make reservations at www.a-lodge.com or 303/444-0882. The fee for tent sites and van spots is $45 per night.

Directions: From downtown Boulder, head west up Canyon Blvd into Boulder Canyon for 2.5 miles. Turn right on Fourmile Canyon Dr. and the A-Lodge will be the first driveway on your left with a big sign out front.

Contact: Go to www.a-lodge.com or 303/444-0882.

49 RAINBOW LAKES

Scenic rating: 9

north of Nederland

Rainbow Lakes is a former bear-hunting camp at an elevation of 10,000 feet, with direct access to the Indian Peaks Wilderness. The serrated ridgeline of the Indian Peaks runs from Longs Peak to James Peak and contains gorgeous alpine lakes and a handful of glaciers. This wilderness is easily accessible from Denver, Boulder, and Fort Collins. Usage is closely monitored, and permits are required for backcountry camping. You'll see black bears from time to time, and moose are common as well. Campers can take the Rainbow Lakes and Arapaho Glacier Trails for six miles to awesome views of the glacier, and two miles farther to Arapaho Pass. There are nine rainbow lakes, with trail access to four of them. Fishing is available and there is no limit on brook trout, since they are invasive and threatening to the native fish.

Campsites are flat and even, set in in a thick conifer forest. Sites 5, 7, and 15 have the least shade, while sites 16-18 are short, walk-in tent sites.

Campsites, facilities: There are 16 sites for tents and small trailers. There are no hookups.

Picnic tables, fire rings, and grills are provided. Vault toilets are available. There is no drinking water (bring your own or treat the glacier melt in the nearby creek). The facilities are wheelchair-accessible. Trash must be packed out. Leashed pets are permitted.

Reservations, fees: Reservations are not accepted. The fee is $17 per night. Cash or check only. Open June-September.

Directions: From Nederland, take Highway 72/Peak to Peak Byway north for 7.1 miles. Turn left on Forest Route 298. The campground is in 4.9 miles. Multiple signs warn that the road is "rough and narrow," but it's not that bad.

Contact: Arapaho and Roosevelt National Forest, Boulder District, 303/541-2500, www.fs.usda.gov/arp.

50 KELLY DAHL

Scenic rating: 7

south of Nederland

Kelly Dahl is a convenient campground right off the Peak to Peak Scenic Byway. There are a handful of trailheads in the area (none that leave directly from the campground, however). There is also a small stable there where you can hire trail rides. The campground has three loops in a shady ponderosa pine forest. The Aspen Loop (sites 1-20) is shady; sites 10, 11, 14, and 15 are on a beetle-affected, clearcut slope that wouldn't be fun for tents. Site 16 has good shade and views to the north. Fir Loop (sites 21-27) has some very nice, shady sites surrounding a small meadow. Pine Loop (sites 28-46) is similar to Aspen Loop; sites 28 and 30 are next to a playground. If you get tired of camp cooking, the Sundance Café is less than two miles down the highway and is famous for brunch and amazing views of the Continental Divide.

Campsites, facilities: There are 46 sites for tents and RVs up to 50 feet. There are no

hookups. Site 11 is pull-through. Picnic tables, fire rings, and grills are provided. Vault toilets, high-quality drinking water, and an old, simple playground are available. Leashed pets are permitted.

Reservations, fees: Reservations are accepted (and highly recommended) for sites 21-46 only at 877/444-6777 and www.recreation.gov. The fee is $23 per night. Cash or check only. Open May-September. Day use for picnics near the small playground is $5.

Directions: From Nederland, take Highway 119 south for 3.7 miles. The campground is on the left.

Contact: Arapaho and Roosevelt National Forest, Boulder District, 303/541-2500, www.fs.usda.gov/arp.

51 REVEREND'S RIDGE

Scenic rating: 6

in Golden Gate Canyon State Park

BEST (

Golden Gate Canyon State Park has 12,000 acres of pine forests, hills, and meadows just 16 miles northwest of Golden. Activities include hiking, biking, and horseback riding on 35 miles of trails. Ralston Creek and all of the ponds are stocked by the Department of Wildlife. The park's facilities—especially the Red Barn and Panorama Point—are frequently reserved for special events like reunions and weddings. Winter activities include cross-country skiing, snowshoeing, ice fishing and ice-skating.

Reverend's Ridge, a busy campground in the northwestern corner of the park, is also the largest campground in the area. It's very well laid out and organized, with its own office and visitors center. The Elk, Mule Deer, and Raccoon Trails all pass through the

A lone hiker rests atop the Continental Divide in the Indian Peaks Wilderness, just west of Boulder.

campground, which has 10 loops in a seemingly endless lodgepole pine forest. The sites are 20-50 feet apart, so privacy is at a minimum.

Campsites, facilities: There are 59 sites for RVs (up to 35 feet) and 38 sites for tents only. Loops A-E (sites 1-59) have electric hookups and are used mainly by RVs; sites 9-24 and 44-59 are pull-through. Loops F-J are for tents only. There are also five rustic cabins and two yurts for rent. Picnic tables, fire rings, and grills are provided throughout. Restrooms with flush toilets and showers, a laundry room, drinking water, amphitheater, campfire programs and dump stations. Leashed pets are permitted. Sites 21 and 56 and the facilities are wheelchair-accessible.

Reservations, fees: Reservations are accepted at 800/244-5613 and www.cpwshop.com. The fee is $28 per night for nonelectric sites and $36 per night for electric sites. Campers must also purchase a daily vehicle pass ($8) or Annual Parks Pass ($80). Open year-round. The two yurts and five cabins are $90 per night.

Directions: From Golden, take Highway 46 west about 20 miles. Go north on Highway 119 for 3.3 miles. Turn right on Gap Road. In 1.1 mile, turn left at the campground sign. Camper registration is in 0.4 mile.

Contact: Golden Gate Canyon State Park, 303/582-3707, www.cpw.state.co.us.

spruce-fir forest with a small aspen grove next to a meadow; sites 17-23 and 26-25 are walk-ins (35 feet to 0.25 mile). The Conifer Loop (sites 26-35) is the most attractive; sites 29-35 follow a small creek up a slight rise with an aspen grove and a small meadow. This is a great location for families, since small kids can explore without going near the parking lot. Sites 15 and 16 in the Rimrock Loop can accommodate horses and horse trailers. The rest of the sites in this loop are shaded. (For more information on Golden Gate Canyon State Park, see the Reverend's Ridge listing in this chapter.)

Campsites, facilities: There are 35 sites for tents. Picnic tables, fire rings, and grills, and tent pads are provided. Vault toilets and drinking water are available. Leashed pets are permitted.

Reservations, fees: Reservations are accepted at 800/244-5613 and www.cpwshop.com. The fee is $28 per night. Campers must also purchase a daily vehicle pass ($8) or Annual Parks Pass ($80). Open mid-May-mid-October.

Directions: From Golden, take Highway 46 west about 20 miles. Go north on Highway 119 for 3.3 miles. Turn right on Gap Road. The campground entrance is on the right in 3.0 miles.

Contact: Golden Gate Canyon State Park, 303/582-3707, www.cpw.state.co.us.

52 ASPEN MEADOW
🏃 🚲 🛶 🐕 ⛺

Scenic rating: 7
in Golden Gate Canyon State Park

Aspen Meadow is in the northwestern corner of 12,000-acre Golden Gate Canyon State Park. This tent-only campground is a smaller, more primitive alternative to Reverend's Ridge. The Snowshoe Hare and Mule Deer Trails are accessible from the campground, and Dude's Fishing Hole is a short hike away. Meadow, the first loop, has walk-in and drive-in sites in a

53 RIFLEMAN PHILLIPS GROUP
🏃 🚲 🐎 🚐 ⛺

Scenic rating: 6
in Golden Gate Canyon State Park

BEST (

This campground in the northern half of Golden Gate Canyon State Park is only for groups with reservations. It is located in a pine and aspen forest, with dispersed tent camping. It's not the most appealing site, but the park's group facilities are excellent and they have been used by local Boy Scout troops for decades. The

Red Barn and Panorama Point sites can be reserved for group functions. Panorama Point has an extensive deck with views from Idaho Springs to Estes Park. The Red Barn's picnic area can accommodate up to 150 people and has a volleyball court, fishing ponds, and horseshoe pits. It's a long drive from the campground to the Red Barn, but ambitious groups can hike there on the Buffalo Trail. The Snowshoe Hare Trail also passes by the campground and provides access to Dude's Fishing Hole.

Campsites, facilities: There is dispersed tent camping for up to 75 people and 15 vehicles. Picnic tables, fire rings, grills, and tent pads are provided. Vault toilets and drinking water are available. Showers and laundry facilities are available at Reverend's Ridge. Leashed pets are permitted.

Reservations, fees: Reservations are accepted at 800/244-5613 and www.cpwshop. com. The fee is $364 per night for up to 75 people. Campers must also purchase a daily vehicle pass ($8) or Annual Parks Pass ($80). Open February-October.

Directions: From Golden, take Highway 46 west about 20 miles. Go north on Highway 119 for 3.3 miles. Turn right on Gap Road. The campground entrance is on the right in 3.8 miles.

Contact: Golden Gate Canyon State Park, 303/582-3707, www.cpw.state.co.us.

54 COLD SPRINGS
🐕 ♿ 🚐 ⛺

Scenic rating: 7

north of Black Hawk

Cold Springs is a nice stopover campground for travelers exploring the Front Range. The campground is in a forest of lodgepole and aspen. It's a scenic spot with a few views of the high peaks to the east and west, especially from the vista point. The nearest hiking and biking trails are in Golden Gate Canyon State Park. The only

drawback is the ever-present traffic noise, but choosing sites farther from the highway will help. The host here emphasizes that there is no access to four-wheeling trails and ATVs are not welcome. (They should instead try nearby Columbine campground for four-wheeling access and camping.)

Sites 6-8, 14-17, 32, and 33 have views of the high peaks to the south. The tent sites (20-22) are very close to each other and the road. Sites 26-30 are in the aspen grove, and sites 35-38 overlook the highway. Steep stairs climb up to sites 1-5.

Campsites, facilities: There are 38 sites for tents and RVs up to 40 feet. Sites 20-22 are for tents only. There are no hookups. Sites 1-5, 9, 10, 35, 36, and 38 are pull-through. Picnic tables, fire rings, grills, and tent pads are provided. Vault toilets, drinking water, and a playground are available. Leashed pets are permitted. Site 23 and the facilities are wheelchair-accessible.

Reservations, fees: Reservations are accepted for sites 1-24 at 877/444-6777 and www. recreation.gov; the remaining sites are first come, first served. The fee is $22 per night. Cash or check only. Open May-October.

Directions: From Black Hawk, take Highway 119 north for 5.1 miles. Turn left into the campground.

Contact: Arapaho and Roosevelt National Forest, Clear Creek District, 303/567-3000, www.fs.usda.gov/arp.

55 COLUMBINE
🐕 ♿ 🚐 ⛺

Scenic rating: 4

near Black Hawk

Columbine is the gambler's choice campground: You can drive from the campground to Black Hawk's casinos in 15 minutes. The historic mining and gambling town is the main reason to come to this campground, which is otherwise unremarkable. It's a large loop in a lodgepole forest with moderate bark beetle activity. There are no views, and the sites are just 25-50 feet apart. The rocky ground makes it hard to find multiple tent sites.

Campsites, facilities: There are 47 sites for tents and RVs up to 55 feet. There are no hookups. Picnic tables, fire rings, and grills are provided. Vault toilets and drinking water are available. The facilities are wheelchair-accessible. Leashed pets are permitted.

Reservations, fees: Reservations are accepted at 877/444-6777 and www.recreation.gov. The fee is $21 per night. Cash or check only. Open May-October.

Directions: From Black Hawk, take Highway 119 north for 1.9 miles. Turn left on Apex Valley Road. In 2.3 miles, turn left on Upper Apex Road. In 2.4 miles, turn right on Bald Mountain Road. The campground is on the right in 1.3 miles.

Alternately, just continue straight uphill through Central City, past the cemetery, and look for the campground road.

Contact: Arapaho and Roosevelt National Forest, Clear Creek District, 303/567-3000, www.fs.usda.gov/arp.

56 CLEAR LAKE

Scenic rating: 7

south of Georgetown

Clear Lake campground is a short drive beyond the historic mining district of Georgetown, on the western boundary of Mount Evans Wilderness area. It is popular on weekends and fills up with ATV owners, anglers, and Front Range residents looking for a quick high-altitude getaway. The entire road from Georgetown, over Guanella Pass to Grant, was paved in 2015 and should be open, but check for both weather and construction delays if you plan on continuing to the South Park area.

Clear Lake campground is in a narrow valley

forested with spruce, fir, and aspen; it's about one mile above Lower Cabin Creek Reservoir and 10,000 feet above sea level. The sites are large and spaced about 80 feet apart. Sites 1, 2, and 5 are next to the road.

Campsites, facilities: There are eight sites for tents and RVs up to 25 feet. There are no hookups. Picnic tables, fire rings, and grills are provided. Vault toilets and drinking water are available. Leashed pets are permitted.

Reservations, fees: Reservations are not accepted. The fee is $19 per night. Cash or check only. Open June-September.

Directions: From the Georgetown visitors center, turn right on Argentine Street and then left on 6th Street. On 0.1 mile, turn right on Rose Street/Guanella Pass Road. The campground is on the right in 5.8 miles.

Contact: Arapaho and Roosevelt National Forest, Clear Creek District, 303/567-3000, www.fs.usda.gov/arp.

57 GUANELLA PASS

Scenic rating: 8

south of Georgetown

This campground is on the west side of the Mount Evans Wilderness area and a short drive from the spectacular views at the top of the pass. Due to its proximity to Denver, Guanella Pass is usually full during the summer, especially on weekends. Anglers can fish for brookies on the creek or hike a 1.5-mile trail to Silver Dollar Lake. Hikers have several options in Mount Evans Wilderness, which has two fourteeners (Mount Evans and Mount Bierstadt), alpine tundra, arctic tundra, and the Mount Goliath Natural Area, a large stand of bristlecone pines. From the summit of Mount Bierstadt, hikers can follow a horseshoe-shaped ridge another two miles to Mount Evans. Bighorn sheep and mountain goats are frequently sighted in this area.

The campground has two loops, which straddle the road. The first loop (sites 1-7) is on the west side of the road, and the sites are first come, first served. The second loop (sites 8-18) is on the east side of the road beside Cabin Creek. Sites 2, 3, 7, and 14-16 have good views down the valley. Sites 8, 10, and 11 are creekside. Sites 9-12, 14, and 15 are walk-in tent sites.

Campsites, facilities: There are 18 sites for tents and RVs up to 40 feet. Sites 9-12, 14, and 15 are for tents only. There are no hookups. Picnic tables, fire rings, grills, and tent pads are provided. Vault toilets and drinking water are available. Leashed pets are permitted. The facilities are wheelchair-accessible.

Reservations, fees: Reservations are not accepted. The fee is $21 per night. Cash or check only. Open June-September.

Directions: From the Georgetown visitors center, turn right on Argentine Street and then left on 6th Street. On 0.1 mile, turn right on Rose Street/Guanella Pass Road. The campground is in 8.7 miles. Sites 1-7 are on the right, and sites 8-18 are on the left.

Contact: Arapaho and Roosevelt National Forest, Clear Creek District, 303/567-3000, www.fs.usda.gov/arp.

58 WEST CHICAGO CREEK

🏃 ⛴ 🐕 🚗 ⛺

Scenic rating: 7

south of Idaho Springs

West Chicago Creek flows out of the Mount Evans Wilderness area down a narrow valley. The campground is a short distance from the Hells Hole trailhead, which follows the creek to the meadows at its headwaters beneath Gray Wolf Mountain. West Chicago Creek is a quick getaway from Denver, so it's very popular throughout the summer. The camp usually fills up by Thursday evening, but there are five non-reservable sites as well as dispersed camping farther up the road past the official

campground; try your luck there if the campground is full.

The campground is a small loop in a lodgepole forest. An aspen grove borders one side of the campground and covers the slope down to the creek. The sites are just 25-50 feet apart. Sites 11 and 12 have views up the valley of Sugarloaf Peak. Sites 1 and 13-16 are next to the road, which receives a fair amount of traffic on weekends.

Campsites, facilities: There are 16 sites for tents and RVs up to 45 feet. There are no hookups. Site 10 is pull-through. Picnic tables, fire rings, and grills are provided. Vault toilets and drinking water are available. Leashed pets are permitted.

Reservations, fees: Reservations are accepted at 877/444-6777 and www.recreation.gov. The fee is $20 per night. Cash or check only. Open May-September, weather permitting.

Directions: From Idaho Springs, take Highway 103 south for 6.7 miles. Turn right on Forest Route 188, a fairly bumpy dirt road with several hairpin turns that could be difficult for trailers. The campground is on the left in 2.8 miles.

Contact: Arapaho and Roosevelt National Forest, Clear Creek District, 303/567-3000, www.fs.usda.gov/arp.

59 ECHO LAKE

🏃 ⛴ 🐕 🚗 ⛺

Scenic rating: 8

south of Idaho Springs

Echo Lake is on the northern edge of the Mount Evans Wilderness at a stunning 10,600 feet above sea level (the campground is adjacent to the University of Denver High Altitude Laboratory). The Mount Evans Byway is the highest paved road in North America. It climbs from the lake and campground 14 miles farther to the peak (elevation 14,265 feet) and features frequent sightings of bighorn sheep and mountain goats. Peak-bagging hikers take the

Resthouse Trail to the Summit Lake Trail to Mount Evans. Most of the wilderness is above timberline, and the landscape is rugged glacial terrain pockmarked by alpine lakes and arctic tundra. The views plus the wildlife and proximity to Denver make this wilderness extremely popular. Reservations are highly recommended during the summer.

The campground is in a spruce-fir forest beside the highway and a short distance from the lake, which is owned by the City of Denver and open for fishing. The terraced sites are very close together, and the campground is a bit cramped. Sites 11 and 14 have the most privacy.

Campsites, facilities: There are 18 sites for tents and a couple for RVs up to about 30-35 feet, although small RVs fit this campground much better. Sites 1-4 are walk-ins. There are no hookups. Picnic tables, fire rings, grills and tent pads are provided. Vault toilets and drinking water are available. There is a small store at Echo Lake Lodge. Leashed pets are permitted.

Reservations, fees: Reservations are accepted for sites 1-7, 9, 10, 12, 13, and 14 at 877/444-6777 and www.recreation.gov. The remaining sites are walk-in only. The fee is $21 per night. Cash or check only. Open May-September, weather depending (spring snow can delay the opening by a month).

Directions: From Idaho Springs, take Highway 103 south for 13.3 miles. Turn right after Echo Lake Lodge and then make the first left to enter the campground.

Contact: Arapaho and Roosevelt National Forest, Clear Creek District, 303/567-3000, www.fs.usda.gov/arp.

60 CHERRY CREEK STATE PARK

🚶 🚴 🏊 ⛏ 🛶 🏊 ❄ 🐴 ♿ 🚐 ⛺

Scenic rating: 3

in Denver

BEST (

Urban camping at its best, Cherry Creek State

Park is remarkable for its size and proximity to downtown Denver, just 12 miles to the northwest. The park has 4,200 acres of land and an 880-surface-acre lake; the lake and skyline make this a popular backdrop for Denver area weddings. A marina is on the west shore of the lake and a large wetland preserve surrounds the south shore and Cherry Creek. The campground sits back from the east side of the lake and is popular all summer long with Colorado residents and visiting out-of-staters exploring the Front Range. Campers can go horseback riding, swimming, fishing, boating, and hiking or biking on the trail system. The 24-mile Cherry Creek Regional Trail connects the park with Castlewood Canyon State Park to the south. Winter visitors can go ice fishing or cross-country skiing. There's also a model airplane field and shooting range. Plus, the lakeshore offers excellent views of the Front Range.

The campground is very pleasant, considering its size. There are six loops in the main campground, plus a group loop with three sites. There are no views of the mountains, but large cottonwoods provide shade at many of the loops. The loops are mostly designed for RVs, with the exception of the Cottonwood Grove Loop (sites 100-129), which attracts mainly tent campers. The only loop with mountain views is Gold Rush (sites 75-97), but this loop has less shade than its neighbors. It's a real family scene, with kids of all ages taking over the grove on weekends. The sites are close together, but there's room for multiple tents.

Campsites, facilities: There are 152 sites for tents and RVs up to 80 feet. Full hookups are available. Picnic tables, fire rings, and grills are provided. Restrooms with flush toilets and pay showers, a laundry room, drinking water, a boat ramp, an amphitheater, and dump stations are available. The park also offers interpretive programs, a riding stable, a shooting range, and a swim beach. Leashed pets are permitted. Some of the sites and the facilities are wheelchair-accessible.

Reservations, fees: Reservations are accepted

at 800/244-5613 and www.cpwshop.com. A basic site is $28 per night, a site with full hookups is $41 per night. Group sites are $216-432 per night. Campers must also purchase a vehicle pass ($10) or Annual Parks Pass ($83). Open year-round.

Directions: From I-25 in Denver, take I-225 east for 4.0 miles. Go south on Highway 83. The park entrance is on the right in about 3.0 miles. The campground is 0.8 mile after the visitors center.

Contact: Cherry Creek State Park office 303/690-1166; campground office 303/693-3957; www.cpw.state.co.us.

61 CHATFIELD STATE PARK

Scenic rating: 3

near Denver

Chatfield State Park is in Littleton, on the southwestern edge of the Denver metropolitan area. This is a full-service state park, from the riding stables to the marina to the hiking and biking trails. It's also a popular park—there are nearly 1.9 million visitors annually, so if you're visiting on a summer weekend, make reservations. The lake is open to boating, fishing, and swimming. It's stocked with rainbow trout and other species. Bass, catfish, perch, and crappie are common catches in the summer. The park is also a popular hot-air balloon launch site. Wake up around sunrise to catch a glimpse of these beauties taking off.

The campground contains four large loops and 10 group sites on the south shore of the lake. It's overwhelming, to say the least. The loops have a few trees, but shade and privacy are virtually nonexistent. When they're full, all four loops look almost identical. The nicest feature is the views of the foothills and glimpses of the lake. The beach with swimming is a three-mile walk away.

Campsites, facilities: There are 197 sites for tents and RVs up to 45 feet and 10 group sites. Sites 1-51, 66-78, 88-96, 100-102, and 154-197 have full hookups, and all other sites have electric hookups. Most sites are pull-through, a few are back-in. Picnic tables, fire rings, grills are provided. Thirty-four sites in Loops B and D have tent pads. Restrooms with flush toilets and showers, vault toilets, a laundry room, drinking water, an amphitheater, a playground, a volleyball court (bring your own net), and dump stations are available. The park also has a horse stable, model airplane field, restaurant, swim beach, and marina with a small store and boat ramp. There is a gift shop at the park headquarters as well. Leashed pets are permitted. Sites 33, 50, 51, 99, 102, 148, 151, 155, 156, 157, 176, and 177 and the facilities are wheelchair-accessible.

Reservations, fees: Reservations are accepted at 800/244-5613 (in Denver, call 303/470-1144) and www.cpwshop.com. The fee is $36 per night for a site with electric hookups and $41 per night for sites with full hookups (a fee increase may be pending). Group sites cost $200 per night for up to 36 people and six camping units. Campers must also purchase a vehicle pass ($9) or Annual Parks Pass ($80). Open year-round; water is turned off mid-October-April. Dump station fee is $28.

Directions: From Denver, take U.S. Highway 85 south for 10.5 miles. Take I-470 west for 2.5 miles to Highway 121/Wadsworth Boulevard south. The park entrance is on the left in 1.0 mile. Make the first right after the entrance station. The campground is on the left in 3.5 miles.

Contact: Chatfield State Park, 303/791-7275, www.cpw.state.co.us.

62 JELLYSTONE PARK CAMP-RESORT AT LARKSPUR

🚶‍♂️ 🏊 🎣 🐕 🛶 ♿ 🚐 ⛺

Scenic rating: 5

south of Denver

Jellystone Park at Larkspur is a full-service commercial campground right next to I-25 and two sets of train tracks. But rather than a drawback, the campground's location on the highway is its biggest asset—only 30 minutes south of Denver and 30 minutes north of Colorado Springs. This campground could serve as a stopover for travelers coming to or from the mountains, or as a destination in itself. In 2016, the campground was acquired by Sun RV Resorts and completely torn down, reconstructed, then reopened in summer, 2020 as a fully modern, amenity-filled campground. Families like it here because it's close and easy, and there's so much for the kids to do. When we stayed there, my kids couldn't care less about the noise from the highway or rumble of the trains, and they couldn't get enough of the Yogi and Boo Boo characters and all the activities.

Campsites, facilities: There are 287 full hookup RV sites (50 amp, room for slideouts), plus 89 fully furnished cabins, and plans for future glamping sites and other accommodations. There are two snack bars, a restaurant, water park, dog park, mini bowling alley, arcade, rec center, sports courts, fitness center, two pools, and a hot tub. There is a general store and ranger-led activities for kids, including daily flag ceremonies with the campground mascots.

Reservations, fees: Reservations are accepted at 720/325-2393 and www.jellystonelarkspur. com. RV sites start at $61/night. Open year-round.

Directions: From Denver, take I-25 south for about 30 miles. The campground is on your right, at the end of the exit ramp at Exit 174.

Contact: Jellystone Park Camp-Resort Larkspur, 720/325-2393, www.jellystone larkspur.com.

63 INDIAN CREEK

🚶‍♂️ 🚴 🐕 🚐 ⛺

Scenic rating: 7

north of Deckers

Indian Creek is at the northern end of the Rampart Range, a granite uplift that demarcates the eastern edge of the Front Range Mountains between Denver and Colorado Springs. This area of low peaks and steep, forested valleys extends west to the Lost Creek and Mount Evans Wilderness areas. Panoramic vistas are few and far between, but there's good fishing in the creeks and moderate hiking and riding on the trails. Indian Creek is a beautiful little campground full of ponderosa pine, aspen, and wildflowers. The sites are about 50-100 feet apart, encircling two small meadows. Go straight to the back loop for the best combination of scenery and privacy. Sites 5-8 have views of Devil's Head. The Indian Creek Trail is open to hikers, bikers, and riders. This campground is so close to the Denver area that it fills up on Thursday nights, but midweek it's almost deserted. There is also a separate equestrian campground in a small clearing surrounded by ponderosa pines, where the middle of the loop can accommodate corrals. The 7 equestrian sites on the outside of the loop are about 100 feet apart and shady.

Campsites, facilities: There are 11 sites for tents and RVs up to 20 feet. There are no hookups. Picnic tables, fire rings, and grills are provided. Vault toilets and drinking water are available. Leashed pets are permitted.

Reservations, fees: Reservations are not accepted. The fee is $22 per night. Cash or check only. Open early May-early October.

Directions: From Denver, take U.S. Highway

85 south to Sedalia. Go west on Highway 67 for 10.4 miles. The campground is on the right. **Contact:** Pike and San Isabel National Forest, South Platte District, 303/275-5610, www. fs.usda.gov/psicc.

64 FLAT ROCKS

Scenic rating: 6

northeast of Deckers

Flat Rocks is near the northern end of the Rampart Range, a granite uplift that demarcates the eastern edge of the Front Range Mountains between Denver and Colorado Springs. This area of low peaks and narrow, forested valleys extends west to the Lost Creek and Mount Evans Wilderness areas. There's good fishing in the creeks and moderate hiking and riding on the trails, but the biggest draw is the motorized trails. There are more than 100 miles of trails open to ATVs and dirt bikes in the Rampart Range Motorized Recreation Area, so Flat Rocks and other nearby campgrounds are packed on weekends with families, trailers, and four-wheelers. Flat Rocks is on a long, narrow ridge forested with pine trees and scattered aspen. Because of the steep terrain, there is limited tent space at the sites. Sites 2 and 3 are the roomiest. There are great views of the plains from the Flat Rocks overlook. Sites 2, 3, 8, 10, 12, 13, 18, and 19 have partial views to the west.
Campsites, facilities: There are 19 sites for tents and RVs up to 20 feet. There are no hookups. Picnic tables, fire rings, and grills are provided. Vault toilets and drinking water are available. No water is available in the winter. Leashed pets are permitted. Site 3 and the facilities are wheelchair-accessible.
Reservations, fees: Reservations are not accepted. The fee is $22 per night. Cash or check only. Open early May-early December.
Directions: From Denver, take U.S. Highway 85 south to Sedalia. Go west on Highway 67 for

10 miles. Turn left on Rampart Range Road. The campground is on the right in 4.6 miles. **Contact:** Pike and San Isabel National Forest, South Platte District, 303/275-5610, www. fs.usda.gov/psicc.

65 DEVIL'S HEAD

Scenic rating: 8

east of Deckers

Devil's Head, reported to be the hideout of bandits and outlaws in the 1800s, is a prominent peak on the Rampart Range between Castle Rock and Colorado Springs. It's most notable for the lookout tower on the summit; originally built in 1919, it is the last functioning lookout tower in Pike and San Isabel National Forests. The views from the tower extend 100 miles in any direction on a clear day. A steep, 1.4-mile out-and-back trail climbs the peak. It can be combined with Zinn Trail to make a 3.75-mile loop. The trail is very busy, so bikers should ride with caution.

The campground is quieter but just as busy as the ATV hubs to the north. It attracts mainly tent campers and a large group of regulars from the Front Range. It has two loops in a forest of pine and aspen dotted with huge granite boulders. The top loop has five walk-in sites. Site 5 has the best views of Devil's Head. The road to the lower loop (sites 10-21) is very rough, but the sites can accommodate larger groups.
Campsites, facilities: There are 21 sites for tents and RVs up to 22 feet. There are no hookups. Sites 6, 17, and 18 are pull-through. Picnic tables, fire rings, and grills are provided. Vault toilets and drinking water are available. Leashed pets are permitted.
Reservations, fees: Reservations are not accepted. The fee is $22 per night. Cash or check only. Open early May-early October.
Directions: From Denver, take U.S. Highway 85 south to Sedalia. Go west on Highway 67 for

10 miles. Turn left on Rampart Range Road. The road forks in 9.0 miles. Stay right on Forest Route 300. The Devil's Head Recreation Area and campground are in 0.3 mile.

Contact: Pike and San Isabel National Forest, South Platte District, 303/275-5610, www. fs.usda.gov/psicc.

66 GREEN MOUNTAIN
🚶🚴🛶🏕🚐⛺

Scenic rating: 7

northwest of Deckers

Green Mountain is on South Fork Creek, a short distance downstream of Wellington Lake. The campground is in a spruce-fir forest. The sites are large and about 75 feet apart. On the map, this campground looks like it's in the middle of nowhere, but it's actually just about an hour from Denver, and it's just outside the Lost Creek Wilderness. The wilderness has almost 120,000 acres of dense forests, granite domes, and high parks. Mule deer, elk, bobcat, bear, and a healthy bighorn herd thrive there, and there are 100 miles of trails to explore. The Colorado Trail runs past the campground and into the middle of the wilderness area. It connects with the Rolling Creek, Payne Creek, and Brookside-McCurdy Trails. This is a great jumping-off point for exploring both the north and south ends of the wilderness, which may explain the campground's popularity. It frequently fills up midweek.

Campsites, facilities: There are six tent sites. Picnic tables, fire rings, and grills are provided. Vault toilets and drinking water are available. Leashed pets are permitted.

Reservations, fees: Reservations are not accepted. The fee is $18 per night. Cash or check only. Open May-September.

Directions: From Deckers, take County Road 126 north for 11.5 miles. Turn left on Forest Route 550. In 5.4 miles, stay left at the fork on

Forest Route 543. The campground is on the left in 1.6 miles.

Contact: Pike and San Isabel National Forest, South Platte District, 303/275-5610, www. fs.usda.gov/psicc.

67 MEADOWS GROUP
🚶🚴🏕🚐⛺

Scenic rating: 9

northwest of Deckers

As the name indicates, Meadows Group is in a large meadow dotted with pines and bands of aspen. It's a gorgeous location, surrounded by low ridges, with views of Buffalo Peak. The peak is inside the Lost Creek Wilderness, a landscape of granite domes and buttresses that encompasses the Tarryall Mountains, Platte River Mountains, and Kenosha Mountains. Despite the number of peaks, the habitat rarely enters the alpine zone. There are numerous broad valleys and small, steep creeks. Mule deer, elk, bobcat, bear, and a healthy bighorn herd inhabit the dense woods. There are 100 miles of trails to explore as well, and several loops are possible. The Colorado Trail runs through the campground and into the middle of the wilderness area. It connects with the Rolling Creek, Payne Creek, and Brookside-McCurdy Trails. This is a great jumping-off point for exploring both the north and south ends of the wilderness.

Campsites, facilities: There are two group sites for up to 150 people each (maximum trailer length 28 feet). There are no hookups. Picnic tables, fire rings, and grills are provided. Vault toilets and drinking water are available. Leashed pets are permitted.

Reservations, fees: This campground is available by reservation only. Reservations are accepted at 877/444-6777 and www. recreation.gov. The fee is $150 per night. Open May-September.

Directions: From Deckers, take County Road

126 north for 11.5 miles. Turn left on Forest Route 550. The campground is on the left in 5.1 miles.

Contact: Pike and San Isabel National Forest, South Platte District, 303/275-5610, www. fs.usda.gov/psicc.

68 BUFFALO

Scenic rating: 7

northwest of Deckers

Buffalo is about three miles east of the Lost Creek Wilderness, a landscape of granite domes and buttresses that encompasses the Tarryall Mountains, Platte River Mountains, and Kenosha Mountains. The broad valleys and dense forests provide habitat for healthy populations of elk and bighorn as well as some bobcat and bear. The extensive trail system, including a long portion of the Colorado Trail, can be used for weeklong backpacking trips. The Colorado Trail runs through the campground and into the middle of the wilderness area. It connects with the Rolling Creek, Payne Creek, and Brookside-McCurdy Trails. This is a great jumping-off point for exploring both the north and south ends of the wilderness.

The campground is a large gravel loop on a gentle slope. Tall, scattered pines provide shade but only moderate privacy. The sites are 50-100 feet apart. The only landmark is the large granite formation across the valley.

Campsites, facilities: There are 38 sites for tents and RVs up to 22 feet. There are no hookups. Sites 2, 10, 11, 28, 30, and 31 are pull-through. Picnic tables, fire rings, and grills are provided. Vault toilets and drinking water are available. Leashed pets are permitted.

Reservations, fees: Reservations are accepted at 877/444-6777 and www.recreation.gov. The fee is $22 per night. Cash or check only. Open May-September.

Directions: From Deckers, take County Road

126 north for 11.5 miles. Turn left on Forest Route 550. The campground is on the left in 4.9 miles.

Contact: Pike and San Isabel National Forest, South Platte District, 303/275-5610, www. fs.usda.gov/psicc.

69 LONE ROCK

Scenic rating: 7

near Deckers

Lone Rock is in a small meadow with scattered ponderosa pines on the banks of the South Platte River. These are Gold Medal waters, so fishing is limited to artificial flies and lures. This campground is popular because of its proximity to the Front Range. It fills up by Thursday evening, usually with families and large groups. Nearby Cheesman Reservoir used to be a popular destination, but the 2002 Hayman Fire—the largest in Colorado history—closed many trails and campgrounds in this area and drastically altered the landscape. Things are finally growing back and recovering, though. Sites 4 and 7-11 are riverside. Sites 14 and 16-19 are in the middle of the loop. The sites are 50-100 feet apart and set back a bit from the campground road.

Campsites, facilities: There are 19 sites for tents and RVs up to 22 feet. There are no hookups. Sites 8-10, 12, 13, 15, and 16 are pull-through. Picnic tables, fire rings, and grills are provided. Sites 13, 15, and 16 have tent pads. Vault toilets and drinking water are available. Leashed pets are permitted. Sites 13 and 16 are wheelchair-accessible.

Reservations, fees: Reservations are accepted at 877/444-6777 and www.recreation.gov during the summer season (book six months in advance). The fee is $22 per night. Cash or check only. Open year-round.

Directions: From Deckers, take County Road

126 north for 0.7 mile. The campground is on the left.

Contact: Pike and San Isabel National Forest, South Platte District, 303/275-5610, www.fs.usda.gov/psicc.

70 PLATTE RIVER

Scenic rating: 7

near Deckers

BEST (

The South Platte watershed provides more than 60 percent of Denver's water supply. The water quality is closely monitored by the state and the South Platte has been designated a Gold Medal trout fishery. This campground is in the floodplain and on a hillside overlooking the river, which is wide and slow at this point. It's a soothing place to pitch a tent and cast a line from the fishing platform or the shore. Only artificial flies and lures are allowed because of the Gold Medal designation. Sites 1 and 2 are next to the parking lot. Sites 3-8 are on the hill and shaded by scattered pine. Sites 9 and 10 are right next to the water. This campground can be very busy on weekends, but it's quiet midweek.

Campsites, facilities: There are 10 walk-in tent sites. Picnic tables, fire rings, and grills are provided. Sites 1-3, 9, and 10 have tent pads. Vault toilets are available. Leashed pets are permitted. Site 10 and the facilities are wheelchair-accessible.

Reservations, fees: Reservations are not accepted. The fee is $20 per night. Cash or check only. Open year-round.

Directions: From Deckers, take County Road 69 north for 3.9 miles. The campground is on the right.

Contact: Pike and San Isabel National Forest, South Platte District, 303/275-5610, www.fs.usda.gov/psicc.

71 PAINTED ROCKS

Scenic rating: 7

north of Woodland Park

The Manitou Park Recreation Area is heavily used year-round. The five-acre Manitou Lake is a family fishing hole encircled by a hiking trail. Another trail connects the campgrounds and picnic area, and the Centennial Bike Trail runs into Woodland Park. The park's grasslands and pine stands are not especially scenic, but visitors appreciate the proximity to Garden of the Gods, Pikes Peak, Florissant Fossil Beds National Monument, and Colorado Springs. Painted Rocks is the smallest and most attractive campground in the park. It has the same pine and grassland habitat of the other campgrounds, but it's away from the roads, and there are some interesting rock outcroppings in the adjacent meadow. The large sites are about 100 feet apart and are shaded, except for 11-13. Sites 9 and 12-18 have the best views. This campground fills up on weekends with a crowd of regulars.

Campsites, facilities: There are 18 sites for tents and RVs up to 30 feet. There are no hookups. Site 15 is pull-through. Picnic tables, fire rings, and grills are provided. Vault toilets and drinking water are available. Leashed pets are permitted.

Reservations, fees: Reservations are accepted at 877/444-6777 and www.recreation.gov. The fee is $23 per night. Cash or check only. Open May-September.

Directions: From Woodland Park, take Highway 67 north for 6.3 miles. Turn left on Painted Rocks Road/County Road 78. The campground is on the left in 0.4 mile.

Contact: Pike and San Isabel National Forest, Pikes Peak District, 719/636-1602, www.fs.usda.gov/psicc.

72 COLORADO
🥾🚵🛶🐴🚐⛺

Scenic rating: 6
north of Woodland Park

Colorado is the largest campground in the Manitou Park Recreation Area, a broad valley with grasslands and abundant ponderosa pines. This valley is pleasant but not extremely scenic. Nevertheless, it's busy year-round because of the proximity to the Colorado Springs area. This campground usually fills up on weekends. It has two large paved loops in a thin pine forest that provides shade but not much privacy. The sites are 50-100 feet apart and large enough for multiple tents. Sites 5, 11, and 56 are doubles. Sites 1-10 are very close to the road.

Campsites, facilities: There are 80 sites for tents and RVs up to 30 feet. There are no hookups. Picnic tables, fire rings, and grills are provided. Vault toilets, drinking water, and an amphitheater are available. Leashed pets are permitted. The facilities are wheelchair-accessible.

Reservations, fees: Reservations are accepted at 877/444-6777 and www.recreation.gov. The fee is $23 per night. Cash or check only. Open May-September.

Directions: From Woodland Park, take Highway 67 north for 6.0 miles. The campground is on the right.

Contact: Pike and San Isabel National Forest, Pikes Peak District, 719/636-1602, www.fs.usda.gov/psicc.

73 SOUTH MEADOWS
🥾🚵🐴🚐⛺

Scenic rating: 6
north of Woodland Park

South Meadows is the second-largest campground in Manitou Park Recreation Area. It doesn't have views, but the pine forest provides lots of shade and some privacy. The sites are 50-100 feet apart and a nice distance from the road. Hikers and bikers can take the Centennial Trail to Manitou Lake, a family fishing hole, or south to Woodland Park. For more entertainment, campers drive to the Colorado Springs area and Pikes Peak. This campground is extremely busy in the summer because of its proximity to so many Front Range attractions.

Campsites, facilities: There are 64 sites for tents and RVs up to 30 feet. There are no hookups. Picnic tables, fire rings, and grills are provided. Vault toilets and drinking water are available. Leashed pets are permitted.

Reservations, fees: Reservations are accepted at 877/444-6777 and www.recreation.gov. The fee is $23 per night. Cash or check only. Open year-round.

Directions: From Woodland Park, take Highway 67 north for 5.2 miles. The campground is on the left, across from the Pike Community Group campground.

Contact: Pike and San Isabel National Forest, Pikes Peak District, 719/636-1602, www.fs.usda.gov/psicc.

74 PIKE COMMUNITY GROUP
🥾🚵🛶🐴🚴🚐⛺

Scenic rating: 6
north of Woodland Park

Pike Community Group is a large group campground with a steady stream of reservations from the Colorado Springs area. Church groups, Scout groups, and family reunions enjoy this location with its proximity to Pikes Peak, Florissant Fossil Beds National Monument, Garden of the Gods, and the Air Force Academy. The campground is in a grassland with scattered ponderosa pines. It has dispersed tent camping and a large kitchen area. There is frequent traffic noise from the highway. Across the highway, the Centennial Trail connects the campground to Woodland Park and Manitou Lake. The five-acre reservoir is a family fishing destination with a multiuse trail around the shoreline. The views are not exceptional, but there are glimpses of a small peak to the north. This is not wilderness—but it is a good destination for a diverse group.

Campsites, facilities: There is dispersed tent camping for up to 100 people and parking spaces for 48 vehicles. There are no hookups. Picnic tables, fire rings, and grills are provided. Vault toilets, drinking water, a playground, volleyball court, softball field, and horseshoe pits, and dump stations are available. Leashed pets are permitted. The camp host is across the highway at South Meadows campground.

Reservations, fees: Reservations are accepted at 877/444-6777 and www.recreation.gov. The fee is $125 per night for up to 100 campers. Open late May-late September.

Directions: From Woodland Park, take Highway 67 north for 5.3 miles. Turn right at the campground sign. The campground is in 0.5 mile.

Contact: Pike and San Isabel National Forest, Pikes Peak District, 719/636-1602, www.fs.usda.gov/psicc.

🄷🄵 RED ROCKS GROUP
🚶 🚲 🐴 🚐 ⛰️

Scenic rating: 6
north of Woodland Park

Red Rocks is located in a dense pine forest just a few miles north of Woodland Park at an elevation of 8,200 feet. It's farther from the road than nearby Pike Community Group, but there is still a lot of traffic noise, and there are no scenic views. However, the six group picnic areas have a nice communal atmosphere. The nearest activity is the Centennial Trail, a paved hiking and biking trail that connects Woodland Park to the Manitou Lake picnic area. Also, Red Rocks Trail leads to some unusual sandstone formations. Most groups select this site for its location—it's a short drive from Pikes Peak, Florissant Fossil Beds National Monument, Garden of the Gods, and Colorado Springs.

Campsites, facilities: There is dispersed tent camping for up to 100 people. There are no hookups. Picnic tables, fire rings, and grills are provided. Vault toilets and drinking water are available. Leashed pets are permitted.

Reservations, fees: Reservations are accepted at 877/444-6777 and www.recreation.gov. The fee is $125 per night up to 100 people. Open early May-late October.

Directions: From Woodland Park, take Highway 67 north about 3.0 miles. Turn right on Forest Route 335. The campground entrance is on the left in 0.2 mile.

Contact: Pike and San Isabel National Forest, Pikes Peak District, 719/636-1602, www.fs.usda.gov/psicc.

🄷🄶 SPRINGDALE
🐕 🚐 ⛰️

Scenic rating: 6
east of Woodland Park

The highlight of Springdale is the drive there, with its awesome views of Pikes Peak. The campground is in a forest of pine and aspen beside a grassland plateau. All of the sites have good shade and privacy. Sites 7 and 8 feature views across the grassland. Rampart Reservoir Recreation Area is a few miles away. Fishing, hiking, and boating are available in the recreation area, but there are no activities at the campground. It has a weekend crowd of locals and regulars, but it's very quiet midweek.

Campsites, facilities: There are 13 sites for tents and RVs up to 16 feet. Site 7 is walk-in. There are no hookups. Site 6 is pull-through. Picnic tables, fire rings, and grills are provided. Vault toilets and drinking water are available. Leashed pets are permitted.

Reservations, fees: Reservations are not

accepted. The fee is $18 per night. Cash or check only. Open late May-early September.

Directions: From Woodland Park, take Kelly's Road east for 1.0 mile. Turn left on Rampart Range Road. In 1.6 miles, stay right at the fork. The campground is on the left in 2.2 miles.

Contact: Pike and San Isabel National Forest, Pikes Peak District, 719/636-1602, www.fs.usda.gov/psicc.

77 MEADOW RIDGE

Scenic rating: 6

east of Woodland Park

Located in Rampart Reservoir Recreation Area, Meadow Ridge is a modern campground with decent recreational opportunities. The 500-surface-acre reservoir stores water for Colorado Springs, so it can get quite low during drought years. When it's full enough, it's open to wakeless boating and fishing for trout, bass, and perch. There are several hiking trails around the lake, including the Rainbow Gulch, Rampart Reservoir, Aspen Grove, and Nichols Trails. Rampart and Rainbow are also popular with mountain bikers. A one-mile trail connects the campground to the reservoir. The boat ramp is about three miles away.

The campground is on a ridge overlooking the reservoir in a forest of aspen and pine. The sites are terraced and many have stairs. They are 50-100 feet apart. The campground is booked on weekends, and there is only one first-come, first-served site. Sites 7-11 have the most privacy.

Campsites, facilities: There are 19 sites for tents and RVs up to 30 feet. There are no hookups. Sites 6, 14, 16, and 18 are pull-through. Picnic tables, fire rings, grills, tent pads, and lantern hooks are provided. Vault toilets and drinking water are available. Leashed pets are permitted. Sites 12 and 13 and the facilities are wheelchair-accessible.

Reservations, fees: Reservations are accepted at 877/444-6777 and www.recreation.gov. The fee is $23 per night. Cash or check only. Open May-September.

Directions: From Woodland Park, take Kelly's Road east for 1.0 mile. Turn left on Rampart Range Road. In 1.6 miles, stay right at the fork. In 5.3 miles, turn left into the Rampart Reservoir Recreation Area. In 0.8 mile, turn left at the entrance station. The campground is in 0.6 mile.

Contact: Pike and San Isabel National Forest, Pikes Peak District, 719/636-1602, www.fs.usda.gov/psicc.

78 THUNDER RIDGE

Scenic rating: 7

east of Woodland Park

Thunder Ridge is in an aspen and pine forest overlooking Rampart Reservoir. It has less shade than nearby Meadow Ridge, but better views. Sites 7, 9, and 10 have views of the foothills, and sites 11-13 have lake views. The sites are just 25-50 feet apart. Privacy is poor, but the topography is quite hilly. A short trail leads down to the lake, where there are more trails for hiking and biking and good shore fishing. The boat ramp is about two miles away. (For more information on the Rampart Reservoir Recreation Area, see the Meadow Ridge listing in this chapter.)

Campsites, facilities: There are 21 sites for tents and RVs up to 30 feet. There are no hookups. Sites 6, 10, and 11 are pull-through. Picnic tables, fire rings, grills, tent pads, and lantern hooks are provided. Vault toilets and drinking water are available. Leashed pets are permitted. Sites 7, 8, and 21 and the facilities are wheelchair-accessible.

Reservations, fees: Reservations are accepted at 877/444-6777 and www.recreation.gov. The fee is $23 per night. Cash or check only. Open May-October.

Directions: From Woodland Park, take Kelly's Road east for 1.0 mile. Turn left on Rampart Range Road. In 1.6 miles, stay right at the fork. In 5.3 miles, turn left into the Rampart Reservoir Recreation Area. Turn left in 0.9 mile. The campground is in 0.2 mile.

Contact: Pike and San Isabel National Forest, Pikes Peak District, 719/636-1602, www.fs.usda.gov/psicc.

79 MUELLER STATE PARK

Scenic rating: 8

south of Woodland Park

BEST (

Mueller Park is a 5,000-acre park west of Pikes Peak. Its forested ridges are home to bear, elk, bighorn, and mule deer. Pioneers settled the area in the 1860s. Logging and cattle ranching supported residents until the former owners, the Mueller family, turned it into a game preserve. The park is a great destination for families who like hiking and biking; there are 55 miles of trails in the park. Other attractions include nearby Florissant Fossil Beds National Monument and the Pikes Peak massif. Other activities include pond fishing, cross-country skiing, and snowshoeing.

The campground has seven loops, but the ridgeline topography and dense woods separate the loops and make the campground seem smaller than it really is. Most of the loops are best for RV camping, but Turkey Meadow and Prospector Ridge are reserved for walk-in tent camping. Peak View (sites 1-5) and Turkey Meadow (sites 100-109) have views of Pikes Peak. Pisgah Point (sites 70-80) is a group site that's available by reservation only. With its deluxe rustic cabin, ample deck, and space for guests to sleep, this is a popular site for weddings; there are even photographers in the area who specialize in Mueller State Park weddings.

Campsites, facilities: There are 110 sites for tents and RVs up to 60 feet. There are an additional 22 tent-only sites (sites 55-66 and 100-109) and three furnished cabins. All sites (except the walk-in tent sites) have electric hookups and most sites are pull-through. Picnic tables, fire rings, and grills are provided. Tent pads of various sizes are provided at most sites. Restrooms with flush toilets and showers, vault toilets, drinking water, a laundry room, amphitheater, playground, interpretive programs, and dump stations are available. Leashed pets are permitted in the campground but are not allowed on trails or in the backcountry. Sites 12 and 22 and the facilities are wheelchair-accessible.

Reservations, fees: Reservations are accepted at 800/244-5613 (in the Denver area, call 303/470-1144) and www.cpwshop.com. Group reservations are accepted at 719/687-2366. Walk-in tent sites are $28 per night and electric sites are $36 per night. The group campground is $396 per night. Vehicles must also have a Daily Parks Pass ($8) or Annual Parks Pass ($80). Cash or check only. Revenuer's Ridge loop is open year-round. The rest of the campground is open mid-May-mid-October.

Directions: From Woodland Park, take U.S. Highway 24 west for 7.0 miles. Go south on Highway 67. In 0.9 mile, turn right at the park entrance. The campground is 2.0 miles past the fee station.

Contact: Mueller State Park, 719/687-2366, www.cpw.state.co.us.

80 THE CRAGS

Scenic rating: 6

south of Woodland Park

Located between Pikes Peak and Mueller State Park, The Crags looks remote on the map, but it's a high-use campground in the summer. It's in a spruce-fir forest with outcroppings of Pikes Peak granite and a small creek running through it. Most sites are creekside. Sites 15 and 17 are next to The Crags trailhead, a short hike to a rock outcropping with impressive views of the Rockies. Sites 5-7 are walk-ins. Besides the hike, the other nearby attractions are the 55 miles of trails in Mueller State Park and the historic mining towns of Cripple Creek and Victor.

Campsites, facilities: There are 17 sites for tents and RVs up to 20 feet. There are no hookups. Sites 3 and 11 are pull-through. Picnic tables, fire rings, and grills are provided. Vault toilets and drinking water are available. Trash must be packed out. Leashed pets are permitted.

Reservations, fees: Reservations are not accepted. The fee is $18 per night. Cash or check only. Open year-round, road conditions permitting.

Directions: From Woodland Park, take U.S. Highway 24 west to Highway 67 south. In 4.3 miles, turn left on Forest Route 383. This road is very rough. The campground is on the left in 3.1 miles.

Contact: Pike and San Isabel National Forest, Pikes Peak District, 719/636-1602, www.fs.usda.gov/psicc.

81 NORTHERN PLAINS

Scenic rating: 6

in Lake Pueblo State Park

Lake Pueblo State Park is west of Pueblo on the Arkansas River. It is one of the most popular destinations in the state for water sports. The 4,546-surface-acre reservoir is open to waterskiing, sailing, swimming, and fishing. There are two marinas, two boat ramps, and a swim beach with a five-story waterslide. Fish species include trout, walleye, large- and smallmouth bass, crappie, bluegill, and yellow perch, and below the dam there is a stocked fishing pond for kids. There are also 18 miles of trails for hiking, biking, and riding. The park's backdrop includes the Sangre de Cristo and Wet Mountains and Pikes Peak to the north.

The campground is at the west end of the lake near the North Marina and the inlet. The campground includes three loops: Prairie Ridge, Yucca Flats, and Kettle Creek. The Prairie Ridge and Yucca Flats loops are large and fairly cramped. The Kettle Creek loop does not have electricity and has seven walk-in tent sites. There are also three group camping loops.

Campsites, facilities: There are 204 sites for tents and RVs up to 60 feet, seven walk-in tent sites, and three group loops. Electric hookups and pull-throughs are available. Picnic tables, fire rings, grills, and tent pads are provided. Restrooms with flush toilets and showers, vault toilets, laundry facilities, drinking water, an amphitheater, a playground, campfire programs, and dump stations are available. Leashed pets are permitted. Sites 207, 227, 246, 247, 260, 302, 406, 423, 436, 443, 470, 505, and 521 and the facilities are wheelchair-accessible.

Reservations, fees: Reservations are required at 800/244-5613 or www.cpwshop.com. Group reservations can be made at 719/561-9320. Nonelectric sites are $22-24 per night and electric sites are $32-36 per night. Group sites are available. Campers must also purchase a daily vehicle pass ($8) or Annual Parks Pass ($80). Open May-September.

Directions: From I-25 in Pueblo, take U.S. Highway 50 west for 4.0 miles. Turn south on Pueblo Boulevard and go 4.0 miles to Thatcher Avenue. Turn west and drive 6.0 miles to the park entrance.

Contact: Pueblo Lake State Park, 719/561-9320, www.cpw.state.co.us.

82 JUNIPER BREAKS

Scenic rating: 6

in Lake Pueblo State Park

Juniper Breaks is on the north shore of Lake Pueblo, a reservoir on the Arkansas River with nearly 5,000 surface acres. Predictably, it's one of the most popular water-sports destinations in the state. The campground sits on the bluffs overlooking the lake and is surrounded by prairie grass. Most sites have good views of the lake and the Sangre de Cristo Mountains, but shade and privacy are poor. It's a short drive from the campground to the sailboat launching area. (For more information on Lake Pueblo State Park, see the Northern Plains listing in this chapter.)

Campsites, facilities: There are 84 sites for tents and RVs up to 40 feet. There are no hookups. Picnic tables, fire rings, grills, and tent pads are provided. Vault toilets and drinking water are available. Leashed pets are permitted. Sites 114, 116, 157, and 158 and the facilities are wheelchair-accessible.

Reservations, fees: Reservations are accepted at 800/244-5613 and www.cpwshop.com. Nonelectric sites are $22-24 per night and electric sites are $32-36 per night. Campers must also purchase a daily vehicle pass ($8) or Annual Parks Pass ($80). Loop D is open year-round.

Directions: From I-25 in Pueblo, take U.S. Highway 50 west for 4.0 miles. Turn south on Pueblo Boulevard and go 4.0 miles to Thatcher Avenue. Turn west and drive 6.0 miles to the park entrance.

Contact: Pueblo Lake State Park, 719/561-9320, www.cpw.state.co.us.

83 ARKANSAS POINT

Scenic rating: 6

in Lake Pueblo State Park

Arkansas Point is on the rocky south shore of the 11-mile-long Lake Pueblo, a massive reservoir that's also one of the most popular water-sports destinations in the state. This campground is less scenic than the Northern Plains and Juniper Breaks campgrounds on the north shore, but it is next to the South Marina, so it stays busy all summer. It's packed with RVs and families and can be quite loud on summer weekends.

Campsites, facilities: There are 93 sites for tents and RVs up to 60 feet. Electric hookups and pull-throughs are available. Picnic tables, fire rings, grills, and tent pads are provided. Restrooms with flush toilets and showers, vault toilets, laundry facilities, drinking water, and a playground, and dump stations are available. Leashed pets are permitted. Sites 13, 31, 51, and 85 and the facilities are wheelchair-accessible.

Reservations, fees: Reservations are accepted at 800/244-5613 and www.cpwshop.com. Nonelectric sites are $22-24 per night and electric sites are $32-36 per night. Campers must also purchase a daily vehicle pass ($8) or Annual Parks Pass ($80). Sites 1-27, 94, and 95 are open year-round. The rest of the campground is open May-September.

Directions: From I-25 in Pueblo, take U.S. Highway 50 west for 4.0 miles. Turn south on Pueblo Boulevard and go 4.0 miles to Thatcher Avenue. Turn west and drive 6.0 miles to the park entrance.

Contact: Pueblo Lake State Park, 719/561-9320, www.cpw.state.co.us.

84 ECHO CANYON CAMPGROUND

Scenic rating: 7

west of Cañon City

This campground is notable for its proximity to a myriad of fun local activities in the Royal Gorge Region, a relatively unsung destination in Colorado. Within a few minutes' drive, you've got the Royal Gorge Bridge and Park, a kind of amusement park straddling a famous 1,000+ foot deep canyon; there's also the Royal Gorge Route Railroad, with its various dining, wine, beer, murder mystery, and other themed train rides through the canyon; and then there's rafting on the Arkansas River, both family-oriented, flat-water floats further upstream, and Class V routes through the Gorge. There's also a Dinosaur Experience across the highway, helicopter rides, an awesome rock shop, and the town of Cañon City itself, with its quirky Prison Museum, casual restaurants, and even a winery. The campground is owned by the same folks who run the 8-Mile Bar and Grill and Echo Canyon River Expeditions, a professional rafting outfitter, both right across the highway. You may not feel that remote or isolated at this campground, being so close to the road and a small city, but the skies are still clear at night and the view of the Sangre de Cristo mountains to the west is a not too shabby. Plus the sites are clean and well maintained and in addition to tent sites, Echo Canyon offers "Glamping Tent Cabins" that come with queen beds, luxury linens, blankets, pillows, and towels, plus a picnic table and fire ring. (If that's not plush enough, there are fully-equipped luxury cabins, too.)

Campsites, facilities: There are 11 sites for tents, each with a 12-foot-square wood platform with tie-down points for your tent's guy lines. Another five premium sites have electric hook-ups with two standard outlets. All sites have a picnic table, fire ring, cooking grill, and access to a common shower house with flush toilets. Glamping tents come in single or double queen sizes, and all have lights and electricity,

a glamping tent at Echo Canyon Campground in the Royal Gorge Region

an evaporative cooler for hot summer months, free WiFi, patio furniture, and access to the shared shower house and bathrooms.

Reservations, fees: Reservations are accepted at 800/748-2953. Premium tent sites are $49 and wall tents are $149-239. Sites are based on a 4-person occupancy. Groups of 5 or more must rent multiple sites and guest numbers will be verified at check-in.

Directions: Located at 45044 W U.S. Highway 50, about 8.0 miles west of Cañon City. From I-25 south in Colorado Springs, take exit 140 to Highway 115 South. Turn right (west) onto Route 50, continue through Cañon City, then look for campground on your left (south side of the road).

Contact: Tel. 800/748-2953, www.royalgorge cabins.com.

FOUR CORNERS AND THE SAN JUAN MOUNTAINS

In Colorado's southwestern corner, the towering

San Juan Mountains rise above the arid mesas and canyons of the Four Corners region. Ouray is an important destination for rock and ice climbers, as well as jeepers and hot spring soakers, with unparalleled hiking in the Mount Sneffels and Uncompahgre wilderness areas. The Animas River runs through downtown Durango and has excellent fly-fishing and white water. West of town, the La Plata Mountains contain the southern terminus of the Colorado Trail; Junction Creek campground is at the trailhead.

From Durango, the San Juan Skyway heads west toward Ancestral Puebloan archeological sites at Mesa Verde National Park, the Ute Mountain Tribal Park, Hovenweep National Monument, Anasazi Heritage Center, and Chimney Rock Archaeological Area.

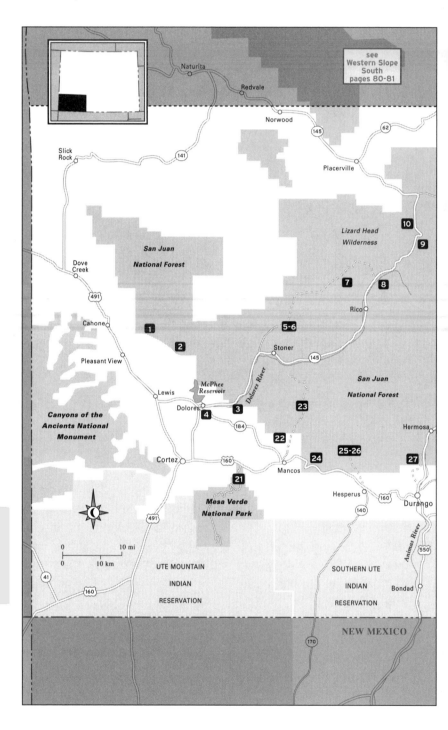

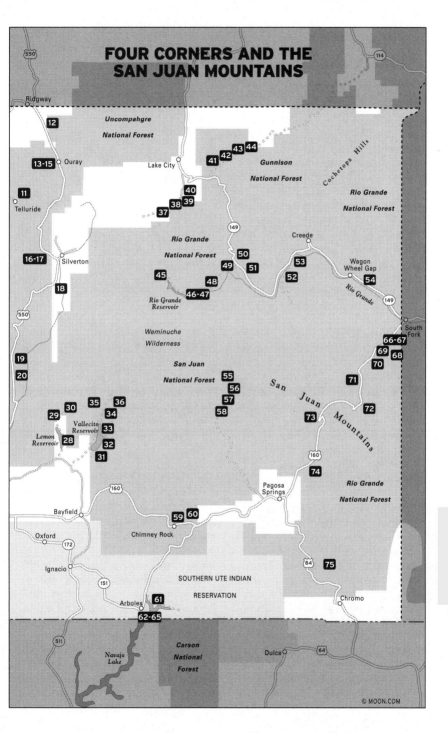

FOUR CORNERS AND THE SAN JUAN MOUNTAINS

1 BRADFIELD

Scenic rating: 7

north of Dolores

The Dolores River was named by the Franciscan friars and explorers Dominguez and Escalante in honor of Our Lady of Sorrows. From its headwaters in the San Juan Mountains, it flows northwest 200 miles to the Colorado River. Below the McPhee Reservoir, the Dolores traverses John Wayne country—beautiful sandstone canyons where cowboys and their herds used to winter. This campground, sometimes called Bradfield Bridge, is named for the Bradfield Ranch, which owned the land until the 1970s. It's set in an appealing meadow with a boat ramp for the river runners—commercial and private—who float downriver on single and multiday trips. The last take-out, Bedrock, is 97 miles (and a few Class IV rapids) downstream. The fishing is good, too. From McPhee Dam to Bradfield Bridge, the Dolores is very popular with anglers looking for native trout. There are very few trees in the campground, but the sites are spaced 100-200 feet apart, which affords some privacy. Site 5 is the best. It's next to the river and surrounded by shade trees.

Campsites, facilities: There are 22 sites for tents and RVs up to 45 feet. There are hand pumps for water. Picnic tables, fire rings, grills, and shelters are provided. Vault toilets, drinking water, a group picnic area, and a boat ramp are available. Trash must be packed out. Leashed pets are permitted. The campsites and facilities are wheelchair-accessible.

Reservations, fees: This is a first-come, first-served campground. The fee is $8 per night. Cash or check only. Open year-round, without water in the winter.

Directions: From Cortez, take I-491 north. From the intersection with Highway 184, continue north on I-491 for 10.6 miles to County Road DD/County Road 15. Turn right on County Road DD and then left on County Road 16. In 2.7 miles, turn right on S Road. In 1.0 mile, turn left at the Bradfield Recreation Site sign. The campground is in 0.5 mile.

Contact: San Juan National Forest, Dolores District, 970/882-7296, www.fs.usda.gov/sanjuan.

2 FERRIS CANYON

Scenic rating: 7

north of Dolores

Ferris Canyon is a smaller version of Cabin Canyon to the west, except it is about 400 yards from the campground to the Dolores. It's about six miles from Ferris Canyon to the McPhee Dam. This whole stretch of river is managed by the San Juan National Forest and is open to anglers. It's very popular with anglers who fly-fish for Colorado River rainbow trout, Snake River cutthroat trout, and brown trout in these waters. Fishing is limited to artificial flies and lures and catch-and-release. The campground is a densely wooded loop with very few users.

Campsites, facilities: There are seven sites for tents and RVs up to 45 feet. Picnic tables, fire rings, and grills are provided. Vault toilets and drinking water are available. Trash must be packed out. Leashed pets are permitted. Site 4 is wheelchair-accessible.

Reservations, fees: This is a first-come, first-served campground. The fee is $10 per night. Cash or check only. Open early May-late October.

Directions: From Cortez, take I-491 north. From the intersection with Highway 184, continue north on I-491 for 10.6 miles to County Road DD/County Road 15. Turn right on Country Road DD and then left on County Road 16. In 2.7 miles, turn right on S Road. In 1.0 mile, turn right on Forest Route 504. The campground is in 6.4 miles on the right.

Contact: San Juan National Forest, Dolores

District, 970/882-7296, www.fs.usda.gov/sanjuan.

3 DOLORES RIVER CAMPGROUND

🏃 🚲 🛶 ⛴ 🏕 🐕 ⚓ ♿ 🚐 ⛺

Scenic rating: 8

east of Dolores

This large, relaxed, family owned property is located on a tree-shaded, mellow stretch of the Dolores River, just northeast of Cortez through the town of Dolores. In addition to tent and RV sites, there are a variety of accommodations—yurts, cabins, vintage trailers, and covered Conestoga wagons. The location is ideal for accessing southwest Colorado's greatest hits, including mountain biking, hiking trails, and jeeping roads, San Juan National Forest, McPhee Reservoir, Canyon of the Ancients National Monument, and Mesa Verde National Park, all nearby. Campers have river access, a river-fed fishing pond, fly fishing on the river, and a very friendly vibe around the campground.

Campsites, facilities: There are 78 sites for tents and RVs up to 45 feet, and 11 sites for tents only. Leashed pets are permitted. There are two bathhouses, laundry facilities, a large common rec hall, food trucks, and social events.

Reservations, fees: Rates start at $30/night for a tent site and go up to $175/ night for a deluxe full service cabin. They accept reservations up to a year in advance, especially for the restored Airstreams, which are very popular.

Directions: Located at 18680 Highway 145, the "San Juan Skyway," on the south side of the road and just east of Dolores.

Contact: Dolores River Campground, 970-882-7761, doloresrivercampground@gmail.com, doloresrivercampground.com.

4 MCPHEE

🏃 🚲 🛶 ⛴ 🚤 🛥 🐕 ♿ 🚐 ⛺

Scenic rating: 4

north of Dolores

McPhee Reservoir, the second-largest lake in Colorado, offers warm- and cold-water fishing. It is stocked with rainbow trout, kokanee salmon, bass, catfish, and pan fish. Shoreline fishing, waterskiing, and canoeing are all popular water sports at McPhee. Fly-fishing and rafting take place on the Dolores River above and below the reservoir. When you're tired of playing in the water, you can explore the numerous cultural and archaeological attractions in the Four Corners region. Mesa Verde National Park, Hovenweep National Monument, Ute Mountain Tribal Park, and the Anasazi Heritage Center are all day trips from McPhee. In the winter, hunters use McPhee as a base camp for hunting elk and deer at higher elevations.

The campground consists of two loops, Pinyon and Juniper, on a hilltop overlooking the lake. Piñon and juniper trees throughout provide more privacy than shade. The sites on the outside of the loops tend to have more coverage and privacy. The walk-in sites are removed from the main loops and have the best views of the lake. The campground is quiet and attracts families and retirees, but it is very exposed and can get quite hot in the summer. There are 13 additional sites on the other side of the reservoir at House Creek campground.

Campsites, facilities: There are 64 campsites for tents and RVs up to 50 feet and 12 walk-in tent sites. There are also 2 group campsites and 2 day-use group sites that can accommodate 30 people each. Some electric hookups are available. Picnic tables, fire rings, and grills are provided. In the Pinyon Loop, sites 7, 20, and 31 have sun shelters. In the Juniper Loop, site 29 has a sun shelter. Restrooms with flush toilets, drinking water, and boat ramps are available. The group sites have a ball field, volleyball posts, and horseshoe pits. Leashed pets are permitted. Juniper 21 and Pinyon 10 are wheelchair-accessible.

Reservations, fees: Reservations are accepted at 877/444-6777 and www.recreation.gov for 50 sites in the Pinyon Loop. Nonelectric sites are $24 per night, and electric sites are $26 per night. Fees are half price when the water is off in winter. Cash or check only. Juniper is open year-round (without water in the winter), and Pinyon is open May-October, weather depending.

Directions: From Dolores, take Highway 184 west for 4.2 miles. Turn right at the McPhee Reservoir sign. Follow the signs 2.1 miles to the campground entrance.

Contact: San Juan National Forest, Dolores District, 970/882-7296, www.fs.usda.gov/sanjuan.

5 MAVREESO
🏕️ 🚴 🛶 🦌 🚐 ⛺

Scenic rating: 7
near Dolores River Canyon

Mavreeso is a narrow campground that parallels the West Dolores River, about 20 miles north of Dolores. The sites are distributed throughout an evergreen forest. The best riverside sites, 6 and 11, are at opposite ends of the campground. Site 14 is the most appealing RV site. The campground isn't striking, but the location is excellent for hikers, mountain bikers, and ATVers, and it's a decent stopover for travelers on the San Juan Skyway. Mountain bikers can do a 25-mile intermediate to advanced loop on the Stoner Mesa Trail and West Dolores Road. Hikers can also explore the Stoner Mesa and Stoner Creek area by trail. Anglers can fish for stocked rainbow, brown, and cutthroat trout along the West Fork, the largest tributary of the Dolores, as well as in Stoner Creek, accessible only by trail.

Campsites, facilities: There are 19 sites for

tents and RVs up to 35 feet. Electric hookups are available at sites 15-18, 10, 13, and 14. Picnic tables, fire rings, and grills are provided. Vault toilets, drinking water, a group picnic area, and a dump station are available. Leashed pets are permitted.

Reservations, fees: Reservations are not accepted. The fee is $24 per night. Electricity costs $6 per night. Cash or check only. Open mid-May-early October. Sometimes this campground remains open through hunting season.

Directions: From Dolores, take Highway 145 north for about 13 miles. Turn left on Forest Route 535/West Dolores Road. The campground is on the right in 6.0 miles.

Contact: San Juan National Forest, Dolores District, 970/882-7296, www.fs.usda.gov/sanjuan.

6 WEST DOLORES
🏕️ 🚴 🛶 🦌 🚻 ♿ 🚐 ⛺

Scenic rating: 7
near Dolores River Canyon

West Dolores is in a beautiful setting on the banks of the West Fork of the Dolores, a first-rate trout fishery. It's a quiet destination during the week, but on weekends, the riverside sites fill up quickly with a mostly local crowd. Hikers will enjoy the miles of trails in the San Juan National Forest. The Stoner Mesa, Stoner Creek, Fish Creek, Calico, and Navajo Lake Trails are accessible from this campground. Mountain bikers can also explore these intermediate to advanced trails. ATV and Jeep owners frequent this campground as well and explore the Forest Service roads up to Groundhog Reservoir and Lone Cone State Wildlife Area. Riverside sites are 3, 4, 8, 9, 11, and 12. Site 15 lacks trees and is the least appealing.

Campsites, facilities: There are 18 sites for tents and RVs up to 40 feet. Electric hookups are available at seven sites. Site 12 is pull-through.

Sites 1, 9, and 14 are double sites. Picnic tables, fire rings, and grills are provided. Vault toilets and drinking water are available. Leashed pets are permitted. The picnic tables and toilets are wheelchair-accessible.

Reservations, fees: Reservations are accepted for 10 of the sites at 877/444-6777 or www.recreation.gov. The fee is $24 per night. Electricity costs $6 per night. Cash or check only. Open mid-May-late September, though this campground may remain open through hunting season without any services.

Directions: From Dolores, take Highway 145 north for about 13 miles. Turn left on Forest Route 535/West Dolores Road. The campground is on the right in 7.2 miles.

Contact: San Juan National Forest, Dolores District, 970/882-7296, www.fs.usda.gov/sanjuan.

⁊ BURRO BRIDGE
🏃🚵🛶🐕🚐🏕

Scenic rating: 10

north of Rico

BEST (

From the south, Burro Bridge is the third campground on West Dolores Road. It is a long haul to get here, but if you prize scenery and solitude over accessibility, then keep driving. (The most traffic I ever saw at this campground was an enormous herd of sheep that passed by after breakfast, driven by two dogs and a cowboy with a ski pole.) Burro Bridge is the ideal base camp for exploring the Lizard Head Wilderness. The Navajo Lake trailhead is a mile up the road. From the lakes, three fourteeners are accessible to experienced mountaineers. Mountain biking is not allowed in the wilderness area, but there are advanced trails south of the campground. The river is about 100 feet down a steep slope; anglers will have to scout for access sites. The campground is full of ponderosa pine and aspen, which are beautiful when the colors change in the fall. Many

sites have views of Mount Wilson. Sites 1 and 11, at either end of the campground, offer the most privacy.

Campsites, facilities: There are 13 sites for tents and RVs up to 40 feet, including two equestrian sites with corrals. Sites 7 and 8 are pull-through. There are no hookups. Picnic tables, fire rings, and grills are provided. Vault toilets and drinking water are available. Trash must be packed out. Leashed pets are permitted.

Reservations, fees: Reservations are not accepted. The fee is $24 per night. Cash or check only. Open late May-early October.

Directions: From Dolores, take Highway 145 north for about 13 miles. Turn left on Forest Route 535/West Dolores Road. In 22.5 miles, stay right at the fork. The campground entrance is on the right in 1.2 miles.

If coming from Ridgway or Telluride to the north on Highway 145, the turnoff to Burro Bridge is opposite Cayton Campground; from there, it is 8.0 miles up Forest Route 535, with a few extremely narrow and steep sections.

Contact: San Juan National Forest, Dolores District, 970/882-7296, www.fs.usda.gov/sanjuan.

⁸ CAYTON
🏃🚵🛶❄️🐕🚐🏕

Scenic rating: 7

north of Rico

At 9,400 feet, Cayton can be a chilly place to wake up. It's not unusual to find patches of snow in June. Nevertheless, this is a popular summer destination, frequented by backpackers and hikers heading into the rugged Lizard Head Wilderness as well as RVers who will appreciate the hookups that were installed during a campground renovation in 2009. The Lizard Head Wilderness encompasses 41,000 acres in the San Miguel Mountains, including three fourteeners and several thirteeners. The Navajo

Lake and Lizard Head Trails are popular destinations. Outside of the wilderness, ATVers and snowmobilers enjoy the Barlow Creek and Divide Roads. There are 60 miles of snowmobiling trails in the Roaring Forks and Barlow Creek Snowmobile Area. The campground consists of two loops beside the Dolores River. Both loops have excellent shade and moderate privacy. Sites 10-20 in the lower loop are closest to the river.

Campsites, facilities: There are 27 sites for tents and RVs up to 35 feet. Pull-throughs are available. Electric hookups are available at most sites. Picnic tables and grills are provided. Vault toilets, drinking water, and a group picnic area are available. Leashed pets are permitted. Sites 5, 6, 10, and 25 are wheelchair-accessible.

Reservations, fees: Reservations are not accepted. The fee is $24 per night for a nonelectric site or $36 per night for an electric site. Cash or check only. Open late May-early October.

Directions: Take Highway 145 south from Telluride. The campground entrance is 9.0 miles past Lizard Head Pass. Turn left onto Forest Route 578 and cross the bridge. In 0.3 mile, stay right at the fork and enter the campground.

Contact: San Juan National Forest, Dolores District, 970/882-7296, www.fs.usda.gov/sanjuan.

9 MATTERHORN

Scenic rating: 10

south of Telluride

Matterhorn is named for the awe-inspiring views of Sheep Mountain to the south. It's a large loop located in an aspen grove between North Fork Creek and Yellow Mountain. This is a gorgeous location. The only drawbacks are the sound of the highway and chilly nights, but at this altitude, the stargazing is unbeatable, and, with a little patience, you'll see several shooting stars. It's a short hike from the campground to Trout Lake, where the rainbows are

morning traffic on the road in the San Juan National Forest

biting all summer. The historic town of Ophir and the Ophir Needles are a brief drive away. The Lizard Head Wilderness is on the opposite side of the highway. Several trailheads into the wilderness are located on the other side of Lizard Head Pass. RV drivers appreciate the full hookups, and tent campers won't want to miss the hike-in sites (11-14). Site 1 is the only unattractive location because of its proximity to the entrance. Sites 10, 17, 19, and 21 are in the middle of the loop and less private than the rest of the campground.

Campsites, facilities: There are 25 sites for tents and RVs up to 45 feet and three walk-in tent sites. Full hookups are available at sites 5, 7, 20, and 22-26. Picnic tables, fire rings, and grills are provided. Tent pads are available at sites 7, 8, 11-14, and 17. Restrooms with flush toilets and showers and drinking water are available. Trash must be packed out. Leashed pets are permitted.

Reservations, fees: Reservations are accepted at 877/444-6777 and www.recreation.gov. The fee is $22 per night for tent sites and $32 per night for sites with hookups. Cash or check only. Open mid-May-late September. They charge $5 per bag of trash.

Directions: From the San Miguel River bridge just west of Telluride, take Highway 145 south for 12 miles. The campground entrance is on the left.

Contact: Uncompahgre National Forest, Norwood District, 970/327-4261, www.fs.usda.gov/gmug.

10 SUNSHINE

Scenic rating: 8

south of Telluride

Sunshine is the closest national forest campground to Telluride, and it's on the San Juan Skyway, so the earlier you arrive at this first-come, first-served campground, the better.

The campground is a paved loop through a pretty aspen grove. A 50-yard trail leads to an overlook with views of the South Fork valley and the snowbound peaks of the Lizard Head Wilderness. And that's just the beginning. From Sunshine, campers can hike or drive up to Alta Lakes. And just a short drive away is a Nature Conservancy Preserve on the South Fork of the San Miguel with excellent catch-and-release fishing. The historic town of Ophir, the Ophir Needles, and wall and crack climbing are a 15-minute drive to the south. And cyclists shouldn't miss the heart-stopping climb up Lizard Head Pass. Sites 1-3 are next to a small wetland. Sites 8 and 9 are next to the overlook trail. Sites 10-12 are right next to the road, but sites 11 and 12 also have the best views of the mountains.

Campsites, facilities: There are 18 sites for tents and RVs up to 35 feet. There are no hookups. Picnic tables, fire rings, grills, and tent pads are provided. Vault toilets and drinking water are available. Leashed pets are permitted. Sites 2-4 and 12-14 are wheelchair-accessible.

Reservations, fees: Reservations are not accepted. The fee is $18 per night. Cash or check only. Open mid-May-late September.

Directions: From the San Miguel River bridge just west of Telluride, take Highway 145 south for six miles. The campground entrance is on the right.

Contact: Uncompahgre National Forest, Norwood District, 970/327-4261, www.fs.usda.gov/gmug.

11 TELLURIDE TOWN PARK

Scenic rating: 5

in Telluride

BEST (

Telluride's social calendar would give Martha Stewart a conniption fit. A typical summer lineup includes the celebrated Bluegrass

Festival, Bike Week, Wine Festival, Jazz Celebration, Mushroom Fest, and the Film Festival. Add to that the endless hiking, mountain biking, and fishing opportunities of the San Juans (and all that Main Street shopping), and finding a place to pitch your tent in a town with only one campground can be pretty tough. If you want to camp at the town park, arrive early. If there's a festival going on, call ahead to check availability. If you do manage to snag a spot, you can sit back and enjoy the scene: Deadheads, prayer flags, family reunions, and VW buses are typical sights. The park is adjacent to Bear Creek Preserve, a 381-acre open space. The San Miguel River Trail and Bear Creek Trail are accessible from the campground. There is no privacy in this campground, but privacy is not the point. Camping in Telluride is a social event, so bring your hiking boots, your hammock, and your happy face.

Campsites, facilities: There are 28 sites for tents and small RVs and 5 walk-in tent sites. There are no hookups. Picnic tables, grills, restrooms with flush toilets and showers, and drinking water are provided. The park also contains a swimming pool, playground, volleyball and basketball courts, baseball fields, tennis courts, a fishing pond, skateboard ramp, disc golf course, and festival stage. Leashed pets are permitted, and leash laws are strictly enforced.

Reservations, fees: Reservations are not accepted. The fee is $19 per night for a walk-in site and $33 per night for all other sites (discounts for seniors age 59 and up). The fees include one vehicle. Additional vehicles cost $6 per night. Cash only. Open mid-May-mid-October. Seven night max stay.

Directions: The town park is located at the east end of Telluride, at 500 East Colorado Avenue. Highway 145 (the only road into town) turns into Colorado Avenue/Main Street. The park entrance is at the Maple Street bridge.

Contact: Telluride Parks and Recreation Department, 970/728-2173, www.telluride.co.gov.

12 ORVIS HOT SPRINGS

Scenic rating: 5

near Ridgway

BEST (

Orvis is a commercial hot springs in the Uncompahgre Valley with seven soaking areas with water temperatures ranging from 98-112°F. The main attraction is The Pond, a deep and wide natural spring pool with amazing views of Mount Sneffels. Visitors can also dip into The Lobster Pot and several pools with waterfalls, or sign up for a massage. The soaking areas are available all night to overnight guests. Clothing is optional, but this is a family-oriented environment. The campsites are in a gravel lot (next to an AmeriGas facility) with pleasant views of the valley and the San Juan Mountains. There are eight wooden tent pads and two ground pads. The springs attract a large crowd of regulars in the summer, so reservations are recommended.

Campsites, facilities: There is vehicle and tent camping for up to 24 people. Tent pads and a group picnic table and grill are provided. Restrooms with flush toilets and showers, drinking water, and a community kitchen are available. Leashed pets are permitted only in the campsites.

Reservations, fees: Reservations are accepted at 970/626-5324. The fee is $37-49 per person per night for adults and $12 per night for children age 4-12. This fee includes access to the springs. Open year-round.

Directions: From Ridgway, drive south on U.S. Highway 550 for about 2.5 miles. Turn right at County Road 3. The resort is on the right.

Contact: Orvis Hot Springs, 970/626-5324, www.orvishotsprings.com.

13 OURAY KOA

Scenic rating: 7

north of Ouray

BEST (

Ouray is the northern gateway to the San Juans, which makes this KOA a destination campground. It's packed all summer and people rave about it, so reservations are strongly recommended, especially for RVs. Families, tour groups, and snowbirds make the most of easy access to the San Juan Scenic Byway and the historic town of Ouray (not to mention the public hot springs, which are four miles south of the campground). From June 15 to August 15, the campground offers breakfast, all-you-can-eat Texas-style barbecue, pizza, and live bluegrass music on weekends. Jeep rentals also are available, as well as yoga decks and a tepee that accommodates groups of around 20 adults. This campground consists of multiple loops on both sides of a small stream. There is not much privacy, but some sites are wooded and others have views of the mountains. The best tent sites, 47-50, are situated in an aspen grove.

Campsites, facilities: There are 80 sites for RVs up to 80 feet and 50 tent-only sites. Full and partial hookups and pull-through sites are available. Picnic tables, fire rings, and grills are provided. Restrooms with flush toilets and showers, laundry facilities, drinking water, a store, free Wi-Fi, meeting room, and playground are available. A hot tub, horseshoe pits, volleyball court, yoga decks, tepee, and restaurant, and dump stations are also available. Leashed pets are permitted. The cabins and some facilities are wheelchair-accessible.

Reservations, fees: Reservations are accepted at 800/562-8026. The tent fee is $39 plus tax per night for two people. The RV fee is $45-63 per night for two people. Additional people cost $5 per night. Furnished tepee and cabins also available. The KOA Value Kard is accepted. Open early May-late September.

Directions: From the Ouray Hot Springs Pool, drive north on I-550 for 4.0 miles. Turn west on County Road 225. The campground entrance is in 0.2 mile.

Contact: Ouray KOA, 970/325-4736, www.koa.com.

14 4J+1+1

Scenic rating: 3

in Ouray

BEST (

Ouray is a historic mining town turned summer destination in the San Juan Mountains. The opportunities for outdoor recreation are endless, including hiking, mountain biking, rock climbing, four-wheeling, and fishing. Ouray has a sulfur-free Hot Springs Pool, which includes a public outdoor park with a lap pool, several soaking pools, a diving area, and three water slides. It's only a couple of blocks to walk from the campground to the hot springs, via a footbridge across the river. The 4J+1+1 is a longtime family-run operation, practically in the center of town. It's a good destination for RVers and families who don't mind the close quarters. The campground itself is fairly cramped. The sites are around a gravel loop with little privacy, but its location makes it easy to rent a Jeep, sign up for a trail ride, go shopping, or visit art galleries. (There are about 20 galleries, pottery studios, and silversmiths in town.) The tent sites are all across the road on a narrow strip of grass, and have small wooden privacy screens.

Campsites, facilities: There are 58 sites for tents and RVs up to 60 feet and 10 sites for tents only. Full and partial hookups and pull-through sites are available. Picnic tables are provided at every site. Fire rings and grill are provided at tent sites. Restrooms with flush toilets and showers, laundry facilities, drinking water, free Wi-Fi, and a playground are available. Leashed pets are permitted.

Reservations, fees: Reservations are accepted

at 970/325-4418. Tent sites are $28 per night for two people. RV sites are $38-42 per night for two people. Additional people over the age of eight are $2 per night. Open early May-mid-October.

Directions: From Main Street in Ouray, drive west on 7th Avenue. After the bridge, follow the road to the right. The campground is on the right.

Contact: 4J+1+1, 970/325-4418, www. coloradodirectory.com/4j11rvpark.

15 AMPHITHEATER

Scenic rating: 8

near Ouray

BEST (

This is one of the busiest campgrounds in the state, especially on July 4th, when the town of Ouray sets off fireworks in the amphitheater, a massive glacial cirque that looms over the town. The campground is on a steep hill below the amphitheater and across the narrow valley of Ouray from Mount Sneffels and an impressive range of thirteeners. The terraced sites are set in a forest of aspen and evergreens and many feature views of the mountains (Sites 7-14, and 25 have the best views. Sites 5, 12, and 16 have no view.) From the overlook, there is a vertigo-inducing view of Ouray, only about a 10-minute drive away, where weary campers can browse art galleries, go on a mine tour, or take a dip in the hot springs. Nearby trails include Portland, Baby Bathtubs, and Upper Cascade Falls. Campers should also head down the hill and across I-550 to Box Cañon Falls Park to view the Canyon Creek waterfall. (There's a $4 entrance fee for a very short hike, but totally worth it to feel the pounding spray of the falls). Many visitors rent Jeeps or mountain bikes to explore the numerous mining towns and four-wheel-drive roads in the area. One of the most popular (and difficult) routes is the Camp Bird Road up to Imogene Pass and then down to Telluride. This route takes about four hours and requires a detailed map.

perched above Ouray and the world, at Amphitheater campground

Campsites, facilities: There are 35 sites for tents and RVs up to 25 feet. Picnic tables, fire rings, and grills, tent pads are provided. Vault toilets and drinking water are available. Leashed pets are permitted. Many sites are wheelchair-accessible, including 16, 17, 29, and 30.

Reservations, fees: Reservations are accepted for 19 of the sites at 877/444-6777 and www.recreation.gov. The fee is $24 per night. Cash or check only. Open late May-mid-October.

Directions: In Ouray, from the intersection of Third Avenue and I-550/Main Avenue, drive south on I-550 for 1.0 mile. Turn left at the National Forest sign. It is 1.0 mile up a very narrow paved road to the campground entrance.

Contact: Uncompahgre National Forest, Ouray District, 970/240-5300, www.fs.usda.gov/gmug.

16 SOUTH MINERAL

🥾 🚴 🛶 🐴 🚐 ⛺

Scenic rating: 8

near Silverton

In July and August, it can be tough to find an empty campsite in this gorgeous valley formed by volcanic activity. The surrounding mountains are colorful and dotted with waterfalls and alpine lakes. The most popular hike, Ice Lake Trail, is a strenuous 4.5-mile climb to a lake surrounded by thirteeners. Clear Lake Trail is equally challenging and rewarding. The Rico-Silverton Trail can be accessed by following South Mineral Road past the campground to Bandora Mine. The eight-mile trail climbs two passes and provides access to Grizzly Peak, Rolling Mountain, and Graysill Mountain. Mountain bikers and ATV owners will enjoy exploring the forest routes. When you're ready for some culture, it's a short drive to Silverton, a National Historic District with good restaurants and mining attractions. The campground is a dirt loop in an evergreen forest, at an elevation of 9,800 feet. Sites 4-6 and 18-20 have the best views. Sites 5, 8, 9, 11, and 14-16 are on the banks of South Mineral Creek. Site 10 is hike-in. Be sure to bring your air mattress—the ground can be quite rocky—and arrive early to beat out the large crowd of regulars.

Campsites, facilities: There are 26 sites for tents and RVs up to 45 feet. There are no hookups. Sites 2, 15, 16, and 30 are pull-through. Picnic tables, fire rings, grills, vault toilets, and drinking water are provided. Leashed pets are permitted.

Reservations, fees: Reservations are not accepted. The fee is $30 per night. Cash or check only. Open mid-May-mid-September.

Directions: From the intersection of I-550 and Highway 110 in Silverton, take I-550 north for 2.0 miles. Turn left on County Road 7/South Mineral Road. Continue 4.6 miles to the campground.

Contact: San Juan National Forest, Columbine District, 970/884-2512, www.fs.usda.gov/sanjuan.

17 SOUTH MINERAL DISPERSED

🥾 🚴 🛶 🐴 🚐 ⛺

Scenic rating: 9

near Silverton

In July and August, it can be tough to find an empty campsite in this gorgeous volcanic valley. If the developed campground at the end of South Mineral Road is packed with regulars, look for a campsite at four pull-offs along the road (two beside the creek, two across the road). You won't be missing out. The floodplain has numerous beaver ponds and amazing views of the igneous peaks and sparkling waterfalls. Two hikes begin at the end of the road. Ice Lake Trail is a strenuous 4.5-mile climb to an alpine lake basin surrounded by thirteeners. Clear Lake Trail is equally challenging and rewarding. Mountain bikers and ATV owners can explore the forest routes. Silverton, a National Historic District with good restaurants and mining attractions, is a short drive to the east. This is free camping at its best.

Campsites, facilities: There are four dispersed camping areas for tents and small RVs. A vault toilet is available at the last pull-off. Leashed pets are permitted.

Reservations, fees: Reservations are not accepted, and camping is free, although camping in the National Forest is limited to 14 days. Open mid-May–mid-September.

Directions: From the intersection of I-550 and Highway 110 in Silverton, take I-550 north for 2.0 miles. Turn left on County Road 7/South Mineral Road. The pull-offs are located at mile 0.5, 0.9, 1.3, and 3.

Contact: San Juan National Forest, Columbine District, 970/884-2512, www.fs.usda.gov/sanjuan.

18 MOLAS LAKE

🚶 🚴 🛶 🎣 ⛵ 🐕 ♿ 🚐 ⛺

Scenic rating: 9

south of Silverton

BEST (

This is a campground of superlatives. At 10,680 feet, Molas Lake is the highest campground in the continental United States, and the views are nothing short of awesome. The park, which has been owned by the town of Silverton for nearly a century, is surrounded by BLM property to the north and east, and national forest to the west and south, including the Weminuche Wilderness, one of the largest wilderness areas in the lower 48. Molas Lake is cradled by high peaks: Engineer Mountain, Twin Sisters, Sultan Mountain, Whitehead Peak, and Snowdon Peak. The drive here on I-550 is part of the San Juan Scenic Byway, often called the most beautiful drive in the country. Every traveler on the byway should reserve at least one night for Molas Lake. There's stocked fishing and boating on the lake and excellent hiking around

the lake as well as on the Colorado Trail. With a shuttle, backpackers can hike 20 miles one-way from Molas Pass to Bolam Pass or make a loop with several connecting trails. Molas Trail leads east from the pass into the Weminuche. It's four miles one-way, and it connects with Elk Creek, the most popular trail in the wilderness area. The Upper Animas, from Silverton to Rockwood Railroad Depot, is considered one of the finest Class IV-V white-water adventures in the country. It's enjoyed by advanced kayakers and commercial rafting companies.

The campground has relatively modern facilities. The campsites are dispersed around the north and east sides of the lake, and they are very diverse. Campers can choose from forest, meadows, and lakefront. Weekends get very crowded, but there is ample privacy midweek. Alcohol is prohibited in the campground.

Campsites, facilities: There are 45 sites for tents and RVs of any length, including several walk-in tent sites. There are no hookups. Picnic tables and fire rings are provided. Vault toilets, coin showers, drinking water, a fish-cleaning station, and a small store are available. Leashed pets are permitted. One site and most facilities are wheelchair-accessible.

Reservations, fees: Reservations are accepted online at www.molaslake.com. The fee is $20-30 per night. Cash or check only. Open late May–early October.

Directions: From Silverton, take I-550 south for 5.2 miles and turn left at the Molas Lake Public Park sign and continue 0.5 mile to the office. The dirt road can be very bad when wet.

Contact: City of Silverton, 970/387-5522, www.molaslake.com.

19 HAVILAND LAKE

🚶 🛶 🚐 ⛵ 🐕 ♿ 🚐 ⛺

Scenic rating: 7

north of Durango

BEST (

Haviland Lake is an attractive destination,

and it's a short drive away from Durango, so it's a convenient stopover on the Million Dollar Highway. The lake is stocked and practically lined with kids fishing with power bait and hauling out trout. It's a good lake for fly-fishing and a beautiful place to paddle a canoe. There's a short interpretive trail for hikers. This is a modern, well-designed facility. There are four interlaced gravel loops on a hillside overlooking the lake. The sites are terraced and have large pull-ins, so they work well for tent camping and RVs. Most of them are screened by aspen, so even when the campground is full, it's easy to find privacy. The campground fills up quickly on the weekends, so arrive early if possible. Most of the campers are retirees and families, but it can get a little rowdy until 10pm when the camp hosts enforce quiet hours.

Campsites, facilities: There are 43 sites for tents and RVs up to 45 feet. Sites 8, 12, 21, 23, 39, and 43 are double sites. Sites 10-16, 19-21, 31, 32, and 39-43 have electric hookups. Picnic tables, fire rings, and grills are provided. Vault toilets and drinking water, a boat ramp, and a group picnic area are available. Leashed pets are permitted. Some sites and all facilities are wheelchair-accessible.

Reservations, fees: Reservations are accepted at 26 of the sites, at 877/444-6777 or www.recreation.gov. The fee is $24 per night, plus an additional $16 for electricity and premium lakeside sites. Cash or check only. Open early May-late September.

Directions: From Durango, take I-550 north for about 24 miles. Turn right at the Haviland Lake sign onto an unmarked road. Stay left at the fork. The campground is in 0.3 mile.

Contact: San Juan National Forest, Columbine District, 970/884-2512, www.fs.usda.gov/sanjuan.

The Durango & Silverton Narrow Gauge Railroad can take you to backcountry campgrounds.

20 CHRIS PARK GROUP

Scenic rating: 7

north of Durango

This group campground is in a sheltered hollow full of ponderosa pines. It's a perfect location for a family reunion, Scout trip, or church event. The three sites have large gravel lots for RVs and dispersed tent camping in the woods. Haviland Lake is accessible via the short Wagon Road Historic Trail. The trout fishing on the lake is good, and it's a nice place to paddle a canoe. Durango is just 30 minutes away, and the Trimble Hot Springs are just outside of town. There are no mountain views from the campground, but the lake is very scenic.

Campsites, facilities: There are three group sites for tents and RVs up to 45 feet. Sites 1 and 2 can accommodate up to 75 people and site 3 can accommodate 150 people. Picnic tables, fire rings, and grills are provided. Vault toilets and drinking water, an event pavilion, horseshoe pits, and a volleyball court are available. Leashed pets are permitted. Some sites and all facilities are wheelchair-accessible.

Reservations, fees: Reservations are required and are accepted at 877/444-6777 and www.recreation.gov. The fee is $100-220 depending on group size. Open mid-May-mid-September.

Directions: From Durango, take I-550 north for about 24 miles. Turn right at the Haviland Lake sign onto an unmarked road. Stay right at the fork. The campground is in 1.0 mile.

Contact: San Juan National Forest, Columbine District, 970/884-2512, www.fs.usda.gov/sanjuan.

21 MOREFIELD

Scenic rating: 4

in Mesa Verde National Park

Mesa Verde National Park contains more than 5,000 archaeological sites, including 600 cliff dwellings of the Ancestral Puebloans. Local cowboys stumbled across Cliff Palace, one of the largest, most impressive of the sites, in the late 19th century. The cliff dwellings and steep canyon formations have amazed archaeologists, photographers, and tourists ever since. If only Morefield were as impressive as the rest of the park. The campground, which is managed by the Aramark concession, feels like an overblown, abandoned subdivision in the desert. The sites are small, cramped, and overgrown, and the facilities are dated. The campground is in a small valley without views and the surrounding hillsides have been ravaged by forest fires. Although the oak brush has filled in a lot, it's still a grim place to camp and only a handful of sites are lucky enough to be enclosed in the oak shade. The best features are the three hiking trails that begin at the campground. The nearest accessible archaeological sites begin 12 miles farther inside the park.

The campground consists of four large paved loops: Pueblo Road, Hopi Road, Ute Road, and Apache Road. Pueblo Road has tent pads. Ute Road has hookups at some sites. The campsites are 15-30 feet apart. Some of them are well protected by small trees and shrubs; most are not. Campers must drive around for a while to find privacy. There is also a group area.

Campsites, facilities: There are 267 sites for tents and RVs up to 40 feet. Full hookups are available at 20 sites. Picnic tables, fire rings, and grills are provided. Restrooms with flush toilets and showers, a laundry room, drinking water, gift store, grocery store, gas station, cafe, amphitheater, telephones, and dump stations are available. There is also a campground restaurant with all-day dining. Leashed pets are permitted in the campground but are not allowed on trails.

Reservations, fees: Reservations are accepted at 800/449-2288 and www.visitmesaverde.com. Sites without hookups are $33 per night and sites with full hookups are $45 per night. 17 group sites can hold up to 25 people. The park entrance fee is $15-25 per vehicle (annual pass $50). The same company manages the Far View Lodge, a hotel 15 miles inside the park. Open late April-early October.

Directions: From the intersection of Highway 145 and I-190 in Cortez, take U.S. Highway 160 east for 9.0 miles. Exit at Mesa Verde National Park. Turn right off the ramp and stop at the entrance station to purchase a park pass. The campground is 4.0 miles past the entrance station.

Contact: Mesa Verde National Park, 970/529-4465, www.nps.gov/meve.

22 MANCOS STATE PARK

Scenic rating: 8

north of Mancos

Mancos State Park has 300 acres of land and a 216-surface-acre reservoir. The park isn't half as spectacular as its surroundings, but it's a great place for children to learn to fish. The reservoir is stocked with rainbow trout, and the dam is often packed with kids casting power bait. Wakeless boating is allowed on the lake. The park also has a five-mile trail system open to hiking and mountain biking, and it is adjacent to San Juan National Forest. Majestic Dude Ranch, located just outside the park, offers one-day and multiday trail rides into the national forest. "Dudes" practice in the park before heading up the mountain. This small park can get very busy on weekends with a largely local crowd. The campground is divided into two loops. The larger loop near the entrance station is situated in a forest of ponderosa pine

Cliff Palace at Mesa Verde National Park

and Gambel oak. The sites are large and fairly private. On the far side of the lake, there are nine sites intended for tent camping, but small RVs and pop-ups can also access this area. (There is no drinking water on this side of the campground.) The tent sites have views of the San Juans to the east, and each site has room for several tents. In the winter, campers can enjoy snowshoeing around the lake and snowmobiling in the national forest.

Campsites, facilities: There are 30 sites for tents and RVs up to 35 feet and two yurts. Sites 1, 9, 16, 25, and 26 are pull-through, but there are no hookups. Picnic tables, fire rings, and grills are provided. Vault toilets, drinking water, a boat ramp, horseshoe pits, volleyball court, a group picnic area, and dump stations are available. Leashed pets are permitted. Site 24A and the facilities are wheelchair-accessible.

Reservations, fees: Reservations are accepted at 800/244-5613 and www.cpwshop.com. The fee is $22-28 per night. Pets cost $10 per night. The yurts sleep six and cost $90 per night. Campers must also purchase a vehicle pass ($8) or Annual Parks Pass ($80). Open year-round.

Directions: From Cortez, take U.S. Highway 160 east to Mancos. Drive north on Highway 184 for 0.3 mile and then turn right on County Road 42. In 4.2 miles, turn left on N Road. The campground is at the end of the road.

Contact: Mancos State Park, 970/533-7065, www.cpw.state.co.us.

23 TRANSFER

🥾 🚴 🐴 🚐 ⛺

Scenic rating: 9

north of Mancos

Transfer is a beautiful, secluded campground on the west slope of the La Plata Mountains. The weddings that take place nearby occasionally in the summer are a testament to the scenic tranquility of this campground, which sits in a grove of aspen trees and wildflowers and couldn't be more peaceful (except on Friday mornings, when a local dude ranch uses the horse corral). From the campground, backpackers, mountain bikers, horse owners, and ATV riders explore the La Platas via the West Mancos, Box Canyon, Sharkstooth, Morrison, and Bear Creek Trails, totaling nearly 50 miles of trails. The 40-mile Aspen Loop Trail, specifically designed for ATVs, is also open to bikes and horses. Most of the sites in Transfer consist of tent and pop-up campers who rarely stay just one night, in part because of the remote location, but also because there's so much to do. Site 10 is one of the larger sites and is only 50 yards up a trail to the West Mancos Overlook, with views of Debe'nsta (aka Hesperus Peak), a sacred mountain to the Din'e (Navajo) people.

Campsites, facilities: There are 12 sites for tents and RVs up to 45 feet. There are no hookups. Picnic tables, fire rings, and grills are provided. Vault toilets, drinking water, a group site with a volleyball court (bring your own net) and creek access, and a horse corral are available. Trash must be packed out. Leashed pets are permitted.

Reservations, fees: Reservations are not accepted; sites are first come, first served. The fee is $16 per night. The group site is $50 per night for up to 60 people. Cash or check only. Open late May-early September.

Directions: From Cortez, take U.S. Highway 160 east to Mancos. Drive north on Highway 184 for 0.3 mile and then turn right on County Road 42/Forest Route 561. This is a gravel and dirt road and can be rough, but it is passable by passenger vehicle. In 10 miles, turn right at the Transfer sign. Turn left after the overlook to enter the campground.

Contact: San Juan National Forest, Dolores District, 970/882-7296, www.fs.usda.gov/sanjuan.

24 TARGET TREE

Scenic rating: 7

east of Mancos

This site was formerly a Ute camp. The campground is named for the trees they used for target practice, and it is still possible to find ponderosa pines with scars from arrowheads and rifles. The abandoned Rio Grande Southern Railroad is nearby; hikers and bikers may enjoy exploring the grade. After exhausting those recreation opportunities, most campers will move on. Target Tree is a convenient stopover between Durango and Cortez, and it is also close to Mesa Verde National Park. The sites are fairly large, private, and have lots of shade. The elevation is 7,800 feet.

Campsites, facilities: There are 25 sites for tents and RVs up to 45 feet. One-third of the sites are pull-through. Picnic tables, fire rings, grills, and tent pads are provided. Vault toilets, drinking water, and a group picnic area are available. Leashed pets are permitted.

Reservations, fees: This is a first-come, first-served campground but it's sometimes possible to reserve via the Dolores Public Lands Office at 970/882-6800. The fee is $20 per night. Cash or check only. Open late May-early September.

Directions: From Mancos, take U.S. Highway 160 east for 7.0 miles. Shortly after the La Plata County line, turn left at the Target Tree Recreation Area sign. The campground is in 0.4 mile.

Contact: San Juan National Forest, Dolores District, 970/882-7296, www.fs.usda.gov/sanjuan.

25 SNOWSLIDE

Scenic rating: 8

west of Durango

The La Plata Mountains were named by Spaniards for the silver ore they found here. Appropriately, the La Plata Canyon has a rich mining history, as evidenced by the historic town of Mayday, which has become a bedroom community of Durango. Enclosed by 12,000-foot peaks, the canyon is narrow and cool. Hikers and mountain bikers can explore several very steep fire roads or drive to the Kennebec trailhead at the end of County Road 124 and take Sharkstooth Trail to Indian Ridge Trail (a part of the Colorado Trail). The views of the Animas valley are spectacular. The campground is the largest and most appealing of two developed campgrounds on this road. There are two very nice tent-only sites by the river, and most of the sites have good views of the La Plata peaks at the end of the canyon. The avalanche path for which the campground is named is just north of the campground. There is fishing on the La Plata.

Campsites, facilities: There are 13 sites for tents and RVs up to 35 feet, including two tent-only sites. There are no hookups. Picnic tables, fire rings, and grills are provided. Vault toilets and a group picnic area are available. There is no drinking water. Trash must be packed out. Leashed pets are permitted.

Reservations, fees: This is a first-come, first-served campground. The fee is $15 per night. Cash or check only. Open mid-May-mid-September.

Directions: From Durango, take U.S. Highway 160 west for about 12 miles. At the Kennebec Cafe, turn north on County Road 124 and drive up the La Plata Canyon for 5.6 miles to the Snowslide sign. The campground is on both sides of the road.

Contact: San Juan National Forest, Columbine District, 970/884-2512, www.fs.usda.gov/sanjuan.

26 KROEGER

🚶 🚲 🛶 🐾 🚐 ⛺

Scenic rating: 7

west of Durango

Kroeger is not quite as roomy or private as nearby Snowslide, and it lacks the excellent views of the La Plata peaks. But if you're looking for a quiet place to pitch the tent or want a base camp for exploring the La Plata region, then Kroeger might be perfect for you. (Due to snow and rain, it can stay muddy until July.) There is fishing on the La Plata.

Campsites, facilities: There are 10 sites for tents and RVs up to 25 feet. There are no hookups. Picnic tables, fire rings, and grills are provided. Vault toilets are available. There is no drinking water. Trash must be packed out. Leashed pets are permitted.

Reservations, fees: This is a first-come, first-served campground. The fee is $20 per night. Cash or check only. Open mid-May-mid-September.

Directions: From Durango, take U.S. Highway 160 west for about 12 miles. At the Kennebec Cafe, turn north on County Road 124 and drive up the La Plata Canyon for six miles to the Kroeger sign.

Contact: San Juan National Forest, Columbine District, 970/884-2512, www.fs.usda.gov/sanjuan.

27 JUNCTION CREEK

🚶 🚲 🛶 🐾 ♿ 🚐 ⛺

Scenic rating: 7

near Durango

BEST (

This campground is hopping all summer long with hikers, bikers, and horseback riders heading out on the Colorado Trail, a 470-mile multiuse trail that is the pride and joy of the Colorado trail system. It travels from Durango to Chatfield State Park in the Denver area. The campground is in a pine forest, with ample shade and fair privacy. It's located just 5 miles northwest of Durango at 7,300 feet elevation.

Campsites, facilities: There are 46 sites for tents and RVs up to 60 feet, including four double sites. There are electrical hookups at 14 sites. Picnic tables, fire rings, grills, and tent pads are provided. Vault toilets and drinking water are available. In the day-use area, there is a group picnic site for up to 65 people, a pavilion, horseshoe pits, and volleyball court. The facilities are wheelchair-accessible. Leashed pets are permitted.

Reservations, fees: Reservations are accepted at www.recreation.gov or 877/444-6777. The fee is $24 per night, plus $5 for electrical hookups. Cash or check only. Open early May-late September.

Directions: From downtown Durango, take I-550 north. Turn left on Junction Creek Road/25th Street/County Road 204. In 3.0 miles, stay left at the fork. The campground is on the left in 2.0 miles.

Contact: San Juan National Forest, Columbine District, 970/884-2512, www.fs.usda.gov/sanjuan.

28 MILLER CREEK

🛶 🚐 🛥 🐾 🚐 ⛺

Scenic rating: 7

on Lemon Reservoir

Located in the Florida River drainage at an elevation of 8,200 feet, Lemon Reservoir is much less developed than Vallecito Reservoir to the east. The fishery was decimated by the Missionary Ridge forest fire in 2002, but it has recovered nicely since then. There is good shoreline fishing at the north end of the lake, and a concrete boat ramp, though both fishing and boating are affected by water levels that vary annually. The lake is also a great place to learn to roll a kayak. The sites at the campground are close together and offer little privacy, but all are close to the water's edge and are quite nice.

Campsites, facilities: There are 12 sites for tents and RVs up to 26 feet, with a few sites that can handle RVs up to 35 feet. There are no hookups. Picnic tables, fire rings, grills, vault toilets, trash service, and drinking water are provided. A boat ramp is available. Leashed pets are permitted.

Reservations, fees: Reservations are not accepted. The cost is $22 per night. Cash or check only. Open mid-May-mid-September.

Directions: From Durango, drive east on Florida Road/County Road 240 for 14 miles. At Helen's Store, turn left on County Road 243. The campground is on the left in 3.5 miles.

Contact: San Juan National Forest, Columbine District, 970/884-2512, www.fs.usda.gov/sanjuan.

29 FLORIDA
🚶 🐴 🚙 ⛺

Scenic rating: 7

near Lemon Reservoir

Florida is two miles beyond the north end of Lemon Reservoir, which makes it a great compromise for families with hikers and anglers. The campground is a small loop in a pine forest alongside the Florida River. Sites 12 and 13 are next to the river. The sites are small, but dense vegetation affords ample privacy. It is quiet and clean but not especially appealing. Two hikes are accessible nearby. The Lost Lake Trail, a 0.5-mile trail to a scenic alpine lake, begins two miles up East Florida Road. The Burnt Timber Trail, which begins at Transfer Park, climbs into the Weminuche Wilderness and connects with Vallecito Creek Trail. Half

of the campground was renovated in 2015 to accommodate larger rigs in bigger sites.

Campsites, facilities: There are 20 sites for tents and RVs up to 40 feet and one group site for up to 100 people. There are no hookups, but some sites are pull-through. Picnic tables, fire rings, grills, vault toilets, trash service, and drinking water are provided. Leashed pets are permitted.

Reservations, fees: Reservations are not accepted (except for the group site). The cost is $22 per night. The fee for the group site is $125 per night. Cash or check only. Open mid-May-mid-September.

Directions: From Durango, drive east on Florida Road/County Road 240 for 14 miles. At Helen's Store, turn left on County Road 243. In 7.0 miles, turn left at the Florida sign. The campground is in 0.3 mile.

Contact: San Juan National Forest, Columbine District, 970/884-2512, www.fs.usda.gov/sanjuan.

30 TRANSFER PARK
🚶 🐴 🚙 ⛺

Scenic rating: 6

near Lemon Reservoir

Transfer Park is a historic site where miners transferred ores and supplies from wagons to pack mules. The campground has two loops separated by a small meadow. The small sites are fairly close together, but there are so few visitors that it's easy to find a bit of privacy. It's a quiet destination for families and large groups. Fishing and boating are available four miles away on Lemon Reservoir. Hikers and horseback riders can head north on the Burnt Timber Trail into the Weminuche Wilderness. While enjoying this area, be aware of burn hazards from the Missionary Ridge fire of 2002, which burned 70,000 acres. Fire-damaged trees can fall without warning after strong winds or thunderstorms.

Campsites, facilities: There are 25 sites for tents and RVs up to 35 feet. There are no hookups. Picnic tables, fire rings, grills, vault toilets, and drinking water are provided. Leashed pets are permitted.

Reservations, fees: Reservations are not accepted. The cost is $20 per night. Cash or check only. Open mid-May-mid-September.

Directions: From Durango, drive east on Florida Road/County Road 240 for 14 miles. At Helen's Store, turn left on County Road 243. In 7.0 miles, turn left at the Florida sign on an unmarked road. Bear left through the Florida campground. The road becomes very rough. The campground is in 1.2 miles.

Contact: San Juan National Forest, 970/247-4874, www.fs.usda.gov/sanjuan.

31 GRAHAM CREEK

Scenic rating: 7

on Vallecito Reservoir

The string of U.S. Forest Service campgrounds along the eastern shore of Vallecito Reservoir offers unparalleled sunset views across the water, plus access to all manner of water and mountain-based adventures. This whole area is really one of the best-kept secrets in Colorado. The area is still recovering from the devastating Missionary Ridge Fire in 2002, but beautiful aspen patches are coming into some of the burn areas and the fishery has recovered nicely. In addition to all the boating, fishing, and hiking opportunities (see other campground listings on Vallecito Reservoir for more information), there is one active dude ranch (Colorado Trails Ranch) for trail rides, as well as Elk Point Lodge and Stables, which offers trail rides and pack trips into the mountains.

Graham Creek is the first campground you come to driving north from the dam. It consists of two loops along the water in a fairly thick pine and spruce forest. The large sites are

anywhere from 30 to 100 feet apart. The hillside sites are about 100 yards from the water's edge. The campground is adjacent to North Canyon, and is run by the same hosts. There is an old boat ramp here, but you can launch small craft (which can be carried). All trailered boats need to be inspected by Colorado Parks and Wildlife for zebra mussels at the station near the marina (on the west shore of the reservoir). For hiking, there is easy access to the North Canyon, Graham Creek, and East Creek trails, in addition to nearby trailheads into the Weminuche Wilderness.

Campsites, facilities: There are 25 sites for tents and RVs up to 35 feet. Six sites are pull-through. There are no hookups. Picnic tables, fire rings, grills, vault toilets, drinking water, and dumpsters are provided. Leashed pets are permitted.

Reservations, fees: Reservations are accepted for 15 of the sites at 877/444-6777 and www.recreation.gov. The fee is $22 per night. Cash or check only. Open mid-May-mid-September.

Directions: From Durango, drive east on U.S. Highway 160 for about 18 miles. Turn north on Vallecito Road/County Road 501. Continue on Vallecito Road for 4.5 miles. Before the dam, turn right on Forest Route 603 to follow the east side of the reservoir. Turn right on Forest Route 603. The campground is on the left in 2.9 miles.

Contact: San Juan National Forest, Columbine District, 970/884-2512, www.fs.usda.gov/sanjuan; http://vallecitolakechamber.com.

32 NORTH CANYON

Scenic rating: 7

on Vallecito Reservoir

This is a quiet, one-loop site on the shore of the reservoir in a pine and spruce forest; sites are slightly more open than neighboring Graham Creek. The large sites are anywhere from 30 to 100 feet apart, with plenty of shade, moderate to great privacy, and wonderful sunset vistas from most sites. There are a few direct access points to the water, which is separated from the campground by willows.

Campsites, facilities: There are 21 sites for tents and RVs up to 40 feet. There are no hookups. Picnic tables, fire rings, grills, vault toilets, and drinking water are provided. Leashed pets are permitted.

Reservations, fees: Reservations are accepted for 12 of the sites at 877/444-6777 or www.recreation.gov. The fee is $20 per night. Cash or check only. Open mid-May-mid-September.

Directions: From Durango, drive east on U.S. Highway 160 for about 18 miles. Turn north on Vallecito Road/County Road 501. Continue on Vallecito Road for 4.5 miles. Before the dam, turn right on Forest Route 603 to follow the east side of the reservoir. The campground is on the left in 3.1 miles.

Contact: San Juan National Forest, Columbine District, 970/884-2512, www.fs.usda.gov/sanjuan; http://vallecitolakechamber.com.

33 PINE POINT

Scenic rating: 8
on Vallecito Reservoir

Pine Point is a small lakeside loop in a mature pine forest with views of the snowy San Juan peaks to the north. Sites 11, 13, 15, 17, and 18 are lakeside. The lake is stocked with native trout species, as well as kokanee salmon and pike. Some anglers fish from the shore, but most fish from boats. There is a trail to the lake but no place to moor boats. Hiking is available less than a mile south of the campground on the North Canyon Trail, which climbs to the ridgeline and features scenic vistas of the reservoir and San Juans. A small store, restaurant, and dump station are available at the 5 Branches RV Park just north of the campground.

Campsites, facilities: There are 30 sites for tents and RVs up to 40 feet. There are no hookups. Picnic tables, fire rings, grills, drinking water, and vault toilets are provided. Leashed pets are permitted.

Reservations, fees: Reservations are accepted for 15 of the sites at 877/444-6777 or www.recreation.gov. The fee is $22 per night, or a few dollars more for lakeside sites. Cash or check only. Open mid-May-mid-September.

Directions: From Durango, drive east on U.S. Highway 160 for about 18 miles. Turn north on Vallecito Road/County Road 501. Continue on Vallecito Road for 4.5 miles. Before the dam, turn right on Forest Route 603 to follow the east side of the reservoir. The campground is on the left in 4.0 miles.

Contact: San Juan National Forest, Columbine District, 970/884-2512, www.fs.usda.gov/sanjuan; also see www.vallecitolakechamber.com.

34 MIDDLE MOUNTAIN

Scenic rating: 7
on Vallecito Reservoir

Middle Mountain campground is in an aspen and pine forest on the eastern shore of Vallecito Reservoir. Fish the reservoir for kokanee salmon, native trout species, and pike. Fishing is possible from the shore, but most prefer fishing from boats. There is a big ice-fishing tournament in February. An interesting half-day trip involves following Middle Mountain Road/Forest Route 724 up the Bear Creek drainage, 12 miles to the old mining town of Tuckerville. Additionally, nearby outfitters offer trail-riding excursions. The sites at the campground are large and set about 50 feet apart, but they are not very private. All of the sites have excellent views of the lake and surrounding ridgelines.

Campsites, facilities: There are 24 sites for tents and RVs up to 40 feet. There are no hookups. Picnic tables, fire rings, grills, vault toilets, and drinking water are provided. Leashed pets are permitted.

Reservations, fees: Reservations are not accepted. The fee is $22 per night, plus an additional $3 for "premium" lakeside sites. Cash or check only. Open mid-May–mid-September, and sometimes without services for hunting season.

Directions: From Durango, drive east on U.S. Highway 160 for about 18 miles. Turn north on Vallecito Road/County Road 501. Continue on Vallecito Road for 4.5 miles. Before the dam, turn right on Forest Route 603 to follow the east side of the reservoir. In 5.0 miles (the road twists through 5 Branches RV Park), turn left on Forest Route 602. The campground is on the left in 0.2 mile.

Contact: San Juan National Forest, Columbine District, 970/884-2512, www.fs.usda.gov/sanjuan; www.vallecitolakechamber.com.

35 VALLECITO
🏃 🛶 🐕 🚐 ⛺

Scenic rating: 9

near Vallecito Reservoir

Many people don't realize this campground exists, and they're missing out. Although not directly on the reservoir, it hugs the banks of the creek and borders the vast Weminuche Wilderness (nearly 500,000 acres), which begins 0.5-mile up the Vallecito Creek Trail. This 15-mile trail climbs 3,840 feet to Rock Lake and offers waterfalls, wildlife viewing, and wildflowers in late summer. It can also be linked with the Pine River Trail to form an epic 50-mile loop. Anglers can fish for trout on Vallecito Creek or drive to the north end of Vallecito Reservoir about 4 miles away.

The campground consists of four loops in a mature ponderosa pine forest: Bear, Wapiti, Deer, and Chipmunk. In Bear Loop, the sites are large enough for multiple tents, and sites 1-10 and 12 are next to Vallecito Creek. In

Chipmunk, the sites are closer together, but this smaller loop is much quieter. Wapiti, located next to the trailhead parking, is the least private of all the loops.

Campsites, facilities: There are 79 sites for tents and RVs up to 40 feet; 16 sites have electric hookups. Many sites are pull-through. Picnic tables, fire rings, and grills are provided. Vault toilets, drinking water, a dumpster, and a group picnic area are available. Leashed pets are permitted.

Reservations, fees: Reservations are accepted for 33 sites at 877/444-6777 and www.recreation.gov. The fee is $24 per night, or a little more for premium creekside sites (4, 6, 9, 10, 12). Cash or check only. Open mid-May–mid-September; sometimes without services for hunting season.

Directions: From Durango, drive east on U.S. Highway 160 for about 18 miles. Turn north on Vallecito Road/County Road 501. In Columbus, stay right at the fork, continuing on Vallecito Road along the west shore of the reservoir. At 9.7 miles past Columbus, turn left on County Road 500. The campground entrance is in 2.6 miles at the end of the road.

Contact: San Juan National Forest, Columbine District, 970/884-2512, www.fs.usda.gov/sanjuan; www.vallecitolakechamber.com.

36 PINE RIVER
🏃 🐕 🚐 ⛺

Scenic rating: 6

near Vallecito Reservoir

Like Vallecito campground to the west, Pine River is a gateway to the Weminuche Wilderness. Backpackers and horseback riders use Pine River Trail to access Weminuche Pass and 10 other trails. It can also be linked with the Vallecito Creek Trail to form a 50-mile loop. Except for the trailhead traffic, this is a very quiet place, and you may not even notice the campground at first. The primitive sites are dispersed on a hillside overlooking a ranching valley with impressive granite cliffs soaring overhead. The sites themselves are rather small and are along the road to the big pull-through parking lot at the trailhead.

Campsites, facilities: There are two sites for RVs up to 20 feet and four walk-in tent sites. There are no hookups. Picnic tables, fire rings, and grills are provided. There is no potable water, but a small creek trickles by the first two sites. There is also a parking lot for hikers and horseback riders. Leashed pets are permitted.

Reservations, fees: Reservations are not accepted. The fee is $15 per night. Cash or check only. Open mid-May-mid-September, and sometimes without services for hunting season.

Directions: From Durango, drive east on U.S. Highway 160 for about 18 miles. Turn north on Vallecito Road/County Road 501. In Columbus, stay right at the fork, continuing on Vallecito Road. At 4.5 miles past Columbus, turn right on Forest Route 603. At Middle Mountain, turn right on Forest Route 602. In 3.8 miles, the road ends at the campground.

Contact: San Juan National Forest, Columbine District, 970/884-2512, www.fs.usda.gov/sanjuan.

37 MILL CREEK

Scenic rating: 7

west of Lake City

The Lake City area is extremely popular with ATV riders and four-wheelers heading out on the Alpine Loop Backcountry Byway, a 65-mile 4WD route that connects Lake City, Ouray, and Silverton. The setting is the high San Juans, dotted with the remnants of the mining boom and basins of wildflowers in July and August. Mountain bikers also travel the Alpine Loop, rated by *Outside* magazine as one of the 10 best rides in the country. The entire route takes bikers four to five days to complete, but day trips to Carson City, Sherman, and beyond are also possible. ATVs can unload in the Mill

setting up camp at Vallecito

Creek campground, so they're a common sight. Anglers also come to Mill Creek for the fishing. North of the campground there is a willow-filled park known for brookies. Waders are helpful. The water adjacent to the campground is faster, and the fishing is excellent.

The campground is on a slope above the Lake Fork of the Gunnison. Most sites are wooded with aspen and spruce, so there is plenty of shade. Sites are about 50 feet apart. Sites 10-17 have great views.

Campsites, facilities: There are 22 sites for tents and RVs up to 45 feet. There are no hookups or pull-throughs. Picnic tables, fire rings, grills, vault toilets, bear lockers, trash disposal, and drinking water are provided. Leashed pets are permitted.

Reservations, fees: Reservations are not accepted. The fee is $22 per night. Cash or check only. Open late May-early September.

Directions: From 2nd Street in Lake City, take Highway 149 south for 2.3 miles. Turn right on County Road 30. The campground is on the left in 10.8 miles.

Contact: Bureau of Land Management, Gunnison Field Office, 970/642-4940, www.co.blm.gov.

38 CASTLE LAKES RESORT

Scenic rating: 7

west of Lake City

BEST (

This campground is on the Alpine Loop Backcountry Byway, a 65-mile 4WD route through the San Juans. This is beautiful high mountain country with excellent fishing, hiking, mountain biking, and especially four-wheeling. ATVs can unload in the campground, which attracts many long-term visitors escaping the heat of the South and Midwest. The other main attraction is the stocked fishing ponds, one of which is reserved for catch-and-release fly-fishing. Sites 2-20 are close together

in an open area; the rest of the sites are in a wooded area with an unusual amount of privacy and shade. Sites 35-43 and 48-50 are next to the pond and have excellent views. The tent sites are also next to the pond and shielded by aspen and spruce. This is one of the nicest private campgrounds in the state.

Campsites, facilities: There are 45 sites for RVs up to 43 feet and 5 tent sites. Full and partial hookups are available, but there are no pull-throughs. Picnic tables, fire rings, and grills are provided. Restrooms with flush toilets and showers, laundry facilities, drinking water, a Wi-Fi hot spot, a playground, pavilion, and store are available. Horseshoe pits, stocked fishing ponds, Jeep rentals, a recreation room, and video rentals are also available. Leashed pets are permitted.

Reservations, fees: Reservations are accepted at 970/944-2622. The tent fee is $29 per night for two people. The RV full hookup fee is $34-37 per night for two people. Each additional person costs $1 per night for kids 12 and under and $2 per night for anyone over 12. Open Memorial Day-October 1.

Directions: From 2nd Street in Lake City, take Highway 149 south for 2.3 miles. Turn right on County Road 30. The campground is on the right in 8.1 miles.

Contact: Castle Lakes Resort, 970/944-2622, www.castlelakes.com.

39 WILLIAMS CREEK

Scenic rating: 7

west of Lake City

Williams Creek is the closest national forest campground to Lake City, so it sees a fair amount of stopover traffic. There are also lots of long-term campers here who come to enjoy the Alpine Loop Backcountry Byway, miles of hiking and biking trails, fishing on the Lake Fork of the Gunnison and Lake San Cristobal, and sightseeing in this historic mining district. ATVs cannot unload in this campground, so it tends to be quieter than nearby Mill Creek. Anglers will enjoy the canyon on the Lake Fork, which extends from the Wupperman bridge upstream for two miles. It's full of deep pools and fair-sized rainbows and brookies. Anglers can also try Williams Creek, but it's brushy and tight. The Williams Creek Trail connects with the Alpine Gulch Trail. Across the road, Camp Trail climbs steeply to join the Colorado Trail.

The campground is on a hill, with views down the valley toward Lake San Cristobal. It is pretty but not jaw-dropping. Sites 6-10 have the best views. The sites are about 50 feet apart in an aspen and spruce-fir forest. Privacy is moderate but not great for tent campers.

Campsites, facilities: There are 23 sites for tents and RVs up to 40 feet. There are no hookups. Picnic tables, fire rings, and grills are provided. Vault toilets and drinking water are available. Leashed pets are permitted.

Reservations, fees: Reservations are not accepted. The fee is $14 per night. Cash or check only. Open late May-mid September.

Directions: From 2nd Street in Lake City, take Highway 149 south for 2.3 miles. Turn right on County Road 30. In 4.0 miles, turn left on County Road 33. The campground is on the right in 6.8 miles.

Contact: Gunnison National Forest, Gunnison District at Lake City, 970/641-0471, www. fs.usda.gov/gmug.

40 WUPPERMAN

Scenic rating: 7

near Lake City

Lake San Cristobal is the second-largest natural lake in the state. It was formed about a thousand years ago by the three-mile-long Slumgullion Earthflow, which is still moving a few feet a year. The lake contains mostly brook and rainbow trout, plus some monster browns and mackinaw. The Wupperman campground is on the high bluffs on the eastern shore of the lake. There are five loops in a semiarid setting. The sites are either shaded or very exposed, with great views. It can be hard to find a flat tent site with shade. Sites 26-31 are in the flats beside the water and have the best fishing and boating access.

Campsites, facilities: There are 28 sites for tents and RVs up to 25 feet and 3 tent-only sites. There are no hookups. Picnic tables, fire rings, and grills are provided. Vault toilets, drinking water, a boat ramp, and a dump station are available. Leashed pets are permitted. Sites 7 and 8 are wheelchair-accessible.

Reservations, fees: Reservations are not accepted. The fee is $15 per night. Cash or check only. Open late May-early September. The campground can be used without services during the off-season.

Directions: From 2nd Street in Lake City, take Highway 149 south for 2.3 miles. Turn right on County Road 30. In 4.0 miles, turn left on County Road 33. The campground is on the left in 0.8 mile.

Contact: Lake City Chamber of Commerce, 970/944-2225, www.hinsdalecountycolorado. us.

41 DEER LAKES

Scenic rating: 9

east of Lake City

The drive up to Deer Lakes, from Forest Route 788 to the campground, offers spectacular views of the peaks of the La Garita Wilderness to the east. The campground is almost as scenic and just as magical. Tucked into an area of rolling hills and small parks between the Powderhorn and La Garita Wilderness areas, Deer Lakes campground is in an aspen and spruce forest beside a series of small stocked fishing ponds. Tall trees block the best views, but they also offer abundant privacy. The area is remote, rugged, and quiet. Hikers and anglers will appreciate this campground, which rarely fills up. The artificially constructed lakes are perfect learning ponds for kids. More advanced anglers can explore Cebolla Creek or hike up to Devils Lake. The Deer Lakes Cutoff (open to bikes) reaches from Deer Lakes to the Powderhorn Wilderness boundary, where it connects with the Cañon Inferno and Calf Creek Plateau Trails (closed to bikes). Sites 7 and 8 are close to the lakes. Sites 4 and 5 offer outstanding privacy and scenery.

Campsites, facilities: There are 12 sites for tents and RVs up to 45 feet. There are no hookups. Sites 10 and 12 are pull-through. Picnic tables, fire rings, and grills are provided at all sites. Sites 1, 4-6, and 12 have tent pads. Vault toilets and drinking water are available. Leashed pets are permitted. Site 8 and the facilities are wheelchair-accessible.

Reservations, fees: Reservations are not accepted. The fee is $12 per night. Cash or check only. Open mid-May-October.

Directions: From 2nd Street in Lake City, take Highway 149 south for 9.6 miles. Turn left on Forest Route 788 (before Slumgullion Pass). In 2.7 miles, turn left at the tent sign. The campground is in 0.8 mile.

Contact: Gunnison National Forest, Gunnison District at Lake City, 970/641-0471, www.fs.usda.gov/gmug.

42 HIDDEN VALLEY

Scenic rating: 6

east of Lake City

Hidden Valley isn't half as enchanting as the name implies. There are four tent sites on the banks of Cebolla Creek. Three of them are accessible via a small footbridge. Scattered spruce provide some shade but not much privacy.

There is fair to poor fishing for brook trout on this portion of the stream. Hiking trails into the La Garita and Powderhorn Wilderness areas are a short drive away, but not within walking distance. The biggest attraction here is solitude. There are few visitors to this remote part of the state, and even fewer visitors to this campground. For more information on the La Garita and Powderhorn Wilderness areas, see the Cebolla listing in this chapter.

Campsites, facilities: There are four dispersed tent sites. There are no hookups or pull-throughs. Picnic tables, grills, and vault toilets are provided. Leashed pets are permitted.

Reservations, fees: Reservations are not accepted. Camping is free but feel free to leave a donation. Open May-September.

Directions: From 2nd Street in Lake City, take Highway 149 south for 9.6 miles. Turn left on Forest Route 788 (before Slumgullion Pass). The campground is on the right in 7.3 miles.

Contact: Gunnison National Forest, Gunnison District at Lake City, 970/641-0471, www.fs.usda.gov/gmug.

43 SPRUCE

Scenic rating: 7

east of Lake City

Spruce campground is in the northern portion of the La Garita Wilderness. The Powderhorn Wilderness begins a few miles away. This remote area offers a true wilderness experience to the adventurous camper, but the narrow, winding road deters the majority of visitors. The creek has good brook trout fishing for experienced anglers in the canyons. Novice anglers will have better luck in the numerous beaver ponds. The campground is in a small park on Cebolla Creek, surrounded by dramatic rock formations. The willowy undergrowth provides more privacy than at Cebolla campground downstream. The sites are 50-100 feet apart and offer lots of room for large groups to spread out. Sites 2, 3, 5, and 6 have abundant shade and privacy. For more information on the Powderhorn and La Garita Wilderness areas, see the Cebolla listing in this chapter.

Campsites, facilities: There are nine sites for tents and short RVs. There are no hookups or pull-throughs. Vault toilets, picnic tables, fire rings, and grills are provided. Leashed pets are permitted.

Reservations, fees: Reservations are not accepted. Camping is free, but you can leave a donation. Open May-September.

Directions: From 2nd Street in Lake City, take Highway 149 south for 9.6 miles. Turn left on Forest Route 788 (before Slumgullion Pass). The campground is on the right in 8.4 miles.

Contact: Gunnison National Forest, Gunnison District at Lake City, 970/641-0471, www.fs.usda.gov/gmug.

44 CEBOLLA

Scenic rating: 6

east of Lake City

This remote little campground is on Cebolla Creek, between the Powderhorn Wilderness to the north and the La Garita Wilderness to the south. The Powderhorn Wilderness ranges 8,600-12,600 feet in elevation. Most of it is a plateau, the largest relatively flat expanse of alpine tundra in the continental United States. This area was summer hunting grounds for the Utes and was used for cattle and sheep ranching in the early 1900s, but it was never widely settled. It's home to beaver, bobcat, mountain lion, bear, mule deer, and elk, as well as bighorn sheep and the occasional moose. The best way to access the interior is with pack animals. The Powderhorn Lakes trailhead is a short drive east of the campground. The Rough Creek Trail begins near the campground and extends 7.5 miles into the La Garita Wilderness. Anglers

can fish for brookies, brownies, and rainbows on Cebolla Creek. Young anglers will have an easier time on the beaver ponds upstream.

The campground is in a spruce-fir forest on the banks of Cebolla Creek in a steep-walled canyon. The sites are about 50 feet apart. There is plenty of shade, and the sun doesn't penetrate the canyon until late morning. Visitors are few and far between, but the campground has a small following of regulars. Campers should come prepared for a wilderness experience.

Campsites, facilities: There are three sites for tents and short RVs. There are no hookups or pull-throughs. Picnic tables, fire rings, and grills are provided. Vault toilets are available. Leashed pets are permitted.

Reservations, fees: Reservations are not accepted and there is no fee. Open late May-early September.

Directions: From 2nd Street in Lake City, take Highway 149 south for 9.6 miles. Turn left on Forest Route 788. The campground is on the right in 9.3 miles.

Contact: Bureau of Land Management, Gunnison Field Office, 970/642-4940, www.co.blm.gov.

45 LOST TRAIL

Scenic rating: 9

west of Creede

BEST (

This campground is on Lost Trail Creek, about a mile upstream of the confluence with the Rio Grande. It's a long, narrow, bumpy road to get there, but it's worth every bit of washboard. Every site has outstanding views of the surrounding ridgelines, which include the thirteeners Pole Creek Mountain and Ute Ridge, as well as the spires of Finger Mesa. The Continental Divide lies to the north of the campground, and the Weminuche Wilderness boundary is just south of the road. This destination campground attracts hikers, anglers, horseback riders, and four-wheelers. The Lost Creek Trail begins near the campground and connects with the West Lost Creek, Heart Lake, Continental Divide, and Colorado Trails. These trails feature open parks, aspen groves, panoramic views, bighorn sheep, and good fishing. Backpackers will find good camping along West Lost Creek and at Heart Lake. The Ute Creek Trail begins a mile east of the campground. This 12-mile trail is a popular route into the Weminuche Wilderness. The Ute Basin has four good fishing lakes below the Continental Divide. There are also views of The Window and the Rio Grande Pyramid. Four-wheelers can take Forest Route 520 to Stony Pass (the old toll road to Silverton) or Forest Route 506 to Beartown and Kite Lake. When you're done exploring, you can kick up your feet at this quiet campground and listen to the bubbling of Lost Trail Creek.

One disappointing development in this area is the arrival of the spruce beetle, which is browning out many of the hillsides. The impact so far is only visual as the beetle activity has not moved into the campgrounds, but visitors may want to call the Forest Service for current conditions while planning their trips.

Campsites, facilities: There are seven sites for tents and RVs up to 25 feet. There are no hookups. Picnic tables, fire rings, and grills are provided. Vault toilets are available, but there is no drinking water. Leashed pets are permitted.

Reservations, fees: Reservations are not accepted. There is no fee. Open mid-May-October or November, weather permitting (no services or water after Labor Day).

Directions: From First Street in Creede, take Highway 149 west for 20.7 miles. Turn left on Forest Route 520. The campground is on the left in 18 miles. This is a rough road, but it is 2WD. It is not recommended for long trailers or RVs.

Contact: Rio Grande National Forest, Divide District, 719/657-3321, www.fs.usda.gov/riogrande.

46 THIRTY MILE

Scenic rating: 8

west of Creede

Thirty Mile is a short walk from the east end of the Rio Grande Reservoir, a 1,196-acre lake with an earthen boat ramp that can accommodate only canoes, rafts, and small fishing boats. Fishing is also possible on the Rio Grande, Squaw Creek, Weminuche Creek, and Little Squaw Creek, all of which are within walking distance of the campground, and kayakers can take their boats on the Rio Grande. Two trails begin at the campground and access the Weminuche Wilderness. The popular Weminuche Creek Trail is a five-mile climb to Weminuche Pass, the lowest point on the Continental Divide within the wilderness area. The Squaw Creek Trail parallels the creek for 10 miles from the campground to the Continental Divide. There is good fishing and frequent elk sightings on this trail. Because of the variety of activities and accessibility, Thirty Mile is a very popular campground, and reservations are recommended. It has four loops in a spruce-fir forest. The sites are large and spaced 25-75 feet apart. Privacy is fairly limited. Sites 2, 3, 5, 6, and 24-26 are next to the river. See the Lost Trail entry in this chapter for more information on the spruce beetle activity.

Campsites, facilities: There are 35 sites for tents and RVs up to 60 feet. Sites 12 and 21 are double sites. Some sites are pull-through. There are no hookups. Picnic tables, fire rings, and grills are provided. Vault toilets and drinking water are available. Leashed pets are permitted.

Reservations, fees: Reservations are accepted at 877/444-6777 or www.recreation.gov. The fee is $22 per night for a single site and $44 per night for a double site. Cash or check only. Open year-round, weather and road conditions permitting. No water or services after Labor Day.

Directions: From First Street in Creede, take

Highway 149 west for 20.7 miles. Turn left on Forest Route 520. The campground is on the left in 11.2 miles.

Contact: Rio Grande National Forest, Divide District, 719/657-3321, www.fs.usda.gov/riogrande.

47 RIVER HILL

Scenic rating: 8

west of Creede

BEST (

River Hill is at the confluence of Little Squaw Creek and the Rio Grande, which offer fair stream fishing. It was closed for two years after the West Fork fire in 2013, but is scheduled to reopen in 2016. The kayaking here is excellent. The six-mile stretch from the campground to Trail 816 offers Class III white water when water is being released from the reservoir in May and June. The nearest hiking trails are Weminuche Creek and Squaw Creek, which begin at the Thirty Mile campground and access the Weminuche Wilderness and Continental Divide.

The campground is in the riparian zone between the forest route and the river. It has a blend of meadows and spruce-fir forest. Most of the sites are shaded. The best sites, 5, 6, and 8-12, are next to the river. This campground is smaller than Thirty Mile and offers more privacy. It's very popular with return campers, and stays about three-quarters full throughout the summer. See the Lost Trail entry in this chapter for more information on the spruce beetle activity.

Campsites, facilities: There are 20 sites for tents and RVs up to 35 feet. There are no hookups. Sites 2, 7, 11, and 13 are pull-through. Picnic tables, fire rings, and grills are provided. Vault toilets, drinking water, volleyball, and horseshoe pits are available. Leashed pets are permitted.

Reservations, fees: Reservations are accepted

at 877/444-6777 or www.recreation.gov. The fee is $22 per night. Cash or check only. Open late May-early September.

Directions: From First Street in Creede, take Highway 149 west for 20.7 miles. Turn left on Forest Route 520. The campground is on the left in 9.8 miles.

Contact: Rio Grande National Forest, Divide District, 719/657-3321, www.fs.usda.gov/riogrande.

48 ROAD CANYON

Scenic rating: 4

west of Creede

This unattractive campground is squeezed between Forest Route 520 and the Road Canyon Reservoir, and it's easy to miss. It looks more like a picnic area than a campground. There are no trees or shade, and the campsites are totally exposed to the road. When the campgrounds upstream are full, there are usually vacancies at Road Canyon. The reservoir has an earthen boat ramp suitable for small boats and canoes. Most of the campers are there for four-wheeling in House Canyon and up Stony Pass, the historic toll road to Silverton. Fishing is poor on Road Canyon Reservoir, but better fishing is available on the Rio Grande and the Rio Grande Reservoir. See the Lost Trail entry in this chapter for more information on the spruce beetle activity.

Campsites, facilities: There are six sites for tents and RVs up to 30 feet. There are no hookups. Sites 3 and 4 are pull-through. Picnic tables, fire rings, and grills are provided. Vault toilets are available. Trash must be packed out. Leashed pets are permitted.

Reservations, fees: Camping is free, and reservations are not accepted. Open year-round, weather and road conditions permitting.

Directions: From First Street in Creede, take Highway 149 west for 20.7 miles. Turn left on

Forest Route 520. The campground is on the left in 6.3 miles.

Contact: Rio Grande National Forest, Divide District, 719/657-3321, www.fs.usda.gov/riogrande.

49 SILVER THREAD
🏃 🚲 🐴 🚐 ⛺

Scenic rating: 6

west of Creede

Silver Thread is a stopover on the Silver Thread Scenic Byway, a 75-mile route from South Fork to Lake City. The scenery of the Rio Grande valley around Creede is spectacular, so if you're heading east on the byway near nightfall, spend the night at Silver Thread so you don't miss some of the best sites on the route. The campground contains open meadows and aspen groves below a hairpin turn in the highway. There is a foot trail to the impressive North Clear Creek Falls, where the creek tumbles over volcanic tuff. Fishing for brookies and rainbow trout is available in the creek and beaver ponds. The only drawback is the proximity of the road. Traffic noise deters many campers, so there are always open sites. Sites 1-4 are in a meadow near the highway. Sites 5, 6, and 9-11 are in an aspen grove. (See the Lost Trail entry in this chapter for more information on the spruce beetle activity.)

Campsites, facilities: There are 10 sites for tents and RVs up to 30 feet, including two double sites. There are no hookups. Sites 1-4, 7, 9, and 11 are pull-through. Picnic tables, fire rings, and grills are provided. Vault toilets and drinking water are available. Leashed pets are permitted.

Reservations, fees: Reservations are not accepted. The fee is $19 per night for a single site, and $38 for a double site. Cash or check only. Open year-round, weather and road conditions permitting.

Directions: From First Street in Creede, take

Highway 149 west for 24.3 miles. The campground is on the right, across from Forest Route 515.

Contact: Rio Grande National Forest, Divide District, 719/657-3321, www.fs.usda.gov/riogrande.

50 NORTH CLEAR CREEK
🚲 🐴 🚐 ⛺

Scenic rating: 7

west of Creede

North Clear Creek is an easily accessible destination for travelers interested in exploring the Rio Grande valley. The campground is in a little park beside North Clear Creek, ringed by a forest of spruce, fir, and aspen. The meadow in the middle accommodates two volleyball courts. The best feature of the scenery is the views of Table Mountain and Snow Mesa. Anglers can fish for brookies on the creek. The sites are well spaced, and the campground seems smaller than it is. Sites 10-20 have the best creek access and shade. Sites 4-8 and 21-25 border the meadow and have partial shade but nice views. Sites 1 and 2 share an aspen grove on a small hill overlooking the meadow. Site 20 is a double site with an extra-large picnic table and room for several tents. (See the Lost Trail entry in this chapter for more information on the spruce beetle activity.)

Campsites, facilities: There are 25 sites for tents and RVs up to 32 feet. There are no hookups. Some sites are pull-through. Picnic tables, fire rings, and grills are provided. Vault toilets and drinking water are available. Leashed pets are permitted.

Reservations, fees: Reservations are not accepted. The fee is $19 per night for a single site, and $38 for a double site. Cash or check only. Open late May-early September, gated the rest of the year.

Directions: From First Street in Creede, take Highway 149 west for 22.9 miles. Turn right on

Forest Route 510. The campground is on the right in 2.0 miles.

Contact: Rio Grande National Forest, Divide District, 719/657-3321, www.fs.usda.gov/riogrande.

51 BRISTOL HEAD

Scenic rating: 7

west of Creede

Bristol Head is named for the 12,706-foot peak to the east of the campground. Most sites have excellent views of this landmark, which marks the northwestern boundary of the Creede Caldera, a 10-mile-wide caldera that was formed 30 million years ago during a massive volcanic eruption. BASE jumpers sometimes use this peak for parachuting into the Rio Grande valley, a surprising sight to most campers. (BASE is an acronym for building, antenna, span, and earth, the four kinds of fixed objects from which BASE jumpers hurl themselves, with small parachutes attached.) Activities include fishing for brookies on South Clear Creek and hiking a short footpath to an overlook with views of North Clear Creek Falls and the North and South Clear Creek Canyons, also formed by volcanic activity and erosion. In addition to these activities, most campers are inclined to just cook and visit. There are two loops that border a meadow. The second loop, sites 9-16, has more trees and shade. The campground is about half full most of the summer. See the Lost Trail entry in this chapter for more information on the spruce beetle activity.

Campsites, facilities: There are 15 sites for tents and RVs up to 35 feet. There are no hookups. Sites 2-7, 9, and 11-15 are pull-through. Picnic tables, fire rings, and grills are provided. Vault toilets and drinking water are available. Leashed pets are permitted.

Reservations, fees: Reservations are not accepted. The fee is $19 per night. Cash or check only. Open late May-early September.

Directions: From First Street in Creede, take Highway 149 west for 22.9 miles. Turn right on Forest Route 510/North Clear Creek Road. The campground is on the right in 0.2 mile.

Contact: Rio Grande National Forest, Divide District, 719/657-3321, www.fs.usda.gov/riogrande.

52 RIO GRANDE

Scenic rating: 6

west of Creede

This campground has seven basic sites on the north bank of the Rio Grande. Spruce trees and willows provide limited shade but no privacy. The campground is completely hidden from the highway, and there is no traffic noise. It's a good destination for small groups interested in fishing, rafting, or tubing on the river. The river has large rainbow trout, brown trout, and native cutthroat, but special fishing regulations apply. The road is not suitable for long trailers or RVs. (See the Lost Trail entry in this chapter for more information on the spruce beetle activity.)

Campsites, facilities: There are seven sites for tents and small RVs. There are no hookups or pull-throughs. Picnic tables, fire rings, and grills are provided. Vault toilets are available. Trash must be packed out. Leashed pets are permitted.

Reservations, fees: Camping is free, and reservations are not accepted. Open year-round, weather and road conditions permitting. No services available after Labor Day.

Directions: From First Street in Creede, take Highway 149 west for 9.0 miles. Turn left on an unmarked dirt road. The campground is in 0.6 mile.

Contact: Rio Grande National Forest, Divide District, 719/657-3321, www.fs.usda.gov/riogrande.

53 MARSHALL PARK

Scenic rating: 6

west of Creede

Marshall Park is on the north bank of the Rio Grande, just seven miles from Creede. This popular campground stays full for most of the summer. The majority of campers stay for a night, but there are also snowbirds who spend several weeks enjoying the Creede area. There is good fishing for rainbow, brown, and native cutthroat, but special regulations apply. The campground is a paved loop around a small meadow. The middle sites (1-3, 8, and 15) are exposed and have no shade. Cottonwoods, spruce, and fir provide shade and privacy at the riverside sites (4-7 and 9-14). Mornings are cool and afternoons are hot. (See the Lost Trail entry in this chapter for more information on the spruce beetle activity.)

Campsites, facilities: There are 16 sites for tents and RVs up to 35 feet. There are no hookups. Picnic tables, fire rings, and grills are provided. Vault toilets are available, but there is no drinking water. Leashed pets are permitted.

Reservations, fees: Reservations are accepted at 877/444-6777 or www.recreation.gov. The fee is $19 per night. Cash or check only. Open late May-early September.

Directions: From First Street in Creede, take Highway 149 west for 6.7 miles. Turn left on Forest Route 623. In 0.2 mile, turn left after the bridge and into the campground.

Contact: Rio Grande National Forest, Divide District, 719/657-3321, www.fs.usda.gov/riogrande.

54 PALISADE

Scenic rating: 5

east of Creede

Palisade campground is two miles downstream of Wagon Wheel Gap and the former location of the Hot Springs Hotel on Goose Creek, now privately owned. As the only campground on the Silver Thread Scenic Byway between Creede and South Fork, Palisade receives a lot of stopover activity, but if you have time to cast a line, the fishing is excellent. This stretch of the Rio Grande is not known for its whitewater, but beginning kayakers and rafters may wish to float it. There are no hiking or biking trails within walking distance, but snowmobilers will enjoy Forest Route 600. This road goes to the Wheeler Geologic Area, an area of volcanic ash carved into tepees and hoodoos by erosion. The road is groomed in the winter, but snowmobilers should check trail conditions at www.sledcity.com. Big cottonwoods as well as willows, spruce, and fir provide ample shade at sites 9-13. Sites 1, 4-6, and 8 are next to the river. Site 1 is a walk-in tent site.

Campsites, facilities: There are 13 sites for tents and RVs up to 36 feet and one walk-in tent site. There are no hookups. Sites 5-8 and 13 are pull-through. Picnic tables, fire rings, and grills are provided. Vault toilets and drinking water are available. Open year-round.

Reservations, fees: Reservations are not accepted. The fee is $22 per night. Cash or check only. Open year-round, weather and road conditions permitting. No services after Labor Day.

Directions: From Creede, take Highway 149 east for 12 miles. Turn right at the campground sign.

Contact: Rio Grande National Forest, Divide District, 719/657-3321, www.fs.usda.gov/riogrande.

55 CIMARRONA

Scenic rating: 10

north of Pagosa Springs

At an elevation of about 8,400 feet on the north end of the Williams Creek valley, Cimarrona campground has spectacular views of the distant Williams Reservoir and surrounding peaks: Toner Mountain, Sugarloaf Mountain, and Cimarrona Peak. The Cimarrona Creek trailhead is adjacent to the campground. The first two miles are easy, but then it climbs steeply past Cimarrona Peak to Squaw Pass and the Continental Divide. Williams Creek Trail begins at the end of the road and continues for 14 miles through the Weminuche Wilderness to the Continental Divide. At 3 miles, the trail passes through an area that looks like a walled garden with unusual rock formations, which could explain the Spanish name for Williams Creek: Huerto, or gardenlike. Both of these trails are closed to mountain bikes, but they are very popular with horseback riders.

Sites 1-5, 7, 20, and 21 are in a meadow with a young aspen grove. These sites have limited shade but the best views. Sites 8 and 10-19 are in a forest of spruce, fir, and cottonwoods. They have ample shade and a little more privacy. Sites 11, 13, 16, and 17 are next to Cimarrona Creek. Site 13 is a family site. The sites are about 100 feet apart. The campground is usually about half full, so it's easy to find a site.

Campsites, facilities: There are 21 sites for tents and RVs up to 35 feet. There are no hookups. Sites 12, 13, and 17 are pull-through. Picnic tables, fire rings, and grills are provided. Vault toilets and drinking water are available. Leashed pets are permitted.

Reservations, fees: Reservations are not accepted. The fee is $22 per night. Cash or check only. Open June-September.

Directions: From U.S. Highway 160 in Pagosa Springs, take Piedra Road/County Road 600/Forest Route 631 north for 22 miles. At the fork, stay right on Forest Route 640. The campground is on the right in 4.0 miles.

Contact: San Juan National Forest, Pagosa District, 970/264-2268, www.fs.usda.gov/sanjuan.

56 TEAL

Scenic rating: 10

north of Pagosa Springs

Teal campground perches on the western shore of Williams Creek Reservoir and features dramatic views of the San Juans towering above the lake. Cimarrona Peak, Chief Mountain, and Toner Mountain dominate the horizon to the north. To the east, Rock Mountain juts out of the surrounding slopes. If you look closely, you can see the profile of the Wounded Warrior peering up at the sky from the south face. Behind the campground, the slopes are covered in aspen groves. Unlike the nearby Cimarrona campground, Teal is almost always full because of the adjacent 343-acre reservoir, which has good trout and kokanee salmon fishing in early summer. Small sailboats and canoes and kayaks are frequently on the lake (and wakeless motorboats). Hikers can drive to the Williams Creek and Cimarrona trailheads.

The campground has two loops. The right loop has just five sites, all with excellent views and lots of shade. The left loop has 11 sites close to the lake. Sites 6-12 overlook the water; they are closer together and have less shade. Campers are also allowed to walk down and pitch a tent in small clusters of pines.

Campsites, facilities: There are 16 sites for tents and RVs up to 35 feet. There are no hookups. Picnic tables, fire rings, and grills are provided. Vault toilets, drinking water, trash pickup, and a boat ramp are available. A dump station is 1.6 miles away. Leashed pets are permitted.

Reservations, fees: Reservations are not

Teal campground on the shore of Williams Creek Reservoir

accepted. The fee is $22 per night. Cash or check only. Open early May-late September.

Directions: From U.S. Highway 160 in Pagosa Springs, take Piedra Road/County Road 600/Forest Route 631 north for 22 miles. At the fork, stay right on Forest Route 640. The campground is on the right in 1.6 miles.

Contact: San Juan National Forest, Pagosa District, 970/264-2268, www.fs.usda.gov/sanjuan.

57 WILLIAMS CREEK

Scenic rating: 7

north of Pagosa Springs

Williams Creek campground is the biggest and busiest in the area. It has six sprawling loops on both sides of the creek in a forest of pine, spruce, fir, and aspen. There are excellent views of the San Juans from the road, but fewer from the campground. It's probably the least appealing of the four campgrounds in this valley, but it's still very popular with families and retirees. Anglers can try stream fishing on Williams Creek, or drive one mile to the reservoir for better luck. The Piedra River is also an excellent trout fishery, but anglers will need to drive south to the bridge on Forest Route 631. Trail 583 begins nearby and is open to hikers and bikers.

Sites are fairly large and spread out. Loop E (sites 1-4, 12, and 13) is in a forest of ponderosa pine on the edge of the meadow. It's popular with RVers. Loop G (sites 5-11) is also popular with RVers. The rest of the loops are in the spruce-fir forest, with good shade and moderate privacy. Sites 50-66 are very close together. Sites 9-11 have the best creek access. Sites 29-49 are in a hilly area, which offers the best privacy.

Campsites, facilities: There are 67 sites for tents and RVs up to 45 feet. Water hookups are available at sites 1-4 and 6-8. Sites 3, 5, 9, 10, 12, 16, 18, 19, 21-23, 27, 29, 37, and 40 are pull-through. Picnic tables, fire rings, and grills are provided. Vault toilets, trash disposal, and drinking water are available. Leashed pets are permitted.

Reservations, fees: Reservations are not accepted. Basic sites are $25 per night; sites with hookups are $20 per night. Cash or check only. Open June-September.

Directions: From U.S. Highway 160 in Pagosa Springs, take Piedra Road/County Road 600/Forest Route 631 north for 22 miles. At the fork, stay right on Forest Route 640. The campground is on the right in 0.4 mile.

Contact: San Juan National Forest, Pagosa District, 970/264-2268, www.fs.usda.gov/sanjuan.

58 BRIDGE

Scenic rating: 8

north of Pagosa Springs

BEST (

Bridge is the least-used campground on Piedra Road, but it shouldn't be overlooked, especially by hikers, kayakers, and anglers, because it has the best access to the Piedra River. The Piedra River Trail begins a couple miles to the south, where Forest Route 631 crosses the river. This trail is 14 miles one-way. Most hikers just hike 3.5 miles to the footbridge and then turn around, but if you continue, the trail passes through two box canyons. The 10-mile stretch of river from the bridge through the Second Box Canyon has Class III white water. Only advanced kayakers should continue through the First Box Canyon. Anglers will enjoy fly-fishing for trout on the river. Access begins at the bridge and extends to the lower boundary of the Tres Piedras Ranch.

The campground is a mile-long spur on the west bank of Williams Creek. This riparian zone is lush with cottonwoods and willows, and many sites have excellent views of the San Juan Mountains to the north. Sites 6, 13, and 19 are the most secluded. Site 7 has the best views.

Campsites, facilities: There are 19 sites for tents and RVs up to 50 feet. There are no hookups. Picnic tables, fire rings, and grills

are provided. Vault toilets, trash disposal, and drinking water are available. Leashed pets are permitted.

Reservations, fees: Reservations are not accepted. The fee is $22 per night. Cash or check only. Open June-September.

Directions: From U.S. Highway 160 in Pagosa Springs, take Piedra Road/County Road 600/Forest Route 631 north for 19 miles. The campground is on the right.

Contact: San Juan National Forest, Pagosa District, 970/264-2268, www.fs.usda.gov/sanjuan.

59 LOWER PIEDRA

Scenic rating: 7

west of Pagosa Springs

Lower Piedra is a very pretty campground in a mixed evergreen and deciduous forest on the banks of the sparkling Piedra River. It's only one mile off Highway 160, yet it feels very remote. The sites are wooded and widely spaced. Sites 1-5 are next to the river; sites 7-11 have the most privacy; and site 14 has a private trail to a stunning knee-deep, turquoise wading pool. Sites 13-15 are set apart from the rest of the campground and perfect for a large group. Located between Durango and Pagosa Springs, this campground makes a good base camp for exploring the southern San Juans. Kayakers and hikers will enjoy the Piedra River. North of the campground, there is a 19-mile stretch of Class IV-V white water early in the boating season. Hikers can check out the river and its interesting geology by setting up a shuttle for Trail 596 (14 miles one-way). From north to south, this is a long but easy hike with access to the Lower Weminuche and Sand Creek Trails.

Campsites, facilities: There are 15 sites for tents and RVs up to 35 feet. There are no hookups. There are no pull-throughs. Picnic tables, fire rings, and grills are provided. Vault toilets

Site 14 at Lower Piedra campground accesses a knee-deep, turquoise wading pool.

and trash disposal are available. Leashed pets are permitted.

Reservations, fees: Reservations are not accepted. The fee is $22 per night. Cash or check only. Open May-late September.

Directions: From Durango, take U.S. Highway 160 east for 37.2 miles. Turn north on Forest Route 621. (If you cross the Piedra River, you've missed it.) In 0.2 mile, turn left and follow the signs to the campground.

Contact: San Juan National Forest, Pagosa District, 970/264-2268, www.fs.usda.gov/sanjuan.

60 UTE

Scenic rating: 6

west of Pagosa Springs

This seldom-frequented campground gets so little use that for years the Forest Service has considered closing it down. With the 2012 National Monument designation of nearby Chimney Rock, the Forest Service hopes the campground will get more visitors. The campground is in a thickly wooded pine forest on the north side of Highway 160, but there's not much traffic noise. Overall, it's a well-spaced campground, with sites anywhere from 50 to 100 feet apart. Sites 1-4 are for tents only, and probably offer the least privacy. Site 16 on the west end of the main loop is the most removed and has the most privacy. The host here also cares for Lower Piedra, a few miles to the west.

Campsites, facilities: There are 26 sites for tents and RVs up to 30 feet. There are no hookups and no pull-throughs; all sites are back-in. Picnic tables, fire rings, grills, and drinking water are provided. Vault toilets and trash disposal are available. Leashed pets are permitted.

Reservations, fees: Reservations are not accepted. The fee is $20 per night. Cash or check only. Open May-late September.

Directions: From Durango, take U.S. Highway 160 east for 43 miles; Ute campground is located on the left (north) side of the highway, a couple of miles before the turnoff onto

Colorado 151 for Chimney Rock National Monument.

Contact: San Juan National Forest, Pagosa District, 970/264-2268, www.fs.usda.gov/sanjuan.

61 ARBOLES POINT

🏃 🚴 🏊 🛶 🚤 🛥 🐕 🚐 ⛺

Scenic rating: 6

in Navajo State Park

This primitive campground offers three tent sites in the piñon-sage flats at the north end of the reservoir, and one RV site in the parking area beside the vault toilet. This is a popular destination for sunbathing teenagers and water-sports enthusiasts. There are views of the western shore and the Arboles community. The tent sites are far apart, partly shaded, and very private. (For more information on Navajo State Park and activities, see the Rosa listing in this chapter.)

Campsites, facilities: There are three walk-in tent sites plus one site for a small RV. There are no hookups. Picnic tables, grills, vault toilets, drinking water, tent pads, and an earthen boat ramp are provided. Restrooms with flush toilets and showers, laundry facilities, and a dump station are available at the Rosa campground. Leashed pets are permitted.

Reservations, fees: Reservations are not accepted. The fee is $14 per night. Campers must also purchase a vehicle pass ($8) or Annual Parks Pass ($80). Open year-round.

Directions: From Pagosa Springs, take U.S. Highway 160 west for 17 miles. Take Highway 151 south for about 15 miles. Turn left on County Road 500/Carracas Road. In 3.5 miles, turn right at the Arboles Point sign. The campground is in 0.3 mile.

Contact: Navajo State Park, 970/883-2208, www.cpw.state.co.us.

62 ROSA

🏃 🚴 🏊 🛶 🚤 🛥 🐕 ♿ 🚐 ⛺

Scenic rating: 8

in Navajo State Park

The 35-mile-long Navajo Reservoir straddles the Colorado-New Mexico border. Three thousand of the 15,000 surface acres are on the Colorado side. This warm-water fishery is also a boating mecca, and everything from houseboats to sailboats plies the waters. Water sports are also very popular. The reservoir is so large that even on holidays it's possible to find a secluded cove for fishing. In shallow waters, there are northern pike, bluegill, catfish, and smallmouth bass. In deeper waters, there are kokanee salmon and lake trout. If you cross the state line, don't forget to follow New Mexico fishing and boating regulations, which are available at the park headquarters and the marina. There are five trails for hiking and biking. Wildlife includes deer, beavers, muskrats, raccoons, foxes, and, of course, shorebirds. Bald eagles nest in the park during the winter. Beginning kayakers and rafters can boat Class I-II water on the Piedra and San Juan Rivers.

This full-service loop is very popular with RVers, but tent campers shouldn't overlook the walk-in tent sites. This campground has the best views in the park. Sites 130-147 have lake views. The setting is piñon-juniper and sagebrush. The only shade is provided by the shade shelters.

Campsites, facilities: There are 39 sites for tents and RVs up to 45 feet and 8 walk-in tent sites. There are full hookups, and most sites are pull-through. Picnic tables, fire rings, grills, and tent pads are provided at all sites. A number of sites have shade shelters. Restrooms with flush toilets and showers, a laundry room, and drinking water are available. A boat ramp, store, and water-sports rentals are available at the marina. Leashed pets are permitted. Sites 103, 105, 108, 121, 128, and 130 and the facilities are wheelchair-accessible.

Reservations, fees: Reservations are accepted at 800/244-5613 and www.cpwshop.com. The basic tent site fee is $24 per night, and the RV hookup fee is $32-41 per night. Campers must also purchase a vehicle pass ($8) or Annual Parks Pass ($80). Open year-round.

Directions: From Pagosa Springs, take U.S. Highway 160 west for 17 miles. Take Highway 151 south for 17.8 miles. Turn left on County Road 982. Continue 1.6 miles to the visitors center. Rosa is across from the visitors center.

Contact: Navajo State Park, 970/883-2208, www.cpw.state.co.us.

63 CARRACAS

Scenic rating: 7

in Navajo State Park

This paved loop is popular with both RV and tent campers. Like Rosa, it attracts a boating crowd because of its proximity to the boat ramp. Sites 60-75 are on the lakeside. There are nice views of the surrounding hills. The setting is piñon-juniper and sagebrush, and the only shade is provided by the sun shelters. (For more information on Navajo State Park, see the Rosa listing in this chapter.)

Campsites, facilities: There are 40 sites for tents and RVs up to 45 feet. Electric hookups are available, and many sites are pull-through. Picnic tables, fire rings, grills, and tent pads are provided at all sites. Sites 51, 57, 61, 64, 67, 70, 75, 84, 85, and 88 have sun shelters. Restrooms with flush toilets and showers, drinking water, and a small amphitheater are available. Laundry facilities and a dump station are available at the Rosa campground. A boat ramp, store, water-sports rentals, and a fish-cleaning station are available at the marina. Leashed pets are permitted. Sites 75, 84, 85, and 88 and the facilities are wheelchair-accessible.

Reservations, fees: Reservations are accepted at 800/244-5613 and www.cpwshop.com. The basic tent site fee is $24 per night, and the RV hookup fee is $32-41 per night. Campers must also purchase a vehicle pass ($8) or Annual Parks Pass ($80). Open year-round.

Directions: From Pagosa Springs, take U.S. Highway 160 west for 17 miles. Take Highway 151 south for 17.8 miles. Turn left on County Road 982. Continue 1.6 miles to the visitors center. Turn right out of the parking lot and stay right at the boat ramp. The campground is on the left in 0.5 mile.

Contact: Navajo State Park, 970/883-2208, www.cpw.state.co.us.

64 TIFFANY

Scenic rating: 7

in Navajo State Park

Tiffany is the original campground at Navajo State Park, but it's been updated with sun shelters and tent pads and is comfortable for tent and RV campers. Sites 22-26 overlook the lake. Sites 27-32 are next to the cabins. The setting is piñon-juniper and sagebrush, and the only shade is provided by the sun shelters. (For more information on Navajo State Park and activities, see the Rosa listing in this chapter.)

Campsites, facilities: There are 24 sites for tents and RVs up to 45 feet and 6 walk-in tent sites. There are also three cabins. There are no hookups, but pull-throughs are available. Picnic tables, fire rings, grills, and tent pads are provided at all sites. Sites 1, 13, 18, 20, 21, and 32 have sun shelters. Restrooms with flush toilets and showers, drinking water, and a small amphitheater are available. Laundry facilities and a dump station are available at the Rosa campground. A boat ramp, store, water-sports rentals, and a fish-cleaning station are available at the marina. Leashed pets are permitted. Sites 13, 21, 31, and 32 and the facilities are wheelchair-accessible.

Reservations, fees: Reservations are accepted

at 800/244-5613 and www.cpwshop.com. The basic tent site fee is $24 per night, and the RV hookup fee is $32-41 per night. Cabins cost $90-120 per night. Campers must also purchase a vehicle pass ($8) or Annual Parks Pass ($80). Open year-round.

Directions: From Pagosa Springs, take U.S. Highway 160 west for 17 miles. Take Highway 151 south for 17.8 miles. Turn left on County Road 982. Continue 1.6 miles to the visitors center. Turn right out of the parking lot and stay right at the boat ramp. The campground is on the left in 0.7 mile.

Contact: Navajo State Park, 970/883-2208, www.cpw.state.co.us.

65 WINDSURF BEACH
🏃 🚴 🏊 🎣 🛶 ⛴ 🏕 ♿ 🚗 ⛺

Scenic rating: 7
in Navajo State Park

This primitive campground is adjacent to the rocky shoreline of Navajo Reservoir, a 35-mile-long lake that straddles the Colorado-New Mexico border. There's no sandy beach here, but the proximity to the water attracts windsurfers, personal watercraft riders, and kids. The campground has views of the steep slopes at the north end of the reservoir. The habitat is piñon-juniper and sagebrush. (For more information on Navajo State Park and activities, see the Rosa listing in this chapter.)

Campsites, facilities: There are 15 sites for tents and RVs up to 20 feet. There are no hookups. Picnic tables, grills, and vault toilets are provided. Restrooms with flush toilets and showers, laundry facilities, and a dump station are available at the Rosa campground. Leashed pets are permitted. Two sites and the facilities are wheelchair-accessible.

Reservations, fees: Reservations are not accepted. The fee is $14 per night. Campers must also purchase a vehicle pass ($8) or Annual Parks Pass ($80). Open year-round.

Directions: From Pagosa Springs, take U.S. Highway 160 west for 17 miles. Take Highway 151 south for 17.8 miles. Turn left on County Road 982. Continue 1.6 miles to the visitors center. Turn left out of the parking lot and continue 0.7 mile. Turn right at the Windsurf Beach sign. The campground is at the end of the road.

Contact: Navajo State Park, 970/883-2208, www.cpw.state.co.us.

66 LOWER BEAVER CREEK
🏃 🚴 🏊 🏕 🚗 ⛺

Scenic rating: 7
south of South Fork

This campground is popular with families with young children. Set in the narrow valley of Beaver Creek, the campground is lightly wooded with mature ponderosa pine, spruce, and fir. Interesting boulders dot the landscape as well, and steep, forested hills ring the horizon. Most sites have good shade. Sites 10, 12, 14, 16, and 18 are next to the creek, but the bank is very steep. Sites 13 and 14 are a double site, and sites 19 and 20 are on a spur very close to the road. Tewksberry Trail begins at the end of Forest Route 355 and offers five miles of moderate climbing to Meadow Pass, between Cattle Mountain and Demijohn Peak. This rarely used trail is open to hikers, bikers, horseback riders, and ATV riders. The scenery is best viewed in the fall. Fair trout fishing is available from the campground on Beaver Creek, and lake fishing is available a few miles upstream on Beaver Creek Reservoir.

Campsites, facilities: There are 20 sites for tents and RVs up to 35 feet. There are no hookups. There are three pull-throughs. Picnic tables, fire rings, and grills are provided. Vault toilets and drinking water are available. Leashed pets are permitted.

Reservations, fees: Reservations are not accepted. The fee is $20 per night for a single site and $40 for a double. Cash or check only. Open mid-May-October or November depending on weather and road conditions. No water or services after Labor Day.

Directions: From Highway 149 in South Fork, take U.S. Highway 160 south for 1.3 miles. Turn left on Forest Route 360/Beaver Creek Road. In 3.0 miles, turn right on Forest Route 355. Make an immediate left into the campground.

Contact: Rio Grande National Forest, Divide District, 719/657-3321, www.fs.usda.gov/riogrande.

67 UPPER BEAVER CREEK

Scenic rating: 6
south of South Fork

Upper Beaver Creek is a pleasant family destination. Except for playing or fishing in the creek, there is little to do in the campground, but there are several trails a short drive away and good lake fishing and boating on Beaver Creek Reservoir, about two miles upstream. Hikers, bikers, and ATV riders can drive to the Tewksberry and Cross Creek trailheads. Despite the limited activities, this campground fills up frequently with regulars from Texas, Kansas, Missouri, and Colorado, perhaps because all of the sites are next to the creek. Sites 1-6 and 10-13 have good shade. The road is visible from sites 4-9. The best tent sites are 2 and 11-13.

Campsites, facilities: There are 14 sites for tents and RVs up to 35 feet, including seven walk-in tent sites. There are no hookups or pull-throughs. Picnic tables, fire rings, and grills are provided. Vault toilets and drinking water are available. Leashed pets are permitted.

Reservations, fees: Reservations are not accepted. The fee is $20 per night, $40 for double sites. Cash or check only. Open late May-early September.

Directions: From Highway 149 in South Fork,

take U.S. Highway 160 south for 1.3 miles. Turn left on Forest Route 360/Beaver Creek Road. The campground is on the right in 3.8 miles.

Contact: Rio Grande National Forest, Divide District, 719/657-3321, www.fs.usda.gov/riogrande.

68 CROSS CREEK

Scenic rating: 7
south of South Fork

Cross Creek campground is at the south end of Beaver Creek Reservoir, near the inlet and adjacent to the Cross Creek trailhead. The lake contains rainbow, brown, and cutthroat trout as well as kokanee salmon. The boat ramp is suitable for small boats and rafts. Fishing is best in May and June, and ice fishing is excellent in the winter. Cross Creek Trail, open to hikers, bikers, and ATVers, is a moderate four-mile climb to Willow Park, with nice views of Del Norte Peak. This trail is popular with big-game hunters in the fall, and the forest routes in this area are groomed for snowmobilers in the winter. The campground is split into two small loops on either side of Cross Creek. Sites 1-3 have views of the reservoir and partial shade. Sites 6-8 are walk-in tent sites in a grassy area with mature spruce and fir. They have limited shade and privacy. Sites 10-12 are best for RVs. This campground sees moderate use throughout the summer. It usually fills up on the weekends.

Campsites, facilities: There are nine sites for tents and RVs up to 30 feet and three walk-in tent sites. There are no hookups or pull-throughs. Picnic tables, fire rings, and grills are provided. Vault toilets are available, but there is no drinking water (during the summer, drinking water may be trucked-in). There is a small boat ramp for wakeless boats. Leashed pets are permitted.

Reservations, fees: Reservations are not accepted. The fee is $20 per night. Cash or check only. Open late May-October or November depending on weather and road conditions. Water and services are not available after Labor Day.

Directions: From Highway 149 in South Fork, take U.S. Highway 160 south for 1.3 miles. Turn left on Forest Route 360/Beaver Creek Road. The campground is on the left in 6.2 miles.

Contact: Rio Grande National Forest, Divide District, 719/657-3321, www.fs.usda.gov/riogrande.

69 HIGHWAY SPRINGS

Scenic rating: 5

south of South Fork

Except for accessibility, there is little to recommend this stopover campground between South Fork and Pagosa Springs. The upper loop, sites 1-6, overlook the road and have very little shade. The lower loop, sites 9-11, are away from the road but very close together. They also lack shade. Site 8, located between the two loops, has the best combination of views and privacy. Good fly-fishing is available on the South Fork.

Campsites, facilities: There are 13 sites for tents and RVs up to 35 feet. There are no hookups or pull-throughs. Picnic tables, fire rings, and grills are provided. Vault toilets are available. Leashed pets are permitted.

Reservations, fees: Reservations are not accepted. The fee is $16 per night. Cash or check only. Open late May-early September.

Directions: From Highway 149 in South Fork, take U.S. Highway 160 south for 4.0 miles. The campground is on the left.

Contact: Rio Grande National Forest, Divide District, 719/657-3321, www.fs.usda.gov/riogrande.

70 PARK CREEK

Scenic rating: 6

south of South Fork

This campground is 0.5 mile upstream of the confluence of the South Fork of the Rio Grande and Park Creek. Most sites are on the west bank of the South Fork, which offers excellent trout fishing. The campground has cottonwoods, willows, spruce, and fir trees. The river sites are well shaded and large enough to accommodate several tents. The sites are 50-100 feet apart but not well screened from each other. Traffic noise from the busy highway can be annoying.

Campsites, facilities: There are 13 sites for tents and RVs up to 35 feet. There are no hookups. Sites 1, 10, 11, and 13 are pull-through. Picnic tables, fire rings, and grills are provided. Vault toilets and drinking water are available. Leashed pets are permitted.

Reservations, fees: Reservations are not accepted. The fee is $20 per night. Cash or check only. Open late May-early September.

Directions: From Highway 149 in South Fork, take U.S. Highway 160 south for 7.6 miles. The campground is on the left after Park Creek Road.

Contact: Rio Grande National Forest, Divide District, 719/657-3321, www.fs.usda.gov/riogrande.

71 BIG MEADOWS

Scenic rating: 6

south of South Fork

This is a busy campground adjacent to popular Big Meadows Reservoir, the largest body of water in the South Fork area. There is fair fishing for stocked rainbow, brook, and native cutthroat trout, and a paved boat ramp that can accommodate small motorboats. Anglers can also hike seven miles to Archuleta Lake, near the Continental Divide in the Weminuche Wilderness. The alpine lake has medium-sized native trout. There is also a two-mile hiking trail around the lake and a 0.25-mile trail to Cascade Falls. ATVs can unload in the campground. Many ATV riders travel from the campground on Forest Route 430 to nearby Shaw Lake.

The campground was impacted by the spruce beetle and lost quite a few trees, which opened up more views of the scenic valley. Privacy varies widely from site to site. There are three meandering loops on a steep hillside. Sites 1-16 are closest to the lake. Sites 17-43 are more widely spaced. Sites 44-56 are farthest from the lake. The campground stays busy all summer, but many sites are not reservable, so it's usually possible to show up on the weekend and find a site.

Campsites, facilities: There are 56 sites for tents and RVs up to 35 feet. There are no hookups. Sites 12, 13, 18, 29, 32, 34, and 48 are pull-through. Picnic tables, fire rings, and grills are provided. Vault toilets, drinking water, a boat ramp, and fishing pier are available. Leashed pets are permitted.

Reservations, fees: Reservations are accepted at 24 of the sites, at 877/444-6777 or www.recreation.gov. The fee is $22 per night. Cash or check only. Open mid-May-October or November, depending on road and weather conditions. No water or services after Labor Day.

Directions: From Highway 149 in South Fork, take U.S. Highway 160 south for 11.3 miles. Turn right on Forest Route 410. Stay left at the fork. The campground is in 2.5 miles.

Contact: Rio Grande National Forest, Divide District, 719/657-3321, www.fs.usda.gov/riogrande.

72 TUCKER PONDS

Scenic rating: 4

south of South Fork

Tucker Ponds are two tiny reservoirs that offer good amateur bait fishing for rainbows. The trail and fishing pier have been designed to accommodate wheelchairs, and the lake is open to hand-powered boats. The adjacent campground is a quiet family destination, though it was practically clear-cut in 2015 due to spruce beetle damage. (It was in pretty bad shape, but many seedlings were planted, so hopefully it will regain some of its canopy soon.) The campground is a loop in a mature spruce forest, which affords excellent privacy. Site 1 has views of the lake. Sites 3 and 5-7 border a sunny clearing in the middle of the woods. Sites 3 and 5, and 9 and 10, are grouped closely together and can be used as double sites. There are few visitors midweek, and the campground is only half full on weekends.

Campsites, facilities: There are 16 sites for tents and RVs up to 35 feet. There are no hookups. Sites 3, 5, 8, and 11-13 are pull-through. Picnic tables, fire rings, and grills are provided. Vault toilets, drinking water, and a wheelchair-accessible fishing pier and boat ramp are available. Leashed pets are permitted.

Reservations, fees: Reservations are not accepted. The fee is $19 per night for a single site and $38 per night for a double. Cash or check only. Open late May-early September.

Directions: From Highway 149 in South Fork, take U.S. Highway 160 south for 13.2 miles. Turn left on Forest Route 390/Pass Creek Road. The campground is on the right in 2.7 miles.

Contact: Rio Grande National Forest, Divide District, 719/657-3321, www.fs.usda.gov/riogrande.

73 WEST FORK

🚶🛶🎿🏕🚗⛺

Scenic rating: 8

north of Pagosa Springs

BEST (

West Fork is north of Pagosa Springs, on the road to Wolf Creek Pass. The campground is in an old forest of spruce and fir so overgrown with hanging moss that it feels primeval. The campground also looks a bit rundown, but the sites are large and fairly private, and it is lightly used. The West Fork of the San Juan River runs nearby but is not visible from the campground. Sites 4-19 are closest to the river. The surrounding valley is gorgeous, but the high trees obscure the views. The river has good-sized rainbow and cutthroat trout. There is also good fishing along the West Fork/Rainbow Trail. (The trailhead is at the end of Forest Route 648.) This trail passes a waterfall and hot springs in the first three miles before continuing to the Continental Divide. Most of the trail is in the San Juan Wilderness and is closed to bikes. On the way out of the campground, there is an excellent view of Treasure Falls.

Campsites, facilities: There are 28 sites for tents and RVs up to 35 feet. There are no hookups. Sites 1, 7, 12-17, 20, 21, and 26 are pull-through. Picnic tables, fire rings, and grills are provided. Vault toilets and drinking water are available. Leashed pets are permitted.

Reservations, fees: Reservations are not accepted. The fee is $22 per night. Cash or check only. Open June-September.

Directions: From U.S. Highway 84 in Pagosa Springs, take U.S. Highway 160 north for 13.6 miles. Turn left on Forest Route 648. The campground is on the left in 1.6 miles.

Contact: San Juan National Forest, Pagosa District, 970/264-2268, www.fs.usda.gov/sanjuan.

74 EAST FORK

🚶🚴🛶🏊🏕🚗♿⛺

Scenic rating: 7

north of Pagosa Springs

BEST (

East Fork is in a forest of pine, Gambel oak, spruce, and fir with dense underbrush, which provides ample privacy. This is the closest public campground to Pagosa Springs, which is a good reason in itself to stay here. Despite its proximity to town, this campground is usually only half full, so it's easy to find a site that suits you. The Sand Creek and Coal Creek Trails begin 2 miles up the road. Mountain bikers frequently ride the East Fork Road up to the Silver Falls guard station, a round-trip of 16 miles. The road travels through the dramatic East Fork Canyon and a pristine high mountain valley. Four-wheelers can continue on this route across Elwood Pass and down into Platoro. In the spring and early summer, kayakers boat from the East Fork confluence down to Pagosa Springs. This 9-mile run has Class IV white water. Anglers can scramble down to the river for some fishing. The best route is a footpath that begins between sites 14 and 15. Site 24 has a private trail down the bank to the river.

Campsites, facilities: There are 26 sites for tents and RVs up to 35 feet. There are no hookups. There are a few pull-throughs. Picnic tables, fire rings, and grills are provided. Vault toilets and drinking water are available. Leashed pets are permitted. The facilities are wheelchair-accessible.

Reservations, fees: Reservations are accepted for 17 of the sites at 877/444-6777 or www.recreation.gov. The tent fee is $22 per night. Cash or check only. Open May-September.

Directions: From U.S. Highway 84 in Pagosa Springs, take U.S. Highway 160 north for 9.6 miles. Turn right on Forest Route 667/East Fork Road. The campground is on the right in 0.7 mile.

Contact: San Juan National Forest, Pagosa District, 970/264-2268, www.fs.usda.gov/sanjuan.

75 BLANCO RIVER GROUP

Scenic rating: 6

south of Pagosa Springs

This campground is a small loop beside the Rio Blanco. In 2012, its six sites were converted into a group campsite for up to 100 people. Most sites are shaded by ponderosa pine, spruce, or cottonwoods, and there is a small meadow and a group pavilion in the middle of the loop. For an interesting day trip, take Lower Blanco Road west to Trujillo Road to Carracas Road, and then return to Pagosa Springs on Highway 151. This route will take you through an area that seems more like New Mexico than Colorado, past the old settlements of Trujillo and Juanita, the landmark Lone Tree Catholic Church, Navajo State Park, and Chimney Rock Archaeological Area.

Campsites, facilities: The group campground has six sites for tents and RVs up to 35 feet. There are no hookups. Picnic tables, fire rings, and grills are provided. Vault toilets and drinking water are available. Leashed pets are permitted. Two group picnic sites next to the campground have banquet tables, volleyball net posts, and horseshoe pits.

Reservations, fees: Reservations are required at 800/320-2646 or 877/444-6777 and www. recreation.gov. The fee is $85 per night. Cash or check only. Open May-September.

Directions: From U.S. Highway 160 in Pagosa Springs, take U.S. Highway 84 south for 15 miles. Turn left on Forest Route 656. In 2.2 miles, turn left into the picnic ground. The campground is on the far side of the picnic area.

Contact: San Juan National Forest, Pagosa District, 970/264-2268, www.fs.usda.gov/ sanjuan.

SAN LUIS VALLEY AND THE SANGRE DE CRISTOS

The San Luis Valley is Colorado's only true desert, enclosed by the Cochetopa Hills and San Juan and Sangre de Cristo Mountains. Campgrounds on the east side of the southern San Juans are only accessible from the San Luis Valley. There are 180 miles of trails; many are accessible from Conejos River canyon, which has several scenic campgrounds. Across the valley, Great Sand Dunes National Park boasts 700-foot sand dunes. The national park campground there is excellent for tents and pop-ups; RVs will appreciate the modern facilities at nearby San Luis Lakes State Park. The park abuts the Sangre de Cristo Wilderness, where hiking is excellent but extremely challenging. The Wet Mountains are a weekend destination for residents of the Front Range, while the Lake Isabel Recreation Area is popular for families and campers. Farther south are the Spanish Peaks, with nearby campground destinations.

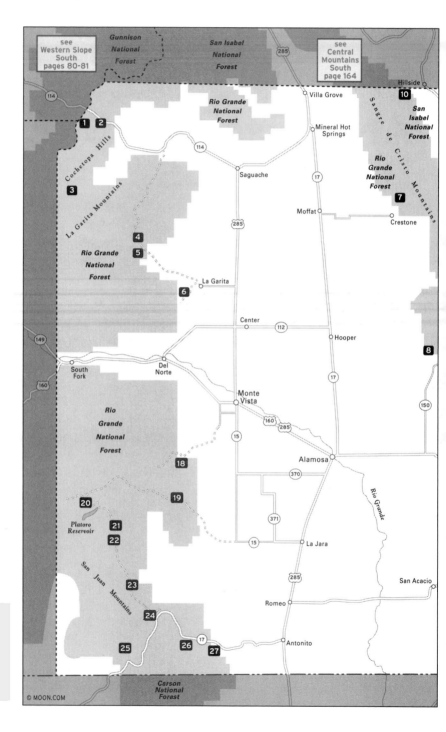

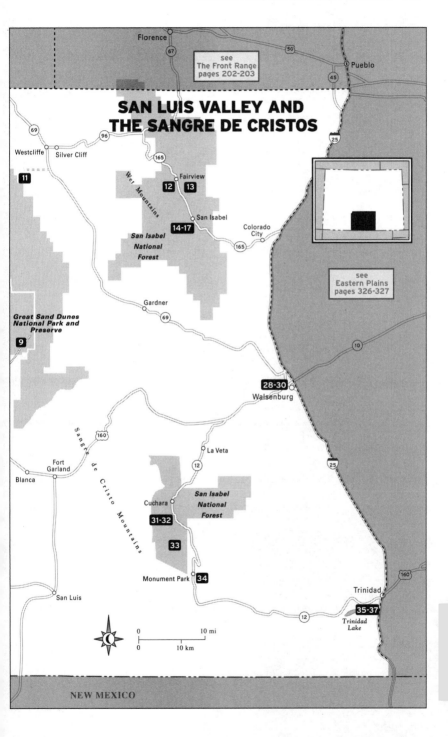

SAN LUIS VALLEY AND THE SANGRE DE CRISTOS

see
The Front Range
pages 202-203

see
Eastern Plains
pages 326-327

Florence

Pueblo

Westcliffe

Silver Cliff

11

Wet Mountains

Fairview

12 13

San Isabel

14-17

Colorado City

San Isabel National Forest

Gardner

Great Sand Dunes National Park and Preserve

9

28-30
Walsenburg

Sangre de Cristo Mountains

Fort Garland

Blanca

La Veta

Cuchara

San Isabel National Forest

31-32

33

Monument Park 34

San Luis

Trinidad

35-37

Trinidad Lake

0   10 mi

0   10 km

NEW MEXICO

1 LUDERS CREEK

🚶 🚵 🐴 ♿ 🚐 ⛺

Scenic rating: 8

west of Saguache

Luders Creek campground is a rare find. Surrounded by the rolling hills and diverse forests of the Cochetopa Hills, the campground is sublimely scenic, small, and remote, set in a wide park banded with aspen and tall spruce. Sites 3-6 are next to the meadow and have good views of the layered hills, an especially scenic sight at sunset. Just a mile to the west, mountain bikers and ATV riders can cross the Continental Divide and hop on the Colorado Trail. This is perhaps the least-used portion of the trail, because it lacks the altitude and views of many other segments, but the mountain biking in this area is excellent. Forest routes make several loops possible around Archuleta Creek and Luders Creek. A good topo map is a must-have on these roads.

Campsites, facilities: There are five sites for tents and RVs up to 25 feet, including three pull-through sites with horse corrals. There are no hookups. Picnic tables, fire rings, and grills are provided. Wheelchair-accessible vault toilets are available. Trash must be packed out. Leashed pets are permitted.

Reservations, fees: Reservations are not accepted. The fee is $5 per night. Cash or check only. Open mid-May-late October, weather and road conditions permitting.

Directions: From Saguache, take Highway 114 west for 21.4 miles. Turn left on County Road NN14. The campground is on the right in 8.7 miles.

Contact: Rio Grande National Forest, Saguache District, 719/655-2547, www.fs.usda.gov/riogrande.

2 BUFFALO PASS

🐴 ♿ 🚐 ⛺

Scenic rating: 7

west of Saguache

The Cochetopa Hills are a rolling landscape of diverse forests and meadows between the Elk and Sawatch ranges to the north and the San Juans to the south. The Continental Divide winds through this area, but the landscape rarely rises above the timberline. Stunning panoramas are visible from Long Branch Baldy (11,974 feet) and Middle Baldy (11,685 feet)—but these peaks are in the heart of an 80,000-acre roadless area and are only accessible via a long hike on the Continental Divide/Colorado Trail.

Buffalo Pass campground is typical of the Cochetopa Hills landscape: towering ponderosa pines intermingled with quaking aspen and arid sagebrush meadows. The sites are about 100 feet apart and have partial shade. Sites 3, 17-19, and 23 have the best views of the surrounding hills, which are scenically silhouetted at sunrise and sunset. The campground is almost empty midweek but can get quite busy on weekends with a local crowd. The area's network of 4WD roads attracts ATV riders and mountain bikers. The Colorado Trail is open to hikers, bikers, and four-wheelers. The trail is accessible about four miles west on Highway 114.

Campsites, facilities: There are 19 sites for tents and RVs up to 35 feet, four of which are pull-through. There are no hookups. Picnic tables, fire rings, and grills are provided. Wheelchair-accessible vault toilets are available. Trash must be packed out. Leashed pets are permitted.

Reservations, fees: Reservations are not accepted. The fee is $5 per night. Cash or check only. Open mid-May-late October, weather and road conditions permitting.

Directions: From Saguache, take Highway 114 west for 26 miles. The campground entrance is on the left.

Contact: Rio Grande National Forest, Saguache District, 719/655-2547, www.fs.usda.gov/riogrande.

🛇 STONE CELLAR
🚴 🐴 🚐 ⛺

Scenic rating: 7

west of Saguache

Stone Cellar is in Saguache Park between the Cochetopa Hills to the north and the La Garita Mountains to the south, a very remote location. The gentle terrain of this area is home to thriving herds of elk, deer, and bighorn sheep. Expect abundant wildlife and very few people in this remote campground. The La Garita Wilderness lies to the south of the campground and offers long backpacking loops through alpine terrain, as well as several virgin spruce-fir forests and the Wheeler Geologic Area, a unique natural formation where wind and rain have carved volcanic tuff into pinnacles and spires. Hikers will have to drive several miles south to the Halfmoon Creek and South Fork Saguache trailheads. Mountain bikers and ATV owners can explore a network of Jeep trails from the campground. A good topo map is a necessity in this remote backcountry.

Stone Cellar is beautiful and isolated. It sits in a meadow with scattered aspen and pine, and a small creek runs through the campground. There are few visitors to this location, which attracts mainly ATV owners and horseback riders.

Campsites, facilities: There are four sites for tents and RVs up to 25 feet. There are no hookups. Picnic tables, fire rings, and grills are provided. Vault toilets and drinking water are available. No water after October 31. Trash must be packed out. Leashed pets are permitted.

Reservations, fees: Reservations are not accepted. The fee is $5 per night. Cash or check only. The Stone Cellar Cabin rents for $50 a night (reserve at www.recreation.gov.) Open mid-May-mid-November, weather and road conditions permitting.

Directions: From Saguache, take Highway 114 west for 21.4 miles. Go west on County Road NN14/Forest Route 750 for 18.7 miles and then south on County Road 17FF for 16.4 miles to the campground.

Contact: Rio Grande National Forest, Saguache District, 719/655-2547, www.fs.usda.gov/riogrande.

🛇 STORM KING
🐴 🚐 ⛺

Scenic rating: 5

west of La Garita

Storm King is a weekend destination for local ATV owners. A network of mining and logging trails crisscrosses the eastern flank of the La Garita Mountains and connects the area to the rolling Cochetopa Hills to the north. The quaking aspen and tall pines provide plenty of shade. The campground is at an elevation of 9,498 feet, at the base of Storm King Mountain. The sites are just 25 feet apart, so privacy is poor on a busy weekend, but midweek the campground is often deserted. The neighboring stream is not fishable.

Campsites, facilities: There are 11 sites for tents and RVs up to 25 feet. There are no hookups. Picnic tables, fire rings, and grills are provided. Vault toilets are available. There is no drinking water. Trash must be packed out. Leashed pets are permitted. Ask about renting the guard station for $50/night.

Reservations, fees: Reservations are not accepted. The fee is $5 per night. Cash or check only. Open mid-May-mid-November, weather and road conditions permitting.

Directions: From La Garita, take County Road G west about 1.0 mile and turn right on County Road 41-G/Carnero Creek Road and continue 14.5 miles to the campground.

Contact: Rio Grande National Forest, Saguache District, 719/655-2547, www.fs.usda.gov/riogrande.

5 POSO

Scenic rating: 6

west of La Garita

Poso is in a narrow canyon on the South Fork of Carnero Creek. The fishing on the creek and in the beaver ponds is fair but challenging. Poso is popular with local church and Scout groups. The sites are shaded by pine and a few aspen and are spaced from 30-60 feet apart. Located on the eastern flank of the La Garita Mountains, there are abundant elk in the area, as well as some moose and bear. Consequently, the campground is very popular with hunters in the fall. There are numerous Jeep trails in the area, but no hiking trails within walking distance.

Campsites, facilities: There are eight sites for tents and RVs up to 25 feet. There are no hookups. Picnic tables, fire rings, and grills are provided. Wheelchair-accessible vault toilets are available. Leashed pets are permitted.

Reservations, fees: Reservations are not accepted. The fee is $5 per night. Cash or check only. Open mid-May-mid-November, weather and road conditions permitting.

Directions: From La Garita, take County Road G west about 1.0 mile and turn right on County Road 41-G. In 10 miles, turn left on Forest Route 675. The campground is on the left in 1.5 miles.

Contact: Rio Grande National Forest, Saguache District, 719/655-2547, www.fs.usda.gov/riogrande.

6 PENITENTE CANYON

Scenic rating: 8

west of La Garita

Penitente Canyon is a nationally renowned destination for sport climbers, with more than 300 routes in the area. The eerie landscape of rhyolite canyons and rock gardens offers mountain biking, hiking, and challenging rock climbing (but watch out for rattlesnakes!). The south-facing walls are climbable year-round. The canyon's proximity to tiny La Garita is also an attractive feature. This historic Hispanic town has a chapel on the National Register of Historic Places and a cooperative art gallery. There is a gas station but no grocery store, so campers should stock up in Del Norte or Center.

The campground is very busy—and hot—in the summer. The best time to visit is in the fall. Piñon and juniper provide limited shade. There are group sites and walk-in sites. Watch for petroglyphs and traces of the Old Spanish Trail in the canyons.

Campsites, facilities: Penitente Canyon has four drive-in sites for tents and RVs up to 25 feet, nine walk-in tent sites, and two group sites for up to five tents. There are eight walk-in tent sites in nearby Witches Canyon. There are no hookups. Picnic tables, fire rings, and grills are provided. There are vault toilets but no drinking water. Leashed pets are permitted. The facilities are wheelchair-accessible. In Witches Canyon, there are no toilets, drinking water, or trash collection.

Reservations, fees: Reservations are not accepted. The fee is $11 per night for a single site (two-tent limit) and $20 per night for a group site (five-tent limit). Cash or check only. Open year-round, weather permitting.

Directions: From La Garita, take County Road G west to County Road 38. Veer left on County Road 38. The main road turns south in

1.0 mile. Stay right and take the middle of three dirt roads. Follow the signs to the campground. **Contact:** Bureau of Land Management, Saguache Field Office, 719/852-7074, co.blm. gov.

⁊ NORTH CRESTONE CREEK

Scenic rating: 9

north of Crestone

BEST (

North Crestone is a one-of-a-kind camping experience. The campground is on the western flank of the Sangre de Cristo range, in the northern San Luis Valley, at the base of Venable Peak, just north of the hamlet of Crestone. Founded as a mining town in 1880, Crestone is now known as the "Shambala of the Rockies," a spiritual center and home to a wide variety of religious and spiritual institutions. South of town, the 200,000-acre Baca Grande subdivision is a complex of shrines, ashrams, churches, monasteries, retreats, and homes. You can get a chakra massage, a tarot-card reading, or a spiritual awakening in these foothills, or you can stick to the campground and the challenging trails of the Sangre de Cristo Wilderness. These peaks—part of the only fault-block range in Colorado—tower 7,000 feet above the valley floor. The contrasts are amazing. The valley is an arid agricultural landscape, while the foothills are covered in piñon-juniper woodlands that rapidly become pine, aspen, and spruce-fir forests laced with steep creeks and cascades. Glacial cirques with alpine lakes are at the top of most creeks, offering good backcountry fishing. The fourteeners south of the campground—especially Crestone Needle and Crestone Peak—should only be attempted by experienced mountaineers. However, hikers and anglers with strong lungs will enjoy the challenging hike up North Crestone Creek, which can be connected with trails down Cotton Creek and Rito Alto Creek. Afterward,

take a dip in Valley View Hot Springs about a half-hour drive to the north.

North Crestone Creek has a wild reputation. It attracts climbers, anglers, and hikers, as well as hippies, yogis, and nudists. The campground is packed on summer weekends—especially during the annual music festival—so arrive early in the week to grab a shady, creekside site. **Campsites, facilities:** There are 13 sites for tents and RVs up to 25 feet, one of which is pull-through. There are no hookups. Picnic tables, fire rings, and grills are provided. There are wheelchair-accessible vault toilets, but bring your own drinking water. Leashed pets are permitted.

Reservations, fees: Reservations are not accepted. The fee is $7 per night. Cash or check only. Open mid-May-late November, weather and road conditions permitting.
Directions: From Crestone, take Forest Route 950 north for 1.2 miles to the campground.
Contact: Rio Grande National Forest, Saguache District, 719/655-2547, www.fs.usda. gov/riogrande.

⁸ MOSCA

Scenic rating: 6
in San Luis Lakes State Park

San Luis Lakes State Park is usually overlooked by visitors to the San Luis Valley, but with spectacular views and excellent facilities, it's the best destination in the valley if you plan on staying more than a week. There are three loops in a high-desert setting, with views of Blanca Peak and the Great Sand Dunes National Park. Shade is nonexistent, and privacy is poor when the park is busy, but otherwise it's a great base camp for exploring this unique landscape. The San Luis Valley was first settled by Spanish farmers in the 1800s, and it remains an agricultural landscape surrounded by the dramatic peaks of the Sangre de Cristo range to the east and the southern San Juans to the south. Hikers and climbers face endless challenges in the Sangre de Cristo Wilderness, and anglers who enjoy backcountry fishing will find numerous alpine lakes at the heads of the steep valleys. More sedentary campers can visit the national park, the nearby gator farm, and the alien-viewing platform in Hooper, or just sit and watch the storm clouds build.

The park has two lakes and a wetlands area that are important for migrating birds. Water levels fluctuate dramatically, so boaters and anglers should call ahead to make sure the boat ramp is open. The four-mile hiking/biking trail is often closed to protect nesting waterfowl. It usually opens after July 4th. Loop A is very popular with RVers, and Loop C is the best loop for tent campers because it's separated from the other loops and has great views. The best tent sites are 2, 4, 7, 25, 27, 33, 37, 38, 39, 42, and 51. No wood gathering or tree cutting is allowed in the park, but you can purchase firewood at the entrance station and park office.

Campsites, facilities: There are 51 sites for tents and RVs up to 45 feet. All sites have electric hookups. Sites 1-7, 11-15, 18-40, 42-47, and 51 are pull-through. Picnic tables, fire rings, grills and shade shelters are provided. Restrooms with flush toilets and showers, vault toilets, laundry facilities, drinking water, a basketball court, a boat ramp, and dump stations, are available. Leashed pets are permitted.

Reservations, fees: Reservations are not accepted. The fee is $20 per night. Campers must also purchase a $36 annual access pass (unless you have a valid Colorado annual hunting or fishing license). Cash or check only. Open early May-early September.

Directions: From Alamosa, take Highway 17 north. About 1.0 mile past Mosca, turn east on 6N Lane. In 7.7 miles, turn left into the state park. The campground is on the left, 0.8 mile after the entrance station.

Contact: CPW at 719/587-6900, www.cpw. state.co.us.

the Colorado Gators Reptile Park in the San Luis Valley

9 PIÑON FLATS

🏃 ❄ 🎣 ♿ 🚐 ⛺

Scenic rating: 9

in Great Sand Dunes National Park

BEST (

The sand dunes became a national park in 2004 to protect the watersheds and mountains that are an integral part of this unique ecosystem. However, Piñon Flats campground (alternately spelled "Pinyon") was built more than 60 years ago. The campground offers views of the park's 30-square-mile dune field surrounded by grasslands and wetlands, and bordered on the east by the high peaks of the Sangre de Cristos—the only fault-block range in Colorado—where the life zones range from montane forest to alpine tundra. The park is a unique experience for hikers, four-wheelers, birders, and naturalists. Most visitors spend a day exploring the dune field and trying to reach Star Dune, the tallest sand dune in North America. If Medano Creek is flowing above ground, plan on some high-mountain "beach" time, splashing in the shallow water at the foot of the dunes (campsites fill up more quickly when this added attraction is present).

Visitors with 4WD can drive the Medano Pass Road, a very rough 22-mile route that connects the sand dunes with the Wet Mountain valley. Hardened backpackers can take the Sand Ramp Trail to the Sand Creek Trail to several alpine lakes. Winter visitors may find enough snow for cross-country skiing, but they should call ahead. The park also offers excellent campfire programs for all ages. Piñon Flats has its own camp store (located at the entrance to Loop 2). You may not collect firewood inside the national park; locally sourced firewood is sold at the camp store and at the visitors center. When closed, the nearest services (a restaurant and small shop) are found at the Oasis, about 4 miles outside the park entrance, which has its own campground and additional lodging options.

Piñon Flats campground has two loops in a piñon-juniper woodland, with sites that are 25-50 feet apart. The piñon-juniper provides some privacy, but the sites are small, and most can only accommodate one tent. It can be a bit noisy in the mornings and evenings, as generators are allowed 7am–8pm. Do not set up your tent outside the provided rock walls. Loop 1 (sites 1-44, first come, first served) is closer to the dunes and has tent pads. Loop 2 (sites 45-88) overlooks the lower loop and the dunes. The sites at the north end of the loops have the best views. The group loop has three sites with dispersed tent camping. Sites B and C have better views. Groups should bring a large tent to provide shade in the picnic area.

Campsites, facilities: There are 88 sites for tents and RVs up to 35 feet and 3 group sites for tent camping only. Picnic tables, fire rings, grills, tent pads, and food lockers are provided. Flush toilets, drinking water, an amphitheater, pay phones, interpretive programs, and dump stations, are available. Leashed pets are permitted. Sites 10, 14, and 63 and the facilities are wheelchair-accessible, and dune-friendly wheelchairs are available at the visitors center.

Reservations, fees: Reservations are recommended and accepted for Loop 2 from mid-May-mid-September at 877/444-6777 and www.recreation.gov. The fee is $20 per night for single sites. Group sites cost $65-80 per night for up to 40 people. Loop 1 is open year-round. The rest of the campground is open from late spring to early fall.

Directions: From Alamosa, take Highway 17 north. About 1.0 mile past Mosca, turn east on 6N Lane. In 16.2 miles, turn north on Highway 150 and continue 5.4 miles to the campground.

Contact: Great Sand Dunes National Park, 719/378-6399, www.nps.gov/grsa.

Great Sand Dunes National Park and Preserve in the San Luis Valley

10 LAKE CREEK

Scenic rating: 7

north of Westcliffe

Lake Creek is in the foothills of the Sangre de Cristo range, at the north end of the grasslands of the Wet Mountain valley. This gorgeous area is not as well known as Colorado's central mountains, but it is popular with southern Colorado residents as well as tourists from Texas and Oklahoma. This campground is just a spur in a dense thicket of Gambel oak and aspen. The majority of sites are well screened and very private, but there are no views from these sites. The campground is best for tents and small RVs. Hikers and bikers can explore the Rainbow Trail, a 100-mile route through the Sangre de Cristo foothills from Music Pass to Salida. This trail skirts the wilderness boundary. Hikers and climbers who want to explore the wilderness are better off staying at Alvarado campground. There has been some bark beetle activity in this area, but so far it has not significantly affected the campgrounds.

Campsites, facilities: There are 11 sites for tents and small RVs. Site 1 is pull-through. Picnic tables, fire rings, and grills are provided. Vault toilets and drinking water are available. Leashed pets are permitted. The facilities are wheelchair-accessible.

Reservations, fees: Reservations are not accepted. The fee is $21 per night. Open late May-early September.

Directions: From Westcliffe, take Highway 69 north for 12.7 miles. Turn left on County Road 198. The campground is on the right in 2.9 miles.

Contact: Pike and San Isabel National Forest, San Carlos District, 719/269-8500, www.fs.usda.gov/psicc.

11 ALVARADO

🚶 🚲 🐕 ♿ 🚐 ⛺

Scenic rating: 7

south of Westcliffe

BEST (

Alvarado is located where the Sangre de Cristo range meets the Wet Mountain valley, a 35-mile-wide grassland with a ranching history. The campground is a short drive from the twin towns of Westcliffe and Silver Cliff, and it sits just outside the Sangre de Cristo Wilderness, so this campground can be very popular in the summer, especially since it was completely renovated in 2007 and 2008. It consists of several loops and spurs in a dense spruce-fir forest with scattered aspen groves. The sites are 20-50 feet apart and shaded.

Venable is one of the best-known trails in the wilderness. Open to hikers and riders, the trail can be turned into a 16-mile loop with Comanche Trail. Mountain bikers and ATVers frequent the Rainbow Trail, a 100-mile route through the Sangre de Cristo foothills from Music Pass to Salida. There has been some bark beetle activity in this area, but so far it has not significantly affected the campgrounds or recreational activities.

Campsites, facilities: There are 43 sites for tents and RVs up to 40 feet, four walk-in tent sites (sites 44-47), and three horse sites. There are no hookups. Sites 18, 42, and E2 are pull-through. Picnic tables, fire rings, grills, and tent pads are provided. Vault toilets are available. There is no drinking water. Leashed pets are permitted. The facilities are wheelchair-accessible.

Reservations, fees: Reservations are accepted for 27 of the sites at 877/444-6777 and www. recreation.gov. The fee is $22 per night. Cash or check only. Open late May-mid-October.

Directions: From Westcliffe, take Highway 69 south for 3.4 miles. Turn right on Schoolfield Road/County Road 140. In 4.6 miles, turn left on County Road 141. The campground is in 2.0 miles.

Contact: Pike and San Isabel National Forest, San Carlos District, 719/269-8500, www. fs.usda.gov/psicc.

12 OPHIR CREEK

🐕 ♿ 🚐 ⛺

Scenic rating: 6

west of Colorado City

Ophir Creek is a remote campground in the Wet Mountains, a narrow range to the east of the Sangre de Cristos. These mountains receive abundant rainfall, and the forests are lush and diverse. This campground has two loops. The lower loop is creekside, and sites 1-6 are in a meadow. Sites 14-16 are walk-ins accessible via a footbridge. The upper loop (sites 23-31) has all walk-in sites. There are no hiking or biking trailheads at the campground, so many of the campers bring ATVs and explore the forest routes that connect this campground with the Lake San Isabel area.

Campsites, facilities: There are 31 sites for tents and RVs up to 30 feet. Sites 8, 9, 14-16, and 20-31 are walk-ins. Picnic tables, fire rings, and grills are provided. Vault toilets and drinking water are available. Leashed pets are permitted. The facilities are wheelchair-accessible.

Reservations, fees: Reservations are not accepted. The fee is $21 per night. Open late May-mid-October.

Directions: From Colorado City, take Highway 165 west for 25.2 miles. Turn left on Forest Route 360 and then left in front of the fire station. The campground is in 0.3 mile.

Contact: Pike and San Isabel National Forest, San Carlos District, 719/269-8500, www. fs.usda.gov/psicc.

13 DAVENPORT

Scenic rating: 7

west of Colorado City

Davenport is a small, isolated campground in the Wet Mountains, a long, narrow range east of the Sangre de Cristos. In honor of the campground's history as the first Forest Service campground, it was renovated in 2010 to restore it to its original design. There's now a group picnic shelter with four fireplaces in the middle of the campground, and several sites have Adirondack shelters and fireplaces. The campground is in a meadow surrounded by spruce and aspen, and the campsites line Davenport Creek. Hikers and bikers will be very happy here. There are several easy to moderate multiuse trails in the area. Squirrel Creek Trail begins at the campground and connects with the Dome Rock, Middle Creek, and Second Mace Trails and Pueblo Mountain Park. The campground receives heavy use on weekends, but it's virtually deserted on weekdays. There has been some bark beetle activity in this area, but so far it has not significantly affected the campgrounds or recreational activities.

Campsites, facilities: There are 12 walk-in tent sites. Picnic tables, fire rings, grills, and tent pads are provided. Vault toilets are available. Leashed pets are permitted.

Reservations, fees: Reservations are accepted for three sites at 877/444-6777 and www.recreation.gov. The remaining sites are first come, first served. The fee is $22 per night. Open late May-early September.

Directions: From Colorado City, take Highway 165 west for 23.9 miles. Turn right on Forest Route 382 and continue 1.3 miles to the campground.

Contact: Pike and San Isabel National Forest, San Carlos District, 719/269-8500, www.fs.usda.gov/psicc.

14 LA VISTA

Scenic rating: 7

west of Colorado City

Lake Isabel is a 37-acre reservoir on the eastern side of the Wet Mountains. The lake is stocked, and the shoreline is easily accessible, with open areas that are perfect for kids learning to fish. Hiking and mountain biking are available on the Cisneros and Charles Trails and on a footpath around the lake. Because of its mountain setting and accessibility, the lake is a very popular weekend destination for families from Pueblo to Trinidad. Reservations are highly recommended in the summer, especially at La Vista, the most modern and scenic campground at the lake.

La Vista has two loops on a promontory overlooking the lake. The lower loop (sites 1-16) is mostly wooded with pine and aspen. Sites 1-10 are attractive walk-in tent sites with good privacy. RV sites 11-16 are very close together. The upper loop (sites 17-29) has mainly RV camping. It has nice views of the surrounding ridgelines. This area has seen mild bark beetle activity, which has not significantly affected recreation so far.

Campsites, facilities: There are 19 sites for tents and RVs up to 50 feet and 10 sites for tents only. Sites 11-29 have electric hookups. Site 15 is pull-through. Picnic tables, fire rings, grills, and tent pads are provided. Vault toilets and drinking water are available. Leashed pets are permitted.

Reservations, fees: Reservations are accepted at 877/444-6777 and www.recreation. gov. The fee is $24 per night for basic sites and $28 for electric sites. A daily pass ($5 per vehicle) for the Lake Isabel Recreation Area is also required. Cash or check only. Open late April-early October.

Directions: From Colorado City, take Highway 165 west for 18 miles. Turn left at the Lake

Isabel Recreation Area. The campground is on the right in 0.9 mile.

Contact: Pike and San Isabel National Forest, San Carlos District, 719/269-8500, www.fs.usda.gov/psicc.

15 ST. CHARLES

🚶 🚴 ♨ 🛶 🛥 🎣 🦌 🚐 ⛺

Scenic rating: 7

west of Colorado City

St. Charles is a small loop on the banks of St. Charles Creek. The forest is especially lush and dense at this campground. Anglers can hike to Lake Isabel, a 37-acre stocked reservoir about a mile from the campground, or try fishing on the creek. The campground is very close to the Cisneros trailhead, a 9.5-mile trail open to hiking, biking, and riding. This trail connects with the St. Charles Trail, a 9.5-mile route that passes by St. Charles Peak. The campground has good privacy and shade. Sites 1-10 are creekside. The best sites for privacy are 2-5 and 11. This area is very popular with Front Range residents, so reservations are highly recommended on weekends. This area has seen mild bark beetle activity, which has not significantly affected recreation so far.

Campsites, facilities: There are 15 sites for RVs up to 35 feet. Sites 6, 10, and 15 are pull-through. There are no hookups. Picnic tables, fire rings, and grills are provided. Sites 4, 5, 13, and 15 have tent pads. Vault toilets and drinking water are available. Leashed pets are permitted.

Reservations, fees: Reservations are accepted for 10 sites at 877/444-6777 and www.recreation.gov. The fee is $22 per night. A daily pass ($5 per vehicle) for the Lake Isabel Recreation Area is also required. Cash or check only. Open late May-early September.

Directions: From Colorado City, take Highway 165 west for 18 miles. Turn left at the Lake

Isabel Recreation Area. In 0.8 mile, turn left at the campground sign. The campground is on the right in 0.2 mile.

Contact: Pike and San Isabel National Forest, San Carlos District, 719/269-8500, www.fs.usda.gov/psicc.

16 PONDEROSA AND SPRUCE GROUP

🚶 🚴 ♨ 🛶 🛥 🎣 🦌 🚐 ⛺

Scenic rating: 7

west of Colorado City

These group campsites offer dispersed tent camping in a spruce, fir, and aspen forest beside St. Charles Creek. The sites are extremely popular with church and Scout groups as well as for family reunions and company events. The campground is a short walk from Lake San Isabel, a 35-acre stocked reservoir with an easily accessible shoreline. The campground is also very close to the Cisneros trailhead, a 9.5-mile trail that connects with the St. Charles Trail. Both trails are open to hiking, biking, and riding. Spruce has a wheelchair-accessible picnic pavilion. This area has seen mild bark beetle activity, which has not significantly affected recreation so far.

Campsites, facilities: These group sites have tent camping for up to 60 people. Small RVs can park in the lot. Picnic tables, fire rings, and grills are provided. Vault toilets and drinking water are available. Leashed pets are permitted.

Reservations, fees: Reservations are required and accepted at 877/444-6777 and www.recreation.gov. The fee is $100 per night (includes 60 people). A daily pass ($5 per vehicle) for the Lake Isabel Recreation Area is also required. Open late May-early September.

Directions: From Colorado City, take Highway 165 west for 18 miles. Turn left at the Lake Isabel Recreation Area. In 0.8 mile, turn left at the campground sign. The group sites are on the left in 0.5 mile.

Contact: Pike and San Isabel National Forest, San Carlos District, 719/269-8500, www.fs.usda.gov/psicc.

Contact: Pike and San Isabel National Forest, San Carlos District, 719/269-8500, www.fs.usda.gov/psicc.

17 SOUTHSIDE

Scenic rating: 4

west of Colorado City

Southside is the last resort campground at Lake San Isabel. Nevertheless, it's frequently full on summer weekends with campers who forgot to make a reservation. The campground is essentially a small parking lot with islands that separate the RV pull-ins. Campers can pitch a tent on the islands at sites 1, 7, and 8, but that isn't recommended for tent camping. The campground is surrounded by a dense spruce-fir forest, and there are no views of the pretty lake that's only a short walk away. The 35-acre reservoir is stocked, and a footpath around the shore makes it very accessible. Hand-powered boats are allowed on the lake as well. Hiking and biking are available on the Cisneros Trail, a 9.5-mile trail through the Wet Mountains. This area has seen mild bark beetle activity, which has not significantly affected recreation so far.

Campsites, facilities: There are eight sites for RVs up to 30 feet. All sites are pull-through. There are no hookups. Picnic tables, fire rings, and grills are provided. Vault toilets and drinking water are available. Leashed pets are permitted.

Reservations, fees: Reservations are accepted at 877/444-6777 and www.recreation.gov. The fee is $20 per night. A daily pass ($5 per vehicle) for the Lake Isabel Recreation Area is also required. Cash or check only. Open mid-April-mid-October.

Directions: From Colorado City, take Highway 165 west for 18 miles. Turn left at the Lake Isabel Recreation Area. The campground is on the left in 0.3 mile.

18 ROCK CREEK

Scenic rating: 6

west of Monte Vista

Rock Creek campground is in a big aspen grove on the south bank of Rock Creek. There is fair fishing in the creek, but the area is most popular with hunters, and horses or ATVs are necessary for rewarding day trips into the mountains. There's lots of shade and heaps of privacy at this rarely used campground.

Campsites, facilities: There are 10 sites for tents and RVs up to 30 feet. There are no hookups. Picnic tables, fire rings, and grills are provided. Vault toilets are available. Trash must be packed out. Leashed pets are permitted.

Reservations, fees: Reservations are not accepted and camping is free. Open year-round, weather and road conditions permitting.

Directions: From Monte Vista, take Highway 15 south for 4.0 miles. Turn right on County Road 29. In 4.5 miles, turn left on County Road 28/Forest Route 265. The campground is on the left in 9.0 miles.

Contact: Rio Grande National Forest, Divide District, 719/657-3321, www.fs.usda.gov/riogrande.

19 ALAMOSA

Scenic rating: 6

west of Alamosa

This campground is on the north bank of the Alamosa River. It's a free campground because there are very few overnight visitors to this valley. Natural contaminants and mining activities have made the Alamosa unfit for recreation. Most of the traffic in this area consists of four-wheelers headed for Elwood Pass and the Continental Divide, the traditional route west for settlers until Wolf Creek Pass opened in 1916. Wildlife-watching is the other main attraction. A herd of about 30 bighorn sheep live on the ridgelines above the river and sometimes come down to the road in search of water. The campground is a small loop shaded by spruce, fir, and cottonwood. It's lightly used and was completely renovated in 2009.

Campsites, facilities: There are five sites for tents and small RVs. There are no hookups. New picnic tables, fire rings, and grills are provided. Vault toilets are available. Trash must be packed out. Leashed pets are permitted.

Reservations, fees: Reservations are not accepted, and camping is free. Open year-round, weather permitting.

Directions: From Alamosa, take U.S. Highway 285 south to Highway 370. Go west on Highway 370 and then south on Highway 15 for 2.0 miles. Go west on County Road 12S/Forest Route 12S for 12.7 miles. Turn left into the campground.

Contact: Rio Grande National Forest, Conejos Peak District, 719/274-8971, www.fs.usda.gov/riogrande.

20 STUNNER

Scenic rating: 9

west of Alamosa

In its heyday, 150 people lived in Stunner and there were 219 mines in the area. But mining never made anyone in Stunner rich, and by 1916, the town was abandoned. Today, almost no traces of the town remain, but the campground merits a visit, and the area, which is at an elevation of 9,700 feet, is especially interesting for amateur geologists. North of the campground, the mineral-rich slopes of Big and Little Red Mountain are a vivid collage of orange, yellow, and red. The runoff from these mountains dyes the Alamosa River almost maroon. (It was these colors that attracted those miners, who were ultimately disappointed.) The campground was completely renovated in 2009. It borders a small meadow above the Alamosa. The sites are shaded by spruce and aspen trees. Due to the remote location, campers here are guaranteed solitude. Most of the traffic in this area is from four-wheelers heading for Elwood Pass on the Continental Divide, the same route used by settlers and the military before the opening of Wolf Creek Pass in 1916. Mountain bikers also traverse this route, and hikers can take Iron Creek Trail to Elwood Pass.

Campsites, facilities: There are five sites for tents and small RVs. There are no hookups. New picnic tables, fire rings, and grills are provided. Vault toilets are available. Trash must be packed out. Leashed pets are permitted.

Reservations, fees: Reservations are not accepted and camping is free. Open mid-May-November, weather and road conditions permitting.

Directions: From Antonito, take Highway 17 west for 22 miles. Continue west on Forest Route 250 for 28.5 miles. Turn left on Forest Route 380. The campground is on the left in 0.3 mile.

Contact: Rio Grande National Forest, Conejos Peak District, 719/274-8971, www.fs.usda.gov/riogrande.

21 LAKE FORK

Scenic rating: 7

in Conejos Canyon

Lake Fork is a family campground in a forest of aspen, spruce, and fir beside the Conejos River, a first-rate trout fishery. This remote canyon is in the southern San Juans. The long ridgelines and 12,000-foot peaks are not as dramatic as the "Alps of America" (the northern San Juans), but the aspen forests and pristine rivers are full of recreational opportunities, and the history of Spanish settlement is also interesting. This canyon attracts repeat visitors from Texas and Oklahoma, and many of these families return to the canyon year after year. In all of the campgrounds in the canyon, it's possible to find three generations of a family enjoying their summer vacation together. In addition to fishing, hikers and bikers can enjoy day trips on the Lake Fork Creek and Bear Lake Trails. Kayakers and rafters can put in at Saddle Creek and boat six miles of Class III-IV water through Pinnacle Gorge. The white water below the gorge is mellower Class II boating.

Sites 7 and 11-17 are next to the river. These large sites have the best shade and privacy and are usually occupied. Sites 1-6, 8, and 9 are in an aspen grove and have partial shade.

Campsites, facilities: There are 18 sites for tents and RVs up to 60 feet. There are no hookups, but pull-throughs are available. Picnic tables, fire rings, and grills are provided. New vault toilets and drinking water are available. Leashed pets are permitted.

Reservations, fees: Reservations are accepted at 877/444-6777 and www.recreation.gov. The camping fee is $19 per night. Cash or check only. Open mid-May-mid-September, without services after Labor Day.

Directions: From Antonito, take Highway 17 west for 22 miles. Continue west on Forest Route 250 for 17 miles. The campground entrance is on the left.

Contact: Rio Grande National Forest, Conejos Peak District, 719/274-8971, www.fs.usda.gov/riogrande.

22 TRAIL CREEK DISPERSED

🚶 🚲 🛶 ⛵ 🐴 🚐 ⛺

Scenic rating: 9

in Conejos Canyon

The area surrounding the confluence of Trail Creek and Conejos River is set aside for primitive camping. There are several dispersed sites for tents and small RVs in a forest of spruce and fir. The campsites are a short distance from the road, but they are completely screened from traffic. It's a gorgeous location above the Pinnacle Gorge portion of the Conejos, but it's a steep scramble down to the river. The mountains across the river are in the South San Juan Wilderness, and there are beautiful views down the valley. The trailhead for the five-mile Valdez Trail is a mile away. Farther down the road, the popular South Fork Conejos Trail begins a 10-mile trek into the wilderness area. The attractions on this trail include narrow canyons, high lakes, and the scenery of a glacial valley. Experienced whitewater enthusiasts can put in for The Pinnacles at Saddle Creek and boat six miles of Class III-IV white water down to the South Fork.

Campsites, facilities: This is primitive dispersed camping. There are no services or facilities. Leashed pets are permitted.

Reservations, fees: Reservations are not accepted, and there is no fee for camping. Open year-round.

Directions: From Antonito, take Highway 17 west for 22 miles. Continue west on Forest Route 250 for 14.2 miles and turn left at the Trail Creek sign. High-clearance vehicles are recommended for this road.

Contact: Rio Grande National Forest, Conejos Peak District, 719/274-8971, www.fs.usda.gov/riogrande.

23 SPECTACLE LAKE
🏃 🏊 🏕 ♿ 🚐 ⛺

Scenic rating: 8
in Conejos Canyon

Spectacle Lake attracts families from Texas and Oklahoma with its good fishing and nearby trails. Anglers will enjoy the Conejos River, and kids love tiny Spectacle Lake. There are two hiking trails within walking distance. The Spectacle Lake Trail is a moderate 1.5-mile day hike that connects with the Valle Victoria and Notch Trails. The Ruybalid Trail is a steep climb through the South San Juan Wilderness to a subalpine lake.

The campground is a riverside loop that is usually less than half full. The sites are shaded by spruce, fir, cottonwoods, and willows. Sites 7-11 are the most private because of dense undergrowth. The sites are 50-75 feet apart, and all have partial shade and nice views of the cliffs on the surrounding ridgelines. Perhaps the only drawback is the open range that surrounds the campground. You could wake up to a cow sedately munching the grasses beside your tent.

Campsites, facilities: There are 24 sites for tents and RVs up to 40 feet. There are no hookups; 13 sites are pull-through. Picnic tables, fire rings, and grills are provided at all sites. Sites 3 and 4 have tent pads. Vault toilets and drinking water are available. Leashed pets are permitted. Sites 3 and 4 and the facilities are wheelchair-accessible.

Reservations, fees: Reservations are not accepted. The fee is $19 per night (includes one vehicle). There is a $5 fee per additional vehicle. Cash or check only. Open late May-early September; no services during hunting season.

Directions: From Antonito, take Highway 17 west for 22 miles. Continue west on Forest Route 250 for 6.2 miles. The campground entrance is on the left.

Contact: Rio Grande National Forest, Conejos Peak District, 719/274-8971, www.fs.usda.gov/riogrande.

24 ELK CREEK
🏃 🏊 🏕 ♿ 🚐 ⛺

Scenic rating: 6
in Conejos Canyon

Elk Creek flows from the Continental Divide through a series of meadows to the Conejos River. The campground is in the small park at the confluence of the two rivers, an attractive location with access to the South San Juan Wilderness via the Elk Creek and Duck Lake Trails. The former is a 13.5-mile trail through the Elk Creek valley to the Conejos Plateau. The latter is a 3.5-mile day hike with scenic vistas and several fishing lakes. Both trails are popular with anglers. You're also near the Cumbres and Toltec Scenic Railroad, a 64-mile narrow gauge steam train along the New Mexico border that makes a great day trip.

The campground has three loops shaded by pine, spruce, fir, and aspen, including an overflow camping space. Small meadows occupy the middle of the loops. The sites are 25-50 feet apart and have moderate privacy. This campground is popular with RVers and families from Texas and Oklahoma. The camaraderie among the regulars (campers who return year after year) will appeal to some and deter others. There are also many campers who are just stopping for the weekend. Sites 11, 13, and 14 are next to the creek.

Campsites, facilities: There are 34 sites for tents and RVs up to 45 feet. There are no hookups. Six of the sites are pull-through. Picnic tables, fire rings, and grills are provided at all sites. Vault toilets and drinking water are available. Leashed pets are permitted. The facilities are wheelchair-accessible.

Reservations, fees: Reservations are not accepted. The camping fee is $22 per night (includes one vehicle). There is a $5 fee per additional vehicle. Cash or check only. Open mid-May-mid-September, no services after Labor Day.

Directions: From Antonito, take Highway 17

west for 23 miles. Just after the Conejos River, turn right on an unmarked dirt road. In 0.1 mile, turn left. The campground entrance is on the right in 0.3 mile.

Contact: Rio Grande National Forest, Conejos Peak District, 719/274-8971, www.fs.usda.gov/riogrande.

25 TRUJILLO MEADOWS
🏕️ 🚲 🛶 🚐 🎣 ♿ 🚙 ⛺

Scenic rating: 8
west of Antonito

This is a destination campground beside the Trujillo Meadows Reservoir in the Rio de los Pinos valley. This *U*-shaped glacial valley offers wide meadows, subalpine forests, wildflowers, and solitude for hikers and anglers. Forest Route 118 continues for four miles past the reservoir to the Los Pinos trailhead. (This section of the road is a rough Jeep trail that is more suitable for hikers and bikers than cars.) This two-mile trail climbs through the South San Juan Wilderness to the Jarosa Mesa and excellent views. The Continental Divide Trail and the Cumbres and Toltec Scenic Railroad cross Highway 17 at the turnoff for the reservoir. Bikers can ride to the trailhead, but hikers will want to drive.

Both loops are in a dense forest of spruce and fir. The sites are grouped in threes and fours, so privacy isn't a problem. The first loop (sites 1-24) is more popular with RVs. The second loop has a scenic overlook of a small waterfall. Site 49 overlooks the lake. The campground was thoroughly renovated in 2010, so the facilities are in great shape, but it has lost most of its trees due to bark beetle activity.

Campsites, facilities: There are 50 sites for tents and RVs up to 40 feet. There are no hookups. Sites 12 and 19 are pull-through. Picnic tables, fire rings, and grills are provided. Sites 41 and 42 have tent pads. Vault toilets are available. There is no drinking water. A boat ramp

and wheelchair-accessible fishing pier are 1.5 miles away. Leashed pets are permitted. Site 21 and the facilities are wheelchair-accessible.

Reservations, fees: Reservations are not accepted. The camping fee is $22 per night. Cash or check only. Open late May-early September. Some portions of the campground remain open for hunting season when road and weather conditions permit.

Directions: From Antonito, take Highway 17 west to Cumbres. Go north on Forest Route 118. The campground is on the right in 2.1 miles.

Contact: Rio Grande National Forest, Conejos Peak District, 719/274-8971, www.fs.usda.gov/riogrande.

26 ASPEN GLADE
🏕️ 🚲 🛶 🎣 🚐 ⛺

Scenic rating: 7
in Conejos Canyon

Aspen Glade campground is a series of loops on the north bank of the Conejos River, an outstanding trout fishery. It can fill up on weekends, but there are usually sites available. Campers go there for the fishing and the hiking. The Sheep Creek and Bear Creek Trails begin at the campground and can be made into a backpacking loop around Osier Mountain.

The A Loop (sites 1-10) is in a meadow near the road. It hasn't been renovated and is the least attractive and private of the loops. The B Loop (sites 11-19) is in a meadow with mature ponderosa pines that overlooks the river. Sites 16-19 have the best views in the loop and more shade. The C Loop (sites 20-32) is beside the river. The sites are shaded by pine and aspen. Sites 20-22 and 24-26 have the best river access and fill up quickly. Sites 8, 11, 17, and 22 have extra-large tables.

Campsites, facilities: There are 32 sites for tents and RVs up to 25 feet. There are no hookups; 7 sites are pull-through. Picnic tables, fire rings, and grills are provided at all sites. Sites

1-19 have tent pads. Vault toilets and drinking water are available. A boat ramp and wheelchair-accessible fishing pier are 1.5 miles away. Leashed pets are permitted.

Reservations, fees: Reservations are accepted at 877/444-6777 and www.recreation.gov. The camping fee is $22 per night. Cash or check only. Open mid-May-mid-September, weather and road conditions permitting. No services after Labor Day.

Directions: From Antonito, take Highway 17 west for 15 miles. The campground entrance is on the left.

Contact: Rio Grande National Forest, Conejos Peak District, 719/274-8971, www.fs.usda.gov/riogrande.

27 MOGOTE

Scenic rating: 6

west of Antonito

Mogote is the first public campground in the Conejos Canyon, but most campers continue up the canyon to Aspen Glade. The valley is much wider at this point than it is upstream, and summer days can be very hot. The first loop (sites 1-21) is in a grassy meadow with tall ponderosa pines. There is not much shade or privacy in this loop. The more popular lower loop (sites 22-41) is beside the river, and those sites are shaded by spruce and aspen. Dense undergrowth provides privacy. Sites 24, 26, and 28-30 are on the river. There are also two group loops (Piñon and Juniper) on the meadows above the river. Scattered ponderosa pines provide partial shade for dispersed tent camping. It's a short walk from these loops to the fishing access. The facilities at this campground were renovated in 2010.

Campsites, facilities: There are 40 sites for tents and RVs up to 45 feet and the Juniper group site with RV and tent camping for up to 100 people. There are no hookups. Many sites

are pull-through. New picnic tables, fire rings, and grills are provided. New vault toilets and drinking water are available. Leashed pets are permitted.

Reservations, fees: Reservations are accepted at 877/444-6777 and www.recreation.gov. Reservations are required for the group site. The fee for a single site is $22 per night. The group rate is $132 per night. Open late May-mid-November, weather and road conditions permitting. No services after Labor Day.

Directions: From Antonito, take Highway 17 west for 13 miles. Turn left at the Mogote sign. The campground is on the right in 0.2 mile.

Contact: Rio Grande National Forest, Conejos Peak District, 719/274-8971, www.fs.usda.gov/riogrande.

28 YUCCA

Scenic rating: 5

in Lathrop State Park

Yucca offers basic tent camping at Lathrop State Park. (For more information on Lathrop, see the Piñon listing in this chapter.) Located beneath the Martin Lake dam, the campground has two small loops in a piñon-juniper setting, as well as two group sites. It's a short walk to the swim beach and the Hogback Trail, but the boat ramp is driving distance. The top of the loop (sites 10-13 and 21) is very close to the highway. The best sites for privacy are 6, 7, 19, and 20. Site 13 is a double site. Group A has walk-in tent camping shaded by large trees for up to 30 people. Group B can accommodate RVs and up to 36 people and it has a covered picnic shelter.

Campsites, facilities: There are 21 sites for tents and small RVs and two group sites. There are no hookups or pull-throughs. Picnic tables, fire rings, grills, and vault toilets are provided. A few sites have afternoon shade structures. Restrooms with flush toilets and showers, drinking water, a playground, golf course, interpretive programs, amphitheater, and dump stations, are available at Piñon campground. Leashed pets are permitted.

Reservations, fees: Reservations are accepted at 800/244-5613 or www.cpwshop.com for the single sites. Group camping reservations can be made at 719/738-2376. The fee is $28 per night for a single site and $60 for a group site. Campers must also purchase a vehicle pass ($8) or Annual Parks Pass ($80). Cash, check, and credit cards accepted. Open late May-early September.

Directions: From I-25 in Walsenburg, take U.S. Highway 160 west for 4.7 miles. Turn right into the park and follow the signs 0.4 mile to the campground on the right.

Contact: Lathrop State Park, 719/738-2376, www.cpw.state.co.us.

29 PIÑON

Scenic rating: 6

in Lathrop State Park

Lathrop was Colorado's first state park. It has two small lakes and about 1,500 acres of high plains grassland. To the south, the Spanish Peaks dominate the horizon. The Utes called these volcanic peaks *wahatoya*, or "Breasts of the World." The land surrounding the peaks was called the Valley of the Rising Sun, and the Utes believed that gods and demons inhabited the area. Lathrop is a weekend destination for residents of Walsenburg and Trinidad. The lakes are stocked with rainbow trout, catfish, tiger muskie, bass, walleye, and bluegill, and they're open to boating, waterskiing, windsurfing, and sailing. There's also a swimming beach with lap lane, a paved trail for hiking and biking, and a municipal golf course.

Piñon was renovated in 2005, and the campsites and facilities got a facelift. The campground has scattered piñon and juniper trees, but privacy is poor. There are four loops. Loop A (sites 22-42) is closest to the water but not recommended for tent camping because the sites are so close together. Loop D (sites 79-103) has the best tent camping.

Campsites, facilities: There are 82 sites for tents and RVs up to 45 feet. Electric hookups are available. Picnic tables, fire rings, grills, and tent pads are provided. Restrooms with flush toilets and showers, drinking water, a playground, a golf course, interpretive programs, an amphitheater, and dump stations, are available. Leashed pets are permitted.

Reservations, fees: Reservations are required at 800/244-5613 or www.cpwshop.com. The fee is $28-36 per night. Campers must also purchase a vehicle pass ($8) or Annual Parks Pass ($80). Cash, check, and credit cards accepted. One loop remains open year-round.

Directions: From I-25 in Walsenburg, take U.S. Highway 160 west for 4.7 miles. Turn right into the park and follow the signs 1.1 miles to the campground on the north side of the lake.

Contact: Lathrop State Park, 719/738-2376, www.cpw.state.co.us.

30 LOS ALAMOS GROUP

Scenic rating: 6

in Lathrop State Park

Los Alamos Group is the newest addition to camping at Lathrop State Park, which opened in 2006. (For more information on Lathrop, see the Piñon listing in this chapter.)

It's a parking lot with a pavilion and an extra-large tent pad on the south shore of Martin Lake. There are a few cottonwoods nearby, but no shade near the tent pad. Campers can enjoy views of the Spanish Peaks, Sangre de Cristos, and Wet Mountains. Hikers can try the three-mile Cuerno Verde Trail around Martin Lake. Martin Lake is itself a popular water-sports destination and is known for its northern pike and saugeye.

Campsites, facilities: The group site can accommodate 50 people or 25 vehicles. Electric hookups are available. Picnic tables, fire rings, grills, and tent pads are provided. Showers, vault toilets, drinking water, a boat ramp, and a dump station are available. Leashed pets are permitted. All of the facilities are wheelchair-accessible.

Reservations, fees: Reservations are required and accepted at 719/738-2376. The fee is $198 per night with electric. Campers must also purchase a vehicle pass ($8) or Annual Parks Pass ($80). Open April-late November.

Directions: From I-25 in Walsenburg, take U.S. Highway 160 west for 4.7 miles. Turn right into the park and follow the signs past the visitors center to the campground on the south shore of Martin Lake.

Contact: Lathrop State Park, 719/738-2376, www.cpw.state.co.us.

31 BLUE LAKE

🚶 🚲 🛶 🎣 ♿ 🚌 ⛺

Scenic rating: 7

south of La Veta

The Utes called the Spanish Peaks *wahatoya*, or "Breasts of the World," a fitting name for these unique peaks that have guided Native Americans and settlers across the plains for hundreds of years. The peaks were formed by molten rock that rose beneath sedimentary rocks, filling vertical fractures. The sedimentary rocks eroded away over millions of years, revealing the volcanic stocks and the rock walls, or dikes, that radiate out from the peaks like giant fins. This area gained wilderness designation in 2000. The peaks are the prominent landmark as visitors drive down Highway 12, "The Highway of Legends," to the Cuchara area on the west side of the wilderness area. There are three campgrounds on the eastern flank of the Sangre de Cristos: Bear Lake, Blue Lake, and Purgatoire.

Blue Lake is in a spruce-fir forest about a mile upstream of its namesake. Cuchara Creek runs through the middle of the campground, and some sites have glimpses of Boyd Mountain, Sheep Mountain, and Trinchera Peak. There are two loops. The smaller loop, sites 14-16, is secluded in a slightly denser wood. Sites 1, 2, and 11-13 are creekside. The campground always fills up on weekends, mostly with Front Range residents and Texans escaping summer heat waves. Campers enjoy fishing on the creek and on Bear Lake, as well as hiking and mountain biking on North Fork Trail and Indian Trail.

Campsites, facilities: There are 16 sites for tents and RVs up to 40 feet. There are no hookups. Picnic tables, fire rings, and grills are provided. Vault toilets and drinking water are available. Leashed pets are permitted. The facilities are wheelchair-accessible.

Reservations, fees: Reservations are not accepted. The fee is $21 per night. Cash or check only. Open late May-early October.

Directions: From U.S. Highway 160, take Highway 12 south for 20 miles. Turn right on Forest Route 422. The campground is on the right in 4.0 miles.

Contact: Pike and San Isabel National Forest, San Carlos District, 719/269-8500, www.fs.usda.gov/psicc.

32 BEAR LAKE

🚶 🚲 🛶 🎣 🐾 🚌 ⛺

Scenic rating: 8

south of La Veta

Bear Lake is an appealing campground on the eastern flank of the Sangre de Cristo range, not far from the Spanish Peaks Wilderness area. (For more information on the Spanish Peaks, see the Blue Lake listing in this chapter.) The campground is in a meadow ringed by a spruce-fir forest. A creek runs alongside the campground, and Bear Lake is a short walk away. The meadow is circled by the forested slopes of Sheep Mountain, Teddy's Peak, and Boyd Mountain. Although there has been some bark beetle activity in the area, it has not been enough to affect recreational activities so far.

Campers will enjoy fishing on the stocked lake and hiking and mountain biking on the Indian, Baker, and Dodgetown Trails. Sites 5-12 are in the meadow and have excellent views. Sites 2, 3, and 13 are creekside. Site 9 is next to the Indian trailhead.

Campsites, facilities: There are 15 sites for tents and RVs up to 40 feet. There are no hook-ups. Picnic tables, fire rings, grills, and tent pads are provided. Vault toilets and drinking water are available. Leashed pets are permitted.

Reservations, fees: Reservations are not accepted. The fee is $21 per night. Cash or check only. Open late May-early October.

Directions: From U.S. Highway 160, take Highway 12 south for 20 miles. Turn right on Forest Route 422. The road ends at the campground in 5.5 miles.

Contact: Pike and San Isabel National Forest, San Carlos District, 719/269-8500, www.fs.usda.gov/psicc.

33 PURGATOIRE

Scenic rating: 7

south of La Veta

Purgatoire is on the North Fork of Purgatoire Creek, just a few miles from the North Lake State Wildlife Area. This quiet campground is in a spruce-fir forest with aspen groves and small meadows. The campground is divided into three loops. The upper loop (sites 5-10) overlooks a large meadow and has the most appealing sites with aspen groves and good views down the valley. Sites 11-15 and 17 are horse sites next to a meadow where horses can graze. Riding and hiking are popular activities, mainly on North Fork Trail, a five-mile

trail that links the Purgatoire campground with the Cuchara Creek area. Fishing is also good on North Lake, but only artificial flies and lures are allowed. Although there has been some bark beetle activity in the area, it has not been enough to affect recreational activities so far.

Campsites, facilities: There are 13 sites for RVs up to 40 feet and 10 tent sites. There are no hookups. Picnic tables, fire rings, and grills are provided. Tent pads are provided at sites 1-10. Vault toilets and drinking water are available. Leashed pets are permitted.

Reservations, fees: Reservations are accepted at 877/444-6777 and www.recreation.gov. The fee is $21 per night. Cash or check only. Open late May-early October.

Directions: From U.S. Highway 160, take Highway 12 south for 31 miles. Turn right on Forest Route 411/North Fork Road. The road ends at the campground in 4.2 miles.

Contact: Pike and San Isabel National Forest, San Carlos District, 719/269-8500, www.fs.usda.gov/psicc.

34 MONUMENT LAKE RESORT

Scenic rating: 5

south of La Veta

Monument Lake is a small, full service summer resort on the Highway of Legends between La Veta and Trinidad. There are excellent views of the Spanish Peaks, massive volcanic stocks with rock walls, or dikes, radiating out from them like giant fins. The stocked reservoir offers good fishing and boating opportunities, and families enjoy the boat rentals and the restaurant and bar at the Southwestern-style lodge. There's RV and tent camping in a pine forest on a hillside above the lake. The sites are only about 15 feet apart, so privacy is poor, but many guests are regulars who return every year and meet up with old friends. The campground is busy throughout the summer, and reservations are recommended. The tent sites are creekside. **Campsites, facilities:** There are 18 full hookup RV sites, 19 partial hookup sites, some basic RV sites, and between 75 and 100 tent sites. The max RV length is 40 feet. Picnic tables and fire pits are provided. Restrooms with flush toilets and showers, a laundry room, drinking water, playground, boat ramp, convenience store, a restaurant, and dump stations, are available. Leashed pets are permitted.

Reservations, fees: Reservations are accepted for RV sites with hookups at 719/868-2226. All other sites are first come, first served. The tent fee is $20 per night (up to six people). The RV fee is $26-32 per night (up to six people). The dump station fee is $5. Open mid-May-late September.

Directions: From U.S. Highway 160 (north of La Veta), take Highway 12 south for 33.2 miles. Turn left at the campground entrance.

Contact: Mike Robb, 719/868-2226, www.monumentlakeresort.com.

35 CARPIOS RIDGE

🥾 🛶 🚤 🐎 🎣 ♿ 🚐 ⛺

Scenic rating: 6

in Trinidad Lake State Park

Trinidad Lake is an 800-surface-acre reservoir stocked with walleye, catfish, trout, bass, crappie, bluegill, and perch. The lake is on the Purgatoire River, west of the historic mining town of Trinidad, where the brick-paved downtown, called the Corazon de Trinidad, is a designated National Historic District, with several museums dedicated to local history. The park is a local fishing and boating destination with 10 miles of hiking and biking trails. It's also a convenient stopover between Denver and Albuquerque.

The campground consists of two loops in a piñon-juniper setting on the north shore of the lake, about 150 feet above the water. Privacy is poor, but the views of the Sangre de Cristos are excellent. The second loop (sites 24-61) is closer

to the lake. It has better privacy and views. The Reilly Canyon Trail connects the campground with the old mining town of Cokedale.

Campsites, facilities: There are 63 sites for tents and RVs up to 45 feet. All sites have electric hookups, and sites 1, 3, 6, and 63 have full hookups. Sites 5, 12, 42, and 61 are pull-through. Picnic tables, fire rings, grills, and tent pads are provided. Restrooms with flush toilets and showers, a laundry room, drinking water, playground, boat ramp, group picnic area, interpretive programs, an amphitheater, and dump stations are available. Leashed pets are permitted. Sites 11, 31, 42, 50, and 63 are wheelchair-accessible.

Reservations, fees: Reservations are accepted at 800/244-5613 and cpwshop.com. The fee is $28 per night for basic sites, $36 for electric hookups and $41 for full hookups. Campers must also purchase a vehicle pass ($7) or Annual Parks Pass ($70). Sites 1-23, 62, and 63 are open year-round, and sites 24-61 are open early May-mid-October.

Directions: From Trinidad, take Highway 12 west for 4.0 miles. Turn left into the park. The campground is on the right in 0.5 mile.

Contact: Trinidad Lake State Park, 719/846-6951, www.cpw.state.co.us.

36 PIEDMONT GROUP

🛶 🚤 🎣 🚐 ⛺

Scenic rating: 6

in Trinidad Lake State Park

Piedmont Group is a new addition to the facilities at Trinidad Lake. (For more information on Trinidad Lake State Park, see the Carpios Ridge entry in this chapter.) The campground sits on a small, wooded bluff below the dam. It lacks the views of the Sangre de Cristos that Carpios Ridge and South Shore enjoy, but it's a small, secluded spot perfect for a family reunion, church group, or other activity.

Campsites, facilities: The campground can

accommodate up to 60 people in tents and RVs. There are no hookups. Picnic tables, fire rings, large grills, and tent pads are provided. Vault toilets and drinking water are available. The boat ramp is a short drive away. Leashed pets are permitted.

Reservations, fees: Reservations are required and are accepted at 719/846-6951 or cpwshop. com. Open early May-mid-October.

Directions: From Trinidad, take Highway 12 west. Turn left on County Road 183 and cross the dam. The gated turnoff for the campground is on the left before the end of the dam.

Contact: Trinidad Lake State Park, 719/846-6951, www.cpw.state.co.us.

37 SOUTH SHORE

Scenic rating: 7

in Trinidad Lake State Park

South Shore is the newest and most scenic campground at Trinidad Lake. (For more information on Trinidad Lake State Park, see the Carpios Ridge entry in this chapter.) It's on a bluff overlooking the lake's south shore. The views of the Sangre de Cristos and the lake are impressive, especially at sunset. There is minimal shade and the campground tends to be quite windy. It's a short walk to the lakeshore, where campers can fish for trout, bass, catfish, and other sport fish. The 2.5-mile South Shore Trail begins near the campground and is open to hiking and horseback riding. It ends at a wildlife viewing area.

Campsites, facilities: There are 10 sites for tents and RVs up to 40 feet. There are no hookups. Picnic tables, fire rings, grills, and shelters are provided. Vault toilets are available. Leashed pets are permitted.

Reservations, fees: Reservations are accepted at 800/244-5613 or cpwshop.com. The fee is $28 per night. Campers must also purchase a vehicle pass ($8) or Annual Parks Pass ($80). Open early May-mid-October.

Directions: From Trinidad, take Highway 12 west for 4.0 miles. Turn left into the park. The campground is on the right in 0.5 mile.

Contact: Trinidad Lake State Park, 719/846-6951, www.cpw.state.co.us.

EASTERN PLAINS

The High Plains extend from the eastern edge of
the Rocky Mountains eastward. One thing here is constant—wind. Highways
are sometimes closed to protect drivers from strong winds that roar across
year-round; blizzards are common, and sandstorms sometimes blow through.

Reservoirs offer the best camping, and campgrounds fill quickly in summer.
Anglers flock to the reservoirs bordering the Arkansas and South Platte Rivers. The John Martin, Sterling Lake, and Bonny Lake Reservoirs are especially
scenic. If you're headed for the mountains and need a place to stay overnight
on I-70, the Strasburg KOA is a great place before climbing the Front Range. On
Highway 50, the John Martin Reservoir is both convenient and scenic. On I-76,
Jackson Lake State Park is the closest public campground to the interstate.

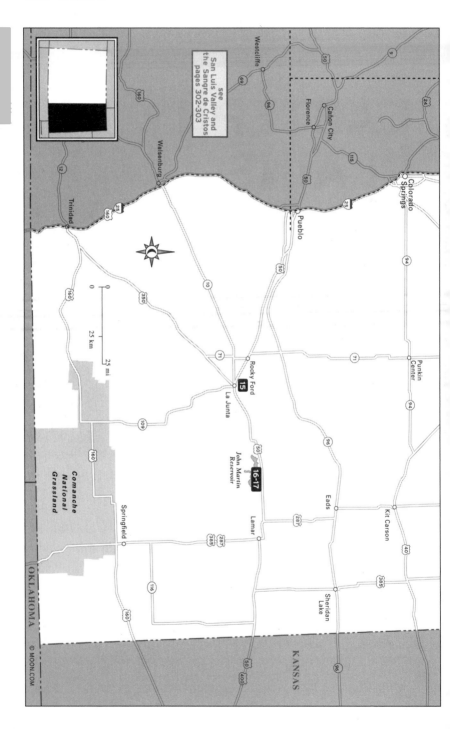

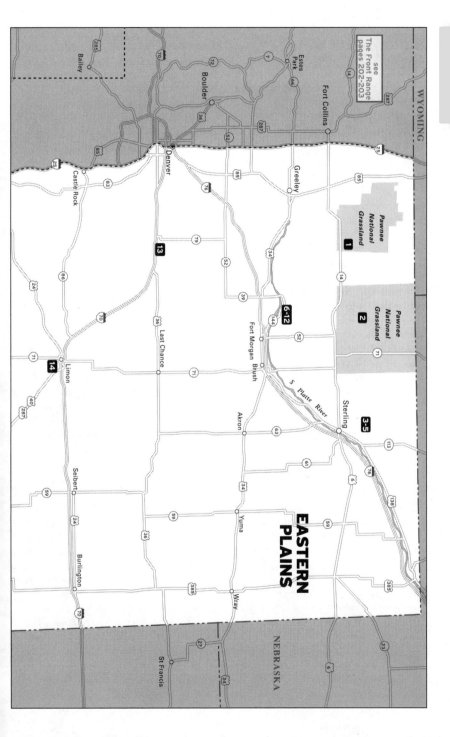

1 CROW VALLEY

🚶 🚵 🐴 ♿ 🚐 ⛺

Scenic rating: 7

in Pawnee National Grassland

After the Homestead Act of 1862, homesteaders flocked to Colorado's eastern plains to claim free land. They plowed up the native grasses, planted wheat, and raised cattle on this harsh landscape. In the 1930s, a series of droughts and characteristic strong winds turned this region, along with the rest of the southern Great Plains, into the Dust Bowl. Topsoil was carried away by wind erosion, burying homes and ruining farms. Many of the settlers gave up their land and migrated farther west.

In some areas, the federal government's new conservation measures included buying land and planting it with native short grasses. As a result, Pawnee National Grassland was created in 1954. The Grassland covers 193,000 acres of public land interspersed with private wheat fields and pastures. It is a haven for migrating birds and bird-watchers who have identified 301 species here. The best months for bird-watching (and good weather) are May and June. A birding checklist and a brochure detailing a 36-mile tour for cars and mountain bikes are available at the campground. A popular and worthwhile hike to Pawnee Buttes is a half-hour drive to the northeast.

The Crow Valley Family Campground is small, scenic, and quiet when there are no large groups present. It is also remote, so be sure to stock up before entering the Grasslands. There are a few cottonwoods for some shade, but not much.

Campsites, facilities: On the main loop, there are 10 sites for tents and RVs up to 35 feet. Sites 4-6 are doubles ("family sites") and can accommodate up to 16 people. The second loop has tent-only camping for groups of up to 100 people by reservation only. Picnic tables, fire rings, and grills are provided. Vault toilets and drinking water are available. Horseshoe pits, a group picnic area, an outdoor farm museum, and a baseball field are also available. Leashed pets are permitted. Site 5 is wheelchair-accessible.

Reservations, fees: Reservations are accepted at 877/444-6777 or www.recreation.gov. Single sites are $14 per night and double sites are $20 per night. The group site is $75-145 per night depending on group size. Open mid-May-early October.

Directions: From Fort Collins, take Highway 14 to Briggsdale. Turn north on County Road 77. The camp entrance is on the left in 0.2 mile.

Contact: Pawnee National Grassland, Pawnee Ranger District office in Greeley, 970/834-9270, www.fs.usda.gov/arp.

2 PAWNEE BUTTES

🚶 🚵 🐴 ⛺

Scenic rating: 8

in Pawnee National Grassland

Pawnee National Grassland is the result of soil conservation policies enacted by the federal government after the devastating Dust Bowl years. When drought and agriculture turned the High Plains prairies into a virtual desert in the 1930s, this region lost several inches of topsoil and most of its homesteaders. Since then, the government has planted native grasses in an effort to restore the land. The birds are thriving here—more than 300 species have been sighted in this area. The best months for bird-watching (and good weather) are May and June. A birding checklist and a brochure detailing a 36-mile tour for cars or mountain bikes are available at Crow Valley (see listing in this chapter).

Plains tribes like the Arapaho, Cheyenne, and Sioux hunted buffalo and antelope in this area. Today, it's a popular hiking destination for Front Range residents. The buttes are the sandstone remains of an ancient sea eroded by wind and rain. You may be tempted to try rock climbing, but the pinkish sandstone is far too soft. A 2.5-mile trail travels from the parking area to the East Butte. A shorter trail goes north to an overlook with views of both buttes. Some of the trail crosses private land—these areas are clearly marked and should not be used for camping. The best camping is around the West Butte. Camping is prohibited within 100 feet of the parking lot and windmills and 200 feet of the overlook.

Campsites, facilities: This is a primitive hike-in campsite in a remote area. There are no facilities. There is drinking water during warm months, but it's best to come prepared. Stock up on gas and water before heading into the National Grassland. Leashed pets are permitted.

Reservations, fees: Reservations are not accepted. There is no fee for camping here. Open year-round, but weather conditions are unpleasant in winter and midsummer.

Directions: From Briggsdale, drive east on Highway 14 for 15 miles. Turn north on County Road 105. In 10 miles, turn right on County Road 104. In three miles, turn left on County Road 111. The trailhead and parking lot are on the right in 5.0 miles.

Contact: Pawnee National Grassland, 970/346-5000, www.fs.fed.us.

3 ELKS

🛶🚐⛴🐕♿🚙⛺

Scenic rating: 6

in North Sterling State Park

North Sterling State Park consists of a 3,000-acre lake and 1,500 acres of land. The reservoir occupies the valley carved by Cedar and Darby Creeks, tributaries of the South Platte. The surrounding sandstone bluffs were first seen by settlers traveling west on the Overland Trail in the mid-1800s. Today, the bluffs are enjoyed by boaters exploring the many inlets of the lake. The hills in this area are sand dunes that were deposited millennia ago by winds from the Rocky Mountains and have since been covered by prairie grass and uncovered by agriculture. On windy days, it can feel more like the Sahara than the High Plains.

Located next to the marina, Elks is very popular with boaters, anglers, and hunters. Sites 5-7, 27-32, and 41-49 are closest to the water and have the best views. Sites 1-21 have tent pads. There are few trees here and very little privacy. The campsites are generally 50-100 feet apart.

Campsites, facilities: There are 50 sites for tents and RVs. All of the sites have 30-amp electrical hookups, and the majority are pull-through. Picnic tables, fire rings, grills, and wind shelters are provided. Restrooms with flush toilets and showers, laundry facilities, and drinking water are available from April-October. Propane gas, a boat ramp, and a convenience store are available at the marina. Leashed pets are permitted. Site 15 is wheelchair-accessible.

Reservations, fees: Reservations are required at 800/244-5613 and www.cpwshop.com. The fee is $36 per night. Campers must also purchase a vehicle pass ($8) or Annual Parks Pass ($80). Open year-round.

Directions: From Sterling, take 7th Avenue/County Road 37 north for 10 miles. Turn left on County Road 46. The park entrance and campground are on the left in 3.9 miles.

Contact: North Sterling State Park, 970/522-3657, www.cpw.state.co.us.

4 CHIMNEY VIEW

🚶🛶🛶🚐⛴🐕🐎🚙⛺

Scenic rating: 6

in North Sterling State Park

Chimney View occupies an exposed, barren hilltop with grand views of the lake and the surrounding farms. Due to the proximity and abundance of sites, the campground looks a bit like a prairie dog colony. On windy days, the hilltop turns into a dust farm. But if you hit it on a calm day, it's a pleasant place for tent camping with all the amenities. The shelter with the laundry room and restrooms is large and clean. The swimming beach is a short walk downhill, and there are several hiking trails leading from the campground down to the water. At night, campers can enjoy stargazing and the nostalgic whistle of the trains crossing the plains to the east. Sites 51, 53, 55, 57, 59, 61, 63, and 65 are closest to the lake and have the most unobstructed views.

Campsites, facilities: There are 43 pull-through sites without hookups. Picnic tables, fire rings, grills, tent pads, and shade shelters are provided. Restrooms with flush toilets and showers, vault toilets, laundry facilities, drinking water, and a dump station are available. A playground and picnic pavilion are a short walk away. A boat ramp and propane gas are available at the marina. Leashed pets are permitted.

Reservations, fees: Reservations are accepted at 800/244-5613 and www.cpwshop.com. The fee is $28 per night. Campers must also purchase a vehicle pass ($8) or Annual Parks Pass ($80). Open early May-late September.

Directions: From Sterling, drive north on 7th Avenue/County Road 37 for 10 miles. Turn left on County Road 46. In 1.9 miles, turn left into the south park entrance. In 0.1 mile, pass the dump stations on the left and turn right into the campground.

Contact: North Sterling State Park, 970/522-3657, www.cpw.state.co.us.

5 INLET GROVE

Scenic rating: 4

in North Sterling State Park

North Sterling Reservoir is a 3,000-acre lake with many coves and abundant wildlife. It's subject to very hot summers and strong winds, but the weather doesn't deter water-sports enthusiasts and anglers. As the name implies, Inlet Grove is situated on an inlet, downhill from Chimney View campground. It is very close to the shore; sites 116-132 are practically touching the water. The campground is a large loop set up for RV camping, fishing, and birding. The South Shoreline Trail begins at the southern end of the campground and follows the south shore of the lake to the end of County Road 29 and a parking lot where hikers who want to do a shuttle can leave a car. Another trail leads up to Chimney View and down to the swimming beach.

Campsites, facilities: There are 46 pull-through sites with electrical hookups (50 amp) for tents and RVs. Picnic tables, fire rings, grills, tent pads, and shade shelters are provided. Vault toilets, drinking water, and a dump station are available. A boat ramp and propane gas are available at the marina. Leashed pets are permitted.

Reservations, fees: Reservations are required at 800/244-5613 and www.cpwshop.com. The fee is $36 per night. Campers must also purchase a vehicle pass ($8) or Annual Parks Pass ($80). Open early May-late September.

Directions: From Sterling, drive north on 7th Avenue/County Road 37 for 10 miles. Turn left on County Road 46. In 1.9 miles, turn left into the south park entrance. The campground entrance is straight ahead in 0.2 mile.

Contact: North Sterling State Park, 970/522-3657, www.cpw.state.co.us.

6 LAKESIDE

Scenic rating: 4

in Jackson Lake State Park

Jackson Lake is a large, shallow reservoir with 11 miles of shoreline. It's popular for its warm water and sandy beaches. Summer weekends can be *very* crowded with water-sports enthusiasts. Water-skiers zip around the lake, and anglers fish for trout, walleye, catfish, perch, and crappie. It's also a convenient stopover for travelers on I-76. The seven campgrounds on the western shore are close together—many of them share facilities—and it can be difficult to tell which campground you're in. Quiet hours are 10pm-6am, but weekend crowds can be quite rowdy (only 3.2 percent alcohol is permitted). Lakeside is a grassy park with more trees than any of the other campgrounds. All of the sites are within 25 yards of the water and are very popular with anglers.

Campsites, facilities: There are 58 sites with electrical hookups for tents and RVs, and 4 sites for tents only. Most sites are pull-through. Site 35 is wheelchair-accessible. Picnic tables, fire rings, and grills are provided. Restrooms with flush toilets and showers, vault toilets, laundry facilities, drinking water, horseshoe pits, and a dump station, are available. A convenience store, propane gas, ATM, boat ramp, and water-sports rentals are available at the marina. Interpretive programs are offered at the visitors center. Leashed pets are permitted.

Reservations, fees: Reservations are required at 800/244-5613 and www.cpwshop.com. The fee is $28 per night for nonelectric sites and $36 per night for electric sites. Campers must also purchase a vehicle pass ($8) or Annual Parks Pass ($80). Open April-mid-September.

Directions: From Fort Morgan, go west on I-76 for 13 miles. Turn north on Highway 39. In 7.0 miles, the road ends at County Road Y.5. Go west for 3.5 miles to the entrance station. Lakeside is the first campground on the right.

Contact: Jackson Lake State Park, 970/645-2551, www.cpw.state.co.us.

⁊ COVE
🚶 🏊 ⛵ 🎣 🚣 🐴 🚐 ⛺

Scenic rating: 4
in Jackson Lake State Park

Cove is a small campground with almost no trees, but it's very popular because it has a sandy swimming beach. It's also a day-use area, so there's not much privacy here. Dense underbrush along the shore obstructs views of the lake. (For more information on Jackson Lake, see the Lakeside listing in this chapter.)

Campsites, facilities: There are 16 sites with electrical hookups for tents and RVs. Picnic tables, fire rings, shade shelters, and grills are provided. Restrooms with flush toilets and showers, drinking water, horseshoe pits, a dump station, and an amphitheater are available. A convenience store, propane gas, ATM, boat ramp, and water-sports rentals are available at the marina. Interpretive programs are offered at the visitors center. Leashed pets are permitted.

Reservations, fees: Reservations are accepted at 800/244-5613 and www.cpwshop.com. The fee is $36 per night. Campers must also purchase a vehicle pass ($8) or Annual Parks Pass ($80). Open April-mid-September.

Directions: From Fort Morgan, go west on I-76 for 13 miles. Turn north on Highway 39. In 7.0 miles, the road ends at County Road Y.5. Go west for 3.5 miles to the entrance station. Cove is the second campground on the right.

Contact: Jackson Lake State Park, 970/645-2551, www.cpw.state.co.us.

🎱 PELICAN
🚶 🏊 ⛵ 🎣 🚣 🐴 🚐 ⛺

Scenic rating: 4
in Jackson Lake State Park

Pelican is very close to the marina, and most of the sites are lakeside. It's usually packed with RVers, water-skiers, and anglers. It's also a short walk away from the beach at Cove campground where there is swimming. The tent-only sites are close to the road but have excellent views of the lake, which can be almost glorious at sunset. (For more information on Jackson Lake, see the Lakeside listing in this chapter.)

Campsites, facilities: There are 33 sites with electrical hookups for tents and RVs and four sites for tents only. Picnic tables, fire rings, and grills are provided. Restrooms with flush toilets and showers, vault toilets, drinking water, volleyball court, and horseshoe pits, and a dump station are available. A convenience store, propane gas, ATM, boat ramp, and water-sports rentals are available at the marina. Interpretive programs are offered at the visitors center. Leashed pets are permitted.

Reservations, fees: Reservations are accepted at 800/244-5613 and www.cpwshop.com. The fee is $28 per night for nonelectric sites and $36 per night for electric sites. Campers must also purchase a vehicle pass ($8) or Annual Parks Pass ($80). Open year-round.

Directions: From Fort Morgan, go west on I-76 for 13 miles. Turn north on Highway 39. In 7.0 miles, the road ends at County Road Y.5. Go west for 3.5 miles to the entrance station. Pelican is the third campground on the right.

Contact: Jackson Lake State Park, 970/645-2551, www.cpw.state.co.us.

9 SANDPIPER

Scenic rating: 4
in Jackson Lake State Park

Sandpiper is a medium-size loop located just north of the marina. The west beach for swimming is a short walk away, at Cove campground. The sites here are roomy, but there is no shade. All of the outside sites are long pull-throughs. Sites 13-15 are lakeside. The ground here is not level, so it's a poor choice for tent camping. (For more information on Jackson Lake, see the Lakeside listing in this chapter.)

Campsites, facilities: There are 28 sites with electrical hookups for tents and RVs. Picnic tables, fire rings, and grills are provided. Restrooms with flush toilets and showers, laundry facilities, drinking water, and horseshoe

pits, and a dump station are available. A convenience store, propane gas, ATM, boat ramp, and water-sports rentals are available at the marina. Interpretive programs are offered at the visitors center. Leashed pets are permitted.

Reservations, fees: Reservations are accepted at 800/244-5613 and www.cpwshop.com. The fee is $28 per night for nonelectric sites and $36 per night for electric sites. Campers must also purchase a vehicle pass ($8) or Annual Parks Pass ($80). Open April-mid-September.

Directions: From Fort Morgan, go west on I-76 for 13 miles. Turn north on Highway 39. In 7.0 miles, the road ends at County Road Y.5. Go west for 3.5 miles to the entrance station. Sandpiper is the fourth campground on the right.

Contact: Jackson Lake State Park, 970/645-2551, www.cpw.state.co.us.

10 FOX HILLS

Scenic rating: 4
in Jackson Lake State Park

Fox Hills is the largest and the most unappealing campground at Jackson Lake State Park. The sites are close together, and there are no trees. Tent campers will probably be uncomfortable here and should head to Northview, Pelican, or Lakeside campgrounds. On the positive side, most of the sites have views of the lake. The swimming beach at Cove campground is a short walk to the south. (For more information on Jackson Lake, see the Lakeside listing in this chapter.)

Campsites, facilities: There are 87 sites without hookups for tents and RVs. Picnic tables, fire rings, and grills are provided. Restrooms with flush toilets and showers, vault toilets, laundry facilities, drinking water, and horseshoe pits, and a dump station are available. A convenience store, propane gas, ATM, and water-sports rentals are available at the marina.

Interpretive programs are offered at the visitors center. Leashed pets are permitted.

Reservations, fees: Reservations are accepted at 800/244-5613 and www.cpwshop.com. The fee is $28 per night. Campers must also purchase a vehicle pass ($8) or Annual Parks Pass ($80). Open year-round.

Directions: From Fort Morgan, go west on I-76 for 13 miles. Turn north on Highway 39. In 7.0 miles, the road ends at County Road Y.5. Go west for 3.5 miles to the entrance station. Fox Hills is the fifth campground on the right.

Contact: Jackson Lake State Park, 970/645-2551, www.cpw.state.co.us.

11 NORTHVIEW

Scenic rating: 5
in Jackson Lake State Park

Northview is the last campground on the western shore of Jackson Lake, and it's the smallest and most appealing in the state park. These sites have the best views of the lake, so it's a very popular campground. Because the ground is uneven, it's more appropriate for RVs than tent camping. (For more information on Jackson Lake, see the Lakeside listing in this chapter.)

Campsites, facilities: There are 10 sites with electrical hookups for tents and RVs. Picnic tables, fire rings, grills, and shade shelters are provided. Vault toilets and drinking water are available, and a dump station for registered campers is at the park entrance. A convenience store, propane gas, ATM, boat ramp, and water-sports rentals are available at the marina. Interpretive programs are offered at the visitors center. Leashed pets are permitted.

Reservations, fees: Reservations are accepted at 800/244-5613 and www.cpwshop.com. The fee is $28 per night. Campers must also purchase a vehicle pass ($8) or Annual Parks Pass ($80). Open year-round.

Directions: From Fort Morgan, go west on I-76 for 13 miles. Turn north on Highway 39. In 7.0 miles, the road ends at County Road Y.5. Go west for 3.5 miles to the entrance station. Northview is the last campground on the right.

Contact: Jackson Lake State Park, 970/645-2551, www.cpw.state.co.us.

12 DUNES GROUP

Scenic rating: 4
in Jackson Lake State Park

BEST (

Dunes is the only group campground at Jackson Lake. Separated from the string of six campgrounds on the west shore, it's more secluded and private than the other sites. The wide-open views make this a popular site for groups and events; it is usually booked out months in advance. The south beach for swimming is a short walk away, and the warm waters of the 2,700-acre reservoir are popular with anglers and water-skiers. There are also interpretive programs at the visitors center. The campground has a large fire pit where as many as 25 people can gather for s'mores and ghost stories. There are also sand dunes bordering the campground where kids romp on sunny days, but beware of windy days when dunes can turn into a miniature Dust Bowl.

Campsites, facilities: There are 18 sites with electrical hookups for tents and RVs for up to 100 people. Picnic tables, fire rings, and grills are provided. Restrooms with flush toilets and showers, drinking water, a group picnic area, and horseshoe pits are available. A dump station is available for registered campers at the north park entrance. A convenience store, propane gas, ATM, and water-sports rentals are available at the marina to the north. Leashed pets are permitted.

Reservations, fees: Reservations are accepted at 800/244-5613 and www.cpwshop.com. The fee is $432 per night for all 18 sites. Campers must also purchase a vehicle pass ($8) or Annual Parks Pass ($80). Open May 1-Labor Day weekend.

Directions: From Fort Morgan, go west on I-76 for 13 miles. Turn north on Highway 39. In 7.0 miles, the road ends at County Road Y.5. Go west for 3.0 miles and turn right at the south entrance to the park. Dunes Group is 0.3 mile past the entrance station.

Contact: Jackson Lake State Park, 970/645-2551, www.cpw.state.co.us.

13 DENVER EAST/ STRASBURG KOA

Scenic rating: 3

east of Denver on I-70

Strasburg is a safe small town, and so is the KOA, only a half-hour from Denver. This convenient stopover on the way to or from the mountains is a beehive of activity. In the summer, there are pancake breakfasts on Saturday mornings and free movies in the evenings. It's a popular place for family reunions, in part because of the meeting room. It's fortunate that there's so much to do at the campground because there's not much to do in Strasburg, and the scenery is mostly granaries and railroads. However, there are plenty of trees onsite, providing much-needed shade during the hot summers.

Campsites, facilities: There are 58 RV sites with hookups, 4 tent sites, and 1 group site. There are also seven rustic cabins that sleep 4-6 people. Picnic tables, fire rings, grills, free Wi-Fi, free cable TV, and an adults-only hot tub are provided. There is a pool, playground, basketball and volleyball courts, a large game room, and a meeting room. There are flush toilets, showers, laundry facilities, drinking water, as well as a store. Bike rentals and propane are available. The management is pet-friendly, but pets should be leashed.

Reservations, fees: Reservations are accepted

at 800/562-6538. The two-person rate is $37 per night for tent sites and $38-45 per night for RV sites. Each additional person is $4 per night. Children seven and under stay free. Group and monthly rates are available. Open year-round.

Directions: From Denver, go east on I-70 for 35 miles. In Strasburg, take exit 310. Turn left off the ramp, then right onto Frontage Road. Turn left on Monroe Street, and the campground is immediately on the right.

Contact: Jeff and Tracy Hastings, 303/622-9274, www.campdenver.com.

14 LIMON KOA

Scenic rating: 3

in Limon

The tiny town of Limon (pop. 2,071) is a spartan stopover point for travelers on I-70. Summer temperatures here regularly top 100°F, and there are few distractions from the heat except for the campground pool, fast-food restaurants, and the Limon Heritage Museum Depot, a short drive away in downtown Limon. There is also a bike path along the river, a golf course on the west end of town, and the Doug Kissel Fishing Pond, a tiny, stocked pond beside the railroad. This family-oriented KOA is very close to the highway and surrounded by fields. There are numerous trees to provide some relief from the heat, but very little privacy. The owners serve a pancake breakfast every day in the summer.

Campsites, facilities: There are 12 sites for tents and 41 sites with full and partial hookups for RVs up to 70 feet. Picnic tables and grills are provided. Restrooms with flush toilets and showers, laundry facilities, drinking water, a convenience store, a diner, a swimming pool, propane gas, tetherball, playground, horseshoes, bike rentals, meeting room, game room, free Wi-Fi, free cable, and dump stations, are available. Leashed pets are permitted.

Bent's Old Fort National Historic Monument is located near La Junta.

Reservations, fees: Reservations are accepted at 800/562-2129. Tent sites are $38 per night for two people. RV sites with hookups are $54 per night for two people. Each additional adult is $4 ($3 for children age 7-17). Group rates are available. Open year-round.

Directions: Take I-70 to Limon and take Exit 361 West. At the Pizza Hut, turn right onto Colorado Avenue.

Contact: Limon KOA, 800/562-2129, www. limonkoa.com.

15 LA JUNTA KOA

Scenic rating: 3

in La Junta

Thanks to the glowing lights of Walmart, flashlights aren't a necessity at this busy KOA. There are a few semi-permanent residents, but this park is mainly for overnighters who need to restock and don't mind the close quarters. What the campground lacks in wilderness and privacy, it makes up for with its proximity to fascinating historical sights along the Santa Fe Trail (Highway 50) and in Comanche National Grassland. Bent's Old Fort, eight miles to the east, was a center of the fur trade in the mid-1800s and a military fort during the Mexican-American War. Today, the restored adobe fort is a national historic site, with tour guides in period clothing. In the Grassland, hikers in Vogel and Picket Wire Canyons can see prehistoric Native American rock art, abandoned homesteads, and the largest dinosaur track site in North America.

Campsites, facilities: There are 56 sites with full and partial hookups for RVs up to 65 feet, four tent sites, and two cabins. Picnic tables, grills, and fire rings are provided. Restrooms with flush toilets and showers, drinking water, a store, propane gas, miniature golf, horseshoes, basketball courts, a playground, swimming pool, meeting room, recreation room, pool table, cable TV, and dump stations are available. Leashed pets are permitted, but some dog breeds are restricted.

Reservations, fees: Reservations are accepted

at 800/562-9501. Tent sites are $30 per night, and RV sites are $37-40 per night for 2-4 people. Each additional camper is $2; children under age 12 are free. KOA Value Kard, AAA, and AARP discounts available. Open year-round.

Directions: The campground is located 189 miles east of Denver. From the junction of U.S. 50 and Highway 109 in La Junta, drive west on Highway 50 for 1.0 mile. The campground is on the left at 26680 Highway 50, next door to Walmart.

Contact: La Junta KOA, 719/384-9580, www.lajuntakoa.com.

16 LAKE HASTY

Scenic rating: 4

in John Martin Reservoir State Park

John Martin Reservoir State Park deserves its moniker "an oasis on the plains." Campers regularly travel from five states to enjoy boating, fishing, bird-watching, and hunting on and around the lake. Hikers and birders will enjoy the Red Shin Hiking Trail (4.5 miles), which begins below the dam, traverses short-grass prairie and wetland environments, and ends at the Santa Fe Trail marker on the north shore. The lake provides nesting habitat for the threatened piping plover and the endangered interior least tern, and it's an important migratory stop for waterfowl and bald eagles. This campground closes in the winter to protect the bald eagles that nest in the large trees scattered throughout the campground.

Located in the shadow of the dam, the campground is a short walk away from two stocked fishing ponds and a sandy swimming beach. Sites 1-29 are the closest to the dam and the least appealing, in part because there are no shade trees at this end of the campground. Sites 30-109 have more shade, and they are closer to the swimming beach. Sites 31-38 are favorite sites and require a reservation for most of the summer. Most of the picnic tables at this campground have shelters, a useful feature when the winds kick up, which they often do. There is very little privacy when it's crowded. Reservations are recommended if you are traveling here in the summer, but you will have the campground almost to yourself in the off-season.

Campsites, facilities: There are 109 sites for tents or RVs up to 60 feet. Sites 59 and 60 are wheelchair-accessible. Every site has electric hookups. Picnic tables, grills, and fire rings are provided. Restrooms with flush toilets and showers, coin-operated laundry facilities, drinking water, dump stations, a playground, and a fish-cleaning station are available. Boat ramps are available at the reservoir. Group camping and picnic areas are available by reservation. Leashed pets are permitted.

Reservations, fees: Reservations are accepted at 800/244-5613 and www.cpwshop.com. The fee is $28 per night. Campers must also purchase a vehicle pass ($8) or Annual Parks Pass ($80). Open year-round; however, only 51 sites are open during winter, and there are reduced services.

Directions: From Lamar, drive west on U.S. 50 for 20 miles. In the tiny town of Hasty, turn south on County Road 24. Follow the signs 2.2 miles to the visitors center, where you can purchase a park pass and camping permit. After the visitors center, go left at the fork. The campground entrance is on the right in 0.9 mile.

Contact: John Martin Reservoir State Park, 719/829-1801, www.cpw.state.co.us.

17 POINT

Scenic rating: 6

in John Martin Reservoir State Park

This campground is popular with anglers, hunters, and birders who travel from five states to enjoy this "oasis on the plains," a year-round migration stop for waterfowl and birds of prey. Located on a peninsula on the north shore, this campground is on a ridge about 0.25 mile from the water's edge and has dramatic views of the lake and the seemingly barren short-grass prairie. Don't let first impressions fool you. The habitat is home to deer, coyotes, rabbits, raccoons, and prairie dogs. For wildlife viewing, try the Red Shin Hiking Trail (4.5 miles), which begins at the Santa Fe Trail marker and ends below the dam. Swimmers must scramble down sandstone cliffs to reach the water, and life jackets are required. There's more room between the sites here than at the Lake Hasty campground—but no trees, a serious drawback when temperatures regularly top 100°F in the summer. There is no shade; bring your own.

Campsites, facilities: There are 104 sites for tents and RVs up to 45 feet, but there are no hookups and no drinking water provided. Picnic tables, grills, fire rings, gravel tent pads, and vault toilets are provided. The boat ramps are nearby. Group camping and picnic sites are available by reservation. Leashed pets are permitted.

Reservations, fees: Reservations are accepted at 800/244-5613 and www.cpwshop.com. The fee is $20 per night. Campers must also purchase a vehicle pass ($8) or Annual Parks Pass ($80). This campground is only open for Memorial Day, Fourth of July, and Labor Day weekends.

Directions: From Lamar, drive west on U.S. 50 for 20 miles. In the tiny town of Hasty, turn south on County Road 24. Follow the signs 2.2 miles to the visitors center, where you can purchase a park pass and camping permit. After the visitors center, follow the Point campground signs for 2.6 miles. Before the boat ramps, turn right onto the dirt road. In 1.0 mile, turn left at the T-intersection. The campground is on both sides of the road in 1.0 mile.

Contact: John Martin Reservoir State Park, 719/829-1801, www.cpw.state.co.us.

RESOURCES

GOVERNMENT RESOURCES

Bureau of Land Management (BLM)
Colorado State Office
2850 Youngfield Street
Lakewood, CO 80215
303/239-3600
www.co.blm.gov

Colorado Dept. of Transportation (CDOT)
Highway and Traveler Information
www.cotrip.org

Colorado Avalanche Information Center (CAIC)
325 Broadway Street, WS #1
Boulder, CO 80305
303/499-9650
www.avalanche.state.co.us

Colorado Parks & Wildlife (CPW)
1313 Sherman Street, 6th Floor
Denver, CO 80203
303/297-1192
www.cpw.state.co.us

Colorado State Government
www.colorado.gov

US Forest Service
Rocky Mountain Regional Office
1617 Cole Blvd
Lakewood, CO 80401
303/275-5350
www.fs.fed.us

LOCAL RESOURCES AND NONPROFITS

Colorado Fourteeners Initiative
(for maps, trail info, and conditions)
607 10th Street, Suite 107N
Golden, CO 80401
303/278-7650
www.14ers.org

Colorado Mountain Club
710 10th Street, Suite 200
Golden, CO 80401
303/279-3080
www.cmc.org

Leave No Trace Center
For Outdoor Ethics
1000 North St
Boulder, CO 80304
303/442-8222
https://lnt.org

The Colorado Trail Foundation
710 10th Street, Suite 210
Golden, CO 80401
303/384-3729
www.coloradotrail.org

The Forest Conservancy
1012 Brookie Drive
Carbondale, CO 81623
970/963-8071
www.forestconservancy.com

Volunteers for Outdoor Colorado
600 South Marion Parkway
Denver, CO 80209
303/715-1010
www.voc.org

Colorado Outdoor Recreation Search and Rescue (CORSAR)

Colorado residents and visitors are served by dedicated volunteer search and rescue teams, but mission costs are often in the thousands of dollars. By purchasing a CORSAR card, you are contributing to the Search and Rescue Fund, which will reimburse these teams for costs incurred if you ever need a search and rescue. Funds remaining at the end of the year are used to help pay for training and equipment for these teams. Anyone with a current hunting/fishing license, or boat, snowmobile, or ATV registration is already covered by the fund. CORSAR cards are available for $3 for one year and $12 for five years, and can be purchased at more than 300 retailers in the state or online at https://dola.colorado.gov/sar/orderInstructions.jsf.

OTHER RESOURCES

CDT Continental Divide Trail
www.continentaldividetrail.org

Colorado Trail
www.coloradotrail.org

Forestcamping.com
www.forestcamping.com

Packed with information on U.S. National Forest campgrounds.

High Rocky Riders
http://highrockyriders.org
An OHV club.

Recreation.gov
www.recreation.gov
The central booking and information site for any campground that accepts reservations.

Stay the Trail, Colorado
www.staythetrail.org
For motor vehicle use maps.

Acknowledgments

Before anyone else, I'd like to acknowledge the two previous authors of *Moon Colorado Camping:* Sarah Ryan, author of the third and fourth editions, and Robyn Brewer, author of the first and second editions. I know that thousands of hours of camping (and driving) around the state were necessary to create this book. I am honored to continue building on their work with the fifth—and now sixth—editions.

I'd like to thank all the campground hosts and park rangers. One of the best parts about writing this book is the opportunity to talk with all of you and to learn from your knowledge and experience. Thank you for your generosity and patience, especially when I showed up out of the blue to your remote corner of Colorado with my notebook and questions.

My wife and three daughters get dragged along on all kinds of "research trips," in all kinds if campers and tents—thanks for coming with me, girls!

I'd like to acknowledge my outdoor/travel editors at The Denver Post: Dena Rosenberry, Danika Worthington, and Barbara Ellis. I mine most of my camping trips for both my monthly "Around Colorado" newspaper column and for this book—it's a nice overlap.

Finally, thanks to the team at Avalon Travel: publishers Bill Newlin and Donna Galassi, and my editors Rachael Sablik, Mike Morgenfeld, Suzanne Albertson, and Darren Alessi, plus all the others who help bring this book into the world. ¡Gracias!

Index

MOON NATIONAL PARKS

ACADIA
NATIONAL PARK

HILARY NANGLE

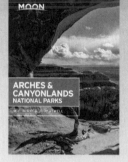

ARCHES &
CANYONLANDS
NATIONAL PARKS

BANFF
NATIONAL
PARK

HIKE · CAMP · KAYAK

ANDREW HEMPSTEAD

GLACIER
NATIONAL PARK

DEATH VALLEY
NATIONAL PARK

JENNA BLOUGH

GRAND
CANYON

KATHLEEN BRYANT

GREAT SMOKY
MOUNTAINS
NATIONAL PARK

HIKE · BIKE · CAMP

JASON FRYE

MOUNT RUSHMORE
& THE BLACK HILLS

Including the Badlands
LAURAL A. BIDWELL

ROCKY
MOUNTAIN
NATIONAL PARK

HIKE, CAMP,
SEE WILDLIFE

ERIN ENGLISH

In these books:

- Full coverage of gateway cities and towns
- Itineraries from one day to multiple weeks
- Advice on where to stay (or camp) in and around the parks

MOON ROAD TRIP GUIDES

Share your adventures using **#travelwithmoon**